THE MOON

MYTH AND IMAGE

THE MOON

MYTH AND IMAGE

JULES CASHFORD

CASSELL
ILLUSTRATED

First published in Great Britain in 2003 by Cassell Illustrated
A Member of Octopus Publishing Group Limited
2-4 Heron Quays, London E14 4JP

A CIP catalogue record for this book is available from the British Library.

ISBN 1 84403 103 9

Designed by Grade Design Consultants, London
Printed in Dubai

CONTENTS

FOREWORD

I thought that whatever of philosophy has been made poetry is alone permanent...
Yeats *The Philosophy of Shelley's Poetry*

This book explores the myths, symbols and poetic images inspired by the Moon, from the earliest Palaeolithic markings on horn and bone, down to the crafted poems of the present. As a study in the history of ideas, the aim is firstly to discover the ways in which stories of the Moon have contributed to the way we think.

The evidence of stories and images from around the world suggests that most, if not all, ancient cultures passed through a stage of interpreting certain aspects of their reality through the Moon. Indeed, the extraordinary and far-reaching powers attributed to the Moon – powers over birth, fecundity, growth, destiny, death and rebirth – amount almost to a world view at the beginning of human history. From a broad perspective, the Moon was just one among many expressions of the culture of the Great Mother Goddess, in which Earth and Moon were understood as one manifestation in dual aspect. But a closer look suggests that the peculiar character of the Moon offered an imaginative scope of its own, both crystallizing the essence of the Goddess myth, and, through the provocative metaphor of the Moon's cycle and phase, exploring ways of thinking about permanence, time and mortality.

The essential myth of the Moon is the myth of transformation. Early people perceived the Moon's waxing and waning as the growing and dying of a celestial being, whose death was followed by its own resurrection as the New Moon. The perpetual drama of the Moon's phases became a model for contemplating a pattern in human, animal and vegetable life, including the idea of life beyond death. It seems that the Moon carried the image of eternity for early people, as well as the image of time. The instinctive identification of the people with their Moon meant that they interpreted the Moon's rebirth as offering a similar promise for human beings in their own waning and death. The Moon then became a visible symbol of hope, the light that shone in the darkness of the human psyche.

* * *

The earliest notations made by human beings in the Palaeolithic age appear to be a record of the lunar cycle, enabling us to measure periods of time longer than 24 hours, which could be reckoned by the Sun. In the Indo-European languages, words for Moon and measurement have the same etymological root, one which extends into a surprising range of words for mind, from memory to mania. Further, the coincidence of the timing of the lunar cycle with the female menstrual cycle suggested a relation between the Moon and the cyclical rhythms of human life, and that relationship entered many dimensions of human experience, particularly those concerned with birth, growth and death.

Many of the myths imply a further idea: that the Moon is reborn out of its own substance, and so is itself the god or goddess of birth and rebirth. The crescent of the Moon was widely believed to be a cup which held the waters of life, both the ambrosial nectar of immortal life, out of which the Moon renewed itself, and the life-giving waters that fell to Earth as dew and rain, or spread across the Earth as seas whose tides waxed and waned to the rhythms of the Moon.

As the giver of birth, the Moon became in many lands guardian of the fertility of humans, animals and plants. Even in the early part of the 20th century, babies were held up to the Moon in places as far apart as India and France, and women would drink water saturated with moonlight in order to conceive. Once the 'powers' of the Moon were asssumed, connections were made between all the phenomena the Moon was thought to influence. Astonishing patterns of correspondence emerge in the symbolism between otherwise disparate things: between, say, bulls, boars and crescents (the horned Moon), black cats and witches (dark Moon), serpents and souls (shedding their skins as the Moon its shadow), spiders and rain (through the spinning lunar Fates); between toads and childbirth (toad-rain-moisture), between hares and death (the hare seen in the face of the Full Moon who dies), and hares who lay the egg of new life (hare-Moon-rebirth), as in modern European folk customs at Easter. Because of this ancient web of associations, the symbolism of the Moon offers a fascinating insight into the symbolic mind.

Each particular phase of the Moon was once widely felt to give a unique and living quality to time. The waxing phase was for growing and the waning for declining. New and Full Moons were for celebration, but Full Moons were dangerous for 'lunatics'. The waning and Dark Moon were for withdrawing, planting root vegetables, cutting wood. The three days of death followed by rebirth is a symbol in many of the world's myths, from the Sumerian Inanna's descent into the Nether World, the Biblical Jonah and the whale, to Christ's Descent into Hell. From African Bushman tales to the Egyptian Mysteries of Osiris and the Eleusinian Mysteries of Greece, the idea of resurrection was found reflected in the Moon's ever-recurring cycle, its eternal return.

* * *

Beginning with the discovery of agriculture, and certainly by the late Bronze and early Iron Age (c. 2000–1250 BC), there was in most parts of the world a change from a purely lunar to a luni-solar calendar, and eventually a reallocation of religious priority from the Moon to the Sun. In a process known as 'solarization,' the Sun officially replaced the Moon in many lands, and many of the Moon's powers and stories were transferred to the Sun, or lost from view. This process, generally speaking, coincided in the west with the rise of the patriarchal cultures over the earlier cultures of the Goddess, when, in a similar way, the stories of the Goddess were obscured or distorted by the dominant mythological perspective. Recovery of all these stories would seem to be essential if we are not to lose the dynamic impulse and original complexity of our ancient inheritance.

* * *

But, perhaps more importantly, the book also asks what these myths and images disclose about human consciousness. This last question may be timely, now that we can stand imaginatively upon the Moon and look back on the Earth, seeing ourselves looking at the Moon. For this is a precise image of the new kind of consciousness which is made possible by achieving a standpoint beyond Earth, allowing us for the first time to see the Earth as a whole. From this magnificent perspective, tribal boundaries, with their warring gods, dissolve into absurdity, even as the smoke of their conflict floats in the air, hovering over regions too small to name, desperate territories on invisible maps.

The other major discovery of the 20th century also made it impossible to think of continents and countries in isolation from each other. As Einstein warned in 1964, 'The unleashing of the power of the atom bomb has changed everything except our mode of thinking, and thus we head toward unparalleled catastrophes.' [1] He was surely signalling that the brilliant experiment in consciousness of the last four thousand years had reached its peak and must now sacrifice its autonomy, if it is not to destroy what it has made.

The great mythologist, Joseph Campbell, has given voice to a vision born of this realization:

> The old gods are dead or dying and people everywhere are searching, asking: What is the new mythology to be, the mythology of this unified earth as of one harmonious being? [2]

The scientific exploration of human consciousness is relatively recent (in contrast to art, which has always held 'as 'twere, the mirror up to nature.'). [3] It began, interestingly enough, around the time that Einstein was speaking, as though the new and necessary focus for the analytic mind was now to be the subject in which that mind inhered. It soon became clear that we understood very little of the way in which a mode of consciousness might change (inevitably inhabiting any paradigm from within). We do not know how mythologies come to be, either new or old, whether they arise spontaneously from the unconscious or whether we can consciously assist new ways of seeing and valuing life to emerge. But by comparing myths from different cultures and times, we have learned that myths make visible to us our deepest longings and imaginings, and so offer one way in which we can apprehend and know our own being.

Since the Age of Enlightenment, it has been a common assumption that the way of thinking about life mythologically belongs to the distant past, such that the speculative thought of modern science and philosophy owes nothing to the 'irrational' intuitions of mythology, and, indeed, is founded on a heroic refusal of them. But, since the work of Jung, Cassirer, Frankfort, Eliade and Barfield, among many others, [4] it has become apparent that speculative thought is an inherent feature of mythical thinking, and, conversely, that mythic images are never absent from any attempt to understand the universe, however rational and empirical it would aspire to be. In this case, there might be something to be learned from the way early people related to the universe.

Before philosophy, and later science, became separate disciplines of their own, the poetic images of myth were the central way in which people addressed the immediate contingencies of daily life, and also thought through the unanswerable questions of life and death. This was speculative thought in that it transcended experience in order to explain and unify experience. Like later thinking, predicated on clear definition and explicit statement, these early modes of thought began with a hypothesis. It may have been a living presence – a goddess or a god; it may have taken the form of an animal or bird, or manifested as Moon, Sun or Earth – but it was no less an attempt to reach for an idea that would reveal patterns and structures and make sense of the world. In this sense myth is not a way of thinking superseded by reflective thought; it is the original and living impulse of philosophy.

Early speculations found their way through an imaginative sympathy, which included the entire relationship of people to their world. And – since this was a mutual process – this sympathy included the way the world related to human beings. For the world of early people was a Thou, not an It, a presence both numinous *and* personal, and so a Subject in the dialectic of thinking, not an inanimate object of thought. What we now call Nature (and forget that the name, and the idea, is a relatively late abstraction) was once not distinguished from humankind: as equally living beings, they belonged to the same continuum of feeling, and did not, therefore, have to be apprehended by different modes of cognition. There was no dichotomy between them. We have always to remember that the ancient imagination was concrete, embedded in and rising out of deeply lived experience, similar, in this respect, to poetry of all ages. It was not that early people did not think philosophically; it was that 'the good,' 'the true' and 'the beautiful' were once good, true and beautiful things, and these 'things' were personalities, activities, cosmic events – all that composes a world of value.

This does not mean that people of long ago imparted human characteristics to an alien universe, personifying it in order to feel more at home in it. Such an interpretation rests on an implicit opposition between Nature and humanity, which western modes of thinking now take for granted but is the very assumption that is up for discussion, possibly the central belief that prevents a change in our world view. So it is not just that early people did not have a category for inanimate phenomena; it is also that this category itself may be provisional and not absolute, a function of a particular stage in the evolution of consciousness, but not universal and necessary. How would we know if we did not call it into question? The point is that in changing a mode of consciousness, all assumptions have to be questioned, and particularly those that the dominant mode of consciousness holds to be self-evident, not least because they have contributed to its position of dominance.

One of the discoveries of Psychology in the last century has been to show us that myths structure our thinking whether we are aware of them or not. We all, as a race, culture, or individual, have a story about the world in which we live and about our place and purpose in it. A myth, in its original Greek meaning – *muthos* – is simply that: a story, one which seeks to render life transparent to an intelligible source. It can be conscious, open to dialogue with other stories, and self-reflective, or it can be unconscious, or less-than-fully conscious, when it is more likely to be understood as literally true and unsusceptible to criticism, usually because it is felt to be vindicated by the Higher Authority who revealed it. What the stories have in common is that they are all constructions of the human psyche. They have to be, because the world is not given as fact but inhabited through interpretation.

The literary critic, Northrop Frye, starts from the premiss that we all live within a 'mythological universe, a body of assumptions and beliefs developed from our existential concerns,' which are so much a part of the way in which we see life that we do not notice them. He then introduces the startling term 'mythological conditioning' to point to how even the most apparently open-minded stories about the world may be partly unconscious, presenting themselves as simple facts validated by perceptions open to all. [5] It is only the existence of contrary stories that may alert us to the partiality of our own, and so to the inevitable partiality of any story. Our imaginations may recognize elements of our myths, or mode of consciousness, when we see them in dreams, or in art and literature, but we may not fully understand the significance of what we see. It would seem that a change of consciousness is not possible without some awareness of our mythological conditioning.

As we all know, it is very difficult to see through family conditioning in individual life, let alone social conditioning in the collective life of the tribe, or the mythological conditioning of the race in the actual time in which we live. The hope for a study of the myths of the Moon is that because we do not 'believe in' the Moon in the way that the Moon was once believed in, we may be able to see something of how 'mythological conditioning' might work. We may get a glimpse of how the human mind thinks when it creates conceptions of reality which it then believes to be true and from which it derives, and defends, its conduct. As myths of long ago, images and stories of the Moon can appear to us now as art, open to scrutiny and debate, while their form – the human search for meaning and intelligibility – may mirror the philosophies of any age.

This book tries to tell the story of the myths of the Moon as a story of human consciousness. Lunar images and rituals still persist in many fields of thought, from religious symbolism, fairy tale and folklore to superstition and unexamined habits of mind, yet their source in the Moonlore of earlier times is not always apparent. The idea would be that if we can trace a custom back to its lunar source, which would be tracing a now secular event back to its sacred original, we might gain a perspective on how we have come to think in some of the ways we do.

CHAPTER 1

THE MOON AND THE RHYTHMS OF LIFE

Sing, Muses, with your sweet voices,
Sing, daughters of Zeus, son of Kronos,
Sing us the story of the long-winged Moon.

Homeric *Hymn to Selene*

When the ancient Greeks looked up from Earth, they saw flashing chariots of light drawn by winged horses and bulls. At night they saw Selene, the Moon, gliding alone through the dark towards the west, floating down to the horizon as Eos, 'rosy-fingered' Dawn, appears in the east, with Helios, the Sun, riding fast behind her, his robe shimmering over his stallions, and his chariot boys, the stars, leaping out of his way.

Selene is the sister of Helios and Eos, all three born to the Titans – Hyperion and Euryphaessa, the 'One Overhead' and the 'Wide Shining one' – Sun and Moon of the older generation who were themselves children of Gaia, Goddess Mother Earth. The Homeric *Hymn to Selene* continues:

Glistening in heaven from her immortal head,
a radiance encircles Earth,
and from her shining light
great beauty comes.
The air, unlit before, glows
with her golden crown,
and her rays are bright as day,
whenever bright Selene
– once she has washed
her beautiful body
in the waters of Ocean
and gathered her garments that gleam so far,
and yoked together her flashing horses,
their necks high-curving –
she speeds them eagerly on, these horses,
their long manes flowing,
at evening, in the middle of the month,
when her great orb swells to the full,
and her beams appear most brilliant,
as there in heaven she grows and grows.

Fig. 1. Selene, Greek Goddess of the Moon. Selene wears the Moon disc upon her head and reins in her prancing horses at the summit of their journey when the Moon is full. The seven arcs along the edge of the circling border below suggest that the Moon may be rising over the waves. Red-figure cup by the Brygos Painter. Vulci. 490 B.C. Staatliche Museen zu Berlin.

Fig. 2. Helios, the Sun, in his chariot. Selene, the Moon, is on the other side of the vase, with Eos, the Dawn, between them. Red-figure vase painting. c. 440 BC. British Museum.

And so she becomes a pledge,
a sign for human beings...[1]

It was told that once Selene fell in love with Endymion, a shepherd boy. She saw him sleeping at night upon a mountain bank and shone her moonbeams over him and kissed him so completely that now he dreams for ever. When Selene disappears behind a mountain, some say she goes to visit Endymion in a mountain cave, but others say she sweeps him up to Heaven where he can still be seen upon the face of the Moon when she is full.[2]

Endymion, the shepherd,
As his flock he guarded,
She, the Moon, Selene,
Saw him, sought him, loved him,
Came down from Olympos

To the glade on Latmos,
Kissed him, lay beside him.
Evermore he slumbers,
Tossing not nor turning,
Endymion the shepherd.[3]

Theocritus, in the third century BC, wrote this version of the tale that was still being told over two thousand years later in Keats' poem *Endymion*:

What is there in thee, Moon! that thou shouldst move
My heart so potently?"[4]

* * *

Stories of the Moon are universal, appearing all around the Earth from the beginnings of human history. The oldest markings on rock, horn, bone and stone suggest that the Moon may even have been the first recorded story of the human race. For the earliest signs known to have been made by human beings mark the tracks of the wandering Moon as it moved silently through the sky.

The ancient watchers of the night skies saw a being of light which was always changing in a way that was always the same. This was a vision renewed so continually that it must have influenced the way people thought. Over many millennia, the alternating rhythm of light and darkness creates in the mind a pattern which becomes a story endlessly told.

Perpetually moving – from crescent to full to crescent to dark to crescent – the Moon tells one fundamental story: birth, growth, fullness, decay, death and rebirth. It is the story of transformation. Like human beings, the Moon is born out of the dark and grows to the peak of its powers when, unaccountably, like them, it begins to wither and decay – to 'fall away', as the Bushmen say – until it dies, vanishing back into the darkness from whence it came. For three nights the Moon is dead and the sky is black. But on the third day the Moon comes back to life; it rises again: it is a 'New Moon'.

Death was not the end for the Moon; it was a prelude to a new beginning that would end in a new death, in an ever-recurring sequence which began again each time at the beginning. Gradually, this rhythm of births and deaths becomes predictable and an image forms of a cycle which stays in the mind as memory. For the cycle, as the invisible totality, can never be seen in any one moment, so it has to be held in the mind as an image of the whole. All that can be seen are the moving phases, following night after night an unerring pattern. Eventually, early people must have come to see and interpret every part of the cycle from the perspective of the whole.

These two points of reference, the cycle and the phase – the one inward and fixed, the other outward and variant – provide an orientation which makes it possible to set the phases in relation to each other, and in relation to the cycle as a whole. This dual rhythm of constancy and change is the beginning of 'measurement', a word with the same etymological root as 'Moon' in many languages. Once the individual phases can be named, and the differences between them identified, a further distinction becomes available – between what came before and what comes after, between present and past and present and future, which is life in time. For while the course of one day can be traced by the Sun, the earliest reckoning of time longer than a day was possible only through the Moon. So the Moon's story of birth, death and rebirth becomes, in its perpetual repetition, the story of time which is lived by human beings on Earth. The Moon's story is then (at the same time) a human story, a story of human consciousness.

* * *

Western culture for the last three thousand years has been predominantly solar-oriented, so it may come as a surprise to learn that Moon worship preceded Sun worship in most if not all parts of the world, at least until the discovery of agriculture, when the Moon was only very gradually superseded in importance by the Sun. Henri Briffault's monumental three-volume work *The Mothers*, written in 1927, brings evidence from beliefs, customs and folklore of every country to show that, certainly before agriculture, and for a long time afterwards, 'the moon, and not the sun, was the chief object of religious ideas and observances, in so far as these ideas assumed a cosmological form and took account of the heavenly bodies.' Consequently, he continues, 'the subsequent development of the religious conceptions of humanity has been profoundly influenced by the character they bore in these earlier phases.'[5] Recent research on the Palaeolithic and Neolithic eras supports Briffault's argument, suggesting that the Moon's role in the evolution of the human mind was older and more pervasive than anyone had imagined.

LUNAR NOTATIONS

For more than 30,000 years Palaeolithic tools and statues lay scattered in the ground, with no one thinking to look for them or dig them up. Then, in 1879, the cave of Altamira in northern Spain was discovered, with paintings of red bulls on the ceiling, and then the cave of La Pasiega in 1911. A year later, in south-western France, three brothers found a cave they named Les Trois Frères, which had animals engraved over the whole of a wall. There were mammoth, rhinoceros, bison, horse, bear, ass, reindeer, wolverine, musk ox, owls, hares and fish – all the animals of the hunt, often with the darts of the hunt flying into them. Over a hundred decorated caves emerged in the next few decades, culminating in the discovery in 1940 of the magnificent cave of Lascaux in the Dordogne. Its curved walls were covered with astonishingly vivid paintings of animals – enormous dream-like bulls and oxen in stately procession across the cave, with little bulls, horses, oxen and deer scampering between their legs, painted around and on top of them, wherever they could go.

Here, demonstrably, was intelligence of a kind undreamed of in our evolutionary theories of human 'development', and so the search for the remains of what might have to be called 'cultures' began. Excavations took place, mainly in France, Spain and Germany, and countless numbers of 'objects' were lifted from the soil and brought to museums: stones chipped into axe heads, bones with holes cut out of them, delicate ivory figures shaped into animal and human forms, pendants with triangles, spirals, meanders and chevrons etched into them, and many pieces of bone and stone with bewildering lines, strokes and notches scratched across them. Placed in glass-fronted cabinets, these unclassified and supposedly unclassifiable objects lay undisturbed and gathering dust. Authorities remained chronically undecided as to whether the lines on the artefacts were random Palaeolithic attempts at making their mark (doodling in a rare moment of leisure), or the incisions of Nature made over the millennia of human neglect.

Into these dusky halls came, one day in 1965, Alexander Marshack, armed with a child's microscope and a question:

> Could the marks, scratches, sequences, and signs of the Ice Age be...notational and, therefore, in one way or another, time-factored and time-factoring devices? If so, dare we assume that we could either 'read' or interpret them?[6]

In his book *The Roots of Civilization*, Marshack describes how he broke the code. In the Musée des

Antiquités Nationales outside Paris, he found a small, flat, ovoid piece of bone, pockmarked with strokes and notches, about 11cm (41/2in) long. The bone was just the right size to be held in the palm of one hand while being engraved by a flint tool held in the other. It came from the Abri Blanchard in the Dordogne, a rock shelter where stones had been engraved with triangular shapes resembling the female vulva, very like many other vulva forms found as far east as Czechoslovakia. This piece of bone had lain, 50 years before, in the same layer of soil as stone blocks painted with two oxen, all dating from the Aurignacian period (c.25,000 BC), and all made by early 'Cro-Magnon Man'.

After painstaking analysis of the notches, and by comparing these to other and later pieces, Marshack realized that he was in the presence of a purposely arranged pattern. This was no ornament or decoration but a carefully designed image, which must have been held in the mind before the sculptor set to work and sustained until the work was done. The final image must, then, have had a meaning, and the meaning must have been known before the work was begun. The bone was structured as a serpentine figure composed of 69 marks, with some 24 changes of stroke, which wound back and forth like a serpent, and – could it be? – also like the turning of the Moon in its waxing and waning. Was Aurignacian Man thinking like Marshack (or was Marshack behaving like a Cro-Magnon)? On closer examination, the differently shaped notches revealed themselves to be similar to crescents and circles, some filled in and others not, as though they were signs for phases of the Moon:

> If this were lunar, the days of invisibility fell at the right, at a point of turning, and the full moon periods fell at the left, at a point of turning, while the half-moons (our 'quarter-moon') all fell in mid-figure. If lunar, we had a visual, kinesthetic, and symbolic representation of the waxing and waning which at any point indicated to the maker where in the lunar month he was, and it did this non-arithmetically. When the maker had finished his notation, the full serpentine figure represented two months or 'moons'.[7]

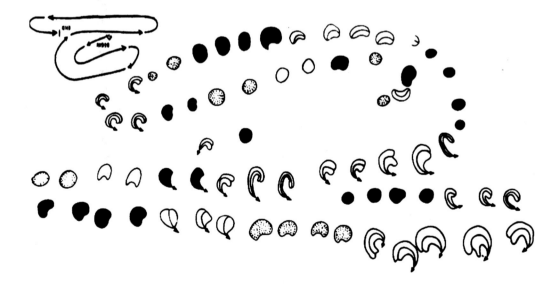

Fig. 3. *Schematic rendering of the engraved marks on the bone from Abri Blanchard as determined by microscopic analysis, indicating the differences in the engraving points and the strokes structuring the serpentine form. c. 25,000 BC. (From Alexander Marshack, The Roots of Civilization, p.48)*

Subsequent finds confirmed his interpretation. It became clear that this system of notation was already evolved, complex and sophisticated, and was being used by other types of *homo sapiens*, such as Combe Capelle Man of the East Gravettian culture in Czechoslovakia and Russia, as well as by other peoples in Italy and Spain. This tradition, Marshack argued, must have been thousands of years old by this point, and appears to be so widespread that the question arises whether its beginnings may not go back to the age of Neanderthal people, who even then buried their dead curled towards the east and sometimes covered them with flowers.[8]

Marshack proposed that civilization took root from these original recordings of the Moon. For these lunar notations were cognitive acts, resting on, and in turn fostering, an understanding of time on which rational thinking depends. They must have laid the foundations for the evolution of all other 'time-factored' modes of thought: astronomy, agriculture, mathematics, writing and the calendar. These achievements would not then have 'suddenly' burst into existence in the Bronze Age, as had previously been assumed, but would have been gestating over immense periods of time.[9]

But what would these turnings of the Moon mean to the people who notched them down, standing at the openings of their caves and looking up, night after night? From this fixed position it would become clear that particular events invariably occurred in the same place in the sky. As Marshack explains:

> The last crescent, sunrise and the rise of the full moon were primary events towards the east; the first crescent and the sunset were primary events towards the west, and here the full moon also sank; when half-moons were highest in the sky, they marked the time of sunset and sunrise....The primary observational dramas were the lunar phases, their general direction of origin and disappearance, and the general westward motion of the moon in the sky.[10]

* * *

The first differentiation it is possible to imagine in the minds of the earliest people is that between light and darkness. The merging of light and dark in dawn and dusk – out of which light *or* dark finally comes – leads the mind to formulate the categories of day and night. The physicist David Bohm has explained how consciousness tends to freeze the continuum of life into concepts and abstractions, replacing the whole with fragmented parts, and flux with stasis (which, expressed grammatically, is to turn verbs into nouns).[11] This predisposes alternating states to be perceived as oppositions, such that where the one is, the other is not. Yet these are 'opposites' more in name than in fact for they complement each other, the one giving way to the other and the other to the one in a continual rhythm which structures the cosmos, if only because the cosmos cannot be imagined without it. The Greek term *cosmos* referred to the universe as an 'ordered whole', though we might refer it rather to the structure of human perception on which the ordering of the whole depends.

Light and darkness were from the beginning mythic realities – full of what would later be called symbolic reference and metaphoric implication, but at the time simply charged with numinous presence. They were never originally the bare descriptive terms they have since become. Even now they continue to structure the popular imagery of modern ethical discourse: in the west, mourners and villains are dressed in black; babies and brides in white. How much closer, then, to the ancient imagination must have been the distinct beings of Sun and Moon, moving through the skies in regular patterns of convergence and divergence, inviting universal speculation as to their meaning.

(*Because the Moon orbits the Earth, it appears to slip eastward from the Sun each day, with the distance between them increasing until Full Moon. After this, the eastward shift brings the Moon back towards the Sun until New Moon when, astronomically, they are in 'conjunction'. The Moon is then between Sun and Earth, and so cannot be seen from Earth.)*

Following the primary perception of light and darkness, the Sun and Moon are the two great structuring principles of human thought. Looking up from Earth, the two orbs of light – one the eye of day and the other the eye of night – present an immediate contrast, for each appears to be the death of the other. And each has a different relation to darkness. The Sun is inimical to darkness, which flees as the Sun advances, while the Moon holds light and dark continually in play. The light of the Sun is forever brilliant; though always in motion, its form never changes. The light of the Moon waxes and wanes as the dark of the Moon wanes and waxes. Darkness inhabits the Moon; it is one of the modes of the Moon's divinity, and out of the darkness comes light. But darkness is the adversary of the Sun, opposed to divinity: it is all that the Sun is not. It shadows the Sun in the evening, floods the sky as the Sun sets, and rules the night when the Sun is gone. The Sun journeys into the night-world and is engulfed by darkness, but by morning the darkness has been vanquished by the Sun.

Inevitably, Sun and Moon were seen in relationship to each other, and that relationship was interpreted on the human model. Were they husband and wife, brother and sister, two brothers, two sisters, mother or father and child? When they moved apart had they offended each other? Was one fleeing and the other in pursuit? Did Sun hunt Moon at the Full, wound and dismember Moon piece by piece, or did Moon suffer a lingering sickness, or receive a punishment for doing wrong? When Sun and Moon came together and Moon disappeared, was Moon dead, or concealed in the embrace of a now-loving Sun? The lives attributed to these celestial beings characteristically dramatize the often troubled relations of the human families dwelling beneath them. Indeed, the multiplicity of interpretation brings to mind Tolstoy's opening in *Anna Karenina* that 'All happy families resemble one another, but each unhappy family is unhappy in its own way.'[12]

Although the Moon is sometimes visible during the day, the Moon was generally named as ruler of the night, in contrast to the Sun as ruler of the day. Psalm 121 says: 'The sun shall not smite thee by day, nor the moon by night.'[13] A fundamental polarity is thus set up between Sun and Moon such that their differences are magnified and, by the same token, their reunion longed for as a reconciliation of cosmic principles, so that all that is separate and alone shall be healed and made whole.

Even though the Sun ruled the day, it was not universally felt to be the cause of light. Since creation myths typically dramatize the stages of human awareness, light was often created before the Sun, as, for instance, in Mesopotamia and the Old Testament. In Genesis, Yahweh creates Day and Night on the first day, after dividing the light from the darkness: 'And God called the light Day, and the darkness he called Night.' But only on the fourth day does he create Sun and Moon: 'And God made two great lights; the greater light to rule the day, and the lesser light to rule the night.'[14] For day appears to be 'there' before the Sun, just as night is 'there' before the Moon; but the Moon comes when it is needed, lighting up the night and letting us see in the dark.

A story about the Sufi 'trickster-sage' Nasrudin, whose attempts to think objectively are designed to mirror our own, may comment:

Nasrudin entered the teahouse and declaimed:
'The Moon is more useful than the Sun.'
'Why, Mulla?'
'We need the light more during the night than during the day.'[15]

Erich Neumann, in *The Great Mother*, explains that 'because of its contrast with the darkness, the light side of the moon and of the stars makes a far deeper impression on man than do the daylight and the sun. For this reason the moon is experienced as forming a totality with the background against which it stands out.'[16] The Moon also stands out as the one who changes over time yet whose changing can be predicted. The Sun's birth and death take place in one day, but for more than one day at a time – for planning ahead – you have to have the Moon, and not just one but two and more.

* * *

The Blanchard bone tracks the course of two Moons, a series of two waxings and wanings, and two periods of darkness or invisibility. Two Moons may have been required to indicate that the first Moon who died was reborn as the second Moon, and also to be assured that the course of both Moons was the same. We are used to thinking of time in astronomical terms, calculating in units from one hour, day, month or year to the next. This requires abstracting from the experience in which the time is lived – 'counting' time. By contrast, measuring the passing of days by the phases of the Moon, and measuring the Moons by the passing of more Moons, means that the idea of 'time' was originally rhythmical, cyclical and concrete: it waxed and it waned. Time was then inseparable from the phases of the Moon's story, and from the way each phase of the Moon's story was experienced as the human story. This means that time was once not a matter of quantity but of quality, not an abstraction but the very structure of life – 'once upon a time'.

About five thousand years or so after the 'inscription' was made on the Blanchard bone, a horn of a bison, crescent-shaped like the Moon, was placed in the hand of a woman, also in the Dordogne, France, in the valley of Laussel, near les Eyzies, just a few kilometres from Lascaux. On a ledge overhanging a high rock shelter with a sheer drop down to the ground, the figure of a reclining woman once soared up out of pink limestone rock. Palaeolithic sculptors had chiselled her with tools of flint out of the soft limestone and sprinkled her with red ochre, the colour of blood.

She is 43cm (17in) high, and was accompanied by other female figures and animals – a horse, a hind and a carnivore – as well as a male figure raising his arm, naked except for his belt. In her right hand she holds up the crescent horn of the bison, which is clearly inscribed with 13 downward strokes; her left hand rests lightly on her swelling belly, which, sloping towards the valley, would have commanded the whole landscape.[17] Her head, distinctly shaped but without features, inclines to the right towards the crescent-shaped horn, as though contemplating the mystery held in the hollow of her hand, to which her other hand also bears witness. The eye of the beholder, following her gaze, is drawn first to the notched horn, so expressively raised, then back to her face for guidance and, finding none, is led down through her arm to her left hand, lying, almost pointing, to her pregnant womb, fingers similarly notched and poignantly separated. The delicately carved vulva and legs seem to slope away, back into the rock from which they came.

Marshack's work suggests that the 13 strokes upon the crescent horn are unlikely to be random. Thirteen is the number of days from the first crescent to just before the days of the Full Moon – the period of waxing; 13 is also the number of cycles that may make up an observational lunar year (a solar year of 365 days measured by the number of Moons). Through the movement of the sculpture and echoing of the motif of notched strokes on the horn and the hand, the artist creates a relationship between the growing of light in the Moon, the growing of the child in the womb, and also perhaps, from the placing of the sculpture as the summit of the landscape, the growing of vegetation in the womb of Earth. Whether this compelling figure is the Great Goddess as Mother of All or the Moon Goddess as Mother of Life, or whether she is the woman whose cycles of fertility are governed by the

Fig. 4. Goddess of Laussel. Limestone bas-relief from Laussel. Height 43cm (17 in.). Dordogne, France. Upper Perigordian. c. 22–18,000 BC. Museé d'Aquitaine, Bordeaux.

Moon, an essential accord between Moon and Earth is proposed and celebrated. As Mother Goddess Moon, pregnant with the world in her waxing mode, she discloses the laws of fertility and growth as cyclical in her own image. As woman, she acknowledges the lunar law on Earth. A more eloquent testimony to the unity of the celestial and earthly orders would be hard to find: 'As above, so below' – as it was elegantly phrased in the Emerald Tablets of Hermes Trismegistos, 20,000 years later.[18]

Campbell, commenting on this sculpture, draws past and present together:

> The phases of the moon were the same for Old Stone Age man as they are for us; so also were the processes of the womb. It may therefore be that the initial observation that gave birth in the mind of man to a mythology of one mystery informing earthly and celestial things was the recognition of an accord between these two 'time-factored' orders: the celestial order of the waxing moon and the earthly order of the womb.[19]

THE MOON AND LIVING TIME

> 'And so from hour to hour, we ripe and ripe,
> And then from hour to hour, we rot and rot;
> And thereby hangs a tale.'[20]

What a later age would distinguish as two separate tales – the Moon making time measurable and the Moon making the growing and diminishing of things in an infinite rhythm – was to an earlier age one comprehensive story of life in time. Mircea Eliade, the great historian of comparative religions, has called it 'living time': time expressed as the rhythms of life.[21] This is the world of Nature, the life-in-time in which all created beings grow and diminish, wax and wane. Eliade shows how the initial perception expands continually until it has become a whole world view:

> Time as governed and measured by the phases of the moon might be called 'living' time. It is bound up with the reality of life and nature, rain and the tides, the time of sowing, the menstrual cycle. A whole series of phenomena belonging to totally different 'cosmic levels' are ordered according to the rhythms of the moon or are under their influence. The 'primitive mind', once having grasped the 'powers' of the moon, then establishes connections of response and even interchange between the moon and those phenomena. Thus, for instance, from the earliest times, certainly since the Neolithic Age, with the discovery of agriculture, the same symbolism has linked together the moon, the sea waters, rain, the fertility of women and of animals, plant life, man's destiny after death and the ceremonies of initiation. The mental syntheses made possible by the realization of the moon's rhythms connect and unify very varied realities; their structural symmetries and the analogies in their workings could never have been seen had not 'primitive' man intuitively perceived the moon's law of periodic change, as he did very early on.[22]

This important passage helps to explain one of the most striking things about what we might call lunar symbolism, but which early people obviously saw as epiphanies of the Moon. Revealed in so many different phenomena, the Moon fosters a vision of the universe as a coherent pattern of relationships, all informed by the same laws which act upon each thing in a similar way. This sets up a system of analogies and correspondences between all levels of life, both visible and invisible. For though the Moon divides and orders temporal phenomena through its distinctive phases, it also unifies them in the larger perspective of its revolving cycles, and this creates reverberations, echoes and harmonies between one part of the whole and another – just as though the universe were one great cosmic web of relationship (as, indeed, modern sub-atomic physics now claims it is).[23] In 'lunar thinking', then, there can be no part without the whole.

Because the Moon, returning to its own beginning, created a cycle, so, analogously, it became the ruler of everything else that was cyclical – the ebb and flow of seas, the nightly dews, the seasonal rains, the flux of rivers and tides of blood. These are the essential waters of life that come and go – in a day, a month, a year and a lifetime. As the cycle of the Moon appeared to correspond so precisely to the monthly rhythms of the wombs of women, it is most likely that women, calculating the timing of their menstrual cycles from Moon to Moon, made the first reckoning of time. Since the timing of birth could also be calculated by the Moon (as ten Moons of 28 days), so the Moon was assumed to govern their phases of fertility and infertility, and, by extension, the creative cycles in all living beings. The Moon was regarded as the primary source of fertility on Earth: the increase and decrease of animals and plants, and all the milk, semen, sap and moisture of growth. As with humans and animals, so with plants: the Moon was the origin of the rhythmic rising and falling of the sap, the seasons of sowing and reaping, the power of growing that came and went in a lunar rhythm.

We might wonder why the source of generation was sought so far away, when all around the Earth

Fig. 5. Phases of the Moon.

was bringing forth life out of itself, or, to speak in the original language, when Mother Earth was bringing forth life out of Herself, out of her inexhaustible womb. One answer is that the Moon was not originally experienced as far away, removed from Earth, but rather as an extension of Earth, a celestial Earth in Heaven. Not so different, as it happens, from Giuseppe Ungaretti's poem, written in the 1960s, after the Moon had shown us Earth:

> What are you doing, Earth, in heaven?
> Tell me, what are you doing, Silent Earth?[24]

In many early cultures, Moon and Earth were believed to be composed of the same substance, such that the Earth Mother and the Moon Mother were alike expressions of the Great Mother Goddess. As the nineteenth-century philosopher of history Bachofen wrote in his book *Motherright*: 'All Earth Mothers lead a double life, as Earth and as Moon.'[25] Earth goddesses were Moon goddesses, and Moon gods were also forms of the Great Mother, either as sons or as consorts, and often both. As Neumann says: 'Everywhere the Great Mother is connected with the duality of moon and earth, and the secret of the earth's fecundation is bound up with the moon and its dismemberment: here the moon is the fructifying as well as the dismembered son.'[26] Even when Moon gods appeared to act autonomously, they did not replace or supplant Mother Earth, as did the later gods of Sun, Wind and Storm, and those still later gods without image or name who transcended Earth and all that therein is. The waxing and waning rhythms of the Moon are easier to isolate and identify than their earthly counterparts spread out across the seasons as summer and winter – the more diffuse and longer-lasting patterns of 'broad-backed' Earth. So it may have been the Moon which first captured and provoked the imaginations of human beings, offering them a habitation in which to explore their own life on Earth and to give that life a name.

* * *

Early human beings saw their own lives reflected in the life of the Moon. The drama of the Moon was the human drama magnified, given dignity and solemnity, and brought into the cosmic drama of all creation. It was different with the Sun. While the Sun was believed to die in the west and be reborn in the east, it was in a sense as unchanged in its dying as in its re-arising. Though it travelled through the black ocean of the underworld, and later fought and overcame the terrible demon of darkness, it did not lose its colour or shape or part of its light, it did not grow old. The Moon, by contrast, suffered painfully the gradual but relentless loss of its own body of light. Just as it had reached its culmination at the full, its shape diminished, its light dimmed, first imperceptibly and then irrevocably, until it was nothing at all, 'mere oblivion': '*Sans* teeth, *sans* eyes, *sans* taste, *sans* everything.'[27] Waning was like ageing. The Moon was like humanity, both caught in the universal law of becoming which ends in death. Tragedy was the fate of the human *and* the lunar condition.

Yet the Moon was also *not* like humanity: it transformed the story of death into a story of rebirth. It brought forth a new Moon. In its perpetual return to its own beginnings, the Moon unified what was broken asunder, and so the Moon held out a promise that death was not final, only a change of form. Death was followed by life as dark was followed by light. Indeed, light came out of darkness, as though the darkness itself had given birth to the light. In this way, duality, made visible as the waxing and waning of the Moon, was both embodied and transcended in the ever-recurring cycle. Analogously, perhaps, life and death might not have to be experienced as opposites, but could be seen as phases succeeding each other in an infinite rhythm. Thus the Moon became an image both of the flux of time and a timeless totality, an image of time and eternity together. It appeared, in its acts of measuring, to create time, and then, month by month, to redeem it.

If the Moon's initial story of being born, growing and dying serves to distinguish the stages of one life-cycle, its complete story, which requires two 'Moons' (one to go and the other to come back) reveals a reality that appears to be greater than time. The paradox arises that, by dying, the Moon is reborn; by going away, it eternally returns, 'time and again'. So if with the awareness of time came the longing for eternity, then the Moon would seem to answer the need it originally provoked. For, in a sense, time *and* eternity come into being together through the Moon. 'May the gods accord me a life renewed each month, like that of the Moon,' it was said in Babylon.[28]

This idea, of the rebirth of life out of death, presses the mind to further reflection, for, in the natural world of the senses, death is everywhere the ending of life and nowhere its beginning. In Oswald Spengler's book *The Decline of the West*, he confronts this paradox:

> We *are* Time, but we *possess* also an image of history and in this image death, and with death birth, appear as the two riddles ... the higher thought originates as meditation upon death. Every religion, every scientific investigation, every philosophy, proceeds from it ... And thus the essence of every genuine–*unconscious and inwardly necessary*–symbolism proceeds from the knowledge of death...[29]

If, as Spengler proposes, we '*are* time', and, as early human beings, identified ourselves with the Moon's temporal rhythm of growing and diminishing, then for our image of history we would look to the Moon's cyclical return. For this alone presents an image of death and birth in one vision, and so offers a perspective on time which consumes what it has brought forth – 'Devouring Time', as Shakespeare calls it in the Sonnets.[30] Eliade observes that:

> It was very probably the image of the eternal birth and death of the moon which helped to crystallize the earliest human intuitions about the alternations of Life and Death, and...the myth of the periodic creation and destruction of the world.[31]

The perspective afforded by the Moon's 'eternal return' is that the death of the individual or of a culture is temporary, and it may even be *necessary* because it is followed invariably by a rebirth. For it is undeniable that the forms of time wear out, break down and grow old; if they are allowed to dissolve into the eternal, to be absorbed back into the primordial unity, they may re-emerge, like the returning crescent, 'good as new'. If they did not die (such reasoning goes), they could not be regenerated. The idea of archaic apocalypses, such as flood or deluge, where the old is obliterated to make way for the new, can be traced to the lunar model of cyclical renewal which gives meaning to catastrophe. In the case of an exhausted or sinful humanity, the deluge is never total (if it had been, how would we know?) Someone always survives – either a lunar animal, like the Maori frog, or a mythical ancestor, like the Hindu Manu, the Sumerian Utnapishtim or the biblical Noah – and a new, revitalized humanity is born from the survivors. It is an optimistic vision because, just as the disappearance of the Moon is not final, so the disappearance of human beings is not final either, neither individually nor as a race: they have a history beyond time.[32]

The most complex and challenging story of the Moon, then, is the story of death and resurrection.

THE DESCENT OF INANNA

The earliest known written myth of the Moon's death and rebirth is the Sumerian poem called *The Descent of Inanna*. Recorded about 1750 BC, it was probably recited or sung for at least a thousand years before that. It tells how the Bright Moon descended into the 'Great Below' and became the Dark Moon: how the Moon died and rose again, and ascended into the 'Great Above'.

Many images converge on the goddess Inanna, who is many things to many people, mostly at the same time. In a religion of immanence, divinity appears whenever life calls out with a peculiar intensity, in the way that 'Zeus', for instance, began as a cry – 'it lightens' – and only later became god of light.[33] (Grammatically speaking, we might say that divinity arises as a verb and only becomes a noun when it has gone).

In the story of Inanna's Descent, she is named as the First Daughter of the Moon god, Nanna, and his wife, Ningal, goddess of the marshes. It happened like this.

In the beginning Nammu, goddess of the primordial sea, brought forth the cosmic mountain An-Ki, Heaven-Earth. An-Ki gave birth to Enlil, Air, who came between Heaven-Earth, making space to breathe for the creation that was to come. An became the Heavens and Ki became the Earth. Then Enlil 'carried off' Earth, the son becoming the consort of his mother, the original son-lover. So Earth, Ki (later called Ninhursag), uniting with Air, became 'Mother of all living'. It was Enlil's second union with Ninlil, Lady Air, which brought forth Nanna, the Moon, and then Nanna's marriage to Ningal which brought forth Inanna, daughter of the Moon, who was also the Evening Star and the Morning Star, and the bright star Sirius.

Other hymns to Inanna celebrate her as the Great Mother Goddess, Queen of Heaven and Earth. The Heavens, she says, are 'set as a crown upon my head' and the Earth 'as sandals on my feet'.[34] As Queen of Heaven, she is the Moon:

> the pure torch that flares in the sky,
> the heavenly light, shining bright like the day.[35]

'Crowned with great horns', she 'flares' in the sky at night. We are to imagine the goddess as the heavens, with the horns of the Crescent Moon as a crown upon her head, the zodiac wound around her body as a girdle and the rainbow strung across the sky as her necklace:

> She made the night come forth like moonlight,
> She made the morning come forth like the bright daylight.[36]

She holds the *me*, the Tablets of the Law, embodying the cosmic order:

Fig. 6. Inanna as Queen of Heaven and Earth, wearing the lunar crescent within her horned crown and holding a cluster of dates, with thick rays flashing from her back like stalks of corn. Fragment of a basalt relief inscribed to Entemena of Lagash, Mesopotamia. Early Dynastic period. c. 2400 BC. Staatliche Museen zu Berlin.

> Begetting Mother am I, within the Spirit I abide
> and none see me.[37]

She is the rain and the power that makes the plants grow:

> I step on to the heavens, and the rain rains down;
> I step on to the earth, and grass and herbs sprout up.[38]

In these images – fragments of other poems – Inanna alone is the Moon, and she was to take over much of her father Nanna's worship. But in the earlier poem *The Descent of Inanna*, Inanna is drawn as one of three children of the Moon god, Nanna, and Ningal, goddess of the marshes; her brother is Utu, god of the Sun, and her sister is Ereshkigal, goddess of the Underworld. Inanna has as her consort the shepherd Dumuzi, the 'Lord of Life', 'Lord of the Flood', the 'Wild Bull', the 'Green One'. Inanna calls him:

> My lord, the honey-man of the gods...
> his hand is honey his foot is honey,
> he sweetens me always.[39]

In one of the poems of their love for each other, Inanna opens her door to Dumuzi:

> Like a moonbeam she came forth to him

> Out of the house,
> He looked at her, rejoiced in her,
> Took her in his arms and kissed her.[40]

Inanna compares the 'untilled plot' of her love to her 'crescent-shaped "Barge of Heaven"... full of loveliness like the new moon.'[41] When Dumuzi becomes her ploughman, new life is awakened through all nature:

> The king's loins! At its mighty rising
> did the vines rise up, did the grains rise up,
> did the desert fill (with verdure)
> like a pleasurable garden.[42]

This is life before death came into the world. But Inanna decides to visit the *Kur*, the Nether World, the place of the dead. It was on the day that the 'Bull of Heaven' died – he who was husband to her sister Ereshkigal – that Inanna, Queen of the 'Great Above', went down to attend his funeral in the 'Great Below' where her dark sister was Queen:

> From the Great Above Inanna opened her ear to the Great Below...
> My lady abandoned heaven and earth to descend to the underworld.[43]

Before she goes, she clothes herself in the seven bright 'jewels' of Heaven – crown, lapis beads, double beads, breastplate, gold ring, lapis measuring rod and line, and the royal robe. But she also takes care that she will come back: she asks her companion, Ninshubur – whose name means 'Queen of the East' – to lament at the houses of the gods if she does not return.

Inanna arrives at the outer gates of the underworld and knocks loudly. Neti, the gatekeeper, asks her who she is. Inanna answers:

> I am Inanna, Queen of Heaven, on my way to the East.[44]

Neti brings the news to Ereshkigal.

> When Ereshkigal heard this,
> She slapped her thigh and bit her lip...
> Then she spoke:
> Bolt the seven gates of the underworld.
> Then, one by one, open each gate a crack.
> Let Inanna enter.
> As she enters, remove her royal garments.[45]

In the image of the Waning Moon slowly losing its light to the dark, Inanna is successively stripped of her seven jewels, one at each gate, until she enters the throne room of the underworld, naked.

> Then Ereshkigal fastened on Inanna the eye of death...
> She struck her.
> Inanna was turned into a corpse,

A piece of rotting meat,
And was hung from a hook on the wall.[46]

After three days and three nights – the time of darkness when the Moon is gone – Inanna has still not returned, so Ninshubur goes to Enlil, god of Air, then to Nanna, Inanna's father, god of the Moon (neither of whom will help), and finally to Enki, the wise god of the Deep Waters. From the dirt beneath his fingernails, Enki makes two creatures, called the *galatur*; to one he gives the water of life and to the other the food of life. Enki tells them:

Go to the underworld, Enter the door like flies,
Ereshkigal, the Queen of the Underworld, is moaning
With the cries of a woman about to give birth...
When she cries 'Oh! Oh! My inside!'
Cry also, 'Oh! Oh! Your inside'...
The Queen will be pleased.
She will offer you a gift.
Ask her only for the corpse that hangs from the hook on the wall.
One of you will sprinkle the food of life on it.
The other will sprinkle the water of life.
Inanna will arise.[47]

It happens as Enki had foreseen. Ereshkigal gives them the corpse of Inanna and they sprinkle the water and food of life over it. Then Inanna arises. But as she is about to leave, the judges of the underworld seize her. They say:

No one ascends from the underworld unmarked.
If Inanna wishes to return from the underworld,
She must provide someone in her place.[48]

The underworld demons, the *galla*, first see Ninshubur, but Inanna refuses. Next they see her son, and then her other son, but she refuses again. Then they see her husband, Dumuzi, seated by the apple tree, 'dressed in his shining *me* garments', and this time she does not refuse:

The galla seized him by his thighs.
They poured milk out of his seven churns.
They broke the reed pipe which the shepherd was playing.
Inanna fastened on Dumuzi the eye of death.[49]

The *galla* drag Dumuzi down to the Great Below. But Dumuzi's sister, Geshtinanna, offers to share his time below with him, so each year he may rise again to Earth and be with Inanna, his love. When, for six months of the year, Inanna mourns the loss of her husband – he who was both the 'Bright-eyed Moon' and the 'Green One' – so the bare land mourns after the harvesting of the crops and the approach of winter. But when the new grain begins to sprout, and the vine and date and apple tree show their buds, it is Dumuzi who at last returns to his love.

Fig. 7. Inanna standing naked in the Underworld, with Nanna-Sin on her left with crescent Moon. Mesopotamian cylinder seal. (From Ward, The Seal Cylinders of Western Asia, p. 211).

* * *

In the Babylonian story, directly inherited from the Sumerian, Inanna was called Ishtar and Dumuzi was called Tammuz (and the two goddesses and gods are often allied as 'Inanna-Ishtar' and Dumuzi-Tammuz). In the later tale, Tammuz takes the place of the Moon Bull, husband of Ereshkigal, as the death that calls the Moon down into the dark. When Tammuz lies dead in the underworld, the upperworld also dies, and the people cry for the death of nature and humanity alike:

> The wailing is for the plants, they grow not;
> For the houses and for the flocks; they produce not...
> The wailing is for the forests; the tamarisks grow not...
> The wailing is for the palace; life unto old age is not.[50]

Ishtar descends to the underworld to awaken Tammuz from the sleep of death, for he had been pierced by the tusks of a wild boar. While she hangs naked for three days and nights, all life in the upperworld is suspended, as though under a spell, until she herself is awakened and has restored to her in seven stages the luminous apparel of the Queen of Heaven. The pattern of this myth is found in many later tales of the interweaving of death and life: Isis and Osiris, Demeter and Persephone, Kybele and Attis, Aphrodite and Adonis (also killed by a wild boar), and even the Sleeping Beauty of the European fairy tale.

* * *

Initially, Inanna's drama enacts the changing phases of the Moon, from maiden (crescent) to woman (full) to waning (unveiling in the 'Great Below') to dark (the three nights when she hangs as a corpse) to returning crescent (when she ascends, reborn, to the 'Great Above'). Her descent, which makes her invisible in the upperworld, makes her visible, imaginatively, in the underworld, giving to the invisible world substance and form, and bringing upper and lower worlds closer together in the mind. But once Inanna has been reborn, and the round begins again, a distinction opens up between phases and cycle, between what we see in the sky and what we have to hold in the mind to make sense of what we see, and do not see. Then the original story seeds a further story: Inanna becomes the Moon in its cycle and Dumuzi becomes the Moon in its phases: he is her son in the crescent, her lover in the full, and the one who dies for her in the waning, in order that she, as the source, may live for ever.

It is the knowledge of the cycle as a whole that names the three days' dark as a fourth phase and not just a void, an absence of light. This fourth phase is embodied in the figure of Ereshkigal who, as Inanna's elder sister, is given as the darkness that was there before the light. Yet Ereshkigal is found giving birth when the rescuers arrive, as though Inanna is to be reborn out of the body of the one into

Fig. 8. The horned goddess, holding grain, receiving the horned grain god with grain sprouting from him. Mesopotamian cylinder seal. c. 2300-2000 BC. (From Ward, The Seal Cylinders of Western Asia, p. 134).

whom she died, in the same paradoxical way that the Dark Moon seems to give birth to the new crescent of light. The dark phase of the Moon may have been understood as the invisible dimension that was the source of the visible – where new life was gestated in the womb of the old – out of which the Old Moon was reborn as the New Moon. So Inanna's descent to the realm of her sister, which makes a link between the Great Above and the Great Below, reunites the two aspects of the one lunar goddess – the realms of dark and light, death and birth – in a single vision.

* * *

It is possible that the capacity for abstract thought was provoked by an interpretation of the Moon's phases as four instead of three. The three visible phases require a fourth invisible phase to lead round again to the beginning in order to complete the cycle and start again. When the dark phase of the Moon is included as the invisible part of the continuing cycle, the Moon has to be thought, not seen: it becomes an idea, not an immediate object of sense. In the language of myth, both Inanna and her sister Ereshkigal are called Queen of the Underworld, but in that underworld the light-world sister Inanna, the Bright Moon, is a corpse not a queen, and the life-principle of the continuing cycle is held *in potentia* by the dark sister, Ereshkigal, the Dark Moon, the only one who can live in the underworld. In the light-world above, Ereshkigal was once a goddess of grain but now lives in the dark as the stage of gestation when the seed of last year's fruit is being transformed into next year's shoot.

This idea – of the transformation of dark into light and death into life – was also explored in the later Greek myth of Demeter and Persephone. Demeter was goddess of the harvest, and her daughter Persephone was the fruit cut from the stem, whose seed falls into the Earth and is lost to light and life. Persephone, who was also called *Kore* – a word which means both 'maiden' and 'shoot' – must live in the underworld for three months of the 'turning year'. The maiden who is seized into the underworld and the seed that is buried beneath the soil, both die and wait for the time of rebirth – the return of *Kore* above the Earth which changes winter into spring.

Given the prevalence of the lunar cross in Neolithic pottery designs, it is likely that the division of the agricultural year into four seasons followed the fourfold division of the cycle of the Moon – Waxing (Spring), Full (Summer), Waning (Autumn) and Dark Moon (Winter).[51] For the construction of a fourth stage to the cycle of the Moon releases the mind from a dependence on the senses, providing a framework of comprehension which allows the Moon to rise again, the year to turn, and the grain to grow.

Fig. 9. Dumuzi rejuvenated on the knees of Ishtar. Mesopotamian cylinder seal. c. 2300–2000BC. The Louvre.

ZOE AND BIOS

Many myths of the Moon are structured on the distinction between the phases and the cycle, which is also the distinction between the parts and the whole. Yet the etymology of the word 'phase', which comes from the Greek *phaino*, 'to show', suggests that the primary distinction is that between the invisible cycle and the visible phase through which the cycle is manifested. This essential paradox, which leads the mind beyond the frame of the senses, is that the cycle, the whole, is invisible yet contains the visible phases, as though the visible comes out of and falls back into the invisible – like being born and dying and being born again.

The rituals surrounding Dionysos, the Greek god of wine, required for their understanding a similar distinction so that life could be conceived in two ways simultaneously: as an eternal whole and a finite part. The Greeks had two words for 'life:' *zoe* (which gives 'zoology') and *bios* (which gives 'biology' and 'biography'). *Zoe* was the word for infinite and generic, non-characterized, life; *bios* referred to specific, individual and finite life. *Zoe* is eternal 'being' that cannot die. *Bios* is the visible manifestation of this eternal life in time which lives and dies. The classicist Carl Kerenyi explains: '*Zoe* is the thread upon which every individual *bios* is strung like a bead, and which, in contrast to *bios*, can be conceived of only as endless.'[52] *Zoe* contains *bios*, as the whole contains the part, but *bios* cannot contain *zoe*, as the part cannot contain the whole, and so cannot expect to understand it. Kerenyi continues:

> A Greek definition of *zoe* is *chronos tou einai*, 'time of being', but not in the sense of an empty time into which the living creature enters and in which it remains until it dies. No, this 'time of being' is to be taken as a continuous being which is framed in a *bios* as long as this *bios* endures – then it is termed '*zoe* of *bios*' – or from which *bios* is removed like a part and assigned to one being or another. The part may be called '*bios* of *zoe*'.[53]

Lest it be thought that these are refinements of language alone, Kerenyi emphasizes that 'the fact that *zoe* and *bios* do not have the same "resonance", and that "*bios* of *zoe*" and "*zoe* of *bios*" are not tautologies, is the linguistic expression of a very definite experience.' Plotinos was able to call *zoe* the 'time of the soul', during which the soul moves on from one bios to another as it is reborn, precisely because this experience was already registered in the Greek language.[54]

For Plato, the soul, *psyche*, could be identified with *zoe*, and so was immortal.[55] *Zoe* is symbolized in the spiral, which, unending and uninterrrupted, permeates all things, as well as in the snakes who regenerate themselves, and also in those myths which show flowering in decay and fermentation, indestructibility in the midst of destruction.[56] In the ceremonial drinking of wine at the festivals of Dionysos, the celebrants believed they were participating in the *zoe* of the god.[57]

Dionysos was himself in nature and origin once a Moon god, as the dismemberment of his body into 14 pieces and his 'second' birth would imply.[58] So it is no coincidence that the Greek terms which belonged to his cult may illuminate the Moon's own dual 'life', and are given dramatic form through the stories of its death and resurrection. For *zoe* is an image of the cycle, and *bios* an image of the individual phases: *bios* is born from *zoe*, dies back into *zoe* and is reborn from *zoe*, as the phases follow each other in the pattern of the cycle. The eternal Moon enters into time but also transcends time, and so may be thought to *transform* time. In this way, in one of the Moon's many metaphors, time is woven with the thread of eternity and so reconciles humanity to death.

This idea underlies many of the Moon's tales, but was most profoundly explored in the west in the great Bronze Age lunar myth of the Mother Goddess and her child.[59] The Great Mother Goddess is an image of *zoe*, the eternal cycle of the whole, imagined as Heaven, Earth and Underworld, and made visible in the perpetual cycles of Moon and Earth. Her son or daughter is an image of *bios*, her mortal form in time. As manifested life, *bios* is subject to the laws of growth, a cyclical process of waxing and waning, expressed in human, animal and plant. Together, *zoe* and *bios* image the two dimensions of life: eternal and transitory, invisible and visible. This primordial pattern could be simply seen in the life of the Moon. As *zoe*, the Mother Goddess gives birth to the child as the New Moon, unites with him or her as the Full Moon, loses her lover or her daughter to the darkness as the Waning Moon, and goes in search of him or her as the Dark Moon. The next cycle begins as the life that was 'found', when *zoe* again gives birth to *bios*, the new life as the crescent of the New Moon. What happens in the monthly round of the Moon happens, analogically, throughout the whole of nature.

With variations, this is the story of Inanna-Ishtar and Dumuzi-Tammuz, the Egyptian Isis and Osiris, the Greek Demeter and Persephone, the Canaanite Baal and Anath, the Anatolian and Roman Kybele and Attis, and the Greek Aphrodite and Adonis. When the daughter or the son-lover dies in the Dark Moon, all nature dies, or seems to die, in the darkness of the month or the winter of the year. After three days or three months the child of the Goddess is reborn, bringing back light and fertility as the waxing of the Moon or as the 'waxing' of the Sun in the springtime of the year. In the myth of Demeter and Persephone, the daughter is the 'part' of her mother which dies, and the reunion of mother and daughter brings the spring. In Greece and Syria the annual rituals of mourning for Adonis, lover of Aphrodite and Lord of Vegetation, lasted three days.

It was the aim of the Mystery Traditions which grew up around these myths to draw the participants into the mythic drama, so they themselves might experience the whole of the cycle, and identify not with the mortal frame, not with *bios*, the form in time that lives and dies, but with the eternal principle that is ever reborn, with *zoe*.

THE DEATH AND RESURRECTION OF OSIRIS

In Egypt, the Moon took many forms, overlapping and merging into each other, all exploring a different dimension of its totality: the Eye of Heaven, Osiris, Thoth, the Left Eye of Horus, Khonsu or Khons, Isis, Hathor, Neith and Aah (often just an epithet meaning 'Moon', added on to other names). However, the oldest living drama of the Waxing and Waning Moon, and the rising and falling Nile on which the lives of Egyptians depended, was enacted through the story of the god Osiris, 'Lord

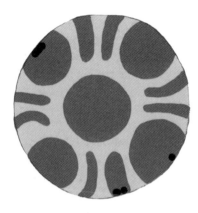

Fig. 10. The lunar cycle as a unit of four: two crescents, opposing each other, and full Moon and new (dark) Moon, represented by the smaller disc. Interior of a Cucuteni dish. Tripolye BII. Nezvisko, upper Dniester valley. c. 4000 BC. (From Marija Gimbutas, The Language of the Goddess, p. 284).

Fig. 11. Lunar cycle as four round Moons around a central Moon. Red painting on white, around the interior of a footed bowl. Cucuteni A. Habasesti, Iasi district, Moldavia. 4400-4200 BC. (From Gimbutas, The Language of the Goddess, p. 284).

Fig. 12. Chinese terra-cotta vase, painted as a full Moon divided into four crescents, surrounded by the pattern of a net, and spirals and meanders, suggesting rain. Found in Pan-shan, Ning-ting, Kanzu Province, China. Neolithic. Museum of Far Eastern Antiquities, Stockholm.

of the Moon'. Osiris is worshipped as the Moon from the oldest Pyramid Texts (c.2500 BC): 'You are born in your months like the moon';[60] 'You appear at the New Moon.'[61] Over a thousand years later, Rameses IV, in a hymn to Osiris, says to him:

> In the days of which it is said that Nut was not yet pregnant with thy beauty, thou didst live nevertheless in the shape of gods and men and mammals and birds and fishes. Lo, thou art the moon on high; thou becomest young at will and agest at will.[62]

But Osiris was also the Nile, the Moon's water on Earth. In the same hymn, Rameses IV continues:

> Thou art the Nile...gods and men live from thy outflow.[63]

This way of seeing the Moon in Egypt lasted for over three thousand years, entering the Greek and Roman worlds, and only ended in the second century AD, when the temples of Isis were closed on the orders of the Christian emperor Theophrastus. The Greek writer Plutarch told the myth of Isis and Osiris in full for the Greeks of the first century AD, finding parallels between Osiris and Dionysos, and Isis and Demeter, as early Christians did between Osiris and Jesus, and Isis and Mary. The story that follows is an abbreviated compilation from Egyptian sources and Plutarch's *Of Isis and Osiris* (though further dimensions of the tale will be explored later).[64]

In the beginning were the dark formless waters of Nun, the 'Great He/She'. Atum, 'the One', rose up out of the waters as the 'High Hill' and shone from the waters as the 'First Light'. Atum created Shu, Air, Space, and Tefnut, Moisture; Shu and Tefnut created Geb, Earth, and Nut, Sky, who lay close together as one. So Shu lifted up his daughter, Nut, and arching her body she rested the tips of her fingers and toes upon Geb, the Earth beneath. Then Geb and Nut gave birth to Osiris, Isis, Seth, Nephthys and Arueris. Osiris married Isis and Seth married Nephthys, and Osiris and Isis ruled the land of Egypt.

Osiris was the first king of Egypt and the creator of civilization. He taught his people how to cultivate wheat and barley and how to transform grapes into wine. He gave laws and 'established justice on both banks of the Nile'. When he travelled to distant lands, instructing the tribes, Isis ruled peacefully in his place. But Seth, his brother, with hair as red as the desert and a brow as black as a moonless night, desired to be king instead of Osiris. When Osiris returned, Seth threw a feast for Osiris but secretly prepared to betray him. In the midst of the banquet, at the height of the celebrations, Seth commanded a magnificent chest to be brought into the room. It had bright pictures painted round the outside and was the size of a man. Seth promised as a jest to give it to the person it fitted. When it was Osiris's turn to try, he lay down inside it, and it fitted him like a coffin. Instantly, 72 conspirators rushed forward and hammered down the lid with long nails, sealed them with molten lead, and flung the chest into the Nile. Then it floated out to sea.

After many days the chest came to rest on the shores of Byblos in Syria. A tamarisk tree grew up around it, and the most wonderful fragrance came from the tree, whose fame spread far and wide. It reached the ears of the king and queen of Byblos, who asked that the tree be cut down and brought to their palace. So the tree, smelling so sweetly, was now, like Osiris himself, cut down in the midst of its life, its branches lopped off. Then it was raised upright to form the central pillar in the palace.

Isis cut off her hair and put on clothes of mourning. She journeyed up and down the Nile, searching for Osiris, asking everyone, had they seen her husband, the sweetest king of Egypt. It was the children who told her they had seen a casket floating by, and now Isis knew where to look. So Isis came to Byblos, disguised as an old woman, and sat down beside a spring. When the queen's servants came to fetch water, she plaited their hair and breathed her divine fragrance over them. The queen, smelling the fragrance on their hair, asked them to bring the woman to the palace to nurse her baby boy. In the day Isis gave the infant her finger to suck, but at night she placed him in the fire to burn away his mortality, while she took the form of a swallow, flying round and round the pillar, singing mournfully.

But it happened that Queen Astarte peeped into the room and saw her child lying in the flames, and screamed. Isis, enraged, seized the child from the fire and flung him away from her, revealing herself as the Goddess. She demanded the pillar to be cut down and placed in a boat on the sea. Alone at sea, Isis opened the lid of the sarcophagus and saw her husband lying inside – dead as the dark Moon. Transforming herself into a kite, she hovered above his outstretched body and with the mighty beating of her wings fanned him back into life. Then she conceived a child from him, Horus. Concealing Osiris in his sarcophagus in the papyrus swamps, Isis hid herself and her child among the reeds. But Seth was out hunting boar in the marshes at the Full Moon, and caught sight of the coffin

Fig. 13. Osiris in the disc of the Moon, wearing the crown of Upper Egypt and holding a sceptre. The cartouche above has the royal name of Unnefer, beginning with the hieroglyph of the Hare. (From John Layard, The Lady of the Hare, p. 146).

Fig. 14. Osiris the Moon god (Osiris-Aah), with crescent and full Moon upon his head. He holds the Djed column in the centre, and rising out of it are the cross with the circle as the sign of life, and above that the sign of strength. The flail and sceptre to the left and right are symbols of his power. Temple of Seti I, Abydos. c. 1300 BC. (From E.A. Wallis Budge, Osiris and the Egyptian Resurrection, i, p. 59).

with Osiris inside it, and slew him again, this time dismembering his body into 14 pieces – the number of nights of the Waning Moon. Then he scattered the pieces all over Egypt, burying them each in a different place. So it was that Egypt became the 'Land of the Moon'.

Then Isis, with her sister Nephthys and the jackal god Anubis, searched again for Osiris, rescuing the fragmented pieces of his body and putting them back together again, except for the phallus which had been swallowed by a fish. So the potency of Osiris was hidden in the Nile, which fertilized new life when it overflowed with his semen each year. When Osiris was again revived by Isis, re-membering the 14 parts of his body as the Waxing Moon, he went to the underworld (as the Old Moon). But each month Osiris is reborn through his son Horus as the New Moon, the new form of himself who takes his place and engages in the monthly battle of waxing and waning with Seth.

The life, death and resurrection of Osiris follows the lunar pattern. Osiris rules for 28 years – a 'Moon' of a life – and then, as all lunar heroes must, he enters the darkness of his own being, murdered on the seventeenth day of the month of Athyr (two or three days after the Full Moon when the Moon visibly begins to dwindle). The ritual emblem of Osiris was the shape of the New Moon.

Isis and Osiris, as goddess and god of the Moon, embodied the ever-renewing cycles of nature, both the waxing of growth – in the Moon, the Nile, the plants, animals and human beings – and the waning of death – when the Moon diminished, the Nile shrank, the plants shrivelled, and animals and people grew old and died. If Osiris is the Moon in all its creative potency, Seth is the opposing principle of destruction, manifest as darkness, desert and drought, both the scorching Sun and the burning winds that sweep across the fields from the hot sands, bringing death. Seth was also, Plutarch adds, that part of the soul which is 'irrational' and 'truculent'.[65] When the Moon was swallowed up by the Sun, people would say Seth had shut Osiris up in his coffin; when the Nile and the plants dried up, they would say that Seth had slain Osiris. But when the Nile began to rise again, people said it was the tears of Isis searching for Osiris, and when the Nile overflowed, and the seed appeared from beneath the black soil, then the people said that Isis had 'found' Osiris, and this was Horus who rose again in his name. Now all creatures who had died lived again, as he did, in new form. The dead were called 'Osiris' and, like him, entered eternity by 'breathing the breath of Isis'. Yet Osiris was not just for those who had died:

Fig. 15. *Osiris arising from within the wings of Isis. Bas relief from the Ptolemaic Temple of Isis at Philae. 323–30 BC. (From Wallis Budge, Osiris and the Egyptian Resurrection, i, p. 59).*

Fig. 16. *Horus protected by the wings of Isis going to take his father's place. Bronze statue. 600 BC. British Museum.*

> Whether I live or die, I am Osiris,
> I enter in and reappear through you,
> I decay in you, I grow in you,
> I fall down in you, I fall upon my side.
> The gods are living in me for I live and grow in the corn
> that sustains the Honoured Ones.
> I cover the earth,
> whether I live or die I am Barley,
> I am not destroyed.[66]

Osiris defeats death, but only because of the love of Isis. It could be said that Isis is the Moon in its cycle, as the eternal life of *zoe*, while Osiris is the Moon in its phases, as *bios*, the form of *zoe* that lives and dies in time. Isis, his sister-wife, becomes his mother who brings him back to life, first giving him the breath of life with the wind from her wings, and then reassembling his dismembered body to make him whole. In the Ptolemaic temple at Dendera there is an inscription which reads: 'He [Osiris] awakes from sleep [of death] and he flies like the bennu bird and he makes his place in the sky as the Moon.'[67] Horus, their son, conceived after Isis had brought him back to life, becomes the *bios* in his father's place, as the form of Osiris that is visibly renewed, battling each month with the darkness of Seth. Horus is addressed as 'the Old Child...the Circulating One...the Moon is thy name.'[68]

Every year, from the Twelfth Dynasty onwards, and probably long before that, there was a festival at the Temple of Osiris at Abydos to celebrate his resurrection and his gift of resurrection for all. The people would come from all over Egypt to participate in the passion of his life and death, and at the culminating moment the king, with the help of four oxen, his arm gripped by the goddess Isis, would raise the trunk of a massive tree to the resounding cry 'Osiris is risen.' The *Djed* column, as it was called, which became, in its rising, the Tree of Life, bore the four crossed branches of the four quarters of the universe and the four phases of the Moon.

In Christianity also, a Tree of Life in the form of a Cross would be raised upright for the two thousand years following, in order to celebrate 'the Resurrection of the Body and the Life Everlasting'. For Jesus, son of the Virgin Mother, Mary, also died, was buried and descended into hell, rising again on the third day, after the pattern of the Moon. Like the others, his resurrection coincides with the Earth's rebirth, with the festival of Easter timed to the first Full Moon after the spring equinox, reflecting the turning of winter into spring.

Fig. 17. Osiris as the Djed column of the Tree of Life, holding crook and flail, with Isis (left) and Nephthys (right), out of which the Sun rises as a hawk to the greetings of baboons. Papyrus of Hunefer. 1310 BC. British Museum.

Fig. 18. Christ on the budding branches of the Cross as the Tree of Life, with Mary and John. Evesham Psalter. mid-13th century. British Library.

CHAPTER 2

THE MOON AND TIME

Time...is a moving image of eternity.
Plato *The Timaeus*

'The moving Moon went up the sky,
And no where did abide...'
Coleridge *The Rime of the Ancient Mariner*

Time was once measured everywhere by the phases of the Moon.[1] More precisely, it might be said that the notion of time came into being when the phases of the Moon fell into a pattern and became measurable. But this was 'time' as a concrete phenomenon, something lived continuously from day to day, or rather from night to night, and then from phase to phase, and so from Moon to Moon. Measurement has now become predominantly a quantitative term – how many days in a month? how many months in a year? – yet the word 'measure' still retains its older qualitative meaning in such phrases as a 'measured dance', in 'due measure', and 'love is the measure of all things'. Ancient measurement contained both meanings: measuring time by counting the phases of the Moon, and also taking time itself as the measure, in the sense of allotting the mode of behaviour due to the time, which was the particular phase of the Moon.

It is unexpectedly difficult to suspend our way of thinking about time astronomically, as though we must take off the watch and then take off the 'watch'. For once the hours, days and months have been detached from the *kind* of hour, day and month it is, they will not 'grow back' into the way they were – the good old days. But if we do not 'suspend our disbelief for the moment', the attitude Coleridge recommends for addressing a poem,[2] we cannot imagine how it might have been to live in harmony with the source of time, when time was not separate from the rhythms of life. For it seems that time once came from the Moon as the *timing* of the Moon's own story, one in which the whole universe participated.

ETERNITY AND TIME

The perennial longing for unity within diversity may once have been orchestrated by the Moon. The perpetual presence of the invisible round in the visible phase evokes the idea of time as the visible form of eternity, or time 'as the moving image of eternity', as Plato puts it in the *Timaeus*.[3] Eternity was not a continual series of moments in time which never ended – that was perpetuity, an infinite multiplication. Eternity was of a different order, an unimaginable plenitude beyond time which time could only serve through *mimesis*, imitation.[4] Shakespeare's Lucrece parodies time in this way, addressing it as 'thou ceaseless lackey to eternity'.[5] For the Greeks, as for others, the cycle or circular movement that brings continual renewal, allowing things to survive by repeating them, was the best possible expression of eternity, which was defined as absolute, immobile and beyond change. Time, by

Fig. 1. Ugra-Tara in the image of Kali. Pahadi painting, Punjab, India. 18th to 19th century. National Museum, Delhi.

contrast, was movement and change – and, for Plato, 'all change is a dying'.[6] So time was an inferior reality that could at best imitate eternity by moving in a circle and gain what identity it could from recurrence – *anakuklosis*, 'eternal return'.[7] The lunar model of early people also gave time a cyclical structure, so that time itself was regenerated at each new birth, and the things of time, the world of nature, along with it.

In early myths, the Moon carries images of both eternity and time in its changeless pattern of changes: it was eternity in the ever-recurring cycle, and time in the phases. In North America the Sioux Indians called the Moon 'the Old Woman Who Never Dies'; the Iroquois called her Aatensic, 'the Eternal One'.[8] For the Egyptians the Moon god, Thoth, was 'the maker of eternity and creator of everlastingness', as well as the 'scribe of time'.[9] Nanna-Sin, the Mesopotamian Moon god, 'ever-renewing himself', 'measured the days of a month'.[10] In Latin inscriptions the Moon was given the epithet of 'the eternal', and in Russia the Moon was called 'the deathless one'.[11] In India Soma, the god of the Moon, is also the name of the ambrosial nectar of immortality which is the food of the gods, and in China the Moon hare pounds the herb of immortality in his crescent cup.[12] In Polynesia, the Moon is perpetually renewed in the waters of *Tane*, the eternal source.[13] In the biblical Psalms, the Moon is offered for comparison as an image of eternity: 'It [David's seed and throne] shall be established for ever as the moon.'[14] In Hottentot and Bushman tales, the Moon would have given immortality to humans if the hare had not lied or squandered the chance.[15] 'Being eternity', by perpetually renewing oneself, and 'bestowing immortality' may not be quite the same, but if the human story can participate in the Moon's story then the difference becomes practically irrelevant.

But the Moon in its phases was also time and, as time, the Moon was never still.

THE MOON AND THE MEASUREMENT OF TIME

For the rational mind, the Moon presents a visible image of the ceaseless flow of time. But for the mythical mind the Moon, measuring time, *makes* time and so ultimately *is* time, as well as the source of time which is eternity. The Indo-European languages demonstrate that terms for the act of measuring come originally from the name of the Moon, not the other way round, as it may now seem to us.[16] Twentieth-century Partridge in his *Origins* writes: 'for Moon, see measure', but one might, more etymologically, say: 'for measure, see Moon', since 'month' comes from 'Moon', not 'Moon' from 'month.'[17] As the philosopher Owen Barfield has observed, 'the farther back language as a whole is traced, the more poetical and animated do its sources appear, until it seems at last to dissolve into a kind of mist of myth.'[18]

The oldest Indo-Aryan root connected with the heavenly bodies is the root *me*, which means 'Moon', and becomes in Sanskrit *mas*, or *masas*, meaning 'Moon', and 'month', while *mami* means 'I measure', *mati* means a 'measure', and *matram* is an instrument for measuring; *ma* means 'time', and 'Moon'. *Ma* or *matar* also means 'mother', in the sense, perhaps, that the mother is the mind and measure of all things for the child, as the primordial Mother is for the race and the Great Mother is for the universe. This is the root of all the subsequent Indo-European languages relating to both Moon and measurement: Greek *mene*, Moon; *men*, month; *metron*, a means of measuring; *metreo*, I measure. Latin, *mensis*, month, *menaeus*, monthly, from which comes *mensura*, measurement, *menstruus*, monthly, *metiri*, to measure, and (surprisingly) *mensa*, table for a meal (held at regular, measurable times). 'Moon' in Latin is *luna*, which is probably a contraction of *leuksna*, from Greek *leukos*, bright, white; Moon goddesses are described as *leukolene*, white-armed. *Leukos* also gives Latin *lux*, *lumen*, light (a possible contraction of *leuksmen* – moonlight, suggesting that 'light' first got its name from

Fig. 2. Hooking spirals move across a field of parallel line bands and circles around the shoulder of the vase. There are thirty triangles around the neck and probably (part of the design being lost) thirty circles beneath the spirals, which may represent the days of the lunar month. Graphite-painted. Karanovo VI/Gumelnita. Tangiru, near Bucharest, Romania, 4500-4300 BC. (From Gimbutas, The Language of the Goddess, p. 282).

moonlight). French follows Latin with *la lune*, Moon, *mois*, month, *mesurer* to measure, and *metre*, a particular length of measurement.

However, the specific measurement of *quality* is clear, for instance, in the Latin *modus*, also meaning a 'measure', hence a measure one should not exceed and so a limit, a manner, a way of behaving, from which comes 'mode' as a way of being and 'moderation' and 'modest' as terms which recognize boundaries. Similarly, the derivation of 'temperance' from *tempus*, Latin for 'time', indicates that this quality of character derives not from 'time' in the abstract, but rather from a practical sense of 'time for', that is, 'in good time', which is 'the right time' and the due behaviour for that time.

In Old English, *mona* is Moon, *monath* is month, *metan* is to measure, and *maeth* is a measure; *mael* is a measure specifically in the sense of a measured length of time or a point in time, an appointed time, hence *mele* (via Middle English *mael*) meaning in English meal-time, a meal. Similarly, in Old Frisian, *mona* is Moon, *meta*, measure; in Old Saxon, *mano*, Moon, *metan*, measure; in Old High German, *mano*, Moon, *mezzan*, measure; in Middle High German, *mane*, Moon, *messen*, measure; in German *mond*, Moon, *messen*, measure; in Gothic *mena*, Moon, *mitan*, measure; in Dutch, *maan*, Moon, *meten*, measure; in Old Norse, *mani*, Moon, *meta*, measure. Moon is *menu* in Lithuanian, *mane* and *maen* in Old High Dutch, *maenon* in Germanic. In English, the etymological relation between Moon, month, matrix, meter, diameter, mensurable, menstrual, measure, immense (unmeasurable), mete out and meal, must now be only too clear.[19]

Martin Nilsson, in his *Primitive Time-Reckoning*, declares that 'the moon is the first chronometer...practically everywhere the month...is denoted by the same word as moon.'[20] Because the Moon could be taken in at a glance, and no glance was the same for long, the Moon drew attention not just to a point of time but to its duration. Nilsson's detailed evidence shows that 'the Indo-European peoples of olden times, and indeed most of the peoples of the globe, count the days from nights', such that 'an inner connection seems to exist between the counting of the days in nights and the designation of the days, or rather the nights, of the month according to the phases of the moon.'[21] The regularity of the Moon's phases which were always there, easy to see, and lasting long enough to record, made it possible to mark off longer periods of time in a way that the Sun did not. Whether for ease of hunting, or the gathering and growing of plants, the nights of the phases were often given separate names, singly or in groups, and these were also the names of the following days – covering the time that in later reckoning became the more abstract idea of 24 hours.[22] Now that our month no longer follows the Moon, it is easy to forget that a long time ago a 'month' would have been a 'Moon', beginning, even called out, when the crescent of the New Moon first glowed in the dark of the western horizon. In ancient Egypt, for instance, the hieroglyph of a Crescent Moon was the abbreviation for the word 'month', and the Chinese also use the same character for Moon and month (beginning at New Moon). The phrase 'many Moons ago' was current even in the twentieth century.

In Sanskrit, the word for 'daily' was 'night by night', *nicanicam*. As one of their hymns says, 'Let us celebrate the old nights (days) and the autumns (years).'[23] Similarly, the Saxon word *den* (day) – as in 'Good den', 'Good day' – really meant 'night', or literally 'Good Moon-day'.[24] In the Persian sacred writings, the *Avesta*, time is counted from nights, as it was in Babylon and in old Arabia, where people would say '70 nights long', 'in three nights', or 'on the first night of Ramadan'. The Polynesians called night *po* and tomorrow *apopo*, the 'night's night', while yesterday was *po-i-nehe-nei*, the 'night that is past'. The North American Indians counted time in nights, as did the Greenlanders, and tribes in many parts of Africa, Asia and Europe.[25] According to Caesar, the Celts 'define all spaces of time, not by days, but by nights, and when they calculate the dates of births, or the beginnings of months or years, they are always careful to put the night before the day.'[26] Tacitus said the same of the Germans: 'They do not reckon time by days, as we do, but by nights. All their engagements and appointments are made on this system.'[27] An old French nursery rhyme from the Loire valley greeted the Moon rising in the evening with 'Good morning, Madame Moon, have you any children to give me?'[28]

In lunar time reckoning, because nights are primary and days come from nights, duration of time is reckoned by nights. Remnants of this way of thinking still exist in the English term 'fortnight' even though 'fortnight', 14 nights, now means 14 days. The less usual 'sennight' (seven nights) is found in the witches' curse in *Macbeth*: 'Weary sennights nine times nine/Shall he dwindle, peak and pine.'[29] In old France, the summer solstice was called *La Lunade*, since it began with the rising of the Moon.[30] Other traces of lunar timing can be seen in festivals beginning on the 'Eve', for many Christian holy days took the same dates as pagan festivals but made them 12 hours later in the clear light of day and changed the names: May Eve (once the Saxons' *Walpurgisnacht* and the Celts' *Beltane*, the 'wearing of the green' in honour of spring), became May Day; Midsummer Eve became St John's Day; All Hallows' Eve (Hallowe'en), from the Celtic *Samhain*, 'Summer's End', and the Feast of the Dead, when the ancestral spirits visited the living, became All Saints' Day on 1 November and All Souls' Day on 2 November. Christmas Eve, the pagan Yule, once called the 'Night of the Mother' and still celebrated with 'Midnight Mass', became Christmas Day. In Holland there is a Santa Klaus Eve on 6 December. Similarly, in Judaism, various festivals and fasts, such as the Sabbath, the Day of Atonement, and the Feast of Unleavened Bread, were arranged to begin and end in the evening, following the original order of creation in Genesis: 'And the evening and the morning were the first day.'[31]

TEMPLES OF THE MOON

The first temple of the Moon was probably a gap between the distant hills of the horizon through which the thin curve of the New Moon appeared as an epiphany. It is likely that stones later marked the place of the vision, and later still that other stones were placed to create a relationship between certain of the Moon's movements and the people gathered on the Earth beneath. These arrangements of stones, which we call temples, may have been the first way of telling time.

Numerous ancient Moon temples are testimony to the union of lunar and earthly life, many of them constructed by the Megalithic people in the fifth millennium BC, and probably long before that: Stonehenge and Silbury Hill in Wiltshire, England, Carnac and Gavrinis in Brittany, France, New Grange and Knowth in Ireland, Callanish on the Scottish Isle of Lewis, and Temple Wood in Argyllshire, Scotland, to name only a few.[32] In the Orkneys, off Scotland, the ancient stone circle is still known as the 'Temple of the Moon'.[33] In 1974 the archaeologist Alexander Thom proposed the theory that Stonehenge, built in three major phases from 3100 BC to 1150 BC, was originally an observatory for studying the movements of the Moon.[34]

The Moon is called 'the wanderer' by many people, and observatories would certainly have been needed to keep track of its very complex wanderings.

(*The Moon rises, on average, nearly an hour later each day, and in its revolution around the Earth it moves eastward in the sky about 13 degrees a day. It moves in an ellipse, not a circle, around the Earth, and the Earth is not at the centre of the ellipse but at one of its foci. So the Moon is closest to the Earth and farthest from the Earth alternately at intervals of about two weeks, travelling fastest when nearest the Earth (perigee – peri, near, Ge, 'earth', Greek), and travelling slowest when farthest from the Earth (apogee – apo 'away', Ge, Earth, Greek). This change of speed of the Moon in its path around the Earth affects the time of rising and setting. Consequently, it is extremely difficult to predict.*)[35]

Yet it seems that in Megalithic times it was usually the extreme movements of the Moon that were significant. On the shores of the beautiful Gulf of Morbihan in Brittany, the Megalithic passage grave at Gavrinis is oriented to the rising sun at the winter solstice, but the main alignment of the tomb is towards an extreme position of the rising Moon. The spirals incised into the stones may imitate movements of creative energy or revolutions of the Moon, as may the left-handed spirals, meanders, and crescents on the stones at Knowth in Ireland.[36]

A stone circle in Castle Fraser in Aberdeenshire, Scotland, has a massive 'recumbent' stone within it, a stone laid horizontally upon the ground. Every 18.6 years the Full Moon seems to roll along the top of the recumbent stone as though it were coming down to Earth. In Scotland several of the stone circles have recumbent stones, all oriented to the rising and setting of the Moon, often on the extremity of its southerly or northerly courses. In the stone circle at Loanhead of Daviot, for instance (fig. 3), the principal megalith plays the role of a near horizon, lying flat between two standing stones which flank it on either side. George Meaden writes that 'if one stands at the centre of some of the circles when the moon is following its most southerly course in the night sky, the moon appears either to rise or set in the direction of the recumbent stone.' And even where 'a recumbent stone was not aligned to moonrises or moonsets the circle builder had set it on an axis to correspond with the moon when it had risen into the sky.'[37] Anyone who lay on the stone at these special times would experience the Moon moving along their body, and it is not difficult to imagine that people may have felt they were absorbing the immense power of the Moon.

These alignments suggest that Megalithic people were practised in keeping track of the Moon, measuring not just the cycles of month or year, but the farthest limits of its movements over long periods of time. But what was the meaning of these measurements for the many people who must have been required to make them possible?[38]

Fig. 3. *The stone circle and recumbent stone at Loanhead of Daviot, Grampians, Scotland. Approx. 20.5 meters across. 2000-1200 BC. Aberdeenshire Archaeological Surveys.*

THE SACRED CALENDAR

From the evidence of all early societies it seems clear that the original intention of calendars was not secular but sacred.[39] They were not simply a recording and predicting of the passing of nights and days, and the setting of boundaries for risings and settings. They caught the moments when time seemed to become transparent to a source beyond it, which was given the name of 'eternity'. We still say 'time stopped' and 'time stood still', as well as 'time flies'. Of course, it is the creatures of time who notice moments of difference which remind them that time has passed and bring time into awareness as an idea. But the source of this awareness – that day has turned into night, that one Moon has become another Moon – appears to come from beyond the divisions of time, from the pattern of the heavens which never changes: 'Thrones have perished, peoples passed from dominion to slavery, from captivity to empire, but the same months of the year have always brought up on the horizon the same stars...', wrote Manilius, the first-century AD didactic poet, possibly of Greek origin: 'Heaven...will remain the same for ever, because for ever it has been the same. Thus it appeared to the eyes of our forefathers, thus will our descendants behold it. It is God, for it is unchangeable throughout the ages.'[40]

Franz Cumont, in his *Astrology and Religion among the Greeks and the Romans*, argues that 'the magic idea of a power superior to man is connected, from the very beginning, with the notation of time.'[41] Cicero, who himself attributed reason to the heavenly bodies, wrote that 'Zeno [the Greek Stoic philosopher] attributed a divine power (*vis divina*) to the stars, but also to the years, the months, and the seasons.'[42] So, long before Kant defined time as an '*a priori* form of intuition' (a category, along with space and causation, of human reason),[43] time 'began' as a being with a personality which was divine and so, to exploit the paradox, eternal. While, for the Greeks and Romans, *all* the heavenly bodies were implicated in the distinctions of time, in the very beginning the one heavenly body of the Moon seems to have been paramount.

Once simple time reckoning had become formalized into calendars, which were instituted and for the most part organized by priests, they were used to indicate the holy days and festivals, and to determine when certain activities would be propitious and when they would not.[44] Time, then, signified a life-value; it was *time for* some things but not for others. The Moon's role in telling the time then entered the realm of sacred literature, which sought to order and comprehend the world:

> God created the moon and appointed its 'houses', it is said in the *Koran*, in order that men might know the number of the years and the measure of time.[45]

A poem from *The Icelandic Edda* declares:

> New Moon and Old were made by the gods
> As a tally of times for men.[46]

Another poem asks:

> Thor: What is the moon called, that men see,
> In all the worlds there are?
> Alvis: *Moon* by men, *The Ball* by gods,
> *The Whirling Wheel* in Hel,

The Speeder by giants, *The Bright One* by dwarves,
By elves *Tally-of-Years*.[47]

The biblical Psalm 104 praises the Lord who 'appointed the moon for seasons: the sun knoweth his going down.'[48] The writer of Ecclesiasticus elaborates: 'He made the moon also to serve in her season for a declaration of times, and a sign of the world. From the moon is the sign of feasts, a light that decreaseth in her perfection. The month is called after her name, increasing wonderfully in her changing.'[49]

In the Temple of Amun at Hibis in Egypt, it was inscribed: 'Moon in the night, ruler of the stars, who distinguishes seasons, months and years: he cometh ever-living, rising and setting.'[50] Very early in Egypt, as elsewhere, the Moon was the chief measure of time for an agricultural people who needed an exact calendar.[51] Of all the many manifestations of the divinity of the Moon in Egypt, Thoth was the Moon in its specific relation to time. He was both 'King of Eternity' and 'Lord of Time', the god of the calendar.[52] He was also called the 'reckoner', the 'determiner', the 'divider', 'lord of measurement and writing', 'scribe of the gods' and 'scribe of time', 'enumerator of the earth and of what is therein, and the measurer of the earth'. His many literate titles are eloquent of the 'god-like' achievement of writing down the phases of the Moon and turning them into a calendar, an art imagined as coming from beyond the time they chart. As the god beyond time, Thoth was the god of wisdom who sustained the cosmic order of the world, while in relation to human beings he was god of fate and regulator of individual destinies: 'Without his knowledge nothing can be done among gods and men', the saying went.[53]

The image of Thoth was found in the bird who was his epiphany. This was the ibis with his great crescent beak, who sifts through the mud, fights off poisonous reptiles and flies to the great beyond, bringing back vision. The black and white feathers of the ibis spoke to Plutarch, among others, of the dark and light phases of the Moon, while the bird's wandering gait and stately flight were evocative of the Moon's passage across the sky. Thoth was sculpted in the shape of the ibis or, more often, drawn in human form as a god with an ibis head, and in his animal form of baboon. When depicted as the reckoner of times and seasons, Thoth wore the Moon crescent and disc upon his head (fig. 4). Thoth, then, was both the Moon itself and, in his eternal role, the Moon's guardian, as when he 'counted', made whole and complete (and so brought back to the full) the *Wedjat*, the Left Eye of Horus which was also the Moon, and was broken into pieces by Seth in its waning.[54]

Thoth was also the inventor of astronomy, mathematics, medicine, reading and writing, and it was his exceptional gift for numbers that was said to navigate the Moon's complex route through the sky. The day of the New Moon, called the 'First of the Month', was sacred to Thoth, and festivals were held at the New and Full Moons (even though a month in the Egyptian civil calendar was 30 days, longer than a lunar month)(fig. 5).[55] Hieroglyphs (which in Greek means 'sacred writings') were known as 'the god's words', and the *Books of the Dead* were said to be 'written' by Thoth 'with his own fingers',[56] as might be expected of one who was both scribe and resurrecting Moon. It was also Thoth who, holding his writing reed and palette in the underworld, recorded the results of the weighing of the heart as the 'scribe of Maat', the goddess who embodied the order and truth of the universe, his female counterpart.[57] Together they assist Re, the Sun, who was the manifest form of Atum, the Great God. 'So important were the moon's phases in determining the rhythms of Egyptian national life,' writes Garth Fowden, 'that Thoth came to be regarded as the origin both of cosmic order and of religious and civil institutions,' presiding over the civil year, law, temple cults and sacred rituals, texts and formulae, especially in Hermopolis (as the Greeks named it, identifying Thoth with Hermes), which was his original home.[58]

Fig. 4. Thoth seated in the crescent-shaped boat of the Moon being presented with the Wedjat-Eye by a baboon, the animal form of himself. The boat floats above the glyph 'Heavens,' and the driftnet ahead suggests that the Moon-boat is flowing with the currents of Heaven. (Nile boats used a driftnet going downstream to the sea and a sail going upstream to the south). The curved stern with notches carved into it, representing broken-off palm leaves, is the sign for 'years,' with each broken-off leaf counting as a day. Sandstone stele of Neferrenpet. Found in Deir el Medina. c. 1320 BC. Egyptian Museum, Turin.

In the Sumerian city of Ur, the great Temple to the Moon was dedicated to the Moon god Nanna, or Suen, meaning the 'Knowing One', later contracted to Sin, still the name for the Moon today among Syrians and Kurds (fig. 6).[59] The Mesopotamian Moon was addressed as the Father who was 'Lord of Heaven, whose sickle shines among the gods', 'Lord of the Month', and 'Lord and Giver of Life'.[60] Other titles were the 'Crescent', the 'New Moon', 'God of the Boat' and the 'Great Boat of Heaven'.[61] Nanna was called 'right god bringing forth day and night, establishing the month, bringing the year to completion'.[62] A hymn to Sin addresses him as the eternal source creating life in time:

> Sin, thou alone givest light from above;
> thou art the light of the world;
> thy light shineth bright as the light
> of thy first-begotten son Shamash [the Sun god].
> Before thee all the gods lie in the dust, O lord of Fate.[63]

The Babylonians, following the Sumerians, called the 12 signs of the zodiac the 'Houses of the Moon', as did the ancient Arabs.[64] In the Babylonian cosmology, as portrayed in their myth of creation, the *Enuma Elish*, Sin again measured time. For so Marduk had decided on the day that he, the new Sun, Storm and Wind god of Babylon, created the world (or rather re-created it) out of the body of his great-great-great grandmother, the Mother Goddess Tiamat, whom he had slain, splitting her body in two pieces, making one into Heaven and the other into Earth. Then Marduk began again and made the constellations anew, fixed the pole star, organized the calendar, and instructed Moon and Sun:

> He bade the moon come forth; entrusted night (to him);
> assigned to him adornment of the night to measure time;
> and every month, unfailingly, he marked off by a crown.
> 'When the new moon is rising over the land
> shine you with horns, six days to measure;
> the seventh day, as half (your) crown (appear)
> and (then) let periods of fifteen days be counterparts,

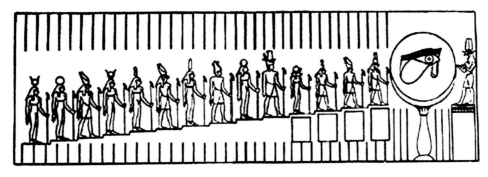

Fig. 5. Ibis-headed Thoth stands by the side of a lotus pillar which supports heaven, while resting on heaven is a crescent, and in it is the Wedjat (or Utchat) of Thoth, as the healed Eye of the Full Moon. Leading up to the top of the pillar is a flight of fourteen steps, one for each of the days of the waxing Moon, with a god standing upon each step, the divinity of the day. The Moon's sky boat sails along the heavens on the left of the picture. Ceiling relief from the Ptolemaic Temple of Horus at Edfu, Egypt. 325-30 BC. (From Wallis Budge, The Gods of the Egyptians, ii, p. 321).

two halves each month.
As, afterward, the sun gains on you on heaven's foundations,
wane step by step, reverse your growth!'[65]

Priests announced the sight of the New Moon when the month could begin. A letter to the Assyrian king Esarhaddon (c.670 BC) from his priest advises him that he 'should wait for the report from the city of Assur and then may determine the first day of the month.'[66] When the Moon was invisible and believed to be dead, it was thought to go to the Nether World to act as judge, and on that day – known as the 'day of lying down' – special offerings were made, often by the reigning queen.[67] There were four or five 'Evil Days' in the lunar month, which were 'interpreted' by the priests, who drew considerable consequences for the people:

An evil day. The shepherd of great peoples shall not eat flesh cooked on coals nor baked bread, nor change the garments on his body, nor put on clean garments, nor make sacrifices. The king shall not ride in a wagon, nor speak as a ruler. The seer shall make no pronouncements in the place of mysteries. A physician shall not lay his hand upon a sick person. It is a day unsuited for doing anything.[68]

Sin may have entered Judaic tradition through his holy mountain, Mount Sinai, known as Mountain of the Moon, first mentioned in Hebrew texts about 1000 BC.[69] It is likely that Mount Sinai, the mountain on which Moses received the Tablets of the Law in Exodus, was the mountain of Sin; and that the golden calf, whose worship so outraged Moses that he made his people grind it to bits, mix it with water and drink it in the manner of an inverted sacrifice, may either have been a statue to the Moon Bull Sin, in his calf form as the New Moon, or else the young bull Horus, son of Osiris, the Moon.[70] When Moses came down from the mountain the second time, the 'skin of (his) face shone', so that he had to wear a veil before his people.[71]

Sin, as the Moon god, was originally the lawgiver to his people (until this role was largely taken over by his son, Shamash, the Sun god), so that, long before the time of Moses, Sinai had been the mountain which received celestial law and conducted it down to Earth. Also, it was from the Moon god's city of 'Ur of the Chaldees' that, according to Genesis, Abraham travelled with his family to

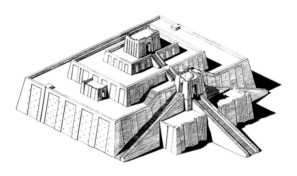

Fig. 6. Reconstruction of the Ziggurat at Ur. Nanna, the Moon god, was said to live in a temple at the base of the ziggurat, except for the three days dark of the Moon when he went to the Underworld. Baked and unbaked brick. 3rd Dynasty of Ur-Nammu Ur, Iraq. c. 2250 BC.

settle in Harran in Assyria, the second most important city where Sin was worshipped, a cult which continued under the Roman Empire and into the early Middle Ages.[72] Harran means 'caravan', a name evocative of long journeys in the desert lit only by moonlight and lasting many Moons before an oasis came into view.[73] Abraham, who became the patriarch of the Jews, is usually placed historically around 1996 BC, the time when Sumerian culture flourished under King Gudea of Lagash (c.2000 BC).[74] There was a tradition that Abraham's original name was Ab-sin, 'Moon-father',[75] or, as Thomas Mann calls him in his novel *Joseph and his Brothers*, Abraham, the 'Moon wanderer'.[76]

In Greece the New Moon, *noumenia*, marking the beginning of the month, was observed as a day of repose and was sacred to Hera and Apollo.[77] In the *Odyssey*, the suitors object that no trial of the bow should be made on the holy day of Apollo.[78] The first of the month is holy, says Hesiod in the eighth century BC,[79] as was the Full Moon day, *dichomenia*. The later Orphic *Hymn to the Moon* registers the complexity of this notion by calling the Moon 'the mother of time, bearer of fruit'.[80]

The Roman month also was originally lunar, and further divided by the phases of the Moon. In Rome, as in Greece, criers watched for the New Moon to begin the month. A *Pontifex Minor* stood on top of the Capitoline Hill and called out, when the Moon appeared, to Juno, Queen of Heaven, who, like the Greek Hera, was seen as the Moon's image.[81] The first of the month was named *kalendae* (after the verb *kaleo*, Greek, *caleo*, Latin, meaning 'to call out'), from which our 'calendar' takes its name. The priest then called out the festivals for the coming month to co-ordinate the days of work and rest, for work was not permitted on the festival days, as many as 109 out of 355 days which were marked *nefas* on the calendars – 'do nothing'. They also announced the *Nonae*, the ninth day before the *Idus*, the Full Moon day. The *Ides* of all the months were sacred festivals when no work was permitted. 'Beware the ides of March', the soothsayer warned Caesar.[82]

In biblical times, in Jerusalem, beacons were lit on the Mount of Olives when the New Moon was sighted by two reliable witnesses, and the news spread (like wildfire) across the hilltops by a chain of bonfires. In China, until recently, the crescent was awaited before the month could start.[83] Even now, the Muslim month can only begin when two trustworthy Muslims witness the New Moon from an open field or the top of a mountain.

But why did the new crescent have to be witnessed in person? Could it not be calculated?

(The Moon takes 27.3 days to travel round the Earth, measured in relation to a fixed star, known as a Sidereal month (sidera, Latin, 'star'); but it takes 29.5 days to pass through its cycle of phases, from New Moon to New Moon, known as a Synodic month, or 'Lunation', until it is again in line with the Sun (synodos in Greek means 'meeting', referring to the meeting of Sun and Moon at New Moon). The discrepancy between the Sidereal and the Synodic months comes because the Earth itself is also moving. The Earth moves through an angle of about 27 degrees along its orbit around the Sun, in the same time as it takes

the Moon to go once round the Earth. So after 27.3 days the Moon has not moved round far enough to be in line with the Sun again because the Earth itself has moved on. So the Moon has to keep on going round its orbit for a further two days before it is in line with the Sun, and the next New Moon occurs.)

Strictly, the New Moon cannot be seen at all, because when the Moon is between Sun and Earth the lighted side is turned towards the Sun, and directly away from Earth. We see it only after it has moved eastward away from the glare of the Sun, a day or two later, when it appears as a thin crescent low in the western sky soon after sunset. Sometimes it can be seen earlier than at other times – hence the uncertainty of predicting it by anything but human sight. So although the extra 2.2 days could have been added on to the Moon's sidereal return, this would still have given only an approximate time of the Moon's synodic return, which was apparently not sufficient. It has to be inferred that the *presence* of the Moon was originally required for 'time' to begin again – or rather that the Moon *was* time made manifest to Earth. It had to be *seen* to be real.[84]

DIVIDING THE YEAR: THE SEASONAL MOONS

The Chukchee reindeer herders in north-eastern Siberia tell a tale of long ago when the Moon offered to measure the year for them and to light up the nights, making them bright as day.

> One night, a tame reindeer, who pulled the sledge for one of the daughters of the herdsmen, looked up at the dark sky and noticed that the Moon Man was getting larger. Then he saw two reindeer pulling the Moon Man's sleigh down to earth.
> 'Watch out! The Moon Man is coming! He'll carry you off,' the reindeer called to the girl.
> 'What shall I do?' asked the terrified girl.
> The reindeer made a hole in the snow with his hoof and told her to jump in. Then he kicked the snow back on top of her so that only her hair showed, looking like a few tufts of grass pushing through the snow. When the Moon Man landed he could not work out where the girl had gone, and so he went away, vowing to return later when she reappeared. The reindeer and the girl rushed back to her father's tent but he was not yet home.
> 'What shall I do now?' the girl asked her reindeer friend, more desperately than before.
> 'A disguise might work,' the reindeer said, 'after all, it did before.' The girl nodded doubtfully.
> 'I'll turn you into a pounding stone,' he said.
> 'No,' she said, 'the Moon Man will know me.'
> 'What about a hammer?'
> 'No, he will know me.'
> 'Then, a tent pole?'
> 'No, he will know me.'
> 'How about a single hair on the hide that hangs over the door?'
> 'No, he will know me.'
> 'There's always the tallow lamp?'
> 'Yes, there the Moon Man will not know me.'
> In a moment she was gone; only a lamp glowed in her place. Just then the Moon Man hurled himself inside the tent and turned everything upside down to find her. But he did not notice the light shining in the middle of the tent, so like his own. His own light was too bright, and anyway he thought the flame would burn him. So he decided to give

up again and go back to the sky. He was just getting on to his sledge when the spirited girl ran out of the tent, calling, 'Here I am!'

The Moon Man rushed back into the tent but she had turned into the lamp again, and he could not find her. He gave up for the third time and was just untying his reindeer when the girl ran out of the tent and shouted again, 'Here I am!'

The Moon Man dashed back into the tent, but by now he was exhausted. Each time he had come inside the tent he had become weaker and thinner. He could not even carry himself back to the sky, let alone carry a girl with him.

The girl was not afraid of him any more, and she tied him up. The Moon Man admitted she had the right to kill him, but begged her to take him inside and cover him with skins. 'I am so cold,' he said.

'How can you be cold?' she asked, amazed. 'You belong outside in the cold outdoor sky.'

'If I must be homeless then at least set me free and I will serve you and all your people forever,' promised the Moon Man. 'I'll be a beacon in the night to guide them and give them pleasure. My light will turn night into day. And I'll measure the year for you.'

The girl waited, still a little distrustful, and the Moon Man went on:

'First, I'll be the Moon of the Old Reindeer Stag,
then the Moon of Bitter Cold Udders,
then the Moon of the Full Udders,
then the Moon of New-born Reindeer Calves,
then the Moon of Water,
then the Moon of First Leaves,
then the Moon of Warm Weather,
then the Moon of Shedding Antlers,
then the Moon of Light Frost,
then the Moon of Pairing Reindeer,
then the Moon of the Reindeer's Winter Back,
then the Moon of Shorter Days.'

'But if I let you go, you'll get strong again, and how do I know you won't carry me off into the sky?' said the girl.

'You are too clever for me,' the Moon Man replied. 'I promise I'll stay in the sky and give you light.'

So she untied him and let him go, and the Moon Man kept his promise faithfully. He shines the months into being and he measures the year. And in case he is tempted into his old ways he grows weak each month, just when he has fully recovered his strength.[85]

In this tale, it is suggestive that the Moon's final gift of measurement comes after he has both waxed and waned – waxed rapacious and waned weak and thin – enacting a full cycle. The names which the Moon gives to the girl show how closely the Moon was involved in the daily life of the tribe. For the story of how the Moon measures the year, and why he grows weaker each month after growing so strong, is also the tale of the kind and magically resourceful reindeer who looks after them, guiding them through dangers, and ultimately giving his own life as food.

The 'Moons' of the North American Indians give the character of their more southern year, one which reflects occupations focused on plants and their cultivation, and the hunting of animals and fish. An eighteenth-century traveller related that the Sioux and Chippewa tribes divided the year into

12 Moon months to which an extra month, known as the 'lost month', was sometimes added. The year began with the first New Moon after the spring equinox: Moon of the Worms (roughly our March); Moon of the Plants (April); Moon of Flowers (May); The Warm Moon (June); Moon of the Roe-buck (July); Moon of the Sturgeon (August); Moon of the Maize (September); Moon of Journeys (October); Beaver's Moon (November); Hunting Moon (December); Cold Moon (January); Snow Moon (February).[86]

Traces of this direct relation between month and season linger in our names for Full Moons: 'Harvest Moon', the 'flame-red' Full Moon in autumn, so large it 'sinks upward' in Ted Hughes's image,[87] and lasting all night so the harvest can be brought in by dawn. Nineteenth-century Scottish Highlanders called it 'Ripening Moon', believing that the crops were ripened by the intensity of moonlight. The Full Moon the following month in the hunting season is still called Hunter's Moon.

THE RECONCILIATION OF LUNAR AND SOLAR TIME

In early times the Moon gave the names to the months, and these names were in turn taken from the changing phases of Nature. For the Moon, which comes round to a new starting point each month, also brings round the cycle of the seasons. Twelve complete cycles of the Moon, sometimes called a lunar year, take 354 days (literally, 29 days 12 hours 44 minutes and 2.8 seconds, rounded off at $29^1/_2$, multiplied by 12, which gives 354 days). This is a little over 11 days short of the solar year of 365 days, which means that, after a few years, the Moons and the seasons get out of synchronization, since the seasons follow the Sun not the Moon (after $2^1/_2$ years, the difference amounts to nearly a full month). Then the names stop working, because the Moon moves ahead of the seasons and starts earlier each year. So the Moon for early spring might be called 'All Leaf Split Moon', but the snow would still be on the ground, just as though it were 'Snow Moon'.[88] An extra month used to be added occasionally to bring the Moon back in relation to the seasons – making a year of 13 Moons – which worked well enough in practice until the Sun was discovered as the sole source of the seasons. Then the question of the harmonization of the old Moon year with the new Sun year became an issue of great symbolic as well as practical importance.

The great calendar debate of antiquity was the fitting together of the old Moon year with the new Sun year, for however the sums were done they did not come out right. Was a Moon month to be 28, 29 or 30 days? And were there to be 13 or 12 months? The Moon of the Chukchee reindeer herders gave them 12 Moons for the year, but in many places the original number of Moons was 13, as on the bison horn of the Goddess of Laussel. Whichever it was to be, there were still days left over when the year of the Sun began again at the winter solstice in the northern hemisphere.

In ancient Egypt there were 12 months with each month rounded off as 30 days, giving an average of 360 days. But as a solar year is 365 days long, the Moon and Sun cycle never corresponded for any length of time. So five days a year had to be intercalated (Latin, *inter*, 'between', *calare*, 'proclaim solemnly'). Plutarch, in his *Isis and Osiris*, tells the story of Thoth playing draughts with the Moon and winning five days from him. Thoth as the eternal Moon is here distinguished from the Moon in its temporal aspect. These became the sacred days, days that did not 'count' – holy days, holidays, days out of time and so suitable for the birth of timeless gods: Isis, Osiris, Seth, Nephthys and Arueris (who does not feature in the drama, and seems to be there to round off the figures).[89]

In ancient Greece, the length of the year had been limited to 12 lunations of 'full' or 'hollow' Moon months (of 30 and 29 days respectively), adding an intercalary month every two years. Geminus writes that 'they sought for a period which should, as to years agree with the Sun, as to months, with the

Moon.'[90] Initially, the Greeks constructed an eight-year cycle called the *octaeris*. In 432 BC the astronomer Meton suggested the 19-year cycle (the one that would be later named after himself), but most cities created their own calendars instead and watched for the rising Moon themselves. Aristophanes, in *The Clouds*, has the Moon itself make a complaint:

> You subvert the calendar and fail to observe her days. When the sacred days are unobserved, the gods go hungry, and it is the Moon they blame.[91]

In the second century BC, two dates were registered, one for the state and one for the deity. In this case the gods, living according to true (Moon) time, would have often 'to go to bed without their supper', as Aristophanes put it.[92]

In Rome, the *Fasti* (calendars), were published in 304 BC, starting the year in March, and any time that had to be intercalated to synchronize the months with the seasons was added in February at the end of the year. But until the end of the Republic the days to be intercalated were the duty of the pontifices, who were lazy or corrupt, and as no one knew whether or when they were going to intercalate a day or not it was impossible to plan ahead. There was even a let-out clause in contracts which read *si intercalat* ('if there is an intercalation'). It fell to Julius Caesar to sweep away the old calendar, extend the year of 45 BC from 355 to 445 days, and begin again on 1 January 45 BC, with a cycle of 365 days, adding another day at the end of the fourth year.[93]

This, with a few adjustments by Pope Gregory XIII in 1582 AD – abolishing ten days, revising the leap years, and changing the new year from 1 March to 1 January – is the solar calendar under which we live today. But when the Gregorian calendar was finally introduced into a reluctant protestant England in 1752, the people of Bristol rioted, protesting at being cheated out of 11 days of life as well as wages.[94]

Robert Graves quotes two English rhymes to show that 'the memory of the 13-month year was kept alive in the pagan English countryside until at least the 14th century.'[95] *The Ballad of Robin Hood and the Curtal Friar* begins:

> But how many merry monthes be in the yeare?
> There are thirteen, I say;
> The mid-summer moon is the merryest of all,
> Next to the merry month of May.

The later ballad changes thirteen to twelve and omits the Moon:

> There are twelve months in all the year
> As I hear many men say.
> But the merriest month in all the year
> Is the merry month of May.

The phrase 'A year and a day', which constantly turns up in fairy tales, often with the sense of forever after – 'and so it continued for a year and a day' – can now be seen to belong to the old lunar calendars of 13 months of 28 days (since 28 days times 13 gives 364 days, with one day left over to coincide with the solar year of 365 days). The extra day which had no month was interposed by ancient calendar-makers between the first and last of their artificial 28-day months.[96]

In the Christian calendar, even the '12 days' of Christmas become transparent to an earlier celebration of sacred time. In 567 AD, the Council of Tours ruled that the 12 days from the Nativity to the Epiphany (the 'showing forth' of Christ) would constitute one religious festival, ending on 'Twelfth Night'. Many folk rituals honour these particular days as special – decorations should not be put up until Christmas Eve and should be taken down by 6 January, or else it is 'bad luck'. In earlier centuries the 'Yule log' of oak was lit on Christmas Eve and kept alight for the whole 12 days of Christmas, and every night the ashes were scattered on the fields to make them fertile. In the Christian calendar, these 12 days constitute the sacred time between divine incarnation and the manifestation of Christ to the world, and so would seem to have a completeness entirely on their own terms. But 6 January was also the day which ended the Roman festival of the winter solstice called the *Saturnalia*, a festival characterized by general license.[97] Since the lunar year falls short of the solar year by 11¼ days, the way to reconcile them is to add these 11 days (say, 12 for the Apostles) to the lunar year. But these days would have been days, as it were, out of time – sacred time – with laws of their own, in which fixed roles and habits of conduct could be disregarded so that new creative energies might break through. Hence the old Roman ritual of King of the Bean in the *Saturnalia*, when the one who got the bean in the cake was king for a day, which was translated into the European Twelfth Night cake which was baked with a bean for the king and a pea for the queen, and lingers on in the Christmas cake when whoever gets the penny gets to make a wish. Fires used to be lit on Twelfth Night in fields and orchards to burn away the dross of the old year, in the guise of fiends, witches and other malevolent beings who might harm the new year's crop.[98]

In folklore, extending from the Highlands of Scotland, through the Celts, to the Aryans of the Vedic Age in India, these 12 days at the beginning of the new year (whenever it was celebrated) were conceived as a microcosm of the whole year, each day corresponding to each of the 12 months, such that the character, and even the weather, could, supposedly, be foretold. (Hence the importance of what 'my true love gave to me' on each of the 12 days of Christmas). The similarity of these 12 days to the five intercalated Egyptian days on which the gods were born is striking. The *practical* considerations of harmonizing two different systems of time and concepts of the year are obvious; but the deeper resonances of the rituals suggest that, long ago, this time was sacred because it was the necessary prelude to the marriage of the Moon and the Sun in the meeting of their days and years, and that these were the precise calculations of an event in which the whole universe participated.[99]

* * *

Yet lunar calendars are still used in many parts of the world. The Hebrew calendar (derived from the Babylonian calendar) is lunar, set within a solar framework, in which the year contains 12 or 13 lunar months, each of which begins with the New Moon. The discrepancy of 11 days between the lunar and the solar year is solved by intercalating a leap year containing an extra month seven times every 19 years, which enables the festival of Passover to fall in spring, and the other festivals to coincide with the seasons. New Year's Day occurs on the day closest to the autumn equinox when the New Moon appears. Prayers are recited at every New Moon, and the congregation is informed of the exact moment when the 'birth' (*molad*) of the New Moon occurred. If, after three days, the Moon can be seen in the night sky, a ceremony of 'sanctification' of the Moon (*kiddush levanah*) takes place out of doors, when each person greets three others with the words *shalom aleikhem*, 'peace be upon you', to indicate, according to the *Dictionary of Jewish Lore and Legend*, that 'the request for God's punishment of one's enemies is not meant to apply to anyone present.'[100] In addition to this, if someone wishes to avoid toothache in the month ahead, it is recommended, the *Dictionary* continues, that the person 'should add the phrase "and I shall have no toothache" to the thrice-repeated request that enemies should not be able to do any harm.'[101] Folklore merges invisibly into religion here, for it is not just the person with toothache but Israel itself who is here identified with, or symbolized by, the Moon: 'The ritual expresses the hope that God will restore the light of the moon to its former glory, and Israel to its former greatness. For in the age of the Messiah the moon will shine as a full moon throughout the month.'[102] There shall be no more waxing and waning in the fullness of time.

It is likely that, before Muhammad, the Arabs had a combination luni-solar calendar, but in 634 AD Muhammad proclaimed that the year should consist of 12 lunar months, counted from one New Moon to the next, and no days should be intercalated at all. The Islamic year is therefore based entirely on the Moon, so the New Year has to begin 11 days earlier each year (according to a Christian calendar). As a rough calculation, it can be said that 100 years of the Muslim calendar are approximately equivalent to 97 years of the Christian calendar. The day begins at sunset, and the festivals return to the same solar season in about 33 years. The crescent is found on the top of minarets, and for the last 200 years has appeared on the Islamic flag, showing a star enclosed within the waxing crescent, which in pre-Islamic symbolism would be an image of creative life.[103]

Even where a solar calendar keeps daily or secular time, the primordial power of the Moon can be intuited in the fact that many of the main religious festivals are still timed to the Moon: Easter, Passover, Ramadan and most Buddhist festivals. Passover falls on the fourteenth day of the month of Nisan – March/April – which on a lunar month is the day of the Full Moon. Ramadan takes place for the whole of the ninth month of the Muslim year. The month of fasting from dawn to sunset ends when the next New Moon appears. Families gather at the Mosque or climb the surrounding hills to watch for the first glimpse of the crescent which begins the three-day Festival of Breaking the Fast. Buddhist festivals are held at New and Full Moons as being times of strength and spiritual power, commemorating the tradition that the Buddha achieved enlightenment at Full Moon.

So whether for influence, correspondence, symbolic harmony or simply wonder, people on Earth have always looked to the Moon for the regulation of their lives, not just for the celebration of rites of passage but for the rhythms of daily life, which were themselves once sacred events timed to the nightly epiphanies of the Moon.

PHASES OF THE MOON AS QUALITIES OF TIME

'Wonder! Rejoice! The Moon has come back to us!' Thus the Bushmen of Namibia would greet the New Moon, blowing on their antelope horns.[104]

When the New Moon appeared in the sky as a thin curve of light against the dark, early peoples across the Earth were waiting. It was the sign that the Moon, and all the different dimensions of life that belonged to it, could begin again. Moon and Earth had, as it were, their beginning together, at the same time. Earthly life took its story from the Moon's story, so the New Moon in Heaven was also the New Moon on Earth. It is not surprising, then, that festivals took place at the New Moon all over the old world: Egypt, Greece, Africa, Mesopotamia, Oceania, Europe, North and South America. New Moon days were days of awe, and so these days were often taboo days of prohibition in which work was laid aside so the celebrations could begin.[105]

Because the Moon was originally a sacred being, it is inconceivable that the Moon was seen merely as a way of making time visible and measurable. This does not mean, however, that the Moon was worshipped whenever it was acknowledged or honoured. We could imagine that, for the early mind, the Moon brought time into being in such a way that it also proposed the way to live in that time: a daily life in harmony with the laws of eternity.

But, as the pre-Socratic philosopher Heracleitus said, 'everything flows and nothing abides', all things are in a state of flux.[106] So it is only time transformed into ritual time that can pin down the continual flux of nature and create *apparent* beginnings and endings within which 'history' may happen, in the sense that Spengler gives to it.[107] In the lunar perspective, change is never final: it is merely a stage in a cyclic pattern which will, in time, give way to its contrary. The change itself will change, and that change will change. Nothing is absolute, but then nothing stays still. It is understandable, then, that the primitive way of stopping the flow was to focus on the dramatic moments of the Moon's cycle, which are the points of difference and discontinuity where something new happens: the first glimpse of the New Moon in the crescent, the perfect orb of the Full, the first loss of light in the Waning Moon, and the total absence of light in the Dark Moon. These are the numinous moments of intensity, when time becomes transparent to its source, and eternity, as it seems, enters into time in the form of a story.

Ritualized time conveys the idea of the *quality* of time. For the time, say, of the New Moon is experienced as qualitatively different from any other time, with a unique character of its own – almost (to use a spatial term) in the manner of a *temenos*. In Greece, this *temenos* was the sacred space 'cut out' around the temple of the gods, which set that space apart from the rest of the land, and within which definite laws operated. Correspondingly, each ritual change of the Moon had its own sacred laws, and these were written into the laws of events on Earth. Earthly affairs are then bound to share in the quality of the time, as they are implicated in the character of the Moon at 'any one time.' What is remarkable is the *range* of implication, extending to everything that grows, which on Earth is everything.

It was, then, a matter of 'common' sense (everybody felt it), as well as a way of living in a sacred world, to put human endeavours into accord with the Moon's energies of increase and decrease, in order to share more immediately in their temporal benefits and later to participate in their powers of renewal in the life eternal. How this lunar energy was interpreted varied, but the effects were held to be similar. Pliny the Elder, the influential first-century AD Roman naturalist, believed the Moon to be a star of breath:

> We may certainly conjecture that the moon is not unjustly regarded as the star of our life. This it is that replenishes the earth; when she approaches it, she fills all bodies, while, when she recedes, she empties them. From this cause it is that shell-fish increase with the increase of the moon and that bloodless creatures especially feel breath at that time; even the blood of men grows and diminishes with the light of the moon, and leaves and herbage also feel the same influence, since the lunar energy penetrates all things.[108]

Plutarch (45–120 AD), on the other hand, believed that the Moon was a planet of water, giving out 'moist heat':

> In general, some things flourish when the moon is waxing, and others when it is waning, since the moisture shed by the increasing light of the moon is beneficial to some things but harmful to others.[109]

Macrobius, a Roman writer and praetorian prefect, writing around 430 AD, also declared that 'the light of the Moon makes moist', adding elsewhere:

There is no doubt that the moon is the author and framer of mortal bodies, so much so that some things expand or shrink as it waxes or wanes.[110]

Scottish Highlanders were saying much the same thing in the eighteenth century.[111]

Ptolemy, in his *Tetrabiblos*, written in the second century AD, taught that the Moon's waxing and waning affected the expansion and contraction of what he called the 'bodily humours' (an idea still prevalent in medieval England up to the seventeenth century), relating the Moon's phase as well as its positioning to the 'character of the soul'. The Moon, he said:

> when at its northern or southern limits, helps in the direction of greater versatility, resourcefulness, and capacity for change... at rising and in the increases of its illumination, towards greater natural endowments, renown, firmness and frankness; and in the waning of its illumination, or its occultations, towards greater sluggishness and dullness, less fixity of purpose, greater cautiousness, and less renown.[112]

But it was not just a matter of expansion and contraction of the Moon's light. The Waxing Moon is seen to rise soon after the Sun sets, softening the difference between night and day, and assuaging the fear of what the darkness might bring. The Full Moon, rising about sunset, shines all night long, setting about sunrise. The Waning Moon, on the other hand, rises later and later each night, leaving the night darker and darker until it does not rise at all. Inevitably, waxing and waning were given opposing meanings around the world, while the Moon itself, capable of both extremes, acquired an ambiguous character, a double meaning which played through life on Earth.

Broadly, those things that were required to grow (sowing, planting, grafting, marrying, conceiving, giving birth, trading, fighting) should be timed for the waxing. Those things that were required to diminish (ills, pains, the sap of a cut branch – anything that would bring benefit by decrease) should be timed for the waning, including felling timber, harvesting crops, mowing the grass, washing linen and treating warts. Again at its most general, participating in the Moon's story meant that New Moons were for beginnings, and the fear and hope of the unknown; Full Moons were for fruition, and the delight and intoxication of fulfilment; Waning Moons were for diminishing, and reflecting upon meaning; Dark Moons were for ending, mourning the death of the old and imagining the form of the new. And New Moons, to go round again, are for the beginning that always comes back and never fails, the second chance, the birth forever arising out of death. So the start of the all-too-temporal enterprise draws power from the Moon's eternal energies which promise to transform time.

This early attempt to comprehend the Moon and Earth as a unity has been called by Frazer (unsympathetically) the 'doctrine of lunar sympathy'. He defines this as:

> the sympathetic influence which the waxing or waning moon is popularly supposed to exert on growth, especially on the growth of vegetation. But the doctrine of lunar sympathy does not stop there; it is applied also to the affairs of man, and various customs and rules have been deduced from it which aim at the amelioration and even the indefinite extension of human life.[113]

The basic idea of waxing and waning in relation to the waters of life, the fertility of humans and animals, the vitality of plants and the vicissitudes of fate, will be explored more fully in subsequent chapters. It is not here the point whether or not any of these beliefs could be said to be true, to any extent or not at all. What is being explored is the Moon as the carrier of these beliefs, and the fundamental ideas involved in asking the Moon to carry them. In this last context, it must be significant that the debate as to the Moon's 'influence' on a variety of earthly phenomena is not decisively closed, not even among scientists, and certainly not among many gardeners, farmers, fishermen, nor among some firefighters, midwives, nurses and surgeons, to name only a few.[114] The language of debate has shifted from light to electro-magnetism, but the debate continues. (For instance, satellites are said by some scientists, but not others, to show that, like the waters of the oceans, land masses are also subject to the pull and push of the Moon, rising and falling as much as one foot, like tides).[115] It is likely that, as so often, interpretation of evidence, and what constitutes evidence, is answerable to more fundamental ideas about the way the universe might be supposed to work, and about the place of human life within the whole of Nature.

The question to be held in mind in the course of this exploration of lunar myths and legends from around the world is, then, what is it about human life that is being made visible in this way? What does it mean that the Moon was once attributed with such far-reaching powers over life on Earth? Frazer writes that from an observation of a natural fact – the increase and decrease of the Moon – 'men have inferred that all things simultaneously wax or wane in sympathy with it.'[116] But we can still ask, *why* did they make this inference? One answer, and the answer many of those who made the inference would give, is that it is true: this is what we see. But much of what is seen is inferred (if not, strictly, all of it), and much of what is inferred is not testable – how would one prove, for instance, that flour rises better at the Full Moon or that the feathers of a duvet lie better in the waning?[117] We might ask, is what is seen governed, wholly or in part, by the argument from analogy – that the rhythmical Moon rules all that is rhythmical, and so is bound to impose its rhythms on everything created? We could further ask, why would anyone *want* to see a relation between Moon and Earth, such that the waxing and waning of the Moon implicate life on Earth in this infinite variety of ways?

The tradition of the Mantras of the Malay Peninsula may point to an answer. They said that in the beginning people did not die but grew thin with the waning of the Moon and waxed fat as it neared the full.[118] People were once, then, imagined to be the same as the Moon, and so perhaps – the thought goes – could be again, or maybe are the same still at a deeper level than now seems apparent. In other words, if early people, thinking about death, saw in the Moon a being who died and came back to life, then the idea of rebirth is given an image: it can be seen with the 'mind's eye' (the meaning of 'idea' in Greek, 'I saw it'). It seems that few people can truly believe in their own death, even though they may accept it, and most religions imagine an 'after-life' as a 'life' after this life (such that death is not a 'real' death), or else a reincarnation, a return to this life in new form. Jung suggests that the idea of life after death is a primordial image, one that belongs to us as part of being human:

> Do we ever understand what we think? We understand only such thinking as is a mere equation and from which nothing comes out but what we have put in. That is the manner of working of the intellect. But beyond that there is a thinking in primordial images – in symbols that are older than historical man; which have been ingrained in him from earliest times, and, eternally living, outlasting all generations, still make up the groundwork of the human psyche. It is possible to live the fullest life only when we are in harmony with these symbols; wisdom is a return to them. It is a question neither of belief nor knowledge, but of the agreement of our thinking with the primordial images of the unconscious. They are the source of all our conscious thoughts, and one of these primordial images is the idea of life after death.[119]

In Chekhov's story *Ward No. 6*, a physician, Andrei Yefimitch, and an old postmaster, Mihail Averyanitch, suddenly find themselves discussing the human soul. The postmaster asks the doctor:

'Then you do not believe in the immortality of the soul?'
'No, my dear Mihail Averyanitch. I do not believe, and I have no reason for believing.'
'I must admit that I also doubt it. Still I have a feeling that I can never die. "Come," I say to myself, "Come, old man, it's time for you to die." But in my heart a voice answers: "Don't believe it, you will never die."'[120]

Later, the doctor makes a friend of the intelligent lunatic Ivan Dmitritch, who tells him he is deeply convinced that 'if there were no immortality it would sooner or later have been invented by the great human intellect.'[121]

NEW MOON

When the Moon grew thin and disappeared, it was thought in many places throughout the world actually to die, and was evidently experienced in early times to be a death as real as the death of human beings. The New Moon phase was often called 'the Moon is dead'.[122] The Nandi of East Africa, for example, named the days 28–30 in terms of the Moon's death: 28, 'the Moon is nearing death'; 29, 'the people discuss the Moon' (discuss whether it is dead), or 'the Sun has murdered the Moon'; 30, 'the Moon is dead' or 'the Moon's darkness'.[123]

All over the world people danced to bring the Moon back to life. The North American Iroquois Indians danced 'for the sake of her health, when she is sick'.[124] The Sakai tribe of the Malay Peninsula thought that the Moon fell to Earth in its time of darkness and needed their magic rites to help her back up to Heaven, so that she and everyone else could live.[125] The Incas of ancient Peru prayed: 'Mama Quilla, Mother Moon, do not die, lest we all perish.' Even in the twentieth century some Peruvian Indians believed that their survival, month after month, depended on the Moon.[126]

So when the silver blade of the new crescent appeared out of the dark it was greeted with joy as a miraculous rebirth that promised the same for human beings after their own waning and death. An old traveller reports how people in the Congo would fall on their knees and cry out, saying: 'So may I renew my life as thou art renewed.'[127] Among the Californian Indians, the old men would summon the young men to celebrate the resurrection of the Moon by dancing in a circle, chanting: 'As the Moon dies and comes to life again, so we also, having to die, will live again.' Other North American Indian tribes stretched forth their hands towards the Moon, ran races and played ball games to speed the Moon's return, for the rising of the New Moon was the banishing of fear.[128]

At the same time the New Moon was a 'nervous' event, a threshold phenomenon which could fall either way, so prayers were recited to make the difference. Even today, when the Nuer tribe in the Sudan see the New Moon, they rub their foreheads with ashes and throw grain at the moon disc, saying a prayer: 'Ah Moon, Daughter of the Sky-Spirit, let us be at peace, we pray that thou mayst appear with goodness. May the people see thee every day. Let us live.'[129] A Bushman 'Prayer to the Young Moon', spoken while sounding the male antelope's horn, was essentially a prayer for food: 'Young Moon!...Thou must speak to me, That I may eat something. Thou must speak to me about a little thing, That I may eat. Hail, hail, Young Moon!'[130] The Chagga of Mount Kilimanjaro also pray to the New Moon, while in Zaire many people still dance and make music all night when the Moon is full.[131] The Ovambo of Namibia used to smear their bodies with white earth and make a wish as they

Fig. 7. The Phases of the Moon, by Athanasius Kircher, 'Ars Magna Lucis,' Amsterdam 1671. Kircher's perpetual lunar calendar, showing the phases of the Moon as two spirals which are mirror images of each other. Luna Crescens, the Waxing Moon, below, expands from the centre, while Luna Decrescens, the Waning Moon, above, contracts to its centre. The cycle of 28 phases of the Moon forms the outer rim of the oval.

danced.[132] Women in many African tribes still cry out and clap their hands and sing.

For the Bushmen, dancing began at the New Moon as an expression of delight.[133] When, in the 1850s, Xhabbo the Bushman was telling the German philologist Bleek why he had to delay his return home, he said:

> Thou knowest that I sit waiting for the moon to turn back for me, that I may return to my place. That I may listen to all the people's stories when I visit them...[Three times he repeats that he is waiting for the Moon. Speaking of himself in the third person as 'a man' as distinct from his name, he adds]: He only awaits the return of the moon; that the moon may go round, that he may return home, that he may examine the water pits...[134]

In the last century, journeys around Africa were commonly postponed till the New Moon.[135] And even after a journey of 19 years, Odysseus was expected to arrive at the New Moon, the holy time.[136] Plato mentions the 'old custom' of mothers and nurses teaching their children to bow down to the New Moon.[137] The Greek etymology of the New Moon is eloquent of days gone by, for *Noumenia* (New Moon) is composed of *nouein*, to nod, stir, awaken, and *menia*, moon, giving the awakening of the Moon, the divine nod of the Moon, and bequeathing, via Latin, the more generalized English term 'numen', adjective 'numinous', intended to signify the coming alive of a divine presence who *recognizes* the worshipper. In the *Homeric Hymns*, Zeus characteristically nods his head as his ultimate sanction, after which no more is said. The extraordinary range and number of rituals governing the correct procedures for observing the New Moon suggest what primitive dread this 'numinous' event inspired. For the New Moon is the first moment of visibility, crossing the threshold between dark and light in the manner of an epiphany.

The belief in the *quality* of time, that is, the *quality* of the Moon – which is to say, its precise phase – had far-reaching implications for the apparently secular affairs of state. In Greece, in 490 BC, the Spartans refused to assist the Athenians against the Persians in the Battle of Marathon because it was against the law to go to battle on the ninth day of the month (the festival of Apollo) unless the Moon was full. So they waited for the Full Moon, by which time the battle was over and won.[138] Caesar reported that in Germany the 'Mothers' (*Matres*), who used to declare by lots and divination whether it was expedient to engage battle, declared that it was not ordained (*non esse fas*) for the Germans to win if they fought a battle before the New Moon (*ante novam lunam*),[139] having to wait, presumably, for their own victory to spring up with the springing-up Moon.[140] Similarly, of German civic life, Tacitus said that 'their meetings are, except in case of chance emergencies, on fixed days, either at new moon or full moon: such seasons they believe to be the most auspicious for beginning business.'[141] As Grimm comments, 'the one would inspire by its freshness, the other by its fullness.'[142]

The New (and Full) Moon was the time for marriages, dreaming of lovers, having babies, divining the future. Plutarch writes that the Athenians chose the days near the conjunction of Sun and Moon for marriages, 'thinking that in nature the first marriage is the conjunction of the moon with the sun.'[143]

Shakespeare's *A Midsummer Night's Dream* is structured on the postponing of the marriage ceremony of Theseus and Hippolyta until the New Moon. The play begins:

Theseus:	Now, fair Hippolyta, our nuptial hour
	Draws on apace; four happy days bring in
	Another moon; but O, methinks, how slow
	This old moon wanes!...
Hippolyta:	Four days will quickly steep themselves in night;
	Four nights will quickly dream away the time;
	And then the moon, like to a silver bow
	New-bent in heaven, shall behold the night
	Of our solemnities.[144]

The dissolution of the human into the fairy world, which shortly follows, takes place, then, in the three days' dark of the Moon, the time of dying to the old outworn forms and the gestation of the new. When Oberon, King of the Fairies, greets his wife, 'Ill met by moonlight, proud Titania',[145] are we to understand the Moon is 'out' in the fairy world, though not in the human world? The implication of the 'old moon' waning slowly in its last four days, and Hippolyta's anticipation of the next Moon as 'like to a silver bow', would suggest that, for humans at least, the night is dark, not moonlit. Does Shakespeare make the fairy world and the underworld equivalent? Certainly, Theseus assumes 'fairy time' to be the time when people go to sleep and dream.[146]

FULL MOON

Full Moons were festival nights and days, times of culmination and fruition: sacred marriages of gods and goddesses, coronations of kings and queens, weddings of men and women, the best time to give birth. As Nilsson says, 'half Africa dances in the light of the nights of the full moon.'[147] So, according to Strabo, did the Celtic Iberians.[148] In Gaelic, the word for 'good fortune' comes from the word for 'Full Moon' - *rath*.

In Euripides' *Iphigeneia at Aulis*, the Full Moon is declared to be the time of marriage. Klytemnestra asks her husband Agamemnon what day is set for the (supposed) marriage of their daughter with Achilles. Agamemnon, who plans to sacrifice Iphigeneia to the Moon goddess Artemis, shields himself behind tradition to deceive her mother and cunningly replies: 'When the Full Moon comes, to bring them good luck.'[149]

A poem from the Greek lyric poet Sappho (c.600 BC) describes a ritual of the Full Moon:

> Off in the twilight hung the low full moon,
> And all the women stood before it grave,
> As round an altar. Thus at holy times
> The Cretan damsels dance melodiously
> With delicate feet about the sacrifice,
> Trampling the tender bloom of the soft grass.[150]

As the Moon at the full was complete, so all its potentialities were at their height: it was either the Healer of sorrows and Muse of poets and dreamers, or the Afflictor of madness or blindness.

WANING MOON

Waning was not the time to begin anything except those things that you also wanted to 'wane'. It had to do with darkness, death, and getting rid of whatever was deemed undesirable. The Nandi's customs can stand for many similar all over the world: they married in the Full Moon and held their rites of mourning in the Waning Moon.[151] In the Dark Moon (the still invisible New Moon), nothing prospered above the ground. The Babylonians fasted, the people of Bali shouted to devils to leave the island, the Tiv people of western Africa, expected to be bewitched.[152]

These, and countless other rites around the world, recall a radically different way of living in time – one that persisted far longer in the history of the race than our own conception of time as a homogeneous medium – given, in the term 'linear', as an invisible line drawn through empty space. The death knell is unwittingly sounded in a poem for children by Robert Louis Stevenson, which begins: 'The moon has a face like the clock in the hall'[153] – that same clock whose face would be covered if there were a death in the house and whose 'hands', once shaped to the heads of arrows, were often believed to stop at the precise time of the death of its owner

* * *

When tribal religions change, beliefs that were once vital to survival and the quality of life die down into folk customs, just as former rituals of war die down into games, the ball replacing the head of the enemy. So what was once taboo – filled with numinosity and fraught with consequence – loses its awesome power, but lingers in later generations as a memory which it is not quite safe to give up – or it will bring 'bad luck'. 'Good luck' may then still come from observing the custom even though the full resonance of its meaning has gone. Later, these customs are relegated to folklore and still later called 'superstitions', which can only 'stand over' (the literal meaning of the Latin) because the world view in which they participated and whose essence they expressed is forgotten – because it is no longer sacred. Take the old British custom of jingling the silver in the pocket at the New Moon so that wealth would increase with the increase of the Moon. If you did not have any silver, or if you did, but did not observe the ritual, then your wealth would decrease, since you would be out of harmony with the Moon's phase. More precisely, your lack of jingle would increase as the Moon increased. In Crete you rub your gold ring with your finger when you see the New Moon, asking for health, wealth and happiness. [154] Bowing, curtseying, blessing and kissing the fingers at the New Moon was common in Ireland, Scotland and England in the nineteenth century, and beyond. (Even my own grandmother would go outside and make a wish to the New Moon – not, of course, wanting to look at it through glass). A popular eighteenth-century book warned:

> To see the New Moon, for the first time after her Change, on the right hand or directly before you betokens good fortune that month: as to have her on your left or behind you, so that in turning your head you happen to see her, foreshadows the worst, especially if you have no money then in your pocket. And to see the New Moon through glass is exceedingly ill-omened, though you may somewhat avert bad fortune by turning over all the money you have.[155]

The nursery rhyme 'I see the moon, the Moon sees me' was once chanted as a charm to avert any harmful effect of the Moon's rays, as the later Christian religion conceived its pagan inheritance. The verse ends 'God bless the priest/that christened me.[156]

DIVIDING THE MONTH

The significance given to the New and Full Moons suggests that, in most places, they were the two conspicuous events in the Moon cycle which were first observed. The month was thereby divided in two, one half of waxing and the other of waning, or, as the Kenyan Masai say, the light and dark halves of the month.[157] This was the simplest, earliest and most prevalent form of division, found among most Indo-European peoples, as well as the Egyptians, Babylonians, ancient Persians, early Greeks and Romans, and others.[158] Hindu and Avesta calendars divided the month into waxing and waning, as did the old Gallic Calendar of Coligny, a long inscription engraved on a bronze tablet where the month is divided into two sharply distinguished halves, with the days of each half month numbered consecutively on the old Indo-European model. Other Celts used terms for two weeks: Welsh *pythewnos*, Irish *coicthiges*, like the English 'fortnight'.[159] In the *Odyssey*, the month was separated into two active phases – *histamenos* and *phthinon* ('rising' and 'fading') – as it was in Colombia, Peru and ancient Mexico, where it was called the Moon's 'waking' and 'sleeping'.[160]

In the next stage of discrimination, the crescent of the Waning Moon is added so that the New Moon becomes the waxing, the Full Moon expands as the culmination, and the third extra phase becomes the waning. The Full Moon then appears as the central point, an independent period between the waxing and the waning,[161] making up the three visible phases of the Moon – a configuration that is repeated constantly in later lunar mythology. This is shown in later Greek terms for the decades (three periods of ten days each) of the month as *men histamenos* (waxing), *meson* (middle) and *phthinon* (waning), which appear in Hesiod's *Works and Days* side by side with the earlier division of the month into two.[162] The month was at one time divided into three parts – usually into decades – among the Egyptians, Greeks, Romans, Chinese, Japanese, the Maori of New Zealand, the North American Zuni Indians and many places in Africa.[163]

The subsequent division of the month into four, giving a week of seven days, was made in two ways.

As may have happened in the Sumerian *Descent of Inanna*, the period of invisibility was added to the three existing phases. Even though not a phase in the proper sense, it was treated as equivalent to the phases so that it could complete the cycle of the month.[164] Probably much later, as cultivation became more common, more frequent market days were needed to sell agricultural produce from the land and to give labourers and animals a break. Since the New and Full Moons, as sacred days, were days of rest when people gathered together, it would have been a simple and expedient act to further divide the two halves of 14 days (as a round figure), making a day of rest, a market day, on every seventh day.

The Babylonian word *Shabbatu* was originally a term for the Full Moon, when ordinary work was forbidden, but was later applied more loosely to the four rest days which closed each week of seven days. More precisely, the Babylonian word *Shabbatu* was applied in two texts to the fifteenth or Full Moon day, while the four 'evil days' – when various forms of abstinence were practised – were named as the seventh, fourteenth, twenty-first and twenty-eighth days of the lunar month.[165] So the Babylonians had seven-day weeks, which followed the lunation, the course of the Moon.

The Babylonian *Shabbatu* is so similar to the Hebrew *Shabbath* that it would be strange if the name had not been picked up during the years of the Exile of the Jews in Babylon from 584 to 534 BC. It is sometimes objected that *Shabbatu* was an evil day for the Babylonians, while *Shabbath* was a holy day for the Jews; but what more understandable than for people in enforced captivity to reverse the religious emphasis of their captors?[166] In any case, the practice of observing the New and Full Moon days is thought to have been in existence long before the Exile, as might be expected for desert nomads moving through the Arabian wilderness.[167] As early as the time of Saul, the New Moon festival was celebrated. David says to Jonathan: 'Behold, tomorrow is the new moon, and I should not fail to sit at meat with the king.'[168] The Full Moon was also given significance by the timing of the great agricultural festivals which were held on that day, as was Passover. The New Moon and the Sabbath are often mentioned together in some of the older parts of the Bible (as though the Sabbath were the other festival and taboo day, the Full Moon one). When the Shunammite mother wanted to ask the prophet Elisha to heal her son, her husband asked her: 'Wherefore wilt thou go to him today? It is neither new moon, nor sabbath.'[169] Amos represents the Jewish traders' concern at the restrictions imposed on them: 'When will the new moon be gone, that we may sell grain? and the Sabbath, that we may set forth wheat...?'[170] Hosea speaks against the unfaithfulness of the people, saying (on behalf of his Lord): 'I will also cause all her mirth to cease, her feasts, her new moons, and her Sabbaths, and all her solemn assemblies.'[171]

The prophet Isaiah points the difficulties of a new tribal religion, whose aim was to withdraw the religious impulse from nature. He begins by denouncing the observance of New Moon and Sabbath ceremonies as empty ritual: 'Bring no more vain oblations; incense is an abomination unto me; new moon and Sabbath, the calling of assemblies – I cannot bear iniquity with the solemn meeting.'[172] But the prophecy ends by invoking those same two events to mark the totality of time within which the Lord will be worshipped: 'And it shall come to pass, that from one new moon to another, and from one Sabbath to another, shall all flesh come to worship before me, saith the Lord.'[173]

It seems that originally the Hebrew Sabbath was an observance of the Full Moon day, and was marked with customs like those of the New Moon day, which were primarily to abstain from secular activities. However, at a certain point – perhaps after the reforms of Ezekial[174] – Sabbath became the festival at the end of each seven-day week. But this was not a week, like the Babylonian week, which followed the Moon. On the contrary, it was a week which followed the life of its people, not the course of Nature. The Hebrew week broke with the Moon in the sky and allied itself to the laws of the tribe, inaugurating a new kind of calendar, still sacred, but proposing a new locus for the sacred: the beauty of Nature was no longer to tempt the people away from the moral law. As Job confesses:

> If I beheld the sun when it shined, or the moon walking in brightness;
> And my heart hath been secretly enticed, or my mouth hath kissed my hand;
> This also were an iniquity to be punished by the judge: for I should have denied the God
> that is above.[175]

The planetary week, where days took the name of the seven 'planets' (Sun and Moon being included as planets), became established as a Roman institution in the first century AD. This meant that the Jewish Sabbath corresponded to Saturn's day at the end of the week, and Saturn was called, by some of the Rabbis, the star of the Sabbath.[176] The abstinence of the New and Full Moon festivals was then intensified for the weekly Sabbath, and restrictions were elaborated more and more minutely, resulting, finally, in the sentence of death: 'Every one that profaneth it shall surely be put to death; for whosoever doeth any work therein, that soul shall be cut off from among his people.'[177] Hence the stoning to death of the man who gathered wood on the Sabbath Day (the man who was to appear many centuries later carrying his bundle of sticks on the face of the Moon – see Chapter 7).

By the middle of the third century AD, the planetary week was prevalent throughout the Roman world and was introduced into India by the fifth century AD. The popularity of the Sun god Mithras led to the substitution of *Dies Solis* for *Dies Saturni* as the first day of the Roman week,[178] and in 321 AD the Roman Emperor Constantine made Sun Day a holiday, declaring that magistrates, artisans and city people, but not agricultural labourers, were to rest 'on the venerable day of the Sun'.[179] Early Christians had initially adopted the Jewish seven-day week, with its numbered weekdays, and placed *Dies Dominica*, the Lord's Day, at the beginning of their week, already long observed as the day on which Christ rose from the dead. But since Christ, the Lord, came to be identified with the Sun as the 'Sun of Righteousness', an affinity was recognized between Roman and Christian holy days, so that the pagan week of planetary correspondence (if not actual astrological influence) entered Christianity under an apparently harmless guise. It was left to the Apostle Paul to remind his flock that these things are but shadows: 'Let no man therefore judge you in meat, or in drink, or in respect of an holyday, or of the new moon, or of the sabbath days: Which are a shadow of things to come; but the body is of Christ.'[180]

MOON DAY

Two thousand years later, the day of the Moon is not the day of rest, but the day that begins the working week: 'Mo(o)n-day', in English, from the Anglo-Saxon *Monandaeg*, is a translation of the Latin *Dies Lunae*, meaning 'Day of the Moon', becoming *Lunedi* in Italian and *Lundi* in French. Not so long ago, this day had not entirely lost its ancient associations, both for good and ill. In 1825, Jamieson, in his *Scottish Dictionary* entry for *Mononday*, voiced his disapproval of superstitious customs: 'Some, who might well be supposed more enlightened, will not give away money on this day of the week, or on the first day of the Moon.' He then took the chance to score one against the Irish, who do not, as they do in Scotland, regard Monday as unlucky:

> The idea is completely inverted in Ireland, Monday being accounted the most lucky day
> in the week...undoubtedly a relique of the ancient pagan worship of the Moon.[181]

In Christian mythology, Sunday, as the day of Christ, is intended symbolically as the eternal centre around which temporal life moves. Monday, then, as the Moon's Day, follows Sunday as an image of time coming forth from eternity; though in pre-Christian mythologies eternity was found in the unchanging cycle of the ever-changing Moon or drunk as nectar from the Moon's crescent cup.

TIME AND ETERNITY

The divisions of time appear either to be endless or to end in a point – a point of time, which then becomes a term of space. The etymology of the word 'time' suggests that once the mind starts dividing and cutting into pieces it cannot stop unless rescued by a different frame of mind. The anonymous sixteenth-century English saying 'Time and tide wait for no man' may illumine this. Partridge, in his *Origins*, writes that the *tides* of the sea were given their name in English in the fourteenth century, because they occurred at regular *times*, though already in Old Norse and Old English 'time' and 'tide' were doublets, that is, words with the same roots but different suffixes.[182] Old words, such as 'eventide', 'betide' and 'tidings', point to their common meaning. In modern Dutch, time is *tijd*, while tide is *getij*. The Old Germanic root is *ti*, corresponding to the Indo-European root *di* (compare the Sanskrit goddess *Aditis*, the timeless one – *a*, 'not' and *ditis*, 'time' – and also Sanskrit *dayate*, 'he divides', and Greek *daiomai*, 'I divide, apportion').[183] In medieval England, as in ancient India, the tides were known to move to the rhythms of the Moon, so the rhyming of 'time' and 'tide' is unlikely to be fortuitous, with the thud of the 'd' evocative of waves falling upon the shore.

Turning to Latin, *tempus*, meaning 'time' and 'season', time divided into seasons and so 'weather', comes from the Greek *temnein*, meaning 'to cut' and so 'to divide' (compare Greek *atomos*, 'indivisible', giving English 'atom', and 'temperate', in the sense of doing things at the right time). The Greek *temnein* comes from the Indo-European root *tem*, with *ten* as a variant, from which comes 'tense' as the grammatical index of time. From the Greek *temenos*, as the 'cut off and so sacred space of a god', comes the Latin *templum*, 'temple', which was also originally a space 'cut off', both on Earth and in the heavens, by the priest or augur, to enable him to collect and interpret 'omens', a term probably composed of *os* and *men*, meaning 'mouth of the Moon'.[184] We still speak of the 'temper' of the time, which may once have been related to the 'mood' of the Moon. This space consecrated to the gods with its own laws and rites then became the structure in which the gods were worshipped, a place where one could 'contemplate', from the Latin *contemplare*, to 'view things together, intensely or far away'. (Compare also *templum*, a 'reverse beam', the English weaving term 'temple', and English 'template'). As Partridge comments, 'One does not need to be a profound philosopher nor even an acute philologist' to be able to perceive the relations between these and other terms, in all of which 'the idea "to cut, to cut out, to cut off", hence of "division, whether spatial or temporal" (the notorious space-time continuum, as valid in language as in science) is either clearly denoted or potently connoted.'[185]

Taking this further, the notion of temporal division, in which a year, week, day or hour is cut into smaller and smaller pieces, implicitly evokes an image of time as a line or length, to be broken up into manageable proportions. If, under the 'space-time continuum', we begin with the less familiar spatial division of a circle, and the idea of time as a 'cutting-out' of space, then the image of a circular Moon, full, round and bright, progressively 'cut out' to yield the phases we call 'time', comes to mind. Dismemberment – the explicit theme of many of the myths of the Waning Moon – is a cutting-up into pieces, taking the members apart. But, if this is a plausible association, then the notion of time as cutting would have originated as a perception of the Waning Moon, not the Waxing, for we do not see the phases of increase as cutting pieces out of the dark but as a growing towards completion in the

Full Moon. In this case, time is not initially presented as an idea of ordering, of setting parameters in order to work the better within them, but as a perception of death, in which what was whole is cut.

In Greek the word for time is *chronos* (from the root to 'wear out', 'grind' or 'erode') and the name of the god who gets time going is Kronos. In Hesiod's story, Gaia, Earth (the first to arise from Chaos), gave birth to Ouranos (Heaven), then to the hills and sea, and then, lying with Ouranos, her son become her lover, she brought forth the goddesses and gods whose names are the familiar forms of nature. But then Gaia (for reasons unknown) gave birth to three ugly giants, whom Ouranos hated and hid inside her, not letting them see the light. Gaia stretched and strained to deliver them but creation was arrested: nothing could come from her, all was dark. Then she who had given birth to everything gave her son Kronos a sickle, and he cut off the genitals of his father, who then lifted himself suddenly off his mother-wife, and creation began again in the space between them.[186] The distinctly visual image of the crescent-shaped sickle slicing through the nether regions of Heaven draws Kronos as the first New Moon curved into black night – the cut that sets the skies moving and time rolling.[187]

It can also be no coincidence that the Greek Moirai, the three spinning Fates who dwell in the Moon, have a name that means 'part' and 'portion', nor that the last of them *cuts* the thread of life with her shears. So to return to the beginning, 'time and tide wait for no man', not only in the sense that rhythms and seasons keep on moving and changing and it is wise to keep up with them, but that in the end they roll over us and beyond us, cutting us off, as the sonnet says:

> Like as the waves make towards the pebbled shore,
> So do our minutes hasten to their end.[188]

'I am Time', declares Krishna in the *Bhagavad-Gita*, revealing himself to Arjuna as Lord of the Cosmos, 'which in its course destroys the world'.[189] The Sanskrit word for 'time', *kala*, also means 'black', and is the root of Kali, the goddess who is the personification of Time in its devouring aspect (fig. 1).[190] Kali, with her necklace of skulls, treading down corpses in an orgiastic dance of life upon death, reveals the 'black' dimension of Time: that is, Time in its pitiless impersonality, its relentless, unstoppable movement which leaves behind only the living memory of successive generations, which, in turn, is superseded by 'history' as the collective memory of what has passed.

Yet Kali, as one of the manifestations of the Great Goddess, Shakti, is also the spouse of Shiva, who is called both Kala, 'The Black One', 'Time', and Mahakala, 'Great Time', which is to say, Eternity.[191] Kali is also, then – the paradox would insist – the Mother who brings forth her children into time, and thereby gives energy and form to eternity, which would otherwise lie quiescent and forever unknown to itself.

Fig. 1 (p.39) shows Kali – called here Ugra-Tara – all in black, standing on Shiva who lies naked save for a loin cloth. She has two pairs of hands: at the lower level, the left hand holds out the bowl that offers life (coinciding with the trunk, leaves and bird of the Tree of Life), while the right hand presents the scissors which are to cut off the threads of that same life. At the higher level, where the hands point upwards, these two facts of life are spiritualized: the right hand wields the sword that cuts through illusion and the left hand clasps the flowering lotus of eternal regeneration. Serpents of transformation adorn her wrists and hair, one twirling up the stem of the lotus flower. The two grey dogs echo these motifs, the dog on the left poised to drink, and the dog on her right gnawing at a severed human arm beside a whitened skull.

In other pictures on this theme, Shiva is drawn twice, in two modes of himself, known as 'Shiva-Shava'. One Shiva rests directly beneath Kali's feet, and opens into life as though waking from a dream. The other Shiva lies below the first and does not touch Kali at any point: sleeping, head turned away, he is as unconscious of death as of life. Shiva is called here 'Shava', 'corpse', the 'Plenitude of the Absolute as Total Void'.[192] The upper Shiva, entering time, wears the Crescent Moon in his hair, the 'crest' of Shiva. Sometimes Shiva is called by a lunar name, *Sakala Shiva*, referring to the Full Moon when filled with all its 'digits'. The lower Shiva is called *Niskala Shiva*, the Moon 'devoid of digits or of constituent parts', which is the Dark Moon. Together, the two Shivas in one are portrayed in the total orb of the Moon, both visible and invisible.[193]

When fully awakened, Shiva is the Cosmic Dancer who balances the opposites in perfect counterpoise, dancing their duality into transcendence. Or, as in fig. 8, again wearing the crescent prominently across his brow and watched over by the crescent-horned white bull Nandi, his earthly vehicle in time, Shiva lies on a couch with the Goddess in one of her other modes of being, here called Parvati. Both Shiva and the Goddess have been changed through their mutual embrace: Kali who transformed him is now transformed herself into the lover through whom his character can unfold. As two aspects of the One being, the image is of reconciliation, revealing the identity between the Absolute and Maya, between Eternity and Time. This perception, the two pictures together suggest, is the goal and gift of contemplation.

Fig. 8. Shiva watches Parvati sleep. Rajput painting. Pahari School. c. 1800. Boston Museum of Fine Arts, Ross-Coomaraswami Collection.

CHAPTER 3

THE MOON AND THE WATERS

The moon, methinks, looks with a wat'ry eye:
And when she weeps, weeps every little flower,
Lamenting some enforced chastity.
Shakespeare *A Midsummer Night's Dream*

When the thin curve of the Crescent Moon rose as new out of the black night, it appeared to many early people to be a cup which held all the waters of life: rain, dew, the moisture of air and cloud, the water of springs, rivers and seas, the sap of plants and trees, and the blood and milk of animals and human beings. Across the continents of the ancient world, tribes sang, danced, painted and wrote of the Moon as the spring and source of water on Earth.[1]

New Moon, appear, give us water! New Moon, come and thunder the waters down for us! Rain for us![2]

So the Bushmen of Angola have sung for thousands of years, praying for rain, wild fruits and game. For the Bushmen, all water came from the Moon, and all creatures, if they are to live, must drink the Moon's water, sipping the dew that hangs from grasses and bushes at dawn and twilight, or sucking it up through long straws from holes deep inside the Earth.[3]

THE MOON AND THE WATERS OF LIFE

In Old European Neolithic art, the Moon had already been vibrantly related to the waters, painted on vases as wavy or jagged lines looking like streams and torrents of rain (figs. 2 and 3). But when, around 3000 BC, cuneiform script appeared in Sumeria and hieroglyphics in Egypt, the lines and streaks painted on bowls and vases could now confidently be read as rain:

I step on to the heavens and the rain rains down;
I step onto the earth, and grass and herbs sprout up.[4]

Thus the hymn to Inanna has her say, she whose earliest name, Nina, meant 'Lady of the Waters'.[5] Inanna's grandmother, mother of the Moon god, Nanna, was the Great Mother Goddess Ki-Ninhursag, herself the daughter of Nammu, the primal sea. Ki-Ninhursag was the Great Cow who encompassed the heavens and the Earth, whose milk fell as celestial food and whose womb opened to give birth to creation. She was also called 'She who gives life to the dead'.[6]

Whenever the Moon was imagined as a goddess, rain came as milk from heaven. Figures of Inanna show her offering milk from her breasts or holding a vessel as the gift of the 'Waters of Life' (fig. 4). A hymn to her goes: 'O Lady, your breast is your field...Water flows from on high for your servant...Pour it out for me, Inanna.'[7]

Fig. 1. Head of the Dancing Shiva, with Crescent Moon in his hair. Bronze statue from Chittoor District, Madras Government Museum, Chennai, Madras, India. Last quarter 11th century AD.

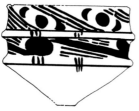

Fig. 2. Right crescent, Full Moon and left crescent, interspersed with wavy lines of water or rain. Upper register of a graphite-painted bowl. Karanovo VI/Gulmenita. Tangiru, near Bucharest, Romania. c. 4500-4300 BC. (From Gimbutas, The Language of the Goddess, p. 284).

Fig. 3. Sonatas of becoming: splitting eggs, crescents, Full moons and snakes as decorative motif on shoulders of late Cucuteni vases. Sipintsi, western Ukraine. 4th millennium BC. (From Gimbutas, The Goddesses and Gods of Old Europe, p. 162).

Fig. 4. Inanna holding the vessel of the waters of life. Sculpture. Palace of Mari, Mesopotamia. Museum Aleppo. c. 1800 BC.

The Sumerian poem known as the 'Langdon Epic' tells of the place 'whence the waters flow from their source, from the moon's reservoir.'[8] Many Mesopotamian cylinder seals link the Crescent Moon with the cup or vase held out by the deity to the worshipper, both containing the waters of renewal. Ultimately, the god or goddess is to embody the particular 'god-like' state of mind of the supplicant, through which transformation takes place.

The Mycenaean goddess in figs 5 and 6, sculpted sometimes as the Full Moon and sometimes as the Crescent, has rain painted upon her 'wings' and upper body, as though falling from her breasts.

Hathor, the Egyptian cow goddess with crescent horns, whose great belly was the heavens and whose four legs stood upon Earth as the pillars of the universe, was also in her nightly aspect the Moon.[9] The deceased were pictured suckling from her udders, or from her breasts when figured in female form. Similarly, Artemis of Ephesus, the Greek Earth and Moon goddess in Anatolia (who became Diana in Roman myth), gave forth milk as heavenly rain from her multiple breasts, as well as earthly food. It was no wonder, then, that this rain was felt to be healing rain, part of the divine substance.

Sometimes the curved cup of the Moon is conceived as a crescent boat sailing across the heavenly sea of the sky, as in fig. 9, where the Mesopotamian Moon god Nanna-Sin meets his priests.[10]

One hymn to Sin thanks him for filling the river:

> When thou floatest like a boat on the waters...
> the pure river Euphrates is filled with water to the full.[11]

The Egyptians also believed that the Sun and Moon used boats to sail around their courses; it was only the later chariot-riding Greeks who saw the Sun and Moon in chariots drawn by horses or bulls.[12]

Figs. 5 and 6. Mycenaean goddess as Crescent Moon (left) and Full Moon (right), with black wavy stripes representing rain. Known as the Psi and Phi statues, after the shapes of the Greek letters. Painted terra-cotta statues. c. 1500 BC. Rijksmuseum van Oudheden, Leiden, Holland.

Fig. 7. Khons with the lunar disc upon his head. From the tomb of Rameses IX, Thebes.

One of the many expressions of the Moon in Egypt was Khons or Khensu, the 'traveller', who was from very early times taken to be a form of Thoth. In the New Kingdom (c.1500 BC), he 'became' the son of Amun and Mut, and Rameses III built him a temple, 'the House of Khensu in Thebes', where inscriptions on the walls address him as 'great god, lord of heaven', and liken him to a bull. He is usually drawn with the head of a hawk, and sometimes shown with a Nilometer in his hand as the one who controls the water of the Nile, which was believed to increase at each New Moon (fig.7).[13]

Osiris was the figure through whom pre-eminently the waxing and waning of the Moon and the rising and falling of the Nile came together as one. When Osiris – as Moon, water and vegetation – was slain by his brother Seth – as Sun, darkness, desert and drought – the Nile waters evaporated and sank into the mud. Then Isis, his sister-wife – she who wore upon her head the circle of the Full Moon within the crescent – filled the Nile with her tears and made it rise again. When the lost Osiris had been 'found' by Isis, the Nile overflowed from his 'thigh' or loins as semen, and his seed covered the Earth, which was Isis, and took root as new plants, their son Horus. The Pyramid Texts say:

> They come, the waters of life which are in the sky.
> They come, the waters of life which are in the earth...[14]
> O Osiris! The inundation is coming.
> Abundance rushes in, the flood season is coming,
> arising from the torrent issuing from Osiris.[15]

According to Plutarch, the Egyptians meant by Osiris the 'lunar world': 'they reason that the moon, because it has a light that is generative and productive of moisture, is kindly towards the young of animal and the burgeoning plants.' This is in contrast to the Sun who parches vegetation and 'in

Fig. 8. Egyptian Moon Boat, with the Full Moon resting upon the Crescent. The two Eyes of Horus are guardians of the journey. The boat steers itself, in the unmanned rudders hanging into the water on either side. (From Maspero, The Dawn of Civilization, London, 1922).

Fig. 9. Sin standing in the Moon crescent boat, with crescent above his head, moving across the heavenly ocean. One priest greets Sin, while the other priest greets the dragon of Marduk, the patron-god of Babylon, with a spade on his back. Neo-Babylonian agate cylinder seal. 2300-2100 BC. British Museum.

many a region overpowers the moon.'[16] 'Not only the Nile,' he continues, 'but every form of moisture they call simply the effusion of Osiris; and in their holy rites the water jar in honour of the god heads the procession.'[17] Isis, as his sister-wife, was also 'none other than the Moon', and was, 'in fact, the female principle of generation.'[18] Plutarch's reliability as an interpreter is confirmed in many Egyptian texts: a Coffin Text of c.1500 BC says: 'Osiris appears whenever there is an outflow [of water].'[19]

In India, it was a common saying that 'the Moon is in the waters' and 'rain comes from the Moon'.[20] The Hindu Moon god Soma (or Chandra, the 'Luminous') was called 'Lord of the Waters', storing the rain and controlling the tides.[21] In an Indian folk tale, the Moon is drawn as a crystal ball containing silver water, with fish and turtles swimming in it, whose shadows appear to us as dark fields upon a milky sphere.[22]

Shiva, in one of his many dimensions, is the Moon god of the mountains. The Crescent Moon resting upon his head catches and filters the flow of the River Ganges, which otherwise would pour down uncontrollably from the heavens and flood the whole of India. Shiva's power draws the great river down through the intricate tangles of his matted hair, separating it into rivulets so it reaches the Earth in small streams, all converging in the lower Himalayas to form the one River Ganges who purifies all creatures (fig. 1).[23]

The Moon's ancient association with water was often rendered by imagining lunar deities as gods and goddesses of the waters, whether in Heaven or on Earth. There were also, more simply, lords and ladies, fathers and mothers, or men and maidens, of the waters. Among the North American Indians, the Moon was called the 'Water-maiden' by the Pueblo Indians, while the Algonquin had the same term for Moon as for water. The Sioux thought the Moon held a pitcher of water, and the Cherokees prayed to the Moon to withhold rain or snow. For the Eskimos, snow fell from the Moon.[24]

In old Brazil, the daughter of the king of the Moon was called 'Mother of Waters' and ruled over rivers and seas.[25] The Spanish Hieronymo de Chaves wrote in 1576 that the ancient Mexicans believed that 'the moon makes all things grow and multiply...and all moisture is governed by it.'[26] In Iran, the Iranian goddess of water, Ardvisura Anahita, was also goddess of the Moon;[27] the Phrygian Moon god Men brought water and rain.[28] The Tartars in Central Asia thought the Moon was full of water, and in China it was said that 'the vital essence of the moon governs water.'[29]

Another expression of this belief was to 'see' pails, pitchers and buckets of water on the face of the Moon (see Chapter 7). These pails were carried either by the Moon deity (as the Maori in New

Fig. 10. Hapy, the Nile god as a form of Osiris, pouring water as the inundation on the grain, whose soul, as another form of Osiris, rises upwards as a bird. To his right, Thoth holds out the palm branch of time to the deceased, showering him with the ankh signs of eternity, transforming the old man into the young hawk-headed Horus, who is Osiris reborn. Bas-relief from the Ptolemaic Temple of Isis, Philae. (From Lucie Lamy, Egyptian Mysteries, p. 6).

Zealand and the Yakuts in Siberia thought),[30] or else by those women and children whom the Moon had kidnapped as they went about their earthly business of fetching water for the night. In Germany, the man in the Moon holds a pitcher,[31] and in old Ireland the people believed the Moon had a well in it.[32] The Nicaraguans carved the Moon as a pitcher of water on their cliffs, and the Mayans drew the Moon with a pitcher in their manuscripts.[33]

With so many men, women and children around the world clutching their pails of water in the Moon, it is not surprising that a common explanation for a sudden downpour was that someone in the Moon had upset their bucket. The coastal tribes of British Columbia thought the woman in the Moon tipped her bucket over every now and then.[34] The Mayan Moon goddess, Ixchel, is drawn pouring water from an upturned pitcher, letting it rain. In figure 14, Ixchel is an older version of the Moon goddess who holds the fertile rabbit, for the Moon is both young and old in turn.

This sample from the tales of many lands shows how widespread was the connection between Moon and water, and how long lasting. Even in classical times, Aristotle, Pliny, Plutarch, Catullus and Macrobius, to name a few, assumed the Moon was the source of all moisture.[35] This idea persisted into the Middle Ages and beyond. In *Hamlet*, Shakespeare has Horatio refer to the Moon as: 'the moist star, Upon whose influence Neptune's empire stands...'[36]

In the Middle Ages, the Old English Friar Bartholomaeus described the Moon as the 'mother of all humours, minister and lady of the sea', while Dalla Porta said that 'the seas and floods, rivers and springs, do rise and fall, do run sometimes swift and sometimes slow, as she rules them.'[37] The occult philosopher Cornelius Agrippa declared:

> Water is the lunar element, the water of the sea as well as that of rivers, and all things humid, the humours of trees and of animals, and more especially those humours that are white, such as the white of eggs, fat, sweat, pituitary discharge, and the superfluities of the body.[38]

Fig. 11. Close up of circle containing Luna as the Water Element. Lausanne Cathedral, Switzerland. c. 1230.

Extending this idea into the medieval notion of the 'humours' brought even the temperament and physique of human beings under the influence: a popular sixteenth-century treatise on hygiene observes that 'the Mone is Ladie of moysture and moveth humours.'[39] Since the 'humours' took their name from the Latin *humor*, which meant 'moisture' (and the way the humours were blended composed the 'temperament', the inner weather, *tempus*, of a person), it is easy to see how the Moon could rule such apparently unrelated matters as moisture on Earth and human disposition. This fusion is evident in Shakespeare's rendering of Queen Elizabeth's grief at her husband's death in *Richard III*:

> Give me no help in lamentation,
> I am not barren to bring forth complaints.
> All springs reduce their currents to mine eyes,
> That I, being govern'd by the watery moon,
> May send forth plenteous tears to drown the world![40]

In the thirteenth-century cathedral of Lausanne, where a magnificent rose window portrays the medieval conception of the universe, Luna is placed in the Element of Water. The whole is composed of a square and a circle, the square at the centre representing all that is earthly and bound by time (including the four elements, Earth, Air, Fire and Water), while the circles disclose the principles that are beyond time. The element of Water is personified in the centre as a goddess who gestures to her breast with all the fullness of antiquity, and is surrounded by four images, the lowest of which is Luna (fig. 11). The three other images come from zodiacal imagery where water is prominent. In the circle on the left is Aquarius, the water-bearer, water pouring from his vase; at the top is Capricorn, the goat who, in early zodiacal images, has the tail of a fish; and on the right are the two fishes of Pisces, the Fishes. Luna, 'in her element' at the lowest point of the circle of the Element of Water, wears a crescent curving round half the waxing circle of her halo. She is drawn by two white horses in a

Fig. 12. The Moon and her attendants. Southern Netherlands 1500–1530, Wool, silk 170 x 465 cm – 5'6" x 15'3". Galerie Blondeel-Deroyan, Paris.

chariot resembling a green and purple tub, propelled by an imposing wheel whose spokes of bright light flash like whirling moonbeams. In one hand she holds the flaming red torch with which she lights up the night, while from the other hand, upraised, fall tiny red circles, sparks or drops from her brilliant fire.

Two centuries later, Luna was still represented as Mistress of the waters in a most unusual and brilliant tapestry entitled 'Allegory of the Moon' (fig. 12). The figure seated in the chariot drawn by two stags against a starry blue sky is identified as Luna by the crescent crown upon her head and by the scroll beneath her chariot. With her right hand she offers the waters of life and with her left hand she holds the bow whose arrows slay. Nymphs from sea, forest, meadow, trees and fountain surround her as an expression of her sphere of influence. Beside Luna's hand flowing with water are three nymphs of the sea, with billowing sail and rudder, identified below their feet as Nereids. Next to them (far left) stand two wood nymphs, named above their heads as Dryads, holding branches of oak, while two Hymnids, nymphs of meadow and flowers, sit upon the ground twining flowers into a crown. On the left of the goddess, beside the bow, are three nymphs called Napeae, who live in fountains and wells, carrying flowers. On the right stand two Hamadyads, tree nymphs dressed in olive-green, holding branches hung with apples. The large rudder, often seen with the goddess Fortuna, is suggestive of the Moon's role in steering the vulnerable ship of fate upon the precarious sea of life. The Moon's ancient powers are re-enacted here not as symbol but as allegory – something which has lost the power to terrify, but still provokes the mind to reflect.

Contemporary language conceals the earlier beliefs in metaphor. Metaphors for the way moonlight is imagined to work are invariably 'wet' and contrasted to the Sun's drying powers. As the Sun's rays burn, parch, dry, heat and warm, so the Moon's liquid rays bathe, splash, wash, intoxicate (like alcohol), quench thirst, dissolve, saturate, cleanse and cool: Oberon, King of the Fairies in *A Midsummer Night's Dream*, speaks of 'young Cupid's fiery shaft/Quenched in the chaste beams of the wat'ry moon.'[41]

THE MOON AND WEATHER

In earlier days, the Moon was commonly observed for signs of weather, as well as for the marking of time. For the Romans time and weather were etymologically linked, pointing to a common origin:

tempus, time, *tempestas*, weather, inherited in the French: *il fait beau temps* (it's fine weather) and *quel temps fait-il?* (what time is it?) A similar link is found in the Greek Horai, the Hours or Seasons, since the word *Hora* was at first nearly equivalent to weather.[42]

The up-turned cup of the Moon is now no longer seen as full of rain, but the idea that rainfall follows the phases of the Moon has not entirely died out (fig. 13). Early and late watchers of the weather can see the look of the Moon changing when the atmosphere changes and the air becomes more transparent. Many sailors and farmers continue to claim that the weather changes as the Moon 'changes' – at New and Full Moons – and folk sayings still abound with lunar weather lore.

Heaviest rain is expected at times of change, just *after* the New and Full Moons (when it rains 'cats and dogs', the Moon's animals), while a halo around the Moon means rain. The Full Moon itself is predictably good: it 'brings fair weather' and 'eats clouds', and a clear Moon heralds frost: 'Clear Moon, Frost soon.'[43] However, again predictably, 'Frost occurring in the dark of the Moon kills fruit and blossoms, but frost in the light of the Moon will not.' The Zuni Indians say: 'The Moon, her face if red be,/Of water speaks she.' The colour of the Moon promises rain, wind or snow:

> Pale Moon doth rain, red Moon doth blow,
> White Moon doth neither rain nor snow.[44]

One Moon a month is more than enough: 'Two full moons in a calendar month bring on a flood.' A second Full Moon in a calendar month is the 'blue moon' of the phrase 'once in a blue moon' (meaning 'hardly ever', or, more exactly, only seven times every 19 years). In many parts of England the rhyme goes: 'Two Moons in May, No corn, no hay.'[45]

Virgil, in the first century AD, claimed in his *Georgics* that 'the Father himself laid down what the moon's phases should mean', so that humans might predict the weather. When the Moon has blurred horns the weather is wet and when it has sharp horns the weather is dry:

> When first at the new moon her radiance is returning,
> If she should clasp a dark mist within her unclear crescent,
> Heavy rain is in store for farmer and fisherman:
> But if a virgin blush covers her face, there'll be
> Some wind – wind always flushes the face of the golden moon.
> And if at her fourth rising (this is a sign infallible)
> She walk the heaven in purity of light, her horns not blurred,
> All that day and the days which follow
> To the month's end you'll fear no rain or wind.[46]

Compare, 1500 years later, Markham in *The English Husbandman*, 1635:

> If when you see the new Moon appear, you perceive that some part of her horns are obscured, or if she be black or discoloured in her midst. If she hang much to the West; if she be compassed about either with thick or waterish transparent vapours; or if she look more than ordinarily pale, all these are infallible signs of Rain. And if it beginneth to rain small and mist-like on the fourth or fifth day of the Moon's age, the Rain will continue all that quarter of the Moon's following.[47]

Many beliefs centred around the crescent as a cup which, if nearly horizontal, would hold water (so the month would be dry), and if tilted toward the perpendicular to the horizon would not hold water (so the month would be wet). This was called a 'dripping Moon', as G. Jean Aubrey noted in 1685:

> Countrymen observe as a certain rule, that a dripping moon (that is, perpendicular) presages wet, especially the Moon being of a cloudy and blackish colour in a clear sky; and that the weather will last so a good while.[48]

In fact, the mind's eye has always to tilt the crescent one way or another to turn it into a cup that could hold water at all. Nonetheless, the difference in perceived tilt gave many people the notion of 'wet' and 'dry' Moons.

The popular Scottish *Ballad of Sir Patrik Spens*, with its lyrical image of the bright new sickle Moon cradling the old black round Moon, is from a sailor's point of view a weather warning:

> Late, late yestreen I saw the new Moon,
> With the old Moon in her arms;
> And I fear, I fear, my Master dear!
> We shall have a deadly storm.[49]

This is Coleridge's version, beginning his *Dejection Ode*. He continues:

> For lo! the New-moon winter bright!
> And overspread with phantom light,
> (With swimming phantom light oe'erspread
> But rimmed and circled by a silver thread)
> I see the old Moon in her lap, foretelling
> The coming-on of rain and squally blast.[50]

The foretelling of a storm becomes for him a metaphor of hope for the ending of the 'void, dark, and drear' of his dejection, with the storm promising the return of his 'shaping spirit of Imagination'.[51]

THE MOON AND DEW

Dew, arising in twilight and lasting till dawn, was generally believed to come from the Moon: 'The heat of the sun dries; that of the moon makes moist', as Macrobius put it in his *Saturnalia*.[52] This contrast makes sense in the tropics, especially in Egypt, where the sun appears to be hostile to life, drying up the drinking pools and scorching the vegetation. In these lands it is obvious that dew and rain bring life for, without moisture, plants, animals and humans die. What is less evident is the further attribution of the source of this moisture to the Moon.

Yet it is a fact that on the nights of the Full Moon the dew lies thickest on the ground, and this finds expression in myths that identify Moon deities with dew. Inanna-Ishtar was addressed as the 'All Dewy One', as well as the 'Green One' and 'Mistress of the Field'.[53] In Greece, Herse, goddess of the dew, was the daughter of the Moon goddess, Selene, and Zeus. Plutarch, labouring under this image, suggests that if the air is seen as 'Zeus', then it is 'liquified by the moon and turns to dew-drops.'[54] The tale of Selene ravished by the Arcadian god Pan, disguising his hairy goatishness with soft white

Fig 13. Assyrian Winged Moon, with streams of water dropping to Earth caught in two cups. Assyrian cylinder, 18th Dynasty. (From Harding, Woman's Mysteries, p. 14).

Fig. 14. Ixchel pouring water from her water jar. Late post-classic Yucatan. Dresden Codex. c. 1300 AD. Sächsischen Landesbibliothek, Dresden.

fleeces so she might to ride upon his back, is the herdsmen's longing for moonlit nights to cover the hills and gullies with sparkling dew (called 'moonwater') so their herds might drink. Pan and Selene were worshipped in caves together, especially in Arcadia and Elis, where Endymion lay sleeping.[55]

Athene had a shrine to the 'All Dewy One', *Pandroseion*, in her temple in Athens, the *Erechtheion*, close to the sacred olive tree, where a dew service, *Hersephoria*, was held at the last Full Moon of the Attic year when dew maidens danced around the statue of the goddess to bring down the fertilizing dew. Statues of Athene's maidens have moon haloes, *meniskoi*, around their heads.[56]

(*Haloes around the Moon are made by tiny ice crystals high above the surface of the Earth which refract and reflect the light of the Moon*).[57]

These ceremonies point to the ancient lunar origins of Athene who, long before her re-appropriation in the mind of Zeus, first appeared in Knossos in Linear B script as *At(h)ana Potinija*, 'Mistress Athana'.[58] Athene sometimes carried the Full Moon instead of the Gorgon's head upon her shield.[59] Her tunics, on vase and sculpture, were often fringed with serpents, while her coins showed the owl, olive and Crescent Moon (fig. 15). Euripides calls both Athene and the Moon *glaukopis*, 'with gleaming eyes', and the Acropolis was once called the *Glaukopion*.[60] Athene's mother was Metis, a word which means the 'wisdom of forethought', 'measuring in advance' (from the Sanskrit root *me*, which gives *metron*, 'rule', 'measure', 'standard'), and Metis was one of the many daughters of Tethys, goddess of the Moon, and the god Oceanos, who circled the Earth like a serpent – the original pair who, in the Homeric story of creation, were the source of all life.[61]

Athene's Etruscan and Roman names pick up her matriarchal inheritance, which links her most obviously to the Moon. The name Minerva, as she was called in Latin, is again connected with the Sanskrit root *manas*, mind, spirit, and the Latin *mens*, whose root is lunar and whose meaning is mind. She first appeared in Etruria under the names of Menrva, Menrfa, Meneruva and Menarva, where she was represented with wings holding a screech owl and may have been the goddess of the thunderbolt. Robert Graves notes that 'this Etruscan Minerva very early merged with the Greek Athena.'[62]

THE MOON AND THE SEA

The sea's a thief, whose liquid surge resolves
The moon into salt tears.[63]

The one indisputable connection between Moon and water is that between Moon and sea and, specifically, between the phases of the Moon and the tides of the sea. At New and Full Moon there are larger tides, known as spring tides, when high water is higher and low water is lower than usual, and in bays and estuaries the difference between high and low water can be as much as several metres, as easily perceptible to the ancient as to the modern eye.

(There are on average two high waters and two low waters in a period of 24 hours and 50 minutes, roughly 6 hours each. As Iain Nicholson, in his Heavenly Bodies, explains it: 'The tides are caused mainly by the gravitational pull of the Moon on the Earth and its oceans. Its pull on the oceans that face the Moon is greater than its pull on the centre of the Earth itself, and this difference in attraction causes the water on the Moon-facing hemisphere to flow into a bulge underneath the Moon. The Moon attracts the solid body of the Earth more strongly than the water on the far side; the water on the far side tends to get 'left behind' and flows into a bulge on that side.' Both Moon and Sun affect the tides, though the Sun's gravitational pull is $^2/_5$ that of the Moon's. So when the Moon is closely lined up with the Sun at New Moon and Full Moon, their tidal forces accumulate, causing bigger bulges and larger tides. When Moon and Sun are pulling at right angles to each other (at First and Last Quarter) their effects partly cancel each other out, producing a smaller bulge and resulting in what are called Neap Tides, where the range is much smaller.)[64]

Nonetheless, it still seems doubtful whether the universal attribution of all other kinds of water to the Moon was invariably the result of a logical inference from watching the tides. Certainly, from very early times it is recorded that the Greeks and the Celts observed the link between the Moon and the tides, as did the Indians from the time of the *Vedas*, the Eskimos, the Maoris of New Zealand, the Andaman Islanders, the Chinese and the Japanese.[65] As Pao P'ah Tsze declared: 'The vital essence of the moon governs water: and hence, when the moon is at its brightest, the tides are high.'[66] Or, in the words of Chaucer, 'The see desyreth naturely to folwen' the Moon.'[67] It is hard to imagine any fisherman who was not aware of the relation of the tides to the Moon for their lives would have depended on their capacity to predict changes, but what of those tribes who lived far from the sea and had different priorities of survival?

The Maoris made the relation between Moon and sea through the tale of Rona, who was called the 'Tide Controller'. She was the daughter of Tangaroa, god of the ocean, who was so large that he only breathed twice every 24 hours.[68] The story is a familiar one around the region. Rona, like the Samoan Sina, was fetching water in her bucket when the Moon went behind a cloud and Rona fell over a root of a tree, swearing at the Moon, calling him a 'cooked-head Moon'. Like other Moons, this Moon took offence easily and raced out of the cloud and caught her with his beams, lifting her up to the Moon where she can be seen to this day, still clinging to her tree and clutching her pail of water.[69] But when Rona was removed to the Moon she brought her power to control the tides with her, the great pail which rocked with the rising and falling rhythms of the sea.

For the Polynesians, the Moon and the ocean were inseparable. The Polynesian Moon goddess, Hina of the two heads and many forms, is called both 'Lady of the Fish', *Hina-Ika*, and 'Lady of the Ocean Waves', *Hina-Te-Ngaru-Moana*. Hina, whose name means 'Moon',[70] was one of the sisters of the Polynesian Sun god, Maui, who made a net with her hair so he could pull the Sun into the world. He then let the Sun fly up into the sky until it reached the west, when he lowered it with the same net into the ocean. Hina-Ika married a fish god, Ira-Waru, who was an even better fisher than the Sun god and invented fishing nets and eel traps, all of them woven from Hina's fine, strong hair, the silvery threads of moon rays shimmering on the sea. Not only can Polynesian fishermen see at nights into the moonlit depths of the sea where their woven nets catch the fish beneath the waves, but each dawn

Fig. 15. Greek coin. One side shows the head of Athene. The other side shows an owl, with olive spray and crescent Moon. Late 5th / early 4th century BC. British Museum.

the silver strands of the Moon's hair pull the Sun up out of the ocean in the east and lower him gently each evening into the west, just as happened in the beginning, for as the Sun goes down the Moon comes up. Hina was also the patron of arts and crafts and guardian of the dead in the underworld.[71]

Many other Moon goddesses are also born from the sea. A late myth draws Ishtar as falling from Heaven into the sea (or the river Euphrates), from where she was brought to shore by water gods or fishes and tended by doves,[72] an image perpetuated in the birth of the Greek goddess Aphrodite.

'Foam-born' Aphrodite is linked to the Moon through her epithet *Pasiphaessa*, the 'All-shining One'. In Hesiod's *Theogony*, Aphrodite was conceived in the lap of the waves which were fertilized by semen from the severed genitals of Ouranos, Heaven, and was 'born in soft foam', as the Homeric *Hymn to Aphrodite* puts it.[73] Aphrodite, the first child of the separation of Heaven and Earth, is therefore the closest to the memory of their union, so love is imagined in the greater context of humanity's longing for reunion with the whole. Understandably, then, Aphrodite was sometimes cast as the eldest of the Moirai, the lunar goddesses of fate.[74]

For the Egyptians, the sea was the salt waste into which the life-giving waters of the Nile dissolved and were borne away – yet another image of Seth slaying Osiris. But when, after Alexander's conquest of Egypt in 323 BC, Egyptian divinities spread into Greece and the Roman world, Isis, who was already goddess of the Moon, destiny and fortune, became also goddess of the sea upon which much Greek and Roman fortune depended. In 'wave-tossed' Delos she was called Isis *Pelagia*, Isis of the Sea, while in Italy she was the protector of navigation, and her spring festival, *Navigium Isidis*, launched the season's ships.[75]

The Virgin Mary inherited the title of Isis, 'Star of the Sea', *Stella Maris*, and was also called 'Mother Moon'. Her name, 'Mary', relates her to the sea through the Latin *mare*, meaning 'sea', while in French 'mother' and 'sea' – *la mère* and *la mer* – are phonetically the same.[76] Some of the oldest goddesses *are* the sea: Nammu in Sumeria, Tiamat in Babylon – the primal ocean as Mother of all. In pre-Columbian Peru, the word for Moon, sea and woman was the same.[77] The Mayan Moon goddess Ixchel was called 'Lady Sea'.

Seafarers and land lubbers alike have drawn analogies between the Waxing and Waning Moons and the flowing and ebbing tide. The flowing tides, like the Waxing Moon, were often believed to bring life in with them, and the ebbing tides, like the Waning Moon, to take life away as they went. Aristotle wrote that animals died during an ebbing tide, and speculated that humans were most likely to die during an ebb tide of the body of water that was closest to them.[78] The metaphor was well known to Shakespeare: in 1 *Henry IV*, Prince Hal and Falstaff, discussing the night's thieving, bandy such phrases as 'Diana's foresters', 'minions of the moon' and 'the fortune of us that are the moon's-men doth ebb and flow like the sea, being governed as the sea is by the moon.'[79] Signficantly, Shakespeare has Falstaff die 'ev'n just before twelve and one, ev'n at the turning o' th' tide',[80] giving him thereby a ritual death, as befits one who was a trickster and kingmaker together.

Dickens' Mr Peggotty in *David Copperfield* (1849) tells the young David that Barkis will go out with the ebbing tide:

> 'People can't die, along the coast,' said Mr Peggotty, 'except when the tide's pretty well nigh out. They can't be born, unless it's pretty nigh in – not properly born, till flood. He's a going out with the tide...If he lives 'till it turns, he'll hold his own till past the flood, and go out with the next tide.'[81]

As a corollary, it was a common belief on many shores around the world that birth at a high tide or a Full Moon brought a lucky life.[82] Keith Thomas, in his *Religion and the Decline of Magic*, mentions an Elizabethan record of the state of the tide on a parishioner's death, adding that these notions, of which there were many, 'were not so much survivals of intellectual doctrines about sympathy and correspondence as the direct product of a life in a primitive world where human dependence on tides and the weather was fundamental.'[83] It would have seemed quite 'natural', then, to live in sympathy with the natural world.

* * *

The hypothesis that all life comes from the sea invites the further hypothesis that all life, at its most fundamental, is receptive to lunar rhythms. Further – the argument goes – the high percentage of water in the human body (around 80 per cent) renders it susceptible to the same ebbs and flows as the tides in the sea. In classical, medieval and Renaissance times, this was a common assumption, especially in medicine, but even now some American and Indian surgeons will not operate at the Full and New Moons, on the grounds that the blood flow, like the tides, is more plentiful at this time.[84] Extending the idea of lunar influence on the fluids of the body into the 'humours' of the mind brought the notion of lunacy coming from the Moon, especially the Full Moon, when its potency is at its height. The challenge of distinguishing symbol from fact, and philosophy from superstition, is made still more difficult when it becomes a matter of the Moon's influence on the 'tide in the affairs of men'.[85]

THE MOON AND THE WATERS OF DEATH

The simplest expression of this idea was that when the moist Moon waxed, the moisture on Earth also waxed, so that plants and animals were then at their juiciest and most active. Conversely, in the Waning Moon, moisture was withdrawn from Earth, and all living things dried out and slowed down. However, once the association between Moon and water becomes constant, the duality of the Moon's powers is brought into play. Then the Moon who brings the waters of life also brings the waters of death. In *A Midsummer Night's Dream*, the quarrel between the King and Queen of the Fairies throws all nature awry, and once the Moon is angry the natural order is displaced. Titania (which is the name Ovid in his *Metamorphosis* gives Diana) says:

> Therefore the moon, the governess of floods,
> Pale in her anger, washes all the air,
> That rheumatic diseases do abound.
> And through this distemperature we see
> The seasons alter: hoary-headed frosts
> Fall in the fresh lap of the crimson rose...[86]

The English term 'mildew' – referring to a white fungus due to an excess of moisture – comes from the Greek *meli*, meaning 'honey', so 'mildew' then becomes 'honey-dew'. Since honey is the image for the sweetness of the Moon's elixir in the *Upanishads*, and elsewhere, the etymology suggests that mildew is in origin the dew from the 'pale' and 'angry' Moon.

The very moistness of the Moon which softens the effects of the drying Sun also dissolves the forms of time, initiating the process of decomposition. In *Anthony and Cleopatra*, Enobarbus, stricken with remorse over his betrayal of Anthony, calls upon the Moon to end his life in this way:

> O sovereign mistress of true melancholy,
> The poisonous damp of night disponge upon me,
> That life, a very rebel to my will,
> May hang no longer on me.[87]

Plutarch, explaining the custom of cutting timber in the Waning Moon, writes that 'the increase of light [in the waxing] makes the trees moister and so prone to decay when cut.'[88] The heat and dew of the Moon, Macrobius continues, 'turn flesh rotten'.[89] For, 'the realm of the perishable begins with the moon and goes downwards. Souls coming into this region begin to be subject to the numbering of days and to time.'[90] As so often, the Moon, as the star closest to Earth, is firstly assumed to share the conditions of earthly life, and then, as a star exalted in Heaven, is assumed to have created them: 'There is no doubt that the moon is the author and contriver of mortal bodies,' concludes Macrobius.[91]

THE DARK MOON AND THE FLOOD

Since the Waning Moon and the ebbing tide come back as the Waxing Moon and the flowing tide, the initial dualism presses towards transcendence of the single round: what is destroyed is recreated. The Moon's dual role of dissolving old forms which have outlived their purpose in order to make way for the new can assume the cosmic proportion of a deluge. The Mayan Moon goddess Ixchel, for instance, whose upturned vessel brings rain, is also drawn as the Old Moon destroying the whole world by water from her open jar.[92] Just as the dark is the prelude to the rebirth of light, so the floods that in the idea of cyclical time periodically submerge and cleanse the Earth are, in the lunar myth, deemed *necessary* for regeneration. Deluges are then understood as a judgement for misdeeds. In this sense floods correspond to the death of the Moon at the end of the cycle, making way for the new. Expectations of a catastrophic change at the end of a millenium, with a different kind of energy becoming available in 'the new millennium', may be interpreted in terms of this ancient lunar tradition.

In Genesis, the flood comes because 'the imagination of man's heart is evil from his youth.'[93] In the earlier Sumerian story of the flood in the *Epic of Gilgamesh*, it is the Moon goddess Inanna-Ishtar who blames herself for causing the flood, and her remorse moves her to save the human race from drowning by interceding with Enlil, god of Heaven. When the deluge came, Ishtar wailed like a woman in travail (just as Ereshkigal had wailed like a woman in travail when Inanna was being reborn from the Nether World):

> The past returns to clay, because I have prophesied evil before the gods! Prophesying evil before the gods, I have counselled the attack to bring my men to nothing; and these to whom I myself have given birth, where are they? Like the spawn of fish they encumber the sea!'[94]

In the biblical story Noah, like Ishtar, saves the types of the world from destruction in his ark – a word which is cognate with the Hindu word *argha*, meaning both 'crescent' and the 'arc' of a circle, like a New Moon boat.[95] As father of the future generations, he is in a sense the generator of new life on Earth, in the manner of lunar ancestors who survive catastrophe and begin again. Campbell, observing the link between the Moon cup's ambrosial fiery fluids and the sacramental intoxicants which are their extract, suggests that this is perhaps why 'Noah, the moon man who had sailed his moon boat on the cosmic sea, planted a vineyard immediately when the waters had abated, became drunk, and lay uncovered in his tent.'[96] Inanna-Ishtar sets the model for Noah and in the same sense is the source of the future: she 'built an ark, a crescent boat in which she could carry a few of her children, the seed of all living things, over the flood which she herself had made.'[97] In Hindu myth the first man, Mani or Manu, also saved creation from a great flood, and was said to be father of the race of man who bear his name.[98]

In this way the Moon becomes the first ancestor of the regenerated race. The Algonquins' hero Manabhozo, identified with the Great Hare, became the tribal ancestor of the human race when he survived the flooding of the world by taking refuge on a mountain.[99] Sometimes the survivor of the flood marries a lunar animal and together they regenerate life. In a Dyak legend, for instance, the flood came about by the slaying of an immense boa constrictor, a 'lunar animal'. One woman survived the flood and mated with a dog, another 'lunar animal', to give birth to a new race.[100]

An Australian version of the deluge myth centres on the frog in the Moon, whose croaking brought down the rain. Dak, the huge frog who was mother of all the other frogs, drank up all the waters in the world. The other animals tried to make her laugh so she would release the waters for all to share, but it was in vain. Only when the sea-eel and his wife writhed their sea-eel dance did the Dak frog burst out laughing, and as she opened her mouth the waters flooded out everywhere.[101] On the other side of the world, in Brittany, the Moon also swallowed the sea, but all it took was a chat with a Breton fisherman who soon persuaded her to disgorge it.[102]

It was also told in Australia that the Moon asked a man for some opossum skins to wear at night because it was cold, but the man refused, so the Moon flooded the whole land to punish him.[103] For this is the Moon's other role: the destroyer of barren and outworn forms *in order that* new forms may emerge. In the Pacific Islands, many tribes conceive themselves as having sprung from some mythical Moon animal which had escaped a great flood, sent to purge humanity for some ritual misdemeanour.[104] Death and rebirth are again, therefore, intimately related in the lunar myth, where both the impermanence *and* recurrence of light and dark continually convey the mind beyond what is present to the senses.

THE MOON IN THE WATER

The Moon's affinity with water was such that Moon and water were often interchangeable. For, while in Heaven the water was in the Moon, on Earth the Moon was in the water, dissolving into lakes, pools and slow-moving rivers, especially on clear nights when the Moon was full. The confluence between Moon and water was also expressed in myths of Moon goddesses and gods bathing, for this was how they purified and renewed themselves, by being submerged, 'drowned' in the water and then rising again.

Artemis, the Greek Moon huntress, was bathing in a lake or river – like the Full Moon floating in water – when the hunter, Aktaion, approached too near and saw the goddess without her veils. Outraged, Artemis turned Aktaion into a stag to punish him, and his own hounds tore him apart – a dismemberment that significantly enacts the phase of the Waning Moon after the full (Ch. 12, fig. 10).[105] D.H. Lawrence's scene in *Women in Love* when Birkin stones the Moon in the lake, repeatedly shattering its reflection while Ursula watches, might be seen as an inversion of this story.[106] In Roman times, when Artemis had become Diana, Lake Nemi near Rome was called 'Diana's Mirror'. A temple to Diana of the Wood stood on top of the mountain, and in the calm, flat water of the round volcanic lake below, the Moon shone like a goddess. Diana's day was celebrated on the Harvest Moon (the Full Moon nearest the autumn equinox), when processions wound for miles around the mountain. According to Ovid, every aspiring keeper of her temple had to kill the priest who was already there, enacting the dark phase of the cycle.[107]

An English folk tale of the 'Dead Moon', caught beneath the water for three nights, comes from Lincolnshire.

> This was a kindly Moon who was concerned about what happened in the bog-lands when the skies grew darker, since she knew that people needed her moonlight to walk through the bogs safely. So, wrapping herself in a cloak with a black hood, leaving only her shining feet peeping beneath the hem, she floated down to the wet and slippery bogs, where witches ride through the air on cats and the red eyes of ghosts gleam in the slimy pools of dank water. Suddenly, Moon lost her balance and slid backwards into the bog. A branch stuck out of the water and she clutched at it but the branch twisted itself round her wrists and held her fast so she could not move. Then she heard a man running in the bogs, crying out as evil spirits pursued him, and to help him she pulled and pulled so fiercely that her hood fell back and her silver light streamed out. At once the man could see which path to take and escaped to safety. But Moon herself was still imprisoned, and the evil spirits pushed her deeper into the water and threw a huge stone over her so her light was covered. Three days and three nights passed. The nights were so dark no one knew what to do. At last the man told the villagers what he had seen, and they consulted the Wise Woman who lived in the old mill. She advised them to carry hazel twigs in their hands and put stones in their mouths and to search till they found three things: a coffin, a cross and a candle. This they did, and finding the great stone which looked like a coffin with two crossed branches and a candle of light flickering up through it, they made the sign of the cross and lifted up the stone. Instantly Moon shone out so brilliantly that all the evil things fled. Moon thanked the villagers and rose up into the sky. And that is why no one goes to the bogs at night unless they go with the Moon.[108]

'Drinking the Moon' is a motif found in many folk tales which play with the idea of the Moon in the water, suggestive of what happens when earlier ways of thinking lose their numinosity and myths of mystery become morality tales. An ancient folk tale, with variations from all over the world, tells of a man who once watched a cow drinking from a pool in which the Moon was reflected. Suddenly a large cloud passed over the Moon in the sky and the 'Moon in the water' vanished. Horrified, the man thought the cow had swallowed the Moon and condemned the Earth to perpetual darkness. So he took his axe and split open the cow to let the Moon out again. Just then the cloud moved away from the Moon, so the man was convinced he had saved the Moon himself.[109]

As the Sufi stories of Nasrudin disclose, an element of this way of thinking is never too far from our thoughts:

Nasrudin was walking past a well, when he had the impulse to look into it. It was night, and as he peered into the deep water, he saw the Moon's reflection there.

'I must save the Moon!' the Mulla thought. 'Otherwise she will never wane, and the fasting month of Ramadan will never come to an end.'

He found a rope, threw it in and called down: 'Hold tight; keep bright; succour is at hand!'

The rope caught in a rock inside the well, and Nasrudin heaved as hard as he could. Straining back, he suddenly felt the rope give as it came loose, and he was thrown on his back. As he lay there, panting, he saw the Moon riding in the sky above.

'Glad to be of service,' said Nasrudin. 'Just as well I came along, wasn't it?'[110]

Tales such as these draw on the idea of 'moonshine' meaning 'appearance without substance', as in the phrase 'that's just moonshine', or in the Shakespearean punchline: 'Thou now requests but moonshine in the water.'[111]

The name 'Moonrakers' involves a story of this kind. Two haymakers from Wiltshire, southern England, returning home late from work with their rakes over their shoulders, caught sight of the Moon reflected in a pond and thought it was a round disc of gold. So, wading into the pond, they tried to rake the gold towards them but without success. Then along came their friends and laughed at the haymakers, calling them 'moonrakers'. In another tale from Wiltshire, the rakers were smugglers. A few hundred years ago Dutch gin was costly in import duty, so the Wiltshire lads used to land barrels of spirits in secluded coves on the Hampshire coast and hide them in ponds and lakes during the day and then fish them out at night. One night at Full Moon they were surprised at their raking by the Customs and Excise men who demanded to know what they were doing. 'Oh,' they said, pointing downwards into the water, "tweren't nothing but a large piece of cheeze.' 'Zo,' the tale comments, 'the exciseman...had his grin at them; but they had a good laugh at he when 'em got whoame the stuff.'[112] In Kentucky, in the 20th century, 'moonshine' was the name for illicit alcohol (borrowed from the local Indians' drink of *Chicha*, made in honour of the Moon), while in Britain the name for whisky secretly distilled in the mountains was 'mountain dew'.[113]

An evocative image of the Moon in the water was given in the seventh century AD by Yang-ti, Emperor of the Sui Dynasty, who wrote:

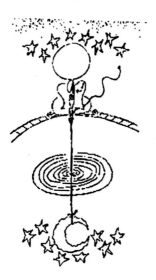

Fig. 16. Nasrudin pulling the Moon from the well. Drawing by Richard Williams and Errol le Cain. (From Idries Shah, The Pleasantries of the Incredible Mulla Nasrudin, p. 43).

The evening river is level and motionless –
The spring colours just open to their full.
Suddenly a wave carries the moon away
And the tidal water comes with its freight of stars.[114]

The Maoris place the Moon's pool not on Earth but in the eternal heavens. They say there is a cloud-land above the heavens called 'the land of the water of life of the gods'. This land has a lake in it called 'the living water of Tane' which renews life. Here is where the Moon goes when it dies, and then it is restored to its path in the sky.[115]

In this case, the Moon shimmering in a pool on Earth is a reflection of the Moon shimmering in its pool in Heaven, such that Earth and Heaven are caught in an embrace of infinitely reflecting mirrors. This mirroring of one world in and by the other dissolves the world into a world of appearances, and so turns the idea of 'reflection' inwards as a way of thinking about what appears. This creates that double reflection which we call consciousness. Julian David, in his discussion of a South African Xhosa tale *Tanga, Child of the Moon*, writes of the Moon reflected in the waters of the river as an image of consciousness:

> When we speak of consciousness psychologically we mean that doubling, that twice-told story or that twice-born life, reflective consciousness, that which is conscious of itself knowing, itself feeling, itself touching, itself thinking. Without that there is indeed consciousness, but it is the consciousness that we call unconscious, the consciousness of *the unconscious*.[116]

So it is, perhaps, that Athene's gift to Perseus is a mirror. By following Athene's instruction to look not at the Gorgon but at her reflection in the mirror, he is saved from being turned to stone, petrified by the Gorgon's gaze (Greek *petros*, 'stone'), for she is the 'evil eye' that slays by sight – a profound image of self-paralysis consequent on gazing fixedly into one's own raw terror. By considering the Gorgon, or rather his fear of her, at one remove, Perseus can gain perspective on his fear while at the same time observing the cause of it. The Gorgon's head, which Perseus severed and gave to Athene

Fig. 17. Lotus and Moon. The Moon is reflected in the water out of which the lotus grows. 14th Century painting by Mokuan, a Chinese Zen priest who lived near Kyoto. (From Awakawa, Zen Painting, p. 111).

to wear upon her shield, was said by the Orphics to be the face of the Moon.[117] In other words, he brings his fear into consciousness and it loses its hold over him.

But of what is Perseus afraid? What does the tale propose as so fearful as to need the ultimate defence of Athene's shield, the 'Moon' worn as a sign upon the Moon? The Gorgons were three sisters whose lunar origins are shown in their names: *Stheino*, 'strong', *Euralye*, 'wide-roaming', and *Medusa*, 'cunning one' or 'mistress', as images of waxing, full and waning. The one known as the 'Medusa', whom Perseus, the 'shining', had to slay, was the only mortal sister out of the three, and as the one who could die embodied the dark, dying phase of the Moon. So, in slaying her, he slays the fear of death which can petrify life. Athene herself, who grants him his release, is then the fully realized perspective on the alternate states of life and death, the Moon beyond the moonshine which is the eternal round beyond the temporal phase.

* * *

Many mythic images survive even when they are disproved as facts about the world, and it may be that their appeal as imaginative truths keeps them alive long after their practical usefulness has gone. It may also be that, long before myth and science were separated and then opposed as different ways of thinking, people could observe connections at a deeper level of relationship, and were better able to make the more minute and complex discriminations on which their lives often depended.

Nonetheless, the continuing debate about whether there is a correlation between lunar phases and life on Earth is not simply to be solved by referring it to the larger dispute between mystics and scientists (which is itself often a question of what constitutes 'evidence'), for scientists with equal access to statistics also disagree among themselves. Even now there is no absolute agreement – and not even with telescopes and computers – as to whether and, if so, how, the Moon and/or the planets affect the weather.[118] The extraordinary prevalence of the myths makes the link between Moon and water (and so rain, storm and wind) predictable in early thought, but does not explain why later thought has not been able unanimously to discount it. As the anthropologist Marija Gimbutas says, 'mythical images last for many millennia.'[119]

In this connection, it may be significant that when, in 1609, surveying the skies above his house in Padua, Galileo took his first look at the Moon through the telescope he had made himself, he saw the dark areas as seas and called them *maria*, a name they still retain on present-day maps – *Mare*

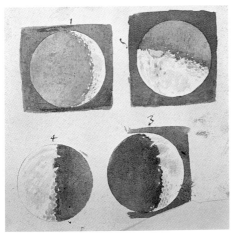

Fig. 18. The Phases of the Moon. Wash drawings by Galileo Galilei. (From Siderius Nuncius, The Starry Messenger, Italy 1610).

Imbrium, for instance, 'Sea of Rains'.[120] Improved telescopes have since shown that the dark patches are merely laval plains between mountains and craters. On the other hand, in March 1998, it was announced by NASA that their *Lunar Prospector* had found water frozen within craters close to the lunar poles, possibly left by bombardments of comets which consist largely of water. This was the dark side of the Moon, constantly turned away from Earth which Galileo could not have seen. The *Times* headline ran: 'Galileo's vision of watery Moon is proved right.'[121]

It may, then, be necessary to go further into the myths to explore the force and persistence of these ideas.

THE MOON AND THE WATERS OF ETERNAL LIFE

The power of this image of the Moon as the source of the waters does not seem to be wholly reducible to the observation that the tides moved to the Moon's phases, dew settled on the ground at night, rainfall appeared to follow the phases of the Moon, and the blood of women ebbed and flowed to a lunar rhythm. Could it have been because of the Moon's rebirth out of its own death that this cup of the Moon's waters was also – or even primarily – the cup of the waters of eternal life, the immortal liquid whose ecstatic promise was tasted each time the Moon reappeared?

SOMA

In ancient India, this sacred drink was called *Amrita* ('immortal' in Sanskrit; *a*, 'not', *rita*, 'mortal'), and also Soma, which was one of the names of the Moon god himself, as well as the name for rain. But what a modern consciousness divides into sacred and profane was originally one indissoluble reality. As Zimmer explains, we are rather to think of the waters circulating throughout the universe and nourishing all living creatures as the counterpart on Earth of the celestial water, the honey nectar of the gods. In an image of the one mystery informing all, *Soma/Amrita* becomes the refreshing rain and dew, which becomes vegetable sap, which becomes the milk of the cow, which becomes blood – and all are differing states of the one elixir, which may also be drunk by mortals after death. The vessel or cup of this immortal fluid, Zimmer concludes, is the Moon, the abode and source of life, which is most conspicuously manifested on Earth in the three sacred rivers – Ganges, Jumna, Saraswati.[122] A Charm from the tradition of the *Rig Veda* clarifies this:

> The rain having rained enters into the moon (for the moon is regarded as the receptacle and main source of the all-enlivening life-sap of the cosmic waters; these in the form of rain feed the vegetable and animal kingdoms, but when the rain ceases the power re-enters the source from which it became manifest, that is, disappears and dies into King Moon, the vessel of all the waters of immortal life); it is concealed; then men do not perceive it.[123]

Another way of phrasing this comes from the *Brihadaranyaka Upanishad*:

> This Moon is the honey of all beings, and all beings are the honey of this Moon.[124]

In eternal life Soma/Amrita is forever full, but in nature, like the Moon, it waxes and wanes.[125] When the Moon is full, the chalice is full with Soma, but – the story goes – the gods need Soma to keep them immortal so they drink a finger of Soma each day until the Moon is empty.[126]

The origin of Soma is found in the story of 'The Churning of the Ocean of Milk' in the *Mahabharata* and the *Ramayana*. In the first days of the world, the gods and the demons, the anti-gods, stopped fighting each other and together churned the cosmic Ocean of Milk so it would yield the potion that granted immortal life – Amrita or Soma. This happened because the gods, gathered at the top of Mount Menu, discovered that by some defect they were not immortal and they became afraid. So they asked Vishnu what to do. Vishnu told them to co-operate with the anti-gods, not fight them. First Vishnu himself took the form of a tortoise and dived into the Milky Ocean to support the weight of the Churning Mountain, *Mandara*, which the gods placed upon his back. The King of Serpents, *Vasuki*, consented to become the churning rope around the mountain, and then together they twirled the serpent back and forth for a thousand years, gods on one side and anti-gods on the other. The mountain whirled so fiercely that trees fell off the mountain and flames came from the friction, which Indra put out with water from his clouds:

> But the various saps exuded from the great trees and the juices from many herbs flowed into the water of the ocean. And from these juices, which had the essence of ambrosia, and from the exudation of liquid gold mixed with the water, the gods obtained immortality. Then the water of the ocean turned to milk as it became mixed with those supreme juices, and from that milk there arose clarified butter.[127]

First to arise from the ocean was 'Soma, the calm moon, with its cool rays, (which Shiva grasped to wear upon his head) and the sun of a hundred thousand rays'. Then the goddess *Sri* (*Lakshmi*), then

Fig. 19. The Churning of the Ocean of Milk. Indian painting, 19th century. Chandigarh Museum, South India.

the goddess of wine, then the milk-white horse of the sun, then the pearl of gems, and the great elephant, *Airavata*. But then there appeared a black poisonous smoke, called 'Black Summit', the highest concentration of the power of death, which Shiva swallowed at a gulp and his throat turned blue. Then came the magic tree and magic cow which grant all desires, and at last the god of healing, *Dhanvantari*, holding the white cup of the ambrosia of deathless life, Soma/Amrita (fig. 19).[128]

There was also a legend that four drops of Soma spilt from the cup and fell into the place where the Ganges and the Yamuna rivers meet and mingle. So vital is this tale to the religious life of Hindus that on 14 January 2001, eight million Hindus bathed in the rivers at Allahabad for the celebration named the 'Giant Festival of the Pitcher of Nectar', *Maha Kumbh Mela*.

Two traditions converge in the meaning of Soma. For it was also said that on Earth Soma was the juice from the milky climbing plant, Soma, which was fermented as a drink and brought ecstasy to those who drank it, releasing them from fear, pre-eminently the fear of death. They were filled with the spirit, with *manas*:

> We have drunk Soma; we have become immortal.
> We have entered into the light, we have known the gods.[129]

Soma was so important in the earlier *Vedas* that it/he is the subject of 120 hymns, and all 114 of the hymns of the ninth book of the *Rig Veda* are addressed to the deity Soma. It is often difficult to separate the plant and the drink from the god, probably because they were originally perceived as a totality. The celestial origin of Soma as 'King of Plants' is shown in the story of the eagle who flew up to the sky and, hurling itself 'with the swiftness of thought', forced the bronze fortress and seized the evergreen plant and brought it down to Earth.[130] Since then the plant grows in the mountains which touch the sky at 'the navel of the earth, on the mountains' and at 'the centre of the world', where sky and Earth interact.[131]

Some commentators consider that it is only in the late Vedic period that Soma became identified with the Moon itself (Chandra being the other Moon god).[132] But Soma held from the beginning all the gifts characteristic of Moon deities: health, fecundity and eternal renewal. 'Have I not drunk Soma?' was the cry of freedom from any limitation.[133] Some passages from the later Vedic hymns and the *Puranas* point to the transition from Soma as ambrosia to Soma as the Moon: 'May the god Soma, he who is called the Moon, liberate me.'[134] As the Moon god, Soma fertilized the whole Earth with his ambrosial moisture which was the elixir above and below: the 'medicine', as it was called. He made the lame walk and the blind see, gave healing to the sick in body and spirit. The drinking of Soma brought inspiration to poets, sexual potency, communion with the gods and immortality.

The key to understanding this seems to lie in the *Stapatha-Brahamana*, where it is said: 'And indeed the Cup of *Soma* is also the mind.'[135] For the image of gods and anti-gods working together to create something new from their opposition offers an image of hope to the mind in conflict with itself. Then Soma, the elixir of life, is the state of being that comes when the mind detaches itself from identification with either pole of opposition, and so is released into a vision of the way between all pairs of opposites: spirit and nature, individual and universe, life and death – 'we have known the gods.'

HAOMA

The Persian equivalent of Soma was *Haoma*, a plant found also on the summits of mountains and brought down to Earth by the birds of Heaven, out of which was made the drink that gave immortality to gods and the gift of spiritual life to humans. The lore surrounding it resembled the kinds of stories which grew up around Soma: it had healing power, it brought fertility to women and husbands to girls.[136] When Haoma was thought of as a god it was personified as Mithra, the son of Ahura Mazda, the Persian god of goodness and light. An alternative tale said that Mithra had to drink Haoma in order to become a god. Zoroaster was born from it, and its fermented juice was drunk in Zoroastrian rituals as the elixir of life, which were said to have been instituted by the progenitor of the human race, Yima, who was immortal. It was said that Haoma 'was the first of the trees planted by Ahura Mazda in the fountains of life. He who drinks of its juice never dies.'[137]

This idea, most fully explored in Hindu thought, is also found in ancient Greece, where the heavenly ambrosia is the nectar that renders the gods immortal on Mount Olympos. The word ambrosia, also meaning 'immortal' (a, not, brotos, mortal) is etymologically related to Amrita. It is curious that the word *soma* turns up in Greek as the word for 'body', including the human body (becoming 'somatic' in English). Partridge, in his *Origins*, does not relate the Greek to the Sanskrit, but lists separately 'soma. 1 – the plant' – and 'soma. 2 – the body.'[138] But it would be strange if there were no connection at all between Sanskrit 'Moon', Soma, and Soma plant, and Greek 'body', given the historical transmission between Sanskrit and Greek, especially as the connection between above and below is already made with the two meanings of Soma – the celestial Moon with its elixir and the earthly plant with its life-giving sap. It is not, then, impossible that the Greek *soma* contained originally an idea of the body – the body of Earth and the body of humans – as being the embodied form of the Sanskrit Soma, the immortal elixir of the Moon. This would mean that the essence of the world was once understood as being composed of heavenly nectar which has solidified into matter, rather in the way that the milky jewel called 'moonstone' was seen as a crystallization of moonbeams. In Greek, *matrix* (deriving from *ma* in Sanskrit, meaning 'mother' and 'measure', and from *mas*, meaning 'moon', the cup of Soma), means both 'mother' and 'matter' – once, as Jung observes, belonging to a common structure of feeling: 'For the root matter is the mother of all things.'[139]

If this is so, then hidden in language is the secret doctrine of the world of the body as saturated with the world of the spirit, a truth which was remembered in the drinking of the plant that was itself the earthly embodiment of the Moon – Soma. This makes intelligible the Platonic idea of knowledge as recollection, a remembering of the original pure Form of which the phenomenal world is a reflection.[140] Ecstasy – standing, Greek *stasis*, outside, *ek*, oneself – brought about by intoxication, itself brought about by the drinking of the Soma plant, then reveals the world in its original 'dissolved' state – as Soma – where it suddenly appears as eternal and unified, in contrast to the secular experience of dismemberment in time.

MANNA

Jewish folklore has its own implicit (and undoctrinal) version of the Moon-dew-honey-elixir complex of ideas in the image of 'Manna', the 'bread from heaven' which the Lord promised Moses to 'rain' down to his people when they were wandering in the wilderness of Sin (the name of the Babylonian Moon god), and which they found in the morning covered with dew:

> And when the dew that lay was gone up, behold, upon the face of the wilderness there
> lay a small round thing, as small as the hoar frost on the ground.[141]

Manna has all the miraculous healing properties of Soma as the immortal dew of the Moon. Manna was created at twilight on the sixth day of creation, and is the food of the angels in Heaven and the righteous (as Soma is also the food of the gods). Manna, which was white and like honey, fell at night and melted when the sun 'waxed hot':[142]

And the house of Israel called the name thereof Manna: and it was like coriander seed, white; and the taste of it was like wafers made with honey.[143]

It did not fall on the Sabbath (obeying the laws of God for the day of rest), left no waste, being entirely absorbed by the body, and ungathered Manna melted and flowed away in streams to be consumed by animals, which were in turn consumed by the children of Israel, who ate Manna for 40 years. A jar of Manna was kept next to the Ark of the Covenant, hidden away before the Temple was destroyed, and is to reappear only in the age of the Messiah.[144] A millennium prophecy in Deuteronomy concludes with the promise that the 'heavens shall drop down dew.'[145]

'Manna' – a word with the by now familiar root of *man* – was a name common to Arabic, Sumerian, Egyptian and Greek, and was generally prevalent in the Sinaitic wilderness as a term for the exudation of the tree *Tamarix gallica*.[146] It was told that when the Torah was given on Mount Sinai, the Israelites died from fright when they heard God speaking to them and it was the 'dew of life' which revived them. This same dew, 'made of the light which was present at creation but hidden ever since, will be used by God in the age of the Messiah when He brings about the resurrection of the dead.'[147]

The cluster of images is strikingly familiar: Manna is covered with 'layers of white dew both above and below', and described by the Rabbis as being 'like pearls', the jewels of the Moon. It is beyond the laws of nature, being eaten but not needing to be excreted. Manna is also like honey, created at twilight, made of light, food for divine beings, raining from heaven yet, as a plant of the same name, dripping from an earthly tree, and, most crucially, this dew is the substance of resurrection. Significantly, perhaps, the *Shekhinah*, the divine presence of God, is also said to be 'like the moon reflecting the divine light into the world.'[148]

Keats picks up similar images in his poem *La Belle Dame Sans Merci*, when he meets a lady, a 'faery's child', whose love allows him to forget death:

> She found me roots of relish sweet,
> And honey wild, and manna dew...[149]

HONEY-DEW

Coleridge's 'honey-dew' in *Kubla Khan* has all the magical properties of *Soma*:

> Weave a circle round him thrice,
> And close your eyes with holy dread,
> For he on honey-dew hath fed,
> And drunk the milk of Paradise.[150]

The Bushmen think of the 'Moon's water' on the bushes as being like liquid honey and also resurrecting the game, or at least keeping it alive, even if it looks as if it has been poisoned. For this reason Bushman hunters were forbidden to look at the Moon while they were shooting, for 'the Moon's water is that which causes the game to live':

> For, our mothers used to tell us about it, that, the Moon's water yonder, (that) we see, which is on a bush, it resembles liquid honey. It is that which falls upon the game. It makes cool the poison with which we shot the game; and the game arises, it goes on,

while it does not show signs of poison; even if it had appeared as if it would die. The Moon's water is that which cures it. And it lives, on account of it...our mothers used to tell us about it, that the Moon, if we had looked at him, the game which we had shot, would also go along like the Moon.[151]

Honey is often indistinguishable from ambrosia in Greece, as it is from Soma in India. Plutarch writes: 'as Athene when Achilles was taking no food instilled into him some nectar and ambrosia, so the moon, which is Athene in name and fact, nourishes her men by sending up ambrosia for them day by day, the food of the gods themselves...'.[152] Euripides likens 'golden Aphrodite' to the bee who makes of the flowering world a sweet honey, reconciling humans to their destiny:

> For her breath is on all that hath life, and she floats in the air
> Bee-like, death-like, a wonder.[153]

This ambrosial tradition persists in our use of the term 'honeymoon' for the time after marriage, Aphrodite's time, when mortals may taste the immortal nectar of the gods, once a 'Honey Moon', lasting a whole month.[154] In French the idea is the same: *lune de miel*.

Zeus was fed on honey in Crete, as was Dionysos. Kerenyi, in his book *Dionysos*, observes that bees were the first source of that intoxication of delight which later issued from the vine. Originally, the nectar of the gods came from those plant juices from which bees make honey. It was not blood that flowed in the god's veins, but a substance called *ichor*, a pale yellow ethereal fluid – just like, it so happens, honey, dew or Soma.[155] Rilke extends the metaphor:

> 'We are the bees of the invisible,' he writes, '*Nous butinons eperdument le miel du visible,
> pour l'accumuler dans la grande ruche d'or de l'invisible.*' ('We deliriously gather the honey
> of the visible, to accumulate it in the great golden hive of the invisible.').[156]

MOON-DEW

Stories of miraculous healing waters are found in folklore everywhere, and these waters are called the 'Well of the World', the 'Well of True Water' or simply the 'Living Waters'. The underlying idea of most quest myths is the search for the 'Water of Life' which transforms the one who goes in search of it, as well as healing the sick, reviving the dead, and granting eternal youth and immortal life. In this Hungarian morality tale the magic elixir is explicitly related to the Moon's own dew. The heroine, called 'Truth', refuses, rather understandably, to admit that 'Falsehood', the name of the villain, is superior. Falsehood retaliates by putting her eyes out. As Truth lies maimed she hears two devils bragging that they have cut off the water from the neighbouring village, and also that they have just killed a physician who had discovered that if the blind washed their eyes in the dew on the night of the New Moon they would be healed. Whereupon Truth rubs the sockets of her eyes with the New Moon dew and her sight returns. Then she runs to the village and tells the villagers how their water may be recovered. So 'Truth' is seen to be true at last.[157]

In Alchemy, dew was one of several symbols of the philosopher's stone in its embryonic stage, often called the 'elixir of the moon' (fig. 20).[158] Senior, in *De Chemica*, brings the traditional imagery of the Moon into his alchemical vision when he writes that 'the full moon is the philosophical water and the root of the science, for she is the mistress of moisture, the perfect round stone and the sea...'[159]

Dew comes up in many a healing cure from folklore: if it is the elixir of the gods, if it is sent by the Moon, then it must have magical powers. A popular cure for gout in Britain was to walk barefoot over the dew-covered grass, but to cure lumbago you had to roll about in the dewy grass when you heard the first cuckoo of the year.[160] The custom of 'May-dewing' – washing in dew, gathered before sunrise on 1 May – was practised up to the twentieth century in Scotland, bringing beauty and husbands to maidens, healing for sore eyes, and a summer of good luck to all.[161] Far away in north-west Amazonia, the Desano Indians still call dew the 'saliva of the Moon', believing that it makes plants grow, fills certain herbs with magical potency, and helps women carry children in their womb. [162]

In one version of the Babylonian myth of descent, Ishtar goes in quest of the Waters of Life from the other side of death in the underworld. If Dumuzi's wounds from the wild boar could be washed in the waters of the marvellous spring, then he would come back from the land of no return. But for Ishtar to return herself, she also must be washed in the eternal waters of the spring, and this is what happens in the presence of the Annunaki, the Laws: 'Namtar (the messenger of Allat-Ereshkigal) poured upon Ishtar the waters of life, and brought her away.' When Ishtar reaches the upperworld she understands that each year she must mourn, and each year she must bathe Dumuzi in the life-giving waters, and he would flourish from springtime to springtime, the time of the "spring".[163]

Ultimately, the idea of the Water of Life refers inwardly to the dissolving of the petrified heart, which brings about a birth at a new level of being – a 'New Moon'. So in fairy tales blindness is often healed through tears of repentance or compassion – like Rapunzel, for instance – for the outer blindness, fully understood, brings the gift of inner sight. Lear says to Gloucester:

> 'No eyes in your head, nor no money in your purse? Your eyes are in a heavy case, your purse in a light, yet you see how this world goes.' 'I see it feelingly.' the blind Gloucester replies.[164]

This thought has a long history. It is possible to look again at the Akkadian seals, such as the one in figure 21 from 2350–2150 BC, where the god Ningizzida, Lord of the Abyss, wearing a crown horned like the Moon, holds out a cup, which the initiate, being led towards him by a second god or priest, also crowned with horns, is about to drink beside the fire altar. Directly above the god's cup hangs the crescent cup of the Moon, source of the intoxicating liquid with which the earthly cup is filled. Campbell points out that the figure to the right with a serpent crowning his head is the porter at the god's gate who, 'admitting and excluding aspirants, is a reduced or preliminary manifestation of the power of the god himself. Hence the contents of his pail must be a reduced or preliminary portion of the ambrosial drink given by the god.'[165] The two together are two levels of manifestation of the one eternal principle. The whole scene is framed by the intertwined male and female serpents of the caduceus, whose union is to signify the transcendence of opposites as the vision which the cup brings to those who drink from it.

Fig. 20. 'Elixir of the Moon.' Codex Reginensis Latinus 1458. 17th c. (From Jung, CW12, p. 214).

Fig. 21. God of the Caduceus. Assyrian Cylinder Seal. From the Diyala Region, Tell Asmar, Iraq. 2350-2150 BC. (From Campbell, The Mythic Image, p. 284).

In Celtic tales, the cup of the Moon becomes the cauldron of rebirth: beneath the waves, Manannan Mac Lir, God of the Sea, served the flesh of pigs that, killed today, were alive tomorrow, and offered an ambrosial ale that bestowed immortality upon all his guests. In what is a deepening of the meaning given to 'eternal' values, Manannan had a golden cup which broke into pieces when lies were told over it, but was restored to a whole when the truth was spoken.[166] The Christian chalice of the Holy Grail comes out of this tradition. In Chrétien de Troye's story, the Grail is the immortal wine of Christ's blood blessed by the Christian sacraments, while in Joseph de Borodin's version the Grail holds the blood of Christ pierced from his side as he hung upon the Cross. In Wolfram von Eschenbach's *Parzival*, the 'Graal' is a stone from heaven which acts like a cup, offering whatever anyone asks of it, whether food or drink, but it may be won only by a man with a compassionate heart.[167]

MEAD

There is also an inexhaustible Well of Wisdom in Norse myth: Odin, or Wotan, called the 'Wanderer' and sometimes imaged as triune, gave an eye for just one sip of wisdom from this well, sunk deep within the roots of the World Tree, the ash Yggdrasil; while above, in Valhalla, the dead warriors drank a heavenly mead which restored them to life and joy (see Chapter 10, fig. 10).[168] Odin's goat also drank from the water of Yggdrasil' and her milk was then drunk as mead by the gods. The mead that was called 'Odin's mead', made of honey and the blood of the wise Kvasir, himself made from gods' spittle, was the source of all poetic inspiration. English and Scottish ballads also tell of rivers of mead flowing in the other world like rivers of fermented honey and water.[169]

The word 'mead', Eliade has observed, can be traced back to Indo-European times. In the *Rig Veda*, Soma is called 'the sweet food honey', the word for 'sweet' being *madhu*, whose cognates are, in Greek, *methy* (an amethyst was originally a jewel that protected against intoxication); in Old Slavic, *medu*, in Icelandic *mjod*, and in Anglo-Saxon *meodu*, a word which becomes 'mead'. This suggests that there was a common Indo-European tradition of a kind of honey mead, attributed to celestial origins, which intoxicated its imbibers with strength, inspiration and the feeling of unity with their gods, which is readily interpreted as immortality.[170]

Archaeologists, excavating the site of Callanish in the Hebridean island of Lewis, off Scotland, have recently found traces of a potent beer made from a honey-based mead and heather, together with numerous drinking vessels, beneath the peat close to the 3000-year-old standing stones, which have a burial cairn at their centre and are aligned to the rising and setting of the Moon.[171] It was surmised that the Neolithic farmers used alcohol ritualistically and, if that were so, there may be yet another, and very early, connection between the Moon and a sacred drink, which the Indo-Europeans knew as Soma.

The eleventh-century Chinese poet Su Tung P'o, dreaming of 'dead kingdoms' and 'friends vanished away in smoke', proposes a toast:

> ...Let people
> Laugh at my prematurely
> Grey hair. My answer is
> A wine cup, full of the
> Moon drowned in the River.[172]

NO WATER, NO MOON

The universal ritual of immersion in water, as a rite of purification, initiation and regeneration, would seem to have its origins in this story of the Moon. For as the flood washed away the old to make way for the new, so, by analogy, the initiates, dying to the old self, were reborn through being submerged, 'drowned', in the Waters of Eternal Life. As the gift of the Moon, the waters brought rebirth after the symbolic death, specifically rebirth into a vision beyond the survival of the ego, a vision in which the greater self of the initiate found itself identified with the greater life: 'That art – Thou!' (*Tat tvam asi!*) was its expression in Sanskrit, the kind of vision, we are to understand, that in the river Jordan was to change the man Jesus into the baptized Christ. The *Amritabindu Upanishad* expresses this as metaphor:

> Being verily one, the Self-of-all-beings-and-elements is present in every being. It is beheld onefold and manifold simultaneously, like the moon reflected in water.[173]

Centuries of Indian thinking would suggest that we are to read this picture of the child Krishna pointing (fig. 22), not as a child mistaking the reflection of the Moon for the real thing which only his mother sees, but as an innate understanding – granted to the child-like mind which the divine Krishna embodies – that this Moon and everything else, the whole world of appearances, is an expression of the Self (*atman*), which, the *Upanishads* teach, is reality.

Fig. 22. The child Krishna pointing to the Moon in the water, while his mother, Yasoda Garhawi, points beyond him at the Moon in the sky. Tempera on paper. Puhari. c. 1790 AD. National Museum, Delhi.

The Zen Master Hakuin wrote a verse to his painting of the monkey reaching for the Moon in the water:

> The monkey is reaching for the moon in the water,
> Until death overtakes him he will never give up.
> If he would only let go of the branch
> and disappear into the deep pool,
> the whole world would shine with dazzling clearness.[174]

A Zen poem, *No Water, No Moon*, takes this image still further, suspecting that even if we appreciate that the manifold is the onefold, we may not be fully experiencing in our hearts the One that is the All that is the None! One night, the nun Chiyona was carrying an old pail filled with water and watching the Full Moon reflected in the water. Suddenly the bamboo strips holding the pail together broke and the pail fell apart. The water rushed out and the Moon's reflection disappeared – and Chiyona became enlightened. She wrote this verse:

> This way and that way,
> I tried to keep the pail together,
> hoping the weak bamboo
> would never break.
>
> Suddenly the bottom fell out.
> No more water;
> no more moon in the water –
> emptiness in my hand.[175]

Fig. 23. Enko ho getsu. *Monkey reaching for the Moon in the water. Painting by the Zen Master Hakuin (1686-1769). Japan 18th c. Eisei Bunko Museum, Tokyo.*

Fig. 24. Enso *(Circle). Brush and ink drawing by Torei, a pupil of Hakuin. The text reads: 'Every family can enjoy a fresh breeze and a bright moon; and the spirit of Zen, too, is present everywhere.' Japan, 19th century. (From Awakawa,* Zen Painting, *p. 91).*

CHAPTER 4

THE MOON AND THE GREAT WEB OF LIFE

All living things are tied together with a common navel cord.
Sioux Elder

Each thing implies the universe.
Jorge Luis Borges

The early perception of the Moon as the measure of rhythms and the creator of cycles weaves together phenomena from many different areas of life, almost in the manner of a web. The metaphor of a web is itself a lunar metaphor, for the Moon is often imagined as a spider spinning life out of its own revolving body of light. Goddesses of Fate, portrayed as dwelling in the Moon, also spin, weave and cut the threads of destiny on Earth. In this perception the great web of space which is the world is spun by the Moon as the Great Spider, just as the tapestry of time is woven as the zodiacal girdle in its endless spinning around the Earth. Here, the universe is conceived as woven together of living things on the same scale of being, all composing a common pattern and all composed of the same thread.

EPIPHANIES OF THE MOON

Wherever and whenever life could be seen in a rhythmical pattern – however imperceptible the rhythms might be – the Moon's presence was disclosed: hibernating bears who disappear in winter and reappear with their cubs in spring; cats whose eyes grow larger and smaller in the dark; frogs swelling up and down; snails pointing and withdrawing their horns from their spiral shells; all the creatures of the sea – mussels, crabs, oysters – drawn back and forth in their tides by the Moon. All these act *like* the Moon and so to the early mind in some sense *are* the Moon. Add to this serpents, bulls, cows, goats, oxen, bison, pigs, boars, hares, rabbits, toads, wolves, dogs, coyotes, jackals, foxes, tortoises, owls, nightjars, spiders...

This does not mean that these creatures stop being what they are; it is rather that they are at the same time *transparent* to something other: to see them in this way involves what Blake calls 'double vision':

> A double vision my eyes do see,
> And a double vision is always with me.
> With my inward eye 'tis an old man grey,
> With my outward, a Thistle across my way.[1]

Fig. 1. Astarte with the Crescent Moon upon her head. Alabaster statue, Babylon. 2nd c. BC. The Louvre.

With the outer eye, all these creatures are simply themselves; but with the inner eye they reveal the Moon. A double vision holds the two eyes together as one.

This is symbolic thinking, which, as Eliade insists, is *not* 'the exclusive privilege of the child, of the poet or of the unbalanced mind.' Rather, he proposes, symbolic thinking:

> is consubstantial with human existence, it comes before language and discursive reason. The symbol reveals certain aspects of human reality – the deepest aspects – which defy any other means of knowledge. Images, symbols and myths are not irresponsible creations of the psyche; they respond to a need and fulfill a function, that of bringing to light the hidden modalities of being.[2]

It would follow that if we ignore or belittle the symbolic life, we ask too much of the rational mind. For reason, which analyses and abstracts – being, as Blake says, only 'the ratio of all we have already known'[3] – cannot on its own sustain an experience of the whole, and inevitably cuts itself off from the deeper levels of the psyche: 'If the symbol is lacking, man's wholeness is not represented in consciousness,' Jung observes.[4] In a symbol – to take it in its original Greek meaning – two terms are 'thrown together' (*sym*, 'together', *bolein*, 'to throw'), such that any one of the two terms can invoke the other because they were originally, and so are essentially, one. Literally, a *symbolon* in Greece was a metal plate which was broken in half so it could be later redeemed, thrown together, to make a whole. But it has to be remembered that what to a later age is a symbol is to an earlier age an epiphany, or rather a hierophany, a showing forth of the sacred.

The classical mythologist Jane Harrison warns that there is no greater bar to understanding mythology than 'our modern habit of clear analytic thought. The very terms we use are sharpened to an over-nice discrimination.' What is needed, she says, is the sympathetic imagination:

> The first necessity is that by an effort of the sympathetic imagination we should think back the 'many' we have so sharply and strenuously divided, into the haze of the primitive 'one'. Nor must we regard this haze of the early morning as a deleterious mental fog, as a sign of disorder, weakness, oscillation. It is not confusion or even synthesis; rather it is as it were a protoplasmic fullness and forcefulness not yet articulate into the diverse forms of its ultimate births.[5]

Yeats reminds us of how far we have come from understanding the past on its own terms: 'Because we have come to associate the ancient beliefs about nature with "savage customs" and with books written by men of science, we have almost forgotten that they are still worth dreaming about and talking about. It is only when we describe them in some language, which is not the language of science, that we discover they are beautiful.' He continues memorably:

> Once every people in the world believed that trees were divine, and could take a human or grotesque shape and dance among the shadows of the woods; and deer, and ravens and foxes, and wolves and bears, and clouds and pools, almost all things under the sun and moon, and the sun and moon, not less divine and changeable: they saw in the rainbow the still bent bow of a god thrown down in his negligence; they heard in the thunder the sound of his beaten water-jar, or the tumult of his chariot wheels; and when a sudden flight of wild duck, or of crows, passed over their heads, they thought they were

gazing at the dead hastening to their rest; while they dreamed of so great a mystery in little things that they believed the waving of a hand, or of a sacred bough, enough to trouble far-off hearts, or hood the moon with darkness.[6]

The constant dilemma in writing about the way people used to think is that the language which describes *how* they thought is not the language *in which* they thought. There is a new level in a modern descriptive language which says – perhaps, initially, must say – *I do not think this now, or not in this way* – hence the 'they' rather than the 'we'. Yet, as Yeats shows, if we cannot think ourselves back into the way they think so that we are actually thinking *their* thoughts as *our* thoughts while we are describing them – or rather reliving them – we will never see what they saw.

Since in a sacred world anything, however small, can disclose the divine and be filled with numinosity, it is possible to build up a picture of that world as much through observing the 'mystery in little things' as by studying its formal divinities, especially when they all flow into each other, back and forth. A pearl can hold the powers of the Moon as vitally as can a hare, a serpent, or a god and goddess, or any other of the creatures whose rhythmic energies weave in the mind an intuition of their fundamental identity. It is as though the web can be entered at any point and the whole pattern is implied in each of its tiniest threads, even though the threads may knot into an apparently autonomous story of their own. The analogies work cumulatively and one analogy serves to invoke others. If, further, the Moon itself becomes a symbol, then it also becomes transparent in its turn.

THE SERPENT

Serpents, sloughing their skin as the Moon its shadow, are believed to be continually reborn like the Moon and so to share in the Moon's powers of renewal. Like the Dark Moon they vanish, leaving their old skin behind in winter and hibernating until spring when they return new-born. In this way they are epiphanies of the self-consuming and self-renewing powers of life, the mystery of an energy beyond the forms of time. As the Moon was thought to be the source of dew, rain, lightning and moisture, so the serpent is found coiling beside springs and fountains, or hanging from the Tree of Life as guardian of the life-giving sap. The serpent becomes the power of the waters: gliding through rivers and pools like an undulating wave, its tongue flickering like lightning as the fertilizing fire within the waters. As both mortal and immortal (continually reborn), the snake could mediate between the living and the dead and so was seen to carry the souls of children waiting to be born.[7]

The serpent in myth may be male or female, like the Moon. Its phallic shape allied it with the Moon as a god, when like the Moon the serpent was regarded as the 'Lord of Women', and so revered or shunned as fertilizer of the womb. Its rising from deep within the Earth united it with the wisdom of Mother Earth and with the Moon as a goddess, sharing in the goddesses' powers of birth-giving and transformation. The Bronze and Iron Age Mother Goddesses of Many Names are always wreathed around with snakes: Inanna-Ishtar of Mesopotamia, Isis of Egypt, Hera and Demeter in Greece, to name a few. Artemis and Hekate, as the specifically Greek goddesses of the Light and Dark Moon, carry snakes like torches; snakes hang from the folds in Athene's robe. If there were any further doubt about the Moon/serpent correlation, Aristotle states as fact in his *History of Animals* that serpents have as many ribs as there are days in the lunar month (200 is apparently a closer estimate).[8]

A serpent coiled at rest becomes a spiral, or, conversely, a spiral in movement becomes a serpent. A spiral is a circle which opens into another circle and so combines a return to the point of origin with movement into another level, as does the Moon. The spiral is also the shape of the seashell, the oyster, the conch and the snail. The earliest known spiral was found in Mal'ta, Siberia, on an ivory belt buckle, with three serpents on the other side (figs 2 and 3). Professor Okladnikov commented that many other details of the find indicated 'the great attention that was paid to the Moon – the crescent-shaped form on the buckle, the half-moon notches on the articles found in Mal'ta, and especially on the figurines of women:...The last fact is especially important because these two images – the Moon and Woman – are connected in mythology. Perhaps the Siberian peoples [of today] possess the key to that phenomenon; their women calculate childbirth by the phases of the Moon.'[9]

The serpentine form of the Blanchard bone may then be no coincidence. Spirals and serpents are interchangeable in the Neolithic age, winding around wombs and phalluses as the energies of fertilization or, with zigzag streaks of lightning, falling from heaven as rain (figs 4 and 5).[10]

In the Irish Megalithic settlements at Knowth, Dowth and Newgrange in the Boyne River valley, an astonishing number of signs and symbols of the Moon and Sun have been exhaustively studied by Martin Brennan in *The Stars and the Stones*, a fascinating book which should be consulted for an understanding of the complex union of this ancient art with astronomy. He gives evidence of the pervasive lunar imagery engraved on the stones, especially at Knowth, the largest passage grave in Ireland, with the two passages aligned to both the sunrise and sunset at equinox. Brennan suggests that, in this and many other cultures, a serpent symbolizes the Moon because the Moon appears to move like a serpent in the sky, weaving above and below the ecliptic every month, as well as winding above and below the celestial equator through the year.[11] The wavy lines of an undulating serpent appear, then, to measure time; each turn is a counting unit of the lunar calendar. Serpentine forms often have between 14 and 17 turnings, 14 for the days of waxing, and 17 for the day the waning is clearly seen to begin. The longest winding snakes have up to 30 turnings, as close a representation as possible of the 29.5 days in a lunar month. A sphere and a snake coil may represent a Full Moon, while opposed crescents with a snake coil in the middle, or opposed crescents alone, depict the whole cycle, and are often found on stones (figs 6 and 7).

The Babylonian boundary stone in fig. 8 shows a huge serpent sipping from the crescent of the Moon, as though it were a cup holding the magical liquid which transforms them both. Here the crescent refers specifically to the Moon-god Nanna-Sin who appears between his two offspring: to the left, Inanna-Ishtar as the Morning Star, and to the right, the solar disc of Shamash, the Sun.[12]

THE BULL AND COW

Other animals become epiphanies of the Moon because they *look* like the Moon. The relating of phenomena according to the similarity of their appearance has been called the 'doctrine of signatures', according to which animals, plants, stones – all the natural world – are stamped with a sign of what they are and what they mean, which in some cases implied what they were 'good for'. If a flower was yellow it was good for jaundice; if it was white like moonlight, it 'belonged to', and acted like, the Moon. Take *Lunaria*, for instance – so called because it has round, white, translucent seed heads, otherwise known as 'honesty', 'money-flower' and 'moonwort' – which excelled in sorceries and 'bringing the dead to life'.[13] The essence of things, in this belief, was visible not hidden, so that the look of a thing was the way it was – a belief that was prevalent in England up to the seventeenth century. This idea had the benefit of freeing the imagination and calling forth the intuition, but it was open to abuse since any limits for the mind could be, by appeal to the same doctrine, overruled. This has always been the challenge of a symbol: how to be open to it and yet to know when to close, and how. Though in our time the challenge is rather how to think symbolically without dismissing the

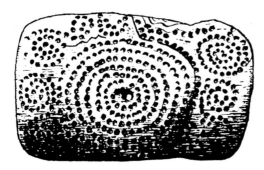

Fig. 2. Schematic rendition of an ivory belt buckle with dotted spiral design, winding seven times from the centre, possibly symbolizing the passage of time. Upper Palaeolithic. Mal'ta, Siberia. c. 16,000-13,000 BC.

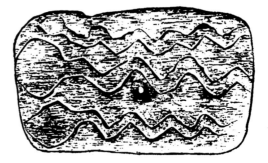

Fig. 3. Other side of ivory buckle, showing three serpents. (From Encyclopédie Illustrée de L'Homme Préhistorique, p. 452)

Fig. 4. Coiled Snake poised above a half-disc and resting between two crescents, probably representing phases of the Moon. The snake coil is flanked by two rain torrents or streams, with two zig-zag signs inside two larger crescents or lens-shaped pointed ovals. A rainbow-shaped rain torrent arches over the scene, with more crescents above it. The two straight lines beneath the two side crescents may represent falling rain. Vase painting, dark brown on buff, with large crescent discs in ochre red. Design flattened out. Dimini culture, Asapi phase, Sesklo, Thessaly, Greece. c. 5000 BC. (From Gimbutas, The Language of the Goddess, p. 286).

Fig. 5. Snake at centre surrounded by black circles as revolving Moons. Graphite painted dish. Tangiru mound, Romania. East Balkan civilization. Mid-5th millennium BC. (From Gimbutas, The Language of the Goddess, p. 283).

Fig. 6. Engravings on curbstones at Knowth. Diagrammatic representation of the Moon phases over one lunar month. The wavy, serpentine line, which extends from the central image, is transformed into crescents and then a full circle or Full Moon on the 14th day. The rest of the month is divided by a line, and towards the end of the month the crescents revert to the wavy line at the last quarter, showing a month of 30 days. Passage Grave culture. Middle of 4th millennium BC. (From Brennan, The Stars and the Stones, p. 146).

Fig. 7. Engraving on curbstones at Knowth. The lunar phases are first counted from right to left, beginning with a right crescent. At the 8th phase, or first quarter, there is a half Moon (in the centre). Circles match phases of the Full Moon. When the count is reversed, the 20th phase represents the half Moon, making the last quarter. Crescents emerge from and disappear into a spiral to represent the unfolding cycle of the month. The bar beneath the wavy line marks off 12 of the 18 turnings, perhaps indicating a year. Middle of 4th millennium BC. (From Brennan, The Stars and the Stones, pp. 148-9).

Fig. 8. Serpent drinking from crescent Moon cup. Kudurru, or Boundary stone, Sumeria, Kassite, 1125-1104 BC. (From Campbell, The Mythic Image, p. 88).

Fig. 9. Horse with mane as horns, and crescent and three round Moons or eggs on its body. Painting on a cave floor. Upper Palaeolithic, Middle Magdalenian. Niaux, Ariège, Pyrenees, S. France. c. 12,000 BC. (From Gimbutas, Language, p. 280).

experience intellectually. As Jung puts it: 'Hemmed round by rationalistic walls, we are cut off from the eternity of nature.'[14]

In early thinking, however, the sharp horns of a bull or cow were seen to match the pointed curve of the waxing and waning crescents so exactly that the powers of the one were attributed to the other, each gaining the other's potency as well as their own. So it was that the horned Moon was incarnate in all horned animals as the source of their fertilizing powers, and particularly in the bull, ox and bison, whose curved horns traced the shape of the crescent as they drew the plough across the fields to make them fertile. This would explain the role of the single horn, held in the hand of the pregnant Goddess of Laussel (Chapter 1, fig. 4), a disclosure of a symbolic relationship between Moon, horn and fertility in existence for at least 20,000 years, and probably many more.

Two horns together placed back to back make two crescents, composing a complete cycle of the Moon. Two horns together set side by side gave the cup and the cornucopia, the horn of abundance. Again, in early forms of thinking a coincidence of shape makes a parallel in kind, and, all things being related, the parallel reveals a unity, which, so it is concluded, means that the Bull is the Moon on Earth and the Moon is the Bull in Heaven. This results in the 'Moon Bull' and 'Moon Cow', the title of many of the Moon gods and goddesses, which became one of the primary cosmological symbols uniting the laws of Moon and Earth, sky and field.

Nanna-Sin, was called the Moon-Bull, where the crescent of the New Moon was seen as the horns of a young bull whose strength grew as the month grew. A hymn to Sin begins:

Proud bull calf with thick horns and perfect proportions, with a lapis beard, full of virility and abundance...[15]

Nanna-Sin's daughter, Inanna-Ishtar, is called 'a splendid wild cow', while in another hymn her body is described as 'covered with scales like a snake's'[16] – the former image allying her with fertility

Fig. 10. Opposed horns and crescents. Some end in discs and some sprout branches, and one has a snake winding upwards. Conical bowls, painted black on red. Cucuteni B. Numbers (1)-(3) from Sipenitsi, 3900-3700 BC; (4) and (5) from Tomashivka, W. Ukraine, c. 3500 BC. (From Gimbutas, Language, p. 294).

Fig. 11. Three stacked bull's heads beneath a Moon crescent. Ancient oriental cylinder seal. (date unknown). Hentze observes that the seal is divided into six spaces with images, with nine Moon crescents in the first space, which means nine Moon orbits. When the seal is rolled, three bull's heads appear, followed by the nine crescents, so that the two partitions appear side by side. Then it is clear that the crescent above the bull's heads is inverted, compared with the nine in the next field, pointing to the changing of the Moon in a new revolution. After the nine crescents follows a field with two crouching human figures. [17] (From Hentze, Früchinesische Bronzen und Kultdanstellungen).

and the latter with rebirth. Other Earth/Moon Cows are 'Cow-eyed' Hera of the Greeks and 'Ashtaroth-Karnaim' (Ashtaroth of the Two Horns), mentioned in Genesis,[18] also known as Astarte, suggesting the goddess was sculpted with a horned crescent Moon upon her head (fig. 1). Ashtaroth was the same Queen of Heaven to whom the women of Israel poured out their drink-offerings, burnt incense and offered cakes, for which they were reproached by the prophet Jeremiah on behalf of his Lord.[19] The Bull's 'Horns of Consecration' which lined the precincts of the Minoan palace at Knossos were also the sign and symbol of the powers of the Moon.[20]

The Egyptian god Ptah from Memphis was said to be incarnate in a black bull engendered by a moonbeam.[21] A similar tale was told of the sacred bull Apis who, Plutarch says, was begotten 'by a ray of generative light which appeared from the moon, and rested upon the cow his mother.'[22] Apis, who carried the lunar disc between his horns, was also the special animal of Osiris, who was himself known as the 'Bull of Heaven' and 'Bull of the Underworld'. After the ritual known as the weighing of the heart, Osiris, as the Moon Bull, carried the deceased on his back to the underworld, ensuring that they would be reborn with him like the Moon (fig. 12). Thoth, who registered the results of the weighing, was called the 'Bull of Truth'.[23]

The cult of the Apis bull was said to have been initiated by Menes, the first Pharaoh, in about 3000 BC. At the great Egyptian festivals a bull, black and white like the Moon, was chosen to represent the incarnation of Apis: it had to be black with a white patch on its forehead and a white crescent on its neck and sides.[24] The bull was led with solemn ceremony to the temple of the living Apis, where it was to be treated for the rest of its days like a king. Anyone who inhaled its breath could prophesy.[25]

In Vedic India the Moon, called Soma, Chandra or Indus, can be represented as a cow or a bull. Since the Moon was the giver of ambrosia, it was to the ancient Indians *like* the milk-giving cow of the heavens, *even though* it was male, and *because* it was male it was also *like* the bull who fecundates the cow. The Moon was the friend of the Sun, Indras – 'Flow, O moon, and envelop Indras', a line from the *Rig Veda* goes – and the two of them went about as bulls to destroy by fire the monsters of darkness.[26]

Fig. 12. Osiris in the form of a black and white crescent-horned Bull, bears his worshipper to the underworld for rebirth. 325-30 BC. (From Wallis Budge, Osiris and the Egyptian Resurrection, *i, p.13).*

In Hindu India the Moon god Soma and the bull Agni were often held to be two forms of one god, while Shiva, who wears the lunar crescent in his hair, took the bull, Nandi, as his earthly vehicle. Shiva also holds the trident of the sea, as does Poseidon, god of the oceans in Crete, Mycenae and Greece, whose animal is also the bull and who sends the fateful bull from the sea to Minos as the sign of his kingship. Dionysos, who marries Ariadne, the daughter of Minos, placing her in the heavens as a wreath of stars, was known as the Bull God.

In Persia, the Moon was called 'the keeper of the seed of the bull'.[27] A myth, older than the Zoroastrian religion of Persia, told how the Primeval Bull deposited his seed in the Moon. Then, in later Zoroastrian thought, this bull – the first animal created – was slain by Ahriman (or Angra Mainyu), the spirit of evil, and then the soul as well as the seed was stored in the Moon. The bull's seed was released when evil first came into the world in the form of death.[28] The myth takes the image of the Moon Bull to explore time: for when the Moon releases the seed into time, as that which is born and dies (as *bios*), it stores the soul for eternal life (as *zoe*), transforming the evil into good. The tale offers a perspective on death, for the soul of the Bull and by analogy the soul of all created beings may share in the fate of the resurrecting Moon which, entering time, yet appears to transcend it.

What is fascinating about the 'primitive mind', as Eliade calls it, is the way nothing stands on its own. Once a living creature, or a stone, or an element of nature such as water has been identified as belonging to the Moon for whatever reason, then all the other so-called lunar qualities belong to it as well. Analogies become affinities which then become symbolically interchangeable. So it is that the bear becomes the ancestor of the human race, an Aztec Moon god is enclosed within a snail, and the moist but modest frog ends up as a goddess of childbirth in Egypt.[29]

THE FROG AND TOAD

Frogs and toads who swell up and down like the Moon also come and go like the Moon, plunging into pools and leaping out again, while on the face of the Full Moon a frog or toad appears which disappears in the Waning Moon. 'On the twentieth day the "toad and hare" wane,' says an old Chinese poem.[30] (The hare will be discussed in Chapter 7). In a work from the Han period (226 BC – 220 AD), the *Huai-nan-zi*, the three-legged toad in the Moon is called the Moon's soul,[31] and in the Guangxi province of China many people of Zhuang nationality still celebrate a toad festival on the first day of the lunar year, praying for a good harvest.[32]

Fig. 13. Two goats flank a central column, with Moons of different sizes, probably representing lunar phases. Painted light and dark-brown on cream. Proto-Geometric. Knossos, Crete. 10th century BC. (From Gimbutas, Language, p. 234).

Fig. 14. Two bulls with crescent-shaped horns draw the Chariot of the Moon in Roman times. The Crescent is often replaced by the Goddess Kybele who is drawn in a similar chariot with the crescent upon her head. (From Lajard, Sur le Culte de Mithra).

Frogs croak more loudly when the rain comes as though they were creatures of rain, whose source was once believed to be the Moon. Virgil names the frogs as one of his sure weather signs for rain, croaking away 'at their old complaint'.[33] The *Rig Veda* says: 'When the waters from the sky fall upon them as they lie like a dried skin in the (dried up) pond, the voice of the frogs rises in concert like the lowing of cows which have calves.'[34] Their croaking around the pool is (respectfully) compared to the chanting of Brahmans at the offering of Soma, and the poem is taken to be a spell for rain.

Frogs and toads – who are usually interchangeable – were believed to bring rain in India, China, British Columbia, Mexico and Chile, among other places.[35] By the familiar logical fallacy *post hoc, ergo propter hoc*, frogs who announced the rain found themselves to be the bringers of rain, and were invoked in spells and charms in times of drought, even beaten or crushed to death slowly so that their croaking would bring the rain down.[36] By contrast, the Maori, who held the frog to be a god of waters, rains and rivers, took care not to harm a frog in case it would cause floods, as it had done in the beginning. In China, frog-spawn was seen falling from the sky with the dew.[37]

There is a chain of analogies here, which can be entered at any point and will invoke the rest of the chain so that the chain gains in strength from each new addition. The mind is working intuitively, moving from an apprehension of the whole to the character of the parts, such that the Moon is seen to reveal itself more and more fully in each epiphany. Thus the frog who appears and disappears into water, as does the watery Moon in the celestial waters, becomes linked with the rain that comes from the Moon and with the fertility that the rain brings down to Earth and with the fecundity of humans and animals, and is finally worshipped in Egypt as Heqet, goddess of childbirth, she who assists births into this world and the next.

Heqet, in the form of a frog, presided over the birth of the life forms that her husband, Khnum, fashioned on his potter's wheel.[38] Frogs were thereby identified with the life that came forth from the dark, muddy waters of the Beginning from which all creation arose and which, in Egyptian thought, re-arises in each new birth. As a hieroglyph the frog could mean 'repeating life', and frogs were found as birth amulets and in tombs of all periods, even mummified frogs, making easier the last birth into the beyond.[39] In later times Heqet was identified with the Mother Goddesses of fertility, and was present when Isis took the form of a bird to conceive the child Horus from Osiris. Egyptian Christians also saw the frog as an image of birth: on a Christian lamp a figure of a frog is drawn with the legend 'I am the Resurrection'.[40] Even today, waxen, wooden and silver toads are presented to the Virgin

Fig. 15. Zoroastrian Moon god in chariot drawn by four bulls. Silver Dish. Iran. 7th century AD. (The Hermitage Museum, St. Petersburg).

Mary in churches in Hungary, Bavaria, Austria and Yugoslavia, a tradition that goes back thousands of years to the cultures of Old Europe where goddesses of birth were modelled as frogs and toads. As an image of the Dark Moon that precedes rebirth, the frog or toad was in other places suspected of incarnating death – sucking blood from people when they were sleeping or stealing the milk of nursing mothers.[41] Either way, the frog and toad are given the powers of the Moon.

A tale from the Kimbundu tribe in Angola draws some of these strands together:

Long ago, the King of the Earth wanted his only son to marry. 'I will help you find a wife,' he said. 'No,' said the Prince. 'I only want to marry the daughter of the Moon King.' The King of the Earth was puzzled, for how do you get to the Moon? He invited all the wise people of his kingdom, but nobody knew, until a little frog spoke up. 'Sire, I will travel to the Moon for you,' he said. Doubtfully, the King gave the frog a letter for the Moon King and sat down to wait until evening. Now the frog knew that the Moon King's water-bearers came down to Earth every morning before sunrise to gather water from a forest spring upon a hill. So the frog hid inside the spring and when the bearers let down the first pail he swam into it before they could see him. When they arrived on the Moon the frog leapt out and said: 'Take me to your king.' The bearers did what he asked, and when the frog finally stood before the Moon King he gave the Moon King the Earth King's letter. The Moon King read it and gave his reply to the frog who went and sat in the empty pail until it was time for the pail to be let down to Earth again. When the pail was plunged into the spring, the frog swam out and jumped all the way to the Earth King's court. 'I am Mainu, the Frog,' he announced himself, 'Ambassador to the Moon King. I bring a message from His Lunar Majesty.' The Earth King accepted the letter gravely, and was delighted to read that the Moon King consented to the wedding of his daughter to the Earth Prince, just as soon as the bride-wealth had been paid. So the Earth King gave the frog a huge bag of gold coins to take up to the Moon in the same way as before. This time the frog was greeted on the Moon in style. He banqueted on pork and chicken, and returned with a message that the Moon Princess would arrive on Earth the night after next. Nobody believed the frog but everybody dressed up just in case, and suddenly they saw the Moon Princess slowly descending down a silver thread woven by the Moon spider and as soon as she touched the ground she married the Prince of Earth.[42]

The anthropologist Gerardo Reichel-Dolmatoff, writing about contemporary Desano Indians in the

Fig. 16. *Liu Hai on the three-legged toad, holding coins as an image of wealth and luck. Bronze statue. Qing, China. 1723 AD. British Museum.*

Fig. 17. *Seti I making an offering to Heqet, the frog-goddess. Drawing of bas relief. Abydos. c. 1300 BC. (From Wallis Budge, Osiris, i, p. 279).*

Amazon rainforest, emphasizes that 'a symbolic or metaphorical relationship is never limited to a one-to-one comparison; symbolic images are always seen as chains of analogies.' The Milky Way, for instance, can be conceptualized in any one of a number of ways: a river, a trail through the forest, a great line of people, a stream of semen, a cast-off snake skin, and so on.[43] 'The categories are interchangeable,' he explains, 'because, on a primary level, a house is a cave, a cave is a womb, a womb is a hearth, and a hearth fire is the sun. And so it does not matter at what point one might begin a chain of symbolic equivalents: with the category of artefacts, of sensory elements, of nature, of supernatural beings, or of myth. The chain is not linear but spirals back and forth from one category to another.'[44]

Compare the twentieth-century Spanish poet Garcia Lorca's poem *Half Moon*:

> The moon goes over the water.
> How tranquil the sky is!
> She goes scything slowly
> the old shimmer from the river;
> meanwhile a young frog
> takes her for a little mirror.[45]

THE BEAR

The bear who follows the lunar pattern – hibernating in the dark of winter and re-emerging in the light of spring – is given divine form as Artemis, one of the goddesses of the Moon in Greece. Artemis was worshipped as the gentle Bear Mother who guards her young with the ferocity of a hunter. On the Acropolis at Athens there was a precinct of *Artemis Brauronia*, where young girls, wrapped in the yellow skins of bears and wearing masks of bears upon their faces, danced to the goddess at the *arkteia*, 'bear-service'. In the *Lysistrata* of Aristophanes, the chorus of women sing of their youth: 'When I was seven years old I became an *Errephorus*, then, when I was ten, I was grinder to our Sovereign Lady, then, wearing the saffron robe, I was a bear in the Brauronian festival.'[46]

The bear has the oldest known history of any animal. Skulls of bears have been found in mountain caves dating to before the last Ice Age, from about 75,000 BC. But this was no random heap of skulls;

they had been arranged in a pattern to express some ritual feeling of the Neanderthal people who had placed them there. Palaeolithic drawings of bears with bleeding mouth, nose and ears may point to an annual sacrifice of the animal, as happened later in the northern hemispheres, particularly among the Ainus of Japan.[47] European folk memories speak of the bear as the ancestress of the human race, the Mother of Life.[48] In Neolithic Europe, bears were the healing image of a safe childbirth for mother and child, as many folktales and sculptures (and teddy bears) show. In eastern Lithuania, a mother confined after childbirth is called 'Bear' (*Meska*).[49] Even the etymology of 'bearing' children is suggestive: the Old European root *bher*, Germanic *beran*, means both 'bear' and to 'bear children', 'give birth', while Germanic *barnam* means 'child', and Old Norse *burdh* means 'birth', itself a word with the root of bear, as is the Scottish word 'bairn'.[50] Compare brown, bruin, Beowulf (Bee-Wolf from the bear's love of honey) and Bavaria, while from the Celtic root *Art* comes the hero Arthur, once the name of a Celtic god of about the sixth century BC.[51] Citizens of the old Celtic city of Bern in Switzerland chose the bear for their name and coat of arms, identifying the bear with the Goddess Artio, the Celtic counterpart of Artemis, as in the old bronze statue, discovered in 1832 (fig. 18). Another patron of childbirth, the Virgin Mary, is honoured each year on 2 February in Acrotiri near ancient Kydonia with a festival to *Panagia Arkoudiotissa*, 'She of the Bear'.[52]

CREATURES OF THE SEA

In ancient China and India the oyster, mussel and pearl belong to the Moon, along with all other shells 'born of water' and 'born of the Moon'.[53] A Chinese treatise from the third century BC reads:

> The moon is the root of all that is *yin*; when the moon is full the *pang* and *ko* mussels are full; all *yin* things are abundant (waxing); when the moon is dark (the last day of the moon) the *pang* and *ko* mussels are empty; all *yin* things are deficient (waning).[54]

Yin, as the feminine energy of the cosmos, is lunar and 'humid'. It is because the Moon is the origin of *yin*, Liu Ngan explains in the second century BC, that the 'brains of fish shrink when the moon is empty, and why the shells of univalves are not full of fleshy parts when the moon is dead.'[55] Also, the 'bivalves, the crabs, the pearls and the turtles, grow and diminish with the moon.' On the other side of the world, Pliny was saying much the same thing in the first century AD: 'The moon nourishes the oysters, fills out the sea-urchins, gives strength and vigour to the mussels.'[56] The snail's shell was the home of Tacciztecatl of the Aztecs, called 'Old Moon God', who carried a white spiral seashell on his back.[57] Among the Aztecs snails used to represent the entire process of fertility, from conception, through pregnancy to parturition, drawing on the resemblance of the snail, oyster and shell to the female genitals. Extending the idea, oysters in Japan and China were believed to promote fertility and easy childbirth[58] and were worn around the waist by the Akamba women until the birth of the first child.[59] They are still eaten as an aphrodisiac. Engaging the Moon's energies of generation also invoked the Moon's other energies of *regeneration*. On many a Roman tombstone a scallop shell was carved to redeem the deceased from his death, and this symbolism of shells and pearls persisted into Christian art – for what nourishes in life may it not yet sustain in death?

THE PEARL

In China the Moon was called 'the pearl of heaven', and 'moon pearl' or 'moon blossom' was thought to

Fig. 18. Deo Artio. *The Goddess feeding her animal, the Bear, who appears to be guarding the Tree of Life in leaf. The Latin inscription says that 'Licinia Sabinella [dedicated this] to the goddess Artio.' There is a slit in the pedestal box for coin offerings. Romano-Celtic bronze statue. c. 200 AD. Bernisches Historisches Museum, Bern, Switzerland.*

fall on the Earth from time to time, making any women who swallowed it pregnant.[60] Dante calls the Moon 'the eternal pearl', while the Gnostics took the pearl as their symbol of the hidden truth, hard to attain.[61] For the Hindus the pearl is 'born of the tears of the god of the Moon: so, as the Moon is the source of eternal ambrosia, the pearl is the antidote to all poisons.'[62] The pearl was also supposed to cure madness, and in Chinese and Arab medicine it was used to cure diseases of the eyes. This healing use of pearls entered European medicine after the eighth century.

Wearing a pearl is healing because it is like wearing a ray of the Moon. A hymn in the *Arthava Veda* praises the pearl for taking away fear: 'I put thee on for life, vigour and strength, for the life of a hundred autumns. May the pearl protect thee.'[63] Covering a dead person in pearls was a gesture of regeneration, for it was designed to unite the deceased with the Moon's powers of renewal.[64] A pearl in an oyster is like a child in a woman's body, said an eleventh-century Chinese text,[65] setting the woman in the cosmological pattern of Moon, sea, water, fertility and regeneration. Aphrodite was called 'Lady of Pearls', and in later art emerged out of the sea in a scallop shell.[66]

By the seventeenth century in Europe, much of the religious import of pearls as Moon-tears had gone yet they were still revered as medicines for just those same areas of the mind and body – madness, epilepsy, fear, melancholy, blindness, love and youthfulness – as had originally belonged to the province of the Moon. Pearls were made into powder which was rubbed on the eyes by the Indians, Chinese and Arabs, and in Europe was thought to cure epilepsy, madness and melancholy (the so-called 'lunar' diseases), along with blindness. Francis Bacon believed the pearl was a drug for longevity.[67] Even now it is a 'precious stone' where the original sacredness of the object is expressed upon another level. Its appeal becomes aesthetic; it serves as a talisman, still retaining that allure which invokes a sense of participation in the pearl's ancient lunar powers. The meaning changes but the image persists, even in the necklaces of shells offered by children on a far-away beach.

THE CRAB

Crabs also rocked back and forth to the tides of the Moon. In 1714 the Alchemical writer Masenius wrote that the crab 'depends on the moon, and waxes with it', and because it sheds its shell it 'signifies resurrection':[68] 'The crab is wont to change with the changing seasons, casting off its old shell, it puts on a new and fresh one.'[69] The natives of the island of Nias in Indonesia tell a tale of origin in which the first people, who were descended from the Moon, became mortal because they ate bananas instead of crabs. Had they eaten crabs first they would have become immortal because crabs shed their skins.[70] In Manipur crabs, when held in a pot of water, bring rain; in the Bahamas they cure earache, and, in South Carolina in 1882, a conjuring man was made invulnerable by holding a crab claw in his mouth, or so he said.[71]

This system of correspondences informs astrological symbolism, inherited from Mesopotamia, through Egypt, Greece and Rome. The zodiacal sign ruled by the Moon is the Water sign of Cancer, the Crab, which lives subject to the lunar sway of the sea and carries its home upon its back. The glyph of the sign of Cancer is a composite figure of breasts and claws, the nourishing of life and the taking of that life away – an image of waxing and waning together. Similarly, the Sun enters the sign of Cancer at its peak just after the summer solstice, when it begins to turn and retreat, and the light loses more and more of its life to the dark. For crabs, moving sideways and backwards, have also their ill-omened aspect, retained in the medical term 'cancer', from the Greek *karkinos*, 'crab', and fostered by the tradition that blamed them for dragging Alexander's ships down into the sea.[72] T.S. Eliot's image is strangely disconcerting:

> I should have been a pair of ragged claws
> Scuttling across the floors of silent seas.[73]

The Moon, as one of the 'seven personal planets', symbolizes in astrology the dimension of the psyche that is closest to the unconscious life: most in accord with the rhythms of the body and the patterns of instinct, and so most sensitive to hidden tides of feeling, evocative of the mother, childhood, and the habits of the past. Astrology follows mythology here by linking the Moon to the earliest experience of the child, recapitulating the childhood of the race. The Moon is 'exalted' in Taurus, the sign of the Bull, ruled by Venus, following on from Hathor-Isis and Inanna-Ishtar, timed to the resurgence of growth in spring.

The lobster appears in the Tarot card of the Moon, in the Major Arcana, Number XVIII (twice times the lunar number nine). In the Marseilles Tarot pack (fig. 19) the Moon card shows a landscape operating at three levels, exploring the relation between Moon and water which are coloured the same dark blue. Two dogs, standing on land, howl at the Moon before two towers, while deep in the water the shape of a lobster lurks directly below the face in the Moon. Drops of blue, red and yellow fall from the Moon to the yellowed Earth, suggestive of 'influence', one blue drop brushing the tongue of one of the dogs as though he is drinking the Moon dew and howling for more. Interpretations range from mystery, intuition, feeling and longing, to deception, confusion and disappointment – evocative of hidden possibilities as yet unborn. The imagery of the card points a contrast between the double towers, dogs, flowers – the dualism of life in time on Earth – and the singularity of the Moon itself between the pairs, with the single lobster lurking in the water below, implying the possibility of reconciling these opposing forces in a new unity.

Waite's twentieth-century Tarot pack (fig. 20) keeps the dualism of dogs and towers but changes the balance of energies, one of the dogs becoming a wolf while the lobster climbs up onto the land, as though these hidden lunar forces can no longer stay submerged beneath the water.

MOONSTONE

Moonstones like pearls are white, the colour of the Moon, and so, it was inferred, partake of the Moon's nature: cooling things, making trees fruitful, bringing luck, curing epilepsy and nervousness. ('White-armed' was a common epithet of Moon goddesses in Greece). These stones, foliated sulphate of lime, were called moonstones or selenite (after Selene) because they were believed to wax and wane with the Moon. They were thought by Hindus to be formed from the congealing of the Moon's life-giving rays and so to contain the essence of healing and fruitfulness. In the fifteenth century, Pope Leo X had a moonstone which he said waxed and waned in brilliance with the Moon (and who would contradict him?).[74] American folklore has it that if a moonstone is held in the mouth at the Full Moon it will reveal the future, while European folklore takes the Waning Moon as the time when the moonstone endows its wearer with the gift of prophecy, while in the waxing it is a potent love charm.[75] Moon amulets, called 'lunuli', took the shape of the Crescent Moon to ward off harm.

THE WOLF AND DOG

I had rather be a dog, and bay the moon,
Than such a Roman.[76]

Thus spoke Brutus to Cassius, proclaiming his principles and disparaging the animal by the contrast. The wolf and wild dog howling at the Full Moon is still a potent image of the Moon's 'attraction' (fig. 21), and no film on werewolves is complete without it, when predictably at Full Moon the man's arms grow furry and before you know it he is a wolf.[77] Yet the wolf and dog's relation to the Moon was once a sign of their affinity with its life-giving force. The Seneca, a Woodlands tribe of the north-eastern United States, tell a different tale of how in the beginning it was the Wolf Spirit who sang the Moon into the sky, and that is why all wolves howl at the Moon.[78]

In the Neolithic age dogs are often drawn with Moons, spirals, plants and trees, even caterpillars, as though like the Moon they stimulate change and growth (fig. 22).[79] For the Inuit, who saw the dog in the Moon, the Moon's 'dog' was an impregnating force, bringing fertility to animals as well as plants.[80] By contrast, for the Hindus the Moon dog was savage and had to be appeased: 'The Moon is that celestial Dog; he overlooks (with an evil eye) the sacrificer's cattle, and that is to their hurt, unless an expiation be made. That is why the people fear the Moon's down-shining, and slip away into the shade.'[81]

The Babylonian seal in fig. 23 registers the ambivalence with which the dog is viewed in myth – tame in the waxing and savage in the waning.[82] More often, the dog (interchangeable with the wolf) stands in for the Waning Moon, leading the way to the underworld – like the Egyptian Anubis, the Jackal-headed god, who, with Wepwawet, the Wolf god, was called the 'Opener of the Way' and Guide of the souls of the dead.[83] This is the dog/wolf/jackal who instigates change by venturing into the unlit, unknown paths which have not been paths before: the way forward is the way lit from within, smelt out with the long nose that is not afraid of the dark. So the dog, friend to the hero, is enemy to the coward.

The guide becomes the guardian in Greece, where the three-headed dog, Cerberus, guards the entrance to Hades, poised on the threshold between life and death. Cerberus was the dog of Hekate, goddess of the Dark Moon, to whom dogs were offered at the crossroads at night and who was once a three-headed dog herself.[84] Hekate's companions, the Erinyes, the three Furies of Retribution who pursued murderers, were sometimes drawn with heads of dogs as well as snakes. Artemis was followed by hunting dogs, as was Hermes, and Selene was invoked as the bitch in the *Magic Papyri*.[85]

In many places 'wolf', the eater of corpses, was the actual word for death.[86] In Norse myth there is a figure called 'Moon's Dog', Managarm, who is the most powerful of all the wolves who threaten Sun and Moon: 'He gorges on the flesh of all that would die, and he will swallow the moon and bespatter the sky and all the air with blood.'[87] Wolves in Scandinavia were called the 'hounds of the Norns', the lunar goddesses of fate, scavenging the battlefields.[88] Though the dog like the Moon leads out of time, it also leads into the eternal realm. Wepwawet leads the procession which begins the Mysteries of Osiris, while Anubis, embalming the corpses, transforms them into the eternal body who may live the life of the universe with Osiris, Moon god of the living dead (fig. 24).[89]

THE CAT

> Look at the cloud-cat, lapping there on high
> With lightning tongue the moon-milk from the sky![90]

From this, an old Sanskrit poem, to Yeats's cat Minnaloushe:

> The cat went here and there
> And the moon spun around like a top,
> And the nearest kin of the moon,
> The creeping cat looked up...
>
> Does Minnaloushe know that his pupils
> Will pass from change to change,
> And that from round to crescent,
> From crescent to round they range?
> Minnaloushe creeps through the grass
> Alone, important and wise,
> And lifts to the changing moon
> His changing eyes.[91]

In this poem Yeats is echoing Plutarch and Cornelius Agrippa, as well as customs from Australia to Russia, Indonesia to Europe.[92] The cat who walks at night and sees in the dark, whose eyes wax and wane, who has nine lives and who was the familiar friend and form of witches, was the Moon's own animal, especially if it was as black as the Dark Moon. In nineteenth century Italy and Germany black cats were kept away from the cradles of children and a black cat upon a sick person's bed foretold death.[93] The Australian aborigines used to identify the Moon with a wild cat, and some North American Indians see a cat in the Moon, unravelling the wool of the waning days. The Norse Moon goddess Freya had her chariot drawn by cats, and in Ovid's *Metamorphosis* Diana takes the form of a cat when the gods flee from the giants.[94] Cats were sacrosanct in Egypt, mummified along with their mistresses and masters, in tribute to the lunar cat goddess Bast or Bastet, who was sometimes identified with the Theban Mut (wife of Amun) and so became the occasional mother of the Moon god Khons or Khensu, and a patron of childbirth.[95]

In Europe there was a widespread connection between cats and rain. A seventeenth-century treatise on agriculture advised: 'The Cat, by putting her Foot over her Ear when washing her face, foreshadows Rain.'[96] In Indonesia, compelling a cat to wash itself was the way to bring the rain down, and in southern Celebes in times of drought a cat was actually conducted around the fields in a sedan chair.[97] As elsewhere, once *one* term of an analogy is made – say, that between the way a cat's eyes grow larger and smaller, most obviously at night, and the way the Moon grows larger and smaller – then the animal assumes the character and role of the whole term of comparison: the cat and the Moon become equivalent. Then the cat washing itself can 'make' the Moon 'wash itself' to release its waters as rain. What begins as analogy ends as identity. So what happens to the cat, the toad, the bull and all the rest of them, happens to the Moon. If a toad cries, the Moon cries – tears of rain.

Fig. 19. 'The Moon.' Marseilles Tarot Pack. 1748 AD.   Fig. 20. 'The Moon.' Waite Tarot Pack. 1910.

THE SPIDER

The spider spinning its web out of its own body is often found as an image of the Moon spinning the threads of time out of its own ball of light, weaving them into the shimmering web of creation. The word 'spider' comes from the Old English word for spinning, *spinan*, as does the term 'spinster', meaning both the one who spins and the one who is single, recalling the virgin spinning goddesses of fate. For the Hopi and the Pawnee Indians 'Spider Woman' was the original weaver of the universe, her eight legs creating the four directions and the four winds of change: she taught the Earth people to weave and herself wove the first alphabet for them to name her creation.[98] In folktales told at Taos Pueblo, New Mexico, it is the 'Spider Grandmother' who befriends the people in unusual ways. In many myths of plains, southwestern and western American Indian tribes, Spider Man or Spider Woman is a creator or a trickster, but almost always a helpful figure and sometimes a medicine man or woman.[99] In the Banks Islands in Melanesia the spider helps the Moon god create humankind,[100] and the Oceanic tribes call her the 'Old Spider'.[101]

Lunar goddesses often assume the form of a spider: Inanna-Ishtar, whose granary is guarded by a huge spider, Neith in Egypt, Holda in Germany, Athene in Greece. In a Greek tale, Athene taught the maiden Arachne to weave, but Arachne wove so finely she was punished by the goddess for rivalling her in her craft. Athene struck Arachne on the forehead, turning her into a spider (the meaning of her name – *arachne*).[102] The etymological root, *rak*, comes from Sanskrit, where it is the name of the Full Moon, *raka*. The *Rig Veda* says that *raka*, the Full Moon, helps the spider to weave the aurora that is woven during the night.[103] Ixchel, the Mayan Moon and Rainbow goddess of fertility, divining and weaving, was also identified with the spider.[104] She was known as *Ix Kanleom*, 'the Spider's Web that Catches the Morning Dew'.[105]

In Angola it was the Moon spider who wove a silver moonbeam for the Moon Princess to climb down

Fig. 21. Aztec dog howling at the Moon. Terra-cotta vase. Colima style. Museum für Volkerkunde, Hamburg.

Fig. 22. Neolithic dogs beside crescent and full Moons. Panels from Cucuteni B vases. Painted black on red. Trusesti, NE Romania. 3800-3600 BC. (From Gimbutas, Language, p. 233).

Fig. 23. Babylonian King, deified as the Moon god Sin, on his throne with two dogs, one coming and one going, suggestive of the waxing and waning Moon. (From Lajard, Culte de Mithra).

Fig. 24. Anubis in his Jackal form with the winged wedjat eye above him. Glazed composite pectoral, Egypt. 19th Dynasty, 1250 BC. British Museum.

from heaven and marry the Prince of Earth. In Borneo the Moon deity becomes a celestial spider to create the world, hanging in the darkness of endless space.[106] In Nias, Indonesia, when the Moon dies, his soul appears as a spider.[107] The Paresi of central Brazil see the Moon as a spider, and the Huitoto give their highest heaven to a spider.[108] In the Loyalty Islands the spider sends the rain on behalf of the Moon,[109] and in many places around the world killing a spider or sparing it, according to culture, is said to bring the rain down. A saying in the United States goes that 'if you kill a spider, it will rain.'[110]

Moonlore persists in the superstitions surrounding spiders, attributing to them the Moon's powers over rain, fertility, health, wealth and omens. In English folklore, small spiders are 'lucky': they are called 'money makers' or 'money spinners', and must *not* be killed – or it will be 'bad luck'. In Polynesia a spider dropping down in front of you is a sign of a present to come. In Tahiti spiders are shadows of the gods and so never harmed. North American Chippewa Indians hang spiders' webs on the hoop of infants' cradleboards 'to catch the harm in the air'.[111] In the twenty-first century, the image of a worldwide web woven by a net of messages spinning around the globe could be seen as a modern equivalent of the ancient idea.

Whatever the emphasis, the spider weaving its miraculous web gives form to a vision of the Moon as spinning with invisible threads a web of relationship between all created beings, bound alike to the cyclical rhythm of waxing and waning as the law and condition of life. The Moon may have once inspired the image, but the image has since taken on a life of its own, as here, in the words of the North American Indian, Chief Seattle: 'All things are connected like the blood that unites us all. Man did not weave the web of life, he is merely a strand in it. Whatever he does to the web he does to himself.'[112]

* * *

It emerges from this pattern of connectedness that what we might call the 'lunar mind' – which we attribute to early people but which, like all mythic images, never completely dies out – gains confidence with each new relationship that can be established. Indeed, once this idea is in place it is almost impossible to disprove it rationally for it composes a world view, a paradigm which includes all evidence, and the criteria for the truth of evidence, within it. Everything then works to confirm it, for the more disparate the phenomena related the more the world discloses itself as a unity – if only in its extraordinary capacity to reveal relationships between elements so apparently unlike each other. Each new thread draws tighter together the composite weave of the Great Web, which then becomes more richly intricate – or yet more illusory.

In this way the Moon has mirrored the images of those who have looked up to it, returning the images with enlarged meaning which are in turn returned, in what becomes an unending process of mutually reflecting mirrors. Ted Hughes captures such a moment of mutual amazement in his poem *Full Moon and Little Frieda*:

> A cool small evening shrunk to a dog bark and the clank of a bucket–
>
> And you listening.
> A spider's web, tense for the dew's touch.
> A pail lifted, still and brimming – mirror
> To tempt a first star to a tremor.
>
> Cows are going home in the lane there, looping the hedges with
> their warm wreaths of breath–
> A dark river of blood, many boulders,
> Balancing unspilled milk.
>
> 'Moon!' you cry suddenly, 'Moon! Moon!'
>
> The moon has stepped back like an artist gazing amazed at a work
>
> That points at him amazed.[114]

CHAPTER 5

THE MOON AND MIND

The Moon became mind, and entered the heart.
Aitareya Upanishad

Atman, the Creator, made Fire, Wind, Sun, Moon, and other divinities. They said to him: 'Find us an abode where we may establish ourselves and eat food.' Atman led a horse to them. They said: 'Verily, this is not sufficient for us.' He led a bull to them. They said: 'Verily, this is not sufficient for us.' He led a person to them. They said: 'Oh! Well done! Verily, a person is a thing well done.' He said to them: 'Enter into your respective abodes.' Fire became speech, and entered the mouth. Wind became breath, and entered the nostrils. The Sun became sight, and entered the eyes...The Moon became mind, and entered the heart...[1]

In this Hindu myth (c. eighth to sixth century BC), it is suggestive that the Moon takes the most reflective abode of all the divinities, becoming 'mind in the heart' – the kind of thinking that is felt throughout the whole being (similarly, the Egyptian hieroglyph for 'thought' was a heart). The Sun, entering the eyes as sight, becomes the power of outer vision, in contrast to the Moon, which, entering the heart as mind, becomes the power of inner vision. So the difference between daylight, where we can see, and the night, where we can only see within, is pointed. The Moon, illuminating the night, then becomes the light in the darkness which we call intuition, a perception beyond the senses, or perhaps perception where the information of the senses is largely unconscious, a seeing in the dark.

Marshack proposed that lunar notations were likely to be the first evidence of cognitive processes in human beings – 'time-factored and time-factoring'.[2] The question presented by the philology of Moon, measurement and mind is whether observation and notation of the Moon did not itself contribute to the development of these and further cognitive processes – for what thought is not time-factored? Did the Moon 'teach us to think'?

THE ETYMOLOGY OF 'MOON'

It is initially surprising how close a relation exists in their etymological history between words for 'Moon' and words for 'measurement' and 'mind.' The extraordinary range of these 'Moon-related' mental activities points back to a time before the mind was differentiated into its various so-called 'functions'. Later thought, for better *and* worse, has made a division between 'thinking' words and 'feeling' words: rational acts of measuring, counting, and relating terms logically, on the one hand, and acts of feeling on the other – purpose, intention, courage – with memory as the underlying structure of the mind on which all mental activities depend.[3] The common 'lunar' root of all these words in Indo-European languages suggests that this distinction between thinking and feeling did not originally exist, as the *Upanishad* above confirms.

Fig. 1. Man looking at Moon. From the Zen 'Ox-herding' pictures. Fhu Bun after Kakunan. Shokokuji Temple, Kyoto, Japan. 1500 AD.

The intriguing idea of words as fossilized poems, or as stories no longer told, might sustain us through a further etymological exploration into the hidden journeys of the 'Moon' in language. If, as Shelley argues in his *Defence of Poetry*, all language in its infancy is poetic,[4] then the origin of a word – the moment of its arising – would hold its most vital meaning, since the word would be closest to the instinctive sources from which it springs. This makes it both animated – alive with implication – and concrete, irreducibly precise. A particular word comes to mind because it is needed to express a particular perception which has not been articulated before, and, as could equally be said, speaking this word creates a new thought. But, as Blake and Shelley insist, the vitality of language soon declines, becoming first generalized and then abstract, by which time the original meaning is obscured and eventually often forgotten.[5]

For Shelley, the original language of the world was poetry, and he brings it to life in images which evoke the ancient celebratory rituals of myth: 'In the youth of the world, men dance and sing and imitate natural objects, observing in these actions, as in all others, a certain rhythm or order.' It follows that: 'In the infancy of society, every author is necessarily a poet, because language itself is poetry...Every original language near to its source is in itself the chaos of a cyclic poem.'[6]

In the Indo-European tradition, the common root of 'Moon' and 'measurement' – *me, ma, men* – extends, fascinatingly, into more complex notions of *mental* activity.[7] Most importantly, Sanskrit *ma*, to measure, seeds the Sanskrit *manas*, which meant mind, in its widest sense of intellect, intelligence, understanding, perception, sense, conscience, will and spirit.[8] *Mata* or *mati-h* was thought, intention, measure, knowledge, and *mantra* was an instrument of thought, a prayer, hymn or text. However, *ma* also means to measure out, to plan (after the manner of a carpenter or house-builder), giving the idea of *maya*, that which is measured out, the phenomenal world of time.[9] *Manu* was the name given to the great teacher who originated Hindu culture, from whom the word 'man' derives, defining 'man' as a thinking being.[10] The Polynesian term *mana*, as the immanent, invisible power of the universe, was believed to have been brought by ancient traders from India.[11]

The speakers of what has been called Proto-Indo-European migrated out of India in waves, beginning well over four thousand years ago, travelling across Asia and Europe, and settling in lands as far apart as Ireland, Scandinavia and Greece. The language groups descended from the Indo-European language are Romance, Slavic, Germanic and Indic, while languages related to these four main groups include Greek, Latin, Armenian, Persian, Germanic and Celtic. This helps to explain the common linguistic roots of many words, especially noticeable in Greek and Latin, one strand of our own inheritance.[12]

In Greek, the Sanskrit root of *me, ma, men* structures a similar range of thought. As well as terms for measurement, the root *me* yields *metis*, wisdom, foresight, shrewdness (also the name of the mother of Athene who becomes in Latin Minerva); *metiesthai*, to meditate, to have in mind, to dream; *menos*, mind, intention, courage, spirit; *menoinan*, to be bent on, eager for, to think of something; *mnasthai*, to be mindful, remember; *mneme*, memory; *Mnemosune*, Greek Goddess of Memory; *mnesis*, remembrance; *amnesis*, forgetfulness (English, amnesia); *anamnesis*, recollection. The root *ma* gives *mainomai*, to think, but also to be lost in thought, and then to rave or rage, which brings in *mania*, madness, possession, frenzy; *mainad*, the raging one, and also *mantis*, seer, and *manteia*, prophecy; *manes*, ancestral spirits, sometimes thought to rage themselves. Also from the same root are *menix*, *menos*, anger, a further meaning of *menos*, above; *menuo*, to announce, inform, reveal; *meno*, remain, linger (the remaining of sensations in the mind), recalling the Sanskrit *man*, to hesitate, remain firm or steadfast, await, linger. (Aristotle saw the origin of remembering and thinking in the remaining of impressions in the mind).[13] Also, *manthano*, to learn; *mathesis*, activity of learning; *mathemata*, mathematics (themes of the mind).

In Latin, the root continues into *menuo*, to indicate, reveal; *maneo*, to remain; *meminisse*, to remember; *rememinissi*, to call back to mind, reminisce; *monere*, to warn, remind (cause someone to think); *mentire*, to mention (bring to mind), and even *mentiri*, to lie. Finally, the one we know best, *mens, mentis* (feminine), meaning mind, becomes mental in English. Latin *luna* gives lunatic, the equivalent of the Greek maniac.

Basically, the roots *me, ma, men* structure words meaning 'to use one's mind' in many ways, and this thinking ranges from simple acts of measuring to the kind of 'measured', meditative reflection whose outcome is wisdom; it extends from logical reasoning through the reasoning of the heart (*'le cœur a ses raisons que la raison ne connaît point'*),[14] to imagination that leads to poetry and prophecy but also to madness and delusion. As Yeats felicitously puts it: 'Our thought and emotions are often but spray flung up from hidden tides that follow a moon no eye can see.'[15] What this common root of Moon, measure, mind and spirit suggests is that originally thoughts arising in the mind – as 'spray' – appeared to the thinkers as revelations from beyond themselves – 'hidden tides' – coming from the realm of the sacred – 'a Moon'.

* * *

In contemporary thought, the word 'Moon' has an outer but not an inner meaning, and the word 'mind' has generally an inner but not an outer meaning. So how, we might wonder, did the outer, ostensive Moon – which we can point at – translate into the inner mind, at which we cannot point? Owen Barfield, in his book *Speaker's Meaning*, argues that 'Words, which for us today have an outer meaning only, formerly had the inner as well.'[16] The same is true the other way round: words which now have an inner meaning, such as spirit, once had an outer meaning, such as wind, air and breath (as in the Greek *pneuma* and the Latin *spiritus*). (The English 'heart' has both inner and outer meanings as concomitant – a 'good heart'). For instance, in the English translation of the third book of St John's Gospel, the term *pneuma* is used throughout, first for 'spirit', then for 'wind', and then again for 'spirit': 'That which is born of the flesh is flesh; and that which is born of the spirit is spirit...The wind bloweth where it listeth, and thou hearest the sound thereof, but canst not tell whence it cometh, and whither it goeth: so is everyone that is born of the spirit.'[17] We would miss the complexity of the original thought if we said that wind was only a metaphor for spirit, as we would if we said that spirit was projected upon wind. The challenge of poetic language is to hold both meanings together, not to separate them into one *or* the other, and then have to devise a way of going back and forth from one *to* the other.

Take, for instance, the Greek word for physical strength *menos* (with its lunar root of *men*), which is at the same time a word for a state of mind. When a man feels *menos* he is aware of a mysterious access of energy which brings confidence, eagerness, a sense of purpose, and the capacity to act instinctively. Homer expresses the power and mystery of this energy by saying that it is given by a god, often as a response to prayer. In the *Iliad*, Apollo puts *menos* into the heart of the wounded Glaucus, and Athene puts *menos* into the chest of Diomede, her protégé.[18]

We might, then, restore to 'Moon' some of its original meaning by seeing it (in contemporary terms) as a poetic image, one which was a focus for inner and outer meanings which were originally inseparable. It would be to split the unity of the poetic image to assume either that the myths in which it occurs are only an unconscious 'projection' of the inner life of feeling upon an inanimate outer world, or that the outer world is so intensely animated that it threatens to engulf any inner life, in which case myths become merely attempts to propitiate the outer powers. It is rather that, as W. H. Auden says, 'human language is mythological and metaphorical by nature.'[19] It is not that myths and metaphors are deliberately added later as human sophistication increases. So describing language in its infancy as 'concrete' is not to say that it is literal, which is something with just one distinct meaning. Barfield elaborates: 'Non-figurative language...is a late arrival. What we call literal meanings, whether inner or outer, are never samples of meaning in its infancy; they are always meanings in their old age – end products of a historical process.'[20]

Restoring the inner and outer meaning to 'Moon' may help to explain why 'Moon' and 'mind' once merged into each other, for the one could not be fully understood without the other. Jung's comment that 'Primordial man projected mind upon the moon'[21] does not answer the question, why the Moon? Did 'primordial man' see mind reflected in the Moon because the Moon had given him reason to reflect? The etymology suggests that Moon and mind reached human consciousness together, so to speak, as the culmination of a long process of mutually reflecting insights. We might hazard that over a period of time perceptions and thoughts became more and more consistent, taking on a relation with each other, finding in the invisible cycle a form to hold them together, provoking, through constant repetition of the visible phases, both anticipation and confirmation. The experience of 'thinking through the Moon' – working out the phases of growing and diminishing, holding the pattern in the mind when the Moon 'dies', predicting when the Moon will be reborn – leads inevitably to the idea of the whole and the part, the whole in the part and the part in the whole. But what is 'the whole'? It is as though the *Upanishad* captures the last stage of this process of awareness, when 'the whole' is both the 'Moon in the sky' and the 'Moon in the mind', when the two distinct sensations merge in a new perception that sees them both at once. This is the moment, caught in the image, when 'the Moon becomes mind, and enters the heart'. Only later does 'mind' become a faculty or a function – a sign instead of an event, as Shelley would say[22] – but once 'mind' was a leap in the heart, just as in ancient Greece an 'idea' first lit up in the mind's eye.

* * *

The Moon's provocative role in human thought is also expressed in the language of myth, which names Moon deities as gods and goddesses of wisdom, arbiters of fate, fortune and justice. A Hindu snake goddess is called Manasa, literally 'mind' and 'thought'.[23] As was explored in Chapter 3, a Hindu ritual of drinking a fermented drink from a plant called Soma, with the same name as the Moon, Soma, brought *manas*, mind, spirit. It was also said that 'when this *manas* was redeemed from death it became the moon.'[24] The *Kaushitaki Upanishad* explains: 'This bright immortal person in this moon, and that bright immortal person existing as mind in the body, both are *madhu*' (soul).[25]

In China the Virgin Mother Moon goddess, Shing Moo, is called 'Perfect Intelligence',[26] while in Egypt the Moon god Thoth was god of writing and wisdom and the spouse of Maat, goddess of truth. Isis and Ishtar are goddesses of wisdom, as is Sophia in Gnostic thought. The dove as the symbol of wisdom is the messenger of many goddesses of the Moon: Ishtar's dove became Astarte's, then Aphrodite's, then Sophia's and lastly Mary's, when it was understood as incarnating the presence of the Holy Spirit.

On the other hand, Moon deities were also credited with bringing lunacy, mania, bad omen and death. The light of the Full Moon was invoked by lovers and poets for inspiration and alternatively feared for its power to send people mad or blind, while the dark of the Moon could kill or heal. The New Moon could enrich or blight the whole of the month to come, depending on whether you saw it before it saw you, and especially if it saw you looking at it through glass. It seems that, at one extreme, the Moon generates 'higher thought' and, at the other extreme, superstition. How can this be?

This vast range of responses may make sense in terms of the difference between the cycle and the phases, since the capacity to apprehend a cycle, as distinct from observing a passing phase, draws on a different level of the psyche. Reflecting upon the cycle as a whole requires detachment and brings perspective, not just in relation to the Moon but as the introduction of a life skill. Holding in the mind what is not present to the eye depends upon the ability to postpone the immediate gratification of instinct, which in turn allows a greater play of imagination and intellect – whereas focusing, without perspective, on each successive phase as it happens, predisposes to identification, all the more so if the phases are believed to thread through the lives of human beings and their world.

In myth, the crucial life-affirming or life-denying difference is always whether the story is taken as a fact, and perceived to be literally and objectively true; or whether it is allowed the play of human imagination and considered as metaphor, holding a poetic and, if the distinction is required, a spiritual, value.

Joseph Campbell has done more than anyone to draw attention to the difference between these two ways of understanding myths (within which he includes religions). For the term 'myth' (when not used as equivalent to untruth) generally refers to a religion that belongs to other people, usually (though not invariably) long dead. No one, at any rate, calls their own religion a myth. Campbell writes:

> Since mythology is born of fantasy, any life or civilization brought to form as a result of a literal mythic identification or inflation, as a concrete *imitatio dei*, will necessarily bear the features of a nightmare, a dream-game too seriously played – in other words, madness; whereas, when the same mythological imagery is properly read as fantasy and allowed to play into life as art, not as nature – with irony and grace, not fierce daemonic compulsion – the psychological energies that were formerly in the capture of the compelling images take the images in capture, and can be deployed with optional spontaneity for life's enrichment. Moreover, since life itself is indeed such stuff as dreams are made on, such a transfer of accent may conduce, in time, to a life lived in noble consciousness of its own nature.[27]

RATIONAL AND INTUITIVE THINKING

When we speak today of the way the rational mind operates, we tend to think of an analytic activity which breaks things down and takes them apart; we also tend to contrast this with the synthetic activity of the intuitive mind, which grasps many disparate elements as a whole. But may not the rational mind act synthetically and the intuitive mind analytically? In other words, these two activities may not originally have been – and may not essentially be – as separate as they now appear. When human consciousness changes, ideas change, and so do the meanings of words and the distinctions made between them. The early myths of the Moon suggest that both these directions of the mind may be pursued together: the capacity to recognize analogies, affinities and harmonies, as in the apprehension of the lunar web, and also the fostering of distinction and division, leading to the ability to count and reason. Which 'direction' is it, for instance, in the first line of Sylvia Plath's poem *The Moon and the Yew Tree?* 'This is the light of the mind, cold and planetary.'[28] Or Wordsworth's Moon, standing 'naked in the Heavens, at height/Immense above my head', looking down upon the lonely mountain in a sea of mist, which appears to him

> the perfect image of a mighty Mind
> Of one that feeds upon infinity...[29]

* * *

Plato, in his *Epinomis*, asks:

> How did we learn to count? How, I ask you, have we come to have the notions of *one* and *two*, the scheme of the universe endowing us with a native capacity for these notions?...And in all this scene, if we take one thing with another, what fairer spectacle is there for a man than the face of day, from which he can then pass, still retaining his power of vision, to the view of night, where all these objects will appear so different. Now as Uranus never ceases rolling all these objects round, day after day, and night after night, neither does he ever cease teaching men the lore of one and two until even the dullest scholar has sufficiently learned the lesson of counting. For any of us who sees this show will form the notion of *three, four*, and *many*. And among these bodies of God's fashioning there is one, the moon, which goes its way, now waxing, now waning, as it lights up one day after another, until it has fulfilled fifteen days and nights, and they, if one will treat its whole orbit as a unity, constitute a period, such that the very slowest creature, if I may say so, on which God has bestowed the capacity to learn, may learn it...I fancy it was for some greater purpose, as well as for this, that when God made the moon in the sky, waxing and waning, as we have said, he combined the months into a year and so all the creatures, by a happy providence, began to have a general insight into the relations of number with number.[30]

Even the slowest creatures, then, learn to divide the orbit or cycle of the Moon. As we saw in Chapter 2, the cycle of the Moon was first cut into two, by the New and Full Moons, then into three, by adding the waning crescent, and then into four, by adding the period of invisibility as a phase. After this, Nilsson observes, there are two ways to go: either you develop more and more elaborately the precise descriptions of the days from the phase and position of the Moon until every day is named, or else you simply number the days. The simple counting and numbering of all the days of the month from the New Moon up to 29 or 30 is the most abstract method, and only found among what he calls the most highly developed peoples.[31]

Even then, counting in early times was never merely numerical, probably beginning as the practical experience of women keeping track of their own cycles by the cycles of the Moon. In much contemporary counting the number is withdrawn from its original context and stands alone, separated from the things being counted. But in early myths the counting takes place within a story which creates or affirms a whole world view, one which places the tribe precisely within Nature. At the same time the story describes and offers an explanation of what we would now name (and so implicitly distance ourselves from) a 'natural phenomenon'.

NUMBERING THE CYCLE

TWO

The difference between light and darkness, which leads to the distinction between day and night, may be found reflected in the light and dark 'halves' of the Moon. Two crescents placed back to back – the waxing crescent facing left and the waning crescent facing right – was the sign for a whole cycle. As Hentze, suggests, all dualisms find in the Moon's phases, if not their historical cause, at least a mythic and symbolic model.[32] Plato made use of the contrast between the Bright Moon and the Dark Moon for his tripartite division of the soul. The soul was composed of a winged charioteer and two winged steeds, one noble and good and the other ignoble and bad. The good horse, who is upright, clean-limbed, and modestly obeys the charioteer, is white with black eyes, while the other, who is crooked of frame, hot-blooded, wanton and hard to control, is black with grey eyes. The charioteer is the intellect, who has to guide these tempestuous horses whose longings diverge.[33] When Christian thought adapted this analogy for its own purposes, it made the white horse 'spirit' and the black horse 'nature', so turning a lively metaphor into a moral judgement.

The simplest division of the year was made into two periods: the bright half and the dark half. In ancient Celtic Ireland, to take one example, the bright half, known as *samh*, summer, began in early May on the feast of *Beltane*, or 'the Sun's Fire'; and the dark half, *gamh*, winter, began in early November on the feast of *Samhain*, which probably means 'Summer's End'.[34] In Greece, too, the year was first divided into two seasons: fruitful and fruitless, followed by the 'Moon year' with three seasons and last the 'Sun year' with four.[35]

The Chinese *yin–yang* symbol in the Sung period (1127–1279 AD), was considered to be a sign of the light and dark phases of the Moon, each containing the other in embryo, both moving and at rest, dividing and unifying (fig. 2).[36] Chuang-hung-yang employs a lunar weaving metaphor when he speaks of the *yin* and *yang* as 'the to-and-fro motion of the shuttle on the cosmic loom.'[37] More generally, the diagram, symbolic of the Tao, represents the continual interplay of two principles that come from the One and yield the ten thousand things of creation: 'In source these two are the same, though in name different. The Moon was *Yin* and the Sun was *Yang*'[38]. *Yang*, corresponding to the waxing phase, was the light, active, hot, dry, positive, beneficent principle, called 'masculine'; while *yin*, corresponding to the waning phase, was the dark, passive, cold, moist, negative and malignant principle, called 'feminine'. However, when considered as a whole in relation to each other, the Moon was *yin* and the Sun was *yang*.

On Malekula, an island in the New Hebrides in Melanesia, the Malekulans in the 1940s still organized much of their lives around the sacred boar, whose shining tusks curve like waxing and waning crescents. This practice will be discussed in Chapter 13, but here the simplicity of the design is evocative of the yin–yang figure (fig. 3).[39]

Many Moon myths have two deities, or a lunar figure with two aspects to them: a bright and a dark. In Greece, Hekate and Artemis were two intrinsically separate goddesses who often came together as a dual Moon goddess: Artemis, young, wild and beautiful, standing at the beginning of the cycle, and Hekate, older, prophetic and deathly, standing at the end. Gimbutas observes that 'whether Artemis and Hekate appear as two goddesses or as one, they both belong to the moon cycle.'[40] However, in the lunar cycle the dark is not only of death, so it is no surprise that Hekate's torches were carried around the fields to make them fertile, and that she was invoked as midwife and nurse at childbirth, bringing visions as well as lunacy and death. Brightness and darkness were in practice shared between the two goddesses, for Artemis, the huntress, slays those mothers she refuses to protect: she could kill as well as save and rear. This complexity speaks of an ancient grandeur, for Hekate and Artemis are both survivals of the Old European Great Goddess in ancient Greece and western Anatolia, who never entirely disappeared when the Indo-Europeans entered Old Europe in the third millennium BC.[41] Their characters may appear to have diminished by the time of Greek culture, but Artemis brought her animals with her down the centuries – bears, dogs, snakes, bulls, stags, does and toads – those creatures, as the Egyptians knew, who do not change but always are.[42]

In Hesiod's *Theogony*, Hekate is given as the original triple goddess, supreme in Heaven, Earth and Sea, allotting victory in war and games, patron of horseman, fishermen and sailors, increasing the

Fig. 2. Zhang Huang, Diagram of the Supreme Ultimate, from the Compendium of Diagrams, Ming Dynasty, Tianqi reign, dated 1623, Woodblock printed book; ink on paper, 26.3 x 15.5cm. University of Chicago Library, East Asian Collection.

Fig. 3. Dual Moon design. AD. 20th century. Malekula. The design inside each crescent to represents a face; the crescents above and below signify the waxing and waning Moon, or the light and dark halves of the Moon. (From Campbell, The Mythic Image, p. 460).

herds and nursing the young. In Hesiod's genealogy, her grandmother was Phoebe, the Titan goddess Bright Moon (who also bore Leto, the mother of Artemis and Apollo), and her mother was Asteria, a star goddess. Hesiod comments that Zeus 'did not snatch away those rights she had under the Titan gods of old.'[43] Apollonius Rhodius also places Hekate at the beginning of things by calling her one of the Daughters of Night.[44] But while her title of threefold goddess remained, the 'three' was subsequently confined to the three phases of the Moon. Hekate, whose name means the 'Distant One' or the 'one who strikes from afar', was also called the goddess 'with the bright headband' – an image evocative of the Moon curved around the black forehead of Night. In the Homeric *Hymn to Demeter*, only 'tender-hearted' Hekate hears Persephone cry out as she is seized into the underworld by Hades, and Hekate accompanies Demeter in her search.[45] But the later Hellenes emphasized the destructive effects of her darkness at the expense of her creative powers until, through Roman Christianity, Hekate was finally relegated to clandestine rites of ghoulish witchcraft and black magic, especially at places where three roads crossed.

In the *Iliad*, Artemis is called *potnia theron*, Lady of the Wild Things, a title which reflects her ancient inheritance from the Palaeolithic hunt. But in her Greek lineage she is adapted to the Olympian family, made daughter of Zeus and Leto, and sister to Apollo. What lingers of her earlier power is her role as huntress, her embodiment as bear goddess, and probably also the monstrous sacrifices of animals and birds which were dedicated yearly to her at Patrae, Hierapolis, Tauris and Messene, as Pausanias saw for himself. He describes 'a hall of the Kouretes, where they sacrifice without distinction all animals, beginning with oxen and goats and ending with birds; they throw them all into the fire.'[46] Yet Artemis pre-eminently captures the beauty of Nature in its original raw state – the miraculous emergence of young creatures from old – all the excitement of the waxing mode of Nature figured in the bright Moon: 'For sucklings of all the savage beasts that lurk in the lonely places, you have sympathy,' sing the chorus in Aeschylus' *Agamemnon*.[47] Artemis was also the Moon in its waning and death. In the *Odyssey*, she shares with Apollo the ministry of death to mortals, in this instance a kindly one: in the fair land of Syria, where hunger never comes, nor sore diseases, but the tribes grow old in their own time, there 'Apollo, Archer of the silver bow, comes with Artemis, and with shafts that hurt not, strikes, and lays them low.'[48] So when, in early Greece, the Moon was divided into two, Artemis and Hekate were the Moon in its dual aspect, which, being both interchangeable, must have confused the assurance of either.

In Melanesia and New Guinea, among other places, there were two contrasting Moon gods, one for the waxing who was bright, good and lucky, and one for the waning who was dark, bad and unlucky.[49] At other times the two are given as the sons of a Moon goddess, who gave birth to them by splitting into two. Here, the mother is evocative of the Full Moon between the waxing and waning, indicative of how the original distinction expands to include a third. She is called, variously, 'Round Head', 'Shining Woman', the 'Old Woman'.[50] Similarly, among the North American Indians, the Old Woman, or Changing Woman, had two sons, one known as the 'White One' and the other as the 'Black One.'[51] Among the Navahos, one was called the 'Controller of Water' and the other the 'Slayer.'[52]

Robert Graves, in his book *The White Goddess*, extended this idea into the structure of the year. He proposed that the Moon goddess herself had three phases: the white goddess of birth and growth; the red goddess of the full; and the black goddess of divination and death. Further, there are two protagonists of the 13-month drama of the year, in which the God of the Waxing Year and the God of the Waning Year compete for her blessing, an interpretation that makes sense of the mythic contest between the two brothers which is only healed when they realize they are one.[53] Parzival and Feirfiz come to mind in Von Eschenbach's *Parzival*, a tale permeated with lunar symbolism.

* * *

Until a distinction between the phases of the Moon and 'the Moon' itself (himself or herself) is made, there appears to be some initial confusion as to how the Moon manages to be both light and dark, or dies and does not die, or nearly dies but doesn't quite. The difference between phase and cycle was explored in the myth of Inanna and Dumuzi (see Chapter 1). Here, the tale of the birth of Inanna's father, Nanna, shows the Sumerian mind working on the same problem but without the benefit of two terms to play with. *The Myth of Enlil and Ninlil: The Moon and his Brothers* explores this question, asking also where did the Moon come from, and why does he have three brothers who live in the dark?

When Enlil, god of Air, son of Heaven (An) and Earth (Ki, Ninhursag), lifted his father from his mother and separated Heaven from Earth, he brought forth 'the seed of the land', all the trees and grains, and 'whatever was needful' for the 'black heads', the people of Sumeria, and indeed humankind as a whole.[54] Now, it happened that, before humans were created, when gods still lived alone in the city of Nippur, Enlil caught sight of the gentle Ninlil bathing in the pure stream, even though her mother, Ninshebarganu, had warned her what would happen:

> In the pure stream, the woman bathes, in the pure stream,
> Ninlil walks along the bank of the stream Nunbirdu,
> The bright-eyed, the lord, the bright-eyed,
> The 'great mountain', father Enlil, the bright-eyed, saw her.
>
> Enlil speaks to her of intercourse(?), she is unwilling...[55]

Enlil called for help, so his vizier brought a boat up alongside her. Then Enlil, 'father of the gods', raped the maiden Ninlil while sailing along the stream, and impregnated her with the Moon god,

Nanna-Sin. But the other gods were so offended by Enlil's behaviour that, even though he was their king, they banished him to the Nether World. The 50 great gods and the seven fate-decreeing gods seized Enlil, saying: 'Enlil, immoral one, get you out of the city.'[56]

When Ninlil began to follow Enlil to the Nether World, Enlil grew perplexed. For his son, Nanna-Sin, whom Ninlil was carrying, was destined to be the luminous body of the Moon, and now would have to live where he was born, in the dark Nether World of his father's banishment for the manner of his begetting. Imprisoned in the dark, how could he be the Moon? So Enlil had an idea. From Nippur to the Nether World there were three beings a traveller had to encounter: first, the Gatekeeper who guards the gates of Nippur, then the 'Man of the Nether World River', and finally the Ferryman. As Ninlil journeyed to the Nether World in search of Enlil, carrying the bright Moon within her womb, Enlil took the form of these guardians, each one in turn, and impregnated Ninlil with three Nether World deities, who would be brothers to the Moon. Now *they* would be able to take the place of their older brother, Nanna-Sin, so that he would be free to ascend to heaven as light.[57]

The numerical composition of three is interesting, as though there were an underworld figure for each of the three days the Moon spends in the dark, releasing him to rise into heaven as its light. This idea may be related to the Mesopotamian belief that anyone who enters and departs from the Nether World must leave someone behind in their place. Death, once met, cannot be dismissed at will, even if you are the Moon. As Graves says, 'myths are the original and living form of philosophy.'[58]

THREE

Why does the chariot of Soma (the Hindu Moon god) have three wheels, and not four? And why is the toad who lives in the Moon in China three-legged? Once the Moon was divided (or classified) into three visible phases, it showed itself, in perfect symmetry, to be a circle at the full, with two generic shapes or forms of movement, precisely reflecting each other on either side: waxing, up to the full, pointing towards the east, and waning, after the full, pointing towards the west. Moon deities were often called 'triform'.

The three visible phases of the Moon are in some places conceived as three different persons: in New Britain, the Full Moon is called the White Woman, and her two sons are the Waxing and Waning Moons.[59] The triune Moon god of the Ashanti is black in two persons and white in the third.[60] In Norse myths the Moon was often given as a threefold deity: *Nyi*, the New Moon; *Mani*, the Full Moon; and *Nithi*, the Waning Moon.[61] The Norns, Norse goddesses of Fate, also numbered three. The pre-Islamic Arabic goddess Manat, whose name means Fate, was threefold, and the Teutonic Moon goddess Holda is triune with two daughters.[62] In Mesopotamia, Nanna was sometimes distinguished as the Full Moon, Sin as the crescent, and Asim-babbar as the New Moon.[63] In Crete, the many triple pillars suggest that the Moon was worshipped there in triple form, as it was in Phoenicia (fig. 4).[64]

The earliest triad of figures dates back to c.13,000–11,000 BC. In a Palaeolithic cave in Angles-sur-Anglin, Vienne, France, three huge rock-carved females soared up over the whole of the back wall in a bewildering composition of great bodies of bellies, loins and thighs, hovering above the horned head of a bull. All three genital triangles are precisely equilateral and distinctly defined, focusing on the mystery of birth.[65] If these could be goddesses of the three visible phases of the Moon, then the bull out of which they rise might symbolize the fourth invisible phase, the Dark Moon where death becomes rebirth. 'The sacredness of the bull,' Gimbutas writes, 'is expressed in particular through the emphasis on horns...Replete with the mysterious power of growth, the horns have become a lunar symbol, which is presumed to have come into being in the Upper Palaeolithic Aurignacian when

Fig. 4. *Phoenician stele of the Moon. The middle column is taller than the other two and surmounted with a circle, suggestive of the Full Moon between the waxing and waning. (From Harrison,* Themis, *p. 192).*

Fig. 5. *Hekate Triformis with her dog. (From Harding,* Woman's Mysteries, *p. 217).*

reliefs of naked women holding a horn begin to appear.'[66] In the Neolithic age the bull and the god were often interchangeable, since the god's principal epiphany then took the form of a bull.[67] A triad of female figures accompanied by a fourth – bull or god – also occurs in classical myth, where Hermes leads the three Horai (Seasons) in the dance, summoning winter to change into spring. *Hermes Psychopompos*, who, as the guide of souls to the underworld, is uniquely allowed to cross the boundaries between life and death, was originally a Moon god, which makes his presence with the three Moon goddesses – Athene, Aphrodite and Hera – at the so-called Judgement of Paris all the more interesting (Chapter 10, fig. 14).

In later times, where the Moon is imagined as a goddess, the three visible phases are often distinguished as the three stages of the biological life of woman: maiden or virgin, bride and/or mother, and old woman or crone. In Greek myth, these three phases were personified as separate goddesses: the New and Waxing Moon was the Virgin – Persephone or Artemis; the Full Moon was the Bride, Wife, Mother or Fulfilled One – Demeter, Hera, Athene or Aphrodite; and the Waning Moon, Hekate, was the Crone or Hag (from *chronos*, 'time', and *hagia*, 'holy', when the light is turned within as the wisdom of age)(fig. 5). Hekate was threefold herself even down to Shakespeare's time – 'And we fairies that do run/By the triple Hecate's team'[68] – as was her three-headed dog Cerberus. The Romans called her *Triformis* and *Trivia*, found where the three ways meet. Selene contained all three phases in one: rising from Ocean she is forever virgin, riding her horses headlong through the dark she is full, shedding her beams on Endymion she is waning, and her darkness is his death.[69]

When the sequential stages of female life are extended to the three structural elements in all life – birth, death and the quality of life in between – the three Moon goddesses become the three Moirai in the Moon, known as the Fates, together with all the other triads through whom their rule is extended: the Muses (who were three before they became nine), the Horai, the Charities or 'Graces', the Erinyes or 'Furies', or, as they are also euphemistically called, the Eumenides, the 'Kindly Ones.' Then there are the Sirens, the Hesperides, the Gorgons, and the Graiai (the 'Grey Ones', sisters of the three Gorgons), who live at the edge of day with one eye and one tooth between them. Harrison summarizes: 'the Moon is the true mother of the triple Horae, who are themselves Moirae, and the Moirae, as Orpheus tells us, are but the three *moirae*, or divisions, *mere*, of the Moon herself, the three

Fig. 6. *A symbol found on the walls of the catacombs in Rome, entitled 'The Kingdom of Heaven.' (From Harding, Woman's Mysteries, p. 223)*

Fig. 7. *Hekate Triformis. Hekate as three in one and one in three. Roman funeral stele, Musée Calvet, Avignon, France.*

Fig. 8. *The revolution of the Moon, where the crescents have become legs moving in a circle from right to left. Coin from Sicily. (From Harding, Woman's Mysteries, p. 223).*

divisions of the old [Moon] Year. And these three Moirae or Horae are also Charities.'[70] The Maenads, priestesses of Dionysos, also numbered three.[71]

The figure three appears in many places around the world, both as a way of identifying the Moon's visible phases and as a way of structuring the month and sometimes the year. Three was a number of growth and completion, which had the status of a law: in terms of things occurring, one or two times might be random but three was not: 'the best of three'; 'One, two, three – go'; (as in 'One for the money, two for the show, three to get ready and go, man, go'); 'for the third and last time', 'going, going, gone'. 'Thrice-noble Lord' leaves no room for doubt, and the cock crowed when Peter had denied his Master thrice. Three was a whole number that was both divisible and indivisible in the sense that it was differentiated and yet remained a unity: it had a beginning, a middle and an end; it was a resolution of opposites: thesis, antithesis, synthesis; creation, destruction, preservation; positive, negative, reconciling. Gurdjieff spoke of 'the Law of Three'.[72] Three was a moving number – mother, father, child – that was also finally at rest – birth, life and death. Three is also given as the number of days when the Moon is gone (though it is sometimes only one or two days missing). But as a whole number of completion it became the number of days in which heroes and saviours are trapped in the underworld (Inanna), imprisoned in the belly of the whale (Jonah), or descend into Hell (Jesus). Paul was blinded, and himself fasted, for three days after his conversion at Damascus.[73]

Three Magi came from the East to visit the Christ child, bearing three gifts. There were three Marys attending the crucifixion – Mary, the Mother of Jesus, Mary Magdalene and Mary of Bethany – a tradition continued in Provence in *Les Trois Saintes Maries de la Mer*, where the black maid Sarah makes up the third, taking the place of Mary of Bethany. In many fairy tales of the three fateful sisters, two are deformed and one is beautiful like the Full Moon, as in the story of Cinderella and the two ugly sisters.[74] In tales of the three wishes, one, the last one, typically redeems the other two; just as the last, the youngest, brother or sister, who is the despised, apparently lazy but essentially intuitive one, breaks through to the magical realm and saves the other two. In British folklore, it was the custom to bow three times to the New Moon. Three was the magic number: 'things always come in threes'; 'third time lucky'; 'if at first you don't succeed, try, try, try again.'

In fact all triune goddesses and gods may be suspected (though not accused) of lunar origins – as, for instance, *Hermes Trismegistos*, the thrice-greatest Hermes of the Gnostics. However, the Sun is also seen as having three modes of being – rising, culminating and setting – suggesting that this is an archetypal pattern of balance and completeness.[75]

The dividing of the Moon's light into three phases may have attuned the human mind to 'think in threes' as a way of defining a whole that could be made intelligible through its parts. This 'three' was then at the same time 'one', the three visible phases and the one cycle, or one Moon manifesting in three aspects, expressing perhaps the earliest trinity that was both Three-in-One and One-in-Three.[76]

But the One, as the cycling Moon, is more than its visible phases because it also becomes invisible and, as it were, exists when they do not. As we saw in *The Descent of Inanna*, the dark Moon becomes another phase of the Moon's continuing cycle, so that darkness and death may be integrated into light and life, and the 'three' may become 'four'.

FOUR

As suggested in Chapter 1, the capacity for abstract thought may have arisen out of the need to comprehend the Moon's phases as four instead of three, when the darkness of the New Moon is counted as a phase even though it cannot be seen. It becomes abstracted from immediate experience and is placed in the mind. In this way the figure four grows logically out of the figure 28, since the dark period becomes a phase only after the cycle of 28 days is registered as permanent.

In the Neolithic, phases of the Moon as four were often drawn on pots as the four arms of a cross within a circle; they also evolve into swastikas, with hooks or wings pointing to the left, representing the monthly eastward course of the Moon, as in the dish from Bulgaria shown in fig. 9, painted in the middle of the fifth millennium BC.

In the early fourth millennium, at Ur, later the chief Sumerian city of the Moon, household vessels were laid in graves, perhaps containing food and drink, to sustain the deceased on the journey through the Nether World towards the new life beyond death. The bowl decorated with Crescent Moons in fig. 10 was found in such a grave, just as 3000 years later many Roman tombstones placed the crescent at the head of their elaborate marble sculptures.

Where three, as the 'visible' number, is taken as the number of time – coming into being, growing and dying, or past, present and future – four is given as the number of space – north, south, east and west, the four directions of the universe. As a number of totality, 'four' also circumscribed the course of the Moon, imagined as a moving figure in space, with the dark period counted as the fourth phase which completes the circle. The 'four' is also the 'One' in the compelling saying of the Alchemist known as Maria Prophetessa: 'One becomes two, two becomes three, and out of the third comes the One as the fourth.'[77]

The swastika or moving cross, with the ends bent to form a hook, can lead either way, to the right or to the left. Generally, the lunar swastikas have left-handed hooks and move in an anti-clockwise direction, from right to left. Later, in Greece, left-handed swastikas thread through the black robes of Artemis and Athene as stars in the night. The earlier unnamed goddesses of the waters also wore upon their gowns the lunar swastikas, interwoven with falling rivulets of water, fish and water birds. By contrast solar swastikas, with right-handed hooks, move from left to right as does the clock, charting the Sun's movement from east to west. They usually appear with Sun gods, such as the Zoroastrian/Roman god Mithras.[78]

TWENTY-EIGHT

It takes the numbering of the whole cycle into 28 to count the nights of the Light and Dark Moons, dividing it subsequently into two halves, giving 13 or 14 each. So 28, making the pattern, in a sense 'comes before' the numbers of its constituent parts.

The Hindu Moon god Soma (or Chandra) was the son of Rishi Atri and Anasuya. Soma married the 28 daughters of the Rishi Daksha, the 'Brilliant', who had emerged from Brahma's right thumb, and had been charged with the creation of all the creatures that moved as well as all those that did not. The trouble was that Soma much preferred his fourth wife Rohini (a constellation known as 'Red Cow'), and this made the other 27 wives jealous. They went to their father Daksha and complained about Soma, how he did not distribute his favours equally among them. Daksha was furious and cursed Soma with leprosy (some say it was consumption), and Soma's bright silvery colour began to fade. When they saw this, the wives took pity on Soma and told their father that this punishment was too severe. Daksha could not recall his curse once he had made it, but he agreed to mitigate it on behalf of his daughters, so the decay would be periodical and not permanent. So now Soma, the Moon, becomes gradually 'grey-skinned' and eventually disappears within 14 days, but then over the next 14 days he slowly recovers his silver colour again. Then he rides through the night sky in a three-wheeled chariot, drawn by ten horses as white as jasmine flowers.[79]

Here the sky is given a structure as the 28 wives (houses) of the Moon, and the days of the Moon's moving on from one person/place to the next are imagined in terms of the trials of ancient domestic life. Is the fourth wife a reference to day four of the Moon, when the crescent of the New Moon first appears over the horizon? In Greek myth, it is the day when Hermes was born to the goddess Maia.[80]

Twenty-eight is the central number in Black Elk's story, when the Sioux Indian chief explains why and how their great ceremonial lodge came to be constructed.

> Long ago, two Sioux Indians were out hunting when they saw a beautiful woman coming towards them, dressed in white buckskin and carrying a bundle on her back. One of the men felt lust for her and told his friend, but his friend said, no, this is no ordinary woman. The woman was now close to them and laid down her bundle on the ground. Then she asked the man who had felt lust to approach her. As he did so, a cloud surrounded them both, and when the cloud lifted there was no man left, nothing but bones consumed by snakes writhing at the feet of the woman.
>
> 'Behold what you see', she told the other man. 'Tell your people to make ready a large ceremonial lodge for me. I want to tell them something of great importance!'

Fig. 9. Painted graphite dish, with a central whirl of crescents turning clockwise around a disc, egg or full Moon. Around the outer edge four crescents create a counter-clockwise whirl, invigorating the central whirl. Karanovo VI. Devetashka cave, central Bulgaria; mid-5th millennium BC. (From Gimbutas, Language, p. 297).

Fig. 10. Painted terra-cotta bowl with round central ring emphasized, possibly as Full Moon, with four groups of crescents, in triple rows, extending outwards in the form of a cross. The crescents are arranged in antithetic positions along the vertical and horizontal axis like the cardinal points of the compass. So called al 'Ubaid ware, found in a grave at Ur, Sumeria. Early 4th millennium BC. Museum of Mankind, London.

The Indian hurried back and related what he had seen, and the Chief, Standing Hollow Horn, made a lodge as the woman had asked. It had 28 poles, arranged around a central pole which was its total support, just as the Great Spirit, Wakan Tanka, was the supporter of the universe. The woman entered by the eastern door and walked sunwise round the central pillar, south, west, north and back to the east again. Then she gave the bundle to Chief Standing Hollow Horn, saying:

'With this pipe you will send your voices to your Father and Grandfather. With this pipe you will walk upon the earth; for the earth is your Mother and Grandmother. Every step taken upon her should be a prayer.'

As she walked away into the distance she became a red and brown buffalo calf. Then she walked a little way and lay down and became a white buffalo calf. Then she walked a little further and lay down and became a black buffalo calf, who turned, bowed to the four directions and disappeared over the hill.

Then Black Elk explained:

'If you add four sevens, you get twenty-eight. The moon lives twenty-eight days and we reckon time by the moon. Each day of the lunar month represents something sacred to our people: two of the days represent the Great Spirit, Wakan Tanka, who is our Father and Grandfather; two, the earth, our Mother and Grandmother; four are for the four winds; one is for the spotted eagle; one for the sun, one for the moon, one for the morning star; four are for the four ages; seven for our seven great rites; one is for the buffalo; one for the fire; one for the water; one for the rock; and one is for man. You should know also that the buffalo has twenty-eight ribs, and that in our war bonnets we usually wear twenty-eight feathers. There is a meaning in everything, and these are the things that are good for men to know and to remember.'[81]

The horned buffalo, with their 28 ribs, who depart and return every year, are assimilated here to the Moon's symbolism of cyclical renewal, together with the ceremonial lodge, the war bonnets, and all who smoke the pipe through the 28 sacred days of each cycle. Further, as one of the 28 supports is the central pole, the axis, the number of poles surrounding it is then 27, composed of three times nine (three times three times three). Black Elk added that the buffalo symbolized the universe in its temporal, lunar aspect, ever dying and ever renewed, but, in his twenty-eighth rib, he was also symbolic of the Great Spirit, who is both the centre that is everywhere and the time that is eternity.[82]

On a lighter note, Plutarch writes that the cat, the Moon's animal, brings forth, so it is said, kittens in ever-increasing number until she has reached 28, 'the number also of the moon's illuminations'.[83]

The Babylonians divided the circle of the zodiac into 28 Mansions of the Moon, as did the Hindus, Buddhists, Persians, Copts, Chinese and Arabs.[84] Later Islamic cosmology also included 28 Mansions of the Moon, from which various systems of numerical symbols were constructed, in order to demonstrate that 'the lunar sphere synthesized the qualities of all the other celestial spheres and transferred their influences to the sublunary world of elements'.[85] The Mayans, who had a very accurate lunar calendar, calculated their lunar month with 29 days, as shown in one of their sculptures of a Mayan scientist seated on a throne symbolizing the lunar cycle. There are 20 Moon symbols in the throne, while the bar and dots compose the number nine.[86] Heroes and Saviours are often found with their lives divided into phases: the first 28 or 29 or 30 years as the cycle of ordinary people, the unconscious life, after which there is a new phase of initiation, which is symbolically rendered as a rebirth. Osiris ruled for 28 years before he became God of the underworld, and Siddhartha spends 29 years of illusory happiness before he leaves his father's palace and encounters sickness and death and lastly a monk who desires neither to live or die. In the subsequent phase he became a Buddha.

* * *

Other 'lunar figures' are seven as the quarter of the lunar month; the nine or ten days to the three-week month, as in Egypt; the ten lunar months of pregnancy (counting 28 days to a lunar month); the 13 months of the lunar year or the days of the Waxing Moon in a hollow month; 14 as the days of the Waxing Moon; 17 as the day on which the Moon can be seen to wane, having seemed to rest for three days at the full. Twelve became a solar number, given as the Sun's annual course through the 12 signs of the zodiac, in the now 12 non-lunar months of 30 and 31 days.

SEVEN

If the lunar cycle of 28 days (to the nearest whole number) is arranged in a circle, and the circle is divided vertically and horizontally, the result is four segments of seven days. When seven became the number of days in a four-week month, the days were accordingly named after the seven planets as the number of completion. For seven is the number of the visible planets, in the original Greek sense of 'wanderers', where Sun and Moon are included with Mercury, Venus, Mars, Jupiter and Saturn. If three and four together compose a unity of time and space, then it is not surprising that seven is everywhere a figure of totality. In proverbial wisdom seven was a lucky number: 'The day that you do a good thing there will be seven new moons.'[87]

NINE

Nine, as a composition of three times three, was also a lunar number: 'Thrice to thine, and thrice to mine,/And three again to make up nine,' chant the three witches in *Macbeth*,[88] servants to the triple goddess Hekate, one third of the triple Moon. The nine Greek Muses were originally three, guardians of night and the stars.[89] Demeter searches for her daughter, Persephone, for nine days and nights, flying like a 'solitary wild bird'.[90] In Christianity, nine choirs of angels surround the throne of the Most High.[91] In late 19th-century Yorkshire, it was said that if you pointed nine times at the Moon you would not go to heaven, while in Derbyshire you could point six times but not seven, but in Lancashire, Worcestershire and Shrewsbury it was a sin to point at the Moon at all.[92]

The ancient mace-head of the pre-dynastic king Narmer in fig. 11 shows the king assimilated to a god seated on a throne at the top of a flight of steps. There are nine steps, corresponding to the days of the Egyptian week, of which there were three in the lunar month. This figure is in turn emphasized by the placing of the three people paying their respects to the king between two sets of three crescent Moons, one shaped as waxing and the other as waning, representing a complete cycle. Osiris is also shown seated at the top of nine steps (Chapter 13, fig. 7).

THIRTEEN/FOURTEEN

The 13 strokes incised on the horn held by the pregnant Palaeolithic Goddess of Laussel are the earliest and most striking representation of the number of days in the waxing phase and also perhaps the number of months in the lunar year.

The division of the cycle of the Moon into two gives the (variable) figure of 14 days of waxing and 14 days of waning. Thoth was represented with the Eye of the Full Moon at the top of 14 steps (see

Chapter 2, fig. 5), as was Osiris. Seth discovered the body of Osiris on the Full Moon, and dismembered it into 14 pieces, as the Moon is broken into pieces as it dies (fig. 12). The Aztec Moon goddess, Coyolxauhqui, was also hacked into 14 pieces by her younger brother the Sun god, Huizilopochtli, who cut off her head, and hurled it up into the sky where it became the Moon.[93]

SEVENTEEN

The seventeenth day in the lunar month is the day the Moon is seen to begin to wane after three days of hardly changing at the Full. In the tradition recorded by Plutarch, it was the seventeenth day of the month on which Osiris was killed – 'on which day it is quite evident to the eye that the period of the full moon is over' – which is why, Plutarch adds, this day is abominated by the Pythagoreans and called the 'Barrier'.[94] Virgil recommended (without giving a reason) that vines be planted on the seventeenth day (rooting down into the dark soil as the Moon began to darken?).[95]

In the land that is now known as 'Old Europe', a rich and graceful civilization flourished long before the Indo-Aryans arrived in the fourth millennium BC. In Rumania, the vase shown in fig. 13 and others like it in Hungary, suggest that the 17 turns of the lunar serpent and the four phases of the Moon are related in Old European thinking.[96] So the beginning of the waning is represented as the dynamic life-force of the undulating serpent and set within the context of two complete cycles of lunar renewal (the circle quartered), both of which have a horn pointing in the anti-clockwise direction of the Moon's movement, and figuring the shape and positioning of the waxing crescent. The narrative of the painting, then, moves the thought of death into life regenerated, from the dark to the bright Moon, and so from time's winter into time's spring.

As we saw in Chapter 4, the wavy lines of the winding serpents on the megalithic stones from Knowth appear to measure time: some of the longest winding snakes have up to 30 turnings, and many of them have 17 turnings, registering the waning of the Moon (fig. 14).[97]

NINETEEN

When Odysseus returns to Ithaca after ten years wandering and ten years before that fighting in the Trojan War, he arrives in winter, at the New Moon, at the feast of Apollo or the solstice festival of the Sun – the time, if any there be, when an old cycle would be closed and a new one would triumphantly begin. For the reunion of Odysseus and Penelope, who has long been weaving and unweaving her lunar web, takes place 'on the twentieth year' (that is, as soon as the nineteenth year is complete), which is when the New Moon coincides with the New Sun of the winter solstice in a once-every-nineteen-years event. Later, in the fifth century, the astronomer Meton of Athens was studying how the lunar and solar calendars might be coordinated (how to match up the 12 lunar months of 354 days with the 364 days of the solar year). This brought him to a formulation of a 'Grand Cycle of 19 Years'. This is explained by Gilbert Murray: 'On the last day of the nineteenth year, which was also by Greek reckoning the first of the twentieth, the New Moon would coincide with the New Sun of the Winter Solstice; this was called the "Meeting of Sun and Moon" (*Sunodos Helion kai Selenes*) – a thing which had not happened for nineteen full years before and would not happen again for another nineteen.'[98] Which is to say, that after 19 years of not coinciding (and so causing havoc with the seasons) Sun and Moon finally met at the same time and made time the same! Starting from now, the phases of the Moon will repeat themselves on the same days as they did 19 years before. Yet how unobtrusively such a momentous event is concealed in the structure of the story's own time.[99]

Fig. 12. The gods of the 14 days of the Waning Moon. Egyptian. (From Wallis Budge, The Gods of the Egyptians, ii, p. 321).

Fig. 11. The mace-head of Narmer as the god-king of nine steps. Pre-dynastic Egypt. (From Briffault, The Mothers, ii, p. 781).

Fig. 13. Central zig-zagging snake (with 17 turns) flanked by two quartered discs, symbolizing the four phases of the Moon, with horns attached to them. Polychrome vase. Cucuteni A, Trusetsi, Moldavia, NE Rumania. 4500-4300 BC. (From Gimbutas, Language, p. 288).

Fig. 14. Winding serpentine forms, with turnings between the numbers of 14 and 17, as the waxing Moon. The upper register of 17 turns begins with a crescent on the left, while above it are carved concentric semi-circles and discs, possibly representing full Moons. Grave culture. Knowth NE 6 and SE 3, Boyne River Valley, Co. Meath, Ireland. Middle of 2nd half of 4th millennium BC. (From Brennan, The Stars and the Stones, p. 202).

The Greek historian Diodorus Siculus also gives the number of 19 years significance in his description of a place resembling Callanish, in an island resembling the Isle of Lewis. In Callanish, there is a megalithic circle of stones which is now agreed to form one of the earliest stone configurations set in relation to the Moon (the term 'lunar observatory' tends to obscure the possibility of religious ritual). Siculus quotes a lost history by *Hecataeus of Abdera*, which describes a voyager around northern Britain who had seen a lunar 'spherical temple' on an island 'no smaller than Sicily'. He continues that 'the Moon as viewed from this island appears to be but a little distance from the earth,' (and so must appear very large), adding that 'the god' visited 'the island every nineteen years' (the 18.61-year cycle of the Moon).[100] Aubrey Burl, in his *From Carnac to Callanish*, comments that the latitude of Callanish is 58 degrees North, which is indeed critical, since nowhere farther south in Europe could the Moon seem to skim the horizon between its rising and setting.[101] Alexander Thom's lifelong work on *Megalithic Lunar Observatories*,[102] showed that contemporary measurements could support the ancient tales. Because of the latitude of Callanish, the path of the Moon at the maximum southern declination skims two ranges of hills, one of which (the south-east) has the appearance of a woman lying upon two pillows. Present-day Gaelic-speaking people call her *Cailleach na Mointeach*, which means the 'Old Woman of the Moors', and English-speaking people call her 'Sleeping Beauty'. The Moon appears from the Sleeping Beauty when it rises at the point of its maximum southern declination (appearing from her knees at one place and from her neck at another), and then, shortly after setting and disappearing from view, it rises again from a V-shaped valley in the south-western range of hills, as though reborn. Many of the stones are aligned to register these events.[103]

FIFTY

It was also told that while the Greek Moon goddess Selene made her nightly visit to Endymion, as he was sleeping his eternal slumber in a mountain cave, she conceived 50 daughters by him, while the river *Menios* flowed softly by. (Selene, whose name derives from *selas*, 'light', had another name, Mene, the feminine form of Men, the name for 'Moon', 'month' and the Phrygian Moon god).[104] These 50 children are the number of lunar months between the Olympic Games, which were held every four years (as they still are today). More exactly, the interval between the Olympic Games was alternately 49 and 50 months, showing that the festival cycle was a period of eight years divided into two halves – the precise period which reconciles the Hellenic Moon year of 354 days with the solar year of $365\frac{1}{4}$ days.[105] (In eight years, the $11\frac{1}{4}$ days by which the lunar year falls short of the solar year add up to 90 days; these 90 days were distributed over the period in three months intercalated in winter; the eight-year period therefore = 12 x 8 = 96 + 3 months = 99 months = 49 + 50). So this figure of four years is precisely half of the eight-year cycle which is the time taken by the Sun and Moon to travel around the zodiac until they reach their original starting point – the same point in the sky from which this cycle began. When Endymion is understood (in one of his meanings) as the figure of the sinking Sun overtaken by the Moon below the horizon (his name means one who 'finds himself within'), it makes sense that his tomb rested at the starting point of the footraces in the stadium,[106] and also that the victors in the two races – one for men and one for women – personified Hera and Zeus in a sacred marriage of Moon and Sun. As Frazer comments, eight years is the time when Moon and Sun 'so to say, meet and mark time together once more after diverging from each other more or less throughout the interval.' Although they are in conjunction once every month (in the dark of the New Moon), their conjunction takes place at a different point in the sky, 'until eight revolving years have brought them together again in the same heavenly bridal chamber where first they met.'[107]

The plot thickens when we learn that Endymion (who in another tale hailed from Mount Latmos in Asia Minor), was also the name of the son of the first king of Elis, who set his sons to run a race for the kingdom at Olympia, and may have reigned for a period of four or eight years after which they had again to stake their right to the throne by winning a chariot race.[108] Furthermore, the games may have originally been instituted in order to *assist* the regular course and activity of the heavenly bodies. The older Women's Games at Olympia date from the earlier system of time-reckoning by the Moon.[109] The daughters of Thetis, goddess of the sea, also numbered 50. At the least, the games speak of a correspondence in feeling between the race on the ground and in the heavens.

These cosmic counting tales, created by minds as yet undivided into rational and intuitive faculties, may help to explain why numbers themselves were symbols with far-reaching powers, as in Pythagorean cosmology. For once the number itself told the tale of the harmonies of the universe.

SHAPING MENTAL IMAGES

The shapes of the phases may also have played their part in the developing of visual forms, from musical instruments to alphabets. Hermes was said to have assisted the three lunar Fates in the composition of the alphabet, invented astronomy, the musical scale and the lyre, with seven strings or three.[110] Musaios, son of Orpheus, whose playing on the lyre enchanted animals, was called the Moon man.[111]

Cirlot, in his *Dictionary of Symbols*, observes that Schneider suggests that the progressive change in the shape of the Moon – from disc shape to a thin thread of light – may have given birth to a mystic theory of forms, which has influenced, the manner of constructing musical instruments. Further, Stuchen, Hommel and Dornseif argue that lunar shapes influenced the characters of the Hebrew and Arabic alphabets, as well as the 'graphic signs' of the Babylonians. Hommel suggests that ten or 11 Hebrew characters resemble phases of the Moon: *aleph*, for instance, which means 'bull', is the symbol of the Moon in its first week and is also the sign of the zodiac where the Moon's mansions begin.[112] Even in English we might loosely describe the crescent as a 'C' – an inverted 'C' for waxing and an ordinary 'C' for waning – a waxing half Moon as a 'D', and a Full Moon as a circle, if not a 'zero' (in Hughes' poem *New Moon in January*), or an 'O' (in Plath's image of the Moon's 'O-mouth', drawing face and mouth as one).[113]

Eliade comments that these parallels or assimilations – if such they be – are not so much classifications as an attempt to integrate human beings and their universe into the same divine rhythm. Letters and sounds here work like images: their innate energies were thought to move people through cosmic levels by magic or contemplation. For example, a person trying to make an image of the divine in Indian yoga is instructed to meditate on an exercise in which the Moon, mystical physiology, the written symbol and the sound value together form a pattern: 'Conceiving in his own heart the moon's orb as developed from the primal sound [*prathama-svara-parinatam*, i.e. evolved from the letter 'A'], let him visualize therein a beautiful blue lotus, within its filaments the moon's unspotted orb, and thereon the yellow seed-syllable *Tam*...'[114]

The thirteenth-century Zen Master, Eihei Dogen, writes more simply:

> The moon
> abiding in the midst of
> serene mind;
> billows break
> into light.[115]

THE LUNAR FRAME

After the more immediately impinging polarities of light and dark, and Earth and sky, the two heavenly bodies which interrupt and point the vastness of space are the Sun and Moon, giving a place for the eye to rest and the mind to start from. As the figure of the Goddess of Laussel implies, it was probably the Moon that first gave the idea of an inherently binding relationship between the heavenly and earthly worlds (provoking and fostering analogies between them), an idea visibly supported by the moving of the tides and the howling of night animals – dogs, wolves, jackals, coyotes and foxes – to the Full Moon. In this way the Moon locates Earth in space and places people at home in their world, as the following images – among countless others – suggest.

Masaoka Shiki:
> Fresh from the Void
> The moon
> On the waves of the sea.[116]

Hitamaro:

> On the Eastern horizon
> Dawn glows over
> The fields, and when
> I look back I see
> The moon setting in the West.'[117]

Pablo Neruda:

> Almost out of the sky, half of the moon
> Anchors between two mountains.
> Turning, wandering night, the digger of eyes.
> Let's see how many stars are smashed in the pool.[118]

However it has been conceived, the Moon is, as it were, the first 'thought' out from Earth, and so the first imaginative standpoint from which to reflect back upon Earth. As our closest neighbour, the Moon has always framed the Earth, giving it 'a local habitation and a name',[119] providing the one 'landmark' shared by everyone in the dark. In a moving poem, *Moonlight Night*, the poet Tu Fu, trapped by rebels and kept apart from his wife, thinks of her gazing into the moonlight on her own, with the children asleep, her black hair wet with dew and her arms chilly with the cold, and asks:

> ...when
> Oh when, shall we be together again
> Standing side by side at the window,
> Looking at the moonlight with dried eyes.[120]

A Zen tale takes the image of the Moon to offer a perspective upon human life, illuminating what things are real and what are not. It is called *The Moon Cannot Be Stolen*:

Ryokan, a Zen master, lived the simplest kind of life in a little hut at the foot of a mountain. One evening a thief visited the hut only to discover there was nothing in it to steal.
Ryokan returned and caught him. 'You may have come a long way to visit me,' he told the prowler, 'and you should not return empty-handed. Please take my clothes as a gift.' The thief was bewildered. He took the clothes and slunk away.
Ryokan sat naked, watching the moon. 'Poor fellow,' he mused, 'I wish I could give him this beautiful moon.'[121]

CHAPTER 6

THE MOON AND THE SUN

Sol gold is and Luna silver we threpe.
Chaucer *The Canon's Tale, The Canterbury Tales*

And pluck till time and times are done
The silver apples of the moon,
the golden apples of the sun.
Yeats *The Song of Wandering Aengus*

The Moon, Sun and starry Heaven appear to exist independently of our cosmologies, even though these cosmologies begin with the human story on Earth. But when the myths of many times and places are read one after the other, so many different Moons and Suns shine out from the pages that it is tempting to wonder whether any of us see the same thing. Yet, as the anthropologist Adolf Bastian (1826–1905) first pointed out, mythic images have both a local and a universal aspect.[1] In their minute particulars they are unique to each tribe, group or culture – sometimes, indeed, almost unrecognizable to those of others. But if the particulars are, as it were, held up to the light and regarded with what Neumann calls an 'archetypal eye',[2] a common pattern comes into view. The immense variety of local detail gradually becomes transparent to a deeper impulse, which has its source in the human imagination. This dimension of the mythic image may be called universal, for everyone on Earth has a story.

Myths of the world are endless, if only because they can never find the beginning. As Wallace Stevens puts it:

...The clouds preceded us

There was a muddy centre before we breathed.
There was a myth before the myth began,
Venerable and articulate and complete.

From this the poem springs: that we live in a place
That is not our own and, much more, not ourselves
And hard it is in spite of blazoned days.[3]

This tells us there is always a story – 'the poem' – about our world, one told so early and so often that we can hardly see it even when we try. And not just one story but many. The human story which is the universal story is often the least visible, for, superimposed upon our shared humanity, there is also the religious story, the race story, the nation, tribe, village and family story, as well as our own personal stories which grow and change, trying to relate to all the rest. While many of these stories may be on their own terms simply a celebration of the wonder of being, they cannot avoid being also an interpretation, and one made on

Fig. 1. God creating the Sun and Moon. Michelangelo,1508-1512. The Sistine Chapel, Rome.

inevitably limited premisses: 'Where were you when the Earth was made?', Job's God asks him.[4]

The Canadian literary critic Northrop Frye, in his book *The Great Code: The Bible and Literature*, coined the phrase 'mythological conditioning' to point to the way our perception of the outer world is invisibly drawn from beliefs which come from the hidden depths of the inner world:

> Man lives, not directly or nakedly in nature like the animals, but within a mythological universe, a body of assumptions and beliefs developed from his existential concerns. Most of this is held unconsciously, which means that our imaginations may recognize elements of it, when presented in art or literature, without consciously understanding what it is that we recognize. Practically all that we can see of this body of concern is socially conditioned and culturally inherited. Below the cultural inheritance, there must be a common psychological inheritance, otherwise forms of culture would not be intelligible to us. But I doubt if we can reach this common inheritance directly, bypassing the distinctive qualities in our specific culture. One of the practical functions of criticism, by which I mean the conscious organizing of a cultural tradition, is, I think, to make us more aware of our mythological conditioning.[5]

We are to understand from this that whatever is waiting to be born into consciousness is likely to be first discovered outside us in our (largely unconscious) interpretations of the world; and it is art or literature – images, stories and poems – which first awaken our imaginations to question the assumptions about the universe on which our interpretations are founded. When we recognize elements of our beliefs as they are mirrored back to us in art, we may grow by becoming conscious of them, observing how we respond to them, how we muse upon them, play with them and make them our own, trying to find the words and pictures that reflect them truly and bring them home.

Jung used the term 'projection' to describe how we 'throw' our perceptions out onto Nature 'on behalf of' our inner life (*pro*, on behalf of, *iacere*, throw, Latin):

> All the mythological processes of nature, such as summer and winter, the phases of the moon, the rainy seasons, and so forth, are in no sense allegories of these objective occurrences; rather they are symbolic expressions of the inner, unconscious drama of the psyche which becomes accessible to man's consciousness by way of projection – that is, mirrored in the events of nature.[6]

While this is remarkably clear, the language of 'projection' may sometimes be in danger of making too radical a division between the outer world and the inner drama of the psyche, almost 'leaving a gap' between them, reminiscent of the gap between God and Adam's finger in Michelangelo's picture of creation. Then Nature and the psyche become different kinds of being, and one or the other is diminished when we speak of either. In a sense we need a language of relationship, one which binds the human psyche to its world just because psyche and world belong to the same reality – even though the psyche in its unconsciousness tends to read one *or* the other as primary, either the world of Nature or, latterly, the human world.

It may be that only the language of poetry can hold the two worlds together in our sympathy. Coleridge, in his *Dejection Ode* presses the paradox when he says:

> O Lady! we receive but what we give,

And in our life alone does Nature live:
Ours is her wedding garment, ours her shroud![7]

Yeats, elucidating Shakespeare's perception that 'the eye, altering, alters all', conveys how humans create their world, yet he does so in such a way that, in his poem, the otherness of that world still beckons:

Our towns are copied fragments from our breast;
And all man's Babylons strive but to impart
The grandeurs of his Babylonian heart.[8]

As he explains in an essay on 'Symbolism in Painting': 'we love nothing but the perfect, and our dreams make all things perfect, that we may love them...and symbols are the only things free enough from all bonds to speak of perfection.'[9] Some of these symbols find expression as goddesses and gods, who have indeed been loved over the ages for their perfection, however idealized they may appear in retrospect and whatever shameful deeds have been done in their name.

The German philosopher Ernst Cassirer proposed that 'man can apprehend and know his own being only in so far as he can make it visible in the image of his gods.'[10] These goddesses and gods, fashioned in the images of those who make them, are not, then, powers who rule over certain provinces of Nature and human life, but ways in which Nature and human nature are revealed – through dream and vision, in ecstasy, confusion or terror. It would follow that the images and narratives of myth are not to be taken literally or treated historically as descriptions of past or present fact; they are rather to be read as *metaphors* of states of being and knowing, revelations which are available to consciousness but not yet wholly accepted as coming from the human imagination. As Campbell has unforgettably said:

Whenever the poetry of myth is interpreted as biography, history or science, it is killed. The living images become only a remote fact of a distant time or sky; furthermore, it is never difficult to demonstrate that as science and history mythology is absurd...[11]

It must be because the source of symbols is obscured in the depths of dream and vision that the images and stories through which they are expressed have first to be discovered outside, in apparently objective circumstance, before they can be reclaimed as belonging to a human experience. Following this through, it means that the human psyche makes itself progressively more visible to itself through the goddesses and gods with which it peoples the universe, a process through which what was unconscious gradually becomes conscious, so enabling a new form of unconscious life to seek expression. Consequently, the character of our divinities will change – must change – as our need of them is outgrown, for even the most religious might concede that our goddess and god images are not to be idolatrously confused with the Source of Creation, necessarily beyond the categories of human understanding. This allows for what might be called the 'dynamic fallibility' of the psyche, which means (to oversimplify) that the psyche grows by getting it wrong, learning from its 'mistakes', as in any other area of activity. But because, in the making of divinities, this wrongness – or, rather, inevitable partiality – is writ so large, the difficulties of moving on from our 'god images' are writ large also, as are the consequences of continuing to hang on to them even when their partialities become clear. Conversely, any image of the divine or sacred, as a culture's most fundamental point of orientation, needs to be continually questioned so it may be the better seen and known, and finally accepted as human, in order to get it less wrong next time. 'Try harder. Fail again. Fail better,' as one of Samuel Beckett's characters puts it.[12] Or, in the closing words of Robert Bly's translation of Rilke's poem *A Man Watching*:

> This is how he grows:
> By being defeated decisively
> by constantly greater beings.[13]

The question that arises from an exploration of these images is, can human beings consciously co-operate with this process? Does an understanding, from our present stories, of what imbalance needs to be redressed constitute in itself, or at least provoke, the future symbol waiting to be born? Or is the nature of a symbol such that we must we stand (helplessly) by while the next stage of our growing takes place through us but without us? In either case, can we welcome our next defeat?

CREATION MYTHS OF MOON AND SUN

Most myths of the creation of the Moon and the Sun present the two heavenly bodies as coming into being together, and only later distinguish between them in terms of authority and influence. Stories of origin address themselves to the simple questions a child (of any age) might ask: Who made the Moon and Sun? Why is the Moon not as bright as the Sun, and why does the Moon lose its light? What are the shadows on the face of the Moon? But, first: Who made the world?

The act of imagining the creation of the universe by those created within it is inevitably doomed. Nonetheless, some story must be found. In the reach for its origins the human mind often seems to set off in one of two apparently different directions, both of which *together* reflect the complexity of consciousness, but when separated emphasize one pole at the expense of the other. These directions (when polarized) lend themselves to being called the 'way of Nature' and the 'way of Spirit'. In the way of Nature, the mind moves backwards to an image of the world as a totally undifferentiated state – imagined as void, formlessness, darkness, silence, vapour, fog, water or sea; when more differentiated, the image of potentiality becomes an egg. This original state, sometimes named as chaos, has then to be energized or organized to let the forms that will become the world appear. Typically, the two heavy elements of earth and water are awakened by the other two lighter elements of air (wind, breath) or fire (heat, light) gently agitating forms out of the original formlessness or exploding them into being by force. Sometimes the 'Spirit' is inherent in the primeval waters (as in the Egyptian dark waters of Nun, which rise as the 'High Hill', or become visible as the 'First Light').[14]

The idea of the Mother Goddess synthesizes these two ways of creation, or rather arises out of an original experience before these categories are solidified and opposed. The Mother Goddess belongs to the way of Nature in that she gives birth to the world from her dark and watery womb, yet she is also of Spirit in that she is imagined as a human figure with more than human capacities – an image both immanent and transcendent. The miracle of animal and human birth is here the inspiration for the birth of the universe. If the act of giving life is foremost, the Mother Goddess is endowed with the loving character of an ideal mother who gives birth for the delight of her offspring. If the act of taking that life away is foremost (in the myth-maker's mind), then she is drawn as an impersonal mother who gives birth indiscriminately ('spawns' life), and abandons her offspring to sickness and death without caring for them personally as individual children.

The cycle of plant life is the model for another kind of creation myth where the universe is imagined as composed of the dismembered pieces of an original goddess, god or primeval being, such that life comes out of their death as a seed flowers from the crushed fruit of the last season's plant.

At the other extreme of this (imaginative, not necessarily historical) continuum, lies the way of pure Spirit, where the imagination moves forwards to an idealized perfection of the human being, to a super-differentiated state – almost in the image of a disembodied human mind. This is imagined as a Supreme Being, a Demiurge, a Transcendent God – a self-created being of pure intelligence and goodness without physical form, typically given as a Father God, as in Genesis. This God creates the world by some act that we recognize as human: he speaks it into being as the Word, or he throws it on the potter's wheel as his craft, or he breathes upon it the breath of life. The Father God makes the world as something apart from himself, in contrast to the Mother Goddess who generates creation as part of herself, out of her own substance.

The challenge for those myths beginning with the way of Spirit is how to embody Spirit back into Nature once it has been separated from it, how to allow the flesh of mortality to take form from such transcendence. The motive given to the God, modelled on the idea of the ideal father, is often intended to be the finest human characteristic – unconditional love. But the world thus created is named as inferior to its Creator, leading to ideas of inanimate Nature, a fallen universe and its human equivalent 'original sin'. It has to be redeemed; it cannot just *be*. So the love was conditional after all, and reward and punishment are not far away. Death becomes the 'fault' of creation so that the unsurpassable goodness of the Creator may be saved, to be worshipped unreservedly. This might suggest that the opposition of Nature and Spirit is misconceived in the first place.

However, there is another kind of story which takes as its starting point the fallibility of such human attempts to imagine the unimaginable, and so builds an awareness of the limits of our thinking into any attempt to formulate beginnings and endings. Such perspectives allow a story to be aware that it is a story, and to tell it anyway. These myths avoid the polarization of Nature and Spirit by invoking the image of consciousness, but not only a human kind of consciousness: rather, a consciousness that is present in all things. To put it the other way, there is nothing that is not consciousness. This consciousness is beyond human categories of time and space, and so beyond the oppositions in which humanity thinks when it thinks about itself. Terms such as the 'Dream Time of Eternity', *In Illo Tempore*, 'In That Time', or the 'Way' that cannot be spoken of or named,[15] offer an image of a state beyond definition. This state includes and comprehends such divisions – or such impossible contradictions – as arise from creatures imagining their own creation, when Nature seeks to become aware of its nature, consciousness becoming conscious of itself.

* * *

Moon and Sun fall into the pattern of creation as among the earliest beings to be created, sometimes before, sometimes after, Earth. Below are just a few examples.

In the Finnish epic *Kalevala* (oral folk songs and poems first written down in 1849), the Mother Goddess is floating in the cosmic waters when her womb is awakened by the wind and impregnated by sea-foam. After 700 years she still cannot give birth and she calls to Ukko, the All-Sustainer, to help her. He sends a bird to rest upon the waves who lays six golden eggs and one egg of lead, which roll about in the water and shatter into bits. Gradually the pieces came together in a beautiful form and the lower half of one egg became the earth and the upper half became the sky. Then:

From the yolk the sun was made,
Light of day to shine upon us;
From the white the moon was formed,
Light of night to gleam above us.

After still more time, the Water Mother gives birth herself to Vainamoinen, the hero, who, after fighting his way out of his mother's womb, floats for five years in the waves and stops at last upon a headland. Then he stands up to see the world:

To behold the moon in heaven
And to wonder at the daylight...[16]

The Polynesians from the Cook and Hervey Islands speak of the Woman of the Very Beginning, Vari-Ma-Takere, who lives in a tiny space at the bottom of the world coconut in the land of eternal silence in the depths of the primeval ocean. Six children are born to her: she plucks three from the left side of her body and three from the right. Avatea, the first child, was the first man on Earth who is also god of the Moon. As he grows, he divides down the middle: the left side is a fish and the right side a human being. Although he was so far down, he begins to move upwards, and, finding an opening to the upperworld, he is given the Earth to live upon, which is called 'Under the Bright Moon'. Of the three taken from the right side of Vari-Ma-Takere, one was female, called Papa, Earth.[17]

The Maoris of Polynesia take the tale forward: the Moon god, now called Vatea, then marries the Earth goddess, Papatuanuku, who swells up with all the waters held inside her body, and then bursts. Two sons stream out of her with the waters: the God of Ocean and the God of Agriculture. The God of Ocean, Tangaroa, is so large that he only breathes twice a day, which is when the tide ebbs and flows. He became the father of gods and humankind, who are therefore the grandchildren of Moon and Earth.[18]

In a Micronesian story from the island of Nauru, there was in the beginning only the sea and Old Spider above it. One day she finds a giant clam and slips inside, where she finds two snails beside her in the darkness. When she gets the shell open again, she makes the smaller snail into the Moon and the larger snail into the Sun.[19]

Dismemberment myths of creation are a way of explaining how the One can become the Many while still remaining the One, and how the universe can be alive while formed from one who is dead.

In the Sanskrit *Rig Veda* (c.1200 BC), creation comes from the dismemberment of the cosmic giant, Purusa. He is dismembered by 'the gods' (who are, in some way not explained, 'already there'). Purusa, called the 'Man', is so large he pervades all time and all matter. He engenders the female Viraj, who in turn gives birth to him. Then he is sacrificed: 'When the gods spread the sacrifice with the Man as the offering, spring was the clarified butter, summer the fuel, autumn the oblation.'[20] From the fat of his sacrifice all living things are born – firstly, verse and chants, then birds, horses, cows, goats, sheep, and then human beings, the Brahmin from his mouth, the people from his thighs and the servants from his feet: 'The moon was born from his mind; from his eye the sun was born. Indra and Agni came from his mouth, and from his vital breath the Wind was born.'[21] Some four hundred years later, the story in the *Aitareya Upanishad* (quoted in Chapter 5), takes this imagery of the outer universe and directs it inward, so that Moon, Sun, Wind and others find their 'abodes' in the human being.[22]

In Norse myth there was in the beginning a primeval cow who was formed from vapours. The tale is told by the Icelandic poet Snorri Sturluson (1179–1241) in his book the *Prose Edda* (so-called to distinguish it from the *Poetic* or *Elder Edda*, which he uses as source material for his own synthesis of the earlier myths). The cow licks the salt from stones and feeds the primeval giant, the frost ogre, Ymir. She licks the ice blocks and in three days a whole man is there. He is called Buri, and he has a son called Bor who marries Bestla, a daughter of one of the frost giants, and they have three sons, of whom one is Odin. But Bor's sons kill Ymir and make the world from his body.

> From Ymir's flesh
> the earth was made
> and from his blood the seas,
> crags from his bones,
> trees from his hair,
> and from his skull the sky...[23]

The sons of Bor make human beings from two trees, and Odin takes Night and her son, Day, and gives them horses and chariots and puts them in the sky to ride round the world every 24 hours. Night rides on Frosty-mane, who bedews the earth with foam every morning; while Day rides on Shining-mane, whose mane illuminates the whole Earth and sky. Then Odin has to guide the course of the Sun and the Moon.

Now, Moon and Sun were once two children on Earth. Their father was a man called Mundilfari, who called his son Moon and his daughter Sun because they were so beautiful. But this angered the gods, and they:

> took the brother and sister and put them up in the sky. They made Sun drive the horses
> which drew the chariot of the sun...Moon governs the journeying of the moon, and
> decides the time of its waxing and waning.[24]

A Chinese myth begins with Yin and Yang, the dual powers of the universe. Their offspring, P'an Ku (or Pan Gu), grows for 18,000 years within a great cosmic egg until it hatches. The dark, heavy parts of the egg sink downwards and become Earth, while the light parts rise up to become the sky. For the next 18,000 years P'an Ku grows ten feet a day and pushes the skies away from Earth until they are fixed. Then he dies and his body becomes the rest of the world: the Sun came from his left eye, the Moon from his right eye, stars from his hair and whiskers, wind and cloud from his breath, thunder from his voice, rain and dew from his sweat.[25]

Slavic myth gives priority to the Sun over the Moon. In the beginning there are two great gods: the White God, Byelobog, God of Light and Day, and the Black God, Chernobog, God of Dark and Night. Against this background of day and night there grows the bright Sky God, Svarog, who gives birth to Sun and Fire, and they reign over the universe as the flaming torch on high, daily lit and extinguished, as they are below on Earth in the hearth fires of human beings. At the beginning of every summer Sun marries Moon, a beautiful young girl called Myesyats, and she gives birth to many stars, but when they are angry with each other there are earthquakes. Every winter Sun abandons her, but every spring he comes back to her. The Ukrainian Slavs see it the other way: their Moon is the husband and their Sun is the wife. A Ukrainian song sings of the heavens as 'the great palace whose lord is bright Myesyats with his wife the bright Sun and their children the bright stars.'[26]

A Wakaranga myth from Zimbabwe makes Moon and the Morning and Evening Stars the creators of vegetation and animals, themselves created by the Great Spirit. The original man was the Moon,

Mwuetsi, to whom the Great Spirit gave a horn filled with ngona oil, and set him at the bottom of a lake. However, Mwuetsi wanted to live on Earth. But when the Great Spirit had put him upon Earth, Moon wept bitterly, for the Earth was bare – no animals, grasses, trees or bushes, and no people. The Great Spirit said to him: 'I warned you. You have begun a path which will lead to your death. But I will give you one of your kind for two years.' So the Great Spirit gave him a wife, called Morningstar, Massassi, and gave her a fire-maker. With the help of Mwuetsi's horn of ngona oil she gave birth to grasses, reeds, trees, and all kinds of plants and flowers. Two years passed, and the Great Spirit summoned Morningstar back up to the sky, and Moon wept for eight days. So the Great Spirit gave Moon another wife called Eveningstar, Morongo. After their first night together, Eveningstar gave birth to cows, sheep and goats; after their second night, antelopes and birds; after their third night, boys and girls. On the fourth day, when Moon again wished to sleep with Eveningstar, the Great Spirit counselled him to let things remain as they were, for the day of his death was approaching. But Moon took no notice, and the next morning Eveningstar gave birth to lions, leopards, snakes and scorpions. Then Moon desired his daughters, and they gave birth to many children, and this made Eveningstar jealous. So she sent a snake to bite Moon and he sickened. At the same time, the clouds stopped shedding their rain on Earth, the lakes and rivers dried up, vegetation withered, and there was famine throughout the land. Moon's children blamed their father for the drought, and they suffocated him and threw him into the sea, and set up another ruler in his place. But from the depths of the sea Moon caught sight of his first love, Morningstar, and he rose from the sea into the sky to be with her. So now he pursues her across the night sky, remembering how happy they were together.[27]

Although Moon is given as the Creator he is still subject to the world of becoming and change. Sharing in the human condition of movement and desire, he claims his destiny even if it means death. First procreating, then sickening (with the rains drying up), and then drowning, he waxes and wanes on Earth before he rises from death as the reborn Moon in the sky, upon which, it is implied, the rains are restored.

In many places, Sun and Moon are the two Eyes of the Supreme Being, as in China and Japan, or the two Eyes of Heaven, as in Egypt. On the Oceanic island of Nias, Sun and Moon were formed from the eyes of the armless and legless being, who was condensed from the thick fog of the beginning. From the heart of this being sprang a tree whose buds were the origin of gods and human beings. In the Cook Islands, Sun and Moon are the eyes of the god Vatea.[28]

In some myths, Moon and Sun begin on Earth and then move into Heaven, in the same way that the Moon and the Sun appear to rise from the Earth every day and every night. The Navaho Indians talk of the First Man and First Woman coming out from the underworld to the surface of the Earth, which was all dark. So they took a slab of quartz crystal and made two discs into Sun and Moon. On the Sun disc they put a mask of blue turquoise so it would give off heat and light, and hung red coral around its rim and on its earlobes, and fixed eagle, lark and flicker feathers to spread the light and heat in the four directions. They took the crystal disc of the Moon and covered it with white shells, and attached the two discs to that place of the sky where they start from – Sun in the east and Moon in the west. But Sun and Moon did not move. Two wise old men offered to give their spirits to the discs to give them life. But which way should they go? First Man noticed that Eagle is guided by his tail feathers, so he tied 12 eagle feathers to each disc to point them to the right paths in the sky. So Sun began his journey towards the west, and, just as he was setting, Moon began his journey towards the east. But at that moment Wind Boy tried to help Moon along, and by mistake blew Moon's 12 eagle feathers across his face, so Moon could not see which way to go. And that is why Moon has an irregular path across the sky.[29]

Fig. 2. Earth and Sky, with Sun and Moon. Navaho pollen painting by Jeff King. c. 1900 AD. (From Maud Oakes and Joseph Campbell, Where the Two Came to Their Father: A Navaho War Ceremonial, *given by Jeff King. Bollingen Series I, New York, Pantheon Books Inc., 1943, p. 95).*

Moon is the Mother of Sun for the Hopi Indians, and for the Snolquamie Indians Moon is the chief of the heavens. Fox, disguised as Beaver, finds Sun hidden in Moon's house, as well as tools for making daylight, and fire inside a smoke hole, which Fox then takes down to Earth for people.[30]

The tribes in Australia tell different tales. The Arunta tribe of central Australia say that a man of the Opossum totem used to carry the Moon around with him in his shield, but in the day he had to put it down so he hid it in a cleft of rock. Then a man of another totem saw the Moon shining through the crack in the rock and ran off with it. The Opossum man could not catch the thief, so he called out loudly to the Moon to rise into the sky and shine for everyone – which it did, and it has been in the sky ever since.[31] The Wongibon of New South Wales say that the Moon is an old man who fell off a rock and hurt his back, before going up to heaven, which is why he walks bowed down. But in Queensland they say Moon is the creator of Sun. Moon created the Sun as a woman with two legs, but she has a great number of arms which dazzle like rays when the Sun rises or sets.[32]

In ancient Greece, there were four different stories of creation, beginning in chaos, darkness or sea.[33] The oldest one is the myth of the indigenous (pre-Hellenic) people of northern Greece, the Pelasgians, who imagine the Goddess of All Things rising naked out of Chaos, and finding nothing but sea. Her name was Eurynome, which means 'wide-wandering' (one of the names of the Moon). Dividing the sky from the sea, she dances towards the south and the wind starts up behind her, and she turns and catches the wind and rubs it between her hands and it becomes a serpent who mates with her and she conceives the life that is to come. Taking now the form of a dove, she lays the universal egg on the waters and Ophion, the serpent, coils seven times around it until it splits, letting forth Moon, Sun, Stars, Earth and all life on Earth, including a man called Pelasgos.[34]

Finally, compare the personified Creator in Genesis with the impersonal idea in the *Tao te Ching*:

> In the beginning God created the heaven and the earth;
> And the earth was without form, and void: and darkness was upon the face of the deep.
> And the Spirit of God moved upon the face of the waters.
> And God said, Let there be light: and there was light.

And God saw the light, that it was good: and God divided the light from the darkness. And God called the light Day, and the darkness he called Night. And the evening and the morning were the first day.[35]

The *Tao te Ching* begins:

> The way (*tao*) that can be spoken of
> Is not the constant way;
> The name that can be named
> Is not the constant name.
> The nameless was the beginning of heaven and earth;
> The named was the mother of the myriad creatures.[36]

THE GENDER OF MOON AND SUN

> That orbèd maiden, with white fire laden,
> Whom mortals call the Moon.[37]

In the West, because of our Judaeo-Christian and classical inheritance, many people tend to think of the Sun as masculine and the Moon as feminine, which is why Shelley's poem above is instantly recognizable. Some go further and consider as anomalies those countries which 'reverse' the gender and see the Sun as feminine and the Moon as masculine, as though gender were given in Nature. An 'alliance' in anomaly has even been implied as an explanation of Germany's and Japan's military alliance in World War II, both cultures having female Suns, 'father' countries and male Moons: the Moon, writes Laurens van der Post, 'by some ominous perversity of the aboriginal urgings of both Germans and Japanese, was rendered into a fixed and immutable masculinity.'[38]

Another way of positing western classical culture as primary has been to assume that 'primitive' people might have a male Moon but 'more developed' people have a female Moon. This issue is complicated by the fact that, as we shall see below, some cultures changed the gender of their heavenly bodies when the Sun took precedence over the Moon, replacing the Sun goddess with a Sun god and the Moon god with a Moon goddess.

Nonetheless, as these stories show, the Moon has been seen as male *or* female, or male on some occasions and female on others (as with the Hottentots and Bushmen, and the Mayans and the Aztecs of ancient Mexico). In the Andaman Islands, among other places, the Moon is male in its waxing and female in its waning.[39] In Melanesia and New Guinea, there are two Moon gods, one bright and one dark.[40] Sometimes the Full Moon is female, mother to two males, gods of waxing and waning, as with the Navaho tribe, among others. Generally, with the North American Indians, as with the Slavs, the Moon was female in some tribes and male in others, though the Indian stories were documented by Christian missionaries whose God and Sun were male, and who may therefore have urged a change of gender along with the change of deity.[41]

The Moon can also take male *and* female form, as with the Egyptians and the Mesopotamians, either alternately or at the same time. In Egypt, Osiris, Thoth, Khons, Horus and Aah are Moon gods, and Isis and Neith are Moon goddesses. In Mesopotamia, the Moon was a god, Nanna-Sin, whose son was the Sun, Shamash, and whose daughter, Inanna-Ishtar, was the Morning Star and also the Moon. In the *Vedas* both Sun and Moon are masculine, Surya and Mas, though in Vedic cult, possibly from an archaic proto-Indo-European tradition, the Sun is feminine, Suryaa, the feminine form of Surya.[42] In Greece many writers spoke of a male Moon, Mene (Homer and Pindar, for instance), though the official Moon was female, Selene. The Orphic *Hymn to the Moon* begins by addressing Selene, and continues 'Mene, waxing and waning, feminine and masculine.'[43] In Aristophanes' argument for the power of love in Plato's *Symposium*, hermaphrodites descended from the Moon 'which partakes of either sex', while males came from the Sun and females from the Earth.[44]

THE MOON AS MALE

For the record, the Moon was male in all the Indo-European languages which followed the course of the Indo-Europeans as they travelled from India to Europe over the millennia from around 2000 BC onwards. It was also male in all the Teutonic and Semitic languages. More generally, the Moon was male for the Ainu, Anatolians, Armenians, Southern Arabians, Australian Aborigines, Balts, Basques, Canaanites, Eskimos, Finns, Germans, Georgians, Greenlanders, Hindus, Hittites, Hurrians, Japanese, Lithuanians, Melanesians, Mongolians, Persians, Phrygians, Poles, New Guineans, North American Indians of British Columbia, the Machivanga of Peru, Scandinavians, Slavs, Tartars and many African tribes, among others.[45] 'Down to recent times,' writes the folklorist Jacob Grimm in the 1870s, 'our people were fond of calling the sun and moon *frau sonne* and *herr mond*.'[46] Bulgarian, Russian and Serbo-Croatian songs call the Moon a father or grandfather. In Basque, the word used for god is same as that for Moon. Usually, though not invariably, where the Moon was male the Sun was female, a goddess not a god. In both Welsh and Irish, the words for Sun are feminine, *huan* and *grian*,

Fig. 3. The Moon god in his chariot. Stone bas relief from Anghor Vat, east gallery, southern half, Cambodia. Early 12th century AD. Photo, Jaroslav Poncar.

as they are for the Moon, *Ilenad* (Welsh) and *gelach* (Irish); however, another word for Moon in Irish is masculine, *Iuan*, also a word for the warrior's halo in battle. The Kenyan Masai have a feminine word for Sun with a male Sun, and a masculine word for Moon with a female Moon.[47] Perhaps this still incomplete list might qualify the many commentaries on myth which begin with 'the Moon is female except...'

THE MOON AS FEMALE

On the other hand, in the West the Palaeolithic, Neolithic and Bronze Age Mother goddesses are all Moon goddesses as well as Earth goddesses, and their consorts are Moon and Earth gods – Isis, Hathor, Nut, Neith, in Egypt, Inanna-Ishtar in Mesopotamia (Sumeria and Babylonia), the Great Mother Goddess of Minoan Crete, and, later, Astarte in Canaan, Aphrodite in Greece, Kybele in Anatolia and Rome. However, attributions of gender in its contemporary meaning are complicated by the fact that some Mother goddesses of the Palaeolithic and Neolithic were given a distinctly phallic neck, as though to emphasize that these sacred images were beyond simple human classifications. Bronze Age goddesses were also occasionally addressed as 'goddess and god', especially when the male was understood as an aspect of the goddess herself.

In Iron Age Greece, many of the goddesses were Moon goddesses: primarily 'white-armed' Selene, Artemis and Hekate, but also 'white-armed' Hera, Athene of the 'gleaming eyes', 'foam-born' Aphrodite, Persephone who holds torches and her mother, Demeter, who holds grain. In Rome, Artemis became Diana, Selene became Luna, Hera became Juno, Demeter became Ceres and Athene became Minerva, while Hekate stayed the same. The three Fates, who were aspects of the Moon, were female in Greek, Roman and Norse myth. This classical inheritance is registered in languages deriving from Latin which still retain gender – *la lune, le soleil*, in French.

The Moon was also female for the Chinese, Polynesians, Indonesians, Etruscans, Rumanians, some North American Indian tribes, the Incas of Peru, Mayans, Aztecs, Brazilians, the Ona and the Yamana and the Selk'nam (or Ona) of Tierra del Fuego, and many others. In Africa, female Moons were found among the Nuer of the Sudan, the Kundu in Cameroon, the Kimbundu of Angola and the people of the Zambezi, among other African tribes.[48]

In the English language, the Moon was originally male and the Sun was female, both in grammar and in myth, and continued to be so until the sixteenth century. In Chaucer and Milton, for instance, the Sun is referred to as 'she'. Bishop Latimer's *Sermon on St Stephen's Day*, in 1552, still calls the Sun feminine: '...Not that the sunne itself of her substance shal be darkened...'; but by the 1607 version *her* had become *his*, in what would seem to be a deliberate doctrinal reversal.[49] However, the male Moon of our ancestors may persist in folklore as the 'Man in the Moon'.

* * *

In many parts of the West for the last two thousand years Sun and Moon have served as absolute paradigms of male and female, almost as though they were given in Nature. Since this is clearly only a relatively late cultural presupposition, we might wonder what this reveals about western culture, specifically about its classic and Judaeo-Christian inheritance, and the subtle way in which natural objects are 'socialized' to reflect and reinforce local custom. The tone of a passage from *The Zohar* (thirteenth century AD) on the relative strengths of Sun and Moon may recall us to the various Houses of God where the pattern of social conduct between the sexes is traditionally handed down:

God made two great lights. The two lights ascended together with the same dignity. The moon, however, was not at ease with the sun, and in fact each felt mortified by the other…God thereupon said to her, 'Go diminish thyself'…Thereupon she diminished herself so as to be head of the lower ranks. From that time she has had no light of her own, but derives her light from the sun…When the moon was in connection with the sun, she was luminous, but as soon as she separated from the sun and was assigned the charge of her own hosts, she reduced her status and her light.[50]

Whichever gender we have given to the Moon, it is instructive to find that other cultures assign an opposite gender, while still attributing to it the same functions of fertility, generation, regeneration, and qualities of mind. That fact in itself may point us beyond the gender of the Moon to its prior role in the imagination of all peoples.

THE MOON AS SYMBOLICALLY FEMININE

But, going beyond modern and western identifications of Moon and Woman, Sun and Man, can we still say, with Jung, Neumann and others, that the Moon is *symbolically feminine* or *archetypally feminine*? The argument for this is that, by contrast with the Sun, the Moon is a vessel, cup or chalice (filling and emptying), which belongs to the night, was constantly related to water (holding it as ambrosia and releasing it as dew and rain), was identified with the Earth and the Great Mother Goddess, and was the presiding force (whether male or female) in the earlier ages of 'matriarchal consciousness.'[51] As Neumann observes, many of the images through which the Moon was worshipped, such as 'Uterus', 'Womb of the Universe', 'Self-generated Fruit', 'Wild Cow', are terms addressed to the Great Mother Goddess, 'who, as the night sky, is also the moon itself to which she gives birth as something male.'[52] (The Sanskrit etymology of *ma*, Mother and *mas*, Moon, masculine, are an example of this). In this case, the Moon, as one among many aspects of the Great Mother Goddess, expresses the feminine dimension given to the image of the divine. Plutarch, for instance, recounts that for the Egyptians the Moon, whether conceived as female or male, embodied 'the feminine principle of Nature.'[53]

Other images addressed to the Moon, such as 'Bull of Heaven', Bull of the Underworld', 'Lord of Women', 'Husband', King' and 'Father', suggest that the male aspect of the Great Mother was differentiated and seen as autonomous, unless the Moon becomes also the 'Son', which recalls us to the greater cyclical reality that grants the changing roles. Still other images make it clear that male and female can coexist together. For instance, Nanna-Sin, Moon god of Ur in Mesopotamia, is addressed as:

> Mighty Bullock, with thick horns…
> Uterus, Womb of the Universe…
> Merciful One, Gracious Father,
> Who holds the life of the entire country in his hand.[54]

The infinitely varied life of the Moon – details of which will emerge in subsequent chapters – might point to how over-simplified contemporary thinking about even archetypal gender has become. In the *Aitareya Brahmana* (a prose compilation belonging to the tradition of the *Rig Veda*), the Moon is both male *and* containing – 'King Moon, the vessel of all the waters of immortal life'[55] – just as Nanna-Sin is both Mighty Bullock and Womb. Conversely, Artemis is both female and a hunter, chalice and blade.

It seems clear that 'the feminine principle', when referred to the Moon, can take male *or* female form, preventing us from identifying the feminine principle with the human female and the masculine principle with the human male. Perhaps we can also let go of the still more limiting assumption that symbols tend to stay the same, not evolving like everything else, on the supposition that they spring uniquely from a core of humanness which structures past and present alike. However, it is no part of Jung's idea of the collective unconscious that archetypal images and symbols should not change,[56] as though the memories of the race were forever imprisoned in their original form, imprisoning in turn the later consciousness (or later ideas about how consciousness works). The essence of the metaphor of the collective unconscious, or the Great Memory, as Yeats would more evocatively call it,[57] is that it is imagined *in relationship* to the consciousness of any age, as a result of which both are continually, albeit infinitely subtly, modified and changed. Symbols are images that are 'living souls', in Yeats's phrase, trailing histories and biographies and memories of past lives; '...an image that has transcended particular time and place becomes a symbol, passes beyond death, as it were, and becomes a living soul.'[58]

The Moon who creates his or her own light is not quite the same Moon as the one who, or rather which, shines with borrowed light, and when this fact about the Moon was understood at different times around the globe the symbol of the Moon gradually changed. Similarly, light and darkness as living images have taken on new cadences of meaning throughout the ages. But what has not changed is the human need to make distinctions by pointing a contrast, and the fundamental division available is that between dark and light in outer and inner worlds. Perhaps this primary distinction between light and dark is where the naming of symbolically masculine and feminine can start from, free from human gendering? As dark is Mother to the light (imagined as 'there first' in creation myths) so perhaps we can say (but only when necessary) that darkness may symbolize the feminine principle, out of which comes light symbolizing the masculine principle (remembering that moving from an image to a 'gendered principle' is always dangerous). The Moon is then gathered to this symbolically feminine night-world as the fluctuating figure which glimmers out of the original darkness – allied to the dark of the womb and the waters, the deeps of sea and earth, and also the depths of the human mind.

Metaphorically, then, the Moon is both at one with and different from the dark places in the psyche, suggestive of the first thought rising out of the unconscious, later to be called intuition. By contrast, also metaphorically, the Sun separates itself from the dark places in the psyche, clarifying what is shadowy and opaque in human thought, offering a brilliance of insight later to be called reason.

It only needs the simple word 'metaphorically' to turn the Sun and Moon into symbols of human consciousness, or rather to reveal what they have been doing all along. For 'daylight consciousness' belongs to the Sun as 'night-time consciousness' belongs to the Moon, and each re-presents to the human mind a different kind of illumination of itself. This symbolization would seem inevitable, for, in contrast to Earth which is experienced as still, both Sun and Moon appear to be moving, as do the thoughts and feelings (e-motions) which make up consciousness. Further, Sun and Moon appear to move each against a different background, one of light and one of dark. It makes sense that they were given separate realities to inhabit, and that the terms 'solar' and 'lunar' consciousness are even now employed to represent different ways of thinking or modes of consciousness, though the meaning of these terms has moved through as many mutations as the meanings of Sun and Moon themselves. The current meaning at any point in history cannot then be 'natural' – inherent in the natures of Sun and Moon – but must be cultural, or rather, culture calling itself natural.

THE 'SOLARIZATION' OF THE MOON

Astonishing as it may initially seem to those of a temperate climate (and a Judaeo-Christian and classical inheritance), it is now undisputed that, of the two heavenly bodies, the Moon not the Sun was the earliest focus of religious life in most if not all parts of the world.[59] Scholars are agreed that worship of the Moon and the orientation of life by the lunar calendar went together, and preceded worship of the Sun and the solar calendar.[60]

It is a measure of how difficult it is to see past our own preconceptions that the relatively late rediscovery of the Moon's precedence was announced with regret or surprise: In the late 1890s the Reverend Timothy Harley conceded in his book *Moon Lore*: 'It seems to be generally admitted that no form of idolatry is older than the worship of the moon.'[61] 'It is a remarkable fact that at first primacy was assigned to the Moon,' writes Professor Franz Cumont in the 1940s.[62] Or take Funk and Wagnall, the authors of the contemporary (and very large) American *Standard Dictionary of Folklore, Mythology, and Legend*, who say, in one entry, that the Moon is 'second to nothing in its influence on worldwide folk belief and practice', and in another that 'throughout the world, the moon is an evil principle or body as compared with the good sun.'[63] This last interpretation might alert us to the extent of 'solarization' in western culture.

The Moon's original power was often attributed to its being the marker, and so in early thought the cause, of time and change, in particular of the changes in women's reproductive life, and so the source of their fertility. But it seems that all means of survival – the success of the hunt, the growth of animals and plants, the continuation of the tribe, the health of babies, the healing of sickness, the granting of longevity and even immortality – all these were once believed to be gifts of the Moon, not the Sun. Although it must have been obvious that, for instance, plants grow towards the Sun, that still left the spirit of growth – that which makes them grow at all – to the province of the Moon. For originally the Moon, with its cyclical rhythms and its powers of renewal, appeared to rule all it surveyed. However, when agriculture became the focus of survival, the Sun was recognized as the source of the seasons which regulated the harvest, so it was inferred that growth came from its light and heat not from the waxing and waning of the Moon. Then the timing of the year began to shift from a lunar to a solar orientation and, as we have seen, a new luni-solar calendar was inaugurated in most places.[64]

But even after the first discovery of the relation of the Sun to the seasons, the Moon was in many places still primary, continuing to play many of its ancient roles for far longer than might have been expected. It may be that the Earth's identification with the Moon was too deeply felt to relinquish centuries, if not millennia, of awe and wonder and a compelling sense of affinity. For, as it was variously expressed in different cultures, both Moon and Earth moved to the same dual rhythm of growing and diminishing – the rhythm, it might seem, of life itself. In Chinese thought, for instance, Moon and Earth were both *yin*, embodying the feminine principle; in Greece the Moon was 'a heavenly Earth'.[65] The Maori experienced the Moon, Hine the 'Woman', as one with the Earth, believing the Moon to be formed out of Earth.[66] This feeling also found expression in the idea that the Moon was the source of all the life-giving moisture on Earth and so the impulse of growth, that which made Earth live. These ideas are typical of many similar and may be understood as answering a need of kinship which the Sun did not satisfy.

This was especially so in hot countries such as India, Mesopotamia, Egypt, Asia Minor and Africa, where the Sun is an enemy at least at its zenith. As late as the first century AD, Plutarch was saying: 'The effects of the Moon are similar to the effects of reason and wisdom...whereas those of the sun appear to be brought about by the power of physical force and violence.'[67] Zimmer writes of India: 'The

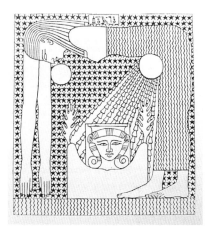

Fig. 4. Nut, the sky goddess, giving birth to the Sun god, whose rays illuminate the face of cow-eared Hathor, here pictured as the horizon between two hills. Painted ceiling relief, Temple of Hathor, Dendera, Egypt. c. 116 BC - 34 AD.

Fig. 5. Seth, after his defeat by Horus, spearing Apophis for the Sun god Re. Papyrus of Lady Cheritwebeshet. 21st dynasty. 1085-950 BC. National Museum, Cairo.

terrible heat of the devouring sun is regarded in India as a deadly power. The moon, on the other hand, conferring the refreshing dew, is the abode and source of life.'[68] In Mesopotamia, also a tropical country, the Moon, Nanna-Sin, was father to the Sun, Shamash, a priority that extended throughout Asia Minor, and was also accorded to the Anatolian Moon god Men. In Egypt, Osiris and Isis never entirely gave way to the later sovereignty of the Sun god Re, for even when the priests came to follow the Sun, the folk continued to follow the Moon.[69] These points of view merged in the image of Osiris as the dead pharaoh, while the living king fashioned himself in the image of Horus who, though in one reading of his name was the son of Osiris (and so the New Moon), became in another reading identified with Horus, the Sun, and later with the blazing light of the Sun god Re. The shift of emphasis may be seen in the two stories of sunrise, one seen from the perspective of the Moon and the other from the Sun, both of which existed side by side without contradiction.

In the Heliopolitan creation myth, Nut was the sky goddess who arched her star-spangled body over her husband Geb, the Earth, resting her feet on the eastern horizon and brushing the west with the tips of her fingers. The Sun was her son, slipping inside her body at night, travelling from west to east to be born from her womb at dawn (fig. 4). This is one of the earliest images of the 'son-lover'.

A similar image gave the heavens the form of the cow goddess, Hathor, whose four legs straddled the Earth as the four directions of space. Her name meant 'House of Horus', and her son was Horus, the golden falcon of the Sun, who in the evening flew into the mouth of his mother and was swallowed deep inside her starry body, where, becoming, as the Egyptians put it, the 'Bull of his Mother',[70] he united with his source and was born again from his mother's womb at dawn. In both these images of sunrise, it is the blood-birth from the Mother which colours the dawn sky red.

In a later story, the drama of sunrise belongs to the Sun god Re. The Great Cow is here called Nut not Hathor (the shared identities disclosing the ephemeral nature of names and forms), and her vast belly carries the two boats of the Sun, one of day and the other of night, with the god himself standing in the lighted boat of day above her forelegs. In the 'night journey of the Sun', Re at sunset travelled in his night boat through the celestial ocean of the Great Cow, where he was attacked by Apophis, the serpent of the darkest hour of night, who threatened to swallow up all the water on which the boat of the Sun sailed. Each night Apophis had to be defeated, and – in a totally different 'solar' meaning to the dawn – it is the blood of the serpent, the blood of battle and victory, which streaks across the sky at dawn (fig. 5). This is no longer the son born of the night, but the son who is hero of the light. The underworld is still conceived as the black belly of the sky goddess, but the dramatic emphasis has shifted from the Mother who bears the Sun to the Sun who rides across the Mother and vanquishes his enemy, the serpent of the dark, who would renew himself instead of the Sun.

* * *

In the Near and Middle East, even when working with the seasons had become crucial to survival, it took the invasion of non-agricultural nomadic tribes worshipping Sun, storm and wind gods to bring about a decisive shift of orientation from Moon to Sun. In the late Bronze Age and early Iron Age, from around 3500 BC onwards, a series of invasions by the cattle-, sheep- and goat-herding people from the broad grassy steppes of the north, as well as the Syro-Arabian desert, had culminated in a change in the rule of Mesopotamia around 2500 BC. The matriarchal, lunar-oriented goddess culture of the Sumerians had now to adapt to the new patriarchal, solar-oriented god culture of the Semitic Babylonians, ruled by their desert kings, of whom the first major one was Sargon of Agade (c.2350 BC) and the second was Hammurabi of Babylon (c.1728–1686 BC).

The key text for the conquest of the Earth and Moon goddess by the Sun and Storm god is the Babylonian epic of creation, the *Enuma Elish* (meaning 'When on High'), which celebrates Marduk's defeat of his great-great-great-grandmother Tiamat. The myth, composed around the time of Hammurabi, was recited for a thousand years in Babylon at the spring equinox, though the version which survived for posterity came from the library of the Assyrian King Ashurbanipal (c.668–630 BC). The significance of the myth lies in the fact that it was the first creation myth to dramatize murder with relish, almost to personalize it, in an age, unsurprisingly, when the god's earthly counterparts were doing the same.

Looking at this myth (mentioned in Chapter 2) more closely, Tiamat is the original Mother of All, pictured as a serpent with the Crescent Moon upon her head. However, this is no longer the magnificent lunar serpent of regeneration, but the dragon-demon in flight who had threatened chaos – an image already resonant of the victor's point of view (fig. 6).

The epic begins gently, with images which still belong to the old Sumeria:

> When the heights of heaven and the earth beneath had not been named, when Apsu, their father [the sweet river waters and the waters that fell from Heaven], and Tiamat, their mother [the salt sea waters] still mingled their waters, and no pasture land had yet been formed, and no gods had been called into being, then were the great gods created within the primal pair.[71]

But the new gods and their children annoy Apsu with their clamour and he wants to be rid of them. Instead it is he who is tricked and killed by his own son, Ea. Marduk is Ea's son, who belongs to the fourth generation of gods from the beginning. It happened like this. Ea's elder brother, Anu, creates fierce winds which 'disturb' Tiamat and monsters come forth from her, threatening, the gods assume, the rest of creation, and so they resolve to destroy her. Marduk's sovereignty is given as a storm god – his weapons are violent winds, tempests, hurricanes, thunder and lightning – but his 'awe-inspiring majesty' is set to dazzle in the image of the Sun:

His figure was enticing, flashing the look of his eyes, manly his going forth. He was a leader from the start...He had four eyes and as many ears, and when his lips moved, fire blazed forth. Each of the ears grew large; each of the eyes, also, to see all. He was prodigious and was clothed with the radiance of ten gods, with a majesty to inspire fear.[72]

Marduk is given the sceptre, throne and ring by the gods, and takes up his bow, spear, mace and thunderbolt. He 'set lightning before him, with burning flame he filled his body', and as he rides on his chariot a brilliant halo shines around his head:

> The lord spread out his net to enfold her.
> The Evil Wind, which followed behind, he let loose in her face.
> When Tiamat opened her mouth to consume him,
> He drove in the Evil Wind that she close not her lips...
> As the fierce winds charged her belly,
> Her body was distended and her mouth was wide open.
> He released the arrow, it tore her belly,
> It cut through her insides, splitting the heart.[73]

Marduk then treads on her legs, crushes her skull, severs her arteries, and splits her like a shellfish into two parts. Half of her he makes into the sky and the other half into the Earth. Then he begins again, establishing the year, making the constellations, appointing the Sun and Moon to their places in the sky, and instructing the Moon on his behaviour throughout the month (see Chapter 2). The god's re-creation by the power of the Word here replaces the original creation by the Mother Goddess, Tiamat, as though the Word has first to destroy the life it would pronounce back into being. Then he wrenches her lifeless body into the despised lineaments of Earth:

> He heaped up a mountain over Tiamat's head,
> pierced her eyes to form the sources of the Tigris and Euphrates,
> and heaped similar mountains over her dugs,
> which he pierced to make the rivers
> from the eastern mountains that flow into the Tigris.
> Her tail he bent up into the sky to make the Milky Way,
> and her crotch he used to support the sky.[74]

In the new ordering of priorities, the mutual process of transformation which had bound Earth to Moon – suggested in the crescent resting on the head of the Serpentine Mother – was no more. The relationship of Moon to Earth, even their implicit rhythmic identity, had been severed. It was as though the Moon was now to be confined solely to the celestial sphere in the name of the new heavenly patterning, which was of a superior order. The fact that Marduk then created humankind out of the blood of Kingu, Tiamat's murdered son-lover (to whom she had entrusted the Tablets of Destiny), suggests, further, that the human psyche had suffered a loss of confidence in itself; for was not life once a gift of the Goddess Mother, from Herself to Herself?

Hammurabi, the warrior-king, took the chance to identify himself with the Sun (as did many kings after him, down to Louis XIV, *Le Roi Soleil*), annexing his own temporal power to the Sun's immortal scope. He had been summoned by name, he declared, by Marduk and Anu (god of the firmament)

Fig. 6. *Marduk slaying Tiamat, with Crescent Moon. Assyrian seal. c. 800 BC.*
(From Jeremias, Das Alte Testament, fig. 14.)

to bring about the rule of righteousness in the land, to wipe out the wicked and evil, to prevent the strong from oppressing the weak, to go forth like the sun over the human race, to illuminate the land, and to further the welfare of mankind.[75]

Campbell comments:

The celestial orb to which the monarch is now likened is no longer the silvery moon, which dies and is resurrected and is light yet also dark, but the golden sun, the blaze of which is eternal and before which shadows, demons, enemies, and ambiguities take flight. The new age of the Sun God has dawned, and there is to follow an extremely interesting, mythologically confusing development (known as *solarization*), whereby the entire symbolic system of the earlier age is to be reversed, with the moon and the lunar bull assigned to the mythic sphere of the female, and the lion, the solar principle, to the male.[76]

This stage in the evolution of consciousness is also typically characterized by the replacing of the myth of the Goddess by the myth of the God. This is to say that the ultimate source of generation – beyond Moon and Sun – was re-imagined as a Sky God, and later a Transcendent God, who called the world into being by word or deed as separate from himself, but did not give birth to the world, as the Mother Goddess had done for millennia before, from her own body as part of her immanent divinity. The universe did indeed fall from grace, but it was the grace of humanity's appreciation of itself as sharing in the divine substance. In other words, the further away the Sun, Moon, goddesses and gods went, the more human beings became alone.

In patriarchal mythologies the sex of the heavenly bodies often changes somewhere along the way, and the Moon god becomes a Moon goddess, wife of the now male Sun.[77] This conversion of the male Moon into a female Moon, and sometimes also the female sun into a male sun, created a new system of priorities – on the grounds, presumably, that whatever was dominant had to be male. Neumann points out how the old Moon myths are subsumed into the new way of thinking:

This trend towards patriarchal consciousness is reflected in the supersession of feminine moon myths by masculine sun myths and can be traced far back into primitive mythology. Whereas the moon myths, even when the moon is masculine, always indicate the dependence of consciousness and light upon the nocturnal side of life i.e., the unconscious, this is no longer the case with the patriarchal solar mythologies. Here the sun is not the morning sun born of the night, but the sun in his zenith at high noon, symbolizing a masculine consciousness which knows itself to be free and independent even in its relations with the self, i.e. the creative world of heaven and spirit.[78]

Furthermore, as Sheena McGrath points out in her book *The Sun Goddess*, once the Sun is declared supreme, other sky and storm gods tend to lose their individual character and are classed as solar, perhaps because of 'syncretizing influences on classical mythology which identified everything important with the sun...Sometimes it is assumed that any sky god is the sun, rather than admit to a sun goddess.'[79] It may then be more exact to see the classical and Christian Sun as co-opted into a patriarchal point of view, and to exclude Sun goddesses in other cultures from generalizations of this kind. For, like the Moon gods, they were to become invisible.

* * *

To summarize, there seem generally to have been four stages to solarization: firstly, the discovery of agriculture, which made the Sun the food-bringer as well as the Moon; secondly, the subordination of matriarchal goddess-oriented cultures to patriarchal tribes, which looked to the impersonal unchanging patterns of the heavens for their model and ideal; thirdly, the development of science, which worked out that the Moon's light was reflected sunlight; fourthly, the advent of Christianity, with its God transcendent and his 'only begotten son' symbolized by the Sun.

What these stages chart is an increasing reliance on the autonomy of the human mind. It is as though human beings pitch their longings beyond the flux of time, testing their dependence on the apparent conditions of life, seeking to be no longer the child of Nature but the master. For, in what might be called a 'solarization of values', an entirely new way of conceiving and relating to life (and to death) was registered.

Cumont points out that 'Sun-worship is essentially a *learned* cult [my italics]: it grew with science itself.' It did not arise instinctively; it had to be calculated. Furthermore, this science was undertaken by the priests, not the people, and was made possible by 'continually placing it [the Sun] farther and farther off in space.'[80] As a 'learned cult', myths of the Sun belong to a later stage in the evolution of consciousness, and it is significant that the learning is only possible when the heavenly bodies are viewed from a greater distance, farther off in space, as a correlative, perhaps, to the consciousness of human beings moving farther and farther away from their immediate experience on Earth. Only then was it possible to conceive that the light of the Moon was reflected sunlight. This was known by the priests in Egypt, and first appeared among the Greek pre-Socratics, particularly Anaxagoras, becoming commonplace in later Greek and Roman thought. Yet any radically new idea is slow to take hold, and it was still being discussed by Augustine in the fifth century AD.[81]

This discovery had the radical implication that the human senses did not yield the truth. Even now it is hard to feel that moonlight does not 'come from' the Moon – that it is just 'moonshine', in the altered meaning now given to the word. Truth, it had to be inferred, must lie elsewhere, beyond the flux of time and the phenomenal world of becoming. This point of view was transmitted to western consciousness chiefly via Plato and Aristotle (who arrived in the west in the twelfth century in Latin translations, some of them from Arabic), and Cicero.

THE MOON AND MUTABILITY

In the *Cratylus*, Socrates, discussing the etymology of the word Moon, *selene*, refers to Anaxagoras's 'recent discovery, that the moon receives her light from the sun.' He adds, 'the light about the moon is always new (*neon*) and always old (*enon*), if the disciples of Anaxagoras say truly. For the sun in his revolution always adds new light, and there is the old light of the previous month.'[82] This last surmise suggests how recent the discovery was! (Anaxagoras died the year Plato was born, in 428 BC).

But in the *Republic*, Plato imagines the image of the Good in the image of the Sun. Coming to the crucial point of his argument – 'what is the nature of the Good?' – Socrates does not define Good but says in effect it acts *like* the Sun. Conversing with Glaucon, Socrates compares the way the Sun and the Good work, the Sun in the visible realm and the Good in the intelligible realm: as the Sun, which is not itself vision, is yet the cause of vision and beheld by means of vision, so the Good is not the same as knowledge and truth but gives to knowledge and truth their reality, being itself their source.[83] Strictly, Plato is only making an analogy between the similar workings of the Sun and the Good, but the cumulative effect, for those less rigorous than Socrates and Glaucon, is to see the Sun as the image of the Good as expressed in visible things, especially when this dialogue is followed by the myth of the Cave in the following chapter. There the Sun is the invisible source of the shadows upon the screen which the uninitiated, strapped to their seats and forced to look forwards at the screen, inevitably take for reality.[84]

Plato's theoretical distinction between the noumenal world of being (the world of Forms) and the phenomenal world of becoming was translated by Aristotle into a practical way of thinking about the world we see. Aristotle (384–322 BC), a biologist and an astronomer, divided the world into two regions: the lower region of continual change – of birth, growing, procreating, decaying and dying – which he called Nature, *Physis* (corresponding to Plato's phenomenal world). The upper region of the regular and permanent movements of celestial bodies, suffering neither growth nor diminution, he called Sky, *Ouranos* (corresponding to Plato's noumenal world).[85] Nature and Sky are here spoken of as two distinct things, composed of different stuff. Nature was made of the four elements, Earth, Water, Fire and Air, so that Sky must be made of something different. But weather, which is changeable, comes from Air which belongs to Nature so that, pursuing the definition, Sky must begin higher up, beyond Air. The substance of Sky he defined as Aether (because it 'runs always', *aei thein*).

Fig. 7. The Phases of the Moon, showing Moonlight as reflected Sunlight. (From A. Cellarius. Harmonia Macrocosmica, 1660).

Aether 'encompasses the divine bodies, but immediately below the aethereal and divine nature comes that which is passible, mutable, perishable, and subject to death.'[86]

What is relevant here is that Aristotle sets the crucial frontier between Sky and Nature at the orbit of the Moon. Contingency and mutability are to belong solely to Moon and Earth, while divinity ('the divine bodies'), that which is imperishable and eternal, belongs to Sky, including the Sun and the stars. Conversely, Nature, all that is below the Moon, is deprived of divinity.[87] While it is alarming to think of the Sun as 'not Nature', it only serves to throw into relief the severity of the definition, which desacralizes the name of 'Nature' and so refuses divinity to life in time. It also pits Sun and Moon against each other, the Sun as eternal and the Moon as mutable along with Earth.

In Roman thought, this position was consolidated by Cicero, who, around 50 BC, wrote his own *Republic*, ending it with a vision, just as Plato had closed his *Republic* with his myth of Er. Cicero's myth is the *Somnium Scipionis*, the Dream of Scipio Africanus the Younger. The young Scipio dreams of his grandfather, Scipio Africanus the Elder, whose essential message (to be given more fully in Chapter 13) reiterates Aristotle's point of view:

> Below the Moon there is nothing but what is mortal and doomed to decay, except the
> souls given to men by the bounty of the gods, whereas above the Moon all is eternal.[88]

A division had arisen in the universe which had once been embraced as a living whole: the Moon and everything beneath the sphere of the Moon, was now to be sharply distinguished from the rest of the universe, not just as of a difference in degree, but of a difference in kind. It was the difference between mutability and constancy. The adjective 'sublunary' (*sub*, 'beneath', *luna*, 'moon') was now the term for the world of contingency and change, and was still a touchstone in medieval and Elizabethan times.[89] When, in Chaucer's *Canterbury Tales*, Nature says:

> Ech thing in my cure is
> Under the Moone that mai wane and waxe[90]

the phrase 'beneath' or 'under the Moon' has a very precise meaning, not comparable to 'under the Sun', as in the generalized term 'everything under the Sun', where no judgement is intended. 'Beneath the Moon' is the place where the elements are improperly mixed together, where uncertainty and doubt prevail, and where nothing stays the same for long. Accordingly, when Lear says to Cordelia:

> ...we'll wear out
> In a walled prison packs and sects of great ones
> That ebb and flow by th' moon,'[91]

he places the eternal realm in their own 'walled prison' and sets the world of court and kings in the mutable realm, tossed about like tides to the Moon.

This division expressed, and in turn fostered, the divisive consciousness which had given rise to it – the latest formulation of the split between Spirit and Nature that had first come in with the patriarchal mythologies of the Iron Age. For above the Moon all was Spirit, and below the Moon all was Nature, given, in its very definition, as divorced from spirit, except for the souls of human beings. Consequently, the uncorrupted and (supposedly) uncorruptible spirit was to be the only standard by which life was measured, and inevitably, therefore, life was found wanting. At root, this was a new formulation of the on-going and never-ending debate about death.

This radical distinction between Nature and Spirit might have been supposed to 'save' life for eternity by confining death to Nature and imagining a place where death was not – Sky, Aether, Spirit, God – where souls could continue to live. But both terms – 'Nature' and 'Spirit' – arise together, in the same moment, as names for a split in the human psyche consequent on a new perception of death as a radical ending, not a phase in the totality of being. The terms, then, point primarily inward not outward, so any attempt to 'find' their realities outside the psyche serves to deepen the split rather than to explore ways of understanding the original dissociation. By contrast, Spinoza's saying, that 'God and Nature are two terms for the same substance',[92] seeks to reunite the terms by referring them back to the human mind which confers names, expressing differing perspectives upon a common ground of being.

* * *

In early times the Moon was Earth's star, a better Earth in Heaven. But when, later, the light of the Moon was discovered to be the reflected light of the Sun, many, if not most, of the powers originally attributed to the Moon were transferred to the Sun, at least as official priestly priorities, though the persistence of the former habits of belief by the folk is astonishing. By Roman times, the Moon's infinite wonder had shrunk, and, for intellectuals at least, it became Earth's boundary, sharing earthly imperfections. Then the Sun, which does not change, served as the model for earthly aspiration, carrying the image of eternity which once was held by the Moon. But when the Moon held the image of eternity for the people who lived beneath it, eternity was not opposed to life and death: it was that in which life and death inhered. Blake's evocative phrase that 'eternity is in love with the productions of time'[93] would have been at home in a lunar cosmology. But the image of eternity embodied in the Sun was opposed to life in time; it promised a perfection free from the vicissitudes of life, so aptly mirrored – now the eye had altered – in the inconstant shapes of the Moon. After that, all was finite beneath the Moon, bound to the laws of becoming and time, which ended in diminution and death. Soon the Moon was considered not just receptive, but dependent, borrowing or even thieving light from the 'glorious planet Sol':

> The moon's an arrant thief,
> And her pale fire she snatches from the sun.[94]

Whereas the Sun is sovereign and offers an ideal for kings who 'observe degree', as Ulysses proclaims to Agamemnon:

> And therefore is the glorious planet Sol
> In noble eminence enthroned and sphered
> Amidst the other, whose med'cinable eye
> Corrects the ill aspects of planets evil
> And posts like the commandment of a king,
> Sans check, to good and bad.[95]

So, when, in *1 Henry IV*, the passionate Hotspur proclaims:

> By heaven methinks it were an easy leap
> To pluck bright honour from the pale-faced moon' [96]

we fear he is doomed, in spite of, or even because of, the enchantment of the image: he aims too far, too high, he is 'reaching for the Moon'. Similarly, in the new climate of belief, to be 'over the Moon' is to have pleasure beyond bounds, beyond what is real.

SUN AND MOON IN CHRISTIANITY

Doctrinal Christianity may have dealt the final blow to the divinity of the Moon, since the symbolism in which Christ's divinity was clothed after his death came from the Sun. In the contemporary Hellenistic world, both the Greek Sun god Helios and the Persian and Roman Sun god Mithras portrayed the celestial drama of resurrection through the risen Sun, reborn from death every dawn and every midwinter at the winter solstice. As Mithras was called the *Sol Invictus*, so Christ was to be the new Invincible Sun, whose birth was to be timed (four centuries after he died) to the winter solstice in the image of the reborn Sun – as was the birth of Mithras. Christ's God was beyond Sun and Moon as the transcendent Creator of the natural world, but the Sun and the Moon played a crucial role in the Christian imagination through the complementary figures of Christ and Mary. They were understood to be figures of divine fulfilment in a higher order of those earlier intimations of pagan antiquity, which now revealed their gods to be but symbols (as, of course, they always had been).

'The true sun is Christ', St Patrick said to his heathen Celts, an identification still present in seventeenth-century England, when a priest new to the English parish of Kidderminster found that some of his flock 'thought Christ was the sun...and the Holy Ghost was the moon.'[97] The early Christian fathers, Ambrose and Augustine, initially envisaged Christ as the Sun and the 'suffering' Church as the Moon, *Luna patiens*, who was the true Luna, as Ambrose wrote:

> When Luna, in whom, relying on words of the Prophets, we see the image of the Church – when this same Luna is reborn to run her monthly course, she is at first hidden by dark shadows. Slowly, however, her horns are filled with light, and then when she stands opposite Sol, she shines again with the brightness of his beams.[98]

But later, as the Virgin Mary grew in the hearts and minds of Christians, she assumed the shining mantle of the heavenly Moon, and with it all the ancient imagery of the lunar goddesses who had gone before her: Inanna-Ishtar, Isis, Astarte, the Virgin Artemis, Persephone, Demeter and Aphrodite, among others.[99] Hekate, the Dark Moon, was officially given to witchcraft and the devil.

In keeping with the transcendent nature of Judaic divinity, Christ was not, of course, the Sun itself, but the 'Sun of Justice', the 'Sun of Righteousness', the 'Dayspring from on High', a spiritualized image which led away from Nature. By contrast, Mary inhabited her lunar role more completely, receiving the names of 'Mother Moon', 'Our Moon', 'Perfect and Eternal Moon', 'Spiritual Moon', 'Moon of the Church', *Stella Maris*, 'Star of the Sea', 'Wide-open Gate of Heaven', *Regina Coeli*, Queen of Heaven, and, more simply, *Notre Dame*, 'Our Lady', as people in France had long greeted the Moon.[100] Even in the twentieth century Cardinal Jean Danielou heard Normandy fishermen calling upon the Virgin for help as the Moon:

> Watch over always, lovely moon,
> the needs of those devoted to you.[101]

The Moon which is filled with light by the Sun and sheds that light into the dark of night became a natural symbol for the Virgin's role in mediating Christ's eternal love to the Christian soul. Mary's splendour, wrote Bernard, 'both shines in the heavens and penetrates into hell, and as it traverses the lands, it causes minds to glow with virtues...'[102] Just as in the pre-Christian world, the Moon was the intermediary between Earth and Sun, so now Mary as the Moon could intercede between the iridescent spheres of pure spirit above and the 'world, the flesh and the devil', the dark sensual earth below. St Bonaventure draws on this analogy:

> As the moon is between the heavens and the earth, so does Mary continuously place herself between God and sinners in order to appease our Lord in their regard, and to enlighten their return to Him.[103]

In the twelfth century Pope Innocent III (1198–1216) urged the sinful to look to the Moon:

> Towards the Moon it is he should look, who is buried in the shades of sin and iniquity. Having lost grace, the day disappears and there is no more sun for him, but the Moon is still on the horizon. Let him address himself to Mary; under her influence thousands every day find their way to God.[104]

Hugo makes the contrast between Christ and Mary explicit by giving the just to Christ as the Sun and the sinners to Mary as the Moon: the Sun, he says,

> is a figure of Jesus Christ, whose splendid rays illumine the just who live in the day of grace; [the Moon] is typical of Mary, whose mild lustre illumines sinners mid the dreary night of sin.[105]

But when Mary became (a figure of) the Moon, the 'light-bearer', as Anselm called her,[106] she brought with her many of the other attributes of Moon goddesses and moonlight. For this was not light as we know it, but beams of immense power, nourishing, fertilizing, purifying, watering: brushing the Earth with dew and rains, harmonizing the tides and the menstrual cycles of women, making them fertile, easing their births and their deaths, protecting their children and all the children of God. It may have been largely through the identification of Mary with the Moon that she assumed so readily the central roles of the earlier goddesses, becoming unofficially a patron of that same carnal world which her incorruptible virginity had supposedly vanquished. (Her virginity, and that of her own Mother – indeed, a whole line of immaculate conceptions – guaranteed for Christian doctrine her exemption from the original sin of concupiscence manifested as lust, in St Augustine's definition).[109]

The 'great wonder' of Revelation, who appeared 'clothed with the sun, and the moon under her feet, and upon her head a crown of twelve stars',[108] was often fused, or confused, with the figure of Mary, as was the 'beloved' of the *Song of Solomon* who 'looketh forth as the morning, fair as the moon, clear as the sun.'[109] But perhaps the greatest effect of the lunar imagery was, subtly and symbolically, to reinstate Mary to the time when the Moon as an expression of the Mother Goddess had been supreme, and the lunar myth of the Mother losing, searching and finding her lost Son had held sway over Egypt and the Near East, long before the Sun had captured the Moon in the imagination of the people.

The older vision, after many centuries of Christian neglect, was drawn, apparently irresistibly, to the figure of the Virgin Mary, reclothing her in the ancient images long after the Book was closed and sealed as Holy Writ. For, allowing the *images* to speak – and not their doctrinal interpretation – Mary, whose name means 'Sea' and whose title is 'Moon', and whose image, like Inanna and Isis before her, is the crescent and the star, appears as a Goddess. As 'Queen of Heaven', she wears a star-spangled robe whose blue is the blue of sky and sea, and, like the Moon, she is the '*Stella Maris*', Star of the Sea, the guardian of childbirth, mediator for the dying and intercessor for the souls of the dead. Legends of the Grain Miracle have fields of corn springing up behind her, and legends of the 'Black Madonna' speak of her healing the sickness of body and soul as the Dark Moon. Like all the triple lunar goddesses, Mary is virgin and mother and crone, though not, in this world at least, bride: she gives birth to her son as the crescent, mothers him at the full, mourns his loss in the three days of death when Jesus is harrowing Hell to awaken and release the buried life, preparing for his ascent as the returning crescent. The three Marys who surround the drama of his passion recall the three visible phases of the Moon, the trinity of goddesses of destiny. In the Greek Orthodox Church, Mary – or the mortal part of her – dies, or rather sleeps, for these same three days (in the darkness of her own Moon) during what is called her 'dormition', before she ascends into heaven to be reunited with her son in a ceremony which is called the 'Coronation of the Virgin', but which resembles in its iconography the sacred marriage rite of Moon and Sun.

The 'revelation' which appeared to St John the Divine, gave licence to Renaissance artists to restore to Mary her ancient power. For Mary, with the 12 stars circling her head like a halo of brilliant light, is reinstated in the tradition of Inanna-Ishtar, who wore as her crown or as her girdle the 12 constellations through which the Moon moved in a month and the Sun moved in a year. Almost entirely circled by a golden crescent, in the *Heures de Rohan* Mother and child in fig. 8, Mary holds the child as the crescent incarnate, or, more scripturally, in fig. 9 she rests her feet upon the down-turned crescent which has grown the black claws and tail of the dragon of sin. The crescent, once worn by Queen Astarte as a celebration on her head, is here relegated, as the rest of Nature, to the place beneath Mary's feet, in the company of the lions, dragons and serpents of the outcast love of this world.

Within the lunar metaphor, Jesus is the incarnation of *zoe* as *bios*, the eternal clothed in the life of time, who gives his life that the unquenchable source may be renewed, and whose individual death is the promise and pledge of eternal life for all. Pictures of the crucifixion often show Jesus attended by Sun and Moon with the Moon full or in eclipse, while a French woodcut of the crucifixion, framed by Sun and Moon above and by the skull of death encircled by a serpent below, has parts of limbs and heads hanging from the cross, which places the sacrifice of Jesus in the tradition of the dismembered gods of the Moon (see Chapter 12, fig. 12). In the Last Supper, Jesus takes for his commemoration the bread and wine as the food and water of life, which are to be transformed into his own body and blood, in the long-observed ritual of re-membering the fragmented light of *bios*, which has continually to be reunited in the human heart with its eternal source, *zoe*.

The understandable ambivalence as to which heavenly body Christ is to transfigure is reflected in the Church's rites of celebration. In the cycle of the Christian year, Christ is incarnated at the birth of the Sun in the winter solstice. Yet the commemoration of the essential drama of his life and teaching, his willing death and resurrection, is set by the Moon: Christ's rebirth at Easter – after his victory over the forces of darkness – is arranged for the day of the Sun (Sunday) following the first Full Moon after the spring equinox. In this way lunar symbolism structures the story of Jesus, casting him as the latest in the tradition of dying and resurrected gods, which, it is implied, had existed for thousands of years in anticipation of this, its final apotheosis. So, in the language of metaphor, Christ *is* the Sun, but he *becomes* the Moon.

THE LOSS OF THE MOON'S STORIES

When the Sun took precedence over the Moon, it often took the Moon's stories along with it, grafting the new life onto the old. Who now would consider the hero myth to be originally a lunar myth? It is the Sun, we are taught, who slays the demon of the dark and is victoriously reborn each dawn and each year; and it is the pattern of the Sun which the hero imitates, descending into the underworld in his war of light against the dragons of darkness and death. But is it not strange that so many hero myths have their heroes dying for three days before they are reborn – imprisoned in the underworld, hung naked upon a hook, swallowed in the belly of the whale, or descending into Hell – those same three days when the Moon is dark and was thought to be dead?

When, in ancient Greece, the Moon was married to the Sun (and, as Harrison adds, 'in true patriarchal fashion sank into wifely subjection'),[110] the heroic mode passed to the gods Zeus and Apollo in their battles with female serpents and dragons, following the blood-stained tracks of Marduk and Tiamat. So the hero myth, in so far as it was given form through the heavenly bodies, was implicitly redefined as the conquest of the Moon (lunar serpents and dragons) by the Sun, replacing the original contest, when the Bright Moon overcame the Dark Moon, which is the story of life overcoming death. In the Christian tradition, the hero myth was further redefined, through such figures as St Michael and St George and their dragons, as Spirit conquering Nature, which became the battle of Good against Evil.

Fig. 8. The Virgin and Jesus within the Crescent Moon. Heures de Rohan, 1415-16. Bibliothèque Nationale.

Fig. 9. The Glorification of Mary. Geertgen tot St. Jans. c. 1490-5. Museum Boijmans van Beuningen, Rotterdam.

It may not always matter whether the Sun or the Moon is taken as the model for the hero, but there is a significant difference of inflection; for if the essence of the hero myth is lunar rather than solar, the final emphasis of the drama falls not on conquest but on transformation. 'Solar heroism' is distinct from 'lunar heroism', as Mozart's and Schikaneder's double ordeal for Taminah and Paminah in *The Magic Flute* would imply: trial by fire and trial by water. To put it another way, heroism of any age may belong to a lunar consciousness as much as to a solar consciousness, with all the difference in feeling that this implies. For while the drama of heroism may appear solar to the modern solar-oriented mind – and so oppositional and inimical to darkness – its roots are irrevocably lunar, meaning that the darkness is a dimension of the total being which the hero has to become in order to know himself.

Elsewhere, stories of the Bright Moon typically became stories of the Bright Sun, while the light of the Moon was allowed to fade, until, deprived of its own inherent drama, the Moon became in feeling more like the Waning Moon for the whole of the month. For, in the next stage of revaluation, new stories arise about the Moon, but are told now from a solar point of view. The Moon comes to be seen solely from the perspective of the Sun, no longer granted even an historical reality in its own right. Consequently, many of the Moon's stories have now to be sought for within official tales, lurking in the structure and imagery, hiding in implication and innuendo, faintly gleaming in gaps and lacunae, or in the curious reasons for the tales at all.

For instance, there is a memory in many disparate cultures of a time when the Moon was once as bright as the Sun, not only in light but also in importance. Then something happened. At one level this is a 'Golden Age' fantasy, which sets perfect balance and harmony at the beginning of the world when imagination and reality are the same; but at another level there may be a sense that values have shifted. In either case, the tales imply, the Moon's dimmer light is not to be taken as a sign of its intrinsic inferiority, and so the dimming of its light requires an explanation.

In a Brahmanical text, it is said that the Sun 'took to himself the Moon's shine; although the two are similar, the Moon shines much less, for its shine has been taken away from it.'[111] Not dissimilarly, the Huitoto of Columbia thought that the Moon was once the Sun and the Sun was the Moon, but they changed places with each other.[112] The North American Indian Pueblo tribes had a legend that the Moon was once as bright as the Sun, but Moon gave up part of her light so people could sleep at night.[113] In Genesis the Sun is the 'greater light' and the Moon the 'lesser light' from the beginning, but in Talmudic literature, which preserves many of the older unexpurgated ideas intact, the Sun and Moon were created equally brilliant.[114] Similarly in Islamic legend, God created Moon and Sun of an equal brightness, but the Angel Gabriel rubbed his wings against the Moon and the Moon lost its shine.[115] In Aztec myth, the Moon and Sun were both made equally hot and brilliant, but one of the gods threw a rabbit onto the face of the Moon so it became pale and cold.[116] Here, as in many other tales, one story explains both the markings on the Moon's face and its demise. Sometimes no reason is given: in the beginning things were as they should be and afterwards it is different. The Maori say that formerly the Moon stretched out its limbs over all time but since then it has withdrawn into the night, although 'to the moon belong the night and the day.'[117]

* * *

We (the 'we' of collective western culture) have long looked at the Moon through the eyes of the Sun, just as we are used to seeing the 'Goddess' through the eyes of the 'God'. These two visions are not everywhere commensurate, since, as we have seen, the God and the Sun are not universally the same, any more than are the Goddess and the Moon. But Neumann clarifies how they could have become related in the West when he says that 'the relatively late astronomical recognition of the moon's

Fig. 10. Moon god or hero holding snakes with crescents on their heads, slaying the sea-dragon. Pottery design, Chimu Indians, Moche IV, Peru. c. 400–500 AD. (From Neumann, The Great Mother, p. 180).

dependence on the sun is the expression and the symbol of the moon's humiliation in the patriarchal world, in which sun and day, like human consciousness in its archetypal masculine expression, have assumed sovereign authority.'[118]

Without assuming an absolute relation, we can at least say that in the same way that the stories of the Goddess have been overlaid by stories of the God, with the Goddess given new, diminished or subversive roles, so have stories of the Moon been occluded by stories of the Sun. It is worth emphasizing how ruthlessly the dominant mode of consciousness – now patriarchal and solar – has excluded and even denigrated the earlier consciousness – matriarchal and lunar – out of which it grew. In both cases, stories are lost or parodied or reinvented, and with the stories a distinct way of relating to the universe disappears, and so a dimension of the human mind atrophies or lies fallow. Indeed, the distortions due to the dominant mode of consciousness are related, for both set us further apart from the original idea that the Earth has – or is – soul, spirit or consciousness, and that life on Earth might simply be good in itself. The idea that the rhythmic patterns of Moon and Earth might reflect a lawful patterning in the consciousness of human beings is also lost, along with the possibility that Nature could be our Teacher.

* * *

It certainly seems that the movement from Moon-orientation to Sun-orientation, from the late Bronze-age onwards, involved much more than a relocation of the source of fertility: it expressed, and in turn continued to foster, a change of values, which subtly but inevitably set human consciousness apart from the world in which it lived and moved and had its being. The philosopher Owen Barfield describes this movement as a withdrawal of what he calls 'original participation' with nature. In his book *Saving the Appearances* he offers a perspective on our mythological history which takes a long view over the past and discerns a pattern that makes some sense of the place of transition in which we now find ourselves. He sees the evolution of consciousness as falling broadly into three different phases or stages, which he characterizes as different kinds of participation of humans with their world (defining 'participation' as an act where self and not-self are identified in the same moment of experience). He calls these phases 'original participation', 'withdrawal of participation' and 'final participation'. He describes the earliest, lunar, goddess-oriented, hunter-gatherer to agricultural phase of human evolution – from, say, the Palaeolithic to late Bronze Age, early Iron Age – as enacting what he calls 'original participation', which he defines as 'the sense that there stands behind the phenomena, *and on the other side of them from man*, a represented which is of the same nature as man. Whether it is called "mana", or by the names of many gods and demons, or God the Father, or the spirit world, it is of the same nature as the perceiving self, inasmuch as it is not mechanical or accidental, but psychic and voluntary.' Barfield defines the 'represented' as 'whatever is *correlative* to the appearance or representations' (or, in plainer language, what the appearance is, or is imagined to be, 'of'). [119]

So, in 'original participation', the reality behind or within all the different kinds of natural life was felt to be the same reality as the human reality. There was a sacred bond between Nature and humanity, which meant that Nature and humanity had the same 'nature', as the words would indicate. Human nature was simply a dimension of the whole of Nature, so humanity and Nature did not have to be apprehended by different modes of cognition. What, in contemporary terms, we would call the objective, natural world, and contrast to the subjective, human world, were once inexorably bound together, so that Nature was more awesome – both loving and terrifying – *and* more personal – peopled with divine presences imagined in human, animal and plant form. This is immanence, where the visible appearance and the invisible source are one and the same. Life carries on, as it were, beyond the senses, doing all the things it does when it can be seen. The human mind can then find itself at home in the invisible world as confidently as it does in its visible surroundings. The words of a North American Indian convey the radical ambiguity of this feeling, both its imaginative freedom and its limitations: 'You ask me to plough the ground? Shall I take a knife and tear my mother's bosom? Then when I die she will not take me to her bosom to rest.'[120]

Earth was the Mother who was like the human mother; the Moon was also the Mother, or the Father, or the Husband, or the Mother with her son or daughter; they were like the human family, only without human restriction. In this way of thinking it does not seem so strange to think that as the Moon died and came to life again, so humans on Earth could also die and come to life again. For, in this vision, there is no *intrinsic* difference between them. It is a world we know as children, and rediscover in theatre, art, fiction and poetry, or whenever the participating mind takes over, delivering us to the shock of union with nature, or with human beings, recalling it later, elegiacally, as a vision that is both real and unreal: more real than unreal or more unreal than real, depending on who we are.

Fig. 11. *Hottentots dancing under the Moon. Engraving from* A Precise and Extensive Description of the Cape of Good Hope *by Peter Kolb c. 1705-13. Beneath a similar engraving of Bushmen dancing a late 20th century comment warns that 'European interpretations of Khoisan dancing under the moon alternated between recognizing the practice as religious and dismissing it as entertainment.'* [121] *In earlier centuries the Hottentots and Bushmen's supposed 'Moon-worshipping' may have been used against them.*

There followed the second stage of the pattern, beginning around 2000 BC when humanity, in different parts of the world, withdrew this immanent divinity from Earth and placed it firstly in the patterns of the heavens, with the Sun as the ruling force, and later in the invisible world, transcendent to all of Nature. Numinosity, especially in the Judaic tradition, was now found in what could *not* be seen or touched, including the invisible world of human beings, specifically in the human capacity to interiorize divinity – as humans conceived it – most obviously as the Word of God in Judaism, but also as the Rational Mind in later Greek thought, and much later as the saving power, as it initially seemed, of Reason in the Age of Enlightenment. Consciousness could then expand inwards, and learn to name and control those outward phenomena whose beauty now appeared alien, detached from human life and concerns. Mythologically, this was the time when Sky, Storm and Sun gods replaced Earth goddesses – Enlil and then Marduk in Mesopotamia, Atum-Re and Ptah in Egypt, Yahweh-Elohim in the Old Testament, Zeus and Apollo in Greece. Typically, the old Mother Goddess – if she was there at all – was seen no longer as life-giving but as dark and chaotic, and had to be slain for the sake of light and order. The story of Adam and Eve in the Garden, which stands at the beginning of our tradition, registers this disruption of the original bond with nature. The solarization of the Moon falls into this stage.

This change in priorities can be glimpsed in the term 'Nature'. In the time of 'original participation', what we now call Nature was a Thou not an It, a personal presence, clothed in numinosity, not an inanimate object. But this 'Thou' was almost certainly not thought of as 'Nature', a term, or rather an idea, first invented by the pre-Socratics to talk about the great variety of phenomena under a single name.[122] The Greek *physis*, from which derives 'physical', became in Latin *natura*, from *natus*, birth, as that which is born (and dies). Yet the underlying idea of unity implicit in the name 'Nature', as in every name, did not always include everything, an omission that Aristotle inherited when he confined Nature to the sublunary, relegating it to the Moon and the Earth beneath. The medieval Christian mind also did not regard Nature as all that God had created: Nature's place was, following Aristotle, below the Moon. As C.S. Lewis points out: 'Nature may be the oldest of things, but *Natura* is the youngest of divinities...'Mother' Nature is a conscious metaphor. 'Mother' Earth is something quite different.'[123] When, in Greek times, for instance, she lies beneath Father Sky, he begets, she bears. You can see it happening. 'This is genuine mythopoeia,' he continues, 'but while the mind is working on that level, what, in heaven's name, is Nature? Where is she? Who has seen her? What does she do?'[124]

It seems that the idea of 'Nature' begins to form once the unified vision of Mother Earth or the Goddess begins to fade. Similarly, the idea of Spirit as a separate entity arises at the same time as a corollary to 'Nature' and in compensation for the loss of 'Mother Earth'. Those of us who assume that what we call Nature can hold all the mythopoeic feeling once given to Mother Earth, the 'Goddess' or the 'Mother Goddess', should perhaps be aware how our very language might be imprisoning us in the oppositions of a later form of consciousness. In *King Lear*, the greeting 'Thou, Nature, art my Goddess'[125] is significantly spoken by Edmund, the man without feeling, whose obeisance to Nature is intended to signal his alliance with the basest instincts of the play, imaged as predatory wild beasts.

Barfield does not mourn this stage in the evolution of human consciousness, seeing it as inevitable and necessary, with a brilliance of its own. This, the 'Passion of the Western Mind', as Richard Tarnas explores it in his crucially important book of the same name,[126] is almost too close to us to allow us to do anything but instinctively celebrate it; yet the warnings of Einstein, and here Barfield, oblige us to realize that it has gone too far. For Barfield, there is a further stage that can 'save appearances', which is to bring back the world into our hearts. This he calls 'final participation', where the old participating consciousness can be recreated at a new level through the Imagination. This will be discussed in Chapter 14.

SOLAR AND LUNAR CONSCIOUSNESS

Thomas Mann, in his *Joseph and His Brothers*, devised the phrase 'lunar syntax' (or 'moon grammar') to describe how Jacob can be telling Joseph about two different men as though they were one person: 'But daylight is one thing and moonlight another...Things look differently under the moon and under the sun, and it might be the clearness of the moon which would appeal to the spirit as the truer clarity.'[127] Yeats's contrast between 'the silver apples of the moon' and 'the golden apples of the sun', in the poem quoted at the start of this chapter, meant still more to the Hermetic Students of the Golden Dawn. For them, Yeats said, 'Solar' meant all that was elaborate and full of artifice, whereas 'Lunar' (which meant Water), was all that was simple, popular, traditional, emotional.[128] For his part, he added, if you wish to be melancholy, 'hold in your left hand an image of the Moon made out of silver, and if you wish to be happy hold in your right hand an image of the Sun made out of gold.'[129]

'Solar' and 'lunar' have inevitably become metaphors for two alternative ways of thinking and being. For where 'solar syntax' divides, 'lunar syntax' merges, and the on-going debate between them reveals contrasting models of value, reflecting in part their different relation to darkness. In solar myths where the Sun is a goddess, she comes bringing gifts of warmth and light, her changing phases – dawn, noon, sunset – are registered and celebrated: gentle at dawn (often called the 'daughter' of the Sun), fierce at noon, reflective at twilight; sometimes reluctant to appear, sometimes diffuse, at other times dancing with her sparkling rays.[130] But even when given a feminine character she has to remain apart, never uniting with darkness, which flees before her as she comes towards it. In solar myths where the Sun is a god, the Sun is seen as heroically independent of his origins, captured, by the human psyche, forever at high noon on a cloudless day. The solar hero slays the dragon of darkness with the lance of his burning rays: he is unvanquished and unmoved.

As the Sun sends the dark away, so the solar view sets life and thought into opposites – light *or* dark, true *or* false, good *or* evil – almost as though they were distinct entities in themselves. The idea that these may be distinctions whose meaning is given by the larger story of life is not a 'solar idea', for the Sun takes itself to be the largest story and so sets the terms for all other stories. For 'solar thinking', a thing *is* or it *is not*: where light is, darkness is not. 'Lunar thinking', on the other hand, points to the fluidity and evanescence of forms: like a candle in the dark or the play of a mask, it allows something to be and not be at the same time. Light and dark are present together in a continuing drama of expansion and contraction. Only at the poles of full and new is there light without dark and dark without light. Symbolically, the Moon evokes the imaginative, contingent, ambiguous world of becoming – the lived-in time – in contrast to the Sun's absolutes of the ideal world of being. The Moon engages with the poetic truths of presence *and* absence, truth *and* falsity, and the ultimate fusion of death-in-life and life-in-death.

Since, in western culture, the Sun is dominant and mostly male, the solar view has long carried the culture's formal identification with its values, allying them with the virtues of clear and distinct ideas, and ultimately with 'reason' as the expression of the highest value. Eliade comments that at the end of this long process of solarization, '*sun* and *intelligence* will be assimilated to such a degree that the solar and syncretistic theologies of the end of antiquity become rationalistic philosophies; the sun is proclaimed to be the intelligence of the world.'[131] In so far as this is taken literally, the Moon, and the Moon's way of thinking, is then seen predominately from the solar point of view – as the opposite of clarity, as irrational and so unreliable – the focus turned now upon the ever-changing phase, not upon its unchanging pattern of return.

From the solar perspective, the Moon, or the lunar point of view, is now revealed to be changeable, inconstant, fickle, faithless, undirected ('mooning about'), confusing, deceptive ('moonshine'), rhetorical ('over the Moon'), unrealistic ('casting beyond the Moon') or fantastic ('made of green cheese'), prone, in its lack of singular definition, to chaos and madness. In sum, the lunar life is swayed by rhythms that offer no release; it cannot be trusted, and it leads to death:

> 'Lady, by yonder blessed moon I vow...' protests Romeo,
> to which Juliet replies:

> 'O, swear not by the moon, th' inconstant moon,
> That monthly changes in her circled orb,
> Lest that thy love prove likewise variable.'[132]

One might ask, when intelligence is imagined in exclusively solar images, what of a lunar intelligence, a sensibility that is holistic, animistic, intuitive, engaging a poetic language of image and symbol, issuing from feeling as well as thinking? What of emotional intelligence, native wit, practical wisdom – the intelligence of the heart? Conversely, from an exclusively lunar perspective, the Sun, or the solar point of view, is blinding, over-simplified, inflexible, intransigent, dogmatic, obdurate, literal, over-idealistic, prone to polarization and abstraction. It seems that the perennial debate between intuition and intellect, passion and order, spontaneity and law, finds expression in the metaphors of Moon and Sun. Where the Moon offers a model of completeness, the Sun offers a model of perfection. Accordingly, the Moon has often been drawn as an image of soul, with the Sun as an image of spirit. Indeed, these metaphors have frequently suffered from the Judaeo/Christian priority of according a higher value to spirit than to soul on the analogy of the Moon only reflecting light from the sun, and not generating it.[133] For the Moon proposes the values of 'cosmic becoming' – a destiny of birth, death and growth out of decay – while the Sun proposes the luminous values of the intellect and of eternal being poised beyond the flux of time and death. Where the Sun is the invincible conqueror of death, the Moon surrenders to death as to the ambivalence of life in time, yet lives to rise again, a drama that comprehends the totality of human endeavour.

Nonetheless, *both* modes of consciousness are necessary for human wholeness, and in the myths and rituals of the world there is everywhere an impulse to bring the Moon and Sun together, either through the Moon's 'sacred marriage' with the Sun, or through the symbolic life which seeks to reconcile lunar and solar ways of being. But in order to try to see both solar and lunar modes from a further position beyond either, it is necessary first to reclaim the lost heritage of the Moon in its myths, legends, rituals, folklore and lingering superstitions, all of which lead back to an earlier, more participative, age. For if it is true that one of the ways in which human beings may come to know themselves is through the images of their goddesses and gods, then these images cannot simply be lost without consequence. Their disappearance or distortion may diminish in turn a vital complexity in the human psyche, one which is necessary for the finest insights to be generated. For a symbol, as D.H. Lawrence has said, 'is not just meaning within meaning; it is meaning *against* meaning.'[134]

Let us return, then, to the days when, as children, we first looked up in wonder at the face of the Moon, and to the time of our forbears upon whose insights we rest, when, in the imaginative childhood of the race, they saw figures upon the face of the Moon and called them real.

CHAPTER 7

THE FACE OF THE MOON

Art thou pale for weariness
Of climbing heaven and gazing on the earth,
Wandering companionless
Among the stars that have a different birth,–
And ever changing, like a joyless eye
That finds no object worth its constancy.
Shelley *To the Moon*

There liveth none under the sunne,
that knows what to make of the man in the moone.
John Lilly Prologue to *Endymion*

Who as a child has not spoken to the Moon as though it were real? When the Moon 'doth shine as bright as day' the shadows strewn across it fall into shapes and take on life as images that mirror the lives of those looking up at them: their dreams and hopes, their doubts and fears, wishing for luck or longing for meaning. All these human qualities compose the lunar drama – the gods, goddesses, people and animals who appear on the face of the Moon. In this way the sketch upon the Moon's face, made through the millennnia by the configuring eye of the human psyche, invites the Moon to participate in the human drama enacted beneath it. As Blake says:

As a man is, so he sees. As the Eye is formed, such are its Powers...To a man of Imagination, Nature is Imagination itself.[1]

Or as the Irish song has it: 'I see the Moon, and the Moon sees me.'[2]

THE MAN IN THE MOON

Girls and boys going out to play in England see the friendly face of the man in the Moon looking down on them, someone who has, like them, to eat up his porridge before it has cooled down:

The man in the Moon
Came down too soon,
And asked the way to Norwich;
He went by the south
And burnt his mouth
With eating hot pease porridge.[3]

Fig. 1. The Japanese Buddhist Moon-goddess Gwatten, whose head is haloed by the Full Moon, holds in her hands a basket, upon which rests a crescent Moon against a black disc, with a white hare sitting inside it. Part of a Sung style Japanese Buddhist painting, by Takuma Shoga, Koy'ogokukuji Temple Museum, Kyoto. 1191 AD.

Fig. 2. The Man in the Moon carrying his bundle of sticks on his back. (From Baring-Gould, Curious Myths of the Middle Ages, *p. 179).*

Fig. 3. Seal, containing a man with sticks on his back within the crescent Moon pointing to two stars, appended to a deed of sale of a barn and four acres of land from Walter de Gendene, clerk, to Margaret, his mother, dated in the ninth year of Edward the Third, with the legend - Te Waltere docebo cur spinas phebo gero, 'I will teach you, Walter, why I carry thorns in the moon' 14th century. [12] (From Baring-Gould, Curious Myths, *p. 186).*

In France the man in the Moon is the black and white costumed clown, Pierrot: '*Au clair de la lune/Mon ami Pierrot.*'

Their European elders, duly instructed in the scriptures, saw in the face of the Moon a morality tale: a man leaning on a fork, carrying on his back a bundle of sticks picked up on the Sabbath day, for which he was stoned to death. The text is from Numbers:

> While the children of Israel were in the wilderness, they found a man that gathered sticks upon the Sabbath day. And they that found him brought him unto Moses and Aaron, and unto all the congregation...And the Lord said unto Moses, The man shall be surely put to death: all the congregation shall stone him with stones without the camp. And all the congregation brought him without the camp, and stoned him with stones till he died.[4]

The original biblical story ended with the man's mortal punishment, but the less rigorous tales of the folk pick him up from the ground and put him in the Moon, where he may continue to live as an example to others (fig.2).[5]

A German folk tale follows the Bible, except that, in the change from Judaism to Christianity, the Sabbath day has moved from Saturday to Sunday. The sentiment, however, has not changed:

> Long ago, one Sunday morning, an old man went into the wood to hew sticks. After he had cut a faggot, he slung it on his staff, cast it over his shoulder, and set off for home. On his way the wood-cutter met a handsome man in his Sunday suit who was walking to Church. The man stopped the faggot-bearer and asked him:
> 'Do you not know that this is Sunday on earth, when everyone must rest from their labours?'
> 'Sunday on earth, or Monday in heaven, it is all the same to me!' laughed the wood-cutter.
> 'Then bear your bundle for ever,' the stranger replied. 'And as you value not Sunday on

earth, you shall have a perpetual Moon-day in heaven. You shall stand in the Moon for
eternity, as a warning to all Sabbath-breakers.'

The stranger vanished, and the wood-cutter was caught up into the Moon, together
with his staff and faggot, where he stands still.[6]

Sometimes, as in Dante's *Divine Comedy*, the man in the Moon carrying the bundle of thorns is
interpreted as Cain, still offering to his god the cheapest gift in the field:

> For now doth Cain with fork of thorns confine
> On either hemisphere, touching the wave
> Beneath the towers of Seville. Yesternight
> The moon was round.[7]

At other times the man in the Moon was seen as Judas, exiled for betraying Christ, or Isaac,
carrying wood for his own sacrifice on Mount Moriah.[8]

In Holland and some parts of Germany, the man in the Moon was a thief. In the nineteenth
century, the North Frisians saw a man who stole cabbages, willow boughs, or sheep (depending on the
district). For the man in the Moon comes from the time when wishes came true, so when the thief
was caught stealing he found himself wished up to the Moon by his neighbours.[9] As the rhyme goes:

> The Man in the Moon was caught in a trap
> For stealing the thorns from another man's gap.
> If he had gone by, and let the thorns lie,
> He'd never been Man in the Moon so high.[10]

The earliest depiction of this thought in England comes in a fourteenth-century seal of a wayward son,
Walter, to his mother, as in fig. 3.[11] Chaucer, writing about 50 years after the date of the seal also refers
to the man in the Moon as a thief. In his *Testament of Cresside*, he calls the Moon 'Lady Cynthia':

> Her gite was gray and full of spottis blake,
> And on her brest a chorle painted ful even,
> Bering a bush of thornis on his backe,
> Whiche for his theft might clime so ner the heaven.[12]

Crime, sin, or the will of Yahweh, were thereby indelibly inscribed upon the European Moon, an
idea whose doctrinal gravity is parodied by Shakespeare in the yokels' play before the Greek wits of
Theseus, Demetrius and friends in *A Midsummer Night's Dream*, all themselves waiting for the Moon
to rise as new before they marry:

Prologue:	This man, with lantern, dog, and bush of thorn,
	Presenteth moonshine...
Moonshine:	This lanthorn doth the horned moon present –
Demetrius:	He should have worn the horns on his head.
Theseus:	He is no crescent, and his horns are invisible
	within the circumference...

Moonshine:	All that I have to say is to tell you that the
	lanthorn is the moon, I, the man i' th' moon, this
	thorn-bush my thorn-bush, and this dog my dog.
Demetrius:	Why, all these should be in the lanthorn; for
	all these are in the moon.[13]

A dog is often given to Cain or the thief for company, as it is in *The Tempest*, where the rogue Stephano plays on the gullibility of Caliban – 'moon-calf', as he calls him:

Caliban:	Hast thou not dropp'd from heaven?
Stephano:	Out o' the moon, I do assure thee. I was the man i'
	the moon, when time was.
Caliban:	I have seen thee in her, and I do adore thee:
	My mistress show'd me thee, and thy dog and thy bush.[14]

Polish children are still told the cautionary tale of Mr Twardowski, a sixteenth-century alchemist, who sold his soul to the devil for a life of riches and thought he could get away with it. When the devil tricked him into keeping his word – reminding him, in Latin, that a man's word is his bond – and was bearing him up (not, we note, *down*) to Hell, Mr Twardowski called as a last resort upon the Virgin Mary. Instantly the devil disappeared and Mr Twardowski went to the Moon. Children of today sing: 'Look, look, Mr Twardowski's on the Moon.'[15] Here, the Moon and Hell appear to be alternatives, at least after the intervention of the Virgin Mary (though the old Polish name for the Moon was Prince – *ksiezyc* – the Prince of Darkness). In parts of medieval Europe the Moon itself was often conceived as the seat of hell. ('Hell' in German means 'light', as does the Dutch *helder*.) Take, for instance, the baleful lines of one M.F. Tupper:

> I know thee well, O Moon, thou cavern'd realm,
> Sad satellite, thou giant ash of death,
> Blot on God's firmament, pale home of crime,
> Scarr'd prison house of sin, where damned souls
> Feed upon punishment.[16]

No wonder the pictures of the Virgin Mary with the Moon beneath her feet are susceptible to opposing readings! Orthodox Christian doctrine places Mary in the eternal realm beyond the Moon as transcending time and mortality (when a Crescent Moon, often etched with the face of a dragon or the devil, is turned upside down (fig. 4). Yet the image of a blue-clothed Virgin Mother soaring into Heaven upon her brilliant sickle (when the crescent curves upwards, with no face except the one rising above it) recalls the folk tradition of Mary as 'Mother Moon' herself (fig. 5). Others say the Moon is Mary Magdalene and the spots are her tears of repentance.[17]

The Moon, in the humanist culture of the west, is often seen simply as a face, as shown in fig. 6.

THE WOMAN IN THE MOON

Outside Europe, many tribal people see a woman in the Moon, typically continuing her earthly work of caring for the child, cooking, sweeping, spinning, beating bark, fetching wood and water – all in a

Fig. 5. *The Virgin Mary within a rising Crescent Moon. Woodcut, Albrecht Dürer. From* Epitome in divae parthenices Mariae historiam, *Nürnburgh, 1511.*

Fig. 4. *The Virgin Mary seated above the down-turned Crescent Moon. Painted statue. Birnau Church, Lake Constance, Germany. c. 1450.*

night's work. In Polynesia, the woman in the Moon is cooking over her oven and stoking the fire with her tongs, or hammering out bark-cloth with a mallet.[18] She is called Rona or Hina, and in Samoa she is called Sina. They all suffered the same fate when they lived on Earth:

> One evening Sina was sitting outside her house, beating bark to make cloth. There was a famine, and her child was hungry, and the rising Moon looked just like breadfruit. 'Why can you not come down and let my child have a little bite of you?' Sina asked the Moon. But the Moon was insulted and swept them both upwards, and now they have to live in the Moon. 'Yonder is Sina,' the Samoan people say, 'and her child, and her mallet, and her board.[19]

The Haida Indians of north-west America tell a similar tale of a woman who offended the Moon, and was removed to the Moon forthwith, together with her pail of water and the berry-bush to which she clung, trying to save herself (fig. 7).[20]

In Longfellow's narrative poem *The Song of Hiawatha* (1855), based on a North American Indian Algonquin legend and written in the metre of the Finnish epic *Kalevala*,[21] Hiawatha's grandmother, Nokomis, was the 'daughter of the Moon'. She had fallen from the Full Moon to Earth when a jealous lover cut through the twisted grapevines on which she was swinging, playing with her women. When she reached the meadow she gave birth to her daughter, Wenonah, among the prairie lilies, as though

Fig. 6. The Face of the Moon. St. Mary's Church, Burnham Deepdale, Norfolk. Medieval stained glass set in an old church with a Saxon round tower and a Norman font. The Moon is at the top of a glass panel set in the porch to the church, with a similar portrait of the Sun on the opposite side. The Moon and Sun porch windows would have come from either side of a crucifixion scene in an East window.

Fig. 7. The Woman in the Moon, with water-pail and berry-bush. Tatoo pattern, Haida Indians, northwest America. (From Jung, CW V, p. 138).

she were already pregnant with life from the seed of the Moon. Nokomis tells the young Hiawatha, son of Wenonah and the West Wind (and so great-grandson of the Moon), that the 'flecks and shadows' on the Moon are signs of a grandmother who had been thrown up there in a fit of rage by one of her warrior grandchildren:

> Once a warrior, very angry,
> Seized his grandmother, and threw her
> Up into the sky at midnight;
> Right against the moon he threw her;
> 'Tis her body that you see there.[22]

The north American Indian Iroquois tribe see in the Moon a woman bending over her hominy pot, weaving a strap for her forehead, with her cat sitting beside her. Once a month she puts down her strap in order to stir her boiling pot of hominy, but then the cat unravels all her weaving and she has to start again. Every month this happens, so her work will not be finished until the end of time. The Shawnee Indians see their Creator goddess with her cooking pot and sometimes a dog beside her.[23]

On the other hand, the Malay fishermen see an old hunchbacked man sitting beneath a banyan tree, plaiting strands of bark to make a fishing line. But there is a rat at the other end of it who gnaws through the line once a month, in spite of the man's cat who watches the rat. The man wants to fish up everything on Earth and reel it back up to the Moon, but he never gets that far because every month he has to begin again.[24]

In many of these tales, the lunar drama reflects the day-to-day life of the tribe, but with the added dimension of measuring the days into months and then extending the months into the perpetual cycle of 'ever after'. In this way, the daily life in time is returned from the Moon cradled in eternity: as below, so above, so below.

When the woman in the Moon is imagined as the wife or sister of the Sun, the markings on the

Fig. 8. Old English Watermark of the Man in the Moon. The lantern slung across his shoulder ends in the crescent, and the two spirals with zigzag lines may suggest the Moon as the source of rain. (From Huxley, The Way of the Sacred, p. 34).

Moon's face often serve as a fable of tribal instruction. The Masai in Kenya see the Sun and Moon as husband and wife who are always quarrelling. After their fights the wifely Moon has a crooked mouth and a missing eye, while the husbandly Sun has no marks at all but is bright with shame.[25] In Tierra del Fuego, the Ona (or Selk'nam) people see the spots on the Moon Woman, Kra, as the marks of a beating that Kran, her husband the Sun Man, gave her when she deceived him and all the men in order to keep power for herself and all the women. [26]

The people of the Zambezi tell a tale of a jealous Moon who is angry with a male Sun:

> Originally the Moon was pale and did not shine, and she was jealous of the Sun with his shimmering feathers of light. When the Sun was away looking at the other side of Earth, she stole some of his feathers of fire for herself. But the Sun came back and discovered it and angrily splashed the Moon with mud, which clings to her forever. Since then the Moon is intent on revenge. Every ten years she catches the Sun unawares and spatters him with mud in his turn. Then large black spots appear on the Sun and for some hours he cannot shine, so the whole Earth is sad and afraid for everyone loves the Sun.[27]

In a Yoruba story from Nigeria the figure in the Moon is the antelope's mother, whom he hid there instead of sacrificing her in a time of famine. She would let down a rope and he would climb up and have a good meal, for honey oozed from springs in the ground and the soil was soft as cornflour and the houses were made from sweet-bread. But he grew fat while the other animals got thinner, and they discovered his secret. So when he was away they called to his mother to let down the rope from the Moon and they all clambered up it at once. But the antelope came back and called out to his mother to cut the rope, and the animals fell to the ground. So now the antelope's mother has to stay in the Moon and on some nights she can be seen there, still waiting to come down.[28]

WATER IN THE MOON

People all over the world have seen water in the Moon, perhaps for the simple reason that they think it is there. The Tlingit tribe of Alaska see children in the Moon bearing water pitchers, and in Germany and England the man in the Moon sometimes holds a pitcher of water, or is drawn with spirals and zigzag lines, suggesting rain, as in fig. 8.[29]

In north-eastern Siberia, the Yakuts say that one night a girl put a yoke on her shoulders with two pails hanging from it and went to fetch some water in the moonlight. But she gaped at the Moon, who was instantly offended and scooped her up, and there she is, still carrying her pails of water.[30] The

Fig. 9. a. Jack and Jill with full pail. b. Jack and Jill with spilt pail. c. Jack and Jill on a see-saw finding their balance. c. 1820. (From Opie and Opie, The Oxford Nursery Rhyme Book, p. 42).

Maori in New Zealand and the Indians of the Gran Chaco say the man in the Moon was kidnapped from Earth as he was drawing water from a well.[31]

A similar tale occurs in Europe, in Scandinavia and Britain. Yet in the familiar English nursery rhyme the Moon is not mentioned. We all know the rhyme:

> Jack and Jill went up the hill
> To fetch a pail of water;
> Jack fell down and broke his crown,
> And Jill came tumbling after.'

But, as the nineteenth-century folklorist Sabine Baring-Gould has argued in his book *Curious Myths of the Middle Ages*, Jack and Jill are names deriving from the Scandinavian *Hjuki* and *Bil*: *Hjuki*, in Norse, would be pronounced *Juki*, which readily becomes 'Jack', while *Bil* becomes 'Jill,', to make the rhyme.[32] The tale concerns the filling and emptying of the cup of the Moon's watery light.

Continuing the tale told by Snorri Sturluson in his *Prose Edda*, the names of the two children whom Mani took from earth were Hjuki and Bil, and he took them

> as they were coming away from the spring called Byrgir carrying on their shoulders the pail called Soegand, suspended from the pole Simul…These children accompany Moon, as can be seen from earth.[33]

But the Norse myth, as Baring-Gould observes, is not just a story which accounts for the spots on the Moon: its deeper significance is related to the Moon's waxing and waning, and points, through the children's gathering and spilling of water, to the belief that rainfall depends on the phases of the Moon. In Scandinavian, the names are resonant: *Hjuki* comes from the verb *jakka*, to 'heap together', 'assemble' or 'increase'; and Bil comes from *bila*, to 'break up' or 'dissolve'.[34] In Sturluson's story, Moon's decision as to 'the time of the moon's waxing and waning'[35] is immediately followed by his removal of the little water-carriers from Earth to Moon, suggesting a link between the lunar phases and water.

In common with many myths where the waxing phase is male and the waning phase is female, Hjuki, the boy, may be read as the Waxing Moon, and his sister, Bil, as the Waning Moon.[36] Similarly, when Jack and Jill go *up* the hill to fetch a pail of water (where the Moon's dew-water would be found most plentifully),[37] the Moon is waxing. But after they have reached the top – the Full Moon – Jack falls down, the water spills out, and Jill comes tumbling after, in the way that one Moon-spot after another dissolves and spills into the dark until there are none, and no Moon, left.

The second verse goes:

> Then up Jack got and home did trot
> As fast as he could caper;
> And went to bed to mend his head
> With vinegar and brown paper.[38]

Putting the two stories together, it seems as if Jack's broken head is bandaged, in the same way that the Moon's 'crown' is covered after its 'fall', and both, after resting, begin to mend again. In these rhymes, water and light are identified so that the loss of moonlight is rendered as the spilling of water, suggesting that the whole Moon is an orb of watery light or glistening dew. More practically, the tale also suggests that there is more rain after the full, a widespread belief of lunar weather lore.[39]

A later poetic version of the Scandinavian myth reminds us that the children will forever be filling their pail from the well of the Moon, for in the Moon the water never runs out:

> Never is the bucket empty,
>   Never are the children old;
>   Even when the moon is shining
> We the children may behold.[40]

FROG AND TOAD IN THE MOON

Frogs and toads, croaking up to the Moon from swampy pools, are also found etched onto the face of the watery Moon as though the Moon's pool of light mirrors the pools on Earth, which themselves mirror the Moon when it is full. Living both on land and in water and so imagined to mediate between them, these moist amphibious creatures croak most loudly when there is rain, which was believed to come from the Moon. Among the North American Indians there are many frog tales. Once two frog sisters were besieged by suitors who cried so much their tears threatened to drown them all, so the frogs jumped onto the Moon and left their suitors behind. Another frog swallowed the Moon who then swallowed the frog back, so now the frog sits weaving a basket. Yet another frog protects Moon and Sun so they will not be swallowed by Bear.[41] There is also a Primeval Toad in the Moon who held all the waters of the world and caused a great flood by discharging them over the Earth.

Further south, the Great Goddess of Mexico, who is the Moon and the ruler of the waters, was pictured as a large emerald frog. In Tibet the Moon is called the 'golden frog' and in China a three-legged toad lives in the Moon, or carries the Moon on its back (fig.11). The Solomon Islanders represent the Moon as a toad, and the Indians of Guiana see a frog in the Moon. What gives life to the faint tracing of the shape of a frog or toad in the Moon is the watery element which both are assumed to share and to be, on that account, bound together as one.[42]

SOOT, ASH, BLOOD AND MUD ON THE MOON

In many stories the smudges on the surface of the Moon are felt to be disfiguring, defacing the otherwise pure sheen of light. In an Eskimo story, Moon and Sun lived as big brother and little sister, as humans on Earth.

Moon fell in love with Sun, his little sister, and sneaked in to lie with her in the dark. Sun could not see who it was so she wiped soot from her lamp across his face. When the lamps were lit she saw her brother Moon with soot on his face, and her face flushed with anger and shame. She cut off her breasts with her crescent-shaped knife and held them out to her brother:

'Here,' she said, 'you seem to have a taste for me, eat these as well!'

Then she grabbed a piece of lamp moss, lit it, and rushed outside, and she ran round and round in a circle until she rose into the air. Moon tried to copy her, but stumbled and his flame went out. Only the embers glowed.

Ever since then Moon gives out light but not heat and tries forever to reach his lovely Sun who forever eludes him, except once a month when he finally catches up with her. This is the time of New Moon when he cannot be seen. After three days Sun breaks free and races off to the west each day with Moon following after her. But he cannot catch her and every day he drops further back, slipping further and further eastward from his sister, so the distance between them becomes greater and greater until Full Moon. Then shifting continually to the east, he comes back to Sun at New Moon.

Moon's light is always pale because his wick burned down to glowing embers in the beginning, and his light is the cold light of winter. Whenever he disappears from the sky in winter, he crosses the sea of ice with his dogs to hunt food for the dead humans in the realm of death. But Sun gives out light and heat, especially in summer when Moon becomes pale in her light, since in the beginning her wick of flame kept on blazing.[43]

Even though their relation is incestuous and so prohibited to the tribe, their celestial union is fruitful, for in Moon's ceaseless pursuit of Sun he spills his semen on Earth as winter snow, and as Sun climbs higher and higher above the horizon in spring her warm rays dissolve the snow and ice, which stream forth like blood. Then seals bring forth their young, and birds and animals appear upon the melting snow, just as though they were the children of Sun and Moon.[44]

The Cherokee Indians have a similar story but with different focus: they see the Moon fleeing from the Sun: Sun goddess Ulenanunhi had a lover who visited her once a month but she never knew who it was. So one night she rubbed his face with ashes, but the next morning she saw her own brother with ash upon his face. He was so ashamed he separated from her, trying to make himself thinner so she could not see him when she approached him in the west. But once a month he visits her in the underworld and so is missing for three days. When the Sun is eclipsed he has dared to meet her in the day.[45] In some South American Indian tales, the Sun-sister smeared not ash but menstrual blood on her Moon-brother's face.[46]

Variations on this story have travelled as far south as Brazil. The problem may present itself as one common to many tribes, for when the Moon visits the Sun at their 'conjunction', the night sky is shrouded in darkness and lovers cannot always tell exactly who is who. In Brazil the shame is reversed: Moon is the maiden who falls in love with her brother Sun, but he passed his mud-blackened hand over her face so when she moved away from him, and certainly by the Full Moon, the marks were clear for all to see.[47]

THE ELIXIR IN THE MOON

There is another kind of story about the markings on the Moon's face, where the concerns of the tribe are left behind to explore ideas of time and eternity in a manner accessible to children and philosophers alike.

Fig. 10. Heng-O, the Moon Goddess. Late Yuan or early Ming Dynasty. c. 1350–1400. Anonymous fan painting; ink and colours on silk, 25.5 x 26.1cm. The Art Institute of Chicago, Samuel M. Nicholson Collection.

The Chinese myth of Heng-O (or Ch'ang O) is one such story which runs through a whole culture, originating probably as early as the fourth century BC,[48] and still found today painted on mirrors in Chinese restaurants many thousands of miles from home.

> There were once nine extraordinary birds who blew fire and formed nine extra suns in the sky, threatening to shrivel up the whole world in their blazing heat. Shen I (or Hou Yi), the Archer with exquisite aim, took his bow and arrow and shot at the birds. When his arrow struck the birds, the false suns turned into red clouds and melted away, leaving the one true sun to shine alone. So Shen I saved the world from burning.
> Then Shen I was sent to do battle with a torrential river. Shooting an arrow into the midst of the waters, he watched them fall back to their source. Now he could see a man clothed in white, riding a white horse with a young woman beside him. This was Heng-O, who was the sister of the Spirit of the Waters. Shen I shot the horseman in the eye, but he shot the woman in the hair. She at once thanked him for saving her life and agreed to be his wife.
> One day he arrived at the palace of Chin Mu, Queen Mother of the West.
> 'I have heard,' said he, 'that you have the herb of immortality. I beg you to give me some.'
> 'I have heard,' said she, 'that you are a great architect. Please build me a palace on the side of the White Jade-tortoise Mountain.'

Fig. 11. T'ang Dynasty bronze mirror. The hare stands on the right pounding the powder with his pestle and mortar. Heng-O is seated on the left. The cinnamon tree with roots below and branch above rises through the middle of the mirror, while at the centre is placed the toad. 618-906 AD. Werner Forman Archive Art Resource, New York.

When the palace was completed she gave him one pill of the special herb.

'This will give you immortality,' she said to him, 'and also allow you to fly though the air. But you must not eat it until you have dieted and exercised for a year.'

He thanked her and took the pill home and hid it under a rafter.

Now Shen I had to go away to the south to subdue a wild man with a chisel tooth. When he was gone, Heng-O saw a beam of white light streaming down from the roof and found herself breathing a delicious fragrance which filled every room. She climbed up a ladder and, following the light, saw the precious pill and swallowed it. Instantly, she became weightless and began floating up to the ceiling as if she had wings.

Suddenly Shen I returned and went to look for his pill, but could not find it. So he called to his wife to ask her what had happened to it. Heng-O was terrified and opened the window and flew out to escape him. Shen I reached for his bow and arrows and set off after her. He saw her rising towards the Full Moon, shrunk to the size of a toad, but just as he was nearly upon her a blast of wind struck him to the ground.

Heng-O kept on flying until she reached a cold, glassy, luminous sphere. Nothing grew on it except a cinnamon tree. As soon as she landed on the Moon she vomited the covering of the pill, which turned into a hare as white as the purest jade. This was the ancestor of the *yin* or the female principle. Heng-O drank some Moon-dew, ate some cinnamon, and made her home in the Moon.

From that time the hare pounds the elixir of immortality with a pestle and mortar, using twigs from the cinnamon tree beside him, since the tree, being evergreen, never dies. Sometimes he is joined by a three-legged toad. Some say that when Heng-O took her first sip of Moon-dew she turned into a three-legged toad and this is the toad that can be seen in the face of the Moon.[49]

In this tale it is the Moon hare who transforms time into eternity through the pounding of the magic elixir in the mortar-cup shaped like the crescent Moon, which is the shape in which the Moon appears to be continually reborn. While Heng-O swallowed just one pill of immortality herself, the

Fig. 12. T'ang Dynasty bronze mirror showing the hare in the Moon pounding the herb of immortality. 700 AD. British Museum.

Moon hare continues to make it for all time. In his book on Chinese bronzes, Carl Hentze describes the 'hare in the moon' as a symbol of resurrection. Referring to the Chinese motif of 'spittle flowing out of a vessel', Hentze links this vessel to the New Moon through the action of the hare:

> Since the hare belongs to the moon, 'immortality' can here only refer to the new rising (or resurrection) of the moon, so that the mortar is evidently the New Moon in which the 'Herb of Immortality' is prepared, that is to say from which rejuvenation springs.[50]

This may be one reason why, even now, every year at the Chinese mid-autumn festival of the Moon on the fifteenth day of the eighth month at the Full Moon of the autumn equinox, the Moon's birthday is celebrated. The eighth month was also the month when the cinnamon tree flowered, which could be seen in the Moon with Heng-O. Women and children in China make little white cakes in the shape of the round Moon and the hare, and offer them to the Moon when it has risen above the rooftops of their homes. In some villages there used to be a 'Moon-cake society' when poor families paid the equivalent of ten pence to the baker every month and on the day of the moon-feast the baker gave every member of the society Moon-cakes. Although the Moon-cake society has now gone, the Moon-cakes are still baked.[51] No one knows how old the ceremony is. According to a traveller to China in the mid-1840s:

> This festival, known as the *Yue-Ping* (loaves of the moon), dates from the remotest antiquity...On this solemn day, all labour is suspended; the workmen receive from their employers a present of money, every person puts on his best clothes, and there is merry making in every family. Relations and friends interchange cakes of various sizes, on which is stamped the image of the moon; that is to say, a hare crouching amid a small group of trees.[52]

In the 1920s, the festival was movingly described as a ceremony of the people, shining on all alike:

The courtyards in millions of small, poor homes are changed to fairyland because the Goddess touches them with her silver fingers. She hides the poverty and ugliness of everyday things. She smoothes away the wrinkles from tired faces, and lends a grace to awkward silhouettess as they approach her table. One after another the women go forward and make their bows. Two candles are lighted because it is customary to offer them in pairs. Bundles of incense sticks are stuck flaming in the family urn, but their light glimmers faintly in the floods of moonshine. The whole service lasts but a few moments and concludes with the pasting of a brilliant poster against the wall of the house – a poster showing the Moon Rabbit under the Sacred Cassia Tree, pounding the Pill of Immortality in his Mortar. Ceremonious salutations are addressed to this quaint little animal figure. Then his picture is taken down and burned. Thus end the religious rites proper to the Moon Festival.[53]

Back in the eighth century, the poet Tu Fu wrote a melancholy poem called *Moon Festival*:

> The Autumn constellations
> Begin to rise. The brilliant
> Moonlight shines on the crowds.
> The moon toad swims in the river
> And does not drown. The moon rabbit
> Pounds the bitter herbs of the
> Elixir of eternal life.
> His drug only makes my heart
> More bitter. The silver brilliance
> Only makes my hair more white.
> I know that the country is
> Overrun with war. The moonlight
> Means nothing to the soldiers
> Camped in the western deserts.[54]

THE HARE IN THE MOON

The Chinese hare in the Moon may have come over from India with the Buddhists in the fourth century BC, but it is more likely to have been already there. For the hare in the Moon is found in cultures as far apart as Mayan, Aztec, Indian, Buddhist, Tibetan, Egyptian, Mexican, Hottentot, Bushman, North American Indian, Teutonic, Anglo-Saxon, Japanese and Indonesian.[55] The ubiquity of the hare in the Moon may seem initially surprising in the West, where we are accustomed to look for a face in the Moon; but look again at any time from the eighth to the fifteenth day, starting with the long ears on the right. Then it is clear why the hare and/or rabbit has played such an extraordinarily prominent role in myths and folklore throughout the ages: as sage or trickster, Creator or thief.

THE HARE IN INDIAN MYTH

A Buddhist tale, attributed to the Buddha himself, tells how, while still a Bodhisattva, he was reborn in one of his incarnations as a hare. He had three friends, a monkey, a jackal and an otter.

Fig. 14. Close-up of Mayan Moon goddess on crescent with rabbit. Diagram of incised ceramic vase. Late Classic. c. 550-800 AD. American Museum of Natural History, New York.

Fig. 15. Aztec Rabbit in the Moon. Florentine Codex. 16th century AD. Bibliotheca Medicea-Laurenziana, Florence.

Fig. 13. Moon and Hares. Utagawa Hiroshige. (1797-1858). Edo Period, 19th century. Tokyo National Museum.

It happened that the hare looked up at the Moon and saw that the next day was a holy day as it was Full Moon. So he advised his friends to observe the holy day by giving food to any beggar they should meet before they, themselves, eat. Each of the three animals managed to trick some human out of food: the otter got some fish, the jackal two meat puddings, a bottle of sour milk and a newt, and the monkey a bunch of mangoes. The hare thought to himself that if a beggar came to him he would offer his own body as food.

Now the god Sakka, the 'Strong' [one of the epithets of Indra], was sitting in heaven on a stone seat covered with a woollen blanket when he felt his seat grow very hot. He decided that this was because of the renunciation of this hare. So he came to Earth in the form of a Brahman to put the hare to the test. Appearing to the other animals, he was offered their food but refused it. Then he stood before the hare and said:

'Wise one, if I could have something to eat I would observe the holy day and so be able to fulfil my duties.'

The Bodhisattva, in the form of the hare, asked the Brahman to fetch wood and make a fire and to tell him when it was ready:

'I will offer myself by leaping into the fire,' he said, 'but when my flesh is roasted you must eat it so you may then fulfil your priestly duties.'

When the fire was burning, the hare, first shaking off any insects from his fur, leapt into the flames like a royal swan alighting on a lotus bed. But it was as if he had leapt into snow. The hare said to Sakka:

'Brahman, the fire which thou hast made, it is too cold.'

Sakka said to the hare: 'Wise one, I am no Brahman. I am Sakka who came to put thy virtue to the test and I tell thee thy virtue shall be known for a whole aeon.'

Then he squeezed the mountain and with the essence of the mountain he painted the hare's image on the disc of the Moon. Sakka went back to heaven and the four friends lived in peace for the rest of their days.[56]

In a simpler version from Sri Lanka, the hare and the Buddha are distinct, and the Buddha puts the hare in the Moon:

The Buddha was wandering through a wood when he met a hare who asked him how he fared.

'I am poor and hungry,' the Buddha replied.

'Art thou hungry?' asked the hare. 'Make a fire, friend, and then kill, cook, and eat me.'

The Buddha thanked him and lit the fire. But as the hare leapt into the flames the Buddha plucked him out unharmed and placed him in the Moon.[57]

John Layard, in his book *The Lady of the Hare*, relates the sacrifice of the hare in such tales to the behaviour of hares in the cornfields which farmers burn at the end of the season. Unlike the other animals, the hare does not run away from the flames but stays hidden in the grass scrub until it is too late, and so is often burned to death.[58] In these stories the hare's characteristic death as the culmination of the harvest becomes a willing sacrifice of himself which brings forth a greater good. Layard comments:

The hare represents the material part, or unredeemed instinct, of the Buddha, Bodhisattva, or god which is transformed into spirit by being translated to the moon, whence it shines down to earth in the form of divine intuition.[59]

If the Sun and the daylight world may be understood as symbolizing the conscious, rational mind, then the Moon, as the 'nocturnal Sun', would suggest itself as the figure of intuition: the thought that sees in the dark and so may see further, or more deeply, because it sees inwardly. Then the light that lightens the darkness may illumine the essences of things that cannot be seen in the clear light of day.

The stories that have gathered around the hare in the face of the Moon may be exploring this faculty of intuition, trying to discover when and how it works – often against the odds, as in this Indian tale.

In the first story of the third book of the *Pancatantram* there were many hares living on the shore of the Lake *Chandrasaras*, which means 'Lake of the Moon'. The King of the Hares was called *Silimukha*, which means 'Stone-Face':

> Now it happened that a drought came amongst them, and many of the other lakes and pools dried up. So the leader of a mighty herd of elephants, *Chaturdanta*, the One with Great Tusks, led his whole thirsty herd into the water of Moon Lake, and they drank deeply. When they had gone, the Hare-King realized that the elephants had trampled many of his subjects to death, and he was very grieved. He summoned his wisest hare, called *Vijaya* whose name means 'Victory', and said to him:
>
> 'Now that the Lord of the Elephants has tasted the water of this lake he will come here again, and then again, and we will all be destroyed. I want you to think up something ingenious, and go to him and convince him that he should go somewhere else to drink. All the other times I have asked you, you have done well.'
>
> The wise hare was glad to help and went slowly on his way, all the time following the large tracks of the elephants through the scrub. He saw the King of the Elephants at the head of his herd and, just as the King was going past a rock as high as himself, the hare leapt to the top of the rock and greeted him:
>
> 'I am the Ambassador of the Moon, and this is what the God of the Moon says to you through my mouth: "My home is a lake called *Chandrasaras*, the Lake of the Moon. Hares live there and I am their king. I love them well, and so I am known as the cool-rayed and the hare-marked. But you have defiled my lake and slain my hares. If you do this one more time you will receive that recompense from me which is your due."'
>
> When the King of the Elephants heard this he was struck with fear:
>
> 'I will never do this again,' he said. 'I must show respect to this awful Moon God.'
>
> The hare said: 'So come, my friend, I will show him to you.'
>
> Darkness was falling when the hare led the Elephant King back to the lake.
>
> 'Look in the water,' the hare said in a hushed tone, and he pointed into the middle of the lake.
>
> The elephant looked down into the water and there he saw the silvery-white face of the Full Moon gazing up at him, marked with the shadowed outline of a hare. The elephant plunged his trunk into the water to show respect to the God and the Moon splintered in pieces all over the lake.
>
> 'What have I done?' asked the terrified elephant.
>
> 'The God of the Moon is angry with you,' replied the hare.
>
> 'Then I vow never to come back again,' the elephant said, walking away from the lake as fast as he could.
>
> Silimukha, king of the hares, was watching, and he honoured the wise hare who had gone as his ambassador to the elephants. After that the hares lived beside their lake in complete peace.[60]

The Moon is so closely allied with the hare in Sanskrit that the words are practically the same. 'Hare' in Sanskrit is *sasa*, and the Moon is called *sasin* – 'that which is marked with the hare'. So it

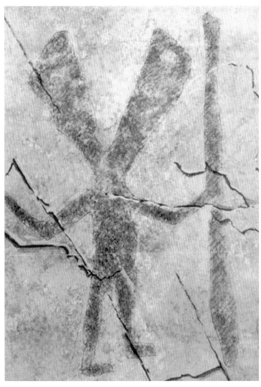

Fig. 16. Ixchel as the Moon goddess, with her rabbit. Painted terra-cotta figurine. Mayan. Jaina Island, Campeche, Mexico. The Art Museum, Princeton University, Griffin Collection.

Fig. 17. The Great Hare, probably Manabozho. Rock painting. Lake Mazinaw, Southeast Ontario, Canada. (From Campbell, The Mythic Image, p. 186).

was said by the people that Chandra, god of the Moon, used to go about carrying a hare.[61] Even today, in some regions of northern India, the hare is embroidered on 'bridal durries', woven rugs which brides from the villages weave especially for their wedding day. Images and designs are handed down relatively unchanged for centuries.[62]

When Buddhism spread to Japan, the Moon hare came with it, as can be seen in the Japanese Buddhist painting on silk in fig. 1, which is one of the screens representing the Twelve Devas.

THE HARE IN AZTEC AND MAYAN MYTH

The hare and rabbit are often interchangeable in myth, though rabbits are not native to India and were not found in Greece or Italy before the first century BC.[63] The theme of sacrifice also appears in an Aztec myth from Mexico which brings in a rabbit to solve the problem of the two Suns, for at one time the Moon was as bright and as hot as the Sun.

> At Teotihuacan, the 'Place Where the Gods Were Created', the gods gathered to create the new Sun. Four earlier Suns and four earlier cosmic ages had ended in destruction, and this was to be the last. But one of the gods had to sacrifice himself in the fire in order to become the Fifth Sun. At midnight, in total darkness before the city's sacred

fire, they tried to decide which one of them it should be. At last two gods offered themselves: *Tacciztecatl*, the arrogant 'Conch Shell Lord', and *Nanahuatzin*, who was diseased and deformed. But when the Conch Shell Lord looked into the abyss and saw the flames raging he shrank back in terror, but the humble *Nanahuatzin* leapt into the blaze without hesitating, and then *Tacciztecatl* found the courage to follow him.

The other gods waited through the dark night for *Nanahuatzin* to appear and at last he arose in the east, transformed into the new Sun, flaming red and swaying from side to side. *Tacciztecatl* was reincarnated as the Moon, and he was just as brilliant as the Sun. But neither of them moved. Then the rest of the gods realized they had to sacrifice themselves as well if the heavenly beings were to move along their ordained courses. But before they died, one of the gods seized a rabbit and hurled it into the face of the Moon and the dark shape of the rabbit dimmed the brilliance of the Moon, and the Moon became cold and pale. The rabbit can still be seen, testimony to the sacrifice of the Conch Shell Lord, and the sign of his undying life in new form (fig. 15).[64]

The Mayans, who lived in Mexico before the Aztecs, also depicted a rabbit in the Moon. In the Mayan stone carving of the Vision Serpent issuing from the mouth of the Celestial Monster shown in fig. 14, the Moon rises between two loops of the serpent's body as the vision appears, while the young goddess seated on the curve of the crescent, leg dangling over the rim, holds a rabbit on her lap. Sometimes she is called Ixchel.[65]

Ixchel's name means 'Lady Rainbow', but she was often depicted as a Moon goddess, especially in northern Yucatan. She was the wife of the sky god and lord of creation, Itzamna, and was herself goddess of fertility, childbirth, weaving and healing, a range of concerns that characterize many of the Moon's divinities.[66] The figurine of Ixchel and the rabbit in fig. 16 was found on the island of Jaina which was a burying place for the dead, suggesting that the deceased were identified with the reborn Moon.[67]

THE HARE IN NORTH AMERICAN INDIAN MYTH

The Creator god of the North American Algonquin Indians, Great Manitou, the Great Spirit, took, as one of his manifestations, the form of a hare. Great Hare, or White Hare, was either himself the Moon or lived in the Moon with his grandmother who was herself the Moon. He was the provider of the waters and the fish, master of winds, and brother of the snow.[68] Other tribes, such as the Ojibwa and the Menomini, identified the Hare with Manabhozo, who was a trickster-hero, credited with initiating the Grand Medicine Society.[69] The Sioux and the Indians of British Columbia also see a rabbit in the Moon.[70]

Contemporary Caribbean-American legends of the mischievous trickster Brer Rabbit, who outwits Brer Fox and Brer Bear every time, were originally brought to America by African slaves from West Africa. They must have found in the American Indian myths an astonishing echo of their own native trickster, the Moon hare.[71]

THE MOON HARE AS A FIGURE OF DEATH AND REBIRTH

Although we may see a hare in the Moon, we can still ask *why* it is there. The hare is fast and fertile; indeed, because of its fecundity ('breeding like rabbits'), it became for the Christian sensibility a symbol of sexual lust – St Augustine's definition of the 'original sin' which brought death[72] – and so

Fig. 18. Saxon 'Idol of the Moon' as a goddess with the head or mask of a hare, holding across her belly a Moon-disc inscribed as a human face, with features resembling her own - as though giving birth to a future form of herself. (From Verstegen, A Restitution of Decayed Intelligence, 1605).

was sometimes put at the feet of the Virgin Mary to signify the triumph of Spirit over Nature, as was the down-curved, dragon-clawed Crescent Moon. But outside Christianity, the fertility of the hare was celebrated for its timely coincidence with the lunar cycle. The hare's 30-day gestation period – covering roughly the course of one Moon – suggested an innate affinity between hare and Moon, such that the hare's act of giving birth continually could be read in the context of the Moon's continual rebirth of itself. In Japan and China hares were supposed to give birth with their eyes fixed on the Moon, and never to close their eyes: 'Two only sleep with their eyes open, the hare and the Moon,' the old Chinese proverb went.[73] It seems as though, in much early thought, the hare's death was felt to be analogous to the Moon's death: a sacrifice which makes possible a new birth.

In many cultures the hare was a taboo animal, not to be hunted or eaten or even named. Countries which once observed the food taboo range from European Russia, to the Baltic, the Caucasus, the Turkish Empire, Spain, India, China, Britain, much of the Near East, as well as Muhammadan Persians, Christian Armenians, and Somalis in Africa, and also in Spain, India, and Britain.[74] Up to Victorian times hares were not killed in Wales or in County Kerry in Ireland. In Leviticus, the hare was named as 'unclean',[75] and Caesar remarks that the Britons regarded it as 'unlawful' to eat it.[76] In Greece, Xenophon writes that hares were protected from being hunted 'for the sake of Artemis';[77] Hekate had hares as well as dogs around her, and her chief shrine was at Lagina, the hare-city.[78] It may even have seemed as if the Moon itself hunted or spared the hare – its earthly form – with the moonlight striking the dark field and the prey suddenly illuminated for the hunters to kill. In those cultures where the hare was hunted, it was often not eaten, as though it were still an uncanny animal, even if the original reason for its numinosity had been forgotten.

In British folklore, a hare or rabbit's foot, the part which touched the ground – and so, perhaps, made a link between Moon and Earth – was considered to be good luck even a few years ago. A correspondent from Norfolk in the *Sunday People* said in 1981: 'I always carried a rabbit's foot for luck until someone said: "Well, the rabbit wasn't lucky, was he?"'[79] Soldiers carried them in their pockets in World War II, and mothers put them into the cradles of new-born babies, traditions possibly dating back to pre-Roman times when the ancient Britons used hares in the rituals surrounding divination and war.[80] Dion Cassius, in his *Roman History*, written in the early third century AD, reports that the British Queen Boadicea began the battle against him by releasing a live hare from her breast, which raced away across the field on what was held to be the auspicious side, upon which the whole multitude shouted with pleasure. Then Boadicea raised her hand towards heaven and said: 'I thank thee, Andraste...I supplicate and pray thee for victory.'[81]

THE EASTER HARE

It is tempting to think that, for the folk imagination, the hare in the Moon embodied playfully the intransigent paradox of birth, death and rebirth, explored more profoundly through the lunar symbolism of the Mystery traditions. Yet we find a hare lurking unsuspected even within Christian ritual. The Venerable Bede, a zealous seventh-century Father of the early Christian Church, in the course of explaining what it meant that April was called *Eostur-monath*, said that Easter took its name from the Anglo-Saxon *Eostre*, who was a Goddess of Dawn, Spring and Fertility, and whose festival was celebrated

Fig. 19. Titian. 'La Vierge au Lapin.' 1488-1490. The Louvre.

in April.[82] The Germans also speak of *Ostermoneth*, and their 'Easter-hare' is central to their celebration of Easter. Grimm gives the goddess a German name, calling her *Ostara*, and labelling her on etymological grounds as 'the divinity of the radiant dawn...whose meaning could easily be adapted to the resurrection day of the Christian God.'[83] Other forms of the Teutonic Moon goddess were surrounded by hares: Holda was followed by a train of hares carrying torches, as was Harke, and the Scandinavian Freya was 'attended by hares bringing her light and bearing her train.'[84]

Some scholars have doubted Bede's credibility, since he is the only one to mention the Anglo-Saxon *Eostre*. But are we to conclude that the Venerable Bede is lying, just because there is no one else to back him up? As Grimm tactfully phrases it, would it not be uncritical to saddle this eminent Father of the Church, who keeps Heathendom at arm's length and tells us less of it than he knows, with the invention of this goddess?[85] Also, Bede, born in 672, lived at the cusp of the changeover from pre-Christian to Christian worship, since the beginning of the Christianization of England took place at the end of the sixth century, and was not completed until around the end of the seventh century; so the pre-Christian, not to say heathen and pagan, goddesses and gods would have been still very much alive in his lifetime. It may even be that the name of *Eostre* was advisedly retained for Easter, since the Dawn and the East and the Resurrection all convey the meaning of life reborn.[86]

A goddess of the Moon with the head or mask of a hare was known to be worshipped by the Saxons. Layard quotes a book, written in 1605, describing 'the ancient manner of lyving of our Saxon ancestors. Of the Idolles they adored whyle they were pagans: and how they grew to be of greater name and habitation of any other people of Germany.'[87] In the chapter relating to the deities connected to the days of the week, the 'Idol of the Moon' is discussed, 'whereof wee yet retain the name of Monday', with the author expressing much bewilderment at the idol's long ears, combined with short coat and pointed shoes.[88] (fig. 18). In Britain, hares had been sacred since the time of the Celts, if not before,[89] and in many parts of Europe cutting the last sheaf at harvest time was called 'killing the hare', when, with all his cover gone, the hare rushed out as though the corn-spirit were escaping to live for another harvest.[90]

Further traces of the earlier sacredness of the hare may be present in Leicestershire in England in two Easter customs described by C.J. Billson in an article on the Easter Hare in *Folklore*, written at the end of the nineteenth century. The custom of 'Hunting the Easter Hare' on Easter Monday took place in Leicester, where a hare was followed to the Mayor's house, followed by a banquet of hare. Similarly, the Hallaton 'Hare-pie Scramble and Bottle Kicking', where the hare was carried in procession on a pole, also culminated in a feast where the hare pie was eaten and afterwards loaves were distributed to the community. These customs, Billson argues, suggest that the hare was originally a divine animal among the 'local aborigines', such that the customs may be 'relics of the religious procession and annual sacrifice of the god' in the springtime of the year.[91] Nothing now remains of their former sanctity except the lust of the chase, but a formerly sacred animal typically remains an uncanny animal in the same way that earlier gods become devils when their worshippers change their faith. On these grounds, as Billson says, 'we may often argue back from the present unpopularity of an animal to its former divinity.'[92]

In England, up to the nineteenth century, hares were frequently taken to be the witch's familiar, and indeed, according to the folklorist W. Henderson, the hare was 'the commonest disguise of the witch in all the northern countries of Europe.'[93] Sometimes the only way to shoot a witch-hare was with a silver sixpence or silver bullet (the Moon's own metal); no ordinary missile would do.[94] Katherine Briggs tells the tale of a farmer whose cows gave no milk, and was told by a wise woman that someone was taking the milk from his cows at night. So, waiting up, he saw a brown hare come into the byre at midnight, and he shot her in her front paw with a silver sixpence, upon which a flood of milk flowed out of her. The next day, stopping at a nearby cottage, he found an old woman huddled by the fire with her hand wrapped up. Insisting on unwinding the bandages, he saw a wound in her hand, with a silver sixpence in the middle of it. After that the farmer's cows gave good milk.[95] In the late nineteenth century the country people of Kerry still thought that hares were inhabited by the souls of their grandmothers[96] – the souls, perhaps, that in earlier myths lived in the Moon with the hare.

This alternation of witches and hares might pass as random if it were not that in many other hare/rabbit customs the hare and rabbit are frequently linked to death, just as they were in the old myths of the Moon. Seamen would not take a rabbit or hare on a boat, and even their names should not be pronounced. In the thirteenth century the hare was called 'the animal that no one dare name'[97] It was ill-omened for anyone to cross paths with a hare on any day of the year, but especially pregnant women whose child could be born with a hare-lip (unless she instantly stooped down and tore her shift).[98] These are accidental meetings, but it seems as if the ill-omen of the hare and rabbit can be turned to good if one deliberately seeks them out (as with the hare's and rabbit's foot). Even now in England some children say 'hares' (or 'rabbits') on the last night of the month and 'rabbits' (or 'hares') on the first day of the new month, to have good luck for the whole month.[99] When the month began with the New Moon, this ritual would have been even more resonant.

In the twenty-first century, the 'Easter Bunny' is fully absorbed into the Christian festival, mostly found modelled in chocolate, along with the Easter egg. In Germany and the Low Countries, the ancient custom of searching for painted Easter eggs hidden around the garden is still one of the excitements of the year for children, who are told that the eggs are laid by the Pasche hare.[100] Yet the connection between the 'Pasche hare' and the 'Moon hare' is long forgotten, and only the imagery reminds us that this Bunny who lays eggs was once the ubiquitous figure of the hare of death and rebirth in the Moon.

In Titian's fifteenth-century painting (fig. 19), the white rabbit has crept back to its original place upon the blue gown of the Moon, whose latest incarnation – the image (but not the doctrine) would suggest – is now the Virgin Mary, she who is called 'Moon of our Church', 'Mother Moon'.[101] The Virgin, with one hand around her baby's head and the other resting upon the white rabbit, brings them into relation with each other, both embodying life renewed. While the baby Jesus gazes raptly at the rabbit, the gaze of the Virgin goes between them both.

THE HARE IN AFRICAN MYTH

In the Buddhist tales the hare's relation with death is a noble one: it offers its life for another. But in Africa the hare is often a trickster who cheats human beings out of immortal life, bringing them death instead.[102]

A Hottentot tale, called *The Origin of Death*, puts the Moon hare at the heart of the matter of death and immortality.

> The Moon said to the Hare:
> 'Go thou to Men, and tell them, "Like as I die and rise to life again, so you also shall die and rise to life again."'
> So the Hare went to Men, and said:
> 'Like as I die and do not rise to life again, so you shall also die, and not rise to life again.'
> When he returned, he told the Moon what he had said.
> 'What,' said the Moon, 'hast thou said that?' And she took a stick and beat the Hare on his mouth, which was slit by the blow.
> And that is where the Hare-lip comes from. The Hare fled, and is still fleeing.

The old man who told the tale said they were angry with the Hare because he brought such a bad message, and therefore disliked to eat his flesh.[103]

Other versions have the Hare overtaking an Insect, or raising his own claws after he was hit and scratching the Moon's face, leaving dark scars.[104] The Zulus' version leaves out the Moon and the Hare, and has the Supreme Being (*Unkulunkulu*) sending the Chameleon to the people, who is outrun by the Salamander who gives the wrong message.[105]

On the other side of the world in the Fiji islands there is a story told so similar to the Hottentot legend that they seem like variations from a single source – though whether the source be a common story-teller or the story-telling mind common to all, who is to say? Participants in this debate often fall along the traditional lines drawn by the difference between empiricists and idealists, and the question is answered according to one's overall point of view. Here, the Fijian rat takes the role of the Hottentot hare:

> Two old gods, Moon, *Ra Vula*, and Rat, *Ra Kalavo*, were discussing the fate of human beings. 'Let them be like me,' said Moon, 'and disappear for a while and then live again.' 'No,' said Rat. 'Let them die as a rat dies.' And so they did.[106]

A tale from the Kalahari desert has the Moon giving a message to the tortoise to take to the people on Earth: 'Tell them that as I dying live, so they dying will live again.' The tortoise was very slow because she kept repeating the message so as not to forget it, so eventually the Moon called the hare and gave her the message as well. But the hare was so hasty she had no time to remember what the Moon said and, though she arrived far ahead of the tortoise, she gave the wrong message to the people.[107]

The assumption in all these tales is that eternal life is in the Moon's power to give – at one level a simpler, more dramatic way of saying that the idea of eternity is made visible through the Moon. It may be that the recurring motif of theft is linked to a perception of the contrast between the death of human beings and the renewal of life in the Moon. In some stories it is the Moon which kidnaps people from Earth, stealing them from their own life, or stealing their own life from them. Kidnapping becomes theft. The idea of the thieving Moon – as in the Scandinavian myth of Hjuki and Bil or the Polynesian myth of Sina or Rona – may eventually become the idea of the thief *in* the Moon. In African stories, where the Moon and the hare are distinguished, it is the hare who is the thief stealing from humans the Moon's supreme gift. The Moon wishes to grant immortality to human beings but the hare gets in the way: he is too hasty, too casual, doesn't care, and the chance is lost. It is not hard to see how a sense of loss turns into an attribution of theft: for if life, once embarked on, feels like a right, then it cannot be taken away without violation – it can only be stolen. Many myths look around for the thief – whether hare, rat, serpent, salamanda, iguana, chameleon, dog or other – anyone who can take the blame and make sense of it.

The Buddhist hare, by contrast, does not forget that life is a gift, and more, that life, given him, is now his to give. By offering his life to one in greater need, as he thinks, he is placed in the Moon as an example, not as a thief but as the bestower of gifts. What he gives others by enacting it himself is thereby suggested as the state of mind embodied in his freedom from attachment to life, which in turn allows release from resentment and fear of death. Is this, then, the elixir of life which the Chinese hare pounds in his lunar cup? The Christian ritual of resurrection which, calling itself 'Easter', retains the name and meaning of *Eostre*, the Dawn goddess with her Moon hare, celebrates a similar gift: the willing sacrifice of Christ on the cross which is to transform death – and life – for his followers.

The central importance of how one regards death is addressed in this Bushman tale, as it was told to the German philologist Dr Bleek in the 1870s. Probably the oldest of all the African stories of the hare, it begins with a prayer to the young Moon:

We, when the Moon has newly returned alive...when we perceive it we shut our eyes with our hands, we exclaim: 'Yonder! Take my face yonder! Thou shalt give me thy face yonder – with which thou, when thou hast died, thou dost again, living return, when we did not perceive thee, thou dost again lying down come – that I may also resemble thee. For, the joy yonder, thou dost always possess it yonder, that is, that thou art wont again to return alive, when we did not perceive thee; while the hare told thee about it, that thou shouldst do thus. Thou didst formerly say, that we should also again return alive, when we died.'

What had happened was this: the mother of the hare had died, and the hare, standing over her, cried greatly, declaring his mother to be 'altogether dead':

The Moon replying, said to the hare about it, that the hare should leave off crying; for, his mother was not altogether dead. For, his mother meant that she would again living return. The hare replying, said he was not willing to be silent; for, he knew that his mother would not again return alive. For, she was altogether dead.
And the Moon became angry about it, that the hare spoke thus, while he did not assent to him (the Moon). And he hit with his fist, cleaving the hare's mouth; and while he hit the hare's mouth with his fist, he exclaimed:
'This person, his mouth which is here, his mouth shall altogether be like this, even when he is a hare; he shall always bear a scar on his mouth; he shall spring away, he shall doubling come back. The dogs shall chase him; they shall, when they have caught him, they shall grasping tear him to pieces, he shall altogether die.
'And they who are men, they shall altogether dying go away, when they die. For he was not willing to agree with me, when I told him about it, that he should not cry for his mother; for, his mother would again live...I said to him about it, that they (the people) should also be like me; that which I do; that I, when I am dead, I again living return. He contradicted me when I told him about it.'
Therefore, our mothers said to me, that the hare was formerly a man; when he had acted in this manner, then it was that the Moon cursed him, that he should altogether become a hare.
...If the hare had assented to the Moon, then, we who are people, we should have resembled the Moon; for, the Moon had formerly said, that we should not altogether die. The hare's doings were those on account of which the Moon cursed us, and we die altogether...[108]

Frazer comments that 'a righteous retribution overtook the sceptic for his scepticism.'[109] But what does it mean that the hare was once a human being until he was cursed by the Moon? The curse of becoming a hare and the curse of death are presented as one and the same, suggesting that we lose our essential humanity when we limit our understanding of life and death to the visible world alone. For the mother of the hare, like Lazarus, was not dead but sleeping, or so the Moon says. Is this, then, a story which, through the figure of the Moon, points beyond the senses, implying that a complete perspective on death would not remain exclusively with our hare sensibility but might include the broader insight embodied in the Moon's vision – he who began life as a feather to brush away the gall of death?

HOW MANTIS MADE THE MOON

The story of how the Moon was made from an ostrich feather by the Bushman Creator god, Mantis, was also told to Bleek. Mantis is actually a Greek term, meaning 'prophet', for the delicately angular green insect we call a praying mantis.

One day Kwammanga-a, son of Mantis, threw away part of his shoe. Mantis picked up the shoe and soaked it in the water that lay between the reeds. Then he went away. Then he came back again. He looked at the shoe in the water and saw it move. Then he went away so it could grow.

When he came back he found the footprints of an animal in the mud. They were the tracks of an Eland, a little deer with straight horns. Mantis sat down by the water and waited. The Eland came to drink at the water. And Mantis called: 'Kwammanga-a's shoe's piece.' And the Eland came up to his father.

Mantis went to find some honey. He cut the honeycomb from the wild bee's nest and put it in a bag and laid the bag down beside the water. Then he called the Eland. And the Eland got up from the reeds and walked to his father, and his father rubbed him all over with honey. Mantis stayed away for three nights, and for three nights the Eland grew and grew till he was as big as an ox. On the fourth day when the sun was rising, Mantis came back and called the Eland, and the Eland rose up and stood before him. Mantis sang:

> 'Ah, a person is here!
> Kwammanga-a's shoe's piece!
> My eldest son's shoe's piece!'

While he was singing, he rubbed the Eland down with honey. Then he went home.

The next morning he asked his grandson, Ichneumon, to go with him to the water. When it was noon and the sun was hot, Mantis told Ichneumon to go to sleep and cover his head. Then the Eland came to drink from the water. But Ichneumon lay awake and saw him.

'That is not Magic,' Mantis said. 'That Eland came from a piece of father's shoe, which he dropped.'

When Ichneumon got home he told his father, Kwammanga-a, and Kwammanga-a said his son should guide him and show him the Eland. So the young Ichneumon guided his father, and his father went up to the Eland in the water and knocked it down while Mantis was not there. When Mantis arrived, he saw Kwammanga-a and the others cutting up the Eland.

Mantis wept for the Eland. He said: 'Why could you not first let me come?'

Kwammanga-a said: 'Tell Grandfather to leave off! He must come and gather wood for us, that we may eat, for this is meat.'

Then Mantis came and said they should not have killed the Eland when he was not looking, for he alone had made it. Then as he went to gather wood he caught sight of his Eland's gall hanging upon a bush. And he said he would pierce the gall open, he would jump upon it. And the gall said: 'I will burst, covering you in.' Mantis left the gall and found wood, but went back to the gall and spoke to it again, and the gall said again: 'I will burst, covering you in.' Ichneumon called to Mantis: 'What are you doing? Why do you keep going to that bush?'

Kwammanga-a said: 'Grandfather has seen the gall. We must go quickly for Grandfather is playing tricks with this thing. Call him so we may leave.'

Then they packed up the meat into the net, while Mantis untied his shoe and put it into the bag. It was his arrow bag which he had slung on next to his quiver. On the way Mantis said: 'This shoe-string has broken.' And the young Ichneumon said: 'You must have put the shoe away.' And Mantis said: 'No, no, the shoe must really be lying there, where we cut up the Eland. So I must turn back and fetch the shoe.'

And the young Ichneumon said: 'You must have put the shoe in, you must feel in the middle of the bag.'

And Mantis felt in the bag above the shoe. He said: 'See, the shoe is really not in it. I must go back and pick it up.'

Then Kwammanga-a said: 'Let Grandfather be! Let him turn back and do as he says.'

Then Mantis turned back. He ran up to the gall, he pierced the gall, he made the gall burst. And the gall broke, covering in his head; his eyes became big, he could not see. And he groped about, feeling his way. He went groping along, groping, groping, and he found an ostrich feather. He picked up the feather and sucked it and brushed off the gall from his eyes. Then he threw the feather up, he said: 'Thou must now lie up in the sky, thou must henceforth be the Moon. Thou shalt shine at night. Thou shalt by thy shining lighten the darkness for men, till the Sun rises to light up all things for men. For thou dost glow for men, while the Sun shines for men. Under him men walk about, they go hunting, they return home. Thou art the Moon, thou dost give light for men, then thou dost fall away, thou dost return to life, when thou hast fallen away, thou dost give light to all people.'

This is what the Moon does: The Moon falls away and returns to life, and he lights up all the flat places.[110]

CHAPTER 8

THE MOON AND FERTILITY

When she in all her virginal pride
First trod on the mountain's head
What stir ran through the countryside
Where every foot obeyed her glance!
What manhood led that dance!
Yeats *The Crazed Moon*

In the metaphor of correspondence or the argument from analogy, as the Moon grew in heaven so was there growing on Earth. The Palaeolithic Goddess of Laussel, whose waxing crescent horn matched her waxing womb, implied a relation between her fertility and the Moon (see Chapter 1, fig. 4). But once the written word appeared, it could confidently be said that many early people did indeed believe that fertility on Earth came from the Moon, just as they believed the Moon was the source of moisture, rain and dew. The Moon was then the origin not only of the waters of life but of the generation of life in humans, animals and plants.

The title 'Mother of Vegetables', 'Mother of Maize', was given to the Moon among the North American Indians, 'Mother of Grasses' in Brazil, 'Lord of Plants' in India, 'Lord of Cattle' in Egypt and Mesopotamia. Where Moon/Earth goddesses brought forth the forms of life, Moon gods fertilized and quickened them. Even the more sober commentators concurred: Cicero writes that the Moon 'contributes strongly by her influence to the growth of plants and the increase of animals',[1] and Lydus that 'the Moon is the principle of generation.'[2]

One of the primary 'arguments' for this was that the reproductive cycle of human females appeared to follow the cycle of the Moon.

THE MOON AND MENSTRUATION

The coincidence of the lunar cycle with the rhythmic cycle of women is so precise as to create in the early human mind an identification between them. No constant correspondence is arbitrary in a unified vision, and so in many places around the world it was inferred that the Moon was the 'cause' of menstruation, and, further, that Moon and women were alike in their natures, embodying the same law. When portrayed as feminine, the Moon's own periodical swelling up and down was the prototype for human females, who followed the Moon's cyclical course through menstruation, pregnancy and childbirth. When portrayed as masculine, the Moon – imagined as god, man, bull, serpent or moonbeam – was supposed actually to enter the bodies of young girls, bringing the first fall of blood and, later, conception and birth.

In many languages, words for Moon, month and menstruation are identical; in other languages, the words are cognate – that is, related – and readily identifiable. Menstruation is frequently spoken of as 'the Moon', which was originally also 'the month'. For instance, Greek: *mene*, moon, *katamenia*,

Fig. 1. Eskimo Mask of Moon as 'person,' holding a water bucket and a dog or polar bear, attached to a leash of sinew thread. The ring around the mask is the 'world circle,' and attached to it by black feathers are the animals the Moon hunts. A blue bird with outstretched wings, the migratory eiderduck, may signal the transition to winter, Moon's season, where the other animals on the mask are hunted: the fox in his winter coat of white, seal, walrus, codfish, flounder, shrimp and humpback salmon. The hands and feet, extending beyond the 'world circle,' suggest the range of his influence, relating it to human life below. National Museum, Copenhagen.

menstruation; Latin: *mensis*, month, *menses*, menstruation, while *menstruum* meant both a monthly payment or term of office and, in the plural, *menstrua*, the blood of the *menses*. *Mensura*, measurement, defines this common idea, since the course of both Moon and menstruation enables the measuring of days and so the calculation of time. Gaelic words for 'menstruation' and 'calendar' are practically the same – *mioach* and *miosachan* – and in Central America the Mayans pronounced their great calendar to have originated in correlating the female menstrual cycle with the cycles of the Moon.[3]

In the Chukchee reindeer herders' story of the *The Girl and the Moon Man*, it was the Moon's attempted abduction of the girl which began the process of negotiation culminating in the Moon's offer to measure the year, so suggesting a relation between menstruation, months and the measurement of time.[4] In Polish, the word for Moon, month and menstruation is the same; in German, *Mond* is Moon, *Monat* is month, *Mens* is menstruation; in French, menstruation is called *le moment de la lune*. In the Congo, the same word is used for Moon and menstruation (*ngonde*), as it is in the Torres Straits, in India, and in western Sudan, among many other places.[5] The Iroquois of North America consider that all menstruation begins when the Moon is new; others that it begins in the waning, still others when the Moon is full, but, whichever phase is selected, a link is assumed.[6]

The English word 'period' comes from the Greek *peri-hodos*, literally meaning 'way round', and so circuit or cycle, so even there the word retains its ancient lunar reference. Aristotle refers to the 'Moon's periods', meaning measuring points of phase or cycle.[7]

INITIATION BY THE MOON GOD

The Mataco Indians of northern Argentina tell a story which holds the Moon responsible for initiating menstruation, and so bringing the female cycle of fertility into being.

> Once upon a time, when the Moon was young, he was a great hunter but a spasmodic eater. When he had caught his game he would eat without stopping, growing larger and larger until he was completely full up. Then he would starve himself and grow thinner and thinner for fourteen days until there was hardly anything left of him at all. Then he started again.
>
> One night he married a girl from the local village, but she died. He married another girl, but she died too. And then another, and another, until people began to wonder what was going on. The strange thing was, all the girls died five days after the wedding. But the Moon could not remember a thing. He only remembered going to bed with his wife and waking up in the morning to find her dead beside him.
>
> Yet the Moon wanted to marry again. This time the girl's family made her promise to stay awake all night and see what happened. They made a plan that she would go home to her family in the day and sleep there instead. At first the Moon was very kind to her. But when the time came to consummate the marriage, being well rested and so wide awake, she got a good look at him. And she saw that the Moon would split her in two, and that must be how his other wives had died. So for both their sakes she left him, and the Moon was alone for many years.
>
> Years later, he went to visit his grandchild who was now fifteen years old (no one was quite sure where *she* had come from). He begged her to come home with him and she agreed, for she lived in another village and had not heard about the Moon's effect upon his wives. One night on the journey, when she was sleeping, he got up to his old tricks again but he only managed to penetrate her halfway. She woke with a scream, torn and bleeding from her wound, but still alive and very angry. And that is why all women have menstruated ever since – because of the Moon.[8]

The metaphor of largeness suggests that consummation with the wives took place at the Full Moon, such that the wives' deaths are incorporated into the shrinking of the Moon, as emblematic of the Moon's own dying in the waning. But the granddaughter was no wife, and the attempted penetration illegitimate and 'untimely'. That the granddaughter survived suggests that the Moon's violation took place in the waning, when the Moon was in his thinning phase. Waning and menstruating are thereby allied, the loss of light in Heaven becoming the loss of blood on Earth.

In many early cultures the Moon was personified as male, and often this male was a wily one who preyed upon maidens, stealing into their chambers at night while they were sleeping, and when they awoke they found they were bleeding. Menstruation, it was inferred, had been initiated by the Moon through intercourse, earning him his title 'Lord of Women'. The Uaupe Indians of the Upper Amazon speak of a girl's first menstruation as 'defloration by the Moon'.[9] The Papuans thought menstruation began when the Moon visited a girl in her sleep, a view common to most Australian aboriginal tribes and to the people of the Pacific islands, for whom the Moon is almost always masculine and the Sun feminine.[10] Intercourse with the Moon god was given as the cause of menstruation in Japan, the Baltic countries, India, Siberia, Greenland and Alaska, and Terra del Fuego, among many others.[11]

A tale from the Urubu Indians of Brazil makes the relation between Moon and menstruation less direct. The tale is a familiar one. There was a man who lay with his sister at night when she could not see who it was. One night she painted his face black. The brother ran away from his village and climbed into the sky where he became the Moon, with the black paint still marking his face. His sister climbed after him and became the Evening Star. The moment the Moon appeared in the sky all the women menstruated, crying: 'Ah we have seen a bad thing.'[12]

Briffault proposes the idea that the Moon was originally personified as male as a way of explaining menstruation:

> The moon is by all peoples in the lower phases of culture regarded primarily as a male; this is doubtless on account of the notion...that menstruation is due to sexual intercourse of the Moon-god with women. In later stages the sex of the lunar power is usually changed, and the moon, the 'Lord of the Women', becomes the chief goddess in mythological pantheons, the Great Mother...The cult of moon deities, whether male or female, is everywhere the special cult of women.[13]

Briffault wrote this in 1927. We would not be so certain today that we knew what the 'lower phases of culture' were, nor how we could define them without presuming the culture out of which we were speaking to be the higher phase. However, the prevalence (though not universality, as he implies) of male Moon gods in earlier times continually needs emphasizing to those cultures which assume that the Moon is female, such that other cultures for whom the Moon is male have 'got it wrong'.[14]

MOON BLOOD

The moisture that filled the Moon in the imagination of early people – whether dew, rain or Soma – could also be interpreted as blood. Blood is the essence of the water of life in the animal kingdom, and the 'Red Moon' was often seen as filled with blood. Ovid may talk metaphorically of 'Diana's chariot stained with blood',[15] but in earlier times the Moon, when imagined as a goddess, was believed by certain tribes actually to menstruate herself – a belief that lasted in some parts of India at least up to the twentieth century.[16] The waning Moon was spoken of as 'sickening' in many places, Switzerland and Mesopotamia among them. Some North American Indians believed that the Moon 'bled' during her waning, as did some European 'peasants', talking of the Moon's 'red rain' or 'heavenly blood'.[17] Ishtar's own 'evil day' was the Full Moon, the *sabattu*, meaning 'heart-rest' (when the Moon appears to rest at the full). On that day the taboos to be observed – not working, not eating cooked food, not going on a journey – were the same taboos enjoined upon the menstruating woman.[18]

'Moon blood' was supposed to fall from the skies upon the place beneath. The Ashanti called the day of the New Moon the 'Day of Blood', while the Yoruba from Nigeria and the Mendis from Sierra

Leone believed that the corn and rice would turn blood red if they worked on the fields that day.[19] The Maori speak of menstruation as 'moon-sickness', *mate marama*, and the African Mbuti (Pygmy) people give the name 'moon maiden' (*matu*) to menstrual blood.[20]

Take 'cow-eyed' Hera with her 'white arms', the old Pelasgian Earth goddess, only late in the life of her worship annexed as Zeus's wife.[21] In Greek tales the Moon is usually called Selene (and also, at particular times, Artemis, Hekate, Athene, Demeter and Persephone), but Hera's rituals show her also to be a goddess of the Moon as well as of Earth.[22] She was known as a single goddess in three phases, corresponding to the three phases of the visible Moon: virgin, *Parthenos* or *Pais* (crescent), fulfilled one, or wife, *Teleia* (full), and widow, *Chera* (waning and dark), after she had left Zeus and returned to her lake at Stymphalos – by which is implied the abstinence of the couple due to menstruation.[23] Greek medicine followed myth, with Galen (the second century AD Greek physician to Marcus Aurelius) declaring that the Moon controlled the monthly period of women. Kerenyi adds that 'the Romans openly assigned the periodicity measured by the lunar month to the woman's nature – *provinciam fluorum menstruorum* – of their Juno' (Hera's Roman counterpart).[24] Hera's statue was bathed as the new-born Moon rose in the sky (rendering her virgin once more), and she was 'married' at the Full Moon; but her statue was bound at the New Moon, in her 'most dangerous aspect', the time when she was invisible and believed to be menstruating.[25]

Less literally, the Moon's affinity with women was taken to mean that, as the Moon lost its light in its waning, so did the women lose their blood in the waning of their own Moon, their own month – an argument which might have seemed to, say, Aristotle, as circular. But that would be to place logic ahead of myth. This is Aristotle himself in *History of Animals*:

Fig. 2. 'The Moon on the Heads of Women.' Anonymous French engraving. Early 17th c. Bibliothèque Nationale.

The onset of the menses develops during the wane of the month; hence the sophistic riddle – the moon too is female because the women's menstruation and the moon's waning occur together, and after the menstruation and the waning both are made full.[26]

Menstruation can, it seems, be used to account for the Moon as male or female, according to culture but, whichever way it goes, Moon and women are connected. Indeed, this connection with menstruation was extended to the whole of the female life of women. A nineteenth-century Maori statement could stand for many similar: 'The moon is the permanent husband, or true husband, of all women, because women menstruate when the moon appears.'[27] When the Tuhoe, a Maori tribe, see the New Moon they say: 'The *tane* [husband] of all women in the world has appeared.'[28] As Esther Harding comments: 'This correspondence between woman and the moon is taken to be absolute proof of the "fact" that they are of like nature.'[29] This idea, and its implications, can still be recognized in customs, proverbs and folk ways whose significance is realized only dimly if at all. For many thousands of years the Moon was the particular deity of women in their specifically womanly role of childbearing: the one who would help with becoming pregnant and giving birth and getting their children to grow. Offering the Moon a central role in the miraculous process of birth becomes more intelligible if we recall that now, as then, the ultimate achievement in any part of it is never our own – gods come forward when humanity steps back, even when the gods are called simply Nature.

In fig. 2, while the men appear to be stumbling or frolicking with their lanterns on uncharted ground, the women, crowned with crescents, dance the round dance of the Moon in an ordered circle before the houses. The contrast between the men and the women, suggests that the men have to make their own light with their lanterns, while the women receive the Moon's gifts directly from the Moon. The moonbeams from the Full Moon, culminating in the crescents upon the heads, draw the dancers ecstatically into the spell of the Moon, turning them into 'loonies', the Moon's people, only later a term of contempt.

A modern North American Indian tale dramatizes a perception of women's affinity with the Moon through the image of an umbilical cord which goes from the Moon to the woman, just as it goes from the woman to her child. As recently as 1981, Leonard Crow Dog, a Sioux medicine man, told a story he said had never been told before but which was as 'old as life'. It came to him in a dream out of the 'World of the Minds', and it went like this:

> Sun created all things, together with the Grandfather Power, *Unknowingly*, who was invisible yet had many forms and who was the Great Spirit yet was also the Sun in part, just as the Sun was part of him. When the Sixteen Hoops came into being, and the Orbits, the Planets, the Stars and the Earth, then the Trees who speak to each other, the Plants and the Four Seasons and the Four Directions – when everything was there – the great Sun said: 'it's time for creating the Birth people, for forming them up in pairs.' A tear from Sun's eye of the universe dropped down upon Earth and turned itself into a blood clot which became Blood Clot Boy. After many aeons, Sun took out one of his eyes and threw it on the wind of his vision and it became the Moon. On the Moon he created woman. In the darkness, at the time of New Moon, Sun touched the woman: 'You are a Moon-maiden,' he told her, 'I want you to walk on Earth.' So Sun made a bridge of lightning from Moon to Earth and the woman walked down upon it. The Great Spirit let blood roll into her, so while she walked on the lightning 'she also walked on a blood vein reaching from the Moon to the Earth. This vein was a cord, a birth cord that went into

her body, and through it she is forever connected with the Moon.' Understanding was given to the man and the woman to know that they were man and woman who could themselves create. The man's understanding came to him through lightning, through the Sun's blood that was in him, and the woman's understanding came to her through the Moon's vein, through 'that birth cord which connects her to the Moon and whose power she still feels at her Moon time.' So the man and the woman brought forth twins who themselves had children who were taught in a vision the way of sacred survival, the dream, the sacred things and understanding. When the First Man and the First Woman imparted this to the many tribes that had sprung from them, the seven million aeons of creation ended.[30]

An immediate exception to the association of 'Moon blood' with women is provided by the Yanomamo tribe of Brazilian Indians, who imagine their Moon full of blood and as ferocious as their own male hunters, such that the Moon is 'in the blood' of the men. One of their creation myths has it that males and females were created from different sources: the males from 'Moonblood' and the females from a fruit (*wabu*). What happened was that one of the Ancestors shot Moon in the belly and his blood fell to Earth and changed into men; but where the blood fell thickest the men were so fierce they all but exterminated each other. When the blood fell in droplets, or when the blood was mixed with water, the men were less violent and more likely to survive. The Yanomamo term for the beginning of time is the 'Time of Moonblood'.[31]

WANING AND MENSTRUATING

It seems, then, that the waning of the Moon and the menstruation of women were once identified, to a greater or lesser extent. Menstruation was the waning of the woman's own Moon (whether or not it coincided with the waning of the actual Moon). This might offer one further perspective on the extraordinary taboos that existed around menstruation in earlier times, horrifying details of which are given in Frazer's *The Golden Bough*.[32] In early thought, the waning of the Moon was the prelude to death in the Dark Moon and so was viewed with alarm and foreboding. Similarly, as Harding points out, menstruation was often regarded as the death of the potential baby, and so, with the typical elaboration of the chain of association, it became also the potential death of other living beings.[33] In Indian myth an analogy was drawn from the creation myth of the Ocean of Milk: as the milk coagulated to form the world, so blood retained in the womb clotted into babies, while blood lost had failed to clot. To the equatorial Desano Indians of the Amazon, for instance, for whom the male Sun is semen and the female Moon a 'blood-bloated liver', every menstruation is the death of a child.[34] Compare the poem *Lesbos* by Sylvia Plath:

> That night the moon
> Dragged its blood bag, sick
> Animal
> Up over the harbour lights.
> And then grew normal
> Hard and apart and white.[35]

Pliny, in his *Natural History*, attributes great powers for good and ill to the hapless woman who is menstruating: her touch can blast vines, ivy and rue, dry up seeds, make fruit fall off the trees, fade

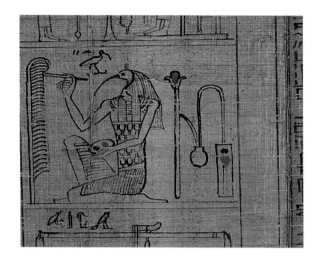

Fig 3.22

Fig 9.1

purple cloth, blacken linen in the washtub, tarnish copper, make bees desert their hives, and cause abortions in mares; but she can also rid a field of pests by walking around it naked before sunrise, calm a storm at sea by exposing her genitals, and cure boils, hydrophobia and barrenness.[36] As with the Moon, the 'waning' can be harnessed to get rid of things not wanted. The Jewish *Talmud* surpasses even this by stating that if a menstruating woman passes between two men, one of them will die.[37] The witches of Thessaly, whom Socrates mentions disparagingly in the *Gorgias* as 'drawing down the Moon',[38] were thought to make their spells from a girl's first menstrual blood shed during an eclipse of the Moon.[39] Dew that dropped for the witches to use in their spells was gathered from the ground as Moon blood. Graves writes that 'the magical connection of the Moon with menstruation is strong and widespread.'[40] A further parallel is found in a text related to the *Manava Dharmasastra*, sometimes called the 'Laws of Manu' (compiled in the second century AD), where it is said that 'A woman in her courses is impure during three days and nights,' but that her sins are taken away month by month,[41] analogous to the idea of the Dark Moon/flood cleansing of the old to make way for the new.

Like the Moon, the menstruating woman was, in extreme cases, given the power of life and death, inviting us in retrospect to note the analogy drawn between them. It seems as if the irrational terrors attributed to the Waning Moon were transferred onto the act of menstruation – the Moon shedding light and the woman shedding blood in the same period of time (or rather, perhaps, in the same imaginative space). Alternatively, it could be that the original fears of menstruation as death were transferred onto the Waning Moon.[42] The divergence of opinion as to which 'projection' was the model for the other serves to highlight the problem in allotting priorities of thought, especially when neither option is susceptible to empirical proof. On the other hand, the very fact that both 'facts' are false leads us back to the human psyche, which may be either finding an outer form to relieve an inner perplexity, or groping, albeit unconsciously, for a truth of a different kind.

THE MOON AND CONCEPTION

In ancient India, Soma, god of the Moon and the waters of life, was also the 'First Husband of Women' as well as the 'Lord of Plants'.[43] This suggests that Soma is the miraculous *power* of growth in the natural world: the elixir as blood, semen, sap and seed, in the waxing mode. This power is miraculous because it transcends human understanding: it may be described, but it cannot be explained.

The *Rig Veda* has the bridegroom in the wedding ceremony acknowledge: 'Soma has acquired thee as his wife.'[44] Then, when the woman becomes a mother, she brings forth, vicariously, the Moon's seed, a new form of Soma. The *Kaushitaki Upanishad* describes the plight of one who, newly born, is asked by a sage: 'Who art thou?' Having returned to Earth as rain from the Moon, he should answer:

> From the wise moon, who orders the seasons, consisting of fifteen parts when it is born, from the moon who is the abode of our ancestors, the seed is derived. This seed, even me, they (the gods) gathered up in an active man, and through an active man they brought me to a mother.[45]

This suggests a further reason why the Moon is the 'real' husband of women. For if, as many cultures believed, the Moon was the abode of souls, and souls went to the Moon to be reborn, then the Moon ultimately is the one who will impregnate the women to bring about the birth of the souls in his care – yet another image of eternity giving birth to time.

Here, Soma's seed, whether conceived as metaphor or fact, belongs to a way of thinking in which the whole of the temporal world is 'seeded' by the eternal world, so that Soma's priority is inherent in the nature of things – of course 'He' would come first. In Persia, also, the *Zend-Avesta* says that Haoma 'gave a good child to those women who wanted a baby, one that would be just.'[46] In one Buddhist legend, Buddha himself was begotten by the Moon from the wife of Brishpati.[47] Other cultures retained the idea of the Moon's fertilizing power but viewed it more as a threat, an idea that makes sense of Laertes' warning to Ophelia in *Hamlet*:

> The chariest maid is prodigal enough
> If she unmask her beauty to the moon.[48]

So the Moon, as Lord of the life of the womb, was for many early people the 'first' father of the new-born child. For this reason the curtains were closed on the nights of the Full Moon in countries as far apart as Australia, Greenland and Brittany, in case the moonbeams, streaming through the open window, were to fertilize chaste maidens as they slept. Women in Greenland would spit upon their fingers and rub the spittle on their bellies before daring to lie upon their backs to sleep.[49] Meanwhile, an earthly husband wishing to father a child upon his wife had to wait until the New Moon in Uganda, the first quarter of the Moon in Texas, and the Full Moon in Vancouver.[50] In Texas, immediately after marriage the North American Indian women would stand naked over a pail of water saturated with rays of moonlight in order to conceive.[51]

Similarly, in central Europe women drank from a well or spring which held the Moon's reflection in order to 'swallow the Moon' and conceive.[52] Breton women would go to the megalithic dolmen of Cruz-Moquen in the town of Carnac and lift their skirts,[53] while in the Loire valley children's rhymes spoke of 'Madam Moon, giver of babies'.[54] In Nigeria some tribes believe that the Great Moon Mother sends the Moon Bird down to earth to bring babies to women – a tale reminiscent of the European stork (a bird that is also black and white) who carries babies to their mothers in its beak.[55] When mothers all over the ancient world held their babies up to the Moon, often calling the Moon 'father', 'grandfather' or 'uncle', they were asking the Moon to help his own child to grow.[56]

Crescent-shaped necklaces – called *lunulae* – have been worn throughout the ages to engage the energies of the Moon in the processes of birth. 'Birth beads', worn as talismans during birth by African slaves in American plantations, were mostly shaped to the Crescent Moon.[57] The prophet Isaiah denounced the daughters of Zion for wearing 'their round tires like the moon.'[58] Early Christian Gauls made Communion cakes in a crescent shape, and they are still made in modern France as *croissants*, 'crescents' (from *croisser*, to grow), colloquially called 'moon-teeth'.[59] 'Crescent' means 'growing' in Latin – from *creare*, 'to create' – as it does still in English, 'increase', 'crescendo'; in Italian, *crescente* means waxing and *decrescente* means waning. In *Anthony and Cleopatra*, Pompey employs the lunar metaphor, though to no avail:

> My powers are crescent, and my auguring hope
> Says it will come to the full.[60]

Zimmer writes that 'sickle of the new moon, swiftly increasing' is in Sanskrit a 'familiar term for the rapidly growing infant.'[61]

In D.H. Lawrence's *The Rainbow*, the Moon is asked to play its traditional role. Ursula, dancing in the darkness with Skrebensky, suddenly turns and sees:

> a great white moon looking at her over the hill. And her breast opened to it, she was
> cleaved like a transparent jewel to its light. She stood filled with the full moon, offering

herself. Her two breasts opened to make way for it, her body opened wide like a quivering anemone, a soft, dilated invitation touched by the moon. She wanted the moon to fill in to her, she wanted more, more communion with the moon, consummation. But Skrebensky put his arm round her and led her away.[62]

* * *

The danger of the Moon's potency was, inevitably, that it could not be controlled. Women in Brittany would cover their bodies so the Moon's rays could not reach them, especially when the Moon was 'horned' (bull-like) in the first and last quarters, in case they would be 'mooned' (French, *lunée*), and give birth to a 'moon-calf', by which they meant a lunatic child.[63] 'Moon-calf', originally a child of the horned Moon Bull, then became a name for someone carried away for love of the Moon ('calf-love'), but, as the sacredness of the Moon declined, it became a term for a misshapen offspring (in some cases thought to be deformed because of a 'malefic' Moon).[64] In *The Tempest*, Stephano, the King of Naples' drunken butler, calls Caliban a 'Moon-calf' because he is deformed, to which Prospero later adds, 'He is as disproportioned in his manners/As in his shape.'[65] Caliban was the son of Sycorax, a witch who could 'control' the Moon, giving a further meaning to 'Moon-calf'. So when Prospero finally claims Caliban as his own moral darkness – 'This thing of darkness I/Acknowledge mine' – the term 'thing of darkness' may have had for an Elizabethan an even denser lunar resonance within it, deepening the moral frame.[66]

THE MOON AS FERTILIZING BULL

Whether for good or ill, the potency of the horned Moon is assumed.[67] No wonder the southern Slavs used to speak of the bridegroom at a wedding as 'Mr Moonshine'.[68] When a husband is pronounced 'cuckolded' (when, like a cuckoo, another takes over his nest), he is often obliged to 'wear the horns' upon his head, as though to acknowledge the priority of the 'horny' Moon.

The idea of the fertilizing Moon taking the form of the supremely potent horned bull has a long inheritance. In Mesopotamia the Moon god Nanna-Sin, also imagined as a bull, was asked 'to renew the seed of royalty eternally'.[69] In Persia the Moon is addressed as 'Thou moon, that dost keep in thee the seed of the bull'; and when this seed had been cleansed in the light of the Moon, two creatures were shaped from it, a male and a female, from which came forth 272 kinds of animals.[70] In Egypt, the sacred bull, Apis, fathered by a moonbeam, was identified with Osiris,[71] who was himself often addressed as a bull, the one through whom 'many conceptions take place':

> Bull, that groweth young in the heaven each day...at thy rising up into the sky wretchedness departs...when thou art seen in the sky on this day many conceptions take place...the Power of Osiris which is Thoth...The Nile appeareth at thy utterance...making all cultivated lands to be green by thy coming, great source of things which bloom, sap of crops and herbs, Lord of millions of Years, sustainer of wild animals, lord of cattle...[72]

Khons or Khensu, the Moon god in Thebes who becomes old and young 'when he pleases', is compared to a fiery bull in his waxing and an old ox in his waning:

> The moon is his form.
> As soon as he has rejuvenated himself

Fig. 3. Ex-voto inscribed in Greek to 'Men Saviour' (top left) and 'Giver of Riches' (top right). The god's head within the crescent rests upon a pole supported by the single-eyed bull's horns which are placed to match the horned crescent above. The animals and birds, clustered around or upon the pine cone, are among his gifts. A caduceus bears witness to his powers of transformation, as do more than 20 Moon Crescents. Marble bas-relief found in Attica. (From Cumont, Le Symbolism Funéraire des Romains).

he is a heated bull.
When he is old he is an ox
Because he causes only darkness.
His waxing moon, however, brings light,
Causes the bulls to cover,
Brings the cows in calf,
And causes the egg to grow in the body.[73]

On the walls of the Temple of the Moon at Thebes, it was inscribed: 'through his agency women conceived.'[74]

The central images of the Phrygian Moon god Men were the crescent and the matching crescent-horned bull, as in fig. 3, where the pine cone, goat, goose, sheep and other animals are the life that the god makes fertile.

THE MOON AS SEDUCING SERPENT

The seductive powers of the Moon were frequently transferred to the serpent who was granted considerable success (and not just in the Garden of Eden), what with his phallic shape, his undulations in trees and pools, and the re-arising of his own life from beneath his old, discarded skin. In the Abruzzi it was said, even in the 1950s, that the serpent copulates with all women, a view astonishingly common among the Greeks and Romans.[75] Pausanias had no qualms reporting that one Aratus of Sicyon was said to be a son of Asklepios because his mother had conceived him from a serpent; the same thing was said by Suetonius and Dio Cassius about the mother of Augustus, who embraced a serpent in Apollo's temple.[76] We are obviously out of the realm of the literal here. What has happened is that serpents have been brought into the fertility and immortality symbolism that surrounds the Moon: they seduce women, bring about menstruation, conception and birth, and carry the souls of children along with them as they slither from place to place. They also bring rain. In the *Borgia Codex* of the Aztecs, a snake wounded by an arrow means rainfall, and in India, according to the *Grhyasutras*, rituals of venerating the snake begin at the Full Moon in the first month of the rainy season, and end at the Full Moon in the first month of winter.[77]

Among the Togos in Africa, for instance, it was still told in the 1950s that a giant snake lives in a pool near the town of Klewe and receives all the children of the town before their mothers do. The supreme god Namu gives them to the snake, who then brings them into the town to be born.[78] In the Mysore province of India, the Komati tribe make snakes of stone to engender fertility in the women, and in some of the Nagpur paintings women are shown mating with cobras. Snakes as consorts of the Great Goddesses, or simply as images of the goddesses' powers of fertility and regeneration, are found wherever these goddesses are depicted, from the Neolithic to the Bronze and Iron Ages and beyond. Remnants of this tradition exist in some central European superstitions, which hold that the hairs of a woman 'under the influence of the Moon' will turn into snakes if they are pulled out and buried.[79]

Many of these ideas can be traced in the continuing story of the snake-haired Gorgon, whose severed head was received from Perseus by Athene, who wears her snakes hanging from her gown. Athene gives two phials of the Gorgon's blood to Asklepios, god of healing: with blood from the veins on the left of the Medusa's body, Asklepios could raise the dead, and with blood from the right (or was it the left?) he could instantly destroy – a startling image of the duality of the Moon/serpent powers. The snake who is the 'familiar' of Asklepios, never absent from him or his wife, Hygeia, is then the lunar snake with the Moon's powers of life and death (Chapter 11, fig. 3). Two serpents intertwined around a central pole – the two forces yoked in perfect equilibrium – is still the sign of healing today, known as the *Caduceus*.[80]

In Greece, it was Hermes who held the caduceus wherever he went, he who was called the messenger of the gods but was once a Moon god and a daemon of fertility. Apollo, bewitched by Hermes' singing, gave him the caduceus as the magical wand that guides souls to the underworld and back. This movement between life and death refers to the state beyond the opposites of waxing and waning, as might be expected from the vision of male and female serpent in embrace, creating the third term, the life renewed. A stylized caduceus was often drawn as two facing crescents above a circle, suggestive of the cycle that rests beneath and so supports the phases, in the way that a perspective upon the waxing and waning of vicissitudes can lead beyond them.

THE LUSTY MOON

The Balts' way of understanding the Moon's relation to generation was to see the Moon as a seducer. The Balts' Moon god was called *Meness* in Latvia and *Menuo* in Lithuania, both names still close to the original Indo-European, apparently because Christian missionaries found the Baltic languages so unspeakable that the pagan religion lasted longer there than anywhere else in Europe. Both the Latvian *Meness* and the Lithuanian *Menuo* behave in the same way: they are married to *Saule*, the Sun goddess, and seduce the Sun maiden, her daughter, who is the younger form of the Sun herself as dawn and spring when the Sun is gentle and fresh.

Saule had three husbands – *Dievs*, the sky father, *Perkons*, the storm and rain god, and *Meness* himself – though the three husbands may once have been the triple Moon god in his phases of waxing, full, and waning.[81] Earth is the daughter of Sun and Moon, while Sun's other children are the stars. It was the

Moon's seduction of the Sun maiden, Sun's lovely daughter, which destroyed the 'first spring', the original dreamtime. For the Sun maiden was betrothed to *Auseklis*, god of the Morning Star, but *Menuo* seduces her while her mother is not looking:

> The Moon wedded the Sun
> In the first spring.
> The Sun rose early at dawn,
> The Moon wandered alone
> Courting the morning star.
> Perkunas was wroth,
> He cleft the Moon with a sword.[82]

This clefting of the Moon by the storm god breaks the Moon into the pieces of its waning, which are gathered together again by the forgiving Sun maiden, though the violence leaves its mark upon the Moon god's face. In another version, Moon's wife, *Saule*, dismembers him for violating her daughter:

> The Sun shattered the Moon
> With a sharp sword
> Because he stole the bride-to-be
> Of the morning star, Auseklis.[83]

After this, Sun and Moon divorce and live on their own. Now Menuo rides through the night in a starry robe on a chariot drawn by black horses, protecting travellers like himself from harm. But once upon a time Moon and Sun used to travel the skies together, side by side.[84]

In Greenland, the Moon's seductive powers can be put to good use, for Moon who made the sea-tides and gave women menstruation was also happy to offer impregnation when it was required. Once a woman who was barren was running away from a cruel husband who beat her when she met the Moon outside in the dark. He invited her for a ride on his sledge and took her up to his house in the sky. There, he made sure she became pregnant and then sent her back home, barren no longer.[85]

The correspondence between the Moon and 'Moon blood' meant that the Moon could withhold fertility as well as grant it – 'unloosing their moons, month after month, to no purpose', as Plath puts it in her poem *Perfection*.[86] Another poem, *Childless Woman*, begins:

> The womb
> Rattles its pod, the moon
> Discharges itself from the tree with nowhere to go.[87]

In *Three Women*, the childless woman is talking of the Moon:

> It is she that drags the blood-black around
> Month after month, with its voices of failure.
> I am helpless as the sea at the end of her string.[88]

* * *

Folklore is permeated with remnants of the Moon's ancient powers. Crediting the Moon with knowing who the true love is to be, and asking the Moon to reveal it in dreams, was common throughout Europe. In nineteenth-century Scotland, many women would curtsey to the New Moon and in England they would bow to the New Moon three times, some saying 'Lady Moon I hail thee,' while others, sitting astride a stile, would add:

> I prithee good Moon, declare to me,
> This night, who my Husband must be.[89]

Across the sea in France, girls were singing:

> *Lune, lune, belle lune,*
> *faites me voir en mon dormant*
> *le mari que j'aurai de mon vivant.*[90]

Customs of marrying only at Waxing or Full Moon, hiding from moonlight at Full Moon, hoping to give birth at a Full Moon, and taking cover from an eclipse if pregnant, lead back to a time when waxing and waning could mean life and death. Inevitably, interpretations of dreams followed these hopes and fears. In *A Treatise of the Interpretation of Sundry Dreams* (1601), it is said: 'Hee which seeth his image in the moone, not hauing children, doth foreshew the birth of a sonne to ensue; but to the woman like dreaming, to haue a daughter.'[91]

The 'silver sixpence' in the familiar wedding rhyme slips the Moon back into a modern marriage ceremony under the guise of good luck, silver being the Moon's own metal: 'Something old, something new, something borrowed, something blue, and a silver sixpence in her shoe.'

THE MOON AND CHILDBIRTH

The very pregnant Palaeolithic Goddess of Lespugue (fig. 4), found buried in a ditch near the cave of Lascaux in France, has ten vertical lines from waist to buttocks, suggestive of the ten months of pregnancy, counting by Moons. Turn her the other way up – the body tapers to a point at both ends – and these lines become strands of hair, allowing her to appear as the dual goddess of light and dark. Whichever 'end' of her was placed in the Earth (allowing her to stand upright) became fruitful, the dark changing into its own light and the light changing back into dark, like the waxing and waning of the Moon.

As the Moon, pre-eminently in the heavens, was the one who grew old and then new again, appearing to give birth even to itself, it makes sense that the Moon should have become the model for giving birth on Earth. Moon deities were invariably patrons of childbirth, whether conceived as male or female: Phrygian women in childbirth called upon their Moon god, Men, as 'the Deliverer',[92] while Mesopotamian women called upon Nanna-Sin and Inanna-Ishtar.

Inanna-Ishtar was called the 'opener of the womb of all women' (as was Ki-Ninhursag, her grandmother, before her), and Mesopotamian women would go to the sacred 'cow byre', the temple of Inanna, to give birth under her protection.[93] Pregnant Mayan women went to the sacred island of Ixchel, their Moon, Rainbow and Snake Goddess, to have their babies, or they put an image of Ixchel under their beds at home.[94] The upturned jar which Ixchel holds (see Chapter 3, fig. 14), signalling the falling of rain, also portrays the vase of the womb opening its waters, letting the birth begin. Ishtar, Isis, Heqet the frog goddess, Bast the cat goddess, Neith, Hathor, Artemis, Hekate, Hera, Diana, Juno-Lucina (Juno the light-bringer), Freya, Holda, the Virgin Mary – all are goddesses whose help is invoked at the time of birth.

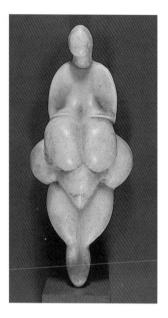

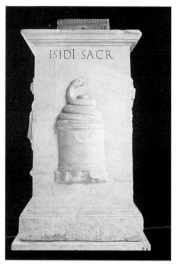

Fig. 4, a. Goddess of Lespugue, front. Mammoth ivory statue. c. 20,000 - 18,000 BC. Height 5 1/2 in. (14 cm). From Haute-Garonne, France.

Fig. 4, b. Goddess of Lespugue, back. Musée de l'Homme, Paris.

Fig. 5. The Basket of Isis. Marble altar. Two ears of wheat sprout from the cup of the crescent Moon, while the coiled serpent rises from the basket as the transforming power of the Goddess. From Caligula's Temple to Isis, Rome. 1st century AD. Museo Capitolino, Rome.

'May Artemis, the far-darter, look with blessing upon the child-bed of women,' the chorus prays in Aeschylus' *Suppliants*.[95] The women in Euripides' *Hippolytus* also sing: 'I felt this thrill, this chill, in my own womb, but I cried to the heavenly archer, goddess Artemis, who presides over childbirth.'[96] It was the cry of women in the raw animal moment of birth which called Artemis away from the wilderness of sky and mountain down to the inhabited plains. In the hymn of Callimachus she says: 'Upon the mountains I choose to dwell, and I mingle amongst city-folk only when women in the anguish of travail call upon my help.'[97] 'Helper in pains whom no pain touches,' the *Orphic Hymn* invokes her.[98] Helpless babies also cried to her to care for them, so she was the *kourotrophos*, 'nurse of children'.

The Polynesian Moon goddess in her full phase – Hina-Keha, 'Bright Lady' – was also goddess of childbirth, whose magic formula for an easy delivery was still being used by women in New Zealand early in the twentieth century. The story went that, in her 'dead' phase (when she was the 'Indigo Lady', Hina-Uri), the Moon goddess drifted down into the sea and became entangled with weeds. The tides washed her ashore inside a matted heap of seaweed and kelp, and she lay there trapped, waiting to be delivered. By good fortune an Earth man discovered her and thought she was a woman. They fell in love (though he was already married), and in due course Hina was ready to give birth to her son, Tuhuruhuru. But the birth became difficult, so she composed a special chant and, while she was reciting it, was delivered of the baby quickly and safely.[99] As the dark Indigo Moon, she possesses the secret of new life, for even when she is submerged in a sea of darkness and smothered in seaweed she is soon to be reborn. In this way the Moon's secret of rebirth becomes the world's gift of birth, for all babies are born into life out of the dark waters of the womb.

In the seventeenth century, Indian women in Peru used to pray to the Moon to give them an easy delivery;[100] in Ireland, two centuries later, Ulster midwives were still chanting to the woman in labour a song called *Moon of the Four Quarters*. The midwife marked the four corners of the house with the crosses of Brigit, the fire goddess, queen of the Sun's cardinal movements; then, on the threshold, the midwife sang:

> Four corners to her bed.
> Four angels at her head.
> Mark, Matthew, Luke and John;
> God bless the bed that she lies on.
> New moon, new moon, God bless me.
> God bless this house and family.[101]

'To this sound,' Michael Dames comments 'the newborn child entered the world.'[102]

BIRTH AND THE PHASES OF THE MOON

Many myths point to the Full Moon as the time of easiest childbirth for the mother and the most fruitful entry into Earth for the child, participating in the Moon's fullness of light and life. Plutarch, for whom the gods are both real presences *and* ideas and principles, understood the Moon's control over moisture as leading to the Moon's role in childbirth: 'The moon is also said to assist in easing childbirth, when it occurs at full moon, by making the pains gentler by releasing moisture. For that reason...Artemis who is none other than the moon is called *Locheia* [midwife] and *Eileithyia*' [goddess of childbirth, literally, 'she who comes in need'].[103] European women called upon the Moon as the 'Moistener' and the 'Dew-bringer', while in Greece among many other places it was once believed that waxing gives an easy birth and waning a difficult one.[104] Even today, many people claim that there are more births at the Full Moon.[105]

Folklore is in no doubt of the wisdom of harmonizing with the Moon when human nature needs all the help that Nature can offer. So the assumption that 'childbirth is easier during the waxing moon than during the waning phase' was confirmed by the assurance that 'people cannot die when the Moon is rising, unless it has passed full and is on the wane.' Birth at a Full Moon or a full tide brought a 'lucky life'.[106] Following this logic, it was not a good idea to be born when the Moon was dark: 'No Moon, no man', was the phrase current in Cornwall at least up to the 1920s,[107] and put into the mouth of Timothy Fairway in Hardy's *Return of the Native*. Fairway is talking to a young man, Christian, a 'faltering man with reedy hair', who introduces himself as the man no woman will marry, adding that his mother said there was no moon when he was born. Mr Fairway's response was not encouraging:

> '"No moon, no man." 'Tis one of the truest sayings ever spit out. The boy never comes to anything that's born at new moon. A bad job for thee, Christian, that you should have showed your nose then of all days in the month.'
> 'I suppose the moon was terrible full when you were born?' said Christian, with a look of hopeless admiration at Fairway.
> 'Well, 'a was not new,' Mr Fairway replied with a disinterested gaze.[108]

Such beliefs ramify: West Virginians, recalling life back home in Scotland and Ireland, used to say: 'If a baby is expected, it will be born right after the Moon changes'; 'if the moonbeams are strong at the time of a child's birth, he will always make friends easily.'[109] Similarly, in the old Arab tradition, a dream in which a pregnant woman sees a beautiful crescent is interpreted as 'will have a nice baby'; but a husband dreaming of 'a crescent looking red' means 'wife will have a miscarriage'.[110]

The very young were thought to be especially vulnerable to the particular phase of the Moon. Lithuanians used to wean boys on a Waxing Moon so they would grow strong, and girls on a Waning Moon so they would become slender and graceful.[111] On the other hand, in Greece, nurses were careful not to expose young children to the loosening effects of the Moon (at the full), since, like green wood, they have enough moisture in them already, and would be thrown into spasms and convulsions.[112]

THE MOON AND THE FERTILITY OF ANIMALS

Nanna-Sin's power to renew himself was shown each time he reappeared as a new crescent:

> ...lamp appearing in the clear skies,
> Sin, ever renewing himself, illuminating darkness,
> bringing about light for the myriad people.[113]

Nanna-Sin's city, Ur, was situated on the lower Euphrates along the edge of the marshes, where orchardmen and cattlemen lived together on the riverbanks, hedged around with reeds. It was probably the orchardmen who saw their god as a 'fruit self-grown', and the cattlemen who saw him as a 'frisky calf of Heaven' as well as a herdsman himself, tending his own star herds in his crescent boat: 'Calf of the crown, when for the calves thou carest.'[114] In the minds of his worshippers Nanna-Sin was thus eminently suited to promoting the fertility of cattle and plants, especially as they already looked to him for the spring floods on which that fertility depended.

In a Sumerian song, Nanna sends a message to his wife Ningal, goddess of the marshes, asking her to join him at the top of his ziggurat at Ur. He tells her of the delicious food he has prepared for her. Ningal answers that she will come to him only when he has filled the rivers with water and the fields with grain, and when he has put stags in the forest and plants in the desert, and when he has made honey and wine plentiful in the orchards, got cress to grow in the garden and given long life to the palace. Only then, Ningal says:

> In your house on high, in your beloved house,
> I will come to live...
> Where cows have multiplied, calves have multiplied,
> I will come to live,
> O Nanna, in your mansion of Ur
> I will come to live,
> O lord! In its bed I for my part
> will lie down too![115]

In some parts of Lapland, at least before the 1950s, it was the custom to sacrifice a reindeer calf and hang the hide inside the tent and, outside on the roof, to hang a ring of copper tied to a copper chain so that the fertilizing rays of the Moon could fall upon it. For then the Moon would help the reindeer cows to give birth to their calves easily and would protect them from injury while they were with calf. The animals sacrificed to the Moon were never black and never males. As soon as the Christmas New Moon was visible, complete silence was observed in the tent. The women were forbidden to weave and the men to do any noisy work. A ring of copper was placed in the smoke hole of the tent to draw the moonbeams down through it; for if they could not get through, the Moon would be angry and would have to be

Fig. 6. The Cow jumping over the Moon. 1880. (From Johnsons, Nursery Rhymes, 1880).

placated with sacrifices.[116]

In Ireland, rituals to the New Moon were specifically linked to the well-being of cattle. The seventeenth-century traveller William Lithgo was obviously not a native:

> 'They also at the sight of each new moon (I speak it credibly) bequeath their cattle to her protection, obnoxiously imploring the pale Lady of the Night that she will leave their bestials in as good a plight as she found them, and if sick, scabbed or sore, they solicitate her maiden-faced majesty to restore them to their health.[117]

In present-day St Lucia, an island in the Caribbean, some of the hill farmers still believe that if a cow mates in the first phase of the Moon she will bring forth a male calf.[118]

Folk remnants of the Moon's fertilizing powers may also lurk in the familiar cow of childhood who jumped over the Moon.

> Hey diddle diddle, the cat and the fiddle,
> The cow jumped over the moon.
> The little dog laughed to see such sport,
> and the dish ran away with the spoon.

The lunar symbolism established so far allows us to speculate that this milk-giving cow is less fanciful than she used to seem. In the Scandinavian *Manavegr*, the Milky Way was known as the 'Moon Way',[119] and in Celtic lands it was called the 'Track of the White Cow'.[120] The English word for 'galaxy' comes from the Greek word for mother's milk – *gala* – where the silvery-white stars appear as drops of milk sprinkled across the night sky. Either 'cow-eyed' Hera spurted forth the galaxy as she suckled the infant Heracles, or it was Rhea, wife to Kronos, suckling Zeus, or, as the Ionians said, it was their own Moon Cow, Io, 'the Moon', whose milk streamed out into the dark.[121] The popular saying that 'the moon is made of green cheese', used first by Sir Thomas More (1478–1535) and then by the French wit François Rabelais (1495–1553), presents itself as an iconoclastic image of the Moon's yellowy face blotched with shadow like an overripe cheese dotted with green mould.[122] But actually a 'green cheese' is a new cheese, one that has not yet aged or been cut, and in earlier days would have resembled the Full Moon in colour and shape. Yet even this homely image draws on the idea of the Moon as curdled into a ball of cheese from its own milk, out of which the Milky Way was made. As Job said to his God: 'Hast thou not poured me out as milk, and curdled me like cheese?"[123]

It may then be that the once perplexing nursery rhyme turns out to be an eighteenth-century play on lunar imagery: the White Cow, leaving a trail of her star-milk across the sky as though suckling her children, the stars. The Moon Cow may have been the self-fertilizing mother or she may have been impregnated by the Moon Bull, recalling the Egyptian Horus who flew at night into the mouth of Hathor, the Cow, and became 'the Bull of his Mother'.[124] The other animals in the nursery rhyme, the cat and the dog, are both lunar animals, while the dish evokes the crescent cup of the Moon which gathers the ambrosial milk, and perhaps the spoon, scooping it out, just rhymes.

A poem from the Sanskrit gives the image a haunting quality:

> Black clouds at midnight;
> Deep thunder rolling.
> The night has lost the moon;
> A cow lowing for her lost calf.[125]

THE MOON AS THE HUNTER

Those who hunt their prey in the light of the Moon may come to see themselves as prey for the hunting Moon, when it arches its waning crescent as a bow or hangs as a sickle in the darkness. For the crescent that in the waxing is a cup of potent waters, or a bow 'new-bent' for change, becomes in the waning 'thinned/To an air-sharpened blade',[126] poised to cut down the lives it once had grown.

Many of the Moon gods and goddesses are portrayed as hunters as well as givers of fertility, as though in the waxing they give life and in the waning they slay. It all depends whose life it is. For the Bushmen, the life of their game animals was thought to depend upon the Moon,[127] just as the Inuit hunters shared their fish, birds and animals with the Moon who both created and hunted them.[128] In New Guinea, while the men went out hunting, the women stayed behind to sing to the New Moon for the success of the hunt.[129] In England, the large Full Moon after the autumn equinox, known as 'Hunter's Moon', recalls a time when activities were timed to the Moon not the month, and when silver bullets were preferred over lead bullets for witch-hares and infidels.[130]

Inanna-Ishtar, who opened the wombs of women, also carried the bow of Sirius. 'Which of your lovers did you ever love for ever?' asks Gilgamesh, fearing to be discarded, or sacrificed, in his turn.[131] The star Sirius was called the 'Bow Star' in the image of Inanna-Ishtar in her hunting mode, since its rising at sunrise in high summer brought intense heat and drought: water dried up, plants withered, and the people fell beneath the arrows of hunger, thirst and disease. The vegetation of the Earth – in the image of the goddess's 'son', Dumuzi-Tammuz – died and went down to the Nether World where Ereshkigal, the Dark Moon, was queen.

Artemis, 'who roves by night', glancing 'with her starry eye',[132] was the Hunter Goddess as well as Goddess of Wild Animals and Childbirth. She could have inspired the saying of Heracleitus: 'Life: a name for the bow is life, but its work death.'[133] In the *Iliad*, Hera accuses Artemis of hunting women in childbirth: 'A lion to women Zeus has made you, and granted you to slay any at your pleasure.'[134] The clothing of women who died giving birth was offered to Artemis at her temple in Brauron, where young girls danced to her in the costumes of bears.[135] When Artemis is angry, then either, Callimachus says, 'the women die in child-bed, smitten by her shafts, or if they survive, bear children that cannot live.'[136] Without the idea of the light and the dark Moon – the cup and the bow as one, or Artemis and Hekate as one figure – it is initially baffling to see why the goddess who protects women in childbirth should also be the one who slays them, unless it be that both life and death are under her protection, and the protection of the goddess cannot be taken 'for granted' – until she grants it. In a trice Artemis could turn into Hekate and reverse her gifts: This is the 'two-fold torch', of which Sophocles writes,[137] bringing light *or* darkness, easing the young into life or hunting them down.

It is surely no coincidence that Artemis of the silver bow and 'moaning arrows', goddess of the wild, untameable domain of Nature, should be the most feared goddess in the Greek pantheon. She received greater sacrifices than any other god, for hers was the raw, volatile dimension of life farthest from human ordering. She was the image of the light of life that could, unaccountably, go out. How remote this idea seems from the familiar domestic ritual of a child having to blow out *all* the candles on a birthday cake in one go. Yet this was originally a Greek rite to celebrate the birthday of Artemis when, on the sixth of every month, candles were arranged on altars in the temples and special cakes were baked in the shape of the Moon. At the height of the ceremony, all the candles had to be blown out at once with one breath to ensure that Artemis would look kindly upon her worshippers.[138]

The symbolism of the single breath is suggestive of the one completed round of the cycle, while the absolute darkness that is left when the lights are extinguished is evocative of the dark phase of the Moon, which must be fully accomplished for the crescent to reappear as the next 'birth' of Artemis, who might then herself be wished 'many happy returns' (with some relief) for if *she* does not 'return' then neither, it may be, do we.

The Roman counterpart of Artemis, 'smiter of deer', was Diana who, like most of the other Roman deities, initiated no radically new stories but assumed the character of the Greek model, becoming at once more concrete and more abstract, as the vital presence of the divinities moved away.[139] Cicero offered an etymological pun upon her name: 'Diana is associated, it is thought, with the moon...she is called Diana because at night she makes the day (*dia* for 'shining' and *diem* for 'day').'[140] Diana is rarely drawn without a stag or hound beside her, bow and arrows slung across her shoulders, an image which continued to inspire artists up to the Renaissance and beyond. Ben Johnson hails her under the name of Cynthia in his play *Cynthia's Revels*:

> Queen and Huntress, chaste, and fair,
> Now the sun is laid to sleep,
> Seated in thy silver chair,

Fig. 7. Artemis as huntress. Attic pelike. c. 380 BC. British Museum.

State in wonted manner keep:
Hesperus entreats thy light,
Goddess, excellently bright.[141]

The Germanic sky and Moon goddess Holde, Holle, Holl or Hel, who rode upon the wind and bathed in lakes and streams, had the by now familiar fusion of qualities which give life and take it away. She presided over the cultivation of flax and spinning of it into thread, yet was also leader of 'the furious wild hunt'. The souls of unbaptized babies – as later Christian theology saw it – went to Holde's realm after death (later to be known as 'Hell'). There they followed after her in the wild hunt through the sky and over the fields, which would then yield double the usual harvest.[142]

Reichel-Dolmatoff describes how, for the Desano, a tribe of the Tukano Indians of the north-western Amazon, the phases of the Moon regulate both hunting and sex, constituting a calendar for birth control, the protection of game and the restriction of the production of many materials. The Desano watch the lunar phases very closely, considering them to be correlated with female fertility and the growth cycles of animals and plants. Sexual intercourse is prohibited between New Moon and first quarter, and also during the waning of the Moon and the three nights of darkness. He writes:

> This cycle is geared to hunting and fishing activities; fishing is said to be most profitable in dark nights, between new Moon and first quarter, but when the Moon becomes brighter, hunting and fishing must be interrupted, to be resumed during the waning and dark nights. Shamans say this programme is quite intentional, to keep the men away from the women at night. Older women support the shamans, and both are blunt about the birth control aspects of them.[143]

In 1924 some Eskimos from the island of Nunevak, off the west coast of Alaska in the Bering Sea, called properly Nunivaarmiut, spoke to the explorer Knud Rasmussen, sharing their stories with him and eventually showing him their sacred masks. He learned that while both Moon and Sun were related to the annual cycle of hunting and fishing, it was the Moon to whom the shamans travelled during a seance if the hunting failed, to ask for help with the hunt and for fine weather and good health. The shaman would wear

Fig. 8. Diana the Huntress. Marble statue, Germain Pilon. Mid-16th century. The Louvre.

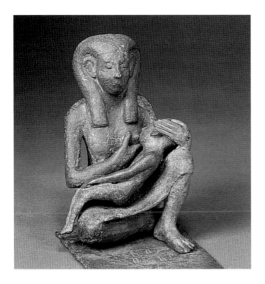

Fig. 9. *Isis nursing Horus. Copper statue. 2040-1700 BC. Staatliche Museen zu Berlin.*

Fig. 10. *Mary nursing Jesus. Painting on wood. Sandro Botticelli. c. 1470. Musée du Petit Palais, Avignon.*

the mask at the Full Moon to ally himself with the 'Moonman', since Moon loved to hunt all the animals dangling from the 'world circle' on his mask (fig. 1).[144] An essential rite of the hunt, then, was imaginatively to identify oneself with the Moon as the greatest hunter, taking on his knowledge and his power. Shamans from neighbouring Canada and Greenland said they knew, from their own journeys to the Moon, that Moon created life – both on the Earth and in the sea – through his 'dog', which could also transform itself into a polar bear.

Winter, the time of the seal hunt, belongs to the Moon, while summer, the time of the caribou hunt, belongs to the Sun. Every month and every year, Moon and Sun relive their unhappy love affair when Moon received the marks of soot upon his face.[145] In winter, Sun turns pale and loses height until the middle of winter when she gains in beauty and strength, becoming irresistible in spring when Moon's desires are aroused again. In summer, when Sun is at the height of her power, Moon grows pale and weak and bides his time until winter.[146]

THE CYCLE OF REBIRTH

A child born of a goddess is a child born from the eternal realm. In lunar symbolism, this is the crescent of the new cycle, figured through the ages as the reborn Dumuzi, Tammuz, Horus, Attis, Dionysos, Persephone, Adonis and Jesus, to mention only those whose names we know. Whether the divine child is read as an image of humanity cradled in the lap of the Great Mother, or as the returning springtime of Nature in bud, shoot and leaf, and all the lambs, kids, foals and calves of the season's new mothers; or whether it is read as an image in the heart, born from the vast deeps of the Great Memory or the World Soul, it is an image which clothes each child entering the world. In the Sufi poet Rumi's poem, the Angel Gabriel says to Mary:

> O Mary! Look well, for I am a Form difficult to discern.
> I am a new moon. I am an Image in the heart.[147]

CHAPTER 9

THE MOON AND PLANTS

The moon like a flower,
In heaven's high bower
With silent delight
Sits and smiles on the night.
Blake *Night*

Many people who would not now suppose the Moon to hold water, rain or dew, nor believe it to be the fertilizing power in human and animal conception, will yet sow their seeds in the waxing and full of the Moon, and harvest their fruits in the waning.[1] The connection made between the Moon and the patterns of growth in plants seems to have survived longer than any other (except perhaps lunacy). And to bewilder those who dismiss such practices as at best wishful thinking and at worst craven superstition, a television series in 1999, entitled *Supernatural: The Unseen Powers of Animals*, declared that the Moon 'really does have a profound influence on plants.'[2] In the 1950s, experiments suggested that the rising and setting of the Moon affected the rate at which carrots and potatoes took in oxygen, and subsequent experiments claimed that many plants grow better at some times of the cycle than at others, some germinating more quickly at Full Moon (radishes and forest seedlings), and others absorbing minerals more easily at the New and Full Moons.[3]

More recent research has shown that tree stems follow the daily lunar cycle by swelling and shrinking, just as the tides do, and, like the tides, tree stems have two 'high tides' a day. The modern explanation does not implicate the Moon's pull on the water inside the tree but the Earth's magnetic field, which pulses to a lunar rhythm and is strongest when the Moon is directly above or below it.[4] The Moon also creates tides in the crust of the Earth, which bulges towards the Moon when it passes overhead, as though there were waves in the body of Earth. The research purports to show that Moscow rises and falls twice a day by as much as 0.5m (20in), while Europe and North America are pulled towards each other and then pushed apart by 20m (65ft). This would explain why there are more earthquakes around Full and New Moons than at any other time in the lunar cycle.[5] It should, perhaps, be left open, in view of the last five millennia's lunar claims, as to whether we should consider this research to be entirely valid on its own terms, or to be but one more stage in our incomplete understanding of our interrelationship with the rest of creation.

The assimilation of the cycles of plant life to the cycles of the Moon has a long and ancient history, which was originally founded on the imaginative power of analogy rather than hypothesis and experiment (though one might ask, where does a hypothesis come from?). To a mind attuned to celestial cycles, vegetation waxes and wanes like the Moon. So the plant, like the crescent, emerges as a shoot from the dark underworld of death, flourishes like the Waxing Moon to its full flowering and fruit, when, shedding its flower, leaves, fruit and seed, as the Moon its light, the plant finally disappears back into the darkness from which it came. In the New Year of the following spring, the seed returns, reborn like the New Moon. This pattern of thought comprehended both lunar and vegetative life

Fig. 1. 'The Starry Hall of the Queen of the Night.' Aquatint by C.F. Thiel after Karl Friedrich Schinkel's set design for Mozart's opera The Magic Flute. 1815. University of Cologne, Theaterwissenschaftliche Samlung.

as one process, drawing on the Moon's other spheres of influence: light was life because it was moisture and fertility. Plutarch says: 'The Moon, having the light which makes moist and pregnant, is promotive of the generating of living beings and of the fructification of plants.'[6] But it may be that the underlying reason why this moist light was 'pregnant' was because it came from, contained, or itself *was*, the water of eternal life which had the power to bring vegetation back from death.

If it were simply, as Ptolemy says in his *Tetrabiblos*, that the Sun heats and dries, while the Moon humidifies,[7] then this original preference for the Moon as the source of growth might be less likely to prevail in temperate climates. For the burning Sun, which deals death to plants in hot countries by drying up their water, brings elsewhere seasons of fruitfulness and relief from bitter cold. But in many cooler countries also – even in ice-covered Greenland – the Moon was attributed with the power of growth even though the Sun warms the land and melts the snows, after which shoots appear above the ground. Eliade argues that the relation between Moon, rain and plant life was made before the

Fig. 2. *Beanlike plant within oval discs or eggs, possibly representing Moon phases, connected by undulating snakes. Painted black on red. The vase as a whole configures the process of regeneration. Cucuteni B, Koszylowce, Galicia, W. Ukraine. c. 3500 BC. (From Gimbutas, Language, p. 222).*

Fig. 3. *Plant or tree inside circles, connected by undulating snakes, and interspersed with round discs, probably representing phases of the Moon. Terra-cotta vase, painted brown on red. Mycenaean. 14th c. BC. (From Gimbutas, Language, p. 222).*

discovery of agriculture in the Neolithic Age (8000–3500 BC), being derived, like all things cyclical, from the law of universal fertility found in the Moon.[8] But, surprisingly, even when people began growing and cultivating plants for themselves, and saw the dependence of their plants on the seasons brought by the Sun, the belief in the Moon's powers did not die out for a long time. Apart from the fact that it is always difficult to change beliefs and withdraw projections even when we know they are wrong, one reason for this delay may be that the Moon was still believed to be the source of water which the Sun dried up. Another reason may be that this water was ambrosial water, holding the secrets of the life-force and its renewal, a code still untapped.

MOON DEITIES OF WATER, PLANT AND TREE

This relation between the Moon and plant life was expressed mythologically in the depiction of Moon deities as gods and goddesses of vegetation, typically the plant which above all others sustained the tribe. The 'Old Woman who never dies' of the North American Indian agricultural tribes was the 'Mother' of corn and vegetables.[9] The ancient Mexican Great Mother, who was goddess of the Moon and the Waters, was also 'She of the Maize-plant'.[10] The Persians said that the Moon 'flows towards the pastures to give food',[11] while in Deuteronomy the Moon is called the bearer of 'all things precious'.[12] Torches of the Moon goddess Hekate were carried around the fields after sowing to make them fertile.[13] Porphyry (233–304 AD) writes of his countrymen that 'the power productive of corn-crops, which is Demeter, they associate with the moon as her productive power', adding that 'the moon is also a supporter of Kore; they set Dionysos also beside her.'[14] Up to the nineteenth century in many places around the world, the Harvest Moon, rising as the Sun is setting, was thought actually to ripen the crops by shining all night.

Where rice was the staple food, as in the islands of Indonesia, the Moon contained the rice spirit and had to be appeased with sacrifices. The people of Mori in central Celebes believed that the rice spirit *Omonga* lived in the Moon and ate up the rice in the granary if he were not treated with respect.[15] The Tomori People of Central Sulawesi performed sacrifices to Moon for rice.[16]

In Peru, the story goes that the Moon gave cultivated plants to mortals, instructing a young girl whom he married. He caused her to be fertilized by a fish, and she brought forth four children: the daytime Sun, the Sun Under the Earth (the Sun at night), the Morning Star, and the Nocturnal Sun (the Moon), which was invisible but lit up the stars. This last child was so hot he burnt his mother's

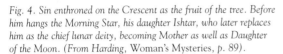

Fig. 4. Sin enthroned on the Crescent as the fruit of the tree. Before him hangs the Morning Star, his daughter Ishtar, who later replaces him as the chief lunar deity, becoming Mother as well as Daughter of the Moon. (From Harding, Woman's Mysteries, *p. 89).*

Fig. 5. Moon-man with 'saladberry bush' and bucket. Wooden model of the crest of North American Haida Indian Chief, 'He Whose Voice is Obeyed.' From Skidegate, Queen Charlotte Island, British Columbia.

womb and she died. The girl's mother was angry with the Moon and told him to eat his wife's corpse, since her soul had gone to the underworld. This the Moon did, and so he became an eater of corpses and moved far away from Earth.[17] As with other myths, the Moon is linked both with the discovery of plants and with death and decomposition.

The Mesopotamian Moon god Nanna-Sin was hailed as the 'Green One', the 'Creator of the Grasses' and 'Lord of Vegetables', as were Inanna-Ishtar and Dumuzi-Tammuz after him. Inanna-Ishtar was called 'Mistress of the Field', 'She of the Springing Verdure', the 'Green One', 'Mother of the Vine-stalk'.[18] Sin was himself conceived as a fruit, the 'fruit which brings forth from itself', and in a Babylonian seal his crescent is drawn resting on a field.[19] A hymn to Sin goes:

> As for thee, thy decree blows above like the wind,
> and stall and pasture become fertile!
> As for thee, thy decree is accomplished upon earth below,
> and the grass and green things grow![20]

Sometimes Sin is represented as the trunk of a tree, with branches and leaves growing from him, like the Green Man of later European lore (fig. 4). Cuneiform inscriptions state that the healing herb of Sin 'is cut after sundown and before sunrise when one has veiled one's head and made a magic circle of flour around the healing herb.'[21]

So often glimpsed between the tangled branches of trees, as though resting in the boughs on its way down to Earth, the Moon had in many countries its own Moon Tree in which the fructifying dew was gathered and transformed. Sometimes this tree was also seen in outline in the Moon's orb. This gives the idea of the Tree of Life whose sap never runs out and whose fruit is, as Neumann puts it, 'the precious fruit of the full moon'.[22] In many lands – Polynesia, Melanesia, Moluccas, China and Sweden, among them – trees were seen in the Moon of the kind that gave evergreen its name: as often as they were cut down each month, the next month they would grow again, as did the cinnamon tree in the Chinese Moon.[23] For whatever grew on the Moon would be nourished by its ambrosial water and would never die. In fig. 5, which shows the crest of the North American Haida Indian Chief, 'He Whose Voice is Obeyed', the man in the Moon holds a 'saladberry bush' in one hand and a bucket of

Fig. 6. Shrine of the Sacred Moon Tree, with crescent beneath the altar and a worshipper seeking help. The tree leans towards the supplicant as if in answer to the prayer. Minoan gem from Crete. (From Harrison, Themis, p. 190).

Fig. 7. Sacred dance of three priestesses beside an altar containing three upright crescents and three down-turned crescents. Gold seal ring found at the Mycenaean cemetary of Aidonia, near Nemea, Peloponnese, Greece. c. 1,500 BC.

water in the other, while the lunar bear clambers up the column.

The bundle of thorns for firewood or the thorn bush, carried in Europe by the man in the Moon, takes on a more than biblical meaning when it is realized that thorn bushes were sacred to the Celts and the Teutons, only to be cut for sacred purposes and used for cremating the dead.[24] In the South Pacific, according to Captain Cook, 'the spots observed in the moon are supposed to be groves of a sort of trees which once grew in Otaheite, and, being destroyed by some accident, their seeds were carried up thither by doves, where they now flourish.'[25] Indeed, Plutarch finds the Moon an ideal habitat:

> What wonder then if on the moon there grow roots and seeds and trees that have no need of rain nor yet of snow but are naturally adapted to a summery and rarified air? And why is it unlikely that winds arise warmed by the moon...and by scattering off and diffusing dews and light moisture suffice for the vegetation and that she is herself not fiery or dry in temperament but soft and humidifying?[26]

In Cameroon, the identity between Moon and tree is complete: a Moon priest can take the Moon down from the sky and plant her in his garden, as if she were a banana tree.[27]

In Iroquois myths, a luminous tree once lit the upperworld, and when the Moon came down to light up the Earth she did all the things the first tree used to do.[28] In South America the sacred pachimba-palm tree is thought to have fallen from the Moon (and, when chewed, to grant magical gifts), while in the Admiralty Islands the coconut palm is said to be the same as the Moon.[29] In New Britain the Full Moon is supposed to have come out of a sugarcane.[30] It seems as if the Moon is identified with each tribe's most important source of food, as a way of attributing generation to the Moon for the fruits of the Earth.

In the Minoan gem from Crete (fig. 6), the Moon rests beneath the tree, in the centre of a sanctuary as the invisible source of growth. 'The cult of the moon in Minoan times,' Harrison comments, 'is a fact clearly established,' while the conjunction of Moon and olive tree points forward a thousand years to Athens, to the *Pandroseion*, the Moon shrine in the Acropolis, Athene's temple.[31]

The ancient *Hymn of Eridu* (from the people who were later called Chaldeans, 'Moon-worshippers', and founded the city of Ur) places the white-rooted Moon Tree at the centre of the Earth, like the *Axis Mundi* of the Tree of Life:

Its root of white crystal stretched toward the deep...Its seat was the central place of the earth; its foliage was the couch of Zikum, the primeval mother. Into the heart of its holy house which spreads its shade like a forest hath no man entered; there is the home of the mighty mother who passes across the sky; in the midst of it was Tammuz.[32]

Here, Tammuz is given as the sap and fruit of the tree – 'in the midst' – source of the immortal juice as the ever-recurring New Moon, 'the Wanderer', 'my Lord the Honey-man', as Ishtar calls him.[33] The 'mighty mother who passes across the sky' would be Ishtar as the Moon, who reunites with her son-lover when she comes 'home'. The Moon Tree which brought the Moon dew down to Earth was common in Babylonia and Assyria, sometimes abstracted into a pole or three pillars or a cross, or modified into a lotus or fleur-de-lys.

As we have seen, the common belief was that when the moon waxed, moisture on Earth below also waxed, such that the sap rose and fell in a lunar rhythm. Plants, like animals, were thought to be at their juiciest in the waxing, and so to grow faster, while during the waning, living things dried out and slowed down. As the *Zend-Avesta* says: 'When the light of the moon waxes warmer, golden-hued plants grow on from the earth during the spring.'[34] Plant juices were seen as the concentration of lunar power, as were the fluids that exuded from their stems and leaves – the resins, gums and incense – so that pressing the juices out of the plant, fermenting and then drinking them, was to imbibe the divine essence of the moist Moon. Osiris, Inanna-Ishtar, Tammuz and Men, as well as Dionysos, are identified with the cultivation of the vine. The South American Huitoto thought that the Moon itself waxed by drinking *chicha*, a kind of beer, which was the blood of the Moon.[35]

MOON PHASES AND EARTH

In an intellectual climate when the Moon set the time and the weather, gave the rains and dews, and was the source of all growth, it would seem foolhardy not to profit from the timing of its own rhythms of energy; but, more likely, it would have been unthinkable to ignore the celestial pattern. Light was moisture was growth, on Earth as it was in Heaven, and, more precisely, waxing light in heaven meant waxing moisture and growth on Earth, a process that went into reverse in the waning.

To summarize again, the primitive assumption behind this idea of 'lunar sympathy' is that what happens to the Moon happens to Earth. The gelding of animals, the shearing of sheep, the cutting of corn and cutting down of trees – these are 'waning' activities, for both the Moon and the animal, tree and plant are losing something, breaking into pieces together. Conversely, when the Moon is growing, earthly matters grow: planting, putting eggs under the hen, grafting, the mating of animals – these are the 'waxing' activities of increase. This idea contained the related idea that not only does everything grow better in the waxing, but that living things are also stronger and more resilient, less vulnerable to harm and decay. It followed that, in the waning, living things grew weaker and diminished, and so were more likely to become ill and die.

We need not be surprised, then, that the sowing of seed took place in the Waxing Moon and that these same plants would be harvested in the Waning Moon. This was the way to work in accordance with the laws of fertility, and these laws were originally felt to be in the dominion of the Moon. Many classical authors in their different ways drew on this basic idea – Hesiod, Aristotle, Hippocrates, Plutarch, Horace, Pliny, Galen, Virgil, Cato, Varro, among others. Hesiod's poem *Works and Days*, written in the eighth century BC, is the earliest work in the West to advise farmers how to work with the phases of the Moon. 'Avoid the thirteenth of the waxing month for sowing; it is best for setting plants.'[36] Onions were the odd one out, sprouting in the waning and withering in the waxing.[37] Roman writers, such as Pliny and Cato, also recorded rules of planting and harvesting by the Moon, distinguishing primarily between the activities proper to waxing and waning.[38]

While the aim was to harness the Moon's power of growth for human ends, the interpretation of the means often varied. To take some examples: sheep must be sheared in the Waxing Moon so their wool may grow again as quickly as possible, but hay and grain must be cut under the Waning Moon so they do not ferment or sprout; trees must be felled under the Waning Moon when their moisture would be dried out – if felled under the Waxing Moon they would go on growing and the wood would not mature. This custom was given the status of law in pre-Revolutionary France, where it was prohibited to cut wood except in the Waning Moon. Fruit should be gathered and cattle gelded in the Waning Moon. But pigs must be killed in the Waxing Moon, for if they are killed in the Waning Moon then 'the bacon will waste away with the moon'.[39] Horses and mares must be put together in the increase of the Moon. Root crops must be sown in 'the dark of the moon'. In *Tusser's Husbandry* (1580), the lines for February go:

> Sowe peaseon and beans in the wane of the moone,
> Who soweth them sooner, he soweth too soone;
> That they with the planet, may rest and rise,
> And flourish, with bearing most plentiful wise.[40]

But what, then, of the cottager who has a different rhyme?

> Sow new beans when the moon is round
> They'll pod down to the ground...[41]

The Old Farmer's Almanac, still in use in America, makes the general notion clear:

> Plant flowers and vegetables which bear crops above the ground...during the LIGHT of the moon; that is, between the day the moon is new and the day it is full. Flowers which bear crops below ground should be planted during the DARK of the moon; that is, from the day after it is full to the day before it is new again.[42]

It is as though a Light Moon would encourage plants to grow upwards into the 'light' of air, and a Dark Moon would draw plants downwards into the dark of the soil. Like is to create like, but of what is this likeness composed? Even today, a Welsh adage for planting potatoes is not to plant until Good Friday, the day when Christ descended into the darkness of hell. Yet the date of Good Friday can vary from 19 March to 21 April, since the timing of Easter is set by the Moon, giving a long variation for potatoes. Lunar 'superstitions', as they were called by sceptics, were often mocked: 'He (the superstitious man) will not commit his seed to the earth when the soil, but when the moon requires it',[43] though superstition, dismissed by Dr Johnson as 'vulgar philosophy', was to Yeats 'popular poetry'.[44]

Given the basic assumption of 'sympathy', these principles are intelligible on their own terms, but sometimes the sheer density of detail reads as though the Moon were asked to serve as the guide and governor of all earthly affairs, releasing the dilatory from uncertainty and indolence alike. These, for example, are the duties to be found for *The English Housewife* in March 1683:

> In March, the Moon being new, sow Garlic, Chervil, Marjoram, white Poppy, double Marigolds, Thyme and Violets. At the full Moon, Chicory, Fennel, and Apples of Love.

At the wane, Artichokes, Basil, Cucumbers, Spinach, Gillyflowers, Cabbage, Lettuce, Burnets, Leeks and Savory.[45]

The hint of a paradigm comes when we remember how one aspect of the Moon's qualities characteristically invokes the rest. Recalling the Moon's power of decomposition – the way, as Pliny said, it disengages moisture from bodies, putrefies, thaws ice and 'unstiffens everything with moistening breath'[46] – it is fascinating to come across the folklore of a small deciduous fern called *Botrychium lunaria*, or Moonwort, also called 'unshoo-the-horse' because it drew the nails out of the shoes of any horse who trod on it. The seventeenth-century herbalist Nicholas Culpeper quoted commanders in Devon who found 30 horse shoes pulled off the feet of the Earl of Essex's horses, for no known reason.[47] No reason is given either for the other qualities of Moonwort: that if it were gathered by moonlight and pushed into keyholes it unlocked doors, loosened nails on hinges, and turned quicksilver into the precious metal.[48]

The folklore of the mandrake plant is also eloquent of long-lost sources. Etymologically, it is the 'man-dragon' (Greek, *drakon*, 'dragon, serpent'), so called because of the large forked root's resemblance to the forked human being. But it may once have come from the 'Moon-dragon' or 'Moon-serpent' (or the man-in-the-Moon-dragon), if its attendant lunar symbolism of death and generation is anything to go by. Literature of 30 centuries – from the Bible to Persian legends, Machiavelli and Shakespeare – has regarded it as a magical plant, and until the end of the Middle Ages there was no plant more highly prized, used as amulet and talisman, adorning the shields of warriors and wrapped around the necks of babies. It was the cure for epilepsy, a sickness supposedly 'caused' by the Moon. Mandrake was believed to have sprung from the semen of a man hanged on the gallows – and so to be born from death – yet it also brings conception and fertility – and so gives birth to life. It shrieks when it is uprooted, and can only be uprooted by a dog who, burrowing in the dark, dies a sacrificial death when he hears the shriek that releases the plant from the underworld.[49]

Mandrake, also called mandragora, was deadly poisonous yet had magical powers to reveal treasures, give prophecies and provide invulnerability. Its magical ancestry was pointed by calling it the plant of Circe, who drugged her victims in the *Odyssey* (and also by identifying it with the herb moly which Hermes gave to Odysseus to undrug them).[50] It was soporific: 'Give me to drink mandragora,' sighs Cleopatra, 'That I might sleep out this great gap of time/My Anthony is away.'[51] It was also an aphrodisiac: Aphrodite was given the title of *Mandragoris*, and the plant was called 'love apples'. Yet both Circe and Aphrodite have lunar associations, the one through her spinning and the other through her name of *Pasiphaessa*, the All-Shining One. In Palestine and the Near East, well into the twentieth century, mandrake was credited with the power to cure barrenness. The Arabs call it the 'devil's candle' because it shines at night.[52]

* * *

Some gardeners, farmers and herbalists still 'swear by' the timing of the Moon, planting in the waxing not the waning, cutting in the waning not the waxing, and gathering herbs under the Full Moon with the dew upon them, when they will be 'most potent'. In Shakespeare's day this was commonplace: Laertes, thinking of poison, talks of 'all simples that have virtue/Under the moon',[53] while the Players dramatize the poison that killed Hamlet's father as 'midnight weeds collected/With Hecate's ban thrice blasted, thrice infected'.[54] In *The Merchant of Venice*, Jessica, sitting with Lorenzo in the moonlight, remembers Medea, who could heal or poison: 'In such a night Medea gather'd the enchanted herbs/That did renew old Aeson'.[55] Gathering herbs by moonlight with the dew on them was still the custom in Culpepper's time.

Today, Emerson College in Sussex, England, teaches 'Bio-Dynamic' gardening, which is the practice of sowing, planting and transplanting according to the Moon, on the assumption that as the Moon affects the tides it similarly affects the expansion and contraction of liquids in the cells of plants.[56] Seeds are planted in the Waxing Moon and transplanted in the Waning Moon. Further, plants grown for fruit should be planted in a different lunar cycle from those grown for flowers, leaves or roots. These practices are based on the ideas of the late nineteenth-century German philosopher and mystic Rudolf Steiner, who in turn was influenced by the holistic world view of Goethe. In the Loire Valley in France, two wines are now cultivated with Bio-Dynamic methods, using a lunar calendar. Whether the outstanding results of this method are due to lunar timing, organic soil or human care is still under debate.[57]

When it is tentatively put to these and other modern gardeners that they might be enthralled in an ancient myth, they understandably respond with a zealous empiricism – precise and practical evidence of a lifetime's experience – as people close to the rhythms of the Earth have always done.

But now, they can call upon the Grunion fish and the Palolo Samoan worm.

The Grunion fish of California (*Leresthes tenuis*) depend for their survival on a precise timing to the phases of the Moon (fig. 8). In the months from March to August, shortly after the Full Moon, the grunion, riding the crest of the waves of the ebbing tide, are carried onto the shore where they lie for a moment, and then fling themselves into the next wave and are borne back out to sea. In that one moment the grunion lay their eggs in the wet sand, where they will be safe for two weeks because the waves will not come in so far again until the next spring tide. When the waves return in two weeks, at the New Moon, the larvae are ready, and at the first touch of the water they break out of the eggs and are carried back through the surf.[58]

The Palolo worm (*Euncie viridis*), which lives in the crevices of coral reefs in the South Pacific, also reproduces in synchrony with the Moon's time. Male and female worms never meet, but mate at a distance by concentrating eggs or sperm into the hind parts of their bodies, adding an eyespot, and then breaking them off and sending them to the surface of the sea to join with the equivalent parts of the other sex. Obviously, they all need to do this at the same time, and it is the Moon that gives the signal. Each November, at dawn, when the Moon reaches its last quarter, all the worms cast off their hind parts, and around the reefs of Samoa and Fiji masses of copulating eggs and sperm colour the blue sea red. Their timing is so predictable that the local people mark it as the beginning of their

Fig. 8. Californian Grunion fish stranded on the shore between waves, the females laying their eggs in the sand. Discovery Images, Jeff Foott Collection.

New Year, taking to their canoes and celebrating 'the great rising.'[59]

Correspondences between the Moon and these sea creatures, as well as experiments on the Earth's magnetic rhythms, make it seem plausible that some at least of the old plant customs rest on plain and simple empirical evidence (if such a thing in this context can still be said to exist). Yet many of the related connections appear to reach back to a deeper mythopoetic way of thinking, in which the primary impulse is to harmonize with the Moon for a more fundamental reason: to banish death by uniting imaginatively with the processes of rebirth. In the *Arthava-Veda*, the Moon god Soma says to mortals: 'Do not die! I free thee from all evil and disease and unite thee with life. Do thou rise up with life; unite thyself with life, with the sap of plants.'[60] Human beings, in this view, symbolically identifying themselves with 'the sap of plants', may yet 'rise up with life' in a new spring.

THE DARK MOON AND WINTER

The crescent which, in the waxing, ploughs the earthly fields in the form of the crescent-horned bull, becomes in the waning a silver sickle poised to harvest the seed it has sown. Saturn, the old agricultural god who became Time, the Reaper (modelled on the Greek god *Kronos* whose name means 'Time'), is often depicted with his scythe shaped to the curve of the waning crescent.

The dark of Moon and winter is both the end and the beginning of the round. The *Katapatha Upanishad* says: 'when during the night he can be seen neither in the east nor west, it is because the Moon (*Soma*) is visiting the world below, entering its waters and plants.'[61] The complexity of this relation between Moon, water, plants and human beings becomes clearer through the idea of Soma. For Soma is a synthesis of different but related levels of being, all of which are given the same name: the eternal waters of the Moon, the earthly plant, the intoxicating drink, and the Moon god himself, who is 'Lord of Plants' and 'Supervisor of Herbs', as well as the 'First Husband of Women'. This suggests that while Soma is the power that makes things germinate and increase, it is also, or *primarily*, the eternal ambrosia which continually rescues life from death.

The New Moon festival of the Pygmies in Africa suggests how the Moon governs and relates the different cosmic levels of rain, plants, animal and human fecundity, as well as the souls of the dead. Their festival of the New Moon is set just before the rainy season. The Moon – called *Pe* – is believed to be the 'principle of generation and the mother of fecundity', as Eliade describes it.[62] Only the women can celebrate the Feast of the New Moon, just as only the men can go to the Feast of the Sun. Because the Moon is both 'the mother of living things' and 'the refuge of ghosts', the women smear themselves with white clay and vegetable juice, looking like ghosts in the moonlight. Then the women dance and pray to the Moon, and when they tire of dancing they drink a powerful liquid made from fermented bananas and call upon the Moon to give the tribe lots of children, as well as fish, game and fruit, and to keep away the souls of the dead. The men are silent, neither dancing nor accompanying the ritual on their tom-toms.

The perception here is the lunar perception: that life comes from death. At the time when the New Moon has just risen from death, so the women, putting themselves in accord with the Moon, 'play' dead by dressing up as (and so dramatically becoming) the ghosts of humans and plants together as one – smearing themselves with vegetable juice and white clay. The dance of death is then the prayer for life, addressed to the Moon Mother who has both in her keeping.

A similar convergence of ideas is expressed in a creation myth of the Tupis of Brazil, whose Moon is 'Mother of Grasses and Vegetables'.[63] They say that once a young man, white and shining, appeared to a young woman who then became pregnant without intercourse. She gave birth to a child who was white as snow, but after a year he died. A plant rose from the child's grave which bore fruit, and when the people tasted it they felt as if the spirit of a god had entered into them. This was the first manioc plant – the food of the tribe. The white and shining man is like the Moon in its waxing, and the child, white like moonlight, dies like the Moon after one 'round' of life (our term 'annual' comes from the Latin word for ring, *annus*). Out of his death comes the plant that gives food.

In Japan, it is the Moon god who first visits and then kills the Food goddess, releasing Earth's food from her broken body; but this alienates his sister the Sun. For once they were as one, Sun and Moon, the two eyes of the heavenly being, *Izanagi*, looking together out of the face of the heavens. A Shinto myth from the *Kojiki*, 'Record of Ancient Matters' (an oral tradition first written down in 712 AD), tells how in the beginning seven generations of deities emerged from the primeval oily ocean, the last of which were the brother and sister *Izanagi* and *Izanami*, who descended from Heaven on a rainbow bridge which lay above the waters. Learning from the water wagtails how to make love, they brought forth islands, trees and mountains. But when *Izanami* gave birth to Fire she was burnt to death and had to travel the long winding road to the Land of Darkness, the Land of Roots, *Yomi*. *Izanagi* followed her to bring her back, and they met at the gate between the two worlds. *Izanami* told him she had eaten of the food of the dead and so was not free to go, but agreed to ask the gods of the underworld to release her as long as he promised not to look at her. But *Izanagi* broke his promise, and humiliated her. For he looked at death only through the eyes of life, and so he saw his wife as a decomposing corpse and, forgetting who she was, he fled from the horror of it. Izanami was enraged and set the Thunders and Demons of the underworld after him. Using all his magic, Izanagi managed to escape and rolled a boulder across the entrance to *Yomi*, sealing it for ever. To cleanse himself of pollution, *Izanagi* bathed in a river and in the sea, and deities of river and sea arose. Then he washed his left eye, and *Amaterasu*, the Sun goddess, was created; then he washed his right eye, and *Tsuki-yomi*, the Moon god, was created; then from his nose came forth *Susanowo*, Storm, Earthquake and Ocean god. This is how Sun and Moon became the left and right eye of *Izanagi* in the heavens, born, as with the Bushman tale, only after his vision of death.[64]

Amaterasu lived in peace with her other brother, the Moon god Tsuki-yomi, until that day when she asked him to visit the Food goddess, Ukemochi, to see that all was in order. When she heard he was coming, Ukemochi offered him food from her body. She turned her face to the land, and rice poured from her mouth; she turned her face to the sea, and fish leapt out of her mouth; she turned her face to the mountains, and meats spilled from her mouth. This was the feast she prepared for him. But Tsuki-yomi was horrified. He drew his sword and struck her dead. As Ukemochi lay dying, cows and horses appeared out of her head; grain sprouted from her forehead; rice plants sprang up from her belly; silkworms threaded out of her eyebrows. When the Sun goddess Amaterasu heard what Tsuki-yomi had done, she was incensed. So, when she is awake the Moon god leaves the heavenly palace, and only when she goes to sleep does he dare come back.[65]

If fire brought the destructive principle into being in the first story, resulting in the creation of the underworld, then in the second, the Moon god brings death to Earth almost in the form of a revelation: that food comes from the death of others, that life lives upon life. However, this new stage of awareness appears to make possible the next stage: the setting into motion of time. Moon separates from Sun, and they each move through the heavens along their own particular course. After this, Tsuki-yomi was sent down to rule the land of the dead, hence his name, *Tsuki*, (meaning Moon') and *Yomi* (meaning 'of the Dead'). By contrast, the splendour of the Sun as the Great Mother Goddess persists in Japanese lore to this day.[66]

In the Indonesian archipelago, Ceramese myths make an intrinsic connection between the death of the Moon and the birth of plants, presenting the first death in the world as a murder, though a murder necessary for the sake of future procreation. The myths centre around two maidens who are essentially one: *Rabie*, the Moon-maiden, and *Hainuwele*, whose name means 'coconut-palm branch', sometimes called *Rabie-Hainuwele*.

Rabie, the Moon-maiden, was wooed by Tuwale, the Sun-man, who desired the divine maiden in marriage. But her parents, not finding him good enough for their daughter, placed a dead pig in her place in the marriage bed. So Tuwale returned the bridal portion and went away. A few days later Rabie left the village and stood upon the roots of a tree but, while she was standing there, the roots sank into the ground and Rabie sank with them, crying for help. Nothing the villagers did could prevent her from sinking deeper and deeper. When she had gone down as far as her neck, she called out to her mother: 'I am dying. It is the Sun-man, Tuwale, who has come to claim me. Kill a pig and celebrate a feast for me. But in three days, when evening comes, look up at the sky and you will see me shining upon you as a light.' And when her mother and her relations had slaughtered a pig and celebrated the death feast for three days, they looked up and saw for the first time the Full Moon rising in the east. In another story the Moon-maiden hides in a pond after her marriage with the Sun-man, and goes on living as a pig with her child.[67]

The second, related myth starts with the father, *Ameta*, whose name means 'dark' or 'night'. He went out hunting with his dog, who scented a pig in the wood and followed it to a pond, upon which the pig ran into the water and was drowned. Ameta fished out the dead pig and found a coconut on the end of the pig's tusk, which was strange because there were no coconut palms on Earth. When he got home, he covered it up, as they did with new-born children, and planted it in the ground. In an amazingly short time it grew into the first coconut palm, reaching its full height in three days and blossoming in another three days. A drop of Ameta's blood fell on one of the leaves, and in twice three days the maiden Hainuwele was formed. After another three days she was ready to marry. So there was held a great dance, the Maro Dance, in which men and women danced in a ninefold spiral that composed a labyrinth. Hainuwele stood in the middle of the labyrinth beside a big hole dug in the earth. In the convolutions of the spiral dance the dancers pressed towards her, closer and closer, until she was finally pushed into the pit, her cries drowned by the deafening Maro chanting. Earth was heaped upon her and stamped down over the pit with the dancing feet. Then the buried parts of her body turned into things that had not existed before on Earth, especially the tuberous fruits which feed the people.[68] The resemblance of this tale to the Greek myth of Kore-Persephone astonished those who first heard it in the 1930s, members of an expedition organized by Frobenius.

In the Polynesian myth of *Hina and the Coconut*, a specific relation is again made between the Moon's death and the food that gives life to the tribe. *Hina* – or *Ina*, as she is called in yet another variant, this time from the Cook Islands – is the goddess of the Moon who in other tales appears on the face of the Moon. Here she is a beautiful maiden who used to bathe in a certain pool, where a great eel also swam and frequently curled himself around her as he swam past. One day he threw off his eel form and revealed himself to be a man, called *Tuna*, the Eel or the Phallus. They became lovers, and Tuna would visit her as a man and leave her as an eel. But after a while he told her that he had to leave her forever; he would come in his eel form in a great flood of water, and she was to cut his head off and bury it. He came the next day and, sorrowfully, Hina did as he had asked. Each day she visited the place of the buried head until a shoot appeared which grew into a beautiful tree that bore fruit: the coconut. When it is husked, every nut shows the eyes and face of her lover, the Eel.[69]

The Great Eel is the local version of the lunar serpent, who comes in a flood like the Moon at the full. The familiar mythological image of the divine being whose dismembered body becomes food for the Earth is found in many plant-oriented cultures in the tropics, from Oceania to Egypt to Greece.[70] What is striking is that this dismembered being so frequently takes its reference from the Moon, as though the Moon's dismemberment and the healing of the fragmented pieces in a new whole offered a way of coming to terms with the inextricability of life and death.

DYING AND RESURRECTED GODS

All dying and resurrected Gods were once gods of the Moon. When Moon gods extended into the new agricultural realities, their ancient form was found anew in the rising and falling seasons as the yearly counterpart of the cycle of the Moon. The Moon, who in many places used to stand alone, here splits into the Father and the Son, with the Father becoming more remote and the Son assuming the rhythmical life and death of the phases. The Goddess Mother embodies the inexhaustible creativity of the eternal whole, which appears both in the cyclical revolutions of the Moon and the cyclical womb of Earth.

Plutarch, naming Osiris as the Moon and a god of vegetation, explains that Osiris is for Egypt what Dionysos is for Greece: they were both portrayed in the form of a bull, both dismembered and revived, both lords of moisture and the vine, both honoured with ivy as their sacred plant. Speaking of the Greeks, Plutarch says: 'Dionysos they call *hyes* ("the raining one") since he is the lord of the nature of moisture, and he is no other than Osiris.'[71] Affinities between the different gods were easily recognized and welcomed in the past (a way of thinking known as 'syncretism'). Indeed, it is a feature of 'Nature' deities, in contrast to 'tribal' deities, that they embody a shared reality in human experience: a perception of the immanent divinity of the created world. Campbell points out that people from one race or country will hail the *Nature* gods and goddesses from another race or country with a sense of knowing them already: 'the one you call X, we call Y.'[72] Each implicitly gains from the other's existence. This is, of course, quite different from the distressing experience of a meeting of *tribal* gods, or (which appears to be the same thing) inter-tribal interpretation of gods, whose adherents believe that their god or god-like interpretation is superior and the others' is 'heresy,' (a term originally meaning in Greek 'to choose', *airesis*).[73] But then the difference between Nature and tribal deities is also the difference between Earth and territory, the same soil seen in differing ways.

OSIRIS

So it is that Osiris can be seen in Dumuzi-Tammuz, Dionysos and Hades; Dionysos can be recognized in Soma and Osiris, and can share in the rituals of Demeter and Persephone; Orpheus recalls Dionysos, and Men can be found in the 'Bacchic rites' and identified with Attis, while the cries for 'Tammuz, that is to say Adonis', the dying Lord, can be heard echoing for Jesus, the Lord, coming (as St Jerome himself observed) almost from the same grove.[74]

By the same token, the mothers and lovers of these dying and resurrecting gods are kith and kin, the Great Goddess of Many Names, whose epiphany is the Full Moon. The second-century AD Roman writer Apuleius, who was himself an initiate of the Mysteries of Isis, brings this image to life in his book *The Golden Ass*. Lucius, whose name means 'light', is a man whose own true nature is obscured, and who explores the darkness of his being in the condition of an ass. After submerging himself seven times beneath the waves, with 'tears running down my hairy face', he prays to the goddess Isis to transform him (in an ironic metaphor of initiation) from an ass into a human being. Hardly has he closed his eyes when a vision appears to him, Isis rising from the sea, wrapped in a mantle of deepest black, embroidered with stars, and in their midst a Full Moon breathing forth 'flaming fires':

> Her hair, long and hanging in tapered ringlets, fell luxuriantly on her divine neck; a crown of varied form encircled the summit of her head with a diversity of flowers, and in the middle of it, just over her forehead, there was a flat circlet, which resembled a mirror or rather emitted a white refulgent light, thus indicating she was the moon.

Vipers rising from the furrows of the earth, supported this on the right hand and on the left, while ears of corn projected on either side...her mantle of the deepest black...was wrapped around her...while a part of the robe fell down in many folds, and gracefully floated with its little knots of fringe that edged its extremities. Glittering stars were dispersed along the embroidered extremities of the robe, and over its whole surface; and in the middle of them a moon of two weeks old breathed forth its flaming fires.

Then she addresses Lucius:

I am Nature, the universal Mother, mistress of all the elements, primordial child of time, sovereign of all things spiritual, queen of the dead, queen also of the immortals, the single manifestation of all gods and goddesses that are...Though I am worshipped in many aspects, known by countless names, and propitiated with all manner of different rites, yet the whole round earth venerates me. The primeval Phrygians call me Pessinunctica, Mother of the gods; the Athenians, sprung from their own soil, call me Cecropian Artemis; for the islanders of Cyprus I am Paphian Aphrodite; for the archers of Crete I am Dyctynna; for the trilingual Sicilians Stygian Proserpine; and for the Eleusinians their ancient Mother of the Corn. Some know me as Juno, some as Bellona of the Battles; others as Hecate, others again as Rhamnubia, but both races of Aethiopians, and the Egyptians who excel in ancient learning and worship me with ceremonies proper to my godhead, call me by my true name, namely, Queen Isis.[75]

So it was that 'the sun shone at midnight'. The initiated state, it is implied, is to include the ability to see through the many names into the one face of Nature who is the universal Mother. Apuleius's magnificent image was the model for Mozart's Queen of the Night in *The Magic Flute* (fig. 1).

One of the titles of Osiris was 'Lord of Everything'. As lunar god of moisture and generation he was the lord of vegetation, who died as the falling grain in the harvest and was reborn in the growing grain of the following season. When the corn was cut the people wept as though the body of the god were being threshed into pieces, and reapers called on Isis to mourn and summon her husband back home: 'Come to thy house, beautiful one!'[76] In later times crescent-shaped figures of moist earth and seeds were made when Osiris was 'found', when his semen, as the Inundation, flooded the fields. So, also, models of Osiris were filled with earth and planted with barley, and placed in the burial chambers of the royal tombs. When the barley began to sprout the deceased person was resurrected, in the same way that Osiris was reborn in the grain.[77] These 'Osiris-beds', as they were called, re-emerged in Greece as the 'Gardens of Adonis', which were shallow baskets of lettuces and wheat, grown to live and die in eight days when, along with his effigy, the dying plants were cast beneath the waves to rise with the god in three days' time.

The waning of Osiris was also expressed in the cutting down of the Tree of Life, since, like Tammuz and Dionysos, Osiris was the life-force of the tree. His coffin is enclosed by the tamarisk tree which is then cut down to form a pillar for the king's palace. Isis in turn cuts down the pillar to release the coffin from its trunk, after which Horus, is conceived. The Tree of Life is raised up again by Isis and the Pharoah as the *Djed* column on the day that celebrates the resurrection of Osiris.

There is a remarkable sequence of engravings in the Ptolemaic Temple of Isis in Philae, which relates Osiris as Moon god to the growth of plants. Imagine standing in the Temple of Isis looking out through an opening that was once a gate called Hadrian's Gateway, which faces the island where

Fig. 9. *Osiris in the character of Menu, the 'god of the uplifted arm,' and Harpokrates, sitting in the disc of the Moon, from the 3rd day of the new Moon until the 15th day (each of the 12 stars signifying one day). Below, the Crocodile god, Sobek, bears the mummy of Osiris on his back. To the left stands Isis, identified by the head-dress of the throne upon her head. Bas-relief (left of Hadrian's Gateway). The Ptolemaic Temple of Isis at Philae. (From Wallis Budge, Osiris and the Egyptian Resurrection, i, p. 21).*

Fig. 10. *Hapi, the Nile god as a form of Osiris, concealed in his cave, encircled by a cobra, pouring water for the inundation. The rocks above are the Nile rocks. Bas-relief (first right of Hadrian's Gateway). The Ptolemaic Temple of Isis, Philae. (From Lamy, Egyptian Mysteries, p. 5).*

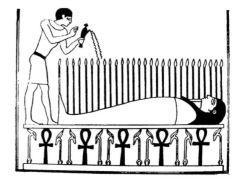

Fig. 11. *Cow-headed Isis watering the plants growing in a sacred lake, out of which rises a man-headed hawk as the soul of Osiris: 'This is the soul of Osiris speeding upwards.' Bas-relief (second right of Hadrian's Gateway). The Ptolemaic Temple of Isis at Philae. (From Wallis Budge, Osiris, i, p. 8).*

Fig. 12. *Priest watering the grain growing from the body of Osiris. The ankh sign for life and the was-sceptre of strength are carved beneath him. Bas-relief (third right of Hadrian's Gateway). The Ptolemaic Temple of Isis at Philae. (From Wallis Budge, Osiris, i, p. 58).*

Osiris was believed to be buried. On your left is a relief of the dead Osiris being carried to the underworld on the back of a crocodile, while above are inscribed the 12 stars of the Waxing Moon, visible from the third day after the New Moon (fig. 9). On the right of the gate are scenes of rebirth. First, an engraving of the Nile God Hapi, a form of Osiris, pouring water for the inundation (fig. 10); beside this scene stands the cow-headed Isis pouring a libation on the plants, bringing the Inundation which releases the soul bird of Osiris, making them grow (fig. 11). Next to this scene is a priest watering the plants growing from the body of Osiris (fig. 12).

A *Spell for Becoming Barley* expresses the relation between the eternal principle and life in time:

> I am the plant of life
> which comes forth from Osiris,
> which grows upon the ribs of Osiris,

which allows the people to live...
I am life appearing from Osiris.[78]

DIONYSOS

Dionysos, as Plutarch has said, is, like Osiris, the lord of moisture and generation. It was not originally that the god was a manifestation of the vine; rather, the vine was one of many manifestations of Dionysos in concentrated form – 'a drink that is poured out, a god for a god.'[79] So the Greek Dionysos and the Roman Bacchus are comparable to Soma, gods all of the liquid of intoxication, whether Soma, mead, beer or wine, juice of herb, honey, barley, rye or grape. As Euripides has Dionysos say of himself, 'All the barbarians dance his rites.'[80] Since Dionysos came from northern Thrace, where there was beer but not wine, it is likely that fermentation of the grape was a late 'gift' of the god as he moved south.[81] Even though the later form of the god became autonomous, and was specifically identified with wine and its revelations, the images surrounding Dionysos reveal him to be in origin a Moon god who was also a god of vegetation.[82]

The story may be unique but the pattern is familiar: 'twice born', form-changing, the 'nocturnal one', giver of prophecies, leader of the Muses, 'the physician', god of the sea, god of fruits, god of the phallus, figured as a bull, dismembered, rent and devoured in the first flowering of his youth, re-membered by his Goddess Mother, and annually, or three-yearly, reconstituted in his rites. On his death a pomegranate sprouted from his blood, coming from the tree sacred to Tammuz and Adonis, the fruit which bound Persephone to Hades. For though the fruit of the pomegranate tree, once opened, spoils immediately – heralding death – its black seeds, packed so densely together, evoke the souls of the myriad dead stored safely in the underworld, awaiting rebirth. In Christian art a pomegranate often adorns the cloak of the Virgin Mary as a promise of resurrection.

While Dionysos holds up the cup of ambrosial nectar as the one who seasonally empties and fills the cup, Semele, his mother, a goddess of Earth, points to her own closed mouth, perhaps to indicate that one may not speak of the Mysteries, perhaps to emphasize that the source of transformation is ultimately within. Graves observes that Semele's other name is Selene.[83] In Roman times, Cicero, in common with Ulpian and Eusebius, said that Dionysos was the son of the Moon (Selene).[84]

Semele was the daughter of Cadmus, whose mythical ancestress was Io, a Moon goddess also named as one of the mothers of Dionysos, who is assimilated to Isis in Egypt and Hera in Greece, and who was transformed by Zeus into a cow to conceal her from Hera. Semele, like the three Maenads who followed Dionysos, was called *Thyone*, the 'raging one', and *Hye*, the 'rainy one'.[85] Semele loved 'thunder-loving' Zeus, and one of the Theban stories went that Semele conceived Dionysos with Zeus, but (beguiled by Hera) she demanded that Zeus reveal himself to her in his true nature. Zeus in anger appeared before her as thunder and lightning, and Semele was consumed in flames. Hermes snatched

Fig. 13. Dionysos and Semele, crowned with garlands of ivy leaves, surrounded by clusters of grapes. Cyclix, Greek. c. 550 BC. (From Campbell, The Mythic Image, p.197).

the six-month-old baby from the burning womb of his mother, sewed him into Zeus's thigh for the last three months, delivered him himself and then gave him to the nymphs of the grottoes to nurse him. So Dionysos was called 'twice-born' and 'child of the double door', though he always remained his mother's son. This was the version of Apollodorus and Apollonius Rhodius.[86]

Nonnos, a writer in the fifth century AD, tells a more ancient tale which comes from Crete. 'Night-shining Dionysos', as he calls him, was born as a horned infant and was made 'king of all gods' by his father Zeus, after which he spent his time contemplating his image in a mirror. But the Titans, at Hera's request, cut him up into pieces – some say 14 – and then devoured him. His heart alone remained, and that was consumed by his mother from whom he was born again.[87] In still other versions, Dionysos is called Zagreus, the 'great hunter', and given as the child of Persephone and Zeus, who had assumed the form of a snake and visited his daughter in a cave one night.[88]

In Greek art Dionysos is shown under three aspects: infant, young man and old man. He was worshipped as threefold at Athens, and in Patrai is represented by three statues. The early Homeric *Hymn to Dionysos*, possibly seventh-century BC, says, ambiguously, 'As these things are three...'[89] At Delphi, Dionysos embodied the voice of *Pytho* the serpent, whom Apollo officially overthrew, and the oracles were delivered from 'the grave of Dionysos', which was the omphalos (the navel of the world) itself. Plutarch comments that 'Dionysos had as much to do with Delphi as Apollo',[90] while many centuries later Nietzsche argued that the birth of tragedy was made possible by the continuous and mutual destruction of the principles embodied in Dionysos and Apollo, energy and form.[91]

It may be no coincidence that tragedy emerged as a universal form of drama from within the cult of Dionysos, he who wears the mask of the Moon's dual powers, and whose rites of intoxication reveal the unfathomable mysteries of life and death inextricably entwined. Tragedy celebrates both the exuberance of the life-force and its shattering defeat, opposites transcended and reconciled by being re-enacted, with passion and self-consciousness, from within the human experience.

ORPHEUS

Orpheus was also dismembered, torn limb from limb by Maenads who threw his head into the river Hebrus. Orpheus, son of the Muse Kalliope and the Thracian King Oeagrus, was a poet and musician

Fig. 14. Orpheus, holding up his lyre, being torn apart by Maenads. Painted dish by the Louvre painter. 480-470 BC. Cincinnati Art Museum.

Fig. 15. Orpheos-Bakkikos crucified, with the crescent at the apex of the cross. Arranged in a crescent above are the seven stars of the Pleiades, known as the Lyre of Orpheus. Haematite cylinder seal. c. 300 AD. (From Campbell, Creative Mythology, p. 9).

who enchanted the hearts of wild beasts, and freed the trees and rocks from their places to follow him. Apollo gave him the lyre, which Hermes had once given to him, and the Muses taught Orpheus how to make music as sweet as the song of nightingales. When his severed head plunged into the river, it floated and sang all the way to the sea. The waves carried it to the island of Lesbos, and laid it to rest in a cave sacred to Dionysos. There it prophesied night and day until Apollo (losing his suppliants at Delphi), stood over the head and commanded it to cease. The Muses collected his limbs and buried them beneath Mount Olympos, where nightingales now sing more sweetly than anywhere else in the world. His lyre became a constellation in heaven, the Pleiades.[92]

But was Orpheus murdered by Dionysos, as some think, setting his Maenads upon Orpheus because the poet had mysteries of his own, without orgy and blood sacrifice? Or was Orpheus a priest of Dionysos (both coming from Thrace), such that their fates were identified by later generations?[93] Plato disparages certain fake mystics who show piled-up books of Musaios and Orpheus, whom they say are sons of the Moon and the Muses.[94] Plato's perspective is not entirely clear from his tone, but the passage shows that the relation of Orpheus to the Moon was often made, as it was for Dionysos. Proclus, in his commentary on Plato's *Politics* writes: 'Orpheus, because he was the principal in the Dionysian rites, is said to have suffered the same fate as the god'[95] (both journeying to Hades, Dionysos to raise Semele and Orpheus to bring back Eurydice, with her lunar name of the 'wide-ruling one'); while Apollodorus declares that Orpheus 'invented the Mysteries of Dionysos.'[96] Certainly, the love of the Muses was common to them both, as though Orpheus embodied the poetic dimension of the earlier god and gave it a life of its own. The Homeric *Hymn to Dionysos* concludes with words that could have been said of Orpheus: 'Anyone who forgets you, forgets sweet song.'[97]

The unique crucifix amulet in fig. 15 names the figure in Greek as *Orpheos-Bakkikos*, identifying Orpheus with Bacchus by name, and both of them with Jesus in the role of crucified god. Surmounted by the seven stars of the Pleiades, Orpheus's own lyre, the crescent rests on top of the cross as the fruit on the Tree of Life, proclaiming that the gift of this particular death is life renewed. The maker of the amulet has been accused of aiming for a 'multiplied potency' by conflating the three figures or, worse, of indulging in 'indiscriminate syncretism'.[98] But could it not be that the artist chose to emphasize the identity of the three saviours to point the mind beyond the forms assumed separately by each one of them, so suggesting, as Campbell did in the title of his four great books on myth, that these three figures, and all others like them, are but the *Masks of God*?

Fig. 16. The Moon god Men with crescent, his left foot resting on a bull's head, holding a sceptre and a pine cone. Bronze statuette. Antalia. Rijksmuseum van Oudheden, Leiden.

Fig. 17. Men, with Phrygian cap, holding pine cone and thyrsus, his left foot upon a bull. The inscription in Greek reads: 'Agathapous of Kaouala offers his prayer to Men.' Marble bas relief. Greek. 2nd century AD. British Museum.

MEN AND ATTIS

The Moon god Men from Asia Minor was also identified with Dionysos. In *Dionysiaca*, Nonnos has 'Bull-faced Mene' say:

> I love the grape and tend the Bacchic rites, for the earth can ripen no fruit save after receiving the bright germinating dew of the moon...I lead the raging choruses; Bacchic Mene am I, not merely because I accomplish in the Aether the cycle of the months, but because I excite mania and rule the raging spirits.[99]

Men, the Phrygian Moon god, was worshipped as a healer and a deliverer of babies, and was often called 'The Saviour'.[100] After the Hittite empire collapsed in the twelfth century BC, he emerged in Anatolia as a synthesis of the many Moon gods in the area, becoming as important to the Anatolians as Nanna-Sin had been to the Mesopotamians.[101] He was known as *Menotyrannos*, 'Men, the Lord', *Men Ouranos*, 'Men of the Heavens', and *Men Katachthonios*, 'Men of the Underworld', suggesting that he was a god of death and rebirth. Romans often called him Lunus. He was also the ruler of water, rains, rivers and plants, and, like Dionysos, was frequently figured as a bull (Chapter 8, fig. 3). Bulls drew his chariot across the heavens, and the god himself was portrayed standing on the head of a bull (fig. 16); many coins have the god on one side and a bull on the other; sometimes he was sculpted riding upon a cock. In his waxing phase he would accept sacrifices of bulls, fruit or cakes.

Men, in his aspect of dying and rising god, was often identified with the Phrygian god Attis, who was the son-lover of the Great Mother Kybele, the 'All-nurturing One', 'Mother of All the Gods', whose cult spread from Anatolia to Greece and then to Rome, where it became part of Roman state religion under the Empire.[102] Sometimes Kybele wears the crescent upon her head as her crown as

Fig. 18. 'Exaltation of a Flower.' Demeter and Persephone reunited. Marble stele, 460 BC. The Louvre.

Fig. 19. Dionysos offering the cup to Demeter. Stone stele Greek from Locri, S. Italy. 470-60 BC. Archaeological Museum. Reggio de Calabria.

does, on occasion, her son. Sculptures of Men show him wearing the pointed Phrygian cap (which Attis and Mithras also wear and which was passed to Hermes), or else a conical bonnet, holding the sceptre of power in one hand and the pine cone of rebirth in the other (fig. 17).

The death and rebirth of Attis was enacted in Rome in the 13 days from 15 to 28 March, the days from full to dark, coinciding with the change of seasons in spring. Whether he was killed while out hunting, like Adonis, by a boar (the animal Seth was hunting at the Full Moon), and whether the crescent-shaped sickle which castrated him was held by his own hand or that of others, is sufficiently unclear to be probably beside the point. In his rites a pine tree, evergreen like the ivy of Dionysos, was hewn down, wrapped in mummy clothes and hung with ribbons and violets; at his death, violets flowered from his blood as anemones sprang from the blood of Adonis. On 24 March, three days after the equinox, a bull was sacrificed, while priestesses called *Melissae*, bees, like those attending Demeter, Persephone and Artemis, served the ritual feast. The relation of the sacrificed bull to the bee becomes clear in a remark of Porphyry's which, incidentally, points to the unbroken line of the Mystery traditions, the same, often bewildering, imagery re-emerging in different cultures:

> The ancients gave the name of *Melissae* ('bees') to the priestesses of Demeter who were initiates of the chthonian goddess; the name *Melitodes* to Kore herself; the moon (Artemis) too, whose province it was to bring to the birth, they called *Melissa*, because the moon being a bull and its ascension the bull, bees are begotten of bulls. And souls that pass to the earth are bull-begotten.[103]

The priestesses, serving the food of the feast, had symbolically in their care the souls of the dead awaiting rebirth. Similarly, when the priests endured their own castration they were but returning their fertility to the Earth from whence it came, that the Earth might again bring forth her food for the good of all. Attis was laid in his grave on the eve of the next day and a vigil was observed throughout the night until his resurrection the following day, when the Festival of Joy, the *Hilaria*, was celebrated with much hilarity among the people: 'Be of good heart, you novices, because the god is saved. Deliverance from distress will come for us, as well,' the high priest chanted.[104]

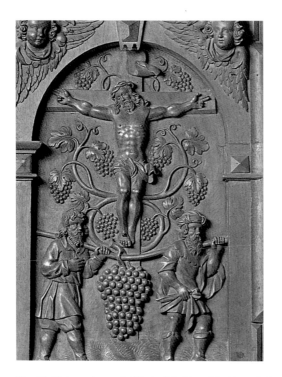

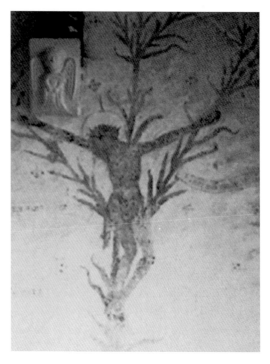

Fig. 20. Christ as the mystical Fruit of the Vine. Wood bas-relief panel. 1553-1619. Cathedral de Valère, Sion, Switzerland.

Fig. 21. 'The Lily Cross.' Mural altarpiece. Godshill Parish Church, Isle of Wight. 14th century.

DEMETER AND PERSEPHONE

The myth of Demeter and Persephone threads through all the stories of rebirth in Nature, which were at the same time metaphors for the soul's transformation. The Eleusinian Mysteries which dramatized the Mother, Demeter's, loss and finding of her daughter, Persephone, deserve a chapter in their own right, but here it may be enough to point to the lunar inspiration of the myth.[105] Mother and maiden were called 'the two goddesses', or the *Demetres*, suggestive of one reality displayed in two guises – the Mother as the cycle and the child as the phases: born, growing to her full stature, then seized by the darkness (personified as Hades, lord of the underworld), dying as the darkening Moon, the falling seed and the failing life. In the underworld of the Dark Moon, married to Death, Persephone rules with Hades, eating the honey-sweet seeds of the pomegranate, until, her imprisonment ended, she returns as the crescent and the flowering spring, when maiden and Mother again become one (fig. 18). The drama identifies with the Mother, and specifically the Mother's love for her child. For Demeter is both the source of all – the Great Mother – and also the human mother who loses the one she loves, and goes to search for her until she finds her and brings her back. It is Demeter whose rage compels Zeus to send Hermes to release Persephone from the cold grip of Hades, and because of her that 'she who shines in the dark' (the meaning of *Persephone*) and 'the maiden shoot' (the meaning of *Kore*) come back as the New Moon in the sky and the new plant on the Earth. The three days' dark of the Moon become the three months' dark of the year as winter, the time Persephone is condemned to live with Hades because she ate of the seeds of the dead. As Kerenyi observes, 'The idea of the original Mother-Daughter goddess, at root a single entity, is at the same time the idea of *rebirth*.'[106]

In the Eleusinian rites, held in the Waning Moon, a child is added to the original two who are one: at the culminating point in the ceremony, a priest calls out 'The Great Goddess has borne a sacred child. Brimo has borne Brimos.' 'Brimo' means the 'raging one' or the 'mighty', recalling Demeter's mighty rage which brought Persephone back to life, and also the rage of Semele, the mother of Dionysos, who in another tale was the son of Persephone. There is a wondrous confusion of names and roles here, all pointing to a shared inheritance, a mystery explored in different but related ways. A statue of *Iacchos* (another name for Dionysos), crowned with myrtle and bearing a torch, was carried in procession from Athens to Eleusis, with crowds lining the route shouting his name ecstatically. Dionysos, who in the role of his Cretan counterpart, *Zagreus*, was dismembered and reborn, is here gentler, more amenable to the culture of the two goddesses, in his role of the mystical child at the breast. Plutarch observes that 'the ancients worshipped Dionysos and Demeter together' (fig. 19),[107] and here the Eleusinian and Dionysian mysteries are united in the figure of the child of the vine, the grain, the Moon and the year. The final moment at Eleusis was the holding up of an ear of wheat.

* * *

The grain and the vine were handed on to the Christian Mysteries in the image of Christ's body and blood, which were to be eaten and drunk in rites that, as in the earlier Mysteries, were to transform the participants.

> And as they were eating, he took bread, and blessed, and broke it, and gave it to them, and said, 'Take; this is my body.' And he took a cup, and when he had given thanks he gave it to them, and they all drank of it. And he said to them, 'This is my blood of the covenant, which is poured out for many. Truly, I say unto you, I shall not drink again of the fruit of the vine until that day when I drink it new in the Kingdom of God.'[108]

In the Gospel of John, this imagery is given form in the words of Jesus:

> 'Except a corn of wheat fall into the ground and die, it abideth alone; but if it die, it bringeth forth much fruit.'[109]
> 'I am the true vine, and my Father is the husbandman...I am the vine, you are the branches. He who abides in me, and I in him, he it is that bears much fruit, for apart from me you can do nothing.[110]

What was once ancient belief – that the Moon was the power which made the trees and plants grow – offers itself to the Christian tradition as the lunar symbolism of death and rebirth. So Christ, hanging from the Cross as the Tree of Death, becomes the mystical fruit of the vine, the lily or the evergreen through which it becomes a Tree of Life. In the myths that grew up around the Gospels, the Cross of wood on which Christ was crucified was set up on the site where the Tree of Knowledge stood in the Garden of Eden, the place of the original sin of humanity, for which it was forbidden to eat of the fruit of the Tree of Life. Christ's sacrifice on the Tree of the Cross, his arms resting on its outstretched branches, transforms the Tree of Knowledge into the Tree of Life, whose flowering and fruit, which is himself, is to heal the incarnate world of sin and death.

CHAPTER 10

THE MOON AND FATE

My days are swifter than a weaver's shuttle.
Job 7:6

O Fates, come, come, Cut thread and thrum...
Shakespeare *A Midsummer Night's Dream*

Had I the heaven's embroidered cloths,
Enwrought with golden and silver light..
Yeats *He Wishes for the Cloths of Heaven*

For the rational mind, the Moon presents a visible image of the ceaseless flow of time. But for the mythical mind, the Moon, measuring time, *makes* time, and so, ultimately, *is* Time itself. In many ancient cultures the Moon, as the cause of time in life, was also the cause of the time allotted to live, measuring out to people their fate, the length and pattern of their span of days, and even their share of good and evil – which is to say, the *quality* of their lives. In a related idea, the Moon was often imagined to reel out strands of time from its shining ball, the way a spinner spins thread. Then the Moon, as the spinner of time out of itself, becomes the weaver of the web of the phenomenal world and so the spinner of the threads of fate and the weaver of individual destiny.

The three visible phases of waxing, full and waning, when reflected back upon human life, chart the course of a life in three stages: being born and growing up; being fully who you are; growing old and dying. In Greece, as we have seen, the three visible phases were personified as separate goddesses: the Virgin Artemis and Kore/Persephone for the Waxing Crescent Moon; Demeter, Hera, Athene, Aphrodite and Phoebe as the Full Moon; Hekate as the Waning Moon. But almost invisibly behind, or within, these goddesses gleamed the shadowy outlines of the three 'Fates', the *Moirai*, who were older than all the goddesses and gods.

THE MOIRAI

Born from underworld and night as the first glimmer of light to arise from the dark, the Moirai reflect that initial moment of insight when birth and death and the passage between are seen in their entirety, as parts of a whole and as a whole that is apportioned.[1] This means that for the first time birth and death meet face to face, and an irreversible boundary forms in the mind, setting a limit on individual lives, offering them a share in the whole but not everything. The name *Moira* means 'part', 'share', 'portion' or 'lot', and refers firstly to the Moirai themselves as figures of the three 'parts' of the Moon,[2] and further to their triple role of apportioning to mortals (and to gods) their lot in life, their beginning, middle and end.[3] No wonder the Orphics called the Moon by the most ancient and fearsome name: the 'Gorgon's head'.[4]

Fig. 1. Artemis holding spindle. Ephesos. Ivory statue, 7th c. BC. Archaeological Museum, Istanbul.

The lunar origins of the Moirai were celebrated by the Orphics, who sang of them as clothed in the 'white raiment' of moonlight.[5] In the Orphic *Hymn to the Fates*, these 'daughters of darkling night' were addressed as those

> Who in the heav'nly lake (where waters white
> Burst from a fountain hid in depths of night,
> thro' a dark and stony cavern glide,
> A cave profound, invisible) abide.[6]

Fig. 4. The Double Maat and the Weighing of the Heart. c. 1450 BC. The Louvre.

mathematics, in that crucial moment of cultural mutation met the earlier-known mystery of biological death and generation, and the two joined. The lunar rhythm of the womb had already given notice of a correspondence between celestial and terrestrial circumstance. The mathematical law united both. And so it is that, in all of these mythologies, the principle of *maat*, *me*, *dharma*, and *tao*, which in the Greek tradition became *moira*, was mythologically felt and represented as female.[22]

The idea of a power beyond the gods whose decrees are unalterable is common to many cultures, and it is surprising how frequently this ultimate power – often called simply 'Fate' – has been connected, directly or indirectly, to the Moon. The idea of the law as the one, the cycle, and its incarnation as the three, the figures of the phases, may be behind this way of thinking about fate, as for instance *Moira*, the one, and *Moirai*, the three. If the Moon is seen to 'give' time, it makes sense that it should also allot the quality of time given, and even in some cultures evaluate how that time was 'spent'. Many lunar deities are lawgivers, particularly in the Dark Moon phase, when they are assumed to be lighting up the underworld and so presiding over the life after death. In Mesopotamia, 'the laws' – known as the *me* – belonged at one time to Inanna-Ishtar (who bewails the loss of them), and she was called both goddess of Fate and the 'spinning goddess', while Nanna-Sin, her father, gave the laws in the underworld when his light was gone from the sky: 'Father Nannar...lord that decreest fate...lord of the net.'[23] A hymn to Ishtar, the 'mighty Queen of Heaven', ends: 'May she fulfil the decrees (of fate) at the dark of the moon.'[24]

In Egypt, Maat was the goddess who embodied Truth and the Right Ordering of the Universe, wearing upon her head the white plume of the ostrich feather. As the spouse and female counterpart of the Moon god Thoth, she stood with him in the boat of the Sun god, Re, when he rose above the waters of the abyss for the first time. Since then Maat and Thoth travel each day with the Sun in his boat, which always follows the 'unalterably right' course.[25] The name of Maat meant 'that which is straight', referring first to a straight rod which the craftsman required to keep things straight, and then to the rule or law by which people were to be kept straight. So the physical meaning merged into the moral meaning, as it does in many languages (Greek *orthos* means both straight and right, *kanon* means a straight rod and a 'canon'; even the English 'ruler' has a double meaning, as does the word

Fig. 5. Penelope at her loom. Telemachos stands beside her with two lances. Red figure vase by Skyphos, the Penelope painter.. 440 BC. National Museum of Archaeology, Chiusi, Italy.

'straight'). After death, the heart of the deceased was placed in the scales of judgement to be weighed against the feather of Maat, the feather of Truth. If the heart was as light as the feather, then the deceased could enter the presence of Osiris, Judge of the Dead.[26] Maat was then the standard which a soul had to meet to be deemed worthy to have an after-life.

In many depictions of this event, the soul-bird watches the ceremony from the top of the scales, while ibis-headed Thoth, standing with raised quill, inscribes the judgement as law. In fig. 4, Thoth takes his other form of baboon to watch over the weighing of the heart. The heart is here placed in the balance against an emblem of Maat – not just her feather, as is more customary – while a double figure of Maat, with feathered head-dress, awaits the result. The Hall of Judgement was called the 'Hall of the Two Maat Goddesses', that is, the two goddesses of Truth, one presiding over Upper Egypt and the other over Lower Egypt, a synthesis that, like the double crown of Osiris, symbolized a spiritual union in which opposing principles were reconciled. In this papyrus, the other small feathered head, both resembling and facing Maat, placed on top of the scales where the soul-bird usually sits, may embody the wish of the deceased person (on the left) that his soul may indeed be 'maat', that is, straight and right, and so at one with the rightness of the universe.

In Greece, the Moon goddesses, as well as the Moirai, were weavers: Artemis, Athene, Aphrodite, Persephone and the Nymphs were all spinstresses, as were many of the fateful figures in the life of Odysseus. Penelope, Odysseus' wife, weaves a web of deceit for her suitors, telling them she has to wait before choosing anyone for marriage until she has finished spinning a shroud for Laertes, Odysseus' father, in preparation for his death. After the fourth year the suitors discover that she unravels at night – 'when torches have been placed by her' – what she has spun by day.[27] Symbolically, then, in the image of the Moirai, Penelope, the 'Veiled One', weaves and unweaves her loom of time to postpone the finishing of the work, for a choice between the suitors would mean the death of Odysseus as her husband – the cutting of the last thread (fig. 5).

In a sense, Odysseus is brought to Penelope through the actions of two other goddesses who also spin his fate, Calypso and Circe. The book opens with Odysseus imprisoned in the cave of Calypso, and Hermes later meets her singing at her loom, 'weaving with a golden shuttle'.[28] Later, Circe's enchantment is specifically linked to her weaving, since it is the voice of her singing as she weaves 'a

Fig. 6. Minoan Labyrinth with crescent Moon at centre. Cretan coin. Knossos. (From Goblet D'Alviella, The Migration of Symbols, *p. 71).*

great imperishable web' that entices Odysseus' comrades to call to her and enter her house of polished stone, upon which she drugs them and turns them into swine.[29] Yet it is Circe who, mastered by Odysseus with Hermes' help, sends Odysseus to the underworld to consult Teiresias, and so indirectly conveys him to Penelope, home to their olive-tree bed. So, after 19 years, is the marriage of the Sun and Moon accomplished (Chapters 5 and 6).

A ball of silver thread in the darkness is the central image in the myth of Theseus and the Minotaur, the thread that Ariadne gave to Theseus to guide him through the labyrinth to meet the Bull of Minos at the centre. The Greek story pits Theseus, as son of the king of Athens, against the Cretan King Minos, drawing Theseus as the hero who slays the Minotaur to free the Athenians from paying (the lunar) tribute of seven youths and seven maidens to feed the Minotaur every eight years. But an older Minoan sensibility shines through the symbolism, where all the female characters have names of the Moon and all the male characters names of the Sun.[30] Then it appears that Theseus is under the protection of a long line of Moon goddesses: *Telephaessa*, the 'far-shining one' (also called *Argiope*, the 'white-faced'), is the mother of *Europa*, 'she of the wide eyes', who was carried across the sea to Crete by Zeus in the form of a bull. 'In other words,' Kerenyi says, 'the face of both mother and daughter was that of the moon.'[31] Europa's son, Minos, married *Pasiphae*, 'she who shines for all', who was herself the daughter of *Helios*, the Sun, and *Perseis*, the Moon, the 'shining one', whose other daughter was Hekate, and who gave her name to Persephone. The daughter of Minos and Pasiphae was *Ariadne*, the 'one visible from afar',[32] who was originally called *Ariagne*, the 'holy and pure one', a superlative form of *hagne* (the origin of the English word 'hag'), which was one of the names of Persephone as queen of the underworld, herself also a spinstress, weaving shrouds for the dead.

From this perspective, Theseus is spun into the darkness by Ariadne's ball of silver thread, in the way that skeins of light unwind from the ball of the Moon until all is gone. In the dark heart of the labyrinth Theseus slays death in the form of the ever-dying, ever-renewing bull (not merely the monster it appeared to later Greek eyes), after which the thread spins him out again into the light, as though spinning him along a journey of death and rebirth. The eight-yearly ransom of 14 Athenian youth to the Bull of Minos coincides with the octennial cycle in which the Sun and Moon, revolving in their separate cycles, return 'to the same heavenly bridal chamber where first they met.'[33] (Chapter 5).

The Minoan labyrinth is often drawn with a Crescent Moon at its centre, and was said to be originally not a maze but a spiral, one of the oldest images of the rhythmic Moon (fig. 6).

THE PARCAE

In Roman times, the Moirai become the *Parcae* (from the Latin *parere*, 'to give birth'), emphasizing their lunar role as birth goddesses who spin their 'gifts' into the child when it is born. The Roman poet Catullus (87–54BC) writes of the Parcae at the marriage of Peleus and Thetis, spinning their

Fig. 7. The Romano-Celtic Triple Matronae, with baby, napkin and materials for bathing, as though bringing forth the child into the human world. Sandstone bas relief. Vertault, Musée de Chatillon, France.

threads while singing a prophetic song of the great Pelides, as the divine guests sit and banquet.[34] With the spread of the Roman Empire, the Parcae entered northern Europe, and even in the eleventh century, long after the Christian faith had become the official doctrine, a certain Bishop Burchard of Worms was obliged to rebuke women for continuing to believe in 'three women', known as the Parcae, who affected the future of a child. He added regretfully that laying three places at table to welcome them was a common custom.[35]

THE MATRONAE

The Parcae were often identified with the *Matronae*, the 'Mothers', where a Latin name was given to the three Celtic goddesses, who were usually seated, offering cornucopias of gifts from their capacious laps, and sometimes carrying a spindle or balance (fig. 7). It was the Matronae who, according to Julius Caesar in his *Gallic War*, declared 'by lots and divinations whether it was expedient to join battle or not.'[36] Worshipped by Romans, Celts and Germans, they were also known to the Anglo-Saxons: the Venerable Bede refers to them when he speaks of the night before Christmas as *Modraniht*, the 'Night of the Mothers'.[37] In Bohemia, even in the early part of the twentieth century, there was a custom of laying the table and lighting the lamps when a child was born, so that when the 'Three' visited at night, they might feel welcome and favour the child with their gifts. In Greece, honey was left for the three Moirai as their favourite food, and in French folklore the fairies (whose name comes from the Latin *fata*, 'fates'), continued to preside at the birth of a child and decide its destiny.[38]

In Christian myth, the three Moirai, Parcae and Matronae, survived as the three Marys and the three daughters of Holy Sophia, and even as Faith, Hope and Charity. In *Les Saintes Maries de la Mer*, in the Camargue in southern France, the black maid Sarah composes the third dark figure who, with the two bright Marys – Marie-Jacobe and Marie-Salome – composes the lunar trinity. Frequently the old classical imagery persisted into Christian times as allegory, officially stripped of its numinosity but still evocative of the ancient mystery.

THE NORNS

The three Norns of Germanic and Scandinavian myth also spin, weave and tear the web of life, transparent, like the Moirai, to the three visible phases of the Moon and, further, to the structure of incarnation. The Norns, called *Urd*, *Skuld*, and *Verdandi*, are interpreted variously as 'Fated,

Happening and What Must Be'; 'Fate (*Urd*), Being (*Verdandi*), and Necessity (*Skuld*)';[39] 'Past, Present and Future'; or 'Origin, Becoming and Debt'. Urd was old, Verdandi was young and lovely, but Skuld was easy to offend, and might rip up the webs of the other sisters when they were nearly done.[40] Some tales made Skuld the same person as the goddess Hel, and her name has the meaning of a debt, and may subtly remind of the death that is 'owed' to birth.[41] The Norns first appear in the *Voluspa* – translated (again variously), as the 'Wise Woman's Prophecy', the 'Prophecy of the Seeress', 'or the 'Song of the Sybil' – which is the early part of the great Old Norse poem the *Poetic* (or *Elder*) *Edda* of c.1000 AD. In Taylor and Auden's translation of the *Edda*, which they call *The Elder Edda*, Skuld comes second and is called the 'scorer of runes', while in Hollander's translation of the Edda, which he calls *The Poetic Edda*, Verdandi is second and Skuld third.[42] This is Taylor and Auden:

> I know an ash-tree, named Yggdrasil
> Sparkling showers are shed on its leaves
> That drip dew into the dales below.
> By Urd's Well it waves evergreen,
> Stands over that still pool,
> Near it a bower whence now there come
> The Fate Maidens, first Urd.
> Skuld second, scorer of runes,
> Then Verdandi, third of the Norns:
> The laws that determine the lives of men
> They fixed forever and their fate sealed.[43]

The Norns, like the Moirai, are older than the gods, and live in the 'Well of Fate' or 'Spring of Destiny', a spring deep in the Earth beneath the roots of Yggdrasil, the World Ash Tree, sprinkling

Fig. 8. The Moon standing behind the spinning Fates, whose spindle has seven spheres. French, 16th century. Illustrated manuscript by Thenaud, Traite de la Cabale. Bibliothèque Nationale.

their magical liquid over its branches, continually rescuing it from the decaying of time, though in the end the tree is to fall. The Icelandic poet and scholar Snorri Sturluson, who was also a Christian, writes in his *Prose Edda*, compiled from earlier sources in the 1220s:

> It is said further that the Norns who live near the spring of Urd draw water from the spring every day, and along with it the clay that lies round about the spring, and they besprinkle the ash so that its branches shall not wither or decay. But that water is so sacred that everything that comes into the spring becomes as white as the film (which is called 'skin') that lies within the eggshell...The dew which falls from it to the earth is called honey-dew by men, and bees feed on it. Two birds are nourished in the spring of Urd; they are called swans, and from them have come birds of this name.[44]

The subtle connections between Moon, dew, honey and ambrosia are present in the detail: the magical water, which falls from the lower branches of the World Tree, is white (the colour of moonlight); it becomes bees' honey, and has the power of resurrection. Nowhere does this part of the text say that this has anything to do with the Moon, even as a memory, yet the imagery is fascinatingly familiar, relating the Norns to the Moon through ambrosial elixir as well as through the spinning of destiny and law. In another poem, however, the Norns are specifically related to the Moon.

The opening verses of *The First Lay of Helgi* describe the Norns coming to the birth of a child who is to be a king, spinning the threads of his destiny beneath the Moon:

> Then was Helgi, the huge-hearted
> Born in Bralund to Borghild.
>
> Night had fallen when the Norns came,
> Those who appoint a prince's days:
> His fate, they foretold, was fame among men,
> to be thought the best of brave kings.
>
> There in Bralund's broad courts
> They spun the threads of his special destiny:
> They stretched out strings of gold,
> Fastened them under the hall of the moon.[45]

In the fortune of battle, the Norns take the form of the three 'weird sisters', *Disir* or 'Valkyries', who weave the 'girdle of victory' and the 'woof of war', spreading it over the battlefield as an invisible cloth.[46] The poem *Njals Saga* gives a chilling vision of war, sung by the Valkyries themselves even as they weave it:

> A loom has been set up, stretching afar and portending slaughter...and a rain of blood is pouring. Upon it has been stretched a warp of human beings – a warp grey with spears which the valkyries are filling with weft of crimson. The warp is formed of human entrails and is heavily weighted with human heads...we are weaving, weaving the web of the spear.[47]

Here, it is the Valkyries who weave the fighting as it happens, binding the fighters to the pattern of their loom. Their name means 'choice of death' (*kjora*, which gives *kyries*, means 'choice', and *val* means 'death'),[48] such that, in the name of Odin, god of wisdom, they choose the warriors who are destined to be rewarded with death in battle. Wolves, who descended on the battlefields at the end of the day, were known as the 'hounds of the Norns'.[49] The Celtic counterpart of the Valkyrie were the Morrigan, 'Great Queen', single or triple, goddess or goddesses of death who took the form of a raven, a bird also familiar at battlefields. King Arthur's nemesis, his sister Morgan la Fée, takes her name from them – la Fée, meaning 'the Fate', *Fata Morgana*.[50]

People who simply died of old age or disease went to the realm of the goddess Hel. But valiant warriors were uniquely favoured by Odin, who sent the Valkyries (riding the clouds and dropping dews upon the Earth), to escort the fallen heroes to *Valhalla* – the Hall of the Slain. There the Valkyries are transformed into handmaidens who wait at the table of the fallen, pouring mead into their goblets and placing the flesh of wild boar upon their plates, which never runs out. To be offered a cup of mead from a Valkyrie (fig. 9) was to be invited, willing or not, into immortality.

The power of belief in the Norns persisted even into Christian times (coming later to Scandinavia than anywhere else in Europe, in the tenth to eleventh centuries). The clash between the old native and new Christian culture is shown in this Nordic tale of a bard called, appropriately, *Nornagesta*, who possessed the gift of youth. A dispute at his birth also initiated his destiny, because Skuld, here the last of the Norns, was insulted. In a fury she declared that the babe would live only as long as it took for the bedside candle to burn down. Everyone began to mourn, until one of the other Norns simply put out the candle, on the grounds that, if it did not burn, it could not burn down. When he grew up, Nornagesta carried the candle with him wherever he went. But when he was 300 years old he was forced to become a Christian, and, to prove that his conversion was real, he had to light the candle stub. Which he did, and, when it burnt out, he dropped dead – confirming, had anyone doubted it, that the power of the Norns was greater than that of their Christian successors.[51]

Originally, there was one Norn, called Urth ('Fate') in Old Norse, Wurd in Old High German, and Wyrd in Anglo-Saxon. Wyrd later became the three-in-one Goddess Wyrd, who was also called the Norns' mother,[52] so the classical triad of the Moirai may have inspired the one to become three. Campbell points out that Wyrd may be etymologically related to the German *werden*, 'to become' or 'to grow', which implies an inherent, inward destiny, locating the 'Fates' in the individual heart. The word is further associated with the Old High German *wirt, wirtel*, 'spindle', suggesting a spinning and weaving of destiny, and also to the German *eerde*, 'earth', suggesting that human destiny is spun from the same fabric as the Earth by the original spinner of time and fate, the Moon.[53]

Fig. 9. Valkyrie offering a Cup of Mead. Silver statuette. Found in a grave, Koepingsocken, Oland. 11th century. Historiska Museum, Stockholm.

The Anglo-Saxon word *wyrd* meant 'destiny', often in the sense of haunting doom, and became 'weird' in English as something strange and inexplicable, but also magically powerful.[54] In Anglo-Saxon poetry, every person's fate is 'woven', *gewith*, and in *Beowulf* (the oldest extended story in Northern European literature) the warriors are given 'webs of war-speed' by their god.[55] Beowulf, when an old king, foresaw the imminence of his death in the feeling that *wyrd* was close to him. He ordered a shield, wrought in iron, and he made the man who had taken the golden cup from the dragon serve as his guide. Then he sat down on the foreland, with 11 other friends, making himself the twelfth and his guide the thirteenth, and he bade his companions farewell:

> His heart was sad,
> uneasy and death-ready: *wyrd* immediately nigh.[56]

THE WEIRD SISTERS

In *Macbeth*, Shakespeare has transformed the Norns of the Well of Fate into the three 'Weird Sisters' around a cauldron of doom, the witches who at night upon a blasted heath prophesy to Macbeth the fate he has conceived already in his heart. That Shakespeare intentionally linked his Three Sisters to the ancient Fates is suggested in *The Merchant of Venice*, in Launcelot Gobbo's playful pretence to his blind father that he is dead:

> The young gentleman, according to Fates and Destinies and such odd sayings, the Sisters Three and such branches of learning, is indeed deceased; or, as you would say in plain terms, gone to heaven.[57]

Through the echoing imagery of Macbeth and the witches, Shakespeare takes on the question as to whether the Weird Sisters predestine Macbeth or, more subtly, reveal to him the depths of his own character as his destiny. The three witches introduce the theme:

> Fair is foul, and foul is fair;
> Hover through the fog and filthy air.[58]

Macbeth's first words are ominous in their repetition, yet still inconclusive, the balance between foul and fair not yet tipped:

> So foul and fair a day I have not seen.[59]

But Banquo takes us deeper into Macbeth's heart:

> Good sir, why do you start and seem to fear
> Things that do sound so fair?[60]

How free is the will when the web is woven; how binding is the pattern of the weave? Which is again to ask, who weaves the cloth?

THE SPINNING MOON

The image of the spinning and weaving Moon moves back and forth across the world, from India to Europe, from Brazil to the North American Indians, and gypsies everywhere. In many places the Moon was conceived as the Great Spider, as shown in Chapter 4. In other places, the metaphor of spinning prevails on its own: in the *Mahabharata*, two women spin and weave the nights and days on the loom of the year, using threads that were black and white.[61] In Sumatra, among the Batak people, the Moon spins cotton, and in a German folk tale even the Moon-hare wove cloth on Earth for a certain old lady, who wove faster than anyone else.[62] In German and Slavonic tales, a woman who worked at her loom on the Sabbath was transported to the Moon (company for the men who gathered sticks and stole vegetables).[63] Shakespeare picks up the image of weaving in *All's Well That Ends Well*, in the commentary of a French Lord:

> The web of our life is of a mingled yarn,
> good and ill together.[64]

In Egypt, weaving was invented by Neith, a huntress goddess of the Moon, whose emblem is a shield with crossed arrows and who sometimes holds a shuttle. Wallis Budge suggests that her name may be connected with the root *netet*, to knit and weave, and her special knots and cords were used in ceremonies of death, when a piece of woven linen was placed in the hand of the deceased.[65] Neith was also described as 'Net, the Cow, which gave birth to Re' (the Sun god), placing her at the beginning of things, like the goddess Maat.[66] The dual image – weaver and hunter – suggests that she both spins life into being and cuts it off with her bow and arrows, but, like the resurrecting Moon, she also weaves the dead into eternity. Neith was called 'the oldest one', and was often identified with Hathor, Nut and Isis in Egypt, and with Athene in Greece. Plutarch refers to an inscription on a statue of Athene, 'whom they believe to be Isis', in the temple of Neith-Isis at Sais, in which the weaver of the cosmic veil declares: 'I am all that has been, that is, and that will be. No one has yet been able to lift the veil which covers me.'[67] As Shelley puts it in the first line of his poem *Sonnet*: 'Lift not the painted veil which those who live / Call Life'.[68]

A similar range of reference might be implied in the curious Greek spherical stone called the *omphalos*, the 'navel' of the Earth. It was found in Delphi, a word meaning both 'womb' and 'dolphin', which was originally the sanctuary of Gaia, Mother Earth, before it was appropriated by Apollo. It was said that 'the omphalos of Earth is the tomb of the Python', the daimon-snake of an earlier age who embodied the fertility of Earth and Moon, and who was a form of Dionysos.[69] Plutarch writes that in Orphic tradition the Delphic oracle was held by Night and the Moon.[70] The stone is sculpted with a net of fillets carved on its surface – an *agrenon* – like a woven net covering the Earth.

Among the North American Indians, the Moon is called the 'Ancient Spinstress' by the Navaho and the Ojibwa, while the Iroquois see an old woman weaving on the face of the Moon.[71] Ixchel, the Mayan Moon goddess, was a weaver, often drawn with her spindle.[72] The Scandinavian lunar goddess, Freya, was also a spinstress, as were the Teutonic goddesses Bertha and Holda, and Holda was the patroness of weavers in medieval Europe. Freya's distaff was the constellation of Orion, which in Sweden today is called the distaff of the Virgin Mary.[73]

The connection between the weaving on the loom and the pattern and span of life may have one source in the fact that spinning and weaving were the work of women who, as mothers, also spun the tissue of their children out of the loom of their wombs. (In Dutch the word for tissue is *weefsel*, meaning something woven). The cutting of the umbilical cord at birth had its counterpart in the cutting of the thread at death when the weaving of life's work was done. Here, this image of the

Fig. 10. Neith, Net, or The Lady of the West, with bow and arrows. (From Wallis Budge, The Gods of the Egyptians, i, p. 451).

woman's body and craft becomes transparent to the essential mystery of the unmanifest becoming manifest and taking form in space and time.

THE VIRGIN MARY AS WEAVER

> She, wild web, wondrous robe,
> Mantles the guilty globe.

So wrote Gerard Manley Hopkins in his poem *The Blessed Virgin Compared to the Air We Breathe:*[74]

The Virgin Mary is also sometimes drawn in the image of a spinstress who spins and weaves the redemption of the world in her womb.[75] In an apocryphal tale she is drawn as the weaver of the veil of the temple,[76] and the spinning wheel itself has two parts called the 'maiden' and the 'mother of all'.[77]

In a twelfth-century Coptic manuscript Mary's spindle is eloquent of the angel's message (fig. 11); while in fig. 12 two angels feed the thread into her hands, drawing it over her womb. The three imposing figures are related through their clothes, the hanging gowns in red and blue, and their outstretched hands, the two angels pointing towards the Virgin in the centre, who guides the thread with her hands. It is as though a vase painting of the three Moirai has been transformed into a Christian sensibility, with meaning at once entirely new yet hauntingly the same. Here are the three Fates spinning the destiny of the world which the weaving of Mary's body is to accomplish.

In a later fifteenth-century picture from Germany, Mary, seated, spins thread from a spindle into her womb, the thread passing directly through the brow of the baby Jesus curled up inside her, while God watches, equidistant from both of them, weaving eternity into time (fig. 13).

Mary, as the mother who wove God's child, became by the Middle Ages the Mother who mediated between God and all his children. The relation between Mary and God was often compared with the way in which the Moon reflects and softens light from the heavens, releasing it at night and illuminating the darkness of the Christian soul. Here, the Moon's traditional role of determining destiny persists in the image of the 'influence' of Mary, inspiring and comforting travellers on their journey, lost and lonely in the dark.

SPINNING AS DESTINY IN FAIRY TALES

The European fairy tale of the Sleeping Beauty, or Briar Rose, is also permeated with lunar symbolism, having at its heart a spindle of great power. The young princess was forbidden to spin, and all the spindles in the country were destroyed, because at her christening she was cursed to die from a prick of a spindle at the age of 15 by the thirteenth 'Wise Woman' whom the king and queen had omitted to invite. (The tale is reminiscent of the Greek myth of Zeus and Hera's wedding feast, to which one of the goddesses was not invited, and also of the Nordic tale of Nornagesta). The 'gift' of the 'wicked' thirteenth Wise Woman was death, but was changed from death to sleep by the good twelfth Wise Woman, who had not yet made her gift. But when the princess is 15 – the number of years matching the number of days makes this the first day of the Waning Moon – she discovers a secret room in an ancient tower where an old woman sits spinning. For at this time of the cycle the spinning goddess of the Moon begins to loosen the threads, to undo what until then has been perfectly woven.

The princess, pricked by the spindle, falls into a deep sleep, as does her whole world. Like the Moon, she does not die but is kissed awake by the prince, who scales the thicket of briars 100 years later (a century is analogous to a complete cycle). In some versions, spinning is then resumed and the Wise Women weave her a wedding veil. The uninvited guest at the feast was the goddess of the Dark Moon or the last of the Fates, the 'wicked fairy god-mother', whose gift of cutting the thread of life has to be accepted as the final bond with fate. Every rose has its thorn, but in this fairy tale the deathly curse is transformed into a sleep from which the maiden eventually awakes, just as the Moon, the original spinner, continually awakens from its sleep of death.[78]

Two other tales from Grimm point to this archaic relation between spinning and destiny. A spindle, shuttle and needle, in the tale of that name, were once given to an orphan girl by her dying god-mother, and, with her last protector gone, they actively create her fate themselves. The spindle goes to fetch the king's son, the shuttle weaves a marvellous carpet, and the needle sews a beautiful home in which to welcome him. They are called into autonomous life by a little song the girl sings, one 'the old woman had occasionally sung',[79] the 'little song' evocative of the singing of the sirens and the spinning of fate in Plato's *Republic*.

There are also three spinners in Grimm's playful tale of the transformation of a lazy girl into a prince's bride. The spinners are ugly, often a sign in fairy tales of being forgotten and undervalued. Seeing the girl listless at the window, they offer to do prodigious amounts of spinning for her (which the Queen, the Prince's mother, has demanded as a prerequisite for their marriage). But in return she must acknowledge them as her cousins and not be ashamed of them. 'The first had a broad flat foot; the second had a lower

Fig. 11. Annunciation. The Angel greets Mary as she is spinning. Illustrated manuscript, Coptic. 1179-80. Bibliothèque Nationale, Paris.

lip so big that it hung down over her chin; and the third had a broad thumb.' They spin vast quantities of fine flax for her and the girl keeps her promise in return, so the three old maids arrive at the wedding party in outlandish costumes. 'Good Lord!' said the bridegroom, 'However did you get such ungainly cousins?' He went over and asked the first: 'How did you get such a broad foot?' 'By treading,' she replied. He asked the second: 'How did you ever get that hanging lip?' 'By licking,' she replied. And he asked the third: 'How did you get that broad thumb?' By twisting thread,' she replied. 'In that case,' declared the prince, 'my beautiful bride shall never touch a spinning wheel again.'[80]

THE VEIL OF MAYA

The ambivalence found in many tales towards the lunar Fates, who end the lives they begin, is evoked in the image of the spider's cycle of spinning a beautiful web and then using it to entice, entangle and kill. In Hindu myth, the spider symbolizes Maya, who spins the illusions of time and weaves the Web of Fate.[81] Zimmer describes Maya in terms eloquent of the Moirai. Maya is:

> In substance one, yet in form and functions three, by virtue of the mirror trick that breaks the All into the Many. Maya is the Mother. Maya is the charm by which life is forever seducing itself. Maya is the womb, the nourishing bosom, and the tomb.[82]

This Great Mother, Weaver of the World, is often called *Kali*, the 'Dark Lady', whose 'gift of life' to the supine Shiva, and their subsequent embrace, was shown in figs 1 and 9 in Chapter 2.

Maya means 'illusion', a term that comes, like 'Moon', from the verbal root *ma*, to 'measure, measure out, form, create, construct, exhibit, display'. *Maya* refers, Campbell says, to 'both the power that creates an illusion and the false display itself.'[83] (Hence the complication of the thought.) The

Fig. 12. Annunciation. Mural painting from the Church of San Pedro de Sorpe, Spain. 12th century. Museo de Arte de Cataluna, Barcelona.

Fig. 13. The Virgin Mary spinning the child in her womb. Upper Rheinish Master. c. 1400. Gemäldegalerie, Staatliche Museen zu Berlin.

magician's art, for example, and the illusion he creates by means of it, are both *Maya*, which is thereby said to possess three powers: a Veiling Power, which conceals the true essence of things; a Projecting Power, which creates all appearances; and a Revealing Power, which art, ritual and meditation can make known, by enabling the illusory phenomena to be viewed in such a way that *they themselves* reveal what they usually veil – 'Thought hid in thoughts, dreams hid in dreams,' in Yeats's image.[84]

It seems to be a condition of the Revealing Power that first the Veiling Power has to be understood. Art and literature have always sought to make us aware that there is a veil or a shadow between ourselves and life, between our understanding and reality. The veil of Maya, the veil of Isis, the words on the temple of Neith-Isis, 'no one has lifted my veil' – all these remind us that we do not, initially perhaps cannot, see things as they are. Plato's allegory of the Cave proposed that all we see are shadows falling on a screen which we cannot but take for real, so imprisoned in our perceptions and ideas that we are ignorant of the light shining from behind us from a source we cannot turn and see. Awareness of this – turning around (the etymological meaning of 'conversion') – is the starting point of any growing: to know you are a fool is the beginning of wisdom, as Socrates said.

* * *

But what, then, of individual 'fate'? Is it already spun, or written, before it gets to us (Atropos sometimes holds a scroll), either randomly, or, as Plato says, willingly chosen by the soul before incarnation? Is there a reason for the way inheritance – of gene, gender, family, tribe, race – relates to what we experience as the chance of event and environment? We may ask how the ancient beliefs surrounding the Moon have contributed to the western tradition of thinking upon these insoluble questions.

The Fates, as Moirai, Parcae, Matronae or Norns, may at least be understood as determining the biological destiny of human beings, personifying the stages of birth, growth and death, common to all living beings. But they obviously meant more than this to the people who believed in them, and not just as a way of deferring to the incalculable, unpredictable elements in any person's life, which, then as now, got the name of good and bad 'luck'. It is as though, in the moment of becoming aware of the inevitable limitation on life, there arose in the heart a complementary image which was *personal*, and took feminine form as identifiable figures, one for each phase of life. As if, in the veiling, projecting and revealing powers of the *image*, the terror could, as it were, be named and find a home. The idea of the Fates may provide a habitation for the mind, primarily in those areas of life over which it has least control: most obviously, birth and death, where the thread of life is spun and cut. But the middle Fate, she who weaves the pattern of what is lived (and what cannot be lived), and whose art must be invoked for an enriching life, she also is given a character, as a way, perhaps, of acknowledging and accepting the impersonal dimensions of life that come as 'gifts', those things which are beyond our own capacity to give (or take away from) ourselves. Here is Yeats:

> All perform their tragic play,
> There struts Hamlet, there is Lear,
> That's Ophelia, that Cordelia;
> Yet they, should the last scene be there,
> The great stage curtain about to drop,
> If worthy their prominent part in the play,
> Do not break up their lines to weep.
> They know that Hamlet and Lear are gay;
> Gaiety transforming all that dread.[85]

* * *

Nonetheless, such a vision, like the revealing power of Maya, is not always available, and then it is significant that the symbolism of spinning, twisting, binding and cutting may emerge as imagery of protest against the apparent absence of an ethical universe, where freedom is found in the ability to throw off the woven web of destiny. The link between spinning and the Moon is here only implicit.

Aeschylus, for instance, the earliest Greek dramatist who stands at the beginning of the western tradition, conceives of fate in the image of a 'net' or 'snare' thrown over human beings from the realm of the gods, all that is 'given' to the person in both character and circumstance. Cassandra is spoken of by the Chorus as 'caught in the snare of fate', and she in her turn sees a vision of Agamemnon's death under his robe as a 'net of Hades'.[86] Sophocles in *Oedipus Rex*, suggests there is no choice except through awareness – as Oedipus, unaware of who his parents were, could not be said to have chosen to murder one and marry the other, but pollutes his city until he accepts responsibility for his unconsciousness, for all he did not and could not know.[87]

In Aeschylus, the limitations upon human choice were simply named as tragedy: 'Which of these courses is without evil?' cries Agamemnon, when the wind will not blow his ships to Troy unless he sacrifice his daughter, Iphigeneia at the altar of the Moon goddess Artemis. This was the sacrifice demanded by the priest of Artemis because one of his men unwittingly pursued a deer into her forest and violated her shrine. When he returns from the war ten years later, his wife, Klytemnestra, takes her revenge for the murder of their daughter, Iphigeneia, and murders him. The perspective is given by Aigisthos (Klytemnestra's lover), who speaks of Agamemnon as 'lying in the woven robes of the *Erinyes*',[88] the three Furies, who are the dark retributive face of the Moirai, holding, as they say of themselves, the 'memory of evil' and carrying the 'mind of the past'.[89] Later, in the *Eumenides*, Athene pits a different kind of intelligence against the Furies to release Orestes from the curse of his inheritance (murdering his mother for murdering his father for murdering his sister), but has to concede that no household will prosper without their blessing.[90] Euripides, in his play *Orestes*, has Orestes' sister Electra talk of 'the father of Atreus for whom the weaving Fates wove the thread of war.'[91]

Looking through a lunar lens at this familiar story, it becomes suddenly no coincidence that it is Artemis, as goddess of the Moon in her hunting mode, whose rage initiates the fateful conflict that circumscribes the beginning and the end of the war. The ancient power of such beliefs is suggested by the fact that not once does anyone question the goddess's demand for sacrifice, as conveyed through her priest Calchas. In Euripides' *Iphigeneia at Aulis*, Calchas, about to slay Iphigeneia, runs around the altar with a knife, crying:

> O child of Zeus, O slayer of wild beasts
> You who turn your disc of shining light
> Through the night's shadows, receive this sacrifice
> Which we make to you...And grant
> That ungrieved now the fleet may sail.[92]

Artemis intervenes in the sacrifice as the knife falls, substituting a deer for the girl, who becomes her priestess instead (as though recalling the moment in Greece when human sacrifice passed to the sacrifice of animals). Certainly, it was Artemis, 'the lady with the golden spindle', *christelakatos*, as Homer calls her,[93] to whom animals and birds were piled high on heaps of sticks, burnt to honour her that she might favour those who lit the flames (fig. 1).

Even the abduction of Helen by the Trojan Paris is underpinned with lunar symbolism. Helen, daughter of Leda and the Swan, sister of the Heavenly Twins, Castor and Pollux, and wife of Menelaos, the 'Moon-man' (as the etymological root of his name *men* would imply), was born from an egg which had fallen from the Moon. Helen was identified with Nemesis – the role she plays in the Trojan War – and the Gnostics regarded her name as identical with that of Selene, the Moon.[94] The 'Judgement of Paris', as Harrison has shown, is by no means a 'vulgar beauty contest' between three goddesses, Hera, Athene and Aphrodite.[95] On the contrary, it is a judgement *upon* Paris by the three goddesses, all related to the Moon, who are to allot to him his particular destiny. The goddesses stand before him with all the grim severity of the three Moirai, one of which will choose *him* and present him with the apple that seals this particular destiny as his own. Aphrodite's girdle, whose magical invitation no one could resist, may carry the deeper meaning of fate for Paris in his supposed 'choice' between three different goddesses carrying three different kinds of destinies. The insistent presence of Hermes, god of imagination, suggests, rather, that a transformation is taking place in Paris's life over which he has little control. In the vase painting shown in fig. 14, Paris tries to escape the three formidable figures advancing upon him but is prevented by Hermes, who, crossing the threshold between the visible and invisible worlds, compels Paris to face who he essentially is. For Paris, then, the oldest of the Moirai puts her girdle on.

Similarly, it may be no coincidence that it is the lunar goddess Athene, who can release Orestes from the unending net of retribution, mediating between the old Furies and the gods Zeus and Apollo, figures of the new order. Athene herself knows the mind of the past, yet, in her new role as 'daughter of the Father', she may transcend the inevitability of the cyclic round at a new level. That is to say, here the lunar imagination comprehends both fate and its transcendence in the dual image of phase and cycle. The *Erinyes* concede the loss of their power: 'The powers of the grey old time are overthrown...Thou art hounding us down, O new God, us, the old ones...It is the old law, the immemorial right, which you are tearing down, you new Gods...tearing out of my hands.[96]

Two thousand years later only the rope is left. The man called 'Lucky' in Beckett's play *Waiting for Godot* has a rope around his neck from which he cannot break free. Lucky, the obedient slave of Pozzo, arrives instead of Godot (thereby symbolically replacing him) to meet the two tramps Vladimir and Estragon, who are waiting for Godot to make sense of why they are waiting. Only when Lucky's hat is put on his head and he 'thinks', does he jerk against his rope and shout:

> Given the existence as uttered forth in the public works of Puncher and Wattmann of a personal God quaquaquaqua with white beard quaquaquaqua outside time without extension who from the heights of divine apathia divine athambia divine aphasia loves us dearly with some exceptions for reasons unknown but time will tell...[97]

In some productions, Lucky struggles against a net which covers him.

THE WHEEL OF FORTUNE

Sophocles draws on the figure of the changing Moon to explore the impermanence of fate:

> But my fate circles on the shifting wheel
> Of God's reversal, and still suffers change.
> Like to the pale moon's face, that cannot stay
> For two nights ever in the same aspect,

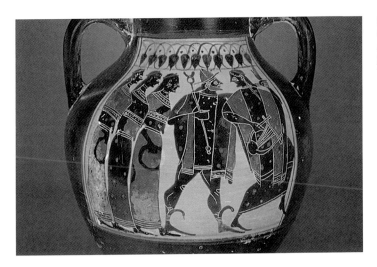

Fig. 14. Paris with Hermes and the three goddesses, Hera, Athene, Aphrodite. Black figure vase painting. Etruscan. 6th c. BC. The Louvre.

> But first comes issuing from the dim, then grows
> With lovelier countenance waxing to the full,
> And every time she shows herself at her loveliest,
> She lapses and fades, and comes to nothingness.[98]

Here, the image of fate circling on a wheel that keeps moving is referred to the endless round of the Moon's waxing and waning, pointing to the lunar origins of the familiar Wheel of Fate or Fortune. The revolving wheel entered many cultures as a way of contemplating the vicissitudes of life from a perspective beyond them, beyond the ups and downs, the good or bad luck.

The Greek goddess of Luck – the goddess *Tyche*, whose name means 'Fortune' – was sometimes identified with the Moirai as the mightiest among them.[99] In Roman thought, *Tyche* became the goddess *Fortuna* – sometimes in triple form – whose Wheel of Fate went on turning, like the Moon and the year. But when the Roman armies entered the Celtic countries they found that one of the pre-Roman Mothers or Matronae already held the wheel upon her lap. In Gaelic, the word for wheel or circle, *rath*, is applied to 'fortune', since the Full Moon when the circle was complete was the most propitious – *ata rath air* – while the Waning Moon is called *mi-rath*, and one who is unfortunate is called *at a mi-rath air*.[100] Although, in Celtic myth, the wheel was mostly a solar symbol, there were also tales of a great silver wheel ridden by heroes, which dipped into the sea on its way to *Emania*, the Moon's land of death.[101]

The richness of the original conception of the wheel as a gift, along with the cornucopia of plenty, was gradually lost, and the symbol of the wheel was later more narrowly interpreted as the impersonal wheel of time which, turning ceaselessly, rolls some people upward towards good luck and others downward towards bad. The Tarot cards kept the image of the Wheel of Fortune alive, virtually unchanged, long after the Romans had left Gaul, Germany and Britain, though by the fourteenth century the Tarot was banned in France, Germany and Italy.[102] Sometimes Fortuna was depicted as blindfold because she did not reward the good and punish the bad, so her choice of lucky and unlucky people did not reflect an ethical universe. (Job, in a different context, protested likewise to his God: 'Thou knowest that I am not wicked; and there is none that can deliver out of thine hand.')[103] The 'Wheel of Fortune' – the tenth card of the Major Arcana in the Tarot – offered a meditation on the inevitability of change, such that the meditator, casting the cards in private ritual, might identify with

Fig. 15. The Wheel of Fortune. King, Queen, noblemen and serfs. From the manuscript of John Lydgate's Troy Book and Story of Thebes. England, c. 1516–1523. The rich red gown of the goddess on top of the wheel contrasts with the goddess behind or within the spokes who wears a sombre blue flecked with gold circles of dots like stars. The two figures are evocative of the bright and the dark Moon, both turning the wheel of fate. British Library, London.

the reality beyond change, not with the changes themselves. Thus the inscription on the Sufi ring, given by the sages to calm their restless king, read: 'This too will pass.'[104]

The wheel, whose inner centre is still and whose outer rim is moving, has inspired Buddhist thought as an image of the way of escape from appearances and the way towards the 'centre', where, with the revealing power of Maya, illusions can be seen to be illusions. So, similarly, has the image of the knot (fig. 18). An early Buddhist text indirectly relates the inspiration of the wheel to the round Moon: 'The heavenly treasure of the Wheel...appeared to the king on the day of the full moon.'[105] The 'Wheel of Law, Truth and Life' is one of the eight emblems of good luck in Chinese Buddhism.[106] A similar purpose seems to be behind what Yeats called his 'parable of the moon', in which he depicts the 'Great Wheel' as a model that offers an understanding of one's type and stage in life.

Yeats takes the cycle of the Moon as the counterpart of the cycle of a human lifetime (averaged out at three score and ten) (fig. 16). In his book *A Vision*, composed in part from automatic writings given to his wife, he proposes a pattern, at once mythological and psychological, in which the mortal temporary self emerges, like the Moon, out of darkness and returns to it at the end (when, in the terms explored here, *bios* is dissolved back into *zoe*):

> How it is whirled about,
> Wherever the orbit of the moon can reach,
> Until it plunge into the sun...[107]

Birth begins with the New Moon becoming visible, and the fifteenth day of the Moon cycle corresponds to the thirty-fifth year of a life, the time when Moon and human are at their peak. Subsequently, waning sets in, with a biblical Dark Moon due at three score years and ten. As Yeats describes it in his book *Wheels and Butterflies*, he saw in the changes of the moon all the cycles: the soul realizing its separate being in the full moon, then, as the moon seems to approach the sun and dwindle away, all but realizing its absorption in God, only to whirl away once more: the mind of a man, separating itself from the common matrix, through childish imaginations, through struggle...to roundness, systematizing, until at last it lies dead, a spider smothered in its own web.[108]

His poem *The Phases of the Moon* draws the character of the phases as the character of types of people, who can be waxing or waning types, oriented outwards in the waxing or inwards in the waning, predisposed to a life of public service or personal whim. The poem is structured as a dialogue between two people, Robartes and Aherne, and recalls the precision of earlier times when each day of the Moon's phases had a specific name and character, here symbolizing the stage of a life and the type of a person:

Robartes:
Twenty-and-eight the phases of the moon,
The full and the moon's dark and all the crescents,
Twenty-and-eight, and yet but six-and-twenty,
The cradles that a man must needs be rocked in;
For there's no human life at the full or the dark.
From the crescent to the half, the dream
But summons to adventure, and the man
Is always happy like a bird or a beast;
But while the moon is rounding towards the full
He follows whatever whim's most difficult
Among whims not impossible...
Under the frenzy of the fourteenth moon,
The soul begins to tremble into stillness,
To die into the labyrinth of itself!...
And after that the crumbling of the moon:
The soul remembering its loneliness
Shudders in many cradles; all is changed...

Aherne:
Before the full
It sought itself and afterwards the world...[109]

When the soul reaches the full dark, it is 'Insipid as the dough before it is baked.' But this is not the end of a life or of a civilization:

When all the dough has been so kneaded up
That it can take what form Nature fancies,
The first thin crescent is wheeled round once more.

The crescent to the full was the phase of complete 'subjectivity', and the full to the dark was the phase of complete 'objectivity'. As a way of determining the nature and degree of subjectivity and objectivity, Yeats proposed, within the circle of the Moon, a further symbol of two interlocking triangles or 'cones': the *Will* and *Creative Mind* cone, and its opposite the *Mask* and *Body of Fate*.

This long poem, and the whole complex book, requires a study of its own,[110] but what is interesting mythologically is how the cycle of the Moon is still being related to the cycle of human life and to the greater cycles of civilizations, as though destiny were delivered by the Moon along with time.

Astrology also takes its reference from this idea of the quality of time, specifically the quality of the moment of birth when the infant takes its first breath into the phenomenal world and enters time. The birth chart is a map of the position of all ten 'planets' at this moment (including Moon and Sun). Astrologers read the particular phase of the natal Moon at the moment of birth as predisposing to a particular kind of orientation to life and, as with Yeats, the Moon's relation to the Sun is taken to be an important part of the astrological composition of a person's character (whether, for instance, it is a 'Waxing Moon' ahead of the Sun, as for example, Sun in Aries, Moon in Leo, or a 'Waning Moon' behind the Sun, as, for example, Sun in Libra, Moon in Virgo).[111]

New and Full Moons in the natal chart are points of particular emphasis. In a New Moon, the Moon and Sun are 'conjunct' – the Moon lying between Sun and Earth, so it is invisible, with no 'light of its own'. Astrology interprets this in terms of the harmonizing of the energies of Moon and Sun, just as many myths of Moon and Sun dramatize this time either as a period of mutual peace – when brother and sister stop fighting, or husband and wife come together in embrace – or as a period of death when the Moon is slain by the Sun. In a Full Moon, the Moon is 'in opposition' to the Sun – lying in a direct line on the other side of Earth, in the opposing zodiacal sign to that of the Sun, and completely illuminated. 'Sun opposition Moon' is understood to mean that the energies of Sun and Moon are clearly distinct and so may conflict with each other, bringing their essential independence into awareness. In many myths Moon and Sun, being then both 'equal' in light and farthest apart, as it were call each other out, disclosing the 'otherness' of the other. If they are brother and sister, the guilty tale of incestuous markings on the Moon is revealed; if husband and wife, it is often the time of the 'sacred marriage' when the separate energies of the cosmos are brought back into balance. But this balance of energies is both exactly timed and forever in motion, for immediately afterwards the Moon begins to lose its light. (There are many variations to these myths as we have seen, but here the point is simply to draw attention to the parallels between astrology and myth.)

When asked whether he believed in the actual existence of his circuits of Sun and Moon, Yeats answered:

> If sometimes, overwhelmed by miracle as all men must be when in the midst of it, I have taken such periods literally, my reason has soon recovered; and now that the system stands out clearly in my imagination I regard them as stylistic arrangements of experience comparable to the cubes in the drawings of Wyndham Lewis and to the ovoids in the sculpture of Brancusi. They have helped me to hold in a single thought reality and justice.[112]

SPINNING TIME AND KNOTTING DESTINY

What does it mean that the Moon which spins time also spins destiny? Time as linear – the thread that is spun and then cut – is hereby brought into relationship with time as pattern – how that thread is woven in the life – and it is these two senses of 'time' which combine to give the idea of the *quality* of time. Later Greek thought distinguished *chronos* (the passage of time) from *kairos* (experienced time or 'opportunity'), and the modern mind too separates time and destiny – asking, rather, what do we make of the time allotted to us – as in E.M. Forster's distinction of 'life lived in time' and 'life lived by value.'[113] Yet we still on occasion refer to the old idea of a certain time having a distinctive quality, and even imply that time itself has a quality except when we abuse it and see only quantity, reducing it to a series of undifferentiated moments. In *Macbeth* these two kinds of time are contrasted, for only when life has lost its value – when 'fair' is 'foul' and 'foul' is 'fair' – does Macbeth experience time as a meaningless line ending in death, in which there is no 'time' to register the death of his wife, because there is no quality left:

> She should have died hereafter;
> There would have been a time for such a word.
> Tomorrow, and tomorrow, and tomorrow,
> Creeps in this petty pace from day to day
> To the last syllable of recorded time;
> And all our yesterdays have lighted fools
> The way to dusty death. Out, out, brief candle![114]

Time that has value is often celebrated, or the loss of it mourned, in imagery that once belonged to the spinning goddesses of the Moon. It seems that myths of the Moon still underlie some of the ways in which we think about free and determined will, wondering what draws a life into its distinctive shape. For the Moon, as spinner of fate as well as time, throws into focus those experiences in which the threads of time are knotted into a person's destiny. Yet, for the most part, the ancient lunar source is long forgotten, and perhaps the imagery is less rich for being unlocatable except as 'superstition'.

We still talk, for instance, of the 'knots', 'bonds' and 'twists' of fate, the 'ties' of friendship, the 'bond' of marriage, 'tying the knot', marriage 'bands', the bonding between mother and child – all of them love knots, places in the web where the threads are tied into time and become the unique pattern which defines and binds people, ties them down, each to their individual destiny.[115] 'My word is my bond,' as the saying goes. Even the word 'destiny' comes from the Latin verb *destino*, which was used of binding and whose primary meaning was 'to fix'.[116]

In a remote Tibetan village, a ceremony of marriage still exists where the boy and girl tie two ropes together into one plait and then burn them, offering the smoke up to the Moon.[117] The Chinese 'Old Man in the Moon', *Yueh Lao Yeh*, who holds in his hands the power of marriages, was said to tie together the feet of the future husband and wife with an invisible red cord which never breaks. The proverb says, 'Marriages are made in Heaven, but prepared in the Moon.'[118] The Aztec marriage union was ritually expressed by the tying together of the couple's clothing in a knot by the old matchmakers (fig. 17).[119]

In Europe, bed sheets for the wedding night were deliberately knotted to make for a happy marriage,[120] and in the seventeenth century it was recommended that, in order to 'tie a man not to meddle with a

Fig. 16. The Great Wheel. From the Speculum Angelorum et Hominum (The Mirror of Angels and Men). 16th century. (From Yeats, A Vision, p. 66.)

woman, *et contra*', the wedding should include a ritual in which a piece of cloth with three knots tied in it was placed over the hands of man and woman, upon which the priest said: 'Whom God hath joined together those let the Devil separate, until these knots be undone.'[121]

We say, of an unavoidable event, that it is 'bound' to happen, that fate lies 'in the lap' of the gods (as the spindle lies in the lap of the spinner), that death is a 'winding sheet', a noose, a rope, a cord, that an illness is 'fatal'. The Hindu death god, *Yama*, led away the deceased in bonds, with a noose,[122] while in war a spell was chanted to send the enemy into the 'net of Indra'.[123] The Norse goddess Hel used a cord, the German death goddesses had a rope.[124] The Kogi Indians are said to attach a twisted cord to the dead person to lower him standing into the grave, and after seven days it is cut and he falls back into the womb of Earth.[125] As children, we cross our fingers for a wish to come true (hoping for the best); we cross them behind our backs when we don't mean what we say (to unbind the oath); and, wagering our innocence, we 'cross our hearts and hope to die' to convince someone we are telling the truth. We tie a knot in a handkerchief to remember something (to twist the thought into time), and we hold up crossed fingers towards a spell or a danger (to tighten the weave to our wish). Rituals were performed in honour of Hekate at the crossroads, and it is there, where the crossing roads knot, that Sophocles has Oedipus kill the bad-tempered stranger who was his father – the act which, all unknowingly and perhaps for that very reason, binds and seals his fate.

The cross is a knot which *unites* contrary forces in dynamic relation, and for this reason, was a symbol of both life and eternity in Egypt, among many other places. Although Christians would later hold up 'their' Cross as an image of the Crucifixion to ward off the devil, it had long been a universal symbol, and in fact the Cross did not feature in Christian art until 600 years after the death of Christ. Early Christians depicted Christ as the Good Shepherd carrying a lamb, like Hermes. Even the 'Hot Cross Bun' of Easter was preceded in Greece and Rome by cakes, marked with a cross, eaten at the festivals of Artemis and Diana, also celebrated at the vernal equinox. There, the quarters made by the cross signified the quarters of the Moon, an image of the renewal of cyclical time in the spring of the year.[126]

* * *

R.B. Onians, in his *The Origins of European Thought*, argues that these spinning, knotting and binding images are not just figures of speech. Rather, they are

> allusions to one of the images under which a whole people interpreted life and saw the working of fate, the action of the gods in things human...a popular belief of what actually happens on that plane where divine and human meet – the mystical and, to the unprivileged eye, invisible. It is in short a part of the national religion, of the philosophy of the race...a mode of conceiving divine causation.[127]

The 'nervousness' about knots appears to turn up, as we might expect, on momentous occasions when life is about to change irrevocably. Pliny's advice for a prospective father at childbirth was to untie his own girdle and then to tie it around his wife, saying, 'I have tied it, and will untie it,' in order to hasten delivery, after which he leaves the room.[128] In England, midwives would make a point of unknotting good luck cords and lengths of string (perhaps to invite the baby to come and make its own knot into time).[129] Old British marriage customs have the bride standing beside the altar with an untied shoe, and the groom tying up the lace as the knotting of their marriage.[130] On the other hand, a knot you haven't tied yourself is suspect: if you happen to find a strange knot on your clothes, you must quickly untie it, for it could have been tied by a demon (anticipating the dismissive phrase 'get knotted').[131] The first knot most people tie is the knot of their shoelaces, and here augury is rife. If your shoelace comes undone at the start of a new enterprise, it 'spells' disaster; but if you find your shoelaces already done up on shoes you have yet to wear, it will bring good luck.[132] Yet the 'right' knot could heal warts and sprains. *Shetland Lore* of 1932 observes: 'Wise women...could cure sprains by a woollen thread spun from black wool and tied in an "aaba k-not" for each day in the moon's age...'[133] The significance of the knot appears to depend upon who tied it, and why, and whether it was tied in grass, garters, girdles, sheets, shoes or shrouds.[134] Cord-amulets, girdles, wreaths, crowns, necklaces and bracelets could all have the function of conferring life and luck by winding a bond of protection around the wearer. Knots could help or hinder, bless or curse, but whatever meaning was given to them they were understood as events which changed the course of life.

Escape from the bonds of fate we express as 'loopholes' (where the web is not woven too tightly); we seize the opportunity – Latin *porta*, 'gate', the opening in the net, the gap in the boundary. In Greek the term *kairos* meant literally the space between two posts, the way through the opposites. This is the sense in which crisis is opportunity, the rupture in the pattern of the weave which gives the chance to slip – 'in the nick of time' – through the time-bound knots into the unbound or timeless reality where we spin our own yarns and weave our own tales to the pattern of the heart.

* * *

The idea that the Moon weaves into the cloth of life its distinct and unique quality of time makes sense of the rituals found all over the world in which human affairs are set in accord with the cyclical drama of the Moon. It may be tempting to dismiss all these customs as magical thinking, in its limiting sense, and then to analyse them as fantasies of fear and hope. Yet the assumption on which they are based – that there is one reality which relates all natural life, both above and below – is one inherent to the mystical tradition, and also newly discovered, or rediscovered, by modern physics at the sub-atomic level of life, where the threads of the web are invisible to the human eye.[135] So the image of the cosmic web spun by the Moon – an image of the 'veiling' and 'projecting' aspects of Maya – may also turn out to hold the 'revealing' power of Maya, a power which allows those same illusions to disclose something about the nature of reality.

For, according to the Gnostic hymn:

> ...what you see outside you, you see within.
> It is visible and it is your garment.[136]

Fig. 17. *Detail of Aztec marriage in which the clothes of bride and groom are symbolically tied. Codex Mendoza. 16th Century. Bodleian Library, Oxford.*

Fig. 18. *Buddhist endless knot. (From Julien, The Mammoth Dictionary of Symbols, p. 227).*

CHAPTER 11

THE FULL MOON

...All light
All ten thousand miles at once in its light!
Tu Fu *The Full Moon*

After a lustre of the moon, we say
We have not the need of any paradise.
Wallace Stevens *Notes Toward a Supreme Fiction*

The beauty of the Full Moon moves the human imagination even now, so in earlier times with nothing but stars, fires and candles to light up the night, the Moon must have been overwhelming. It is not surprising that the rays from the Full Moon were once felt to be physical and palpable, carrying such magical potency that they could fertilize or blind, intoxicate, inspire or make mad. To absorb the full power of the Moon's beams, people have lain for hours on the ground beneath them: women to conceive, witches to cast spells, shamans to 'fly', the sick to be healed. Moonbeams dissolved in water would be drunk, food placed on the moonlit rooftops of houses would be eaten, and pools shimmering with moonlight would be bathed in. However the Moon could be ingested – by skin or mouth, breathing it, drinking it, eating it, washing in it, dancing in it – anything so long as it penetrated the core. Opinions around the world varied as to whether the Full Moon rays were blessed or dangerous, or whether, indeed, they were simply and indifferently powerful, and could act for good or ill. The scope for the human mind was at its maximum: waxing and waning were clearly one thing or the other, but the Full Moon could be either or both, depending at least in part on whether it was regarded with a 'waxing' or a 'waning' eye.

Chukchee shamans in north-eastern Siberia were among those who stripped naked and let the moonlight fall upon their bodies to gain the power of casting spells.[1] In the nineteenth century, witches in the Shetland Isles would lie all night in the Moonlight, amassing their powers.[2] Muslims in India would 'drink the Moon', filling a silver bowl with water and holding it in the light of the Full Moon until the rays saturated the water; then it was drunk at a gulp to cure palpitations and disorders of the nerves.[3] Hindus placed food on the housetops 'to lengthen life', as did the Chinese.[4] Across the world in Full Moon Brittany, women 'drank the Moon' to help them conceive, while in Greenland they covered their bellies with spittle to keep the Moon away.[5] Sailors refused to sleep in the full moonlight on an open deck at sea in case they would go blind.[6] Quartz crystals are still today placed in the full moonlight to activate their healing powers.

In Northern Ireland in the 1930s, in Munster, the older inhabitants living round the sacred lake of Lough Gur still remembered a time when the Full Moon healed the sick:

> On the night of the full moon, the people brought their sick close to the lake so that the moonlight shone brightly on them. The old people called this night 'All Heal', and if a sick person was not better by the 8th or 9th day of the moon, he would then hear

Fig. 1. Full Moon over Wilmington, near Honiton, Devon, England. 28th January 2002. Photograph by Richard Austin.

the *Ceol Side* which Aine [the Sun goddess] would sing to comfort the dying.[7]

In Pliny's day, the Celts believed the Moon to be a great healer. He describes a Druid ceremony of harvesting the mistletoe, whose moon-white berries they revered as the 'sap of the oak':[8]

> Hailing the moon in a native word that means 'healing all things', they prepare a ritual sacrifice and banquet beneath a tree and bring up two white bulls, whose horns are bound for the first time on this occasion. A priest arrayed in white vestments climbs the tree and with a golden sickle cuts down the mistletoe, which is caught in a white cloak. Then finally they kill the victims, praying to God to render his gift propitious to those on whom he has bestowed it. They believe that mistletoe given in drink will impart fertility to any animal that is barren, and that it is an antidote for all poisons.[9]

Fig. 2. William Blake. 'I want, I want.' Engravings of 'The Gates of Paradise.' No. 9. 'On the shadows of the Moon/ Climbing thro' Night's highest noon.' 1793. Fitzwilliam Museum, Cambridge.

It would seem that the Moon was expected to provide whatever was needed from the extraordinary range of gifts it had been given – rain, dew, fertilization, conception, easy childbirth, growth for children, animals and plants, food from hunting, health, long life, inspiration for poets, immortality, and not least a lunar lottery of wealth: all that was felt to be missing from an earthly life. This was known to sceptics, doubtless then as now, as 'crying for the Moon'.[10]

The American poet e. e. cummings plays with this feeling in a poem which begins:

> who knows if the moon's
> a balloon, coming out of a keen city
> in the sky – filled with pretty people?
> (..., where
> always
>   it's
>   Spring) and everyone's
> in love and flowers pick themselves.[11]

Nonetheless, we may ask, what do these customs say about human longing? Praying to the Moon at its junctures of change – the New Moon as it is reborn and the Full Moon when it is most itself – suggests that at the deepest level people were praying to be included in the Moon's own miraculous process of transformation. The ultimate prayer was, perhaps, for the Moon to transform death into life.

THE FULL MOON AS THE MUSE

The crescent is the Moon of growing, and up to the full the Moon is, as Plutarch puts it, 'of good intent'.[12] But any ambivalence towards the Moon reaches a crescendo at the full, and then the Moon in its culmination is either a Muse whose beauty inspires visions beyond mortal boundaries, or else a cold implacable being whose relentless gaze brings madness. And who is to say, on all occasions, which is which?

> The lunatic, the lover and the poet
> Are of imagination all compact...[13]

Inspiration has ever appeared to the eye of the disengaged beholder to be a form of madness, while the distorted truths of madness serve to question the social norms concealed within collective definitions of sanity. Ecstasy, common to both inspiration and madness, allows in both states a leaving of oneself and worldly things behind. So the initiates at the Eleusinian Mysteries were required to close their eyes, ears and mouth, not just to prevent them from revealing the secrets to others (who would not understand them since they had not lived through them), but rather to achieve that closure of the mind to all random sense which renders the person 'virgin': closed to distraction and open to revelation. This ecstasy, then as now, was assisted through intoxication, and, in rituals held invariably at Full Moon, the inebriating drinks – Soma, Haoma, Ambrosia, the Mexican Pulche, honey, dew, mead and wine – were drunk by mad and sane alike as the liquid essence of the Moon. Even without fermentation, the Moon could come to mind, as Yeats recalls: there were always times and places for the old Celts, for people who 'lived in a world where anything might flow and change', when they were dancing 'among the hills or in the depths of the woods, where unearthly ecstasy fell upon the dancers, until they seemed the gods or the godlike beasts, and felt their souls overtopping the moon.'[14]

In Greece, the Muses come from the goddess Memory, whose name in Greek, *Mnemosune*, reminds us that, etymologically, 'memory' (*mne* = *mene*) comes from 'Moon'. *Mosune* means a 'wooden house' or a 'tower', so the goddess may be the 'House of the Mind and/or the Moon'. Mnemosune is the figure of the beginning with her face turned towards humanity: memory as the condition of self-consciousness. She was a child of the first parents, daughter of Gaia and Ouranos, Earth and Heaven, and later, when she lay with Zeus for nine nights together, she conceived nine Muses near the top of Mount Olympos, though in Hesiod's own country, Boeotia, some thought they were originally three: *Melete*, 'Practising', *Mneme*, 'Remembering', and *Aoide*, 'Singing'.[15] The Muses could assume the shape of birds and, when they sang, seas and rivers and stars, everything stood still. Poets and Musicians claimed that they only repeated what the Muses told them 'through their lovely mouths',[16] and through the Muses they listened to the voice of Mnemosune herself.

Goddess Memory was not, of course, conceived as an inexhaustible store of all the facts in the world, but as the figure of origin pregnant with all the forms that are to come. This was what, later, the Neoplatonists called the *Anima Mundi*, Renaissance artists *Memoria*, Jung the *Collective Unconscious*, and Yeats the *Great Mind* or the *Great Memory*, which, he adds, 'is still the mother of the Muses, though men no longer believe in it.'[17] The Great Memory, Yeats explains, is 'the memory of Nature herself', of which our own memories are a part, in a continuous process of mutual exchange. We can reach this Memory through imagination by engaging with symbols, for Memory is 'a dwelling-house of symbols, of images that are living souls.'[18] These symbols are partly hers and partly ours, for 'whatever the passions of man have gathered about, becomes a symbol in the Great Memory,' and, surely, 'imagination is always seeking to remake the world according to the impulses and the patterns in that Great Mind, and that Great Memory?'[19]

Harrison writes that Mnemosune is 'the remembering again, the *anamnesis*, of things seen in ecstasy when the soul is rapt to heavenly places.'[20] Plato's term, *anamnesis*, she continues, is a more accurate

Fig. 3. Asklepios and snake healing the dreamer. In the background the man lying asleep is being licked on his shoulder by a snake while dreaming that he is standing before the god who is touching his shoulder in the same place. The two images, snake and god together, suggest what the artist saw healing to be: a transformation of the whole being, instinct and mind in accord. Votive relief of Archinos dedicated to the oracle god Amphiaraos at Oropos, Attica, Greece. c. 380-370 BC. National Archaeological Museum, Athens.

word for the mythological Mnemosune, because it insists on a re-enactment of a prior knowledge. Harrison proposes further that Plato borrowed much of his imagery from the lunar death and rebirth rituals of the Mysteries since the essence of his idea of memory was a relation to the timeless: 'Plato's whole scheme alike of education and philosophy is but an attempted rationalization of the primitive mysticism of initiation, and most of all of that profound and perennial mysticism of the central *rite de passage*, the death and the new birth, social, moral, intellectual.'[21] Similarly, in the Orphic Mysteries, when an initiate died he had a tablet hung around his neck directing him to drink of the cold water flowing from the Lake of Memory, and to avoid Lethe, the Well of Forgetfulness.[22]

Mnemosune has Hermes as one of her 'followers', and in the Homeric *Hymn to Hermes* Mnemosune is the first to be invoked by the god, still a mischievous child, on his tortoise-shell lyre (the lyre which he gives to Apollo, who gives it to Orpheus). Only after celebrating Mnemosune does Hermes call forth all the immortal gods and the black earth, singing of their origins and the order of their birth in the making of the world.[23] Memory here is the living tradition which structures and ritualizes the present, like the Aboriginal 'Dream-time of the Ancestors', when the patterns of the world were created such that any new creation has to return to the source.[24]

Dream oracles were also to be found in temples to the Moon. In Sin's sanctuary at Harran, King Esarhaddon, who ruled Assyria around 680–699 BC, was told in a dream to conquer Egypt, which he did.[25] In the Peloponnese, a dream oracle was dedicated to Helios the Sun and Pasiphae the Moon (mother of Ariadne), and Hekate was honoured on an altar to Asklepios in the fourth century BC, before his first temple was built.[26] The lunar origins of the healing power of Asklepios (whose father, Apollo, united with Koronis, the Moon in her black 'crow' phase), are suggested in the central ritual conducted in his temples at Epidauros and elsewhere. This was the 'temple sleep', the *incubatio*, when the patient hoped to invoke the god or his snake in his dream, and to wake up healed.[27]

In China there is a legend which traces the origin of theatre to the Moon. In the eighth century, on the fifteenth night of the eighth Moon Emperor Ming Huang asked a priest of what material the Moon was made. 'Would Your Majesty like to see for yourself?' the Sage replied, and learning that His Majesty would indeed like to see for himself, he threw his girdle into the air and it became a bridge by which Sovereign and Sage travelled to the Moon. They saw Heng-O, the Moon Hare and the Cassia Tree, and then the Moon-fairies sang and danced for them. Returning to Earth, and quite an adept at the lute himself, the Emperor taught these same songs and dances to his people, and so the Chinese theatre was born.[28] The Romans conceived of the circus as having for its patron the Moon goddess, Luna;[29] while Virgil in his *Eclogues* claims that 'songs can even draw the moon down from heaven.'[30]

* * *

The affinity between the night Moon and the imagination in all its forms has been consistently registered throughout the ages, and especially by the Romantic poets and painters, for whom the Moon became a symbol of imagination.[31] Thus Keats, flying to his nightingale 'on the viewless wings of Poesy':

> Already with thee! tender is the night,
> And haply the Queen-Moon is on her throne,
> Cluster'd around by all her starry Fays...[32]

The Mediterranean Moon in Malta inspired Coleridge to extremes of worship and contemplation. Watching the Moon across Valletta harbour from his garret window, he sees a Moon 'blue at one edge from the deep utter Blue of the Sky, a mass of pearl-white Cloud below, distant and travelling to the Horizon.' He finds himself stretching forth his arms to embrace the sky 'and in a trance I had worshipped God in the Moon: the Spirit not the Form.' On another night he muses:

> In looking at objects of Nature while I am thinking, as at yonder moon dim-glimmering thro' the dewy window-pane, I seem rather to be seeking, as it were *asking*, a symbolical language for something within me that already and forever exists, than observing anything new.[33]

Neumann links the Moon symbolically to the creative process:

> The creative process takes place not under the burning rays of the sun but in the cool, reflected light of the moon when the darkness of unconsciousness is great: night, not day, is the time for begetting. Darkness and stillness, secrecy, remaining mute and veiled, are a part of it. For this reason the moon as lord of life and of growth is opposed to the death character of the devouring sun. The nocturnal moistness of the moon-night is the time of sleep, but also that of healing and recovery. ...The power of sleep that regenerates the body and its wounds and the restoration that runs its course in darkness belongs to the night domain of the healing moon, as do the happenings in the soul that let a person 'grow beyond' an insoluble crisis through the dark processes perceived only by the heart.[34]

As Wang Wei, the eighth-century Chinese poet-painter, said:

> In the deep bamboo forest I sit alone.
> Loudly I sing and tune my lute.
> The forest is so thick that no one knows about it.
> Only the bright moon comes to shine upon me.[35]

Lorca has a poem called *The Moon Rising*.

Fig. 4. Thoth as the inspiration of the scribe Nebmeroutef. Sculpture, schiste. 1391-1353 BC. The Louvre.

When the moon rises,
the bells hang silent,
and impenetrable footpaths
appear.

When the moon rises,
the sea covers the land,
and the heart feels
like an island in infinity.

Nobody eats oranges
under the full moon.
One must eat fruit
that is green and cold.

When the moon rises,
moon of a hundred equal faces,
the silver coinage
sobs in the pocket.[36]

* * *

Many Moon gods and goddesses acted as Muse. In Egypt, for instance, the saying went:

The finger of the scribe is the beak of the ibis,
Beware of brushing it aside.[37]

The beak of the ibis belonged to the Moon god Thoth. He was the patron of scribes, poets and artists who, as the poem suggests, understood their inspiration as being sent by the god. In the

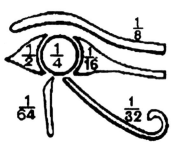

Fig. 6. *The Eye of Horus, composed of separate elements which the Egyptians used for writing the fractional parts of the grain measure. The individual fractions, added together, made 63/64ths, just short of completeness. But the missing portion, the element necessary to achieve wholeness, was magically supplied by Thoth, who created 'with his fingers' the 'sound eye,' revealing the whole to be greater than the sum of its parts. In this way the lunar Eye measures volume, that is, three-dimensional space, as well as time. (Lamy, Egyptian Mythology, p. 16.)*

Fig. 5. *Thoth holding the Eye of Horus. Bas relief. Ptolemaic. c. 330 BC. British Museum.*

sculpture shown in fig. 4, the scribe, Nebmeroutef, seated cross-legged, holds his scroll over his knees, while on a dais above him, apparently unnoticed (for the scribe has eyes only for his manuscript), there sits Thoth in his other form of great baboon, staring intently down upon him. The inscription round the dais reads: 'Thoth brings Maat into being every day' – Imagination brings Truth into being continually (it could be Keats speaking).[38]

Ganesha, the Hindu god with an elephant head and only one tusk, son of Shiva and Parvati, is also involved with the Moon. God of thresholds, standing at the door of house or sanctuary, his role was to create or remove obstacles that all may be well within. So he was god of prudence, with the wisdom of foresight. Brahma gave him the task of transcribing the *Mahabharata*, using as a pen his broken-off tusk that he had once hurled at the Moon, which is why the Moon loses its light from time to time. The art of the scribe and poet is related thereby to the order of Nature, and in particular to the order of the Moon.[39]

What happened was this. Ganesha had eaten too much on his birthday, and he was riding on his rat in the moonlight when he saw a huge snake lying across his path who would not move. At the last moment the rat had to leap to one side, and Ganesha fell off and his belly burst. Ever resourceful, he picked up the snake and rolled it round and round his gaping belly so nothing would fall out. As he was getting back on his rat, he heard great peals of laughter echoing through the sky. It was the Moon jeering at him. Ganesha was so offended he broke off one of his tusks and hurled it at the Moon (who hid behind the clouds), and Ganesha cursed him: 'Let no one look at your face on my birthday. If anyone, knowingly or unknowingly, looks at you, they will be completely misunderstood in the family circle and neighbourhood for no reason whatsoever.'[40] Concealed in the tale is the theme of death and rebirth through the snake as the earthly form of the Moon.

The relation between the Moon and Shiva, Parvati and Ganesha, once made, is liable to turn up anywhere. There is a huge cave inside a mountain at Amarnath in north India, with an imposing ice formation ending in a cone of ice, which is a representation of Shiva. On the right a block of ice represents Ganesha, and a smaller one on the left represents Parvati. People who go as pilgrims to this shrine believe that the ice formations wax and wane with the Moon, reaching a climax on the day of the Full Moon and disappearing completely when the Moon is dark.[41]

THE FULL MOON AS THE HEALED EYE OF HORUS

The idea of the Full Moon as itself healed of fragmentation and darkness, and so able with its restored light to heal others, also comes from Egypt. The Moon is here the physician that heals itself.[42]

In Egypt, the Full Moon was a time of joy because it was the time that the Moon was 'restored' to its true nature, 'healed' by Thoth, guardian of time and timelessness, god of the eternal order. For, in yet another lunar myth, the falcon-headed High God of Heaven, Horus, had two eyes: his right eye was the Sun and his left eye was the Moon. This story of the Moon merged into the story of Isis and Osiris and their son, also called Horus. (As Frankfort warns, the Egyptians 'admitted side by side certain *limited* insights, which were held to be *simultaneously* valid, each in its own proper context, each corresponding to a definite avenue of approach.')[43] Now, after Osiris has been slain by Seth for the second time, and his body dismembered into 14 pieces, Horus, his rapidly full-grown son, determines to avenge his father, and dares Seth, the principle of darkness, to deadly combat. In the course of their battle, they lose their 'human' forms, passing three days and three nights in an indiscernible state, until Isis releases them. At the crucial point in the battle Seth tears out the Eye of Horus and plunges the sky into darkness (Horus the son having dissolved into Horus the Sky god, so that his/their left eye has become the Moon). Thoth finds the pieces, counts them and makes them whole, and then restores the Eye to Horus. In the *Coffin Texts* Thoth says:

> I came seeking the Eye of Horus,
> that I might bring it back and count it.
> I found it [and now it is] complete, counted and sound,
> so that it can flame up to the sky
> and blow above and below...[44]

During this 'great quarrel' of light and dark, described in the New Kingdom text of *The Contendings of Horus and Seth* (c.1500 BC), the alternating fortunes of Horus's Eye symbolize the cyclical phases of the Moon. So when the Eye is dismembered and emptied of light – flung by Seth beyond the world's edge – the Moon is gone and the sky is dark; and when the Eye is found, scattered in fragments in the outer darkness, and pieced together to form a whole, the Moon becomes full, and the dark is vanquished. So the Full Moon was the time when the Eye that was the Moon was 'filled', 'healed' and 'made whole' by Thoth, he who was also called the 'Silver Sun' and the 'Physician of the Eye of Horus' (figs 5 and 6).[45]

The tale of Thoth re-membering the dismembered fragments of the Eye of Horus is a re-enactment of the re-membering of the dismembered body of Osiris by Isis, with the help of Nephthys and Anubis. Returning to the story of Osiris, it is Horus who now descends to the underworld and presents his father with the sacrificed Eye, which grants him eternal life. By analogy, this 'Great Left Eye' was offered to the embalmed pharaohs to ensure their resurrection in the world beyond:

> Take to thyself the Eye of Horus, which is free from Seth, and which thou shalt take to
> thy mouth, and with which thou shalt open thy mouth.[46]

The 'remembered' Eye was known as the *Wedjat* Eye, 'the whole or restored one', and was widely used as a talisman – the 'Good' Eye set against what may have been the original image of the 'Evil Eye', the Dark Moon. The *Wedjat* Eye was sculpted into amulets, fashioned into jewellery, painted on the outside of boats and coffins, and painted on boats laid inside coffins, anywhere, in fact, where the

Fig. 7. The Left Eye of Horus, the Wedjat Eye, between two cobras in a papyrus boat. Above the Eye is the lunar crescent, containing a darkened disk inscribed with the figures of Thoth and Horus who are blessing the Pharaoh in the centre, himself crowned with a crescent. The boat is held up by the winged scarab beetle, Khepri, a form of the Sun, Re, in his arising. Pectoral jewel of gold and precious stones from the tomb of Tutankamun. c. 1350 BC. Egyptian Museum, Cairo.

journeyer was fearful of his journey and longed to 'see' – for the Eye was a prayer – the way ahead.[47]

The intriguing etymology of the term 'remembering' is brought into almost physical relief with the dis-membering and re-membering of the Eye which is the Moon. A 'member' is a part of the whole, especially a limb of the human body, hence a person in a group, and probably derives from Sanskrit *mas*, 'flesh',[48] which makes dismemberment a tearing of limb from limb, a breaking into pieces of a living body. The Full Moon, as the image of the pieces put back together, the severed limbs re-membered, also serves as an image of what remembering means as an act of mind: the gathering together of disparate elements to form the original whole, which can then be imaginatively experienced as present. 'Recollection' carries the same idea, coming from *re-colligio*, 'to bind back together'. It was earlier suggested that the idea of time arose as an idea of waning, when what is whole is cut, and here again a similar motif occurs. For waning, as dismembering, is analogically a forgetting, when the whole is lost and all that is present are parts without a context, limbs without a body. Going back to the idea of the awareness of time and death creating an eternity that was lost but not forgotten, the further implication is that the Full, whole, Moon is translucent to the eternal by bringing back into the mind, remembering, the image of the Great Memory, the original whole.

THE FULL MOON AND LUNACY

However, the Full Moon which was the muse of poets and lovers was also the 'muse' of lunatics, and especially the midsummer Moon: 'Why, this is very midsummer madness,' Olivia responds to the melancholy Malvolio's uncharacteristic behaviour in his cross-garters and yellow stockings.[49] In Dryden's *Amphitrion*, the question is asked: 'What's this midsummer moon? Is all the world gone a-madding?'[50] Even Queen Elizabeth I puns to the Earl of Leicester: 'Rob, I am afraid you will suppose by my wandering writings that a midsummer moon hath taken large possession of my brains this month';[51] here she draws on the medieval idea that a wandering Moon could bring a 'wandering of wits' as well as a propensity to travel to many strange lands.[52] The phrase, ''Tis midsummer moon with you' was a pleasant way of saying 'you are raving mad', a view generalized in Rowley's pithy aphorism from *The Witch of Edmonton*, 1658, put into the mouth of young Banks: 'When the Moon's in the full, then wit's in the wane.'[53]

The connection between the Moon and the inspired or deranged mind has been sealed in western European languages for over 2000 years. The Greek for 'madness' was *mania*, from the Sanskrit root of *ma*, 'Moon', from which we get 'maniac'. The term 'lunatic' comes from the Latin *lunaticus*, deriving directly from *luna*, which meant both 'Goddess of the Moon' and 'Moon', together with *tic*, which meant 'struck'. 'Lunacy' was originally ecstatic possession by the Moon goddess, which could bring revelation *or* madness, as could the Greek *mania*, which also gives 'mantic', prophetic. 'Enthusiasm' comes from *en theos*, 'the god in' (us), or possibly (us) 'in the god', just as 'inspiration' comes from *inspirare*, breathing in a god or being breathed in by a god – the difference between those two experiences probably being the difference between being sane or mad. In Greek the word for lunatics was *seleniazomenoi*, after the Moon goddess Selene. Lunatics were later called 'silly', a word that may derive from Selene, especially as it once meant 'blessed' (rather like the word 'giddy', which once meant 'god-struck').[54] In the New Testament, Matthew describes Jesus as healing *seleniazomenoi*, translated as 'lunaticks' in the Authorized King James Version (1611),[55] but as 'epileptics' in the Revised Version of 1881, since epilepsy was believed to be caused by excessive moisture on the brain, and so made worse at the Full Moon.[56] For the same reason, Aristotle declared that convulsions in babies were 'worse during full moon'.[57] In Milton's *Paradise Lost*, the Angel Michael, revealing the fallen future to Adam, shows him a place of sickness, containing, among other maladies:

> Demoniac frenzy, moping melancholy
> And moon-struck madness.[58]

Less than 200 years ago, in Britain, the Lunacy Act of 1842 defined a lunatic as a demented person with lucid intervals during the first two phases of the Moon, and 'afflicted with a period of fatuity in the period following after the full moon.'[59] Even in the 1940s, a soldier charged with murdering a comrade at the Winchester Assizes pleaded as his defence 'Moon madness', an affliction which came over him at each Full Moon.[60]

In German, *mondsüchtig* ('moonsickness') is the word for 'madness'; in French, to be mad is *avoir des lunes*; in Italian, *lunatico*; in English, 'lunatic' or 'loony', and sometimes 'moon-struck'. A translation of St Matthew's Gospel by Sir John Cheke at the beginning of the seventeenth century, intent on replacing 'foreign' with 'native' words, rendered 'lunatic' as *moond*.[61] Leave out the hard-to-pronounce 'n' and you have the origin of 'mood', with its connotations of moody and moodiness – all changeable states of humour (from Latin *humor*, 'moisture'), supposedly influenced by a changing phase of Moon. To quote the influential Francis Bacon: 'It is like that the brain of man waxeth moister and fuller upon the full of the moon...It is like, also, that the humours in men's bodies increase and decrease as the moon doth.'[62] By such reasoning Bacon inferred that his own intellect grew as the Moon waxed full. 'Influence' (like 'humour') is itself originally a watery term (deriving from *in* and *fluere*, 'to flow'), referring to a supposed ethereal fluid 'in the air' flowing from the Moon and stars, given great consequence in medieval times. Such is the (Renaissance Florentine) derivation of the English word 'flu', *influenza*.

'Moonish' in Shakespeare meant 'changeable' – 'I, being but a moonish youth...be...changeable'[63] – and *lune* meant a fit of temper or irrational frenzy – 'These dangerous, unsafe lunes i' the' King, beshrew them!' says Paulina of King Leontes in *The Winter's Tale*.[64] Furthermore, the activity known to many as 'mooning about' is usually conducted in a mood and condoned by the idea of 'going through a phase'. In French, *etre bien/mal luné* means 'to be in a good/bad mood' – the more usual word is *l'humeur*. *Comment est-elle lunée ce matin?* (literally, 'how is she mooned this morning?') translates as 'what sort of a mood is she in this morning?' *Il est encore mal luné* means 'he's still in a bad mood.' In Italian the phrase *aver la luna* means to suffer a nervous attack. In German, *laune* also means 'whim', 'caprice', 'fit of frenzy', anything unpredictably changeable and so apparently irrational, perhaps one of the less visual sources for the contemporary term 'mooning', meaning 'to expose the buttocks'.

In Greece there were, as anywhere else, true and false Muses, just as there were true and false birds of augury, and two kinds of dreams: dreams from the Gate of Horn, which spoke the truth, and dreams from the Gate of Ivory, which would deceive (a Greek etymological pun on the common roots of 'ivory' and 'deceive', *elephas* and *elephairo*; by contrast, the word for 'horn', *keras*, was related to the word *karanoo*, which meant 'accomplish').[65] Mistaking one for the other would radically confuse, as would taking the figures of a dream or vision literally, and treating them as objective realities. Perhaps the attribution of both kinds of 'Muse' to the Moon leads ultimately – through the experience of enchantment – to the human mind as the source, if not of 'influence', at least of an interpretation which itself influences the way we relate, not least to the Moon itself. Jung observes:

> The moon, too, is a disturber of sleep, and is also the abode of departed souls, for at night the dead return in dreams and the phantoms of the past terrify the sleepless. Thus the moon also signifies madness ('lunacy'). It is such images as these that have impressed themselves on the mind, rather than the changing image of the moon. It is not storms, not thunder and lightning, not rain and cloud that remain as images in the psyche, but the fantasies caused by the affects they arouse....Hunger makes food into gods.[66]

Along with moods and madness, the Moon was charged with sending nightmares, a term coming from the Old English 'night' and '*mara*', a spectre, such that the nightmare was a spirit or incubus who pressed on the chest of people as they slept. The spirit came to be thought of as a witch, and in France this spirit-witch was called Diana, who, in Roman times, was believed to send mad anyone who incurred her wrath.[67] In Greece and Rome, Hekate is sometimes shown riding a horse (hence the confusion between spectre and female horse, *mara* and *mare*); she brought dreams and nightmares, as well as night-time apparitions, such as the *Empusa*, a kind of incubus which sapped the dreamer's energy as did, it was supposed, the Dark Moon from which it came.[68] Even Hippocrates, who was called the father of modern medicine, subscribed to this.[69] Sleeping in moonlight is also dangerous in Jewish legend, because *Agrat Bat Mahalat*, the Queen of Demons, concubine of *Samael*, the King of Demons, is about at that time, stalking the earth for her prey.[70]

So it was inevitably at the Full Moon that Robert Louis Stevenson's Dr Jekyll committed murder as Mr Hyde.[71] Just as wolves howled at the Full Moon, so the Full Moon was thought to elicit the wolfish appetites of human beings, and during the Inquisition in fifteenth- and sixteenth-century Europe men were accused of being werewolves, women of being witches, and all of them of being heretics to the Holy Church. In the twelfth century, only 900 years ago, one Gervais of Tilbury could write, apparently without empirical qualm, that 'in England we often see men changed into wolves at the changes of the moon.'[72]

Such a climate of preconception goes some way to explaining how the horrors of the Inquisition went unchallenged. Those who can readily accept men turning into werewolves and lunatics at Full Moon are less likely to be astonished at the further idea that devils themselves are subject to lunar influence, and especially those devils who molest lunatics in the first place. The infamous duo Sprenger and Kramer, who pursued many people to their death, declared in the *Malleus Maleficarum* ('The Hammer against Evil-doers') in 1486:

The stars can influence the devils themselves. [As proof of this] certain men who are called Lunatics are molested by devils more at one time than at another; and the devils...would rather molest them at all times, unless they themselves were deeply affected by certain phases of the Moon.[73]

This ecclesiastical style of reasoning echoes that of St Jerome, who (while translating the Bible from Hebrew into Latin) was more concerned to transfer power from the Moon to the Creator than to trouble how he did it: 'Lunatics were not really smitten by the moon, but were believed to be so, through the subtlety of the demons, who by observing the seasons of the moon, sought to bring an evil report against the creature, that it might redound to the blasphemy of the Creator.'[74] A somewhat different tone from the American song *It's That Old Devil Moon in Your Eyes*.[75]

'Moon-struck' didn't just mean going mad, it could also mean going blind. A *Sailor's Word Book* of the nineteenth century defines 'moon-struck' as 'an influence imputed to the moon...by which fish become spoiled. Human beings are also said to be injured by sleeping in the moon's rays.'[76] In Egypt, Greece, Armenia, Brazil and many other places, sleeping with the moonlight falling on the eyes was believed to weaken the sight.[77] 'Moon blindness' also afflicted horses, who got 'moon-eye', but it could be cured by washing the eyes in moon-dew (especially on May morning), and by rubbing the eyes with powdered pearls or nine hairs from a black cat.[78]

In this Kalahari Bushman tale, the moon's light splintering into the eye of Mantis blinds him. Here Mantis does not act like the creator of the Moon but like one of its all-too-human creatures.

Mantis wanted to catch the Moon so he could sit on it and cross the sky each night, and all the animals would say: 'There is the Mantis travelling on the moon.' But the Moon was so difficult to catch because it never stayed still. When it peeped over the horizon it was too large, and when it was high and white it was too far away. Once it got caught in the branches of a camelthorn tree, and Mantis flew with a whirr and a click of his wings up the camelthorn tree, but then the Moon moved on to the baobab tree. As the Moon waned it rose later each night, and Mantis got drowsy with watching and missed it, and then there was no Moon at all, and the desert creatures were uneasy in case it did not come back. Then Mantis tried to catch the new young Moon but it was too fast for him, and even the acacias with their sharp thorns could not hold it. So he made a noose out of dry grass to trap the Moon inside it, and then he made a stake to pierce the Moon and hold it, and then he made a reed-feather to twist around the Moon and stop it. But nothing worked. The Moon became full again, and Mantis followed it to see where it went when it sank beneath the horizon. He saw a waterhole, trampled by many hooves, and there at the bottom of the waterhole lay the Moon, caught at last in the water. Many times Mantis tried to pry the Moon out of the water but he could not do it, and in his anger he cursed the Moon and hurled a rock at it, and the stone shattered the reflection of the Moon and thousands of splinters of moonlight pierced his eyes so he could not see. He crept up the thorntree and when the moon rose he folded his front legs and held them out in prayer, begging the Moon to give him back his sight. He bent his head and swayed gently on the twig – he was only a little insect, he did not want to ride on the Moon any more. When daylight came, Mantis opened his eyes. He could see! He could see the birds flying, and the shadows of their wings flying behind them on the dusty earth, and then he knew that the Moon had taken all the splinters out of his eyes. So that is why all his children, and all his children's children, pray to the Moon.[79]

It is as though the Moon, whose splintering beams had blinded him at night, had also healed him with its early morning dew.

* * *

The Full Moon is still credited by some with powers to change human behaviour, which are just as vehemently denied by others. Experiments are interpreted both ways: what is self-evident to some is regarded as flawed to others: either the hypotheses have biased the results, or the statistical sample is too small, or the scope of the experiment too narrow, or the evidence 'anecdotal', and in any case the observer is never wholly independent of the observed (nor, one might add, of what is not observed).[80] Selective memory can work for either hypothesis. Why is it so difficult to agree?

What, for instance, are we to make of Laurens van der Post's tale *A Bar of Shadow*, where the Japanese guard Hara, 'a moon-swung, moon-haunted, moon-drawn soul', committed his most savage acts in the Full Moon (though in van der Post's book on Jung he said the worst time was in the Waning Moon).[81] What about the many people who say they 'feel different' at Full Moon?

As suggested earlier, the persistently divergent points of view eventually give rise to the idea of a paradigm from which the view arises. The question of how Earth relates to Moon has ultimately to draw on the wider issue of how Earth relates to the universe as a whole, and, most broadly, whether the emphasis falls on relationship or uniqueness. Even within this spectrum, there are further priorities of thought or 'lifestyles'. A matter so apparently straightforward as 'change' can be governed by what James Hillman has called 'archetypal fantasies',[82] such as, for instance, the question as to whether character and action are shaped more by external forces than by individual choice and will. Is change of behaviour brought about more by influences beyond our control – genetic coding, social conditions, family upbringing, and so on, extending to electro-magnetic fields? Or is change brought about more by human beings working upon their own attitudes and beliefs, altering their behaviour from within themselves? Or does the very idea of change for the better depend on a 'developmental' fantasy, whereas, for those with a 'golden age' fantasy, change can only be for the worse? Where does the ultimate authority reside? The simple act of looking up at the Moon and down upon ourselves may reach into these fundamental orientations to life, affecting how we interpret what we see, and even predisposing what we see – 'As a man is, so he sees'[83] – rendering statistical surveys for either side shallow and inconclusive.

THE MOON AND MAGIC

Magic and moonlight have always gone together, both shifting the borders of the mind and dissolving the distinctions that underpin the habits of the day. In Harrison's definition, magic is the 'handling of the sacred, the manipulation of *mana*',[84] and so magic merges into religious ritual as the invisible, unfathomable dimension that brings about change where rational means fail. Magic works by enchantment – both within and without religion – quickening the heart to believe in impossible visions, and 'under the influence' to fall in love with them, so they are more likely to 'come true'.

The original source of magic is, of course, Nature. But in the narrower sense anything can be magical in a magical world – a glance, a flight of birds, an animal falling sick, the butter not churning, a certain configuration of clouds, a colour of the Moon – all that is sudden, unexpected, and for which no apparent reason can be found. The usual suspect is the person most feared or the thing least understood, to whom most power is thereby given, albeit unconsciously. In many cultures this was the Moon, and often also its supposed representatives on Earth – women – to whom magical powers were generously attributed in early thought, along with the further possibility of becoming witches when things went wrong. The *Arthava-Veda*, the Vedic treatise on magic, sets this up, ominously, by saying that women's beauty derives from the Moon, and can be increased by eating the flesh of the Moon-hare.[85]

If this seems a long time ago, there is Pope John XII in the tenth century accusing witches of 'riding with Diana'.[86] Similarly, German women suspected of being witches were said to 'ride with Holde', the Germanic Sky and Moon goddess, who flew through the air and disappeared under water.[87] Witches in Germany were accused of changing their form by dancing in the moonlight, and especially on Mondays.[88] All the witches' 'familiar' animals are lunar animals: cats, dogs, frogs, serpents, and especially the hares into which they could turn in a trice. Even the 'witch's broomstick' was seen in the Moon at rest from sweeping.[89] By John Clare's time, tales of witches belonged to the lost magic of childhood, as he recalls in his *Shepherds Calendar* (1827), when his mother would tell him tales of witches riding on sheep-trays from the fold:

> To join the midnight mystery's rout
> Where witches meet the year about
> And how when met with unawares
> They instant turn to cats or hares
> And race along with hellish flight
> Now here and there and out of sight...[90]

Coleridge, in 1851, tells it from the cat's point of view: 'Why should Brigit's cat be worried? Why, to be sure, she's black, an imp of darkness, the witch's own familiar; nay, perhaps, the witch herself in disguise.'[91]

In some places, Ghana for instance, the word for Moon and magic is the same; in other places, such as Brazil, magic was initiated by the chewing of a particular bark which fell from the Moon.[92] Words of magical power come from Moon gods and goddesses: Thoth taught Isis the magic words which enabled her to revive Osiris, and to bring Horus back to life when he was stung by a scorpion. The Norse Moon goddess Freya, she of the chariot of cats, was Mistress of Magic and Prophecy. The Greek prophetesses were called 'Sibyls', but were once one Sibyl and, according to Pausanias, 'Sibyl' was another name for Artemis, which may be why Plutarch says the face of the Sybil can be seen in the Moon.[93] 'The ancients,' comments the Roman Lydus, 'regarded the Moon as the leader in all divination.'[94] The medieval occultist Cornelius Agrippa (1486–1535) popularized these ideas by arguing that while magical power comes from all heavenly bodies, it is only through the intermediary of the Moon that it can be transmitted to the inhabitants on Earth.[95]

By extension, magical potency was ascribed to whatever took the shape of the crescent, starting with the horn upon which the Moon had set its signature. Crescent horns adorned the heads of gods and the helmets of warriors, and were more generally used to ward off the 'evil eye'.[96] In Naples, lacking a suitable horned object, even the saying of the word *corno* would do; this was accompanied by the *mano cornuta*, the vertical or outward hand gesture where the index and little finger make 'the horn'. When pointed towards the chin it is to insult a man for being cuckolded – 'An old cuckold with horns on his head.'[97] Even Moses acquired horns, though whether by accident or design is debatable. In Hebrew, a 'radiated' and a 'horned' head are signified by the same word, so when Moses descended from Sinai, the Mountain of the Moon, he was described as *cornuta fuit facies ejus*, according to the Vulgate (the fifth-century Latin translation of the Old and New Testaments), to be later commemorated in Michelangelo's statue of Moses (see fig. 8). The cornucopia – the horn of abundance – thereby suggests itself as lunar in origin, as does the horseshoe, hanging, points upwards (so the luck will not fall out), on doors, stables and barns in the British countryside even to this day.[98]

The line between magic and oracular foretelling is difficult to draw – if it can be drawn at all – and both practices were attributed to the Moon. Take the medicine shield of Chief Arapoosh of the Crow North American Indians, which had the black figure of the 'Moon as an Above Person' painted upon it. The Chief said that, during a vision quest he had when he was young, he was visited by a figure in black who was the spirit of the Moon. The Moon spirit told him that he was Arapoosh's own spirit guardian and would protect him from harm. So before any battle, the shield would be consulted by rolling it down a row of lodges until it fell over. If the spirit of the Moon was uncovered, the figure pointing upwards, they would win; but if his face was hidden, pointing downwards, the fight would be abandoned.[99] The similarity to 'heads or tails' is arresting (fig. 9).

Many Shamans invoke the Moon to bewitch them into a new vision, and this may be why the shamans of the Lapps painted the lunar crescent on their magic drums. The Moon was the chief of *manitus*, or wizards, for the North American Shamans. For the Eskimos, shamanic power came from the Moon, since when the shaman fell into trance his spirit was 'transferred' to the Moon through magical flight (his body remaining on Earth bound with ropes). Sometimes a shamanic master obtained a mystical faculty called *qaumaneq* for his disciple from the Spirit of the Moon.[100] In one tale a Baffinland Eskimo shaman was carried to the Moon by his helping spirit, who was a bear, and there he met the man in the Moon and his wife, the Sun.[101] In other Eskimo tales, the Moon was the abode of dead souls, so it may be that the shamans went to the Moon to learn about death in order to see life from the 'other side'.

A tale of magic which, to unbelievers, is called sorcery, and to believers, miracle, and to the *Concise Encyclopedia of Islam*, allegory, comes into a story of the Prophet Muhammad. The text in the Koran says:

> The hour of Doom is drawing near, and the moon is cleft in two. Yet, when they see a sign, the unbelievers turn their backs and say: 'Ingenious sorcery!'[102]

Fig. 8. Moses. Sculpture by Michelangelo. 1513 -16. San Pietro in Vinculi, Rome.

Fig. 9. *The Moon as an Above Person.*
The medicine shield of Chief Arapoosh of
the North American Indian Crow tribe.
Painting on bison hide, with parts of bird
and animal. Polychrome mineral painting.
Montana, USA. c. 1830. Museum of
the American Indian, Heye Foundation,
New York.

A story grew up around this that Habib the Wise asked Muhammad to prove his mission by cleaving the Moon in two. So Muhammad raised his hands to heaven and commanded the Moon to do what Habib had asked. The Moon accordingly descended to the top of the *Kaaba* (the ancient stone building containing the black stone, said to have been built by Ishmael and Abraham), and circled it seven times. Then, floating down to Muhammad, it slipped inside his right sleeve and came out of his left sleeve, inserted itself into the collar of his robe, dropped to the skirt and clove itself into two plaits, one appearing in the east of the skies and the other in the west. Ultimately, the two parts reunited.[103]

* * *

What to some is divine epiphany and to others magic, is to yet others superstition, but while the classifications reflect a descending hierarchy of value, the experience common to all is the assumption that the 'laws of Nature' have been suspended. Superstition (like myth) tends to belong to 'other people' rather than the speaker, and it is, of course, easier to see what we might want to call superstitious practices in others than in ourselves. Nowhere is this more evident than in a 'change of numinosity', when, as the Indian scholar Ananda Coomaraswamy, puts it, 'The Gods of an older religion become the Devils of one that supersedes it.'[104] The deeper impulses that accord value are indirectly visible in the apparently incidental imagery that surrounds the main tenets of faith. Take, for instance, the energy that attends the now-unlucky number 13, which confers on the number itself the status of magic.

Thirteen is a number of the Moon (13 lunar months in a year), while 12 is a number of the Sun. In the Christian tradition, the old lunar number 13 became a 'pagan' number and so unlucky, while the solar 12 was affirmed as the number of completeness, the 12 signs of the zodiac through which the Sun passes in its cycle of the year. Christ's title as the *Sol Invictus* conferred divine status on the new way of dividing time according to the Sun, such that the old lunar time became devilish – 13 was called the 'devil's dozen' or the 'baker's dozen' (12, and one for the devil), and became the number that dare not speak its name. Christ was reckoned as the thirteenth among 12 Apostles, from which it was inferred that the number 13 was the number of death (though it could have been just as plausibly inferred that 13 was an eternal number beyond time); alternatively, Judas Iscariot was counted the thirteenth at the Last Supper.[105] For the 'lunar-oriented' Yeats, by contrast, the 'Thirteenth Cycle' in his *A Vision* was given the power to 'deliver us from the 12 cycles of time and space.'[106] It all depends where eternity (and death) are to be located.

Thirteen has stayed unlucky. Some buildings omit the thirteenth floor. Statements containing some such phrase as 'it is traditionally regarded as unlucky for a ship to begin a voyage on the 13th, especially if it happens to be a Friday',[107] compound the problem by not even looking for an explanation. Why, if the thirteenth is a Friday, will the devil win and 'luck' run out?

When 'solar time' became sacred time and 'lunar time' became profane, the day of the Sun became the day of the resurrection, and counting backwards three days meant that Friday was the day that Christ was laid in his grave. But these three days when, in Christian teaching, Christ descended into Hell, are the same three days' dark of the Moon when the Moon was also 'in the underworld', so that concealed within the *Sol Invictus* is the *Luna Renata*! This made Friday the day of death, and with the addition of the even more profane 13, the two clearly made a deadly combination.

In Roman times, Friday (which in English is an abbreviation of 'Freya's day', the Nordic lunar goddess of Fertility), was originally the day of Venus, as it still is in Italian and French, deriving from Latin, *dies Veneris* (becoming in Italian, *venerdi*, and in French *vendredi*). Venus was the goddess of Love, whose counterpart in Greece was Aphrodite, goddess of Love in Nature, and in Egypt the goddess, Hathor-Isis. Whether Egyptian, Greek, Roman or Norse, these were all goddesses of love, fertility and destiny, images of the now-profane love of what the Churchmen called 'this world'. Venus' Day was the day of life not death, when fish was eaten because it was sacred to Aphrodite.

But these were the deities of the religions to be replaced by the Christian Church and, as in so many areas of pagan thought, the old images were inverted and the creative life of the old became death for the new. While the Norse and Germans held their weddings on Freya's Day, which was the luckiest day of their week, Churchmen in the Middle Ages denounced rituals held for Freya's Day as 'devil worship', while continuing to eat their fish on Friday – but as a sacrifice.[108]

The orienting points of 'left' and 'right' are also still given magical properties. In classical augury (reading the signs from birds), birds seen on the left portended ill-luck. Latin for 'left' is *sinister*, Italian, *sinistra*, French, *sinistre*, with all the double meanings that it holds in old English folklore where the devil is always to be found on the left of anyone or anything. If you spill salt at table, it is bad luck – even an omen of death – unless you throw a pinch of salt over your left shoulder 'right into the devil's eye'. It is unlucky to look at the Moon over your left shoulder, but lucky to see it over your right shoulder.[109] The 'left-handed strokes of fortune' were ill-omened, unpropitious, a left-handed compliment is insincere. Can all this be just because, as the *Oxford English Dictionary* has it, the right hand is that which 'is normally the stronger of the two' – the most dextrous, from *dexter*, Latin, 'right'?[110] But that would hardly leave the other hand as sinister, or explain the double meanings of 'right' – as in right side and right conduct – and French, *droit* – as in right side and law, i.e. *le droit*.

It may come as no surprise to find that 'the right' was associated with the Waxing Moon and 'the left' with the Waning Moon. The Waxing Moon, as Funk and Wagnall put it, is the right-hand moon because the curve of the right-hand index finger and thumb follows the curve of the waxing crescent; similarly, the curve of the left hand finger follows the waning crescent.[111] Even starting with the Moon as the circle of the Full Moon, the side we call right (the right of the circle) can be seen to fill up with light/life in the waxing, while the left side is seen to lose its light/life in the waning. This allocation of value is borne out in many myths. The Hindu Goddess Kali ('Black Time') was divided into her right and left sides: on her right side she was universal mother and benefactress, while on her left side she was a furious ogress who brought death. In New Britain, there were two gods, one bright, *Kabinana*, the Wise, and one dark, *Karvuvu*, the Fool. *Kabinana*, the Wise, was called the 'Right-hand god' (and tried to give immortality to humans) but *Karvuvu*, who was called the 'Left-hand god', prevented it.[112] Plutarch tells how the Pythagoreans classified a variety of terms under two categories: 'under the good they set Unity, the Determinate, the Permanent...the Right-handed, the Bright; under the bad they set Duality, the Indeterminate, the Moving...the Left-handed, the Dark, on the supposition that these are the underlying principles of creation.'[113] Again, right-handed and bright are set against left-handed and dark. In some contemporary thought, left enacts, or symbolizes, the unconscious; right, the conscious mind.

Old English, Kentish and German use the same words for 'left' as they do for weak, worthless and diseased, terms also applied to the Waning Moon (Old English *lyft*, as in *lyftadl*, 'left-disease, paralysis'). Graves refers the left/right dichotomy to planting lore (though it could be extended to the related issues of life and death):

> since the rate of plant growth under a waxing moon is greater than under a waning moon, the right hand has always been associated with growth and strength but the left with weakness and decay. Thus the word left itself means in Old Germanic, 'weak, old, palsied'. Lucky dances by devotees of the Moon were therefore made right-handed or clockwise, to induce prosperity; unlucky ones to cause damage or death were made left-handed, or 'widdershins'. Similarly, the right-handed fire-wheel, a swastika, was lucky; the left-handed (adopted by the Nazis) unlucky.[114]

More generally, the Sun moves to the right, clockwise, and while the Moon also travels from left to right, as it grows older and weaker it rises every night a little farther to the left. So even on another way of calculating, the left and the Waning Moon are linked. No wonder the left was where the devil was hiding. At least you knew where he was!

THE MOON AND BLACK MAGIC

> Upon the corner of the moon,
> There hangs a vaporous drop profound:
> I'll catch it ere it come to ground.[115]

This is Hekate, in her reduced role as Mistress of the three witches in *Macbeth*. As Goddess of the Waning and Dark Moon, Queen of the Night, Lady of Crossroads and Death, she was the patron of magic in late Greek, and Roman and Christian lore. Here, she draws down the 'vaporous drop', a drop of dew or blood believed to fall from the Moon as the water of death, in direct reversal of the Moon's gift of the waters of life. Out of this same drop, 'distill'd by magic sleights', shall come artificial sprites who are to confuse Macbeth so completely that he will spurn fate, scorn death, and believe in his own hopes beyond all fear, wisdom and security. Sorcery was practised in the Dark Moon, while the blackest magic was saved for the eclipse of the Moon: 'Gall of goat, and slips of yew/Sliver'd in the moon's eclipse',[116] as the witches chant around the bubbling cauldron from which Macbeth is soon to drink. This was black magic, belonging to the black Moon. Apollonius Rhodius, in his *Argonautica*, written in the mid-third century BC, has the Moon musing somewhat unsympathetically on Medea, one of Hekate's priestesses, in her anguish for Jason. 'So,' says Lady Moon,

> 'I am not the only one to go astray for love, I that burn for beautiful Endymion and seek him in the Latmian cave. How many times, when I was bent on love, have you disorbed me with your incantations, making the night moonless so that you might practise your beloved witchcraft undisturbed!'[117]

Here, it is implied that Medea could actually take the light of the Moon away, as could the witch Sycorax in *The Tempest*, Caliban's mother, who was so strong she 'could control the moon, make flows and ebbs...'[118]

In magical thinking, the lunar cloth of life can be untied and rethreaded by the weaving and binding of spells on Earth. For the Moon which allots destiny may be invoked to change that destiny – or so runs the lore of Ceremonial Magic which, literalizing the symbol, tries to appropriate the Moon's powers of life and death for itself.

The primitive thought within this kind of magic seems to be to pull the Moon closer to Earth, on the assumption that its influence would be correspondingly greater and might be more easily co-opted. Othello, hearing of the murder of Rodrigo, exclaims:

> It is the very error of the moon,
> She comes more near the earth than she was wont,
> And makes men mad.[119]

Plato, in the *Gorgias*, talks dismissively of 'those Thessalian witches drawing down the Moon',[120] while Pliny believed that 'Orpheus was the first to carry the craft [of calling down the moon] to his near neighbours', adding that of course the whole of Thrace, which was the home of Orpheus, was 'tainted by magic.'[121] The Greek poet Pindar says that Aphrodite, the Bright Moon, taught her son

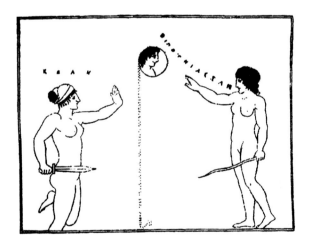

Fig. 10. Priestesses drawing down the Moon, with the Moon's face mirroring the face of the priestess. Greek vase painting, 2nd. c. BC. (From Roscher, Über Selene und Verwandtes. p.209).

Fig. 11. Thessalian Moon Oath. Terra-cotta vessel, Greece. 400 - 380 BC. British Museum.

Jason how to 'draw down the dark moon' when he needed magic powers, that dark Moon who was also called Aphrodite *Melaina*, 'the black one'.[122]

The Greeks had a spell called *diabole*: slandering your enemies to the Moon, and imploring the Moon to punish them. In later Europe, magical textbooks, called *Grimoires*, were popular in the seventeenth to nineteenth centuries. A singularly uncharming spell from the *Grand Grimoire*, entitled 'To Cause a Girl to Seek You Out, However Prudent She May Be', begins (after copious rituals) with an instruction to recite the following:

> I salute and conjure you, O beautiful Moon, O beautiful Star, O bright light which I hold in my hand!...I conjure you again by all the divine Names of God, that you send down to obsess, torment and harass the body, spirit, soul and five senses of the nature of N, whose name is written here below, in such a way that she will come to me and accomplish my will...[123]

It was no better in India. In the *Upanishads*, the faithful are exhorted to 'worship on the day of the full moon as it is seen in the east, saying, "Thou art Soma, the king, the wise, the five-mouthed, the lord of creatures...Do not decrease by our life, by our offspring, by our cattle; he who hates us and whom we hate, decrease by his life, by his offspring, by his cattle."'[124] (As St Augustine was later to say, 'Error has no rights', fathering, thereby, the Holy Church and the Inquisition together.[125])

* * *

However, the Moon's magical power could also be 'white', invoked to bless and not to curse, especially in the days of the white, bright, Full Moon, and the first glimmer of New Moon which casts the darkness behind. The ritual of 'drawing down the Moon' is still practised in modern witchcraft, known as *Wicca* (from Anglo-Saxon for 'witch'), where it is a sacred ritual of uniting the divine with the human feminine, but without the sinister implications ascribed to the Thracians (if, indeed, they ever merited them). Ronald Hutton, in his book *The Triumph of the Moon: A History of Modern Pagan Witchcraft*, gives Gerald Gardner's description of a midwinter ceremony in which the goddess of the Moon is invoked into the high priestess, who stands in the centre of a circle beside a burning cauldron. Witches, led by a high priest, dance in a circle around her in a rite called the 'Cauldron of Regeneration and the Dance of the Wheel'.[126] Margot Adler, in her book *Drawing Down the Moon*, describes the modern enactment of the ritual of 'drawing down the Moon' as one in which the Wiccan priest '*invokes* into the priestess (or... *evokes* from within herself) the Goddess or Triple Goddess, symbolized by the phases of the moon.'[127] This is the Goddess of a Thousand Names of whom Apuleius speaks, and the invocation is reminiscent of the words of Isis two thousand years before: 'Listen to the words of the Great Mother, who was of old also called Artemis, Astarte, Melusine, Aphrodite, Diana, Brigit and many other names...'[128]

In the Greek vase painting in fig. 12, Hekate holds the torches which sustain light and life in the darkness, and assists Persephone to rise up from the underworld as the returning crescent. The presence of Hermes suggests that a change of state is taking place between death and life. The familiar reference of the picture is to Persephone's ascent as spring after her three months of dark in winter, but the drama of rebirth may have begun with the rising of the New Moon out of the darkness of its three days of death at the end of the waning.[129] All three goddesses of the Moon are present: Hekate, the Dark Moon, draws Persephone upwards with the power of her torches, the light held in the dark. Behind Hekate stands Demeter as the Full Moon, when mother and daughter will embrace as one;

now Demeter gazes with awe at her daughter arising as the New Moon. Hermes, guide of souls who, moving between life and death creates the passage between them, is here the image of that moment of transformation, from Hekate to Persephone, from Dark to Light. This, to early people and to children of all ages, and certainly to the artist of the picture, was magic.

THE SACRED MARRIAGE OF MOON AND SUN

On the fourteenth or fifteenth night, there is a moment of perfect balance when the rising Moon, lifting above the horizon in the east, faces the setting Sun falling below the horizon in the west. In certain months of the year, the two orbs appear so similar in light and size that at first sight they look the same, as though the Sun of night had met the Moon of day. So when these two great lights are equally poised across the rim of Earth – the one rising, the other setting – many people throughout the world's history have thought they were witnessing the sacred marriage of Moon and Sun.

In ancient China the Full Moon was the time when the principles of *yin* and *yang* were reunited. The Chinese story of Heng-O and Shen I continues when Shen I, the hunter, flies from the Sun to the Moon to visit his wife. When, originally, Shen I was pursuing his wife up to the Moon, he found himself suddenly swept away by a hurricane onto a high mountain, and there the God of the Immortals spoke to him:

> 'Do not be angry with your wife; you too will become immortal. I myself loosed the whirlwind and brought you here. Heng-O is now an Immortal in the Palace of the Moon. You shall be rewarded with the Palace of the Sun. Thus the *Yin* and the *Yang* will be united in marriage.'
> Then he offered him a red sasparilla cake, with a lunar talisman marked upon it.
> 'Eat this cake,' he said. 'It will protect you from the heat of the Sun. And if you wear this lunar talisman, you may go at will to visit the lunar palace of Heng-O. But she may not come and visit you.'
> That is why the light of the Moon has its birth in the Sun, and why the Moon changes shape in proportion to the light of the Sun and the Moon's distance from the Sun.
> Shen I was carried to the Sun on the celestial bird, the cock of heaven, and landed about mid-day. But he soon became lonely and flew to the Moon on a ray of sunlight to find his wife freezing in the great cold.
> 'Do not be afraid,' he said, 'let not the past annoy you.'
> He cut down some cinnamon trees and made them into pillars, and built her a beautiful palace which he called the 'Palace of Great Cold'. When he returned to the Sun he built himself a palace, which he called the 'Palace of the Lonely Park'.
> Ever afterwards – from the forty-ninth year of the reign of Yao (2309 BC) – on the fifteenth day of every Moon, Shen I visits Heng-O in her palace, which is why the Moon shines so brightly when she is Full. This is called the conjunction of the *Yang* and *Yin*, the male and female principles.[130]

When *yin* and *yang* are united in a person, enlightenment comes. The Chinese character *ming*, which means enlightened as well as brilliant and bright, is drawn as a union of the images of Moon and Sun. As Rose Quong explains: 'Nothing could shine as brilliantly as these two heavenly lights, so man combined the sun and the moon...Lao-tse said: "He who knows others is clever; he who knows himself is enlightened (*ming*)."'[131]

Fig. 12. The Return of Persephone. The rising of Persephone as the New Moon, with Hermes, Hekate and Demeter. Red figured, Bell Krater by the Persephone Painter. From South Italy, Terracotta, c. 440 BC. The Metropolitan Museum of Art, New York.

In Greece, the union of the Full Moon and the Sun was one form of that sacred marriage which in many parts of the ancient world was celebrated at midsummer when the Sun was also 'full', at the height of its powers. The marriage of Selene and Helios was greeted with the sound of clashing shields by the Kouretes (young men), who danced at their wedding as they also danced for the Sun when he rose each dawn and for the Year God when he was annually reborn in spring.[132]

In fig. 13, it is as though the artist is looking with the eye of the dolphin across the sea from west to east and back from east to west, imagining the setting Sun and the rising Moon united in a single chariot, borne over the waves by the dolphin who makes of himself a boat to carry them. Helios, crowned with a halo of rays, sits beside Selene, who wears the crescent horns upon her head, her long hair hanging down in curls like the manes of her horses. Two pairs of horses, prancing in opposite directions, draw the chariot, the short-cropped pair on the left belonging to Helios and the day, the curly-maned pair on the right belonging to Selene and the night. The legs of the horses and the spokes of the wheel intertwine like reeds on the rim of the distant horizon, while the inner horse from each pair has turned to face each other, as though the marriage is taking place in the breathless moment between day and night. Behind the horses, as though disclosed by their parting, Sun and Moon gaze at each other in union, both holding the horses' reins and guiding the chariot together. In front of the chariot stands Pan, god of wild nature, his cloak billowing in the wind like a sail upon the sea, while, holding a quadruple torch, he leads the horses of the Sun. At the back of the chariot, a dancing *Koures*, with his sword still uplifted, has just clashed his shield to greet the celestial couple, announcing their marriage as they floated by.

An even older alliance – of Selene and Zeus – is mentioned in the Homeric *Hymn to Selene*, which tells of Selene (whose name comes from *selas*, 'light'), uniting with Zeus and bearing a child called *Pandia*, whose name means the 'wholly bright', an image of the radiance of the Full Moon.[133] At the festival of *Pandia* in Athens, round Moon cakes were shared and eaten by the people. As we saw in Chapter 10, many Greek stories were structured on the coming together of the solar hero with the lunar heroine: Odysseus and Penelope, and Theseus and Ariadne, for instance. The bulls who, in some pictures, draw Selene's chariot across the sky, are all that are left in Greece of the old stories about a

Fig. 13. Red-figured krater of the marriage of Helios and Selene. Greek, from Basilicata, S. Italy. Late 4th c. BC. The Louvre.

cow-shaped Moon goddess who consummated her marriage with the bull of the Sun.[134]

In North American Indian and Eskimo tales, the Full Moon was also a time of harmony, when husband and wife, or brother and sister, came to rest together for three days (the period when the Full Moon appears to be still) before they once again parted and moved away.[135]

In many places the sacred marriage of Moon and Sun was also celebrated at the time of New Moon, when the Moon is astronomically 'in conjunction' with the Sun. For these three days of nuptial ceremony the Moon is invisible – veiled in the heavenly embrace. In later Greece, Plutarch claimed that the Moon rushed to conjunction with the Sun so that she might be fructified by his light – which is why Greek weddings were held on Dark as well as Full Moons.[136]

The mythic image of the sacred marriage is found also in the marriage of Earth and Heaven, Goddess and God, *Luna* and *Sol* in alchemy, and the caduceus of female and male serpents intertwined. All these marriages symbolize, at a different level, the union of lunar and solar consciousness, however these terms were originally conceived. Common to these different images is the idea that the union of two apparently contrary principles creates the third term which reconciles them. This, the 'child' of their union, brought fertility to the land and vision to the heart. The transforming perception shared by all these traditions appears to be a new perspective on the terms that had presented themselves as opposites, a perspective which discloses their opposition to be ultimately an illusion, consequent on the limitations of the mind's dualistic thinking.

From the Bronze Age onwards and probably long before that, the intention of the rituals held on Earth to celebrate the union in Heaven, was also to reunite the outer world of Nature and the inner world of human beings. Campbell writes that the fundamental idea was that:

> the inward turning of the mind (symbolized by the sunset) should culminate in a realization of an identity *in esse* of the individual (microcosm) and the universe (macrocosm), which, when achieved, would bring together in one order of act and realization the principle of eternity and time, sun and moon, male and female...and the two serpents of the caduceus.[137]

But why is such a reconciliation so necessary? Why is this identity so difficult, even impossible, to realize? The problem of self-consciousness is that it continually undermines the ground of its own being. Whatever the subject thinks about becomes an object, different from, apart from, the subject, even if the subject was thinking reflexively, about himself or herself. When Adam and Eve eat the apple which 'opens their eyes' and gives them knowledge of good and evil, they look at themselves and see that they are naked. Body and mind, or body and soul, have split apart, so that the instinctive harmony with Nature, the formerly unquestioned bond of identity, is lost in the very act of becoming aware of it. Another way of putting this is to say that the conscious mind alienates itself from its source in unconsciousness, which merges into, or is a part of, all life. For the irrevocable consequence of perceiving and naming the difference between light and dark, from which the endless stream of 'opposites' arises – good and evil, I and thou, mind and body, Spirit and Nature, life and death, conscious and unconscious, and so on – is that the perception, once made, cannot be reversed. Those who have become self-conscious can make further refinements, perceiving ever finer and finer distinctions, but they cannot reach back into the unified world in which the original perception took place. The perception itself, originally so great an achievement, finds itself exiled, as it were, from the exhilarating insight of its own begetting.

Yet it seems that whenever the mind finds itself with opposing terms – whatever names it gives to them – it seeks to bring them back together, as though to restore a wholeness which 'feels as if it ought to be there'. The irony is that the mind that thinks in 'opposites', born of consciousness as its supreme act of differentiation, soon longs for its own dissolution in a new unity, in order to recover the original feelings of participation which were lost in the very moment of knowing them. Adam and Eve's self-awareness was followed by their expulsion from the Garden of Eden, the Tree of Life rendered forever unreachable by the eating from the Tree of the Knowledge of Good and Evil. In this sense consciousness is a tragic act, in that it is necessary and creates value yet its consequences are inevitable and irrevocable, both unforeseen and unforeseeable. As Rilke writes:

> Ah, whom can we ever turn to in our need?
> Not angels, not humans, and already
> the knowing animals are aware
> that we are not really at home in our interpreted world.[138]

This is far from the literal Judaeo-Christian rendering of consciousness as a curse, an unforgiving 'fall' from grace brought about by sin. It may be that consciousness is experienced in retrospect – and how else? – as the first sacrifice wrenched from human beings before they understood what it meant. The dying gods also are sacrificed, and Jesus Christ, perhaps the latest incarnation of this archetype of dying and resurrected god, is celebrated as offering of himself a *willing* sacrifice – understanding what it means. One of Blake's 'Proverbs of Hell' – 'If the fool would persist in his folly he would become wise'[139] – might suggest that consciousness, persisted in, would heal itself. Such, at any rate, we might read from the multitude of myths that look forward to a new union of that which has been sundered. In the tale from the Jewish *Midrash*, told in part in Chapter 6, the symbolism of union, disunion and reunion falls into the familiar pattern of the dynamic of consciousness, as expressed here through the the images of Moon and Sun: Moon and Sun, who were equal and together in the beginning, are unequal in the present, but will again be equal and reunited in the end. For though the Sun has become the sole ruler in the heavens, giving clarity and order, this at the same time disturbs the harmony which had existed in the beginning. God, however, makes a promise to the Moon:

In days to come shalt Thou again be great like the Sun; and the
Moon's radiance will be as is the radiance of the Sun.[140]

* * *

Yoga invokes the symbolism of Sun and Moon to convey the practitioner's mind beyond the
dualities of time into an eternal present. The meditating yogi, whose mystical body becomes a
microcosm of the universe, is said to breathe in the Sun and breathe out the Moon, and so to unite
in himself the two polar currents from which all contraries proceed. The 'serpent power' of *Kundalini*
is expected to rise up the central channel of the spine as the Yogi brings into harmony the two polar
currents or spiritual channels – one solar, the other lunar – on either side of the spine's central
channel (fig. 14). 'Thus,' Eliade comments:

> 'the breathing rhythm of the yogi ultimately enters into the rhythm of Great Cosmic
> Time....unifying these two polar currents is equivalent to the unification of the sun and the
> moon, that is the abolition of the cosmos, the reunion of contraries, which amounts to
> saying that the yogi transcends both the created universe and the time that governs it.'[141]

In the third-century AD Elamite bowl shown in fig. 15, the Sun and Moon are poised in
equilibrium around the central Tree of Life, the *Axis Mundi* (the place where 'the moon does not wane
and the sun does not set'),[142] with the lunar serpent of transformation on the trunk as the sap of life,
which rises and falls but never runs out.

As discussed in Chapter 6, Christianity also draws on the symbolism of Sun and Moon, portraying
Christ in the image of the male Sun, the bridegroom, and either the Church or the Virgin Mary as
the female Moon who was his honoured bride.[143] A poem by Anastasius Sinaita, writing in the seventh
century, calls his Church 'Ever-shining Selene', and addresses her in this image:

> Thou consort and fellow-traveller of Christ the Sun
> Who, as thy bridegroom, clothes thee with light...[144]

Later the bridal symbolism passed to Mary who, though his mother on Earth, became his bride in
Heaven. Christian doctrine may call the picture in fig. 16 the Coronation of the Virgin, but the image

*Fig. 14. Yogi meditating in Kundalini Yoga, uniting the solar and
lunar polar currents as a reunion of Sun and Moon. (From
Cook, The Tree of Life, p. 113).*

*Fig. 15. The World Tree with Sun and Moon. Detail of Elamite
bowl. Late Sassanian, 226-641 AD. (From Cook, The Tree
of Life, p. 114).*

speaks of a sacred marriage of hitherto contrary principles, a union which reconnects symbolically the two realities of *zoe* and *bios*, eternity and time, or the divine and the incarnated. It is this vision which, in the Gnostic *Gospel According to Thomas*, heals the wound of consciousness and gives it a home. Jesus says:

> When you make the two one, and
> when you make the inner as the outer
> and the outer as the inner and the above
> as the below, and when
> you make the male and female into a single one,
> so that the male will not be male and
> the female (not) be female...
> then shall you enter the Kingdom.[145]

In fig. 17, Christ is himself beyond the oppositions of Sun and Moon, as the figure in whom they are reconciled, or the image of the state of mind which reconciles them.

* * *

In the fifteenth and sixteenth centuries, one of the secret challenges to the Church's orthodoxy was alchemy, which was presented as a quest for the Elixir of Life or the Philosopher's Stone that would transmute base metals into gold. One way of expressing the goal of the Work was through the union of Sol and Luna, Sun and Moon, without which the Elixir could not be found. Rendered psychologically, the Work would transform what is base in the inner world – the *prima materia*, which is the chaos where opposites conflict – into a vision of unity where conflicts are reconciled. And the outer could not happen without the inner, nor the inner without the outer. In this way Nature and Spirit were to disclose their essential unity, a heresy in relation to the Church's literalized teaching of a fallen universe where Nature's spirit had been cursed to dust by Yahweh. In alchemical symbolism, the inner work of the alchemist was designated as Spirit, and the outer material upon which he worked was Nature, in which the Spirit was imprisoned and concealed but could be released and revealed by the alchemist's work upon himself.

Alchemists described their work in many different ways and under many different guises, since the central tenet of the work – that divinity was hidden in Nature – was in direct contradiction to the official Church's definition of divinity existing necessarily beyond Nature, in Nature's transcendent Creator. Certain things are constant, though. There were three or four stages to the work: *Nigredo*, or blackening; *Albedo*, or whitening; *Citrinitas*, or yellowing (occasionally omitted); *Rubedo*, or reddening. In the course of these four stages the four elements would be transmuted: earth would become water, water would become air, and air would become fire. Omitting here the considerable complexity of the texts,[146] it is still possible to follow the course of the work through the changing relationship of King and Queen, who embodied the alchemist himself and his mystical sister on the earthly plane, and Sol and Luna on the celestial plane. Sol and Luna represented the masculine and feminine principles, whose reconciliation in the sacred marriage meant that the work was complete. The continuous principle of transformation was portrayed in the quicksilver spirit of Mercurius (the latest incarnation of the winged psychopomp, Hermes), who was himself both the beginning and the end of the Work as well as the means by which that end was achieved. Mercurius was also known as the 'circle of the Moon', as well as the 'heavenly dew'.[147]

Fig. 16. The Coronation of the Virgin, 1358. Christ crowning the Virgin Mary, with the images of Sun and Moon beneath their feet. Paolo and Giovanni Veneziano, (active 1321–1358). Frick Gallery, New York.

In the first stage of the Work – the *Nigredo* – the opposites are imaged as King and Queen in conflict, embodying the celestial opposition of Sol and Luna. In fig. 18, the Sun carries the Moon on his shield, as the Moon carries the Sun on her shield, so that the lances of both Sun and Moon strike their own image on the shield of the other, suggesting that this conflict is ultimately within.

In the next stage of the Work the opposites are dissolved, each losing their separate identity. This is rendered as the King and Queen in the Mercurial Bath – the Solution, where earth becomes water. In the mid-sixteenth century Alchemical engraving shown in fig. 19, from the *Rosarium Philosophorum*, *(Rose Garden of the Philosophers)*, the text in German below the figure reads:

> O Luna, folded by my embrace
> Be you as strong as I, as fair of face.
> O Sol, brightest of all lights, known to men
> And yet you need me, as the cock the hen.[148]

In some texts there is a second and a third *coniunctio* known as a 'lunar rebirth' and a 'solar rebirth'. In fig. 20, in the lunar rebirth, King and Queen, united as a winged hermaphrodite, rise together out of the cupped Moon, holding serpents. The lunar tree, with fruits round like Full Moon eggs, echoes the motif of the chicken hatched from the lunar egg which endows the King-and-Queen with the power to fly, to rise above their earlier polarized condition.

Fig. 17. Christ drawing out a soul from the golden dragon of the Sun and the silver dragon of the Moon. North Wall fresco, Abbey Church, Brauweiler, Germany. 12th century.

Fig. 18. Luna (left) on a griffin fighting Sol (right) on a lion. The conflict of opposites as the first stage of The Work. Aurora Consurgens, the 'Rising Dawn.' 16th century. Zentralbibliothek, Zurich.

Just as in the *Upanishads* the soul in its journey after death progressed from Moon to Sun, so alchemical symbolism follows a lunar rebirth with a solar rebirth: 'Here the lunar life completely ends. The spirit into heaven deftly ascends', goes the motto from the *Rosarium's* fourteenth woodcut, which shows the fixation of the yellowing transformation process as it turns into the reddening of the next stage. The underlying idea is that purification consists in the removal of the 'watery' elements of the 'Philosopher's Stone'. Fabricius comments: 'The stone in its moist and lunar form is less refined than the stone in its dry and solar form.'[149]

The *Rosarium* ends with the resurrection of Christ from his tomb. Other alchemists imagine the final stage of the Work as a heavenly marriage between Sun and Moon (fig. 22), or as that marriage internalized within the alchemist, or else as the opposites reconciled within Mercurius, the 'world-creating spirit concealed or imprisoned in matter', as the alchemists conceived him (fig. 23).[150]

The contest between the lunar griffin and the solar lion is also found in the fight between the lunar unicorn and the solar lion, a later version of the Moon-bull and the Sun-lion. We all know the rhyme:

> The lion and the unicorn
> Were fighting for the crown.
> The lion beat the unicorn
> All round the town.

The single horn of the unicorn is the heavenly horn of the Moon, which is 'beaten', extinguished by the Sun. On the analogy of the lion climbing a tree to escape his horned pursuer and then leaping down to kill him, the myth suggests that the Lion-Sun flies from the rising Unicorn-Moon and hides behind the tree of the underworld. The Moon, sinking in its turn, is caught in this underworld tree and slain.[151] Adopted as the royal arms of Great Britain in 1603, the heraldry celebrates, probably without knowing it, the immemorial interplay of the bodies in the heavens.

In the magnificent tapestry of *La Dame à la Licorne* (fig. 24), the lion and the unicorn, holding flags adorned with white crescents, are brought into harmony with each other as the lady's '*seul désir*' beyond the temporal world of the five senses, as depicted in the five earlier tapestries. Jung comments that lion and unicorn are allegories of Christ and the Church, and also 'stand for the inner tension of opposites in Mercurius', as do the Sun and Moon, King and Queen. Mercurius, he explains, is 'the hermaphrodite that was in the beginning, that splits into the classical brother-sister duality and is reunited in the *coniunctio*, to appear once again at the end in the radiant form of the *lumen novum*, the stone.'[152] This movement – from unconscious unity, through the opposition of consciousness to unconsciousness, to a new conscious unity in which this opposition is reconciled – was Jung's chief symbolic model in his later life for what he called the journey of individuation.

* * *

The marriage of Sun and Moon – either visibly, as equals across opposing horizons, or invisibly, conjoined in the darkness of black night, or, still more invisibly, in harmonious rapport within the human imagination – signified for much of the ancient world a miraculous union of eternity and time. Once the Moon had become the lesser light, it took the role of time and the Sun took the role of eternity. In this conception of their union, or reunion, the Sun, as the illuminating light of eternal being, becomes one with the Moon as the illuminated light of the field of time. Eternal and temporal life are thereby revealed to be not fundamentally opposed, but formed from one single essence which manifests in dual aspects. But since the light of the Moon is in fact the reflected light of the Sun, the temporal life is shown, by analogy, to be the reflection of eternal life, the mirror through which the eternal may see its face in time. In Egypt this perception was rendered in the drawing of a Left Eye (the Moon) at the centre of a rounded hand mirror (fig. 25).[153] Thus the beholders, looking in the mirror in the course of daily life, saw their own faces as one with the face of the Moon, receiving and reflecting the light of the Sun, the eternal principle operating in time:

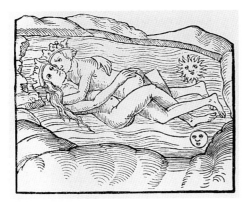

Fig. 19. Coniunctio sive coitus. King and Queen united in the 'Maternal Sea' with Sun and Moon. Rosarium Philosophorum. 16th century. (From Jung, CW 12, p. 330).

Fig. 20. Lunar Rebirth. Winged hermaphrodite with Moon Tree and Serpents. 10th woodcut of the Rosarium. 'Wondrous hatching of a silvery egg.' (From Fabricius, Alchemy, p. 130).

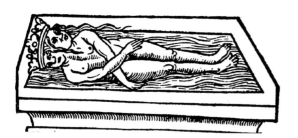

Fig. 21. Solar Rebirth: Spiritual ascent into heaven. King and Queen in bath with spirit ascending into heaven. 14th woodcut of the Rosarium. (From Fabricius, Alchemy, *p. 152).*

Fig. 22. The heavenly marriage of Sol and Luna, encompassing the globe of Earth, within a wedding ring of golden stars. (From Jung, CW 12, p. 125).

Fig. 23. Mercurius as 'uniting symbol.' Valentinus, 'Duodecim claves,' in Musaeum Hermeticum (1678). (From Jung, CW 12, p. 292).

> Light of the night, image of the Left Eye...
> who rises in the east while the sun is in the west...
> the left Eye receives the light of the right Eye (the Sun).[154]

Like the Chinese *ming*, the Eye becomes a complex symbol, in which the Eye of the Moon, knowing its source, becomes the Eye of inner illumination.

* * *

A *Tao* tale invokes the passing of the Full Moon to offer a perspective on time and transience. It was 1081, and the seventh Moon was just on the wane. Two friends had gone by boat to see the Red

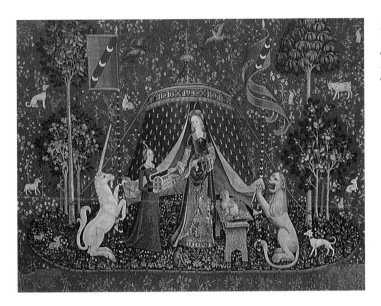

Fig. 24. The Lion and the Unicorn. 'A Mon Seul Désir,' title of the sixth and last tapestry entitled La Dame à la Licorne. End of 15th century. Musée de Cluny, Paris.

Wall, and one of them tells the tale. He had filled his friend's cup and asked him to play to the bright Moon upon his flageolet, while he himself sang a sad song, ending with 'Great heroes dead, where are you now?' His friend accompanied him so delicately that he asked him to explain his art. 'Alas', his friend replied, 'life is but an instant of Time. I long to be like the Great River which rolls on its way without end. Ah, that I might cling to some angel's wing and roam with him for ever. Ah, that I might clasp the bright moon in my arms and dwell with her forever. Alas, it only remains for me to enwrap these regrets in the tender melody of sound.'

'"But do you forsooth comprehend," I enquired, "the mystery of this river and of this moon? The water passes by but is never gone: the moon wanes only to wax once more. Relatively speaking, Time itself is but an instant of time; absolutely speaking, you and I, in common with all matter, shall exist to all eternity. Wherefore then the longing of which you speak? ... The clear breeze blowing across this stream, the bright moon streaming over yon hills, – these are ... the eternal gifts of God to all mankind, and their enjoyment is inexhaustible. Hence it is that you and I are enjoying them now."'

His friend smiled, threw away the dregs from his wine-cup and filled it again to the brim. They lay down to rest in the boat: for streaks of light from the east had stolen upon them unawares. [155]

Fig. 25. Egyptian Hand Mirror with the Moon-Eye at the centre. (From Lamy, Egyptian Mysteries, p. 16).

CHAPTER 12

THE WANING MOON

And like a dying lady, lean and pale,
Who totters forth, wrapped in a gauzy veil...
Shelley *The Waning Moon*

Crazed through much childbearing,
The moon is staggering in the sky...
Yeats *The Crazed Moon*

Waning, like growing old, has always called for explanation as the first intimation of mortality. In myth and folklore, the fact of death for human beings is typically explained, or explained away, as an error or flaw that got in the way of the true scheme of things. Death comes as a consequence of, say, a trivial mistake (when the hare, lizard, or chameleon gets the message wrong),[1] or an unfortunate coincidence (when the serpent is the only one awake to answer the question, 'who wishes not to die?').[2] Or else it is due to an unpredictable moment of malice (when the dog deliberately gives the wrong message after being refused a gourd of milk),[3] or an inability to solve a problem (such as what to do with the skin of old age).[4] Or it is the result of a trick (when the serpent or lizard steals the immortality instead).[5] Alternatively, death comes as a punishment for a flaw in human nature ('original' sin),[6] or maybe it is just because of an error of vision (when the Bushman hare-man insists his mother is not sleeping but dead).[7] Or, as a last resort, death is put down to some unaccountable evil which spoils everything when there is nothing and no one to blame. Very rarely is it allowed to belong to the true nature of things.

At an earlier time in human consciousness, it was generally the vision of the Moon's death and rebirth which carried peoples' reflection on death. Or rather, it was the *interpretation* of the Moon's disappearance and reappearance *as* death and rebirth which allowed these reflections to take place. It was as though a 'real-life' drama were unfolding on an apparently objective stage, upon which the characters of the human story played their parts. The crucial challenge of the plot was, of course, that while Moon, Sun, people, animals, plants and everything else, except perhaps stones, appeared to die, only Moon and Sun were seen to be reborn.

People in earlier times grieved for the death of the Moon as they grieved for the death of their loved ones. Waning was like ageing and disappearing was like dying, a universal law which encompassed the Moon no less than humanity. In the Waning and Dark Moons, tragedy appeared to be the fate of the lunar and the human condition alike.

In the waning, the Moon rises later and later each night (as though running out of its strength), and each night there is less and less of it until finally there is nothing at all. For three dark nights only the stars come out. Then (imagining the first time), a curved gleam of light announces that the Moon is born again. If the Moon and humanity were truly the same, then humanity also would be born again after its own death. From one side of the world to the other, the cries of people greeting the first

Fig. 1. Coyolxauhqui Dismembered. 1469 AD. Volcanic tufta relief. Templo Mayor. Institute Naçionale de Antropologia e Historia, Mexico City.

glimpse of the returning crescent reveal how deeply they had identified with the Moon. No one knows how far back that 'first time' was – though it must have been a long time before whole cycles of the Moon were carved upon the horns of animals, and that was around 30,000 BC. Yet as recently as the nineteenth century AD, old men among the Californian Indians were still dancing in a circle to the New Moon as it rose again, saying:

> As the Moon dieth, and cometh to life again, so we also having to die will again live.[8]

Somehow, for tragedy to be transformed into myth, humanity and the Moon had to become one. Yet the mythic vision, which offers the promise of a life beyond death, depends not only upon the peoples' *wish* to be the same as the Moon but also upon that wish *being believed to be true*. But this is a distinction of contemporary consciousness, which separates – indeed, must separate – what to an earlier mind would

Fig. 2. Three altars to the Moon deity in triple form. The Waxing Moon is indicated by the crescent resting upon first stone on the left, the Full Moon by the horns on the larger stone in the middle, and the place of the Waning Moon is taken by the dog who looks toward the Full Moon as if waiting to bite a piece out of it. Mesopotamian Altar.(From Harding, Woman's Mysteries, p. 217).

have been inseparable. As Harrison says, we need to 'think ourselves back into the primeval fusion of things, a fusion always unconsciously present in the mind of poet and primitive.'[9] In ritual, this *participation mystique* which united people with their Moon took place in a vivid present, in the singing and dancing and acting, the wearing of masks, the miming and chanting – what in a different context we would call prayer. It is the rituals which, as it were, *compel* the fusion to become alive in the present moment. But in the stories, this union of humanity and Moon typically belongs to an earlier age, a 'Golden Age' when things were as they should have been, before anything went wrong. Then it was that the people died when the Moon died, and when, after three days, the Moon was born again, the people also were born again, as though they had gone to sleep for three days and now it was time to wake up.

THE BOND WITH THE MOON

In the Caroline Islands in the eighteenth century, it was said that in the olden days death was only a short sleep. People died on the last day of the Waning Moon and came to life again, refreshed, three days later when the New Moon appeared, just as if they had awakened from a good sleep. But then, 'somehow', an evil spirit appeared, who contrived that when people slept the sleep of death they should wake no more.[10] A similar story is found among the Cheyenne North American Indians who thought that when the 'Wise One Above', who was the Moon, first made people they did not die forever: 'When they died they were to be dead for only four nights, and then they would live again.'[11] The Australian Aborigines also believed that people used to die for three days, like the Moon, and then rise again after the third day.[12] But when it came to what went wrong, each tribe had a different reason. The Wotjobaluk claim that when people died in earlier times the Moon used to say (robustly): 'You up-again,' and they all got up again and went about their business. But there was an old man who said, 'Let them remain dead.' And then none of them ever came back to life any more, except the Moon, who went on getting up again as he always had done.[13]

Other tribes believed that they lost the Moon's goodwill towards them. In the Kulin tribe of central Australia, the Moon wanted to give the people a draught of water which would let them return to life again after they died. But the bronze-winged Pigeon would not consent to this, and the Moon became very angry. Among the tribes of New South Wales, the Moon asked some men to carry his serpents for him, but they were afraid and the Moon said: 'As you would not do what I asked, you have forever lost the chance of rising again after you die.' The Arunta of Oceania said that the Moon used to live amongst them, but died and was buried, and after three days rose again as a young man. The people ran away, and the Moon said: 'Do not run away or you will die altogether; I shall die too but I shall rise again in the sky.'[14]

No one knows why, in the Fijian story told in Chapter 7, the Rat, who wanted human beings to die like rats, prevailed over the Moon, who wanted them to be reborn like itself.[15] In many other tales, also, it is the Moon who tries to give immortality to human beings – preserving the bond – but is prevented by the folly of the messenger or of those who receive the message. The hare, for instance, was sometimes the foolish messenger (as in the Hottentot tale), and at other times (as in the Bushman tale) the one too foolish to understand the message the Moon was giving him: that his mother would rise again as the Moon himself did.[16] Variations on this myth can be found all over Africa. The Wa-Sania of East Africa, for example, believed that human beings did not die until the lizard said to them: 'You know that the Moon dies and rises again, but human beings will die and rise no more.'[17]

Often there are two messengers, one for immortal life and the other for death. Inevitably, it seems, the messenger with the message of death reaches the people first and the second messenger cannot reverse it. The messengers are typically animals or reptiles, perhaps because their message concerns that which we have in common with animals and reptiles. The Bantu, for instance, have the lizard as the messenger of death and the chameleon as the messenger of life, while the Basuto have the lizard for life and the chameleon for death.[18] It does not seem to matter who brings the message: death comes at the last.

In East Africa, the Nandi tribe put the dog in the way of people's bond with the Moon. One day the dog came to the first people on Earth and said: 'Everyone will die like the Moon, but unlike the Moon you will not come back to life again unless you give me some milk to drink out of your gourd and beer to drink through your straw.' But the people laughed at the dog and gave him the milk and beer on a stool, to drink like a dog. The dog drank the milk and the beer, but was angry at not being served like a human being and went away, saying: 'All people will die, and only the Moon will return to life.'[19] What is interesting is that the people who wanted to be like the Moon did not want the dog to be like them, yet the dog, who undoubtedly brought the message from the Moon, is often the personification of the Moon in its waning phase. If the Nandi dog is, at a deeper level, the figure of the Moon in its waning, then the possibility is left open that the verdict of death comes in answer to a lack of generosity of vision (as with the Bushman Hare-man), suggesting that the waning must be taken along with the waxing, all creatures being equal under the Moon.

SLOUGHING THE SKIN OF DEATH

If we humans were more like the Moon, the next argument implicitly goes, then we could slough away the skin of old age, as the Moon sloughs its shadow and the serpent its skin. The problem of renewal in time is then transferred to the wrinkled skin of an ageing body, which seems to defy a vision of being born again like a baby. In Melanesia, 'casting off one's skin like the Moon' is the phrase for eternity; so the missionaries, trying to explain that God is eternal, found themselves saying: 'He sloughs his skin like the Moon.'[20] The tribes of Queensland, Australia, assumed the Moon shed its skin each month, as did the Huitotos of the Upper Amazon. In the Congo, the Baluba tribe thought that the Moon god and his two wives were the first people who renewed themselves by changing their skin, like serpents. The Algonquin Moon goddess, Aatensic, was represented either as an old woman or as a serpent.[21]

There is a common story, told across the islands of the Pacific from the Banks Islands, New Hebrides and New Guinea to the Admiralty Islands and in the mountains of Central Celebes, which addresses the problem from the common-sense view of a child. The Celebes' version, as told by the Dutch Missionaries of the nineteenth century, went that in the old days, when people still dropped their old wrinkled skins, stepped into water and came out again good as new, there was an old grandmother who loved her grandchild. Once she went to bathe in the water and hung up her old skin in a tree. Then, transformed into a young girl, she came back home but her grandchild did not recognize her: 'You are not my grandmother,' the little boy said. 'My grandmother was old, and you are young.' And he would have nothing to do with her. So the grandmother left the house, took her skin off the tree, and went back into the water and came out old again. But ever since then people have to stay with the skins they were given, and must die.[22]

An adult variation on this theme from the Admiralty Islands has the old woman returning from the sea ravishingly young and, as she passes her two sons, one of them says to the other: 'Well, she may be your mother, but she's going to be my wife.' But his mother overheard him and quickly put her old skin back on.[23] The 'Old Woman' of all these tales is one of the names for the Moon, also known as the 'Mother', Our Grandmother', 'Shining Woman', 'Round Head' and 'Skin-changing Woman'.[24]

The ancient Greeks had the same word for old age as they did for the cast-off skin of a serpent – *yeras*.[25] The tale of Glaucus, the infant son of King Minos of Crete, turns on this perception. One day Glaucus fell into a huge *pithos* filled with honey and died. Minos called the wisest man he knew, Polyidos, who sat beside the little body not knowing what to do. Suddenly a snake slid on top of the child, and Polyidos ('Seer of many things') seized a stone and killed it. But then another snake appeared and, seeing its comrade dead, went away again. It soon returned, carrying in its mouth some herbs, which it laid over the dead snake who instantly came back to life. Polyidos then took up the herbs and rubbed them into the body of Glaucus, who came back to life too.[26]

Instead of trying to become like the Moon, the deceased in the Egyptian *Book of the Dead* prays for eternal life by praying that he may become a serpent: 'I am the serpent *Sata*, whose years are many,' he says. 'I die and I am born again, and I renew myself, and I grow young each time.'[27]

Frequently, the serpent, who changes his skin with ease, is accused of stealing the immortality that was intended for human beings. In the *Epic of Gilgamesh* from second-millennium BC Mesopotamia, a serpent takes the herb of immortality from the hero Gilgamesh while he is sleeping. What had happened was that Enkidu, Gilgamesh's friend and brother, hurled the thigh of the Bull of Heaven in anger at the Moon goddess Ishtar, who took his life to avenge the insult. So Gilgamesh, searching for the eternal life his brother was denied – 'because of my brother I am afraid of death' – travels through the mountain of the underworld to Utnapishtim, the Old Man who survived the Great Flood, to ask him what to do. Utnapishtim puts him to trial: can he stay awake for just seven nights, not much, if he wants to stay awake for all eternity? But Gilgamesh cannot stay awake for one night, let alone the

Fig. 3. *Waxing Moon (above) and Waning Moon (below). English Watermarks. (From Bayley,* The Lost Language of Symbolism, *p. 180).*

Fig. 4. *Western Eskimo Moon Mask in the form of a seal. The two faces suggest the different characters given to the Waxing and Waning Moon. American Museum of Natural History, New York.*

seven nights required of him, and wakes each morning to find a loaf of bread outside his door. After one week there are seven loaves, and Gilgamesh must accept his fate. As he leaves in despair for home, Utnapishtim's wife slips him the Herb of Immortality, called the 'Old Man Become Young'. On his way back, Gilgamesh falls asleep (again), leaving the precious herb upon a rock beside him. But the ever-watchful serpent rises from the sea and swallows it, stealing Gilgamesh's last chance. So Gilgamesh wakes to find the dead skin of the serpent lying on the rock where once the living herb had been. 'Everlasting life is not your destiny,' the gods tell him in a dream.[28]

Even in Genesis, where the life-giving power of the serpent has been subverted, it is the serpent, hanging from the Tree of Knowledge, who whispers of immortality and so brings death. As Frazer observes, all that is missing for this story to 'complete its resemblance' to similar myths of serpents, humans and everlasting life, is the serpent eating of the fruit of the Tree of Life and attaining immortality itself.[29] Instead, the serpent, along with Eve, whose name he shares – the Hebrew *Hawwah*, Eve, is very close to the Arabic and Aramaic word for serpent – [30] and together with Adam and the rest of Nature, receives the curse of death from Yahweh who, like the angry Moon, reserves immortality for himself alone.

THE MOON AS THE DEALER OF DEATH

Paradoxically, the Moon who is celebrated as the source of eternal renewal may also be feared as the cause of death. Yet, on reflection, it makes sense that the one allotted the power to give life is also implicitly attributed with the power to withhold that gift, which is effectively to deal death. It is the paradox of all external authority, that the powers come dual: granting and refusing, doing good and evil and, as here, offering life and death, capable of doing either or both. If the Moon's relation to humanity is viewed as that of an authoritarian parent to a helpless child, then the Moon is understood as refusing the longed-for bond between them – not allowing people to be immortal like itself – either because it is angry with them or because it does not care. Arrestingly, the Greek word for Moon, *men*, is also the root of the verb 'to be angry', 'to rage', *menaio*, as though there may once have been a link between the ideas of Moon, time, death and rage. ('Do not go gentle into that good night,/Rage, rage, against the dying of the light...')[31]

Rage, when denied, often becomes the imagined rage of the other towards oneself (rituals to protect the living against the supposed rage of the newly dead are well known in cultures such as Malekula, for instance).[32] So it may be that the rage at death that was originally human became the Moon's rage at human beings which gave them death. Soma is called the 'raging one', as well as 'healer and seer', as was the Egyptian Khons, and the three Maenads, priestesses of Dionysos, as well as the three Erinyes.[33] The word 'shaman' also means the 'raging one'. Furthermore, the old phrase 'with a wanion' – as in Shakespeare's 'Come away, or I'll fetch th' with a wanion',[34] which fell out of fashion in the seventeenth and eighteenth centuries but was revived by Sir Walter Scott, means 'with a vengeance', 'with a curse'.[35] 'In a wanion' (a variant, as in 'he's in a wanion') is evocative of 'in a bad mood', or perhaps just 'mooned'.

The Maoris called the Moon the 'man-eater', the source of death.[36] In equatorial Africa some tribes said the Moon 'looks down over our country and seeks whom she may devour, and we poor black men are very much afraid of her on that account, and we hide ourselves from her sight on that night' (the night of invisibility).[37] In Central Asia the Tartars thought a giant lived in the Moon who ate people.[38] The Tupi tribes of Brazil believed that 'all baneful influences, thunder and floods proceed from the Moon.'[39] In some shamanic lore, the Moon steals souls, and it is a shaman's task to journey to the Moon and bring them back. A South American Taulipang myth tells how the Moon had carried off the soul of a child and hidden it under a pot. The shaman went to the Moon, found the pot, and freed the child's soul.[40]

In Polynesian myth the Moon goddess, Hina, is portrayed as relentless in her unconcern for humankind (when she is not helping them to give birth). Maui, the ancient god, implored his mother Hina, the Moon, to give people the gift of immortality. 'Let humans die and live again, as you, the Moon, die and live again,' he said. But Hina replied: 'No, let them die and increase the soil and never rise to life again.' Maui kept trying: 'Let death be very short; let the people die and live again, and live for ever.' But Hina said: 'Let death be very long, that the people may sigh and sorrow.'[41]

In a Japanese tale, a girl was once found in a bamboo field, no taller than a hand. She was called Kaguya. When she grew up she was the fairest in the land and all the princes wooed her, and even the Emperor himself sought her hand. But when the Emperor came to the bamboo field to bring her home to his palace, she was nowhere to be found. Tsuki-yomi, the Moon-king, who had long watched over her beauty, had sent down a silver throne for her at midnight and taken her back up to his own palace, a vast circle made of white crystal. Thirty princes lived there together, 15 wearing robes of white, 15 wearing robes of black, and each of them ruled the Moon for one day. In vain did the Emperor's guards shoot their arrows at the Moon. Kaguya was never seen on Earth again.[42] It was the same in Greece: when Selene kissed Endymion she gave him death as well as everlasting life.[43]

Tales of the kidnapping Moon in Europe, the offended Moon in Samoa and North-west America, and the hunting Moon in Greece, Rome and the Near East, may be seen as the Moon bringing about death.[44] Here, the contrast drawn between human beings and the Moon implicitly accuses the Moon of breaking the original bond, leaving them to die alone. Yet was it not also the Moon who held out the promise of eternal life? It may be that, in the childhood of the race, the awe felt towards the Moon was originally too overwhelming to draw distinctions, so that the Moon could strike with life and death at any time, whenever it wished. But once differentiation was possible, and life was ranged into pairs of opposites – light and dark, life and death, good and evil – it is likely that the Moon's 'nature' was also divided into two. Then the duality of the Moon's 'gifts' could be simply separated into waxing and waning: the waxing – when the Moon is, as Plutarch puts it, 'of good intent' – and the waning, when the Moon is of ill intent, for, as he adds, 'in the waning the Moon brings sickness and death.'[45]

At least the Moon's moods were clear for all to see. In Melanesia, in the *Old Woman and the Skin* tale, her two sons were two Moon gods, one the god of the Bright Moon and the other the god of the Dark, Waning Moon. The Bright Moon god was wise, good and lucky, while the Dark Moon god was foolish, bad and unlucky.[46] In New Britain, an island in the Bismark archipelago, east of New Guinea,the same two gods existed with different names, Kabinana, the Wise, and Karvuvu, the Fool. It comes as no surprise that Kabinana, the Wise, the 'Right-hand god', intended the message of immortality to go to humankind, but Karvuvu, the Fool, the 'Left-hand god', gave the message to the serpent instead.[47] Symbolically, in the form of the wily serpent, the scaly lizard or the witless hare, it is as though the Moon in its waning steals immortality from humans, hunting them down with silver beams like arrows, or swallowing them back into the darkness of its own death.

If, once, it was widely believed that the Waxing Moon gave life and the Waning Moon gave death, then the apotropaic rituals surrounding the Waning Moon become intelligible, for how else to ward off the harm it might do? Early Jewish lore said that the forces of evil increased in the Waning Moon, and, according to some Jewish mystics looking at the Moon at all was prohibited, though one might glance casually at it when the *kiddush levanah*, blessing of the New Moon, was recited (*levanah* is Hebrew for 'Moon').[48] Even in the nineteenth century in various places around the world, when the Moon waned journeys and weddings were postponed, babies were hidden and not weaned, and planting was suspended (except for root vegetables whose energy goes downwards into the dark).

Many superstitions of later times are resonant of this ancient fear, even though the original feeling and the world view which fostered it are long forgotten. The folk belief that people and animals are more likely to die in a Dark Moon or an ebb tide may be a remnant of this idea. Even in the 1970s, in Cornwall, south-west England, the fishermen would say that life came in with the flowing tide and went out with the ebbing tide.[49] In Robert Burns' melancholy lines:

> The wan moon sets behind the white wave,
> And time is setting with me, Oh![50]

Language has petrified some of these thoughts in their original form, like fossils revealed after only a little scraping. 'Waxing' and 'waning' are Old English words in origin: the verb 'to wax' comes from Old English *weaxan* and Old High German *wahsan*, both meaning 'to grow, to increase', related to Latin *auxi*, 'I caused to grow'. The verb 'to wane' comes from Old English *wanian*, Old High German *wan*, Old Norse *vanr*, meaning 'to lessen, to decrease, to dwindle', where the decline in light and size is also a decline in power, and comes to mean defective, lacking, diminished. Keats, in his poem *Lamia*, draws upon this analogy to show Hermes approaching his lost nymph:

> ...she, like a moon in wane,
> Faded before him...[51]

'Wane', shortened to 'wan', was also used as a negative prefix, meaning 'not', 'un-', 'without', 'bad' or 'wrong' (rather like the modern slang 'dis'), as in *wanhope*, meaning 'despair' (now rare in English but still used in Dutch); *wanchance*, meaning 'misfortune'; *wandought*, meaning 'puny', 'feeble'; *wansonsy*, meaning 'mischievous'; as well as the more obvious *wanweird*, *wanhap*, *wanruly*, *wanrest*, *wanthriven*, *wanthrift*, *wanwordy*, *wanworth*, and even *wanton* (Old English *teon*, meaning 'train', 'discipline').[52] Still in use in German is *wahnwitz* and *wahnsinn*, meaning 'madness', and, in Dutch, *wanorde*, meaning 'chaos', and *wanbeleid*, meaning 'unruly'. 'Wane' must have had both a common and an unambiguously pejorative meaning to become so readily simplified into a common negation – 'wan-'. Also, many of these 'wan-' words are words where rule and order have gone, and chance (and fear of the unknown) takes over. Thus King Henry, in the opening line of *1 Henry IV*: 'So shaken as we are, so wan with care...'[53]

Further, 'wane' enters one of our most commonly used words: 'want'. The Middle English word 'want', coming from 'wane', in its original sense of 'lack, deficiency', is still obvious in the meaning given to a phrase such as 'being in want and penury', and in the nursery rhyme 'For want of a horse, the kingdom was lost.' (Compare French, *il me faut*). 'Wane' is also related to the Latin *uanus*, meaning 'empty', 'without substance', hence 'vain', and has Indo-European cognates, such as Sanskrit *unas*, 'defective', Greek *eunis*, 'deprived', Gothic *wans* and Old Nors *vanr*, 'defective', *vanta*, 'lack'. *Uanus* yields 'vanish', 'vaunt', and is related to *uacere*, 'vacant', and *uastus*, 'vast', 'devastate', 'waste', 'wasteland'.[54] 'In vain' and 'vainglorious' carry the negative meaning of the prefix 'wan', but the term 'vanity', as meaning 'without substance', resounds with echoes of an earlier time when the Moon's rhythms were an intrinsic part of thinking about life. The waning of the Moon, so soon after its waxing, had (at least etymological) implications for the *evanescence* of created forms: 'All is vanity,' saith the preacher.

On the other hand, the waning was the time to harmonize with the waning of earthly things: the time when wood was cut, crops were harvested, and afflictions were presented to the Moon that they might diminish with the diminishing light: 'As the moon decreases, so may my pains decrease also,' as they said in Germany.[55] Even in the waning the Moon could heal, by taking the disease away with it as it went. Many southern Slavs and Italians used to believe that a person suffering from warts, boils, swollen glands, goitre, varicose veins, and even less visible afflictions, could touch the affected part at the moment the

Moon was changing and the Moon would carry it off, taking upon itself the sickness and leaving the person behind cured.[56] This concrete reading of the Moon's waning anticipates the later symbolic tradition of the Saviour who took upon himself the sins of the world that it might be redeemed.

DEATH AS PUNISHMENT

A further refinement on the notion of death given to humans by the Moon, or by any other deity, is that death is a punishment for a flaw in human nature. Enkidu was arrogant; the Bushman man-hare was obstinate; Eve was greedy, Adam was weak, and both were disobedient; the Nandi were unkind; the Arunta, cowardly; Epimetheus ('Hindsight') lacked foresight, opening Pandora's jar and letting out death, while his brother Prometheus ('Foresight') was ineffective.[57] Mothers of children nursed by goddesses are too ignorant to trust the goddesses' methods: they scream, and immortality is lost.[58] All the human fallibilities are represented here: fear, hubris, disobedience, impatience, inattention, ignorance, or, as with Gilgamesh in the oldest story, simply the weakness of the flesh, the weariness of the body he was given, the condition of being human.

In a Tiwi myth from Oceania, death comes as a curse upon the race because the mother neglected her child through adultery with the Moon. Again, it is the Moon who, preying on human weakness, is responsible for the outcome of death. What happened was this. *Bima* was married to *Purukapali*, the great ancestor. When the Moon-man, *Tjapara*, met *Bima*, he took her off into the bush to make love, and she left her baby boy behind, all alone, and stayed away far too long. So when *Purukapali* came back he found the little boy dead. Horrified, he sought out *Tjapara* and killed him. Then, lifting up his son in his arms, he walked backwards into the sea, pronouncing the curse of death that became the law: 'As my son has died and will never return, so shall all men.' *Purukapali* never came back, nor did his son, but the Moon, *Tjapara*, came back from the dead after three days.[59]

DEATH AS A CHOICE

Just occasionally, death is presented as a choice: in the Malay peninsular, in the island of Nias, in Celebes, the Gilbert Islands and Madagascar, human beings had to choose between the Moon and the banana.

The Mantras of the Malay peninsular, who thought that, in former times, people did not die but grew thin and fat as the Moon waned and waxed, were faced with a dilemma. The trouble was, the population increased to such an extent that the son of the first man had to ask his father what to do. 'Leave things as they are,' replied his father, an easy-going man. But his younger brother said, 'No, let people die like the banana and leave their children behind.' The issue was put to the lord of the underworld, who decided for death. From then on people ceased to renew their youth like the Moon, and instead propagated, grew old and died like the banana.[60] Death is here brought into the perspective of the whole through the idea of inheritance and the quality of life.

These myths, addressing the most profound question of the human condition, often seem to trivialize their subject, perhaps understandably since no answer to the question has been found. The immense range of mythic replies to the challenge of responding to the fact of death appear to fall into the same pattern of responses to an intractable problem in life: denial, dissociation, fantasy, rage (turned inwards as guilt and outwards as blame), resignation, apathy, despair. It is the task of the finest myths to move the human mind forward from these positions, to see if it is possible to achieve a perspective beyond both birth *and* death, comprehending the two together in a greater whole, so that life may be lived without fear. But one further group of myths appears to hold the mind back from exploring this possibility, and that is when the people's concern for their own death is transferred to the death of the Moon.

THE DYING OF THE MOON

An instinctive identification with the Moon requires that the Moon itself should not die like human beings, for then human beings would die like the Moon. The circularity of such an argument is less evident when the subject of it appears to be the last hope. For it seems that, drawing on the identity that existed imaginatively between humans and the Moon, and notwithstanding some stories to the contrary, many people continued to regard the Moon's rebirth as the best, if not the only, hope they had for being reborn themselves. So it was crucial that the Moon should be kept alive.

'Mama Quilla, Mother Moon, do not die, lest we all perish!' the ancient Peruvians cried. 'So may I renew my life as thou art renewed!' Thus the women of Luango in the Congo greeted the Moon as it rose again. 'He is risen! God has made thee rise again; God make all of us rise again!' prayed the Christian Abyssinians to the New Moon.[61] Briffault comments that 'the power of men to survive every month, or the hope that they will survive after death, is regarded as being derived from the moon, and as dependent on the moon's faculty of being born again after dying every month.'[62]

What was needed as a way of surviving the chaos of oncoming darkness was that the Moon's waning should become intelligible. Then the alarm at its disappearance could be allayed by a story which would explain what was happening and so keep the promise of the Moon's rebirth alive. In striking contrast to the relatively light-hearted myths of humans dying by mistake, error or flaw, the Moon's own sickness unto death frequently allowed the expression of a profound sense of violation. It is almost as though the strictures on grief are lifted, and what has been denied may be, in displacement, openly experienced and explored. Perhaps rage at the death of the Moon can be more deeply felt because it is not final, and not ours. For the dying of the Moon's light is never the outcome of an apparently casual mistake or heartless trick, but most often the result of being eaten, swallowed or sliced into pieces by an implacable opponent – either the burning Sun or a devouring monster or ravenous dog, or some other unspeakably ferocious being. Alternatively, the Moon dies through the wasting away of an illness, or starvation, or from a curse, or from an emptying of ambrosial liquid. There were many different kinds of explanation which accounted for the Moon's loss of its form, light and life, but all of them predicted its return and reassumption of life, light and form. So that if the Moon had to die, at least it would not be for long.

Let us review some of the tales. In a continuation of the Maori tale of the Moon who kidnapped Rona with her water bucket, her husband, also called Rona, went to the Moon in pursuit of his wife. He ate the Moon, who ate him back, and now they spend their lives eating each other, which is why the Moon diminishes. Then they both bathe in the living waters of *Tane*, regaining their vigour, and their struggle begins again.[63] Here, the male Rona, may be a disguised version of the Dark Moon swallowing the Bright Moon in their perpetual conflict.

A contest between two aspects of the Moon deity can be seen in the tablet shown in fig. 5, where the Babylonian Sin wrestles with the Dark Moon, the other part of himself, figured as a lion or dog. In an Akkadian myth about a dragon *Labbu*, Sin is asked to 'slay the *Labbu*', a word meaning 'the raging one' and often used for 'lion', recalling the myth of the seven devils (one of whom is called *Labbu*) who surrounded the Moon and caused its period of darkness at the end of the month. However the darkness is conceived, it has to be fought and overcome if the Bright Moon is to survive, a story that later passed to the Sun.[64]

Where the male Moon is seen in relation to the female Sun, he is often thought to shrink with shame at some act he committed when he was waxing – incest, rape or murder.[65] This is often reversed when the Moon is female and the Sun male, and the female Moon withdraws in grief, dying for three days, as in the West Ceramese tale of Tuwale, the Sun man, and Rabie, the Moon maiden.[66]

Fig. 5. The contest between the Babylonian Moon god Sin and a lion or dog as the dark Moon. The Moon god is shown in the sign of Taurus (right), with the Pleiades on the left. Astronomical tablet. Persian period. (From Langdon, The Mythology of All Races, v, p. 305).

The Moon was frequently thought to be sickening in the waning, as in Dryden's eighteenth century metaphor:

> So sicken waning moons too near the sun
> And blunt their crescents on the edge of day.[67]

The Sumerians called the dark days of Nanna-Sin 'the days of lying down', as though he were ill. The Vedic god Soma was cursed with leprosy by his father-in-law, and so became 'grey-skinned'[68] or, as we might say in English, 'wan' – a word meaning 'grey', 'black', 'dark', with the later sense of 'pale' connected with 'dark' via the idea of 'lack' and 'deficiency' of colour, as in, of course, 'wane'.[69] In another image, the cup of the Moon filled and emptied with Soma, as the immortal liquid rhythmically sipped by the gods; or else Soma, as the Moon, fills up with the souls of the dead, carrying them onwards to the Sun; as the souls leave the Moon-boat one by one, Soma becomes empty again.[70] In a Hindu tale, the Moon was cursed by Ganesha for laughing at him.[71] The Moon of the Mataco Indians starved himself thin.[72] When imagined as a goddess, the Moon was often believed to be menstruating, shedding its liquid light as blood.[73] Or the Moon is seen as serpentine, progressively peeling off layers of light as a serpent its skin.

Sometimes waning is expressed in the metaphor of the shedding of veils of light, like Inanna-Ishtar removing her seven bright jewels of Heaven as she descends from the Above World to the Nether World until she is naked (dark). When she ascends she reclothes herself with her jewels and veils of light.[74]

The Moon's disappearance is occasionally attributed to its being trapped on Earth, buried beneath lake, river or sea, where before it floated in the water at the full. In another Polynesian story, Hina, the Moon, in her 'dead' phase, lies entangled by weeds in the sea until a man frees her, becoming her lover. After giving birth to a son, she returns to the sky – the cycle completed.[75] In England, the Lincolnshire Moon was caught beneath the water of the bog, giving no light until she was released by the villagers.[76]

More simply, the Moon loses her shining clothes on Earth and has to reclaim them before she can return to the sky. A Japanese version has a fisherman finding a robe of white feathers on the shore. A shining girl rose from the sea and begged him to give it to her, for without her plumage she could not go back to her home in the sky. When he restored to her the feathered robe, she unfolded her white wings and flew away to the Full Moon.[77]

Often the Moon's disappearance and reappearance are dramatized as two figures of the Moon, one of whom is lost and then found by the other. Plutarch says that the Egyptians spoke of Osiris as 'lost' and 'found' by Isis, just as, later, Persephone was 'lost' and 'found' by Demeter. As Seth imprisoned his brother Osiris in a dark coffin, so Hades imprisons Persephone in 'Hades', allowing her to return with Hermes only after Zeus, in response to Demeter's threats, intervenes. Seth, it will be remembered, hunting boar with his dogs at the Full Moon, tears the body of Osiris into 14 pieces, one for each day of the Waning Moon. Here Seth plays the part of the Dark Moon dismembering the Bright Moon, piece by piece, night by night. The funeral rites of Osiris, conducted at Dendera, were celebrated during the nine days of the Waning Moon, the last third of a three-week month.[78] As Plutarch describes it:

> On the nineteenth night they go down to the sea; the priests and wardrobe attendants bear forth the holy shrine with the golden caskets, wherein they pour drinking water. Thereupon those present raise a cry that Osiris has been found. With the water they knead fertile soil, spices, and precious gums, and out of this they make a figure in the shape of a lunar crescent. This they dress and adorn.[79]

WANING AS DISMEMBERMENT

Dismemberment is the most prevalent metaphor for the way the Moon, night after night, loses some of its precious life-giving light until all of it is gone. The most common interpretation of the Moon's dismemberment is that it is slain by the Sun because they cannot co-exist.

In the full, the Moon appears to be equal in shape, size and brilliance to the Sun. The fact that the Moon begins to wane immediately after facing the Sun directly at the full gives rise to the idea that the Sun wounds the Moon to death, in the same way that the Sun's rays dry up water and scorch vegetation on Earth. The Bushmen, hunters themselves, saw the Waning Moon as pierced by the knife-rays of the greatest hunter of all, the Sun. The Sun cuts and cuts until almost all of the Moon is cut away and only one little piece is left. The Moon who, in Bushman stories of origin, was formed by Mantis from a feather or an old shoe, is here given as a man who has incurred the wrath of the Great Hunter and must beg the Sun to spare him a little piece of himself for his children – 'O Sun! leave for the children the backbone!' The Sun consents, and the Moon goes painfully away, and from that small piece he starts to grow until he becomes whole as a Full Moon, when the Sun starts his stabbing and cutting again.[80] The North American Dakota Indians, keepers of grain, saw the Moon as nibbled by many mice, while the Klamath Indians of Oregon referred to the Moon as 'the one broken to pieces'.[81]

The mythic image of the Lame Hero or Maimed King is often related to the Moon. The Chinese flood hero, Yu, became lame from a sickness which shrivelled half his body, and Noah also was lamed, according to folk legend, when struck by the paw of a lion, the beast of the Sun, while floating in his ark upon the sea. In the Grail Castle of Eschenbach's *Parzival*, there are two Maimed Kings: the one old, hidden in an inner sanctuary, invisible to the world, corresponding to the Dark, old Moon, Titurel; and the other young, the Fisher King, corresponding to the New, visible Moon, first seen on the water of a lake, whose pain is greatest 'at the time of the change of the moon'. This is the present king of the inexhaustible vessel of the Grail, whose immortal food and drink, like that of the Moon's, is continually refilled.[82]

* * *

A further group of myths falls into the pattern of that familiar ritual of dismemberment by the family. In Latvian myth, the Moon, Meness, was cut into pieces by his wife, Saule, the Sun, for having been unfaithful:

> The Sun shattered the Moon/With a sharp sword.[83]

Alternatively, the Moon was cut into pieces by Perkons the thunder god (Lithuanian, Perkunas), one of Saule's three husbands, because he had seduced her own daughter:

Perkunas was wroth,/He cleft the Moon with a sword.[84]

In Aztec legend, the Moon goddess Coyolxauhqui had her whole head cut off by her half-brother, Huitzilopochtli, the merciless Sun, Storm and War god, at the very moment he was born.[85] This original decapitation is re-enacted more slowly every month, as pieces of the Moon's body are sliced off by the Sun, one night at a time, until nothing remains.

In the beginning, the Earth goddess, Coatlicue, Mother of all the gods – 'she who has a skirt of serpents'[86] – lived in the place where the world began, on top of Coatepec, 'Serpent Hill'. One day she was sweeping in the yard when she was visited by a feather falling from heaven:

> At once Coatlicue gathered it up;
> She placed it in her bosom.
> When she had done sweeping,
> She sought the feather, which she had placed in her bosom,
> But she saw nothing there.

> At that very moment Coatlicue became pregnant.[87]

Her daughter, Coyolxauhqui, enraged that her mother had dishonoured her children, incited her star-brothers, the 'Four Hundred Southerners', to kill their mother before she could give birth. But one star got a message to Huitzilopochtli, then still a babe in the womb, and he comforted his mother from deep inside her (wise beyond his years):

> Be not afraid, I know what I must do.

Suddenly Huitzilopochtli sprang forth from his mother's womb, fully armed, war stripes covering his body. Feathers shot out from his forehead, shot out from his ears, shot out from his feet. Eagle feathers covered his side as a shield, darts and a fire-stick poised in his hand. Instantly, he struck off the head of Coyolxauhqui. Her body dropped and broke into 14 pieces:

> The body of Coyolxauhqui
> Rolled down,
> It fell to pieces,
> In diverse places fell her hands,
> Her legs, her body.

Then he slew the stars. He utterly 'annihilated them'.[88]

Thus is the Sun born in the manner of a true Aztec warrior, advocating Jung's claim that 'the starry vault of heaven is in truth the open book of cosmic projection.'[89] The Sun was the Aztecs' chief tribal god, born to vanquish the Moon and stars, and to banish darkness with all the burning ferocity of the mid-day Sun.[90] The violence of the Sun's actions then offered a celestial model of behaviour which would vindicate those same Aztec customs on Earth which – it might be said – had created the celestial model in the first place. Aztec Suns do not just 'come up' when the Moon and stars 'go out'.

The name of the Sun, Huitzilopochtli, coming from *huitziln*, meaning 'hummingbird', suggests that he was the true son of the falling feather which impregnated his mother by lying against the skin of her

Fig. 6. Coatlicue, with skirt of intertwined serpents and necklace of severed human hearts and hands, and a head of two facing rattlesnakes. Two crescents back to back protude like tusks. Andesite sculpture. Tenochitlan. Late 15th century. Museo Naçionale de Antropologia, Mexico City.

Fig. 7. Huitzilopochtli, in the form of a hummingbird, poised for battle at the top of Templo Mayor, the pyramid that symbolized Coatepec, 'Serpent Hill,' the sacred mountain of the beginning of the world. The mountain with serpents leaping out of it stands below as the origin, while the pyramid rests upon it as its human construction. From the Codex Azcatitlan, a manuscript made after the Spanish conquest with Nahuatl captions. Biblithèque Nationale.

breasts – an unexpectedly lovely image of the creative powers of Great Mother Earth. Holding this image of conception through to his birth, we can see the Sun rise out of the body of Earth over the breast-hills of her horizon. Soon the rays of the Sun will resemble the long piercing beak of the hummingbird.

The remarkable sixteenth-century stone carving shown in fig. 1 dramatizes the fragmentation of the Waning Moon. It was discovered, only in 1978, in the 'Templo Mayor', once the central temple of the Aztecs in their old capital city of Tenochtitlan, 'Place of the Fruit of the Cactus', whose ruins now lie beneath Mexico City. Constructed as a stepped pyramid symbolizing Coatepec, the Sacred Mountain of the Beginning, the temple depicted the entire world, such that its four sides represented the four directions of the universe. It had a double shrine at the top, dedicated, on the left, to Tlaloc, god of Rain and Agriculture, and, on the right, to Huitzilopochtli. Coyolxauhqui's head was found at the bottom of the temple stairway which led to Huitzilopochtli's shrine, a place where many victims had been sacrificed, as though in imitation of that original murder. For if the tribe's war against its enemies is seen as identical with the Sun's war against the dark – Huitzilopochtli being god of both Sun *and* War – then it follows, with inexorable tribal logic, that the living hearts ripped from those fallen in battle are destined to keep beating as the rhythm of the Sun in its movement across the sky.

George Elder, in his *Archetypal Body*, has commented of this sculpture that, even out of the violence of dismemberment, the artist has sculpted an image of a 'transformed body', in which the broken members of Coyolxauhqui are arranged to form 'a "wholeness", a circle of parts that seem strangely still alive.'[91] The body may be in bits, but the serpents are alive and writhing as the life-principle beyond death, knotting themselves around her severed arms and legs and twining around her waist as a girdle, looped inside a skull. One single serpent rises from her feathery crown. Like the fringe of serpents in her mother's skirt – that Great Mother who gave birth to All – the serpents then

Fig. 8. *Coyolxauhqui as the Full Moon with golden bells upon her face and her ear-rings shaped as the glyph of the Moon. Jade sculpture. 1400-1521 AD. Peabody Museum of Archaeology, Harvard, Cambridge.*

Fig. 9. *Sun Bird eating the Moon Bull. Terra-cotta plaque from Sumeria. c. 2500 BC. University of Pennsylvania Museum, Philadelphia.*

refer the death back to the inexhaustible source of life. As the Moon's monthly drama of dismemberment (given in the figure of the 14 pieces), we might expect the artist to achieve an equipoise between life and death, a composition in which the Moon's death is lawful yet not final.

Corresponding to the Moon's dual potentiality for good or ill, or perhaps to the difference in human feeling between waxing and waning, there is another version of this myth in which the Moon goddess is not to blame. For there Coyolxauhqui – or 'Golden Bells', as her name means – heard her brothers plotting against her mother and ran ahead to warn her. But Huitzilopochtli had just been born, and when he saw Coyolxauhqui running breathless into the cave he took her for a killer and killed her first. Then he went out and slew all the stars as well. After the battle he came proudly back to his mother, but she told him that his sister had always been a good girl and never did anyone harm. So Huitzilopochtli picked up Coyolxauhqui's inert body and cut off her head, and he threw it high up into the sky where the golden bells of her cheeks would forever shine.[92] The face of Coyolxauhqui shown in fig. 8 is serene and as round as the Full Moon.

In Sumeria, the slaying of the Moon by the Sun was represented as the Solar Lion slaying the Lunar Bull.[93] The crescent-horned Moon bull in fig. 9 is shown grandly poised upon the mound of Earth, the smile of ages on his beatific face, while the diminutive lion-headed eagle of the Sun gnaws at his back. The monthly bite of the lion-bird seems hardly to graze the body of the bull, whose confidence in the eternal round beyond the vicissitudes of time remains supreme. And in rituals all over the Near East and Crete, the bull was ceremonially slain as the son-lover of the Goddess, for the Moon bull, as the figure of the temporal phases, gives his life for the sake of the infinite source, intuited in the perpetually unchanging cycle of the Moon and the seasons, and imagined as the Great Mother Goddess of Many Names. The bull, too, had many names: Dumuzi, Tammuz, Nanna-Sin, Osiris, Apis, Khons, Dionysos, Men, and all those nameless animals – bulls, goats, pigs and horses – ritually chosen to embody the New Moon, the New Year and the spirit of rebirth in all of Nature.

Artemis, the Greek Moon goddess, whose hounds are stars in the waxing and dogs of the hunt in the waning, was bathing in the river Partenius – like the Full Moon floating in water. But the hunter, Aktaion,

Fig. 10. Artemis shooting Aktaion. Attica Red Figure Bell Krater by the Pan painter. Early classical period c. 470 BC. Museum of Fine Arts Boston.

leaning against a rock near Orchmenus, caught sight of the goddess and did not turn his face away, but gazed at her without her veils. Artemis, instantly turned huntress, transformed Aktaion into a stag and his own hounds, not knowing him, tore him apart as their prey.[94] Such is the usual reading of the tale.

But in the vase painting shown in fig. 10, the imagery points to an older story suggestive of a dismemberment after the Full Moon. Artemis aims her bow and arrow at Aktaion as though herself launching the two dogs that are biting his belly and neck, and it may be no coincidence that her priestesses were known to wear the masks of hunting dogs, while men attending one of her festivals wore stags' antlers on their heads.[95] There is an affinity between the two figures on the vase: a doe's skin hangs down the back of the goddess as the animal form she often assumed, while Aktaion becomes a stag – her stag – the male version of herself, personifying the horned god. Aktaion then plays the role of the son-lover who becomes her consort at the Full Moon and is sacrificed as the Waning Moon, torn to pieces by the dogs of darkness, so the goddess Moon may return renewed from her immersion in the eternal waters. Autonoe, Aktaion's mother, reassembled the pieces of his dismembered body, as Isis had done for Osiris.[96] Autonoe was also sister to Semele, the mother of Dionysos, and present in Euripides' *The Bacchae* at the dismemberment of King Pentheus.

Aktaion's supposedly improper gaze upon the naked body of Artemis has all the overtones of a late secular interpretation of an earlier rite of sacred marriage, heard about or glimpsed but no longer understood. The union of doe and stag recalls the Minoan festival of the sacred marriage between cow-goddess and bull-god, which the king and queen enacted in cow and bull skins to celebrate the octennial reunion of Sun and Moon. Aktaion had 50 hounds, a ritual number suggestive of the 50 months which make up four years – half that time – and commemorated in the 50 months' interval of the Olympic Games, held every four years. Significantly, Hekate's dog, Cerberus, was at first 50-headed, like the pack of hounds that tore Aktaion apart, though later Cerberus became three-headed like his mistress Hekate, who was none other than Artemis in her waning phase. Indeed, Hekate, as Harrison observes, 'was once a three-headed dog herself', called 'She-wolf' and 'Bitch'.[97]

The tale of Endymion and Selene may also belong to this tradition, in yet another of the story's meanings. For Endymion, who had the by-now-magic number of 50 children with Selene, also dies from his encounter with the Moon, and the shepherd, like the hunter, is often pictured with his

Fig. 11. Selene waking Endymion. Bronze Mirror with bas-relief. c. 310. BC. National Museum, Athens.

hound. In fig. 11, Selene, in a swirl of her mantle, arm raised to strike, appears to be hunting Endymion herself, while he, half-kneeling, awoken from sleep, turns to look behind him, as though taken by surprise. Eros, poised above Endymion, has already disarmed any resistance he might have, by giving his sword to Selene. Is this love or death?

LUNAR MYSTERIES OF DISMEMBERMENT

Myths of devouring, decapitation and dismemberment dramatize the death of the Moon as murder. And as the Moon's life is felt to be like human life, so the Moon's death can represent human death, and allow the expression of the feeling that the death of human beings is also murder. But the fact that the Moon's light comes back out of its own darkness invites the perception that, though all death may feel like murder, it may yet bring life with it. This perception is also afforded by the idea of the cup of the Moon containing the elixir of its own immortality which, as Soma, streams throughout the Earth and compels a feeling for life as a whole.

From this perspective it appears that life lives off itself, in the sense that all life feeds on life. Humankind, as part of life, has also to feed off life and kill to live, transforming those animals and plants which are called, like Soma, food. So a synthesizing insight becomes available of the mutuality of life and death in the universe: that life comes from death and death comes from life. For in all creation death brings life in the form of food, and that same life will offer itself in death as life for others. It is as though life sacrifices itself for Life.

Hence the importance, in the western Mystery traditions, of the idea of the *willing* sacrifice of the gods for humanity, for there this natural process of mutuality is made conscious and embraced on behalf of the whole. Dismemberment can then be seen as a metaphor for life in time, the condition of all created beings. The further distinction between *bios* – the particular individual life – and *zoe* – the non-particular, supra-individual life of the cosmos – makes possible the idea of transformation from one level to another. Then what, at the level of *bios*, appears as dismemberment, appears, at the level of *zoe*, as transformation. The challenge of the Mystery rituals was to shift the consciousness of the participants from *bios* to *zoe*, from looking at life in pieces to experiencing life as one complete whole.

* * *

Most myths begin with a time and place that is beyond pain and death, when the highest hopes for life are realized and where that which is desired may be explored and achieved. Eliade calls this *in illo tempore*, 'in that time', the 'mythical time...when the foundation of the world occurred.'[98] This is the 'Garden of Eden' for Jews and Christians, the 'Dream-time of the Ancestors' for Australian Aborigines, the 'Golden Age' for Greeks and Romans, 'in the beginning' for the writer of St John's Gospel – the 'once upon a time' of fairy tales. This stage of myth is typically followed by a drama which is to explain why this is no longer the case: what went wrong and why. As we have seen above, some myths end at this point, leaving the emphasis on the tragedy of the human condition, without attempting to move towards a resolution, either one that imagines a different kind of ending or one that invites a change in attitude to what is beyond change.

Myths, like poems and people, may be naïve, complacent, self-righteous and querulous, or complex, inclusive, courageous, loving and generous – sharing their perplexity, not masking it. To oversimplify into two extreme poles, myths may celebrate and explore the universe for the sheer wonder of it, trying to understand why and how it is wondrous, or they may be more concerned to explain the workings of the universe, primarily in order to organize the tribe, giving it order and charting its course. Many tribal myths assume they do all of these things together, and move without reflection from one pole to another – from the pragmatic to the mystical – on the assumption that the way the tribe needs to be ordered reflects the natural order. This position lends itself to the belief that other tribes with different modes of operation have, as it were, got the universe wrong. It would seem, then, only righteous to enlighten them, for the 'Supreme Being' – under whatever name – would be thereby reinstated along with the tribe which understood this Being so supremely. Hence the 'holy wars' of history which continue to erupt whenever tribal consciousness claims to speak for human consciousness, and dismisses the voices of other human beings as less than fully human. Myths are then typically invoked to justify the tribe's pursuit of power, which is one reason why the term has got itself a bad name, often used interchangeably with fiction in the sense of falsehood, that is, a lie – 'Pity 'tis, 'tis true, and true it is 'tis pity.'[99]

As constructions of the human psyche, the priorities of myth will inevitably differ and their value is by no means equal, though they may all receive the same name of 'myth', or in the case of one's own myth, 'religion' (which, by contrast, is simply defined as divine revelation). Consequently, it is not always, or perhaps ever, possible, or even desirable, to withhold a value judgement on the myths of the world – phrase it as carefully as we may – though it is necessary to offer reasons for valuing one myth over another (not least when the myth *is* someone's religion – as all myths are, or were). While this may be contentious, it could also be seen as the on-going debate of culture, and it may be more fruitfully conducted at the level of comparative mythology – which finds it easier to suspend disbelief, as Coleridge recommended, if only for the simple reason that it does not *have* to have belief to begin with.[100] The contribution that a study of myth has to offer to the cultural forum arguably lies in its claim that *all* myths and religions, call them what you will, offer the possibility that human beings may come to know some aspect of themselves more precisely. For these goddesses and gods, cows, bulls, stags, dogs and myriad creatures of the heavenly deep enact upon their celestial screen the conflicting perspectives upon being human that come from those creatures who live beneath it, in love with life and aware of their own death: 'the soul fastened to a dying animal', as Yeats has it.[101]

The metaphor of dismemberment in its widest meaning runs through the Mystic traditions – those traditions that celebrated the Mysteries of a god or goddess who died and was resurrected, whether it be Inanna-Ishtar and Dumuzi-Tammuz, Isis and Osiris, Kybele and Attis, Aphrodite and Adonis, Persephone, Dionysos, Orpheus or Jesus. Many of these gods were actually dismembered in their stories – even Jesus is occasionally represented in art as the wine trampled in the wine press or with limbs suggestive of dismemberment dangling around him as he hangs upon the Cross, which flowers as the Tree of Life through his death (figs 12 and 13). However, almost all of these figures descend into the underworld of death for three days – dying as the Moon dies – and rise again on the third day as the New Moon rises again on the third day.

Fig. 12. The Crucifixion. Woodcut. Rennes, France. c. 1830. (From Watts, Myth and Ritual in Christianity, p. 155).

The 'mystery' of the Mysteries was primarily the resurrection after death of the god or goddess (or the half-human, half-divine being who became, through resurrection, a god or goddess). But the deeper mystery was perhaps the fact that those who participated in the passion of the divine being, by ritually re-enacting it, became themselves free of the fear of death. In those Mysteries where the bodies were ritually torn apart in gruesome act or mime, or symbolically broken as a vessel, it was as though the subsequent act of re-membering the bodies metaphorically enabled a remembering of the source, a dying and rebirth into the Great Memory. These traditions, as suggested earlier, are essentially lunar traditions, and, when not taken literally, the Moon or the lunar drama becomes a symbol and is no longer required to be a visible actor in the sky.

This will be discussed in Chapter 14, but for the moment we could say that all of these myths work from an understanding of both an eternal source and a life in time, which corresponds to the lunar model of the cycle and the phases. The cycle which, as an imaginative inference, is invisible in itself yet immanent in the visible phases, is not, however, to be identified with the eternal source, as though they were on the same plane of imagining; rather, the cycle becomes a *metaphor* for the eternal source, just as the lunar phases become a metaphor for the phases of human life and the waxing and waning of all created beings.

It is the task of the finest myths to move the mind away from an identification with our mortal frame, and unite it, or reunite it, with the eternal source which transcends the life in time. For,

Fig. 13. Christ in the Wine Press, carrying his Cross. Stone painted statue. 1650. Kreuzkapelle, Ediger Eller, Germany.

considering creation as a created being, we cannot initially do otherwise than view the whole as a mighty sum of its parts, and can never see the parts falling into place from the view of the whole. Our best effort is then no more than a piecing back together of separated parts – like putting back together the bodies of Osiris, Dionysos or Orpheus – which gives us back the god but not his meaning, not the reason he was dismembered and then re-membered, not the life-force of the drama which is the human story. The descriptions of the *Mystes* suggest that they are firstly shocked out of the literal mind which reduces experience to preconceived categories, and then precipitated into an altered state of consciousness which accepts metaphor as reality. After participating in the Eleusinian Mysteries many people – Sophocles, Pindar and Cicero among them – said they were no longer afraid to die. The question posed by the testimony of the *Mystes* is, then, did the practice of the Mysteries compel a vision of a state of being beyond the opposites of life and death, I and Thou, and Thou and That? And if it did, how did they know? As Eliot says:

> Except for the point, the still point,
> There would be no dance, and there is only the dance.
> I can only say, *there* we have been: but I cannot say where.
> And I cannot say, how long, for that is to place it in time.[102]

CHAPTER 13

THE DARK MOON AND DEATH

…the cold spirits that are born
When the old moon is vanished from the sky
And the new still hides her horn
Yeats *The Double Vision of Michael Robartes*

There's a moon in my body, but I can't see it!
A moon and a sun.
A drum never touched by human hands, beating, and I can't hear it.'
Robert Bly *The Kabir Book*

THE MOON IN ECLIPSE

In an eclipse, the Full Moon (entering the Earth's shadow) suddenly goes dark, and the lower rim turns blood red. Then, as now, this was a different kind of darkness from the gradually increasing darkness of the Waning Moon, which over the centuries had fallen into a pattern of expectation and so become lawful. Instead, the abrupt blackening of the bright Full Moon meant for many early people that the natural order had been violated and life was doomed.

The word 'eclipse', coming from the Greek *ekleipsis*, means 'omission' or 'abandonment', suggesting that people felt abandoned by their Moon and Sun, as though the bond between them and humanity had been broken. Today, an eclipse of the Sun might seem the more dramatic – witness the anguish shown in India at the solar eclipse of 1995 or the excitement in Cornwall in 1999. But in earlier times, especially in 'lunar cultures', an eclipse of the Moon would have meant – if only for a few minutes – that the water and food of life were gone, as well as the hope of life renewed.

Rituals all over the world testify to the horror of the Moon dying unlawfully, interrupting the cycle for no reason. People everywhere tried to help. The Masai threw sand in the air, the North American Indians banged and rattled pots and pans; some lit fires, others shot flaming arrows at the Moon to slay the predator of the Moon's light: the Kamchatkans brought fire out of their huts and offered it up as a prayer; the Orinocans buried their fire underground so it would not go out if the Moon's fire went out.[1] Romans threw firebrands high in the sky and paraded with lighted torches, while Hindus beat pots and pans with their spoons. The Chinese banged on mirrors, to scare the dragon that was eating the Moon into disgorging it. In Chinese, the word for 'eclipse' – *shih* – means 'to eat'.[2]

Even when an eclipse could be predicted, it was still viewed with alarm. The Babylonian priests of Uruk, who could anticipate at least some of the eclipses, set up altars and shouted at the Moon, begging that their city be spared catastrophe. They took their copper trumpets, harps and drums out of the temples and paraded them along the streets. Yet the mere foretelling of an eclipse was nothing to its meaning, which could vary from one city to another. Naturally, each king needed to know how

Fig. 1. Dante and Beatrice standing in the Heaven of the Moon. Bibliotheca Apostolica Vaticana, Rome.

his own city would fare. Thus a placatory astrologer to his king:

> On the fourteenth day an eclipse will take place; it is evil for Elam and Aharru [two cities], lucky for the king, my lord; let the king, my lord, rest happy. It will be seen without Venus; to the king, my lord, I say 'there will be an eclipse.'[3]

In Delhi, in the solar eclipse of 24 October 1995, many of the ancient rituals persisted unchanged. Indian astrologers said that anyone touched by the Moon's shadow (as it crossed the Sun) would suffer ill-fortune: pregnant women, in particular, could give birth to a deformed child. Thousands plunged into holy rivers to be cleansed; many did not eat. The fact that the eclipse coincided with the annual Festival of Light, *Diwali*, brought the contradictions between light and darkness to an unusual pitch. In Cambodia, at Anghor Vat, monks, wearing special eclipse glasses, tried to see if the Sun was eating the Moon or – which would be worse – if the Moon was eating the Sun.[4]

Fig. 2. Lunar Eclipse over Tashkent on December 16, 1880. (From Flammarion, L'Astronomie).

Being eaten was the most prevalent explanation for an eclipse, understandably, perhaps, since this was the original human terror against which there was no defence. Identification with the Moon's untimely death makes Moon and tribes one against a common enemy: both may become the prey of monsters, hunted down in their prime. Then it is that the Moon bleeds (in its reddish colour) as humans do, and dies without ritual from an unexpected attack. Lunar predators around the world, massed together, draw the imagination far back into the terrifying aspect of primeval life: survival in the dense forests and open plains, especially at night. The eclipsing Moon revolving around the Earth is eaten, variously, by jaguars, lions, rattlesnakes, wolves, huge dogs, large fish, fire-dogs, giant birds, snakes, gigantic bats, ants, dead spirits, dragons, vampires, werewolves, witches, man-eating monsters, or just unspecified beings with unpronounceable names.[5]

The old Scandinavians filled their skies with ravenous wolves, forever ready to pounce. In one of the poems of the *Elder Edda*, Moon is perpetually chased by *Hati*, the wolf whose name means 'Hatred' and whose father is the terrible Fenrir Wolf (fig. 3). Sun, who follows Moon, is endlessly chased by Skoll, the wolf whose name means 'Repulsion'. Both wolves, whose mothers are giantesses, long to devour Moon and Sun and, in the end just before the Twilight of the Gods, *Ragnarok*, it is written that they will.[6] Every now and then, *Hati* and *Skoll* catch up with Moon and Sun and, in anticipation of that end, they take a large bite out of them and an eclipse comes. When the people see this they shout and beat their kettles to scare the wolves away. *Hati*, Moon's wolf, may be the same as *Managarm*, Moon's dog, whom Snorri Sturluson describes: 'He gorges on the flesh of all that would die, and he will swallow the moon and bespatter the sky and all the air with blood.'[7]

In Rumanian folklore, eclipses come about because Sun and Moon are eaten by dog-like creatures with sucking mouths, called *varcolaci*. The Sun and Moon are in especial danger if women spin at night without a candle when the Moon is out. Then the *varcolaci* can fasten themselves onto the thread, and climb right up to the Moon and bite her, 'so she appears covered with blood, or till none of her is left. But if the thread is broken their power is broken and they go to another part of the sky.'[8] The *varcolaci* are related to vampires, one of whose earliest meanings (from the Serbian) was a dragon who ate eclipses.[9] The Altaic Tartars also thought an eclipse was caused by a vampire who lived on a star.[10]

* * *

Continuing the Hindu story of *The Churning of the Ocean of Milk*, when *Amrita* or *Soma* finally appeared, and before anyone could get to it, a monster called *Rahu* stole the first sip of the divine liquor and swallowed it. The Sun and Moon told Vishnu who in one stroke beheaded him, but not before the Soma drink had passed through *Rahu's* mouth and neck, making them immortal (fig. 4).

The rest of his body decayed instantly and fell to Earth. But the severed head, ravenous for another taste, at once began to chase after the elixir of Soma, which was also the Moon, and has been hunting it ever since. When *Rahu* catches up with it and gulps it down, an eclipse comes, but the Moon passes so quickly through the mouth and neck – there being no body, and so no stomach, to retain it – that it soon reappears. Then the chase starts again.[11] Another version has it that *Rahu* chases the Sun and Moon out of revenge because they informed on him.[12] Again, it is hatred that destroys the moral order of the world.

Rahu was called the Eclipse Demon (astronomically, the 'Ascending Node' of the Moon), while the other half of his body was called *Ketu* (the 'Descending Node' of the Moon). The nodes (from Latin, *nodus*, knot) are the points where the Moon in its orbit crosses the ecliptic, the plane of the Earth's orbit around the Sun. The time taken by the Moon to circle back to the same node is called the draconic month (from the Greek *drakon*, meaning 'dragon'). In Europe, the Ascending Node of the Moon is still known as the 'dragon's head' and the Descending Node as the 'dragon's tail', testimony to the ancient idea of eclipses brought about by celestial dragons.[13]

(*An eclipse of the Moon only occurs when Sun, Moon and Earth lie almost exactly in a straight line. The Sun and Moon appear to be about the same size: though the Sun's diameter is 400 times that of the Moon, it is also 400 times further away. An eclipse of the Moon would happen at every Full Moon (and an eclipse of the Sun at every New Moon), were it not for the (roughly) five-degree tilt of the Moon's orbit, relative to Earth, which means the Moon usually passes a little above or below the shadow of the Earth. But when the Moon is close to one of its nodes, the line between Sun, Moon and Earth is almost straight, and so the Full Moon passes through Earth's shadow and 'gets caught' in the cone of shadow cast by the Earth.*[14])

Some tribes thought an eclipse was a private matter between Moon and Sun when they could finally get together in peace. The Bangala of Africa believed that the Sun loves the Moon so much he is always pursuing her across the heavens, but in an eclipse he catches up with her at last, and the two lovers forget themselves in mutual passion, concealed in darkness.[15] This view was shared by the Alaskan Tlingit Indians and the Australian Aborigines,[16] while the Eskimos, for whom Sun and Moon are brother and sister, thought they had met in secret to embrace in the dark, breaking the tribe's taboo. On the other hand, the Arawaks of Guiana, South America, believed that an eclipse was the result of 'hand-to-hand' combat between Sun and Moon, or else that Moon had fallen asleep in the path of Sun and was overtaken before it could get out of the way. The noise the Arawaks made was not intended to scare away monsters but to wake the slumbering Moon.[17]

* * *

However it is interpreted, an eclipse portends no good to Earth. Thucydides describes how, in August 431 BC, the Athenian army was on the point of sailing to engage with the Syracusans when, suddenly, the Full Moon was eclipsed. The mass of the army was greatly moved and called upon the generals to wait. Nicias, the commander (being, Thucydides comments, 'too much under the influence of

Fig. 3. Fenrir Wolf. Detail of engraving on Rune Stone. Skaane, Sweden. This is the Great Wolf released after the other two wolves, Hati and Skoll, have swallowed Moon and Sun in Ragnarok. Kulturen Museum, Lund, Sweden.

Fig. 4. Rahu as a head swallowing the Moon. Thai painting. late 19th century, (From H. Ginsburg, Thai Manuscript Painting, p.95).

divination and omens'), insisted they remain thrice nine days, as the soothsayers prescribed – with the result that the less superstitious Syracusans attacked first and won the battle. The Athenians never regained their former strength – an example of the course of history being influenced by a belief in the power of the Moon.[18]

In *King Lear*, Shakespeare parodies Gloucester's conventional ideas by having him espouse them before his son, Edmund's, scepticism, instead of searching his own heart for what is wrong:

> These late eclipses in the sun and moon portend no good to us...Love cools, friendship falls
> off, brothers divide: in cities, mutinies; in countries, discord; in palaces, treason; and the
> bond crack'd twixt son and father. This villain of mine comes under the prediction.[19]

Christian iconography also recognizes an eclipse as a sign of the suspension of the natural order. In the depiction of Christ's crucifixion, the Moon is often either waning or eclipsed, and placed on one side of the Cross, balanced by the Sun on the other side. The Second Coming of Christ, as described in the Gospels, is to be signalled by a darkening of Sun and Moon: 'Immediately after the tribulation of those days shall the sun be darkened, and the moon shall not give her light, and the stars shall fall from heaven and the powers of the heavens shall be shaken.'[20] Similarly, in the vision of the Apocalypse in *Revelations*, 'the sun became black as sackcloth of hair, and the moon became as blood; and the stars of heaven departed as a scroll when it is rolled together.'[21]

As might be expected, folklore follows the traditional fear of eclipses by predicting bad weather: 'The weather following an eclipse of the Moon is tempestuous and not to be depended on by the husbandman.' There will be winds, but no rain.[22] But the red Moon itself heralded death. In Shakespeare's *Richard II*, a Captain in the army, waiting for Richard, says:

> 'Tis thought the king is dead; we will not stay.
> The bay-trees in our country are all wither'd,

And meteors fright the fixed stars of heaven,
The pale-fac'd moon looks bloody on the earth,
And lean-look'd prophets whisper fearful change...
These signs forerun the death or fall of kings.[23]

Ovid mentions Luna's chariot 'stained with blood' as one of the signs sent by the gods to forewarn mortals of Caesar's death.[24] The Ona shamans of Tierra del Fuego respond to a red Moon by flying to the Moon to appease her, for red is the colour of her displeasure and she can send life or death at will.[25] A halo around the Moon can also be a sign of death. The Spanish poet Lorca writes simply:

The moon has a halo,
my love has died.[26]

THE MOON AND SACRIFICE

In an eclipse of the Moon or Sun, some people in earlier times did not just bang pots and shoot arrows in the air – they also killed living beings and offered them up to the Moon to save the world from chaos, calling it sacrifice. In Mexico, for instance, dwarfs and people with deformed backs were quickly slain; among the North American Indians, dogs were beaten and babies made to howl.[27] The trouble was, it always worked.

The darkening of the Full Moon in an eclipse is over so soon that, retrospectively, it seems as if it had been saved from death. But when, in the waning, after losing more and more of its light to the dark, the Moon fails to appear at all, then – such reasoning goes – it must now have lost the whole of its light, and, light being life, the Moon must be dead. The fear displayed in an eclipse was also found in the Dark Moon, and many, if not most, cultures engaged in some kind of ritual, either dancing, singing or a day of rest. But some tribes made sacrifices to the Moon, as they did in eclipses, either to propitiate the one who brings death, or to assist the rebirth of the one who dies, whose return from death is felt to be necessary for the tribe's own continuing life. In many places, it was apparently thought that offering the death of one being – animal or human – would allow the return from death for many other human beings, substituting one for the other as though they were interchangeable. Kings and queens could take either role, the slayer or the slain. The rationale for this appears to be that if someone dies like the Moon dies, then someone else can live again like the Moon lives again. Thus the identification with the Moon is complete in every chilling detail.

On Malekula, an island in the New Hebrides in Melanesia, much of a man's life is devoted to preparing for the journey after death. This takes the form of bringing up a boar whose tusks are to curve precisely into lunar crescents, so as to become the Moon in all its phases. John Layard, in his book *Stone Men of Malekula*, describes in the 1940s a culture living in perpetual fear of the after-life. When a Malekulan dies, he begins his journey to the land of the dead but has to confront a monster before he can reach it. The otherworld is guarded by a Female Ghost who draws a labyrinth on the ground and, as the deceased approaches, rubs half of it out. He must know how to reconstruct the labyrinth to get past her, and he must also offer a boar for the guardian to eat instead of himself. And only a boar that he has personally bred from the age of six, and repeatedly consecrated – the sum of his life-effort – only that boar will do. Initially, the upper canine teeth of the boar are ceremonially removed so that the lower tusks grow unimpeded, curving thereby outward, down and around, circling back and penetrating the lower jaw, forming a ring, and sometimes eventually two or even three rings, when it is proudly known as a 'three-circle tusker'. The animal lives in such pain that it cannot possibly thrive, but its thinness is taken as evidence of a radiant spirituality. Layard explains:

> The really fundamental concept of the tusks is not that they should form a spiral but simply that they should be curved or crescent shaped, thus representing, on one symbolic level, the waxing and waning moon, both represented together on either side of the mouth of the same sacrificial animal...The black body of the boar between them corresponds to the 'new' or 'black' invisible moon at the time of her apparent death.[28]

Both man and boar are identified with the Moon: the boar dies as the Moon dies, swallowed by the goddess guardian of the underworld so that the man may live in the after-life, as the waxing crescent of the returning Moon. The greater the sacrifice – the higher the number of tusked moon circles – the greater the magical power for the man and his family, in this life and the next. Sometimes a young boy was sacrificed along with the boar.

Moving to Africa, to what the German anthropologist Frobenius called the 'South African Eritrean zone', we find a ritual of regicide related to the Moon. Frobenius observes that the timing was crucial, and the deaths of the king and his consort were invariably timed for the New (Dark) Moon. Indeed, he adds, 'the king representing the great godhead even bore the name "Moon"; while his second wife was the Moon's beloved, the planet Venus.'[29] After the strangling, the remains of the 'heavenly couple' were buried in a mountain cave, from where they were to be resurrected as the New Moon and Venus. Here it is as though the king serves his tribe as the sacred victim who dies as the Moon, so that in three nights' time, when the Moon comes back round the mountain, the king and his consort, the Evening Star, will rise from the cave of Earth to fructify the land as the reborn Moon. The parallels with the creation myth of the Wahamarunga of Zimbabwe are unmistakable.

In the Sudan, the regicide took place every seven years (up to 1812), before the falling of the first rain and before the sowing of the first seed and also on a night of the Dark Moon, after which the bones were gathered into the hide of a bull.[30] Frobenius comments that these African rites:

> ...compel us to reconstruct an image that resembles that of the Sumerian and the Indian Dravidian lore of life and the gods as closely as one egg resembles another. The moon-god imaged as a great bull; his wife, the planet Venus; the goddess offers her life for her spouse; and everywhere this goddess, as the Morning Star, is the goddess of war, as Evening Star, a goddess of illicit love, and a universal mother besides...[31]

Frobenius suggests that the skies, with their astral dramas, were imitated so precisely by these cultures that the celestial patterns must have become the model and destiny of life, and may even, ironically, have inspired the earliest form of a state.

In a cave in Zimbabwe, an extraordinary painting was found in the nineteenth century which seems to show a ritual sacrifice taking place. Frobenius interprets this scene of death and celebration as a late version of the Bronze Age ritual regicide, which was explored by Frazer in *The Golden Bough*:

> Here lies the king in the typical posture of the dead in the rock-painted 'Pietas' of this region. The ornamental waist-band is typical; likewise, the body wrapped in tight bands. Over the face there is a horned mask. The upper hand clutches an unidentified object. On his lifted knee is a little bird. There are a number of striding or soaring

human figures round about, and to the right, beneath him, lies a larger figure among what appear to be rocks. Meanwhile, beneath and set apart from this whole group by a number of wavy parallel lines, is a confused multitude of folk amid gift-offerings. Such wavy parallel lines, as may be judged from other examples in this region, are meant to represent the shoreline of the mythical other-world sea: the Dsivoa (fig. 5).[32]

The royal tombs of Ur, Sumerian city of the Moon god Nanna, also bore the signs of grisly sacrifice. Leonard Woolley, who excavated the tombs, describes a piteous pageant of courtly life: King A-bar-gi buried with 68 women arranged in rows, dressed in cloaks the colour of blood, and adorned with great lunate earrings and necklaces of blue and gold. Queen Shub-ad, shrouded in a mass of beads of gold, silver and lapis lazuli, was buried later in the grave above her king, just like, as Campbell observes, 'when the Moon sets and the planet Venus follows.'[33] One of the harps had a golden bull's head upon it, with its eyes, beard and horn tips made of lapis. This was the original Moon Bull, Campbell concludes in his review of Woolley's findings, who as 'symbol of the lunar destiny of all things and the mathematics of the universe...sang to these people the song of their dreams.'[34]

By the First Dynasty in Egypt, the ritual of sacrifice had passed from the Moon king of the pre-dynastic age to the Moon bull who could serve in his place. After living for 25 years with all the ceremonies pertaining to a king, the Apis Bull was slain, embalmed and buried in a rock-cut tomb, known as the *Serapeum*, and laid to rest in the necropolis of Sakkara (where many of them can still be seen in their original graves). A new bull was immediately chosen, black like the black Moon with white marks on his neck and forehead, who was to incarnate yet again the principle of eternal life out of which the temporal comes, just as the new white Moon is born out of the darkness of the old.[35]

As we saw in Chapter 12, the waning of the Moon was originally felt to be a disturbance in the 'natural order' of things, defined, implicitly, as an order in which the Moon would forever shine and people would live for ever. It makes sense, once the waning has continued to its end and the worst predictions have come true, that there should be a common grief and an attempt to bring the Moon back to life. But what is there to do or give? The Bushmen gave their dancing, the North American Indians their dancing and singing, the Greeks their animals and birds, the Malekulans their boars, the Aztecs their enemies, and the early Sumerians and former Rhodesians their kings and queens. But is it – can it ever be – enough? *Do ut Des*, 'I give that Thou might give', is a formula that, focusing more upon what comes back than what is given, cannot fail to fear the disparity between the little 'I' of the request and the greater 'Thou' that may, or may not, grant it.

However, since, against all probability, these rituals were so manifestly successful – since the Moon's death was in fact continually followed by its rebirth – the further idea may have arisen: that death is *necessary* for life, or, more precisely, that the death of the part, a particular death, is necessary for the life of the whole. In exoteric thought – what we might call 'tribal' or 'ego' thinking – this leads to the death of others, characteristically justified as the victory of good over evil. Hence the 'other' tribe, the 'enemy' of the state, the 'heretic', the 'witch', the 'scapegoat', the 'soul-less' animal – wherever the death of another can substitute for the death of oneself. In psychological, esoteric or mystical thought, sacrifice leads to the willing giving up of a part of oneself for the good of the whole. This idea is explored through the Mystery traditions, where the death of the goddess or god or animal is disclosed to be but a manifestation in time of a deeper timeless stratum.

Campbell, in one of his last books, *The Inner Reaches of Outer Space*, extends this argument into the field of consciousness itself:

Fig. 5. "The Moon King and His People." Rock Painting. Diana Vow Farm, Rusapi District, Zimbabwe. From the Frobenius Institute, J.W. Goethe University, Frankfurt-am-Main.

The moon, ever dying and ever renewed, is symbolic of consciousness incarnate in all living beings, suffering in each the pains of desire for the passing gratifications of temporal life, subject in each to death, and yet through death's progeny renewed. It is thus the celestial sign of the necessity of sacrifice; for with each giving of itself to death, lunar life (as distinguished from the term of a single lunation) is sustained.[36]

THE MOON AS ANCESTOR AND JUDGE

When the Moon rises from the dead on the third day it brings with it the idea that it can vanquish death, and even transform death into life. So for the Moon death is not final, and to the Moon the dead of the Earth may go, that death, as it were, may be in its safe-keeping, and life may go on, if not for the body then for the soul. There will at least be a 'life-in-death'.

No 'savage', as Frazer casts those of an earlier age, believes that death is final, only a change of form.[37] So the dead could be imagined as living another kind of 'life' on the resurrecting Moon, shuffling off this mortal coil as the Moon sloughs its shadow and the snake its skin. As the Moon reclaims its own light after its three nights of death, so it may be that the soul likewise will reclaim its body and return to Earth after its time of death is done. Indeed, it seems that the 'primitive' in people of any age cannot help expecting to live for ever, and imagining one's own death is less difficult if there is a home to go to, food and water for the journey, and the prospect of being welcomed by those who have gone before. Such a home was once the Moon.

The Moon in a sense is the first to die, and as the first of the Earth to die is the ancestor of the tribe, it makes sense that the ancestor will inhabit the Moon, from where he can continue to give guidance and law to his inheritors – a brilliant constellation of memory. The *Kaushitaki Upanishad* says that the Moon is 'the home of our ancestors',[38] and death in earlier times was often imagined as joining the ancestors, evocative of the Judaic idea of being gathered to 'Abraham's bosom'. Abraham, who hailed from Nanna-Sin's two cities of Ur and Harran, and whose original name was *Ab-sin*, 'Moon-father', was summoned to father a people at the age of 75, becoming thereby the ancestor of his race.[39]

Sometimes the Moon is directly spoken of as being itself the ancestor of the tribe, suggestive of the very ancient origins of Moon worship.[40] Osiris and Isis were regarded as the ancestors of the kings of Egypt throughout the Dynastic Period, and Osiris later became the great ancestor of all Egypt, with whom Egyptians hoped to be reconciled at death. Kings 'drank at the breast' or 'sat upon the lap' of Isis who wore the throne upon her head, receiving from her their right to rule.[41] In some myths, as in the Arunta myth from Oceania, the Moon was originally the first person ever to live on Earth who, when he died, went to Heaven and became the Moon.[42] The tribe and the human race are generally assumed to be the same, since the myths of each tribe characteristically place themselves at the centre of the world, and so take themselves to be the first people on Earth, from whom all others are descended, (Adam and Eve may come to mind; though, as Black Elk says, 'anywhere is the centre of the world.').[43] The Incas believed they derived from a union of Sun and Moon. Mama Quilla, the Moon, married the Sun and gave birth to a little Sun and Moon: Mama Ogllo, the Moon-maiden (whose name means 'egg'), and her brother, the Sun-man. Sister and brother united to found the Inca royal line at Cuzco, the 'Navel', the place which, in Inca cosmology, is the centre of the world.[44]

The Bushmen called the Moon the 'Great Chief', and 'Our Grandfather';[45] the Algonquin called the Moon goddess Aatensic 'Grandmother',[46] and the various mothers around the world holding up their babies to the Moon, are also acknowledging a lunar inheritance. Soma, or Chandra, was the ancestor of the lunar race of kings, from which Krishna, the eighth avatar of the god Vishnu, was descended.[47] Manu, who saved humankind from the flood and so was, like Noah, the progenitor of his descendants, gave his name to the human race, *manava*.[48] The kings of Burundi in Africa derived their ancestry from the Moon deity, believing that the king would return to the Moon when he died.[49] The Mongol conqueror Genghis Khan (1167–1227) traced his ancestry to a king who had been conceived by a Moon-ray.[50] Sometimes the Moon is the women's ancestor and the Sun is the men's.[51] Even local myths (though all myths are local) draw on this idea. St Maedoc of Ard Ladran, Ireland, who built a church on the Leinster shore, was conceived when his mother saw the Moon entering the mouth of her husband, while her husband, in the same moment, saw a star entering the mouth of his wife.[52]

The Moon in many lands was lawgiver and judge of the dead, as the tribal ancestor had been to the living on Earth. In most Eskimo cultures, for instance, it is the Moon, as the watchful eye of Heaven, who ensures that the tribal taboos are observed down on Earth, though on the island of Nunevak this role is taken over by his close ally the Wolf-Spirit.[53] There is a kind of logic in the idea that the Moon when dark above is bright below, bringing light to the underworld and caring for the

Fig. 6. Diagram of bas-relief dedicated to Men Ouranios, 'Men of the Heavens,' found in Athens. The seven-pointed star within the crescent was a common symbol of the union of Sun and Moon, persisting into Roman times. (From Cumont, Le Symbolism Funéraire des Romains, p. 207).

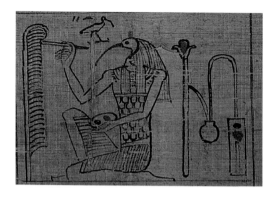

Fig. 7. Osiris as Judge of the Dead in the Hall of Judgement. Tomb of Ramses VI, c. 1135 BC. (From Budge, Osiris, i, p. 42).

Fig. 8. Thoth creating Maat. Papyrus of Lady Taucherit. 1085-950 BC. Rijksmuseum van Oudheden, Leiden.

dead, in some cases according to the lives they had lived. Nanna-Sin, Inanna-Ishtar, Osiris and Isis, Dionysos, Demeter and Persephone, and the Anatolian Men, all are chthonic as well as lunar divinities.[54] For example, *Men Katachthonios*, 'Men of the Underworld', was invoked in epitaphs on funerary monuments all over Asia Minor, from the shores of the Aegean Sea to the mountains of Pont – though, without their sacred literature, none of which has survived, the inscriptions and iconography (written in Greek) tell us only that Men was the protector of the dead, so it is left to comparative lunar symbolism to wonder how and why.[55]

In Sumeria, the Moon god Nanna-Sin decreed the fate of the dead, together with his son, Utu, the Sun god, at the time when, as the Dark Moon, he spent his 'day of rest, sleep, or lying down' in the Nether World.[56] A hymn to 'Father Nanna' goes:

> When you have measured the days of a month
> when you have reached this day...
> When you have made manifest to the people
> your 'day of lying down' of a completed month,
> you grandly judge, O lord, law cases
> in the netherworld, make decisions superbly...
> Just verdicts you put in all mouths,
> make the proper thing apparent,
> the honest hearts you please,
> the administrative decisions you make honestly...[57]

Inanna-Ishtar also 'knew the evildoer':

> Against the evildoer she renders a cruel judgment,
> destroys the wicked,
> She looks with kindly eyes on the straightforward,
> gives him her blessing.[58]

Osiris was Lord and Judge of the Dead in Egypt. Osiris was the 'Lord of *Maat*', a god both just and

Fig. 9. Isis giving the water and food of life to the Heart-soul. The dead were imagined to drink the immortal elixir from the hands of Isis, and also to 'breathe the breath of Isis' in the world beyond this world. (From Budge, Osiris, ii p. 134).

merciful who, innocent of wrongdoing himself, had yet lived and suffered on Earth, and so could understand human weakness. The wicked – those with hearts too heavy or light to be 'equal' to Maat – were to be devoured by the monster *Am-mit* (a hybrid of hippopotamus, lion and crocodile). *Am-mit* sits to the right of the scales, ready for the result of the weighing, as determined by Thoth in his role of 'Lord of the Scales', all in the presence of Osiris.[59]

In fig. 7, Osiris wears the double crown of South and North Egypt (an image of union) and holds a sceptre and the symbol of 'life' in his hands (usually he holds the flail). The scales of judgement stand before him, while the nine steps leading to the throne refer to the nine days of the lunar week, with one of his nine 'Company' of gods represented on each step. In the boat, guarded by two monkeys, is Seth in the form of a pig, recalling the victory of Osiris over Seth.

The feather of *Maat* rests upon the Scales of Judgement as the embodiment of Truth, against which the heart-soul of the deceased is to be weighed. Sometimes the double *Maat* is identified with Isis and Nephthys as the two goddesses of Truth,[60] bringing her more dispassionate standards of right conduct into the living drama of their sorrow. The identity of Thoth and Maat is nowhere more apparent than in this papyrus, when the Moon god Thoth (fig. 8) is shown creating *Maat*, the Law, just as the kings and all their subjects had to 'create *Maat*' every day if they were to live in harmony with the Truth of the universe.

Isis is also present at the judgement of the dead, standing with her sister Nephthys behind Osiris on his throne, as the union of the light and dark halves of the Moon. In their other dual role as Morning and Evening Star (the one star in two appearances), they recall the Rhodesian cosmology further south. Throughout the *Book of the Dead* Isis is spoken of as the nourisher of the dead, the one who takes care of the needs of the deceased, giving him and his soul (who are now one) the water, food and breath of life, and also the compassion due to this new and strange state (fig. 9).

The relation in the after-life between Osiris, the giver of justice, and Isis, the nourisher and comforter, is sometimes echoed in the way Jesus and Mary are depicted in art and ritual. Christian iconography often turns Christ into the remote and stern judge of the quick and the dead, and makes Mary the compassionate intercessor – curiously, given Jesus's articulate vision in the Gospels of the redemptive power of love. On the other hand, it makes sense in terms of the underlying symbolism of Christ as the Sun and Mary as the Moon, whereby union with Christ as the ultimate goal is made possible by the forgiveness and intercession of Mary, who is never far away from us – the Moon still mediating between Earth and Sun (fig. 10).

In Greece, Demeter was called the lawgiver, *thesmophoria*, and in Athens the dead were her children, *Demetreoi*.[61] The Moon was also given as the seat of one of the Furies, who was placed there so that no misconduct on Earth could escape her.[62]

Fig. 10. The Last Judgement. Michelangelo. 1508-1512. Sistine Chapel, The Vatican.

The time of lunar darkness was the time of judgement. Even after 19 years away, Odysseus is expected to arrive to dispense justice in the Dark Moon: 'This very year Odysseus will be here. Between the waning of the old moon and the waxing of the new, he will come back to his home and will punish all that offer outrage there to his consort and his noble son.'[63] When Odysseus has slain the suitors, Hermes escorts them to the underworld, calling forth their spirits with his golden wand, and the spirits follow him, gibbering like bats in a dank and wondrous cave.[64]

In Greece, Sleep, *Hypnos*, is the brother of Death, *Thanatos*, both sons of goddess Night, not only because the dead in their 'sleep of death' resemble the living in their sleep, but also, perhaps, because sleep brings dreams, and dreams draw aside the veil between the worlds of the living and the dead, and between past, present and future. It is as though the dead become visible to the sleeping mind in the way that the Moon makes the night luminous. In fig. 11, the artist has added Hermes to the original tale from the *Iliad*, as though to emphasize the need for a ritual required to enter (or envisage) the realm of the after-life, which the brothers Sleep and Death on their own do not provide. For Hermes *Psychopompos*, 'Guide of Souls', with his ancient wand of intertwining snakes, conducts the souls across the boundary from life to death, in the manner of one who was once a Moon god himself.[65]

All the signs are there. Hermes is born in a cave on the fourth of the month, the first day of the lighted crescent after the three days of dark; he dallies with *Herse*, goddess of dew, Selene's daughter, and he carries a lamb across his shoulders as the increaser of flocks. In Arcadia he was honoured beside swamps and springs, and his *herms*, piles of stones for the weary voyager, pointed the way to the next spring. He is frequently drawn as an old fertility god in ithyphallic mode, and spoken of in epithets that link him to the night: *nuxios*, 'he of the night', and *opopeter*, 'he who sees in the night', or 'companion of black night', as Apollo calls him.[66] The same theme is given implicitly in his most frequent epithet: *Argeiphontes*, 'Slayer of Argus'. Argus was the giant with a hundred eyes, one eye ever

Fig. 11. Sleep and Death transporting the body of Sarpedon to Lycia, under the guidance of Hermes. Signed by Euxitheos (potter) and Euphronius (painter). Calyx krater, red-figured vase, c. 515 BC. The Metropolitan Museum of Art, New York.

open like the light of day (and reason), who guarded the white Moon-cow, Io, at Hera's request because Zeus loved her. Hermes, at Zeus's request, charms Argus to sleep with his flute and then slays him, setting Io free. Argus may be a remnant of an ancient waning Moon god, imprisoning Io as the new Moon, whom Hermes, unexpectedly for the gentle god he has become, has to slay. A later reading would be that Hermes, god of imagination, releases the lunar intuition from a too-watchful eye which inevitably imprisons it.[67] *Propulaios*, 'at the gate', is another of Hermes' names – the one who stands at the gate of the underworld, on the threshold between the human and divine worlds, at the place of transformation. His hat, half black and half white, corresponds to his two-fold nature, alternately dwelling in the luminous heights and in the darkness of the underworld. At every New Moon, Hermes, together with Hekate, another lunar guardian of gates and crossroads, received cakes and smoked offerings, in the hope, perhaps, of a fortunate month.[68]

A trace of the Moon as custodian of the law lingers in the poem *The Freiris of Berwick*, by William Dunbar (1465–1530), suggesting that swearing by the Moon was once an old custom:

> Quhen Symone saw it appinuit on this wyis,
> He had grit wondir; and sweris be the mone,
> That Freir Robert weill his dett had done.[69]

THE MOON AS THE ABODE OF SOULS

Everyone who dies becomes an 'ancestor' to the living, and in the *Kaushitaki Upanishad* it is said:

> All who depart from this world (or this body) go to the moon. In the former, (the bright) half, the moon delights in their spirits [*prana*]; in the other, (the dark) half, the moon sends them on to be born again.[70]

The idea of the Moon as the abode of souls is found among many people: Bushmen, Polynesians, Hindus, Japanese, Babylonians, Egyptians, Assyrians, Phoenicians, Hittites, Anatolians, Manichaeans, Greeks (Orphics, Pythagoreans), Slavs, Gnostics, Romany gypsies, Romans and all over the Roman empire.[71]

In the Egyptian *Book of Respirations*, Isis breathes the wish for Osiris 'that his soul may rise to heaven in the disc of the moon.'[72] The deceased in Egypt was said to 'become Osiris', and so 'to renew his life like the Moon', as it is written on a ritual papyrus on the embalming of the dead.[73] The Moon was called the 'abode of Osiris'.[74] Originally, the Pharaohs claimed immortality for themselves alone and only they could 'become Osiris', though this had changed by the New Kingdom (just as some Polynesian tribes reserved the Moon for their religious or political leaders).[75] In a Pyramid text, the deceased king is called the brother of the Moon, and in an inscription at Abydos, Seti I is greeted:

Thou shalt renew thy youth; thou shalt flourish again like the Moon-Thoth when he is a child.[76]

Pythagoras, according to Plutarch, located the Elysian Fields on the side of the Moon turned perpetually towards Heaven, never visible to human eyes, and this is where the Caesars and the heroes went after death.[77] Indeed, Pythagoras himself was thought by some to be a spirit descended from the Moon.[78] Epiphanius writes that 'the disc of the Moon is filled with souls',[79] while Roman senators, according to Kastor of Rhodes, would wear shoes decorated with ivory crescents (lunules), to indicate that they would inhabit the Moon after they died.[80] In Gaul, the Celts placed the crescent on their tombs, long before the Romans came. And on the urns and gravestones of ordinary Romans, in the countryside and in the towns and especially in the colonies far from home, the crescent was there, the gift and best hope of those left behind.

Selene and Endymion also reappear in the Roman Empire, sculpted on elaborate tombstones as an image of the soul. Like Endymion, the soul has fallen into an eternal sleep from which it will neither wake nor grow old, but may rest peacefully in the Moon's embrace. Lively debates were held on this subject. What is the point of Selene's kiss, demanded Cicero, if the sleeper can never perceive it? But, said the Pythagoreans, the 'sleeper' is actually awake. Souls, they explained, are already familiar with the world of dreams as well as with the souls of the deceased, having many times visited the one and conversed with the other at night while the soul's person was sleeping. Death, they concluded, was not, therefore, a restful sleep but an awakening, where life could be newly perceived as a dream itself, a dream in which the soul believes while still imprisoned in the body but, once set free, can see at last for what it is.[81] The myth, as so often, could support either point of view depending on how it was interpreted, which in turn depended on whether the Moon was envisaged primarily as a place of death or rebirth. Where the emphasis on rebirth was predominant, the deceased was assimilated to the Moon to participate in its renewal. In the relief from Argos shown in fig. 12, the crescent rests upon the head of a woman, who is surrounded on the outside by the signs of the zodiac and on the inside by the seven stars of the Pleiades (suggestive of immortality, as the seven maidens translated into stars after their death). It is open to further debate whether this is Selene, or Sophia, the Gnostic Virgin of Light, or just a girl who died, whose family wished for her a new life like the Moon's.[82]

This thought may have a very ancient lineage, for it is possible that England's Stonehenge may once have housed a festival for the dead in their relation to the Moon. In the second phase of building at Stonehenge (c.2950–2500 BC), a cluster of cremated human remains and a polished stone mace-head were found at the spot which marked the most southerly rise of the Moon in the south-southeast. In north-east Scotland, also, recumbent stones were placed where the Moon would rise or set, and often around the stone were scattered pieces of quartz which glow translucently in a full Moon. Archaeologists Tony Spawforth and Aubrey Burl suggested that aligning the stone with the Moon may have been a way to harness its powers of rebirth, as though the remains were strategically positioned to enable the Moon, at the limit of its trajectory, to sweep up the souls of the dead and take them with it to their final resting place in the Moon.[83]

This suggestion gains credibility from early practices in other parts of the world. For instance, when the Bushmen saw a hollow Moon which was lying down, they understood it to be carrying the dead away. In 1875, a Bushman told Dr Bleek what his parents had told him and what he had observed himself – that when people died the wind blew away their footsteps, their hair became clouds and their gall sat green in the sky:

> ...Mother was wont to do thus when the moon lying down came, (when) the moon stood hollow. Mother spoke, she said: 'The moon is carrying people who are dead...it lies hollow, because it is killing itself (by) carrying people who are dead. This is why it lies hollow...for it is a moon of badness...Therefore ye may (expect to) hear what has happened, when the moon is like this.'[84]

Even in the 1970s, a Japanese sea captain, on hearing from a friend that a mutual friend of theirs had died, sent back a telegram by return, saying: 'Moon rising when sad news arrived so took my shakuhachi [flute] and played to moon where souls of departed rest on their way beyond.'[85]

In 1930s Spain, Lorca's poem *Song of Amargo's Mother* begins with the image of the dead man:

> They carry him on my bedsheet,
> my oleanders and my palm...

and ends with:

> The cross. Don't anyone cry.
> The Amargo is on the moon.[86]

THE MOON AS A STAGE IN THE JOURNEY TO THE SUN

When, in reflections upon death, Earth, Moon and Sun are brought into relation with each other, they are typically drawn in a line of progression which begins with the Earth and ends with the Sun.

Fig. 12. Selene, Sophia, or deceased woman as the Moon. Bas-relief from Argos. 2nd/3rd centuries AD. British Museum.

Fig. 13. Pillar and Moon. Paul Nash, 1932. Tate Gallery, London.

The Moon, as the closest celestial body to Earth, occupies the middle place, and becomes the first stage of a heavenly journey which may continue to the Sun. In this sense, this relation between Moon and Sun is analogous, for a Christian sensibility, to the difference between Purgatory and Paradise.

In the *Upanishads*, the deceased could take one of two paths, in accordance with how they had passed their time on Earth. Both paths led to the Moon and diverged afterwards, one eventually returning to Earth, and the other leading on to the Sun, and then to union with Brahman, after which the long cycle of incarnations would cease.

In the *Brihadaranyaka Upanishad*, the first path, called the 'path of souls' or 'the path of the ancestors', ended at the Moon, and was called the 'road of smoke'. Those who 'conquer the worlds by means of sacrifice, charity, and austerity' (but do not yet have knowledge of 'the True'):

> go to smoke, from smoke to night, from night to the decreasing half of the moon to the six months when the sun goes to the south, from these months to the world of the fathers, from the world of the fathers to the moon. Having reached the moon, they become food, and then the Devas feed on them there, as sacrificers feed on Soma, as it increases and decreases. But when this (the result of their good works on earth) ceases, they return again to that ether, from ether to the air, from the air to rain, from rain to the earth. And when they have reached the earth, they become food, they are offered again in the altar-fire, which is man, and thence are born in the fire of woman. Thus they rise up towards the worlds, and go the same round as before.[87]

In the *Khandogya Upanishad*, being 'eaten' by the Devas is explained as being loved by them.[88] The second path, the 'path of the gods', led first to the Moon and then to the Sun, and was called the 'road of flame'. Those who have knowledge and practise it:

> go to light, from light to day, from day to the increasing half [of the Moon], from the increasing half to the six months when the sun goes to the north, from those six months to the world of the Devas, from the world of the Devas to the sun, from the sun to the place of lightning. When they have thus reached the place of lightning a spirit comes

Fig. 14. The Moon Boat as a Crescent carrying Seven Souls. Indian stele. (From Henderson and Oakes, The Wisdom of the Serpent).

Fig. 15. The Moon as the abode of souls, pictured as a crescent boat sailing above seven stars as the planets. Chalcedon gem. 1st century BC. (From Cumont, Le Symbolism Funéraire des Romains, p. 93).

near them, and leads them to the worlds of the Brahman. In these worlds of Brahman they dwell exalted for ages. There is no returning for them.[89]

Moon and Sun are here conceived as boats carrying souls, moving through the blue-black waters of Heaven. When the Moon waxed it was full of souls, bringing them to the 'aeons of light', which placed them in the 'pillar of glory', their final place of rest.[90] Then the Moon returned to the west for another boatful of souls, now much smaller than before. This lovely image of the Waxing and Waning Moon, swelling up with its load of souls and shrinking when it has delivered them to the Sun, is also found in China. Among the Gnostics, too, the Moon was conceived as a celestial ship bearing the souls of the departed.[91] The Manichaeans, living in the kingdom of the Sassanians in the third century AD, adapted the old Indo-Iranian beliefs about the Moon into their own system. Mani said that the Moon, the 'vessel of light' which wanders through the sky, fills up with souls that it transports each month to the greater ship of the Sun.[92]

The image of a 'Ship of Death' structures one of D.H. Lawrence's last poems:

> ...row, little soul, row on
> on the longest journey, towards the greatest goal...
>
> Oh build your ship of death
> oh build it.
> Oh, nothing matters but the longest journey.[93]

The upward flight of the soul to the heavens is an image of death common to many cultures. In ancient Iran, life after death was imagined as a perilous journey to the Moon, Sun and stars. Ceremonies were conducted for three days after death, dedicated to helping the dead in their journey, which included the crossing of the Cinvat Bridge – razor-sharp to the wicked, broad and flat to the righteous – beginning at the top of a mountain and ending in paradise.[94] After the souls of the dead had crossed the bridge, they continued towards the stars: the good went first to the Moon, and then to the Sun, and the very good entered the eternal light of *Ahura Mazda*.[95]

The Siberian Inuit tribe conceived death as a loss of the soul, which journeys up to the Moon and then onward to the Sun.[96] Gypsies, many of whom came originally from India as slaves, also claimed their own Romany saviour who carried souls to the Moon.[97] Even Jesus was said to have gone on a Moon journey: in the sixteenth-century Digby Mystery Play *Mary Magdalene*, Jesus appears to identify the Moon, his blessed mother, the vessel, and the ship of Noah:

> In the mone I restyd, that never chongyd goodnesse...
> She was the paleys of Phebus brightness...
> My blissyd mother, of demure feminite...[98]

In all these myths, the Moon is both a place – the land of the dead – and an active guardian presence whose role is to receive, purify and regenerate souls.

THE MOON AS THE DOOR TO THE ETERNAL WORLD

The idea of the Moon as a door, gate or mirror, opening onto 'the next' or a further world, is widespread, and then the Moon becomes a dividing line between the temporal world of becoming and the eternal world of being, serving as a place of transition between the two. The passage from the *Kaushitaki Upanishad* quoted above continues:

> Verily, the moon is the door of the *Svarga* world (the heavenly world). Now, if a man objects to the moon (if one is not satisfied with life there) the moon sets him free. But if a man does not object, then the moon sends him down as rain upon this earth.[99]

The Roman Lydus describes Praetextus, the hierophant, as saying that Janus 'sends the diviner souls to the lunar throng'.[100] Janus, or Ianus, the god with two faces, was the guardian of the door, who gave his name to January, the month that faces both ways. His name comes from *ianua*, a door or entrance gate that has two sides, and is also the masculine form of the Roman Moon goddess, Diana, she who was the gateway to life and death.[101] Some Buddhist temples, as some English gardens, have 'Moon doors' or 'Moon gates' as thresholds of initiation from one reality to another (fig. 16).

The rationale for this imaginary line of division is succinctly stated by Cicero: *Supra lunam sunt aeterna omnia*, 'Above [or beyond] the moon all things are eternal';[102] which is to say that only what is beyond the Moon is beyond the phenomenal world of time and change, a distinction inherited from Aristotle.[103] This places the Moon as a mediator between Earth and Sun, not just receiving but also regenerating the souls of the dead so they may continue their journey to the Sun.

Plutarch, in his dialogue, 'Concerning the Face which Appears in the Orb of the Moon', concludes with a story, given, after the model in the *Timaeus*, by a stranger from a place no one knows. This stranger gave the tale to Sulla, the last of the speakers, who passes on the idea that the Moon should be especially honoured because it is the home of the souls of the just, who go there to be purified before going to the Sun. The Moon is also the home of souls that have not yet been born.

A person, Sulla was told, is composed of three factors: Earth furnishes *soma*, the body, Moon furnishes *psyche*, the soul, and Sun furnishes *nous*, spirit or mind, just as it gives light to the Moon herself.[104] These aspects of a person die in stages, each aspect returning to its place of origin. The first death occurs on Earth in the domain of Demeter (which is why the dead are called *Demetreoi*, 'Demeter's people'), when the body separates from *psyche* and *nous*.[105] The second death takes place in

Fig. 16. The 'Moon Door' of a Buddhist monastery, Wu-Shi, China. (From Alistair Shearer, Buddha, *London, Thames and Hudson, 1992, p. 58).*

the Moon, in the domain of her daughter Persephone, who gently detaches *psyche* from *nous*, though the soul clings to dreams and memories of life for some time to come.[106] As the body resolves into the Earth, so the soul resolves into the Moon, once the Sun has taken back the *nous* into itself. But whereas the souls of the just are accepted and soon absorbed by the Moon, those of the unjust she 'thrusts off and sweeps away', condemning them to wander in the region between Earth and Moon until the penalties for their offences are paid. But those who gain a 'firm footing' on the Moon behold first the Moon's 'magnitude, beauty and nature', and this, it is implied, is what begins the process of purification.[107] So Persephone frees the soul to love the 'image in the Sun', through which shines forth the divine towards which all Nature yearns:

> For it must be out of love for the Sun that the Moon herself goes her rounds and gets into conjunction with him in her yearning to receive from him what is most fructifying.[108]

There is, therefore, in Plutarch's thought a hierarchy of Sun, Moon and Earth, with the Moon as the mediator: the Moon is a 'compound and blend of things above and below and therefore stands to the sun in the relation of earth to moon.'[109] Where the Earth takes and the Sun gives, the Moon 'both takes and gives and joins together and divides asunder.' The three Fates are also allocated to these spheres of descending influence: Atropos, 'enthroned in the sun initiates generation', Clotho on the Moon 'mingles and binds together', while Lachesis is placed on Earth, having 'the largest share in chance'.[110] When the Sun with his vital force has again sown *nous* in the Moon, the Moon furnishes new souls who descend to Earth, where they receive their bodies for birth. Here the Moon is fertilized by the Sun, just as the Moon in turn fertilizes Earth.

Plutarch's ordering of Earth, Moon and Sun was inspired by Plato, in particular his vision of the Sun as the image of the Good in the *Republic*.[111] A similar cosmology (applying this hierarchical perspective to gender), appears in Aristophanes' argument on love in Plato's *Symposium*: Aristophanes proposes the idea that once there were three kinds of human beings: 'the male kind originally sprung from the Sun, the female from the Earth, while the sex that was both male and female came from the Moon, because the Moon shares in the nature of both Sun and Earth.'[112] Xenocrates, who directed the Academy from 339 to 315 BC, was the first to propose that the planetary hierarchy of Sun, Moon and Earth could be found as a corresponding triad within human beings – of spirit, soul and body – where the spirit corresponded with the Sun, the soul with the Moon and the body with the Earth.[113] This hierarchical model, where the macrocosm of the universe was reflected in humanity as the microcosm, passed into Roman thought also, and eventually on to Dante.

Cicero's 'Dream of Scipio Africanus the Younger' in his *De Re Publica* presents the young Scipio's vision of his grandfather, Scipio Africanus the Elder, who appears to him in a dream looking, rather alarmingly, more like his marble bust than the old man he once knew: 'Courage, Scipio, have no fear,' his grandfather says to him, robustly, 'but imprint these words upon your memory.'[114]

The young Scipio then finds himself in 'a lofty place, bathed in clear starlight', apparently above and beyond Earth and Moon, and closer to the stars not visible from Earth. The elder Scipio presents to him his father, Paulus, recently escaped 'from the bondage of the body as from a prison' and now living in the Milky Way, who tells him to honour the fatherland and listen to his grandfather.[115] Scipio Africanus the Elder then shows his grandson the nine celestial spheres by which the 'whole is joined'. God is the outermost sphere, the Heaven, which contains all the rest. In it are held the fixed stars in their eternal revolving courses, and, beneath them, the seven other spheres which revolve in the opposite direction from that of Heaven. These are, in descending order, Saturn, Jupiter, Mars, Sun, Venus, Mercury and Moon, who is 'set on fire by the rays of the Sun'. Each sphere has its own sound or note in relation to the speed of its revolution, and all, from high to low, compose a heavenly harmony – with the Moon, as the slowest moving body, having the lowest tone:

> Below the Moon there is nothing but what is mortal and doomed to decay, except the souls given to men by the bounty of the gods, whereas above the Moon all is eternal.[116]

Earth as the ninth and last sphere remains 'ever motionless and stationary' at the centre of the universe. No one on Earth can hear this celestial harmony, for human ears, forever filled with the song of the universe, have now become deaf to it. Leaving his grandson, on the one hand, with the uplifting image of his immortal spirit – which, like God, moves itself – and, on the other, with the salutory image of tormented spirits who gave themselves to sensual pleasures and now must fly about close to Earth for many ages of torture, he departs, and Scipio the Younger wakes astonished from his sleep.

The idea of the song of the universe, composed from the sounds of individual stars and planets and orchestrated into one vast heavenly harmony, has entranced the western imagination – from Plato, through Cicero, the Neoplatonists, to Shakespeare – perhaps because it offers an image of incarnation which still retains the beauty of the whole. We may intuit the harmony even if we cannot hear the sound of the singing. In *The Merchant of Venice*, it is the sweetness of the 'sleeping' moonlight that allows this ancient harmony to reach the lovers. Lorenzo says to Jessica:

Fig. 17. Fragment of a Roman bas-relief from a sarcophagus. Vatican Museum. The veiled female, with a crescent upon her forehead, appears to be the Moon, who is giving a winged, naked child (the soul of the child) to the Sun, identified by the seven rays springing from his head. Vatican Museum, Rome.

How sweet the moonlight sleeps upon this bank!
Here will we sit, and let the sounds of music
Creep in our ears. Soft stillness and the night
Become the touches of sweet harmony.
Sit Jessica. Look how the floor of heaven
Is thick inlaid with patines of bright gold.
There's not the smallest orb which thou behold'st
But in his motion like an angel sings,
Still quiring to the young-ey'd cherubims;
Such harmony is in immortal souls,
But whilst this muddy vesture of decay
Doth grossly close it in, we cannot hear it.
[Enter Musicians]
Come ho, and wake Diana with a hymn...[117]

Though classical sirens have become angels, the song of the universe is still resounding in immortal souls. Lorenzo's thought closes with 'waking Diana', casting off the Muse which the sleeping moonlight brings. But Portia, seeing Lorenzo and Jessica together as the music ceases, remarks: 'The moon sleeps with Endymion, And would not be awaked.'[118]

On a more prosaic level, the division between temporal and eternal, with the Moon as the dividing line between them, became a way of thinking whose hold upon the western mind is registered in Shakespeare's parody of it in *Henry VIII*. Quoth the King:

...I am afraid
His thinkings are below the moon, not worth
His serious considering.[119]

When the Moon is set in relation with the Earth and Sun, as in Plutarch's cosmology, it appears to invite the simple idea of purification, with eternity or Paradise located in the Sun. But when the Moon is set in relation with the whole of the visible and invisible galaxy, as one of nine planetary and starry spheres, then the Moon becomes the outer limit of the phenomenal world, as in Cicero, and so the first of nine stages of the journey from Earth to Paradise, as in Dante. In this case, the Moon offers the first glimpse of Paradise, but from a long way off. Dante's cosmology in *The Divine Comedy* is derived from the intellectual tradition of Plato and Aristotle, St Augustine, and the thirteenth-century schoolmen, Albertus Magnus and his pupil Thomas Aquinas. It proposes nine spheres concentric to Earth, which is still fixed at the centre. Spheres of air and fire surround the Earth, with fire reaching up to the Moon. Beyond the Moon come, in their visible planetary order, Mercury, Venus, Sun, Mars, Jupiter, Saturn, and the fixed stars which inhabit the sphere of the Primum Mobile, or First Movement, which orders and governs the movements of the whole in time and space. Each of these spheres is under the guidance of one of the angelic orders, with a special influence on earthly life.[120]

In this wholly spiritualized universe, souls do not simply go to the Moon and later, perhaps, the Sun. The whole galaxy is alive with souls, dispersed throughout the planets in direct relation to the way they lived on Earth. *Inferno*, Hell, imprisons the unredeemed behind the locked gates where hope is abandoned; *Purgatorio*, Purgatory, guards, on the seven terraces of the island-mountain, the souls purging themselves of the seven deadly sins; *Paradiso*, Paradise, begins the ascent through the spheres

Fig. 18. The Ptolemaic Universe. Orbits of the planets, with Earth stationary at the centre. Engraving by A. Cellarius, Harmonica Macrocosmica 1668.

to the Empyrean Heaven. The Moon, as the first planet out from Earth, is given the first sinners capable of redemption. Souls in the Moon have sinned, but more through infirmity of will and confusion than real wickedness. Souls whose actions were governed by virtuous motives go to the Sun as the fourth sphere, through to Saturn as the eighth sphere. The last two spheres are where the saints and angels meet, and, beyond all these, is the Empyrean Heaven where the Deity abides, and where there is neither time nor place, only light. Thus the universe, as Beatrice explains it to Dante in *Paradiso*, Canto II, is ordered 'grade by grade, each receiving from above and operating below.'[121]

Dante reaches the Moon in the *Paradiso*, the third and last book of *The Divine Comedy* (composed in the years just before Dante's death in 1321). In the *Inferno* Dante had been conducted by Virgil to Hell, entering through the gate at nightfall on Good Friday, and emerging at the entrance to Purgatory on the morning of the third day. Virgil leaves him towards the end of Purgatory, unable to proceed further himself, and now, at noon, the time at which Christ ascended into Heaven, Dante follows Beatrice, his Muse, who leads him to Paradise through the celestial spheres which reflect the spheres of his increasing understanding. While Beatrice stands gazing at the Sun, Dante gazes at Beatrice, and this vision of her brings about his transformation which gives him the power to rise through the spheres. The first sphere is the sphere of the Moon.

In fig. 19 Minerva's golden breath (top left) lifts Dante (in blue) into the air, where he is drawn forwards by Apollo (in golden red), with his black raven beneath him. Apollo points to a star on the far side of the nine Muses, who are themselves pointing to the star, the Great Bear – a literal rendering of lines 8 and 9: 'Minerva breathes, and Apollo leads me, and nine Muses show me the Bears.' The two people in the little bark, who have been following Dante, are now advised to turn back, for he is going into waters never sailed before. If they were to guide their boat into the furrow of his wake, they would be more amazed even than the Argonauts when they saw Jason in Colchis ploughing a field

Fig. 19. *Dante and Beatrice rise towards the Heaven of the Moon. (Paradiso, Canto II). Giovanni di Paolo. c. 1445. (From Pope-Hennessy,* Paradiso: Illuminations to Dante's Divine Comedy by Giovanni di Paolo, *p. 74)*

Fig. 20. *Dante conversing with Piccarda dei' Donati and the Empress Constanza in the Heaven of the Moon. (From Pope-Hennessy, ibid, p. 76).*

with wild bulls (bottom left). Dante's posture, leaning backwards, suggests he also is still caught in the past, fearful of the next stage to which Apollo and the Muses point. A line of cloud runs diagonally through the centre of the picture, separating this first scene from the united ascent of Dante and Beatrice on the right, and illustrating lines 31–33: 'It seemed to me that a cloud covered us, shining, dense, solid and smooth, like a diamond that is smitten by the sun.' Rising together above snow-white mountains, with hands outstretched (as one flies in a dream), they approach the Heaven of the Moon, where the crescent is lighted on the left – the colour, says the *Ottimo Commento*, of white milk – and shaded on the right, illustrating Dante's question about the dark marks on the body of the Moon which make people on Earth tell the tale of Cain.[122]

Significantly, the Moon is brought to life in the traditional images of water and milk, reminiscent of Soma. Dante describes their landing on the Moon through the analogy of water receiving light: 'the eternal pearl received us into itself, as water receives a ray of light and remains unbroken.'[123]

In fig. 20, the figures of two nuns and three naked souls float in the large crescent of the Moon. The nuns, with arms raised in welcome, are greeted by Dante (in blue), with the Sun of love upon his chest, and by Beatrice floating above him (in pink), who is half-hidden in a cloud. Beneath are two small figures, the one on the left gazing into a mirror and the one on the right (in crimson) gazing, like Narcissus, into the mirror of his reflection in the pool. These figures illustrate Dante's confusion as to what is distinct and real (a traditional feature of 'moonshine'). In another allusion to the white, pearl-like, watery nature of the Moon, Dante says:

> As through smooth and transparent glass, or through limpid and still water not so deep that the bottom is lost, the outlines of our faces return so faint that a pearl on a white brow does not come less quickly to our eyes, many such faces I saw, eager to speak; at which I ran into the opposite error to that which kindled love between the man and the spring.[124]

The translator John D. Sinclair comments on Canto III:

> The souls in [the Moon's] sphere, perfected up to the measure of their nature, appear dimly in the Moon's shining substance like reflections in still water, corresponding to something vague and limited in their personalities. And as Narcissus, too credulous, took his reflected face for real, so Dante, too slow of heart to believe, did not know real spirits when he saw them, and he is again corrected for his failure in spiritual perception. He still limits new experience by old...[125]

Dante learns from the nun, Piccarda Donati, that, though infirmity of will in the face of temptation has placed them on the Moon, this same will, tutored by charity, has learned to 'will only what we have and thirst for nothing else.'[126] They do not wish to be anywhere 'better' because where they are is what is best. In this way, personal will becomes one with the divine will, and begins the journey to Paradise. Thus the sin, with awareness, corrects itself.

* * *

Zimmer, in a discussion of 'Death and Rebirth in the Light of India', records a change in consciousness from the 'lunar' to the 'solar' era. Though he is talking specifically of India, a similar change of values took place in the West and in most other cultures throughout the world, when the Sun replaced the Moon as a focus for human aspiration and, in particular, as a way of thinking about death:

> The way of the 'fathers' or 'ancestors', the circuit in the sublunar zone, is the older way. Formerly the moon, continually reborn after total disappearance, was the comforting token that death, like the moonless black night, was but a passage to the rebirth of the infant-crescent, in accordance with the saying: 'Wax and wane.' The recurrent phases of the moon were a visible pledge of eternally renewed rebirth. But this lunar era of the human spirit with its hope of immortality grounded in perpetual alternation, gave way to the solar era, when the unchanging eternity of solar existence was promised to those initiated through 'knowledge'. The moon, formerly a symbol of the supreme consolation and visible hope, now came to stand for the nightmarish vicious circle of death and birth, whence only an esoteric 'knower' could escape into a higher transcendent world.[127]

The newer journey to the Sun offered an image of immortality which had been quite unknown to the earlier Moon worshippers, caught up, as it now seemed, in the endless cycle of death and rebirth. When taken literally, the supremacy of the solar principle in which 'knowledge' was required for 'eternity' meant one more stage in the detaching of human beings from Nature, such that abstract ideas were to

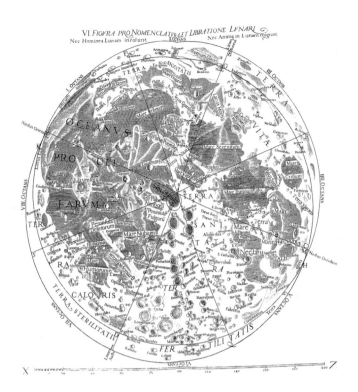

*Fig. 21. Map of the Moon. Engraving by
Giovanni Riccioli, Bologna 1651.
University of Utrecht Library, Holland.*

predominate over lived experience, and something which was once considered a person's birthright now
had to be earned through knowledge, however that was to be defined. But, as Zimmer adds, although 'the
solar principle overcomes the archaic lunar principle', it has to be remembered that both principles –
indeed all doctrines of the cosmos – are symbols of psychic reality. Those, particularly of the Yogic
tradition, who recognised this, understood the innermost self (*atman*) of all living beings as giving rise to
'all the Maya of the world and ego', such that 'all the stages of the journey to it are within ourselves, in
the inner cosmos'.[128] There is ultimately, therefore, no division between them.

Nonetheless, returning to the (apparently) non-symbolic world, the replacing of the lunar with the
solar era still left the Moon in place – albeit erroneously – as one of seven 'planets' moving around an
immobile Earth. This mid-seventeenth century engraving of the map of the Moon shown in fig. 21
still reads like a map of an earthly paradise: a land of peace and plenty, a place of serenity, tranquillity
and fecundity; home for clouds, rains, waters, nectar and manna: *Mare Serenitatis*, *Mare Tranquilitatis*,
Mare Fecunditatis, *Mare Nubium*, *Mare Imbrium*, *Mare Humorum*, *Mare Nectaris* and *Terra Manna*.
Endymion is there, and Hermes, Mercurius, Hercules, Atlas and even Copernicus, whose idea of the
heliocentric universe was first published in 1543, just over a hundred years before.

The revolution in human thought brought about by the general acceptance of the heliocentric
universe in the eighteenth century changed the entire mythic geography of death as well as life. For
the Moon that Galileo first saw through his telescope in 1610 was now entirely displaced from the
pattern of the heavens, The Moon had also inspired Newton's idea of universal gravitation in 1666.
He had worked out that the Moon falls towards the Earth like a ball – or an apple – but goes so fast
that 'she' constantly misses it, going round because the Earth is round.[129] But playing the leading role
in Newton's theory of gravity was eventually to strip the Moon of what was left of its autonomy. It was
relegated to a subservient position, following Earth, with Earth itself no longer the still centre, but

forever moving like the Moon. This displacement meant that the Moon could no longer serve the imagination in the same way, not even as the first stage of a celestial journey where a soul could rest. As Earth's satellite, the Moon became, as it were, inferior to Earth – Earth's wasteland.

THE MOON AS THE WASTELAND OF EARTH

...till this outworn earth be dead as yon dead world
the moon.[130]

This Moon, newly conceived, as in Tennyson's poem above, does not only embody the same circle of death and birth found on Earth (a 'vicious' circle to the 'solar view'); it incarnates more profoundly all the vices of the 'sublunary realm', the realm of decay and dissolution. Sometimes the Christian 'Hell' was placed on the Moon, or else those sins for which Christians believed they 'went to Hell' went to the Moon instead. Even in the 1980s, an Indian guru was advising her devotees not to look at an eclipse of the Moon, because the Moon was coming down to 'eat' the sins of the world.[131] From deity to scapegoat – from hope to the death of hope – is indeed a complete reversal.

In this new way of thinking, the Moon is concretized as the place of death without rebirth. This idea may be intensified by the fact that the far side of the Moon can never be seen from Earth, and so is imagined in perpetual darkness, like some images of Hell and the underworld. For while the Moon is revolving elliptically around the Earth, it is also rotating on its own axis; so one side of the Moon (the 'other side') is forever turned away.

Ariosto's *Orlando Furioso*, a comic poem written in the sixteenth century, catches this sense of the Moon as the place which houses the follies committed on Earth (while, incidentally, in the older tradition, also keeping due account of them). Visiting the Moon, Astolpho finds that bribes were hung on gold and silver hooks, princes' favours were hidden in bellows, and wasted talent was preserved in vases, each marked with a proper name.[132] In Pope's *The Rape of the Lock*, written in 1711, the Moon is the abode of things 'lost on earth', or things sent away to be forgotten. When the Lock, 'obtained with guilt, and kept with pain', disappeared,[133] some people said it had gone to the Moon:

> Some thought it mounted in the lunar sphere,
> Since all things lost on earth are treasured there.
> There heroes' wits are kept in ponderous vases,
> And beaux in snuff-boxes and tweezer-cases.
> There broken vows and death-bed alms are found,
> And lovers' hearts with ends of ribband bound,
> The courtier's promises, and sick men's prayers,
> The smiles of harlots, and the tears of heirs,
> Cages for gnats, and chains to yoke a flea,
> Dried butterflies, and tomes of casuistry.[134]

Giacomo Leopardi, in 1898, also depicted the Moon as the place of vanities, where things well lost on Earth can be rediscovered: tears and sighs of lovers, vain projects, vain desires, gifts offered to princes, and long-forgotten alms.[135] Once the 'light of the world', the Moon is now Earth's 'shadow', the repository of human folly and failure.[136]

The debasement of the Moon is further implied in Gurdjieff's teachings, where it is presented in images evocative of a modern electromagnetic Hell. Gurdjieff, the charismatic spiritual teacher, was saying in the 1950s that 'souls go to the moon'[137] – and saying it apparently not as metaphor but as fact – though with subtly changed meaning. It is rather that 'organic life on earth feeds the moon', which needs it to exist and grow. The emphasis here is on what the souls can do for the Moon not what the Moon can do for the souls. Gurdjieff's student Ouspensky, in his book *In Search of the Miraculous*, quotes Gurdjieff as saying that the energy released at death is attracted to the Moon 'as though by a huge electromagnet, and brings to it the warmth and the life on which its [the Moon's] growth depends.'[138] The Moon is found at the *end* of the 'Ray of Creation', which descends, like the Great Chain of Being, from highest to lowest, and so for the souls that go there the Moon is truly 'the end of the world; it is the "outer darkness" of the Christian doctrine "where there will be weeping and gnashing of teeth."'[139] The Moon is even conceived as predatory: it controls organic life, 'sucking out its vitality', and 'man':

> '...cannot, in the ordinary conditions of life, tear himself free from the moon. All his movements and consequently all his actions are controlled by the moon. If he kills another man, the moon does it; if he sacrifices himself for others, the moon does that also.' [Consequently], 'the liberation which comes with the growth of mental powers and faculties is liberation from the moon.' The 'mechanical part of our life' [where we are not consciously aware of what we do] 'is subject to the Moon. If we develop in ourselves consciousness and will, and subject our mechanical life and all our mechanical manifestations to them, we shall escape from the power of the moon.'[140]

Gurdjieff's sources were ever mysterious and never to be sought impiously, but his image of the Moon does recall the ancient Indian conception of the dead as 'food' for the gods, though without the complementary ideas of love and regeneration for the souls. Here it appears to be the Moon who is regenerated for the sake of the whole of the Ray of Creation. It is as though modern theories of laws of gravity have been drawn irresistibly into the old mythic framework, suggesting that the forms of ancient myth persist as symbols, not only in dreams and visions, but in contexts and ideas when we would have thought them dead and gone.

One such symbol is the three nights' dark of the Moon.

Fig. 22. Le Voyage dans la Lune. Original set drawing by Georges Méliès, 1902. British Film Institute.

CHAPTER 14

THE NEW MOON: REBIRTH

'Luna per omnes menses nascitur, crescit, perficitur, minuitur, consumitur, innovatur.
Quod in luna per menses, hoc in resurrectione semel in toto tempore.'
('The Moon is born every month, increases, is perfected, diminishes, is consumed,
is renewed. As in the Moon every month, so in resurrection once for all time.').
St. Augustine *Sermo CCCLXI: De Resurrectione*

'Jesus said unto her: "I am the resurrection, and the life: he that believeth in me,
though he were dead, yet shall he live."'
John 11:25

**Jesus's death, descent to hell and resurrection were conceived, in the imagery of the time, under
the figure of the setting Sun and its journey through Hades.** Jesus died on the fourteenth of the
month of Nisan, which fell on a Friday (the day of Venus), lay in his grave on Saturday (the day of
Saturn) and was resurrected on the 'first day of the week,' which was Sunday (the day of Helios) as
the risen Sun.[1] The significance of his rising on the third day entered the Apostles' Creed, articulating
the main tenets of Christian belief: '... Was crucified, dead, and buried, He descended into hell; The
third day he rose again from the dead, He ascended into heaven, And sitteth on the right hand of
God the Father Almighty; From thence he shall come to judge the quick and the dead...'[2]

Yet the older figure of the risen Moon lurks, as so often, beneath the later portrait of the risen
Sun. At the deeper level of the imagery, it is as though the ancient lunar imagery clothes the story
of the Resurrection. For 'born of the Virgin Mary' as the New Crescent, Jesus dies at the summit
of his powers at Full Moon, the fourteenth day of the month after which the Moon will wane. In
the figure of the dark Moon, Jesus descends to the underworld and rises on the third day, becoming
the New Moon of the eternal cycle. Krappe observes that all divine heroes rise on the third day
after their death, having their prototype and origin in the disappearance and reappearance of the
Moon:

> *Quoi qu'il en soit, le mythe de la résurrection du héros divin, le troisième jour après sa mort,*
> *mythe bien connu par la légende d'Attis et par l'Evangile, a son prototype et son origine dans*
> *la disparition et la réapparition de la lune.*[3]

The three days descent into the dark entered Christian symbolism originally through the analogy
made between the resurrection of Jonah and Christ. In Judaic tradition, Jonah, fleeing the presence
of his Lord, was cast into the sea in a storm, but:

> The Lord had prepared a great fish to swallow up Jonah. And Jonah was in the belly of
> the whale three days and three nights.[4]

Fig. 1. Earth in Space, as seen by Apollo 17 crew travelling towards the Moon, December 7th, 1972. NASA.

St. Matthew's Gospel, written at least a generation after Christ's death, gives Jesus drawing the analogy himself:

> For as Jonah was three days and three nights in the whale's belly; so shall the Son of Man be three days and three nights in the heart of the earth.[5]

The makers of this 15th century German Bible (fig. 2) obviously wished to emphasize the affinities between Jonah falling into the mouth of the whale, Joseph being cast into the pit and Jesus being laid in his tomb. In fig 3, Samson substitutes for Joseph, Jonah is regurgitated, while Christ is reborn.

Since the Moon could disappear for two or three nights, Jesus's nights of death become, strictly, two nights, rising on the third day. As the lunar gods had illuminated the dead in the underworld,

Fig. 2. Joseph in the Well; the Entombment of Christ; Jonah and the Whale. A page from the Biblia Pauperum, German edition, 1471.

Fig. 3. Samson with the gates of the temple, Jonah coming out of the whale, and Christ arising from his tomb. A page from the Biblia Pauperum, German edition, 1471.

sometimes slaying the monster of darkness, so Jesus is often shown releasing souls from death by spearing the monster of hell, imagined as a whale. Reading the image without the text, Jesus is here cast in the role of the Bright Moon slaying the dragon of the Dark Moon, bringing rebirth.

With this model, it is predictable that Saul's conversion on the Road to Damascus results in three days of blindness and fasting.[6] Similarly, Dante passes through the gates of Hell on Good Friday and reaches Paradise on Easter Sunday (taking, as Christ, three days but only two nights).[7]

The Christian tradition, then, has drawn on a universal symbol of death and rebirth, found all over the world, informing folk-tales and religions alike. Let us review some of its appearances.

* * *

It was for three days and three nights that the Sumerian Moon goddess, Inanna, hung dead as a corpse upon a hook in the Great Below until, revived by the water and food of life, she ascended back into the Great Above.[8] It was for three nights that the Left Eye of Horus was torn into pieces and thrown into outer darkness, when Thoth reassembled it, piecing it together until it was whole.[9] Tjapara, the Oceanic Moon god, who was slain in a death-fight by the man whose wife he had taken, appeared in the sky three nights later, while the mortal drowned in the sea.[10] When the West Ceramese maiden, Rabie, died from her rape by the Sun Man, Tuwale, her family celebrated the death feast for three days, after which they saw for the first time the Moon rising in the east.[11] In Vedic India, the souls who died into the old Moon were reincarnated three nights later in the returning crescent, falling into the wombs of their new mothers as Soma-rain.[12] In ancient Iran, the soul hovered perilously round the body for three days (as though in danger of dying itself), while families conducted ceremonies to help the deceased begin the journey to paradise.[13] The Siberian Yakuts say that 'the future shaman "dies" and lies in the tent for three days without eating or drinking.' Three times the candidate had to undergo this trial, during which he is 'cut to pieces,' as though in imitation of the Moon.[14] The Irish hero, Cuchulainn, fought without stopping from summer to spring in defence of Ulster, then collapsed and slept for three days and three nights while his father from the Other World kept watch over him. He awoke to find his wounds miraculously healed.[15] When the Buddha was dying, the animals of the Earth crowded round him, weeping bitterly. 'Do not weep,' he said to them. 'Look at the moon! As

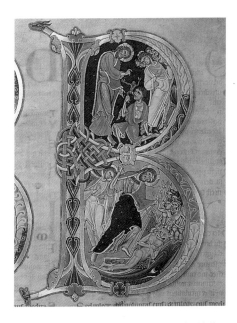

Fig. 4. Christ releasing souls from the mouth of hell, imagined as a whale. Winchester Bible. 12th century. Winchester Cathedral.

Fig. 5. Jason disgorged by the dragon, with the golden fleece hanging on the tree of Life behind. The presence of Athene suggests a lunar pattern to the ritual of release. Attic red-figure vase by the Duris painter. 5th c. BC. Gregoriano Etrusco, Vatican Museum, Rome.

the moon dying renews herself again, so shall I dying be renewed again.'[16] Rituals of mourning for Adonis, lover of Aphrodite, gored to death by the boar, took place over three days: effigies of the god, cast into the waves to the sound of wailing, were rescued three days later with singing and dancing, for had not the god arisen to live again?[17]

THE LUNAR MYTH OF TRANSFORMATION

We may ask, what is going on here? There must be an archetypal model at work which informs all these different stories for some reason beyond that which is given in the stories themselves. The symbol (of death and rebirth) grapples with a contradiction, for at the level of ordinary experience death and life are exclusively opposed to each other - such that where the one is, the other is not. Yet here, at the deepest level, there appears to be a merging into a single reality, as a result of which what *was* death *becomes* life. So - the inference goes - there must be a state from which both life *and* death come. Life and death are the parameters of time as we understand it, so this state must be beyond time, even that from which time also comes, which is to say - to give it a name - eternity. Consequently, the visible Moon - the Moon of the senses - has to make this journey from the temporal to the eternal, to participate in the 'stuff of eternity,' to enter into the sacred realm and become one with the eternal. When 'the eternal' gives birth to the new form of the Moon which is called the New Moon, it imitates the original act of creation in which form came forth from formlessness and light came forth from darkness. For the point about the Moon's death was that it was a return to the original wholeness of the beginning. The old had to die completely, the old structures, the old powers, all had to go before anything new could come. If they did not go willingly, of their own accord, they had to be sacrificed. They had to be absorbed in the primordial unity of eternity out of which all temporal forms arise.

Fig. 6. 'The New Moon...' J.M.W. Turner. Oil on mahogany. 1840. The Tate Gallery, London.

The Moon, then, undergoes a rite of passage from the profane (time, which has worn out) to the sacred (the eternal), which regenerates time, and by implication, the world which cannot be conceived apart from time - making time sacred time and the world a 'brave new world.' This is how it seems to be that the New Moon holds the promise of recreation in the image of the Beginning, *in illo tempore*, which is also, of course, 'the beginning' for the human mind, bound by 'the same' categories of space and time. Nonetheless, those heroes, saviours, shamans - indeed, anyone who endures even for a moment the heroic, shamanic role in their own lives - also follow this rite of passage from profane to sacred to a transformed life in time, in imitation of the way shown by the Moon.

This idea, of the merging of time into eternity, or perhaps the impregnating of time by eternity, can be seen in stories of every plane of being. There appears to be a consistent structure to tales of transformation. The first phase is the dissolution of all forms. On the cosmic plane, order has to collapse into chaos (as in flood, deluge, millennium, apocalypse, or the 'end of the world'); on the tribal plane, the living priests have to be emptied of the present to be filled with the Dream of the Ancestors; on the social plane, norms of conduct have to be suspended or reversed (as in the New Year orgies of the Saturnalia, Twelfth Night, New Year's Eve, and Carnival at the end of the seasonal year); on the individual plane, the conscious self has to lose itself in order to be open to the unconscious; on the vegetal plane, the fruit has to disintegrate in the dense, dark soil (Kore, Persephone, Dionysos), before the seed can be shed, and the life-force return. Festivals of mourning in autumn and rejoicing in spring were intended to assist the life-force in its metamorphosis. This descent into darkness may be conducted through shamanic initiation ceremonies, or the communal rituals of the Ancient Mysteries, or the rite of Baptism (dissolving the forms in water), or through participation in the Mass or Holy Communion, or through the suspension of the individual in ritual prayer, among many other religious forms. Or it may be undertaken in the modern way, mostly without communal guidance, often in the isolation of a private despair.

Many New Year ceremonies used to be timed to the last moonless night before the reappearance of the New Moon. In California, some North American Indian tribes believed that this cosmic timing connected them to the immortal beings who inhabited the world before people did, so that the present tribesmen can re-enact through contemporary ritual the original cosmogonic ceremony inaugurated in the 'Dream-time' by their ancestors. They call it 'putting posts under the world.'[18] Time is again symbolically regenerated by repeating the original act of creation, an aspiration found in the conclusion of many another prayer: 'As it was in the beginning, is now and ever shall be, world without end, amen.'

Another Californian tale centres on the dark time of three days, or three years. A Chumash wizard called Axiwalic fell sick with consumption and left his village to find a place to die. He followed a strange light which led him to some animals who bathed him back to health and sent him home to his village through a spring (baptism through water). When he returned he was amazed to find that he had been gone for three years as he thought it had only been three days.[19] Joan Halifax, in her book *Shaman*, comments of this tale: 'Three days dead, three years dead, like the dark of the moon, is the pause between the personal past and a realized transtemporal life.'[20] The personal and temporal, it is implied, merges in this sacred interval with the impersonal and transtemporal or eternal, and it is this merging that brings about that change of state at a new level which we call regeneration.

But the term 'eternal' is still only an idea, an explanatory hypothesis, as opaque as the condition to which it points, and as unanswerable as any primordial image which will not go away. When a narrative is given to this idea, it is typically represented as a state beyond all opposites, beyond the inevitable dualism of life in time. In ordinary consciousness, differentiation presents us with polarities: life *or* death, time *or* eternity, male *or* female, I *or* thou, Thou *or* That.

It would make sense, then, that, in the imagined dark of the Beginning - before the categories to be called time and space had come into being, and so before consciousness could know itself - there would be a union of realities otherwise experienced in ordinary life as distinct or mutually exclusive. A return to this state would be a return to the state before duality. This means that, to speak in the different language games: mythologically, there would be a union, or reunion, of the human and the divine; psychologically, a reunion of conscious and unconscious; epistemologically, a reunion of reason and intuition as modes of knowing. A male hero would become one with his inner feminine nature and a female hero with her inner masculine nature. Masculine questing consciousness would reunite with the ground of its being, the Feminine. In celestial symbolism this is the Sacred Marriage of Sun and Moon, or Heaven and Earth; in Alchemy this is the *Coniunctio* of Sol and Luna. This Sacred Marriage of hitherto separate, even opposing, realities, it has to be inferred, is what brings about the rebirth at a new level of synthesis, the 'child' of the marriage, the transformed being.

* * *

The Moon's cyclical death and rebirth, which used to be interpreted as promising rebirth after death for human beings, may now be read symbolically, as proposing a structure of transformation in which the individual dies to the old self and is reborn into a new mode of being. It could immediately be objected that, since the premises on which the early inferences were founded are manifestly illusory, there are no grounds for attributing any sense to them at all, symbolically or otherwise. It may also seem ironic that many of the world's religions have drawn on the symbolism of the Moon to explore their insights into the relation of temporal life to eternity, when the symbolism appears to arise merely from the limitations of the human mind. But earlier beliefs, once no longer believed in, can mirror back to us the primordial impulses that were originally behind them, the genuine need of the psyche within the old, literalized, even false, interpretation of the world. Such beliefs lead back to the archetype, rendering it transparent in a way that would be difficult, even impossible, so long as the image through which the archetype is expressed still captures our imagination as objectively true.

What the Moon stories suggest is that the unconscious psyche yearns for transformation. As it is so it sees. Reading the Moon, as the ancients did, as a living being who grows, dies and is reborn, suggests, when mirrored back, that this is how the unconscious psyche sees itself, that ultimately it is interpreting its own reality in this outer pattern. This is to say that, at the deepest level, we could infer that modes of feeling, thinking and being experience themselves as perpetually in movement, growing and diminishing and reforming to a rhythm of their own. Arising from invisible depths, they take on a shape and a character, growing to their most complete manifestation, after which, their purpose done, they start to dwindle, their conviction fades, and (if we would let them) they dissolve back into a deeper stratum of the psyche where they can be re-absorbed, refreshed, and reborn in new form, one more in accord with what has been learned through this latest expression of themselves.

But the temptation of the conscious mind is characteristically to hang on to the old form, to prevent it moving and changing of its own accord (that is, in accord with the laws of the unconscious). Since these laws are not formulated by, and often initially unavailable to the conscious mind, they are vulnerable to being dismissed as arbitrary. For the conscious mind prefers to identify itself with what it knows, with what worked so far, with who it thinks it is or would like to be. The danger, then, may be to arrest the flow of experience, turning it into an idea, confining it to 'culture' and forgetting it is 'nature,' and so must live and die by changing its form. The Moon, Yeats remarks, 'is the most changeable of symbols, and not just because it is the symbol of change.'[21] It is as though the old self, like the old Moon, must die before a new self can re-emerge out of the darkness of its own being, like a New Moon. And not just once, but continually. Goethe's poem: 'Holy Longing' ends:

> So unless you understand this: To die and so to grow,
> you are but a troubled guest on the dark earth.[22]

In *St. John's Gospel*, Jesus, talking of rebirth, appears to be talking of transformation rather than immortality (reading the 'Kingdom of God' psychologically):

> 'Verily, verily, I say unto thee, Except a man be born again, he cannot see the kingdom of God.' Nicodemus saith unto him, 'How can a man be born when he is old? can he enter the second time into his mother's womb, and be born?' Jesus answered, 'Verily, verily, I say unto thee, Except a man be born of water and of the Spirit, he cannot enter into the kingdom of God.'[23]

In the Gnostic *Gospel According to Thomas*, the 'Kingdom of God' is explicitly given as a state of mind:

> His disciples said to him: 'When will the Kingdom come?' Jesus said: 'It will not come by expectation; they will not say: "See, here", or: "See, there". But the Kingdom of the Father is spread upon the earth and men do not see it'.[24]

Paul expresses a similar idea when he says: 'It is no longer I who live but Christ who lives in me.'[25]

Jung, in his *Mysterium Coniunctionis*, explains the alchemical symbolism of the *Coniunctio* in terms of lunar symbolism, making the point that the *Coniunctio* takes place not in the Full but in the darkest night of the New Moon, and it is here that Sun and Moon unite.[26] Von Franz adds: 'the *coniunctio* happens in the underworld...in the deepest depression, in the deepest desolation, the new personality is born.'[27] What St. John of the Cross called the 'dark night of the soul'[28] is, then, a *necessary* stage in the transforming of the personality, not simply an irreparable loss of 'the soul's light' - as it may well feel without the mythic image as guide. T. S. Eliot explores this loss in the *Four Quartets* by showing why everything has to go, even the things that are good:

> I said to my soul, be still, and wait without hope
> For hope would be hope for the wrong thing; wait without love
> For love would be love of the wrong thing; there is yet faith
> But the faith and the love and the hope are all in the waiting.
> Wait without thought, for you are not ready for thought:
> So the darkness shall be the light, and the stillness the dancing.[29]

Similarly, as we have seen, in the Egyptian, Greek and Christian Mysteries, the participants were invited, even compelled, to lose their identification with their mortal frame - which, as *bios*, lives and dies - and find it in their eternal source - *zoe*. What was lost, or sacrificed, was biography, the personal ego, the temporal self, and what was found was that which is beyond the individual at that or any moment in time. As in all true art, perhaps, the people, rapt away from their habitual selves, become - for as long as the rite lasts - gods themselves, participants in 'eternity', entirely convinced by values which transcend the vicissitudes of time. Only when the epiphany is accomplished and the rite is complete, do the priests and the people return to the persons they were before, but, strictly, are no longer, for now they are changed, filled with *zoe*, renewed. The fact that the people went back to the Mysteries in Egypt and Greece year after year (and that the Mysteries themselves lasted for thousands of years) suggests that the inevitable falling back into life in time needs a periodical dissolution into the timeless if the memory of the source is not to fade. Otherwise, the experience may become theoretical, an idea only, the inevitable consequence of knowledge divorced from being. One of the secrets of the Mysteries never to be told (because only to be grasped through an altered state of consciousness) was that, while the slayers or betrayers (Seth, Hades, Judas) are, on the stage, the enemies of those they sacrifice, behind the scenes - where there is no polarity of contraries - slayer and slain are of one mind: sacrificer and victim, hero and dragon, are one and the same. Hence Seth and

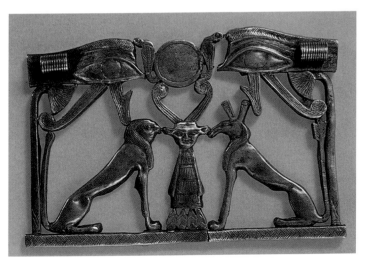

Fig. 7. Horus and Seth flanking the head of Hathor, with Eyes of Sun and Moon above. Gold Pectoral. 12th Dynasty. c. 2050-1750BC. Eton College Library, Meyer's Collection.

Horus face each other as equals, Persephone 'marries' Hades, Jesus 'loves' his enemy and kisses him. Only in ego-consciousness is there separation from one another (fig. 7).

The participants at the Mysteries had to abandon themselves to what would happen, and what happened was a change of vision. For these lunar mysteries do not seem to have been primarily narrative reassurances of a rebirth analogous to the Moon's rebirth: they were essentially possibilities of transformation, which had radical implications for how life was to be lived in the present. 'Osiris is useful here on earth as well as for those who have died,' one Egyptian inscribed on his grave stele.[30]

It is only the experience of the numinous, Jung wrote, which brings about a transformation in a person.[31] Inevitably, what is called *zoe* or the 'eternal self' is indescribable, except in metaphor or analogy, and any attempt to translate it into the language of time results in banality or paradox at best: 'Show me your original face,' the Zen Master demands.[32] Yeats's girl, musing in mirror after mirror, answers an imaginary lover's question: 'I'm looking for the face I had / Before the world was made.'[33] The Egyptians imagined a bennu bird, whom they called *ka*, after the sound the heron makes when it flies away. After the deceased had united with their personal *ba*-soul, in the shape of a bird with their own face, they met their cosmic soul, their *Ka*, the 'Mother of Transformations' (fig. 8).[34] Egyptian Christians transferred the *Ka* to the Holy Spirit, and other Christians conceived of angels – messengers, as the Greek word *angellos* meant, from the divine realm. The Romans had their *genius*, and Blake, for whom 'the Eternal Body of Man is the Imagination,' attributes to all humankind their own 'Poetic Genius.'[35] Throughout the ages the eternal dimension, assigned to humanity by human beings, has also been simply called the soul.

* * *

More generally, a survey of Moon myths suggests that the image of eternity has to be carried by someone or something external to human beings, to enable us to forge a relationship to our own eternal selves. The 'eternal' may be called the Great Mother Goddess, Mother Earth, Moon God or Goddess, Sun God or Goddess, Father God, God, Goddess, Tao, All That Is, or the Good, the True

Fig. 8. The meeting of the person with his Ka in the image of the bennu bird, wearing the crown of Osiris. Tomb of Anhurkhawl, Deir el-Medina, Thebes. c. 1190-1085.

and the Beautiful; it may be mediated through beings who have lived on Earth, such as the Buddha, Christ or Muhammad; or it may be metaphorically located in the human psyche as 'the Self' or 'the Centre' or 'the Soul.' It may also be described as 'the archetype of wholeness'. It may be expressed through values which are considered to belong to human beings by virtue of their humanity, and through which that humanity is defined. Inevitably, there have been numerous expressions of 'the eternal,' just as the idea of 'eternity' has been given many different meanings, but whatever the name the function is similar: the attribution of the highest value, to which all other values are subordinate. This supreme value is invariably conceived as transcendent to time and inviolable, which is to say, sacred (the terms 'eternal' and 'sacred' belong together). Eliade has shown, in *A History of Religious Ideas*, that an experience of a sacred dimension to life occurs in all cultures in every age, early or late. This suggests that 'the sacred' is not a stage in the development of consciousness which human beings outgrow as they become more complex: it is an inherent part of the *structure* of consciousness, possibly the essential part.[36] So when one image of the sacred loses its numinous power, the role of carrier of the sacred is transferred to another image. Someone or something has to carry it: if not a worthy carrier then - as various collective seizures of the race have shown - an unworthy one.

For this reason, it may be that the attempt to understand the source and current of ancient longing is as necessary on a mythic level as the attempt to understand our own outmoded thoughts and actions on a personal level, becoming aware of the deeper impulses that have fuelled them. Otherwise, the danger is that these ancient beliefs (like our earlier now-discarded attachments) will have outworn only their last provisional form. If their springs are not recognized, they will simply reappear in a new, no less opaque, disguise, and the unconscious identification will begin again, with not much more understanding than before. Jung describes the religious feelings that were once 'projected into space as gods, and worshipped with sacrifices' as 'powers' which are 'still alive and active in our unconscious psyche.'[37] They still, therefore, require honouring in some way if they are not to alight anew upon some cause, person, mission, idol or god, anything (to turn to Conrad) which 'you can set up, and bow down before, and offer a sacrifice to...'[38]

* * *

When the Father God took over the role of the sacred from the Mother Goddess, eternity or the sacred was redefined, as it was when (in a parallel way) the Sun took over the role from the Moon and Earth. It seems regrettable that, for these earlier transferences of the sacred to be effective, the previous carrier of the sacred has so far had to be redefined as, at best, inferior and, at worst, destructive to the new order; but so long as this process of transferring the sacred from one image to another takes place unconsciously, it is probably inevitable. Just as, broadly, when the Father God became supreme, the Mother Goddess who had given birth to all life was redefined as chaotic or inanimate (before she became invisible), so, with the rise of the Sun, the Moon, once the hope of rebirth, now promised death. Then Moon, and Earth below Moon (looking down from Highest Heaven), had to carry the pejorative image of time as dissolution and decay - *sublunary* - in contrast to the eternal and immutable Sun who was now the one beyond death. When the Judaic Transcendent God, who was beyond any graven image, turned the role of the Father God into Pure Spirit, eternity was again redefined as beyond anything that could be seen or heard or given a name. The phenomenal and temporal world became 'fallen' - Sun as well as Moon and Earth - so that all of what we now call Nature was desacralized (a loss that remains to this day). The Christian Church, inheriting this tradition, spoke disparagingly of 'this world' in contrast to 'the next,' which was the real world of divine union after death. (Aristotle's adaptation into Medieval Christian thought through Thomas Aquinas meant that the Sun was metaphorically rescued from the curse of the phenomenal world, persisting as a symbol of Christ). The question that arises now, given the general waning of faith in the Christian story as divine revelation, is where will the image of eternity fall next?

We can see from this (extremely over-simplified) pattern that the whole interpretation of our world's structure and value derives from where eternity is located. For it is only 'eternity' - in whatever form it is given - which can be imagined to redeem time and transform death into rebirth. Wherever the sacred is not located, on the other hand, becomes profane.

It now seems clear that all the Moon's ancient powers were derived from its *eternal* being, its capacity for rebirth. The 'water of life' came from the ambrosial cup of the nectar of immortality, which was, of course, the crescent of the reborn Moon. The fertilizing powers over conception and birth came from its ability to give birth to itself, as did its sway over the waxing and waning of plant life, where, most evocatively, new life appears to be born from the death of the old. Its rulership of fate as well as time came from the investing of the Moon's phases with qualities of time, for who better to deliver destiny than the one who can suspend the inexorable laws of its conclusion? Of course, these are sovereignties found in all goddesses and gods in whatever celestial body they are made visible, whatever mound of Earth or height of Heaven. Nonetheless, as beliefs in which few people now believe, they may be viewed with sufficient detachment to be able to mirror the intensity of the unconscious need, however this may appear to the sceptical conscious mind.

MYTH AS SYMBOL AND METAPHOR

Understand that you are another little world, and have within you the sun, the moon, and also the stars.[39]

Thus, somewhat surprisingly, the Early Christian Father, Origen, in the 3rd century AD, anticipating by many centuries Zimmer's analysis of the contemporary state of myth:

All the images and intimations of his depths that man, from the Stone Age almost to the present time, projected upon the shimmering screen of the universe, have flowed back into man himself.[40]

Whether myths are to be called the poetic images of the race, or the collective dreams of the human psyche, or the stories of the tribe, and whether they are to be attributed to the Great Memory, the *Anima Mundi*, the Collective Unconscious, the Imaginal World, or the Soul of Humanity, they may offer us an albeit partial and fleeting glimpse of what it is to be human. For myths can show us how we think, but only if we both engage with them *and* 'see through' them at the same time – the 'double vision' Blake proposed as the way to relate to both art and life.[41] Treat them dismissively, and they are gone; take them literally, and they are in the way. It could be said that the task of mythology is not complete until the myths have become transparent to their source in the human imagination. So goddesses and gods, demons, dragons and the whole pantheon of supernatural beings are in this sense metaphors of states of mind, images of potentialities realizable within us; they are figures of passion which give energy and form to our deepest longings and fears, telling their story, turning them into narratives which test and explore ideas. To try it again, myths are at the least a way of exploring a universal sense of wonder, and apprehending and thinking through the mystery of the numinous (a term which means literally the wink of a god, and, more generally, the coming alive of divine presence). Myths may be read as symbols, whose meaning cannot be known through intellect alone, yet whose multiple meanings unfold the more diligently they are pursued - something that could also be said of dreams, thrown up from the same supra-personal or transpersonal source. For dream, as Campbell has eloquently said, 'is the personalized myth, myth the depersonalized dream.'[42] In their widest reference, myths represent, through analogy, the timeless adventure of the soul.

So it is ultimately an inner drama that is driving those perennial myths which survive through epochs and cultures, not offering solutions - being, generally, insoluble - but requiring ever more baffling complexities of response, ever more depth. 'Primitive man,' (that impossibly unfair but indispensable category), as Jung briskly says: 'simply didn't know that the psyche contains all the images that have ever given rise to myths, and that our unconscious is an acting and suffering subject with an inner drama which primitive man rediscovers, by means of analogy, in the processes of nature both great and small.'[43] But *we* do. Consequently, we can find in the ancient myths a poetic formulation of psychological truths, freed from dogma and schools and doctrines, answerable only to the judgement of an informed heart.

Our age is unique in having the opportunity to understand the essential unity of the human race in its never-ending attempts to understand itself. In the late 18th century, the Sanskrit texts of the Vedas and the Upanishads were translated into English, revealing a common Indo-European linguistic root, which proposed the idea of a common Indo-European family. Then, in 1821, the Egyptian hieroglyphics on the Rosetta Stone were decoded, disclosing a totally unsuspected sophistication of thought some two thousand years older than the Bible. This was followed, in 1850, by Layard's excavations of Babylon which opened up Mesopotamia, and by 1875 Schliemann had uncovered Troy and Mycenae, and inspired Arthur Evans to search for their origins in the island of Crete, which he finally found in the 1920s. At the turn of the 20th century the great Paleolithic caves were discovered, culminating in the find of the cave of Lascaux in 1940, preserved in all its brilliance from 15,000 BC. Mycenaean writing was deciphered in 1954, unlocking the pre-Homeric origins of classical Greece, and in the 1950s and 1960s, the missing Neolithic strata of civilization were put in place by Marija Gimbutas, unearthing what she called Old Europe, while James Mellaart, working in Turkey, once Anatolia, laid bare a place called Catal Huyuk, inhabited since the seventh millennium BC. Then, in 1969, the first image of Earth as a whole planet in space came from the Moon.

All these discoveries have undermined the former assumptions of linear development, in which earlier meant more primitive - 'the dark, backward and abysm of time'[44] - and promoted a spirit of more open-minded assessment as to what composes a cultural life. By comparing the mythic images of these vastly diverse cultures, it becomes undeniable that there are motifs common to all of them - images, rituals and stories, echoing each other as though in dialogue, agreeing or disagreeing on particulars, but always, at the deepest level, as though working on a shared task. Images of the Moon may serve as an example of this. For though the specific ideas focussing on the Moon belong to the local folk in their local landscape, their similarity to those of other groups apparently unknown to them, in many other tribes, times and places, discloses a universal reference. Not surprisingly, it seems, when people are thinking as human beings, not merely as members of a social group, they think in a way that other human beings can recognize, whenever and wherever they live. And thinking as a human being, in this sense, means considering humanity in relation to the universe as a whole.

Perhaps it is just because the reference of thought goes beyond the tribal and self-interested that mythic images in their *universal* dimension have been so often linked with the unanimous tradition of the 'Perennial Philosophy' - the exploration and transmission of primordial truths throughout history, whichever culture and age originally housed them.[45] Coomaraswamy, for instance, writing of the 'Philosophia Perennis, of which the specifically Indian form is Vedic,' calls it 'the heritage and birthright of all mankind, and not merely of this or that chosen people.'[46] It is by no means confined to aspects of the world's great myths and religions; its signature can be found in folklore and fairy tales, legend, custom and rite alike - wherever an underground stream of human wisdom continues to flow.

Can we, then, read back from these ancient myths anything relevant to addressing the questions of our own time, not in terms of what the gods do or don't do, but in terms of what the psyche needs for its growing; or, to speak in the grander Greek meaning of *psyche*, what the *soul* requires? For when myths have lost their ancient power they disengage from the outer world, withdrawing back into the human psyche which once propelled them outwards to contemplate them. And once the soul finds no echo of itself in collective religion, or once the unconscious psyche loses its 'objective correlative,' to expand Eliot's phrase,[47] then the individual has to take the heroic journey within to find new forms, which is to say, new metaphors of reality. As Wallace Stevens writes:

> It is as if there were three planets: the sun,
> The moon and the imagination, or, say,
> Day, night and man and his endless effigies...[48]

NEW MOON

We may ask, then, metaphorically, what is the New Moon of our time? It has to be said that people of all ages have felt themselves to be on the brink of a new world order, and many a personal longing for renewal gains in credibility when represented on the social or cosmic plane. Nonetheless, it is highly probable that so many such intimations of crisis constitute a genuine recognition that collective modes of consciousness are in transition. Furthermore, the fact that many people are speaking of a paradigm shift may be itself the expression of a paradigm shifting, for the mind that reasons and communicates is typically the last aspect of the psyche to know about a change that has already taken place in the deepest springs of its being. Campbell has articulated this perception in the metaphor of death and rebirth:

> The old gods are dead or dying and people everywhere are searching, asking: What is the new mythology to be, the mythology of this unified earth as of one harmonious being?[49]

The astronomer Fred Hoyle declared that 'Once a photograph of the Earth, taken from the outside, is available - once the sheer isolation of the Earth becomes plain - a new idea as powerful as any in history will be let loose.'[50] Ironically, it was the Moon, for millennia a symbol of transformation, which made this new idea possible, providing the standpoint needed to transform our vision - the view of planet Earth as a whole. And from the moment when the Earth could be seen from the Moon - looking like the Moon has always looked from Earth - a new relation to Earth became inevitable. The event, and primarily its image, was greeted throughout the world with the same wonder that abounds in early mythopoetic thought, as though the human imagination had once again awakened.[51] For the first time we were able to contemplate our own home, not forever looking out at somewhere else and far away. At the deepest level, this is an image of consciousness reflecting upon itself, giving form to the idea that human consciousness is Earth's way of knowing itself.

As in early mythopoetic thought, this image allows the Earth to become again both numinous *and* personal, with the radical difference that this Earth is no longer the local piece of territorial earth as in former days but the unified Earth in which everyone shares and for which everyone is, therefore, responsible. Again for the first time, we can experience Earth as a planet revolving in space, putting what we see into accord with what we know, and bringing two hitherto diverging aspects of the psyche into harmony with each other. For though we have known about the heliocentric universe since Copernicus in 1543, most of us still see sunrise and sunset as though our Earth were still the still point of the turning world. But it is possible that, with the vision of our planet floating in the vast, black backdrop of space, its physical boundaries so irrevocably etched against a void, we may finally be persuaded there is nowhere else to go. Here the Moon assumes the role of Wallace Stevens's 'Angel of Reality,' who shows old things anew:

> Yet I am the necessary angel of earth,
> Since, in my sight, you see the earth again,
>
> Cleared of its stiff and stubborn, man-locked set...[52]

Standing imaginatively upon the Moon looking back at Earth, what do we see 'in its sight'? Do we see what Plato saw - a living being, *zoon*, composed of other living beings, bound together in mutual and intimate relationship, all dependent upon one another for survival and value? If we do, we see, then, a community of subjects, not a collection of inanimate objects with only the human mind to bring them to life. From this perspective, the dignity of being a 'subject' is not restricted to humanity but extends to all manifestations of life on the living Earth - animal, vegetable and mineral: in a word, albeit much abused, Nature. Nature becomes then, again, a 'Thou' but a Thou with all the complexity of any personal relationship, which includes the rights and responsibilities common to all communing subjects.

This recalls Barfield's third stage in his pattern of the evolution of consciousness. As mentioned in ch. 6, Barfield called the first stage 'Original (unconscious) Participation,' the second, 'Separation,' and the third 'Final (conscious) Participation.' The first phase could be characterized as an instinctive union with the world, and generally subsumed under the culture of the Goddess; the second involves a radical withdrawal of participation from the world, which is then set in opposition to humanity so that it might be the better understood and controlled. This stage is reflected in the presiding image of the God. The third stage, 'Final Participation,' is defined as a return to the old participative relation to nature, not in the old, original way - which in any case is impossible, consciousness inevitably moving on - but at a new *level*, through 'the Imagination.'[53] This involves, he explains, a dual relation to Nature, which acknowledges our experience of Nature as separate from us, but creates a new poetic union by participating with the natural world, consciously and imaginatively. This brings about a new kind of relationship with Nature, recognizing our essential identity while exploring the specific human role of consciousness within it.

In both of Barfield's two earlier stages, the mythic image is held for the most part unconsciously, in the sense that it is believed in as though it had nothing to do with the human psyche. It is not thought of as a story flowing from human beings, but as the truth about a Goddess or a God - what they said and did. In the third, the present stage, Barfield proposes that we could become aware of our myths by seeing them imaginatively, as stories both provisional and necessary, and that this same imaginative sympathy could return us to participating in a unified Earth in a new mode of being. Barfield's way of restoring poetry to our vision resembles Thomas Mann's way of restoring myth as a 'late and mature' stage in the individual's life, which comes out of the early youthful engagement with myth but renders it conscious, and so can live it and not be lived by it.[54]

Viewing the mythic images of the Moon in the light of different kinds of participation, it would seem that stories of the Moon carry an early stage of exploration of questions about life on Earth. These stories, it could be argued, constitute a necessary stage in the asking of these questions, even though, from a later perspective, some stories are not true and appear to be nonsense, and other stories no longer entrance and so can no longer be told. But it may be possible to save the essence, while abandoning the form in which the essence was originally expressed. In other words, the vision of a unified world, which the lunar myth embodied, is not necessarily disproved because of the simplistic way in which it was once understood; it may rather be that consciousness explored it – perhaps inevitably – at too literal a level. For mythic images do not die out, they merely change their form, and we continue to dream them onwards in new clothes under other names.[55] In the long journey from original to final participation, we might expect that images of a unified world become real at a different level of understanding, so that what was once belief becomes metaphor. The image of the universe as an unbroken wholeness - as composed of a web of relationships, containing an ocean of energy, having an implicate as well as explicate order, being a continual process of movement with no absolute point of rest - these are images from modern sub-atomic physics. Whereas in the myth of the Goddess, of which the myth of the Moon was one expression, these images were believed to be true because all life was of the substance of the Goddess, she who was worshipped under a thousand names. However, the language of the new science might remind us that all the great mystic teachers have had a holistic vision, embodied in a passion for right living: the notion of Buddha consciousness in all things, the Hindu vision of *Thou art That*, and the words of Jesus in the Gnostic *Gospel According to Thomas*:

> Cleave (a piece of) wood, I am there;
> lift up the stone and you will find Me there.[56]

The focus of Barfield's discussion is the evolution of consciousness and how to reunite ourselves with the natural world without forsaking the supreme achievements of the last 2000 years: the persistent differentiation of the human intellect, the hard-won autonomy of human will and reason, wrested from the grip and spell of various religions, the painful creation of interiority and the subjective self, and the forging of the individual in counterpole to the collective norms of the tribe. It was both a condition and a consequence of these discoveries that the objective world would lose its numinosity, and that disenchantment with 'nature' would bring arrogance and alienation, together with a yearning to return to the original ground of being. What, then, can take us forward? Barfield's answer is imaginative participation, but what if the very attribute we need to rescue us has become atrophied over the millennia of its disuse? What, to return to the earlier question, if the last two thousand years of 'mythological conditioning' prevent us from being open to the way out?

Jung uses the phrase 'the inertia of the unconscious' to point to the way in which we may adopt a new position intellectually, but overlook the deeper levels in the psyche which resist change:

> We think we have only to declare an accepted article of faith incorrect and invalid, and we shall be psychologically rid of all the traditional effects of Christianity and Judaism. We believe in enlightenment, as if an intellectual change of front somehow had a profounder influence on the emotional processes or even on the unconscious. We entirely forget that the religion of the past two thousand years is a psychological attitude, a definite form and manner of adaptation to the world without and within, that lays down a definite cultural pattern and creates an atmosphere which remains wholly uninfluenced by intellectual denials. The change of front is, of course,

symptomatic, but on the deeper levels the psyche continues to work for a long time in the old attitude, in accordance with the laws of psychic inertia.[57]

It would seem necessary to take the Hermetic route and 'by indirections find directions out.'[58] In fairy tales the grown-up interpreter is encouraged to look at the structure of the family and see where the imbalances lie; what is missing that the dynamic of the tale is likely to make good? If we look at the Judaeo-Christian 'family' of divine images, we find a Divine Father without a Divine Mother (and not even a Wicked Step-mother to outwit or convert). In the specifically Christian family, there is also a Son (but no Daughter), and a Ghost or Spirit who is Holy but also male. This would suggest that the archetypal masculine has so prevailed over the archetypal feminine that a radical imbalance exists between so-called masculine and feminine values in our time. In a fairy tale we would expect to find (loosely) one or more of the consequences of such an imbalance: an overvaluing of reason over feeling, of intellect over intuition, of spirit over nature, of mind over matter, of the written word over the image, of hierarchy over partnership, of transcendence over immanence, of authority over love.

By analogy, we might expect that in the west we have (collectively) been conditioned by our particular mythologies to assume that the divine, the eternal, the sacred, the holy - call it what we may - is inevitably transcendent, in the sense of being *necessarily* beyond nature. The story of Adam and Eve in the Garden of Eden may still resound with Yahweh's curse, even if we think we no longer hear it. We would, then, be less likely to look instinctively for consciousness in Nature - still less Nature *as* Consciousness, or *Consciousness as Nature* - because we have accorded that prerogative solely to ourselves, on the grounds that only human beings are made in the image of their God (and have souls). We do not read that statement as tautology. We may further assume that Reason, as apparently the closest human relative to transcendence, is our most god-like faculty, and oppose this to other, by definition less god-like, faculties such as Feeling or, worse, Passion and Instinct, which we share with all other creatures. Because of this we may vastly overestimate our power to change the world, or our attitudes, accepting uncritically the derivative myth of Reason and Human Will. We will not be accustomed to distinguishing between different kinds of feelings (as we automatically distinguish between different kinds of reasoning), and so will not be able to recognize and trust *some* of our feelings for intuitive insight, intelligence and moral guidance. We may not, then, instinctively know what Imagination is, and may resist 'final participation' without even being aware of it.

Let us test this. To take one example: it would follow from a perception of a living Earth as a communion of subjects that these subjects are entitled in principle to be accorded the same rights as human beings confer upon themselves. To quote the cultural historian and ecologist Thomas Berry:

> The natural world on the planet Earth gets its rights from the same source that humans get their rights, from the universe that brought them into being.' ... 'Every component of the Earth community has three rights: the right to be, the right to habitat, and the right and responsibility to fulfill its role in the ever-renewing processes of the Earth community. All rights are species-specific and limited. Rivers have river rights. Birds have bird rights. Insects have insect rights. Humans have human rights. Difference in rights is qualitative, not quantitative. The rights of an insect would be of no value to a tree or a fish. Human rights do not cancel out the rights of other modes of being to exist in their natural state. Human property rights are not absolute... Each component of the Earth community is immediately or mediately dependent on every other member of the community for the nourishment and assistance it needs for its own survival. This

mutual nourishment, which includes the predator-prey relationship, is integral with the role that each component of the Earth has within the comprehensive community of existence...[59]

But do we, can we, *feel* this? Is our imaginative sympathy sufficiently *practised* for us to 'widen our circle of compassion,' in Einstein's evocative words? The passage is worth quoting in full:

> A human being is part of the whole called by us 'the universe,' a part limited in time and space. He experiences himself, his thoughts and feelings, as something separate from the rest – a kind of optical illusion of his consciousness. This delusion is a kind of prison for us, restricting us to our personal desires and affection for a few persons nearest to us. Our task must be to free us from this prison by widening our circle of understanding and compassion to embrace all living creatures and the whole of nature in its beauty.[60]

Many individuals, of course, feel such things instinctively, and always have done. The question is addressed only to those times when we think 'collectively,' in Jung's term, meaning when we think as members of a culture, and express the values of that culture rather than our own personal experience. In these moments we may well initially assent with our minds to ideas such as Einstein's and Berry's - since they follow logically and *organically* from the original vision of Earth from the Moon; organic, that is, in the sense advocated by the Romantic poets to explain the way in which one image or thought in a poem comes naturally and inevitably out of the one before: 'Those images that yet / Fresh images beget,' in Yeats's phrase.[61] But, subsequently, do we find ourselves (in a collective moment) returning to the argument with some bewilderment – unable to think it through, unable, ultimately, to *imagine* it in all its ramifications? Possibly the only way it could be sold to us is as 'enlightened self-interest'? Which is to say (to return full circle), by appealing to rational considerations divorced from our sense of value.

But the proposal was presented as an end in itself, as inherently good, without reference to how human beings might benefit from it. It does not say the Earth will be better able to be 'managed' as a resource if it has not been polluted. It says rights belong to all existence as their right, and those who understand this (and are in a position to foster or deny them) have to accept individual responsibility for ensuring that Earth and all Earth's members are no longer deprived of these rights. This is a vision specifically honed to the morality of being a human at this time in our and our Earth's history.

Habits of response, and the mythic structures in which they are, however tenuously, embedded, are extremely difficult to dislodge, as history has taught us many times. A paradigm, such as the Judaeo-Christian myth, and the derivative polarization of Spirit and Nature, which sees Earth and Earth's creatures (except 'Man') as Nature without Spirit, sets up a way of seeing and valuing which cannot be disproved from within the paradigm; it is not falsifiable because it has already subsumed the methods of falsification. But even if we cannot disprove the basic assumptions of the paradigm, we can still recognize and refuse them: arguments that are exclusively anthropocentric, oppositional, mechanistic, materialistic - these we can suspect as belonging to the last stage of the evolution of consciousness, not to the holistic paradigm that is coming into being. Ultimately, one paradigm can only be displaced by another paradigm, a wholly new vision. Richard Tarnas gives a brilliant overview of the way paradigms change:

> Each paradigm is a stage in an unfolding evolutionary sequence, and when that paradigm has fulfilled its purpose, when it has been developed and exploited to its fullest extent, then

it loses its numinosity, it ceases to be libidinally charged, it becomes felt as oppressive, limiting, opaque, something to be overcome – while the new paradigm that is emerging is felt as a liberating birth into a new, luminously intelligible universe.[62]

It is worth considering whether the emerging paradigm is energized by imagining it as being fully operative already, responding *as if* its tenets were true, so that the new way of envisioning life may be explored at the deeper instinctive levels of the psyche. Imagining ourselves into the being of the other – whether that 'other' be humans, animals, plants or the body of Earth – allows us to argue for their rights as if they were our own. Acting *as if*, seeing through the present into the future - this is of the essence of Imagination, which, as Coleridge said, dissolves, diffuses and dissipates what is, in order to create what could be, bringing 'the whole soul of man into activity' in order to do so. Imagination, he continues, 'reveals itself in the balance or reconciliation of opposite or discordant qualities... (It) is the soul that is everywhere, and in each; and forms all into one graceful and intelligent whole.'[63] Imagination is revealed, for instance, in the choice of the name *Gaia* for James Lovelock's theory of 'the Gaia Hypothesis,' since it makes present to the mind and evokes the feeling of the original creative power which once belonged to the ancient Greek Mother Goddess Earth.[64]

Drawing on the lunar pattern of the hero myth, we may remember that the old mode had to be sacrificed before the new could appear. We could 'sacrifice' our reason by temporarily holding it in abeyance (suspending our disbelief) so that feeling and imagination could emerge without comment, without being categorized according to pre-existent ways of thinking. The 'inertia' of the unconscious, of which Jung warns, is now, arguably, manifested in continuing to split off one aspect of life and set it in an absolute hierarchical and oppositional relationship to another, or the rest - whether it be 'Man' over the Cosmos; a particular species, religion, tribe, race, culture, over another; one self over another self; one faculty of the psyche over the other faculties; more generally, it is expressed in separating the part from the whole and the means from the end. All this 'partial thinking' is supported by the habit of reasoning from the senses without reference to the rest of the psyche, and by the language of opposition in which the habit is enshrined and imprisoned. Only poetic language is fluid and flexible enough to allow the emergence of new ideas into consciousness, appealing to feeling and intuition as well as to thinking and reason. This means drawing on a sensibility that might be called lunar because it can rest in ambivalence and sustain contraries until a resolution presents itself in its own time. As Rumi says:

> A new moon teaches gradualness
> and deliberation and how one gives birth
> to oneself slowly. Patience with small details
> makes perfect a large work, like the universe.[65]

So it may be that this 'inertia,' like the dragons of old, can be addressed initially by not endorsing its terms, for ultimately this monster of the dark, like any other, is the outer image of the hero's own fear; here, perhaps, fear of change, particularly fear of the loss of autonomy. But from where does such a refusal come? The power to transform the dragon of inertia - the lunar myth would suggest - comes from a greater allegiance, from an imaginative sympathy for a value discovered beyond one's fear. This is the heroic equivalent of the three days dark, the journey from profane to sacred, when the old forms, or present attachments, have to submit to immersion in the eternal realm where new values are forged. Only these new values can carry the heroes across the lonely threshold of fear and return them to their communities with transformed vision.

Blake and Yeats may serve as spokesmen for the claims of Imagination over Reason. This is Yeats writing about Blake, for whom 'the world of imagination' was 'the world of eternity' and 'Nature was Imagination itself':

> The reason, and by the reason he meant deductions from the observations of the senses, binds us to mortality because it binds us to the senses, and divides us from each other by showing us our clashing interest; but imagination divides us from mortality by the immortality of beauty, and binds us to each other by opening the secret doors of all hearts. He cried again and again that everything that lives is holy, and that nothing is unholy except things that do not live...Passions, because most living, are most holy...and man shall enter eternity borne upon their wings.[66]

Blake even attempts a bridge between the new and the old in his conviction, as Yeats puts it, 'that the sympathy with all living things, sinful and righteous alike, which the imaginative arts awaken, is that forgiveness of sins commanded by Christ.'[67]

For Yeats, as for Keats, the Moon is a muse for Imagination:

> If I look at the moon herself and remember any of her ancient names and meanings, I move among divine people, and things that have shaken off our mortality, the tower of ivory, the queen of waters, the shining stag among enchanted woods, the white hare sitting upon the hilltop, the fool of Faery with his shining cup full of dreams, and it may be 'make a friend of one of these images of wonder,' and 'meet the Lord in the air.'[68]

* * *

In Keats's poem 'Endymion,' the shepherd falls in love with the Moon as the Muse of Poesy, the haunting light that, like 'some shape of beauty,' moves away 'the pall from our dark spirits,' and 'always must be with us or we die.' On a 'magic bed of poppies red' he dreams a vision of the Moon:

> 'And lo! from opening clouds, I saw emerge
> The loveliest moon, that ever silver'd o'er
> A shell for Neptune's goblet...'

The vision comes down to Earth as a maid with 'pearl round ears, white neck, and orbed brow.' Later Endymion swears to Apollo, God of the Sun and the Lyre, that his sister the Moon is 'the gentlier-mightiest':

> 'When thy gold breath is misting in the west,
> She unobserved steals unto her throne,
> And there she sits most meek and most alone;
> As if she had not pomp subservient;
> As if thine eye, high Poet! was not bent
> Toward her with the Muses in thine heart;
> As if the ministring stars kept not apart,
> Waiting for silver-footed messages.
> O Moon! the oldest shades 'mong oldest trees

Feel palpitations when thou lookest in:
O Moon! old boughs lisp forth a holier din
The while they feel thine airy fellowship.
Thou dost bless everywhere, with silver lip
Kissing dead things to life.'[69]

Fig. 9. Crescent Earth. View of Earth as seen from Apollo 12 spacecraft. July 20th, 1969. NASA.

ENDNOTES

FOREWORD

1. Albert Einstein, quoted in the *New York Times* Magazine, August 2, 1964, in *The Expanded Quotable Einstein*, ed., Alice Calaprice, Princeton, Princeton University Press, 2000, p. 184.
2. Joseph Campbell, *The Inner Reaches of Outer Space: Metaphor as Myth and Religion*, p. 17.
3. Shakespeare, *Hamlet*, III, ii, 22.
4. C.G. Jung, *Collected Works*; Ernst Cassirer, *The Philosophy of Symbolic Forms*; Henri Frankfort, *et al.*, *The Intellectual Adventure of Ancient Man*; Mircea Eliade, *Patterns in Comparative Religion*; Owen Barfield, *Saving the Appearances: A Study in Idolatry*.
5. Northrop Frye, *The Great Code: The Bible and Literature*, p. xviii.

CHAPTER 1

1. *Homeric Hymn to Selene*, lines 1–2. (All translations of the *Homeric Hymns* by the author).
2. Apollodorus, *Bibliotheka*, i, 7. 6. Pausanias, *Descriptions of Greece*, v, 1. 3. Scholiast on *Theocritus's Idylls* III. 49. Cicero, *Tuscan Debates*, i, 38.
3. Theocritus, XX. 37–9. Translated version in Rosemary Ellen Guiley, *The Lunar Almanac*, pp. 69–70.
4. John Keats, *Endymion*, III, 143–4.
5. Henri Briffault, *The Mothers*, ii, p. 578.
6. Alexander Marshack, *The Roots of Civilization*, p. 35.
7. *Ibid.*, p. 45.
8. Eliade, *A History of Religious Ideas*, vol. i, pp. 9–12.
9. Marshack, *op. cit.*, pp. 57–79.
10. Marshack, *op. cit.*, p. 127.
11. David Bohm, *Wholeness and the Implicate Order*, p. xi. Cf. an 8th c. poem by Tu Fu: '.Where Dark and Light / Do dusk and dawn unite.'
12. Leo Tolstoy, *Anna Karenina*, pt. 7, ch. 13.
13. Psalms, 121: 6.
14. Genesis, I: 5, 16.
15. Idries Shah, *Pleasantries of the Incredible Mulla Nasrudin*, p. 51.
16. Erich Neumann, *The Great Mother*, p. 57.
17. Marshack, *op. cit.*, p. 333–40.
18. Literally, 'That which is above is like that which is below.' The Emerald Table, attributed to Hermes Trismegistos; in Frances A. Yates, *Giordano Bruno and the Hermetic Tradition*, p. 150.
19. Campbell, *The Way of the Animal Powers*, p.68.
20. Shakespeare, *As You Like It*, II, vii, 26–8.
21/22. Eliade, *Patterns in Comparative Religion*, p. 155.
23. Fritjoff Capra, *The Turning Point, The Web of Relationship*.
24. Quoted in Campbell, *Myths to Live By*, p. 236.
25. J. J. Bachofen, *Motherright*, p. 37. Briffault, *op. cit.*, iii, p. 61. See A. Krappe, *La Génèse des Mythes*, p. 101.
26. Neumann, *op. cit.*, p. 192.
27. Shakespeare, *As You Like It*, II, vii, 165–6.
28. Quoted in Miriam Sachs, *The Moon*, p. 34.
29. Oswald Spengler, *The Decline of the West*, p. 89.
30. Shakespeare, *Sonnet No. 19*.
31. Eliade, *Images and Symbols*, p. 72.
32. Eliade, *The Myth of the Eternal Return*, pp. 86–90.

33. Carl Kerenyi, *Zeus and Hera: Archetypal Image of Husband and Wife*, pp. 3–20.
34. Stephen Langdon, *Semitic Mythology*, p. 97.
35. Thorkild Jacobson, *Treasures of Darkness*, pp. 138–9.
36. Samuel Noah Kramer, *From the Poetry of Sumer*, p. 86.
37. Langdon, *Sumerian and Babylonian Psalms*, p. 13.
38. Jacobson, *op. cit.*, pp. 136–7.
39. Diane Wolkstein and Samuel Noah Kramer, *Inanna: Queen of Heaven and Earth*, p. 38.
40. Jacobson, *op. cit.*, p. 33.
41. *Ibid.*, p. 46.
42. *Ibid.*, p. 46.
43. Wolkstein and Kramer, *op. cit.*, p. 52.
44. *Ibid.*, p. 55.
45. *Ibid.*, pp. 56–7.
46. *Ibid.*, p. 60.
47. *Ibid.*, p. 64.
48. *Ibid.*, p. 68.
49. *Ibid.*, p. 71.
50. Langdon, *Sumerian and Babylonian Psalms*, p. 332.
51. Marija Gimbutas, *The Language of the Goddess*, p. 295–8.
52. Kerenyi, *Dionysos: Archetypal Image of Indestructible Life*, p. xxxv.
53. *Ibid.*, p. xxxiv.
54. *Ibid.*, p. xxxv; Plotinos, *Enneades* III, 7, 11, 43.
55. Plato, *Phaedo*, 105 DE.
56. Kerenyi, *op. cit.*, p. 38; 114–4.
57. *Ibid.*, p. 202
58. 'Dionysos is both moon-god and god of vegetation.' Eliade, *Patterns in Comparative Religion*, p. 162. See also Briffault, *op. cit.*, iii, p. 142–5.
59. See Anne Baring and Jules Cashford, *The Myth of the Goddess*, especially Ch. 4.
60. R. O. Faulkner, *Ancient Egyptian Pyramid Texts*, 732, p. 135.
61. *Ibid.*, 1012, p. 170.
62. Henri Frankfort, *Kingship and the Gods*, p. 196.
63. *Ibid.*, p. 190.
64. Plutarch, *Of Isis and Osiris*, *Moralia*, Bk. V. For an expanded version of this myth, see Jules Cashford, *The Myth of Isis and Osiris*, 1995.
65. Plutarch, *Isis and Osiris*, 371 B.
66. Coffin Text, 330, in R.T. Rundle Clark, *Myth and Symbol in Ancient Egypt*, p. 142.
67. Frankfort, *op. cit.*, p. 195.
68. Janet McCrickard, *Eclipse of the Sun*, p. 197.

CHAPTER 2

1. Martin P. Nilsson, *Primitive Time Reckoning*, p. 148ff: 'The moon is indeed the first chronometer. For (primitive peoples) the moon afforded the only fixed measure of the duration of time.' See also Hutton Webster, *Rest Days*, pp. 173–4ff.
2. Coleridge, *Biographia Literaria*, Ch. XIV, p. 169.
3. Plato, *The Timaeus*, 37, C, D.
4. See C. S. Lewis, *The Discarded Image*, p. 89.
5. Shakespeare, *The Rape of Lucrece*, 967.
6. Plato, *Euthydemus*, 284, D.
7. Henri-Charles Puech, 'Gnosis and Time,' in *Man and Time, Papers From the Eranos Yearbooks*, ed. Campbell, pp. 40–41.
8. Briffault, *The Mothers*, iii, pp. 3–4; ii, p. 601.

9. Wallis Budge, *The Gods of the Egyptians*, i, p. 412.
10. Jacobson, *The Treasures of Darkness*, p. 122.
11. Briffault, *op. cit.*, ii, p. 602.
12. Heinrich Zimmer, *Myths and Symbols in Indian Art and Civilization*, p. 60; John Layard, *The Lady and the Hare*, pp. 125–32.
13. J. White, *Ancient History of the Maori*, ii, p. 87.
14. Psalms, 89: 37.
15. W.H.I. Bleek, *Reynard the Fox in South African, Hottentot Fables and Tales*, p. 71; W.H.I. Bleek, and L.C. Lloyd, 'The Origin of Death,' *Bushmen Folklore*, pp. 57–65.
16. The Indo-European family of languages includes the following: Celtic (Irish, Welsh, Scottish, etc.), Germanic (German, Dutch, English, Norse, Gothic etc.), Italic (Latin, Italian, Spanish, French, Romanian etc.), Greek, Balto-Slavic (Old Prussian, Lettish, Russian, Czech, Polish, etc.), Anatolic (Armenian, Ancient Phrygian, etc.), Iranian (Persian, Afghan, etc.), and Indo-Aryan (Sanskrit, Pali, and the modern languages of northern India, such as Hindi, Bengali, Sindhi, Panjabi and Gujarati, as well as Romany or Gypsy). Zimmer, *Philosophies of India*, pp. 8–9, fn. 3.
17. Eric Partridge, *Origins: A Short Etymological Dictionary of Modern English*, p. 415. For the following etymology, see also the *Oxford Etymological Dictionary*, pp. 587–88.
18. Owen Barfield, *History in English Words*, pp. 87–8.
19. Partridge, *Origins*, pp. 390–4.
20. Nilsson, *op. cit.*, p. 148.
21. Nilsson, *op. cit.*, pp. 13–16.
22. Webster, *Rest Days*, pp. 173–222.
23. Nilsson, *op. cit.*, p. 13.
24. Barbara C. Walker, *Women's Myths and Secrets*, p. 647.
25. Nilsson, *op. cit.*, pp. 13–14ff.
26. Caesar, *Gallic War*, VI, 18.
27. Tacitus, *Germania*, 11.
28. Briffault, *op. cit.*, ii, p. 589.
29. Shakespeare, *Macbeth*, 1, iii, 21–2.
30. Briffault, *op. cit.*, iii, p. 72.
31. Genesis, I:5. Psalms, 55:17.
32. Knowth will be discussed in Ch. 4, figs. 6 and 7.
33. Briffault, *op. cit.*, iii, p. 73.
34. Alexander Thom, *Megalithic Lunar Observatories*, 1978; C.L.N. Ruggles, ed., *Records in Stone : Papers in Memory of Alexander Thom*.
35. Clyde Fisher, *The Story of the Moon*, p. 56.
36. Gimbutas, *The Language of the Goddess*, p. 223.
37. George Terence Meaden, *The Goddess of the Stones*, London, Souvenir, 1991, pp. 184–5ff; Iain Nicholson, *Heavenly Bodies*, p. 58.
38. See also Michael Dames on the Harvest Moon on Silbury Hill, Wiltshire, in his *The Silbury Treasure*, p. 58ff.
39. Franz Cumont, *Astrology and Religion among the Greeks and the Romans*, p. 60ff.
40. Manilius, *Astronomica*, i, 495.
41. Cumont, *op. cit.*, p. 60.
42. Cicero, *De Natura Deorum*, ii, 21; 63.
43. Kant, *Critique of Pure Reason*, passim.
44. Cumont, *op. cit.*, pp. 60–1; Hubbert, *op. cit.*, p. 173.
45. *The Koran*, Sura x, 5.
46. 'The Lay of Vafthrudnir,' verse 25, *The Elder Edda: A Selection translated from the Icelandic*, by Paul B. Taylor &

W.H. Auden, p. 74.

47. 'The Words of the All-Wise,' verses, 13, 14, *ibid.*, p. 80.

48. Psalms, 104: 19.

49. Ecclesiasticus, 43: 6–8.

50. Garth Fowden, *The Egyptian Hermes*, p. 22.

51. Patrick Boylan, *Thoth: The Hermes of Egypt*, pp. 83–6.

52. *Ibid.*, p. 86.

53. Wallis Budge, *Gods*, ii, p. 400; Fowden, *op. cit.*, pp. 2–3.

54. For a fuller account of the Wedjat Eye, see Ch. 11 pp. 280–81.

55. Hilary Wilson, *Understanding Hieroglyphics*, London, Michael O'Mara, 1973, p. 176; Webster, *op cit.*, p. 166.

56. Wallis Budge, *op. cit.*, ii, p. 402.

57. *Ibid.* See ch. 10, fig. 4.

58. Fowden, *op. cit*, p. 22.

59. Jacobson, *op. cit.*, p. 121.

60. Briffault, *op. cit.*, iii, p. 87.

61. Langdon, *op. cit.*, p. 152.

62. Jacobson, *op. cit.*, p. 122.

63. Briffault, *op. cit.*, iii, p. 87.

64. Briffault, *op. cit.*, ii, p. 81.

65. Jacobson, *op. cit.*, p. 179.

66. Jean Rhys Bram, 'The Moon,' in Eliade, ed., *Encylopaedia of Religion*, vol. 10, pp. 84.

67. Jacobson, *op. cit.*, p. 122.

68. Langdon, *op. cit.*, p. 153.

69. Cotterell, *op. cit.*, p. 47.

70. Exodus, 32:1–6. See Bram, 'Moon,' Eliade ed., *op. cit.*, p. 86: 'There is no doubt that the golden calf worshipped in Genesis was a figure of the moon and that Mount Sinai was his home.'

71. Exodus, 34:35. Campbell, *The Mythic Dimension*, p. 50.

72. Genesis, 11:31; Webster, *Rest Days*, p. 240.

73. John Gray, *Near Eastern Mythology*, p. 20.

74. Campbell, *Occidental Mythology*, pp. 115–6.

75. Briffault, *op. cit.*, iii, p. 108, note 4.

76. Thomas Mann, *Joseph and his Brothers*, Ch. 2, p. 7.

77. Webster, *op. cit.*, pp. 169–70.

78. Homer, *Odyssey*, xxi, 258 ff.

79. Hesiod, *Works and Days*, 770.

80. *The Orphic Hymn to the Moon*, 9, line 5.

81. Bram, 'The Moon', *op. cit.*, pp. 84–5.

82. Shakespeare, *Julius Caesar*, I, i, 19.

83. Webster, *op. cit.*, p. 248ff.

84 Nicholson, *Heavenly Bodies*, p. 50.

85. Jeanette Winter, *The Girl and the Moon Man*. (The plot – of the girl's invisibility to the Moon Man – spins on the homely truth of Shakespeare's line, 'When the moon shone we did not see the candle.' *The Merchant of Venice*, V, i, 92).

86. Nilsson, *op. cit.*, p. 190.

87. Ted Hughes, 'The Harvest Moon,' *Selected Poems: 1957–1981*, p. 148.

88. Nilsson, *op. cit.*, pp. 241–81. Guiley, *op. cit.*, pp. 88–9.

89. Plutarch, *Isis and Osiris*, 12, Loeb, p. 31.

90. Bram, 'Moon', *op. cit.*, p. 85.

91. Aristophanes, *Clouds*, 610.

92. *Ibid.*, 618.

93. Bram, *op. cit.*, p. 85.

94. Paul Katzeff, *Moon Madness*, xvii.

95. Robert Graves, *The White Goddess*, p. 96.

96. Graves, *op. cit.*, pp. 94–5.

97. Frazer, *The Golden Bough* (no. 9), Part VI, 'The Scapegoat,' pp. 306–12.

98. *Ibid.*, pp. 313–345.

99. *Ibid.*, pp. 306–12.

100. Alan Unterman, *Dictionary of Jewish Lore and Legend*, pp. 146–7.

101. *Ibid.*, p. 147.

102. *Ibid.*

103. David Ewing Duncan, *The Calendar: The 5000-year struggle to align the clock and the heavens – and what happened to the missing ten days*, London, Fourth Estate, 1998, pp. 175–91.

104. Jan Knappert, *The Aquarian Guide to African Mythology*, p. 166.

105. Nilsson: 'the hailing of the new moon with joy is widespread.' *Op. cit.*, pp. 151–4.

106. Heracleitus, fr. XLI. Cf. 'You cannot step into the same river twice.' fr. 33. See Ananda K. Coomaraswamy, *Time and Eternity*, p. 37ff.

107. Spengler, *The Decline of the West*, p. 89. See Ch. 1, p. 24.

108. Pliny, *Natural History*, Bk II, CII (no. 221), Loeb, p. 349.

109. Plutarch, *Moralia XV*, 111, p. 225; 101, p. 211.

110. Macrobius, *Saturnalia*, vii, 10; *Comment. in somnium Scipionis*, 1, 11, 7. (See also W.H. Roscher, *Uber Selene und Verwandtes* (About Selene and her Relations), pp. 61ff.

111. Grimm, *Teutonic Mythology*, ii, pp. 708–716.

112. Ptolemy, *Tetrabiblos*, III. 13. 168; in Loeb, p. 361. For the persistence of these ideas, see Keith Thomas, *Religion and the Decline of Magic*, p. 351ff.

113. Frazer, IX, 'The Doctrine of Lunar Sympathy,' *The Golden Bough*, Adonis, Attis, Osiris, ii, p. 140ff.

114. Frazer, *op. cit.*, p. 140.

115. John Downer, *Supernatural: The Unseen Powers of Animals*, p. 104.

116. Frazer, *op. cit.*, p. 140.

117. Plutarch, *Table Talk*, III, 10, 659,A, Loeb, p. 277.

118. D. F. A. Hervey, 'The Mentra Traditions,' *Journal of the Straits Branch of the Royal Asiatic Society*, no. 10 (Singapore, 183), p. 190.

119. Jung, *Modern Man in Search of a Soul*, pp. 129–30.

120. Anton Chekhov, *Ward No. 6*, trans. R.E.C. Long, in *Six Russian Short Novels*, selected by Randall Jarrell, p. 323.

121. *Ibid.*, p. 330.

122. Nilsson, *op. cit.*, pp. 155–65.

123. Hollis, *The Nandi*, pp. 95ff.

124. Briffault, *op. cit.*, ii, p. 748.

125. I. H. N. Evans, 'Some Sakai Beliefs and Customs,' *Journal of the Royal Anthropological Institute*, lviii, p. 191.

126. Briffault, *op. cit.*, ii, 654.

127. Webster, *op. cit.*, 141.

128. Webster, *op. cit.*, p. 141.

129. Knappert, *African Mythology*, p. 166.

130. Bleek and Lloyd, *Specimens of Bushman Folklore*, p. 415 (prayer given in 1880 by a man who heard it from his father).

131. Knappert, *op. cit.*, p. 166.

132. Frazer, *op. cit.*, p. 142. For further examples of New and Full Moon celebrations see, Nilsson, *op. cit.*, pp. 151–67; Webster, *op. cit.*, pp. 141–72.

133. G. W. Stow, *The Native Races of South Africa*, London, Swan Sonnenschein Co., 1905, p. 112.

134. Bleek and Lloyd, *Bushman Folklore*, pp. 299–317.

135. Frazer, *op. cit.*, p. 141.

136. *Odyssey*, 14, 162.

137. Plato, *Laws*, X, 887.D,E.

138. Herodotus, *The Histories*, vi, 106.

139. Caesar, *De Bello Gallico*, i, 50.

140. Grimm, *Teutonic Mythology*, ii, p. 714.

141. Tacitus, *Germania*, XI.

142. Grimm, *op. cit.*, ii, 713.

143. Plutarch, *Moralia*, XV, 105.

144. Shakespeare, *A Midsummer Night's Dream*, I, i, 2–11.

145. *Ibid.*, I, ii, 60.

146. *Ibid.*, V, i, 357.

147. Nilsson, *op. cit.*, p. 154. Details in Hubbert, *op. cit.*, pp. 125–172. Celebrations were also held by the Chinese, Egyptians, Babylonians, Iranians, Aryans of ancient India, the Hindus, Buddhists, Greeks, Romans, Arabs and Hebrews, among many others. Katzeff, *Moon Madness*, xiv.

148. Strabo, *Geographica*, iii, 4, 16.

149. Euripides, *Iphigeneia at Aulis*, 717.

150. Sappho, no. 154, and no. 16 (Sappho or Alcaeus), *Greek Lyric: Sappho and Alcaeus*, Loeb, pp. 163, 447.

151. Hollis, *op. cit.*, pp. 52, 60, 71. Webster, *op. cit.*, pp. 131–72.

152. Diana Brueton, *Many Moons*, p. 126.

153. Robert Louis Stevenson, 'The Moon,' *A Child's Garden of Verses*, p. 59. Compare Pablo Neruda, 'The moon turns its clockwork dream.' *Twenty Love Poems*, p. 53.

154. Conversation with Anna Papakaliati-Kaianaki, October, 2000, in Elounda, Crete.

155. From Daniel Defoe, *Memoirs of Mr Campbell* (1732), p. 62, in Opie and Tatem, *A Dictionary of Superstitions*, p. 282; see also pp. 279–283.

156. Iona and Peter Opie, *The Oxford Nursery Rhyme Book*, p. 264.

157. Nilsson, *op. cit.*, pp. 155–67.

158. Webster, *op. cit.*, pp. 183–9.

159. *Ibid.*, p. 185.

160. Homer, *Odyssey*, XIV, 162; XIX, 307. Hesiod, *Works and Days*, V, 780.

161. Nilsson, *op. cit.*, p. 167.

162. Hesiod, *Works and Days*, 765ff.

163. Webster, *op. cit.*, pp. 188–93.

164. Nilsson, *op. cit.*, p. 156.

165. Briffault, *op. cit.*, ii, p. 434.

166. Webster, 'The Hebrew Sabbath,' *op. cit.*, pp. 242–71.

167. Webster, *op. cit.*, pp. 246–50.

168. First Book of Samuel, 20: 5; 24–9.

169. 2 Kings, 4: 23.

170. Amos, viii, 4–5.

171. Hosea, ii, 13.

172. Isaiah, 1, 13.

173. *Ibid.*, 66, 23.

174. Webster, *op. cit.*, p. 253.

175. Job, 31: 26–8.

176. *Ibid.*, p. 244.

177. Exodus, 31: 14; 35: 2.

178. Webster, *op. cit.*, pp. 200–220.

179. *Ibid.*, pp. 122–3.

180. Colossians, 2: 16–17.

181. Jamieson, *Scottish Dictionary*, entry for Mononday, in Opie and Tatem, *op. cit.*, pp. 258–9.

182. Partridge, *Origins*, p. 720.

183. *Ibid.*

184. Old Latin *osmen*, associated with *os*, 'mouth' (Onians, ed. *Dictionary of English Etymology*, p. 626), possibly added to men, 'moon.'

185. Partridge, *Origins*, p. 701.

186. Hesiod, *Theogony*, 116–218.

187. Huxley, *The Way of the Sacred*, p. 192.

188. Shakespeare, *Sonnet 60*.

189. *Bhagavad-Gita*, XI, 32.

190. Zimmer, *The Art of Indian Asia*, p. 94.

191. Zimmer, *op. cit.*, p. 155.

192. *Ibid.*, p. 214.

193. *Ibid.*, pp. 204–9.

CHAPTER 3

1. The Indians of North America and Canada; the Mayans, Brazilian Indians, and Nicaraguans of South America; the Indians, Chinese, Japanese of Asia; the Mesopotamians and Egyptians of the Middle and Near East; the Aborigines of Australia and the Maoris of New Zealand; the Bushmen and Hottentots of Africa; the Siberian Yakuts, the Greeks and Romans, Germans and Scandinavians of Europe. (See Briffault, *The Mothers*, ii, pp. 632–40; Eliade, *Patterns in Comparative Religion*, pp. 159–161; Krupp, *Beyond the Blue Horizon*, pp. 74–5).

2. Knappert, *African Mythology*, p. 166.

3. Bleek and Lloyd, *Specimens of Bushman Folklore*, p. 67.

4. Jacobson, *The Treasures of Darkness*, pp. 136–7.

5. Langdon, *Tammuz and Ishtar*, p. 47.

6. L.W. King, *Legends of Babylonia and Egypt in Relation to Hebrew Tradition*, p. 111.

7. Wolkstein and Kramer, *Inanna, Queen of Heaven and Earth*, p. 39.

8. Eliade, *Patterns*, p. 159.

9. Wallis Budge, *The Gods of the Egyptians*, i, p. 436.

10. See Dominique Collon, *First Impressions*, p. 167.

11. Langdon, *Cuneiform Texts*, 15–17; 16d. Eliade, *op. cit.*, p. 159.

12. Plutarch, *Isis and Osiris*, 34, Loeb, p. 83.

13. Plutarch, *op. cit.*, 43, Loeb, p. 103. Wallis Budge, *The Gods*, ii, pp. 33–37.

14. Faulkner, *Pyramid Texts*, 2063.

15. Faulkner, *Pyramid Texts*, 1944, 2113–2117. Lucie Lamy, *Egyptian Mysteries*, p. 5.

16. Plutarch, *op. cit.*, 41, Loeb, p. 101.

17. Plutarch, *op. cit.*, 36, Loeb, p. 87.

18. Plutarch, *op. cit.*, 53, Loeb, p, 129. Wallis Budge, 'Osiris as a Moon–god,' *Osiris and the Egyptian Resurrection*, vol ii, ch. XII, pp. 384–396.

19. de Bucke, *Egyptian Coffin Texts*, 11, Chicago, University of Chicago, Oriental Institute, 1935–61, p. 104.

20. *Rig Veda*, i, 105, 1; *Aitareya Brahmana*, viii, 28, 15. In the Puranas it is said that the chariot of the Moon consists of water.

21. Krupp, *op, cit.*, p. 75.

22. *Ibid.*

23. Knappert, *Indian Mythology*, p. 224.

24. All these examples, and many more, are cited by Briffault, *op. cit.*, ii, pp. 632–8.

25. Briffault, *op. cit.*, ii, p. 633.

26. Eliade, *Patterns*, p. 159.

27. Eliade, *op. cit.*, p. 159.

28. Briffault, *op. cit.*, ii, p. 636.

29. Briffault, *op. cit.*, ii, p. 633.

30. Krupp, *op. cit.*, p. 74–5.

31. Baring-Gould, *Curious Myths of the Middle Ages*, p. 201ff.

32. Briffault, *op. cit.*, ii, p. 636.

33. Briffault, *op. cit.*, ii, pp. 632–5.

34. Krupp, *op. cit.*, p. 74. See also Briffault, *op. cit.*, ii, p. 632.

35. Briffault, *op. cit.*, ii, p. 636 ff.

36. *Hamlet*, I, i, 118–9.

37. G.B. Dalla Porta, *Natural Magick*, p. 11.

38. Cornelius Agrippa, *De Occulta Philosophica*, p. xxxi.

39. Briffault, *op. cit.*, ii, p. 637.

40. Shakespeare, *Richard II*, II, ii, 66–70.

41. Shakespeare, *A Midsummer Night's Dream*, II, i, 162.

42. Harrison, *Themis*, p. 185.

43. Guiley, *Lunar Almanac*, p. 110. See 'Collectanea: 'Moon Lore from West Virginia,' Folklore, vol. L, 1939, pp. 310–11. (These are largely people of English, Welsh and Scottish descent).

44. De Vries, *Dictionary*, p. 328; Nigel Pennick, *The Pagan Source Book*, p. 94.

45. R. L. Tongue, 'Two Moons in May,' *Folklore*, vol 77, 1966, pp. 41– 4.

46. *The Georgics of Virgil*, trans. C. Day Lewis, lines 427–435, pp. 28–29.

47. Charles Kightly, *Almanack*, entry for June 8.

48. G. Jean Aubrey, *Observations*, 1685; in Kightly, *op. cit.*, entry for August 9.

49. Coleridge, 'Dejection: An Ode' (1802), *The Grasmere Poems*, foreword.

50. *Ibid.*, lines 9–14.

51. *Ibid.*, lines 21; 86.

52. Macrobius, *Saturnalia*, vii, 10.

53. Langdon, *Tammuz and Ishtar*, p. 153.

54. Plutarch, *Orb*, 940.

55. Porphyrius, *De antro. nymph.*, xx; Graves, *Greek Myths*, pp. 102–3.

56. Harrison, *Themis*, p. 191; *Prolegomena*, p. 287; Graves, *Greek Myths*, p. 100.

57. Clyde Fisher, *The Story of the Moon*, p. 96.

58. Harrison describes the birth of Athene from Zeus as 'a desperate theological expedient to rid an earth-born Kore of her matriarchal conditions.' *Prolegomena*, p. 302.

59. Harrison, *Themis*, p. 191.

60. Euripides, fragment (Nauck 997); in Harrison, *Themis*, p. 191. Inanna in her dark aspect was identified with the screech owl, as was Lilith in the Hebrew tradition, and the Comanche Indians also saw an owl in the Moon. Jablow and Withers, *The Man in the Moon*, pp. 15–17.

61. Hesiod, *Theogony*, 52–3. See Ann Shearer, *Athene: Image and Energy*, pp. 23–40 ff for an understanding of the meaning of this goddess in ancient times and modern thought.

62. *Larousse* p. 207.

63. Shakespeare, *Timon of Athens*, IV, iii, 441–2.

64. Nicholson, *Heavenly Bodies*, pp. 66–68.

65. Krappe, *La Genèse des Mythes*, p. 110.

66. Harley, *Moon Lore*, p. 134.

67. Chaucer, *The Franklin's Tale*, F 1052, p. 156.

68. Knappert, *Pacific Mythology*, p. 291.

69. *Larousse*, p. 465; Krupp, *op. cit.*, p. 74.

70. Guiley, *Lunar Almanac*, p. 67.

71. Knappert, *Pacific Mythology*, pp. 114–5.

72. Hyginus, 197; in Briffault, *op. cit.*, iii, p. 89.

73. Hesiod, *Theogony*, 176–210. The Homeric *Hymn to Aphrodite*, lines 4–5; Pausanias, x.24.4 and i.19.2. The goddess Thetis, daughter of Nereus, god of the ocean, was 'silver-footed,' an image resonant of the Moon gleaming on the rippling waves of the sea.

74. Kerenyi, *The Gods of the Greeks*, p.81.

75. Yves Bonnefoy, compiler, *Greek and Egyptian Mythologies*, p. 249.

76. See Jung's discussion of the etymological links between sea, mother, fate and death. Jung, CW 5, p. 250.

77. Katzeff, *Moon Madness*, p. 48.

78. Pliny, *Natural History*, II. C. 1. on Aristotle, in Katzeff, *Moon Madness*, p. 16.

79. Shakespeare, *Henry IV*, I, ii, 25–32.

80. Shakespeare, *Henry V*, II, ii, 11–12.

81. Charles Dickens, *David Copperfield*, ch. XXX.

82. Claudia de Lys, *What's So Lucky About A Four-leaf Clover*, New York, Bell Publishing, 1989, p. 399.

83. Keith Thomas, *Religion and the Decline of Magic*, p. 396.

84. Katzeff, *Moon Madness*, pp. 47–9; 217–22; 237–9.

85. Shakespeare, *Julius Caesar*, IV, iii, 270.

86. Shakespeare, *A Midsummer Night's Dream*, II, i, 103–8.

87. Shakespeare, *Anthony and Cleopatra*, IV, xii, 11–14.

88. Plutarch, 'Fragments,' no. 61, *Moralia*, XV, Loeb, p. 155.

89. Macrobius, *Saturnalia*, lib. VII, cap. XVI. Cf. Pliny, *Natural History*, II, 103: 'The moon by her aspect melts the bodies of wild animals that have been killed and causes them to putrify... thaws ice, and unstiffens everything with moistening breath.'

90. Macrobius, *Commentary on the Dream of Scipio*, I, xi, p. 131. See Jung, CW 14, p. 145.

91. *Ibid*, I, xi p. 131. Plutarch uses the phrase 'moist heat,' in 'Fragments: Other Named Works,' 111, *Moralia*, XV, p. 225.

92. Neumann, *The Great Mother*, p. 188.

93. Genesis, 8;21.

94. Gilgamesh, trans. Maspero, *The Dawn of Civilization*, p. 569.

95. Harding, *Woman's Mysteries*, p. 107.

96. Genesis, 9:20–21; Campbell, *The Mythic Image*, p. 88–9.

97. Harding, *op. cit.*, p. 223.

98. Funk & Wagnall, *Dictionary*, p. 675.

99. Max S.Shapiro and Rhoda A. Hendricks, *A Dictionary of Mythologies*, p. 117.

100. Eliade, *Patterns*, p. 160.

101. Knappert, *Pacific Mythology*, p. 83.

102. H. Krappe, 'The Lunar Frog,' *Folk–lore*, vol. LI, 1940, pp.161–2ff.

103. Eliade, *op. cit.*, p. 161.

104. Hentze, *Mythes et Symboles Lunaires*, pp. 14, 24, ff.

105. Hesiod, *Theogony*, 977.

106. D.H. Lawrence, *Women in Love*, pp. 243–5.

107. Ovid, *Fasti*, III, 275. See Frazer, *The Golden Bough*, pt. 1, vol.1, pp. 1–24.

108. Katherine Briggs, 'The Dead Moon,' *British Folktales*, pp. 21–3.

109. Funk & Wagnall, *Dictionary*, p. 325.

110. Idries Shah, *The Pleasantries of the Incredible Mulla Nasrudin*, p. 43.

111. Shakespeare, *Love's Labours Lost*, V, ii, 208.

112. 1st story: *Notes and Queries*, Ser.4,IV, 1869, 57, (adapted). 2nd story: *ibid.*, 165, (adapted). The first mention of this story comes from Francis Grose, who wrote simply in his *Provincial Glossary*: 'Wiltshire moon-rakers: Some Wiltshire rustics, as the story goes, seeing the figure of the moon in a pond, attempted to take it out.' For the source of this, and many other tales from the British Isles, see Jennifer Westwood, *Albion: A Guide to Legendary Britain*, p. 190.

113. Krappe, *Genèse des Mythes*, p.104.

114. 'Flowers and Moonlight on the Spring River,' by Yang-ti (605–617), Emperor of the Sui Dynasty, in Waley, *170 Chinese Poems*, p. 71.

115. J. White, *The Ancient History of the Maori*, vol. i, p. 142; vol. ii, p. 91. in Briffault, *op. cit.*, ii, p. 657; 673.

116. Julian David, *Interweaving Symbols of Individuation in African and European Fairy Tales*, pp. 78–9.

117. 'The Moon with the Face of the Gorgon,' in Payne Knight, *An Inquiry into the Symbolical Language of Ancient Art and Mythology*, London, Black and Armstrong, reprinted and published by E. H. Barker esq. 1836, p. 130. See Ann Shearer, 'Remembering Medusa,' *Athene*, pp. 60–73; George Elder, *Archetypal Body*, pp. 123–5.

118. Krupp, *op. cit.*, pp. 63–5; Katzeff, *Moon Madness*, xvii–xix.

119. Gimbutas, *Goddesses and Gods*, p. 199.

120. Nicholson, *op. cit.*, p. 69.

121. *The Times*, March 6, 1998.

122. Zimmer, *Myths and Symbols*, p. 60.

123. 'The Dying Round the Holy Power,' *Aitareya Brahmana*, in Zimmer, *Philosophies of India*, pp. 70–1.

124. *Brihadaranyak Upanishad*, 2,5,7.

125. Funk & Wagnall, *Dictionary*, p. 1032.

126. *Rig Veda*, x, lxxxv.5; McGrath, *Eclipse of the Sun*, p. 125.

127. Wendy Doniger, *Hindu Myths*, p. 276.

128. Doniger, *op. cit.*, pp. 274–277. Other versions give a different order. (Cf. Huxley, Rupa, *Myths and Legends of India*, 1–6), *Larousse*, 362–67). Some separate Soma, the Moon, from Amrita, and some do not.

129. *Rig Veda*, 8:48.

130. *Rig Veda*, 8:100.

131. *Rig Veda*, 10:34.1; 82.3. Eliade suggests that, in the frequent sacrifice of Soma by the gods, vestiges of an origin myth can be deciphered where the 'immortalizing' drink was created by the sacrifice of a primordial being. This original sacrifice is reenacted in the ritual squeezing of the plant Soma. Eliade, *History of Religious Ideas*, p. 211.

132. Briffault, *op. cit.*, iii, p. 131.

133. *Rig Veda*, 10:119.

134. *Larousse*, p. 331.

135. *Satapatha-Brahamana*, 9.4.8.

136. Funk & Wagnall, *Dictionary*, p. 479.

137. M. Monier-Williams, *Sanskrit Dictionary*, s.v. 'Soma.'

138. Partridge, *Origins*, p. 640.

139. Jung, *CW V*, xxiv.

140. Plato, *Phaedo*, 72a – 92a.

141. Exodus, 16:4–14.

142. Unterman, *Dictionary of Jewish Lore & Legend*, p. 127.

143. Exodus, 16:31.

144. Unterman, *op. cit.*, p. 127.

145. Deuteronomy, xxxiii: 26–8.

146. Langdon points out that the origin of manna surely lies in Sumerian mythology, where the tree sacred to Anu, god of heaven, grandfather of Nanna, was called the ma-nu, and connected to the tamarisk and date-palm, in turn connected with the herb of everlasting life for which Gilgamesh seeks. On seals Gilgamesh is shown holding a jar of overflowing waters from which this plant springs. *The Mythology of All Races: Semitic*, vol.v, pp. 95–9.

147. Unterman, *op. cit.*, pp. 62; 167.

148. Unterman, p. 181.

149. John Keats, 'La Belle Dame Sans Merci,' verse vii.

150. Coleridge, *Kubla Khan*, lines 51–4.

151. Bleek and Lloyd, *Bushman Folklore*, p. 67.

152. Plutarch, *Orb*, 938.

153. Euripides, *Hippolytus*, 555.

154. There was a time when all the guests at the marriage had also to drink honey for the whole Moon. Peter Lorie, *Superstitions: The Book of Ancient Lore*, p. 224.

155. Kerenyi, *Dionysos: Image of Indestructible Life*, p. 35.

156. *Letters of Rainer Maria Rilke, 1910–1924*, trans. Jane Bannard, pp. 373–4.

157. Harold Bayley, *The Lost Language of Symbolism*, pp. 242–3.

158. Quoted in Biedermann, *Dictionary of Symbolism*, p. 95.

159. Adolphus Senior, *De Chemica*, pp. 35f; in Jung, *CW 12*, p. 404, who comments: 'Being the mistress of moisture, the moon, like Isis, is the *prima materia* in the form of water and thus the mother of the 'Hydrolith,' the water stone-another name for the lapis and hence for Christ. Since the terms *scientia* and *prima materia* are often used as though they were identical, *scientia* or *sapientia* is here identical with the moon, the feminine principle; hence the Gnostic doctrine of Sophia as the mother or bride of Christ.'

160. Opie and Tatem, *A Dictionary of Superstitions*, pp. 245–6.

161. Lorie, *Superstitions*, pp. 62, 68.

162. Campbell, *Atlas*, ii, pt. 3, p.341.

163. Maspero, *The Dawn of Civilization*, pp. 695–6.

164. Shakespeare, *King Lear*, IV, vi, 145–9.

165. Campbell, *The Mythic Image*, p. 284, fig. 253.

166. Campbell, *Creative Mythology*, p. 418. See also Cashford, 'Joseph Campbell and the Grail Myth,' in John Matthews ed., *The Household of the Grail*, pp. 198–217.

167. Wolfram von Eschenbach, *Parzival*.

168. John Grant, *Viking Mythology*, pp. 74–5.

169. Funk & Wagnall, *op. cit.*, p. 697.

170. Eliade, *From Primitives to Zen*, pp. 247–8, note I.

171. *The Times*, 23 February, 1998. (p. 5).

172. Kenneth Rexroth, *One Hundred Poems from the Chinese*, pp. 65–6.

173. *Amritabindu Upanishad*, 11–12; Zimmer, *Philosophies of India*, p. 371.

174. Anne Bancroft, *Zen: Direct Pointing to Reality*, p. 83.

175. 'No Water, No Moon,' *Zen Flesh, Zen Bones*, p. 40. Cf. Zen Master Dogen: 'Enlightenment is like the moon reflected on the water. The moon does not get wet, nor is the water broken... The whole moon and the entire sky are reflected in dewdrops on the grass, or even in one drop of water. The depth of the drop is the height of the moon. each reflection, however long or short its duration, manifests the vastness of the dewdrop, and realizes the limitlessness of the moonlight in the sky.' *Moon in a Dewdrop*, ed. Kazuaki Tanahashi, p. 71.

CHAPTER 4

1. William Blake, *Poetry and Prose of William Blake*, p. 860.

2. Eliade, *Images and Symbols*, p. 12.

3. Blake, *op. cit.*, p. 148.

4. Jung, *CW*, 11, p. 280.

5. Harrison, *Prolegomena*, p. 164.

6. Yeats, *Essays and Introductions*, pp. 174–5.

7. Eliade, *Patterns in Comparative Religion*, pp. 167–171.

8. Aristotle, *History of Animals*, ii. 12. 12; Pliny, *Natural History*, xi. 82.

9. Quoted in Marshack, *op. cit.*, pp. 336–7.

10. Gimbutas, *The Goddesses and Gods of Old Europe*, p. 93–101.

11. Martin Brennan, *The Stars and the Stones*, p. 137.

12. See Campbell, *The Mythic Image*, pp. 88–9.

13. Thomas, *Religion and the Decline of Magic*, p. 224ff; Margaret Baker, *Discovering The Folklore of Plants*, p. 79.

14. Jung, *CW 8*, p. 451.

15. Langdon, *Oxford Editions of Cuneiform Texts*, t, IV, p. 6.

16. Krupp, *Beyond the Blue Horizon*, p. 193.

17. Carl Hentze, *Früh Chinesische Bronzen*, pp. 110–13.

18. Genesis, 14: 5.

19. Jeremiah, 7: 18; 44: 25.

20. Gimbutas, *Goddesses and Gods*, p. 93.

21. Campbell, *Oriental Mythology*, p. 89.

22. Plutarch, *Isis and Osiris*, 43. Wallis Budge, ch. XIII, 'Osiris as a Bull-God,' *Osiris and the Egyptian Resurrection*, i, pp. 397–404.

23. Rosalie David, *A Guide to the Religious Ritual at Abydos*, p. 136.

24. Pliny, *Natural History*, viii, 72.

25. Herodotus, *History of the Persian Wars*, 11, 153.

26. *Rig Veda*, viii, 80, 1, 3; vii. 104, 1. de Gubernatis, 'The Cow and the Bull,' *Zoological Mythology*, i, ch. 1, pp. 1–282.

27. *Vendidad*, xxi. iii. b. 9; in *The Sacred Books of the East*, vol. iv, p. 226.

28. See Madanjeet Singh, comp., *The Sun in Myth and Art*, pp. 235–49.

29. Eliade, *Patterns*, pp. 159; 161.

30. 'Seventeen Old Poems', no. 16, in Arthur Waley, *Chinese Poems*, p. 57.

31. Singh, comp. *Sun*, p. 159.

32. *Ibid.*, p. 165.

33. Virgil, *Georgics*, 380.

34. *Rig Veda*, VII, 103, 2; in J. Muir, *Original Sanscrit Texts*, V, p. 431.

35. Krappe, 'The Lunar Frog,' *Folklore*, vol. LI, 1940, pp. 162–5.

36. Briffault, *The Mothers*, ii, p. 634.

37. Biedermann, *Dictionary of Symbolism*, p. 146.

38. Frankfort, *Kingship and the Gods*, p. 146.

39. Beverly Moon, ed., *Archetypal Symbolism*, p. 75.

40. Wallis Budge, *Osiris and the Egyptian Resurrection*, i, pp. 279– 80.

41. Moon, ed., *Archetypal Symbolism*, pp. 76–7.

42. Knappert, *African Mythology*, pp. 166–7.

43. Gerardo Reichel-Dolmatoff, *Rainforest Shamans*, p. 265.

44. Reichel-Dolmatoff, 'Astronomical Models of Social Behavior Among Some Indians of Colombia,' *Annals of the New York Academy of Sciences*, p. 170.

45. Lorca, *The Selected Poems of Federico Garcia Lorca*, p. 29.

46. Aristophanes, *Lysistrata*, 641.

47. Marshack, *The Roots of Civilization*, p. 237.

48–50. Gimbutas, *The Language of the Goddess*, p. 116.

51. Campbell, *The Way of the Animal Powers*, p. 155ff.

52. Gimbutas, *Goddesses and Gods*, p. 200.

53–55. Eliade, *Patterns*, p. 439; *Images and Symbols*, pp. 125–50.

56. Pliny, *Natural History*, II, 41.

57. Arthur Cotterell, *A Dictionary of World Mythology*, p. 190.

58. Eliade, *Images*, p. 129.

59. Andersson, *Children of the Yellow Earth: Studies in Pre-historic China*, MIT Press, Mass., 1973, p. 304.

60. Donald A. Mackenzie, *China and Japan*, p. 157; Wolfram Eberhard, *A Dictionary of Chinese Symbols*, p. 193.

61. Dante, *Paradiso*, II, 34.

62. Eliade, *Patterns*, p. 439; *Images*, p. 145.

63. *Anhava Veda*, iv, 10.

64. Eliade, *Patterns*, p. 440.

65. Karlgren, *Some Fecundity Symbols in Ancient China*, Stockholm Museum of Far Eastern Antiquities, 1930, pp. 30–6.

66. Eliade, *Images*, p. 131.

67. Eliade, *Images*, p. 145.

68. Jacobus Masenius, *Speculum imaginum veritatis occultae* (1714), cap. LXVII, 30, p. 768. b. Picinelli, *Mondo Simbolico*, Lib. VI, No. 45.

69. Quoted in Jung, *CW 9*, i, p. 342, note 155.

70. Funk & Wagnall, *Dictionary*, p. 258.

71. *Ibid.*

72. De Gubernatis, *Zoological Mythology*, ii, p. 356. He adds that the crab stands for the Sun when it goes forwards and the Moon when it goes backwards.

73. T. S. Eliot, 'The Love Song of J. Alfred Prufrock,'

Collected Poems, p. 15.

74. Funk & Wagnall, *op. cit.*, p. 745.

75. *Ibid*; de Vries, *Dictionary*, p. 328.

76. Shakespeare, *Julius Caesar*, IV, ii, 78–9.

77. The 1997 film 'Wolf,' starring Jack Nicholson and Michelle Pfeiffer, for example.

78. Guiley, *Lunar Almanac*, p. 51.

79. Gimbutas, *Language*, p. 233–4.

80. Birgitte Sonne, *Agayut: Eskimo Masks from The 5th Thule Expedition*, p. 278. (see ch. 8, fig. 1).

81. *Satapatha Brahmayana* xi, 1.5.1,2.

82. See Coomaraswamy, *What is Civilization?* pp. 100–3 for the connections between Moon, dog and hare.

83. Wallis Budge, *The Gods of the Egyptians*, ii, p. 263.

84. Harrison, *Themis*, p. 199.

85. Jung, 'Luna: b. The Dog,' *CW* 14, pp. 146–60.

86. Krappe, *Genèse des Mythes*, pp. 226–8.

87. Snorri Sturluson, *The Prose Edda*, p. 39.

88. Funk & Wagnall, *op. cit.*, p. 798.

89. See Moon, ed., *Archetypal Symbolism*, pp. 99–101.

90. Yogesvara, no. 218, John Brough, trans. *Poems from the Sanskrit*, p. 126.

91. Yeats, 'The Cat and the Moon,' *Collected Poems*, p. 188–9.

92. Plutarch, *Moralia*, XV, 101, Loeb, p. 211.

93. Gubernatis, *Zoological Mythology*, ii, p. 63.

94. Sturluson, *op. cit.*, p. 53; Ovid, *Metamorphosis*, v. 325–32.

95. Wallace Budge, *The Gods of the Egyptians*, i, pp. 444–450.

96. Worlidge, *Systema Agriculturae*, 1697, in Kightly, *Almanack*, 16 March.

97. Briffault, *op. cit.*, ii, p, 621.

98. Buffie Johnson, *The Lady of the Beasts*, p. 212.

99. Funk & Wagnall, *op. cit.*, p. 1074.

100. H.R. Codrington, *The Melanesians*, pp. 159 ff.

101. G.H. Luquet, 'Oceanic Mythology,' in *Larousse*, ed. Graves, p. 457.

102. Graves, *Greek Myths*, vol. 1, p. 98. For Athene as the Moon, as well as Artemis, see Plutarch, 'The Face of the Moon,' *Moralia* XII, 922.

103. Gubernatis, *op. cit.*, p. 163.

104. Miller and Taube, *An Illustrated Dictionary of The Gods and Symbols of Ancient Mexico and the Maya*, p. 156.

105. *The Hutchison Dictionary of World Myth*, p. 106.

106. Briffault, *op. cit.*, ii, p. 624.

107. Briffault, *op. cit.*, iii, p. 624.

108. Briffault, *ibid*, ii, 624.

109. Johnson, *op. cit.*, p. 360.

110. Funk & Wagnall, *op. cit.*, p. 1047.

111. Johnson, *op. cit.*, p. 211.

112. Chief Seattle. The whole passage is quoted in Campbell, *The Way of the Animal Powers*, p. 269.

113. Ted Hughes, *Selected Poems: 1957–1981*, p. 113.

CHAPTER 5

1. *Aitareya Upanishad*, 2: 1–4, trans. Robert Ernest Hume, *The Thirteen Principal Upanishads*, Oxford, 1921, p. 295.

2. Marshack, *Roots*, p. 35.

3. Jung, 'Two Kinds of Thinking,' in *CW* V, pp. 7–33.

4. Percy Bysshe Shelley, *Defence of Poetry*: 'The savage is to ages what the child is to years'. Lines 45–8.

5. Shelley, *op. cit.*, lines 99–108; Blake, 'Marriage of Heaven and Hell,' *Blake's Poetry and Prose*, p. 185. 'Thus,' Blake concludes, 'men forgot that All deities reside in the human breast.'

6. Shelley, *op. cit.*, lines 76–8; 111–8.

7. Partridge, *Origins*, pp. 404–5. Partridge is the source for the following etymology, except where indicated.

8. *Sanskrit Dictionary*, p. 783.

9. Zimmer, *Myth and Symbol*, p. 203.

10. Barfield, *History in English Words*, p. 98.

11. Partridge, *Origins*, p. 375.

12. McGrath, *The Sun Goddess*, p. 10.

13. See Max Muller's discussion on the relation of the root 'man' to meno and maneo, to 'remain,' drawing on Aristotle, in his *Biographies of Words*, p. 24–5.

14. Pascal, *Pensées* (1670, ed. L. Brunschvicg, 1909), sect 7, no. 455. ('The heart has its reasons which reason knows not.').

15. Yeats, 'The Autumn of the Body,' *Essays and Introductions*, p. 189.

16. Barfield, *Speaker's Meaning*, p. 56.

17. Gospel According to St. John, 3: 6–8.

18. Homer, *Iliad*, 16. 529; 5, 125f., 136; See E.R. Dodds, *The Greeks and the Irrational*, p. 9.

19. W. H. Auden, Foreword to Barfield, *Poetic Diction*, p. 9.

20. Barfield, *Poetic Diction*, p. 204.

21. Jung, Lecture VI, 13/11/29, *Dream Analysis: Notes of a Seminar Given 1928–1930*, p. 384.

22. Shelley, *Defence of Poetry*, lines 102–3.

23. Funk & Wagnall, *op. cit.*, p. 671 (also known as 'she who does not cook'!).

24. *Brihadaranyaka Upanishad*, i, 3, 16.

25. *Kaushitaki Upanishad*, 4, 4.

26. Harding, *op. cit.*, p. 101. Gwydion O'Hara, *Moonlore*, pp. 108–10.

27. Campbell, *Oriental Mythology*, p. 96.

28. Sylvia Plath, 'The Moon and the Yew Tree,' *Ariel*, p. 41.

29. William Wordsworth, *The Prelude*, Book XIII, 40–86.

30. Plato, *Epinomis*, 978b–979a, Plato, *The Collected Dialogues*, pp. 1521–2.

31. Nilsson, *Primitive Time Reckoning*, pp. 159; 234.

32. Hentze, *Objets Rituels*, p. 55; Eliade, *Patterns*, p. 183; J. E. Cirlot, *A Dictionary of Symbols*, p. 217.

33. Plato, *Phaedrus*, 246b–253e.

34. Brennan, *The Stars and the Stones*, p. 15.

35. Harrison, *Themis*, p. 189.

36. Campbell, *Oriental Mythology*, p. 24.

37. J.C. Cooper, *Symbolism: The Universal Language*, p. 23.

38. *Tao Te Ching*, 1. 3.

39. John Layard, *Stone Men of Malekula*.

40. Gimbutas, *Goddesses and Gods*, p. 197.

41. *Ibid*., pp. 196–200.

42. Frankfort, *Ancient Egyptian Religion*, p. 13.

43. Hesiod, *Theogony*, 422–3.

44. Apollonius Rhodius, *The Voyage of Argo*, 3. 467.

45. The *Homeric Hymn to Demeter*, lines 57–8.

46. Pausanias, IV. 31. 7. See also VII. 18. 12; IV. 32 6.

47. Aeschylus, *Agamemnon*, 133 ff.

48. Homer, *Odyssey*, XV, 407ff.

49. Briffault, *The Mothers*, ii, 683.

50. R.H. Codrington, *The Melanesians*, pp. 168–9; 150–6.

51. Briffault, *op. cit.*, ii, 729–33.

52. W. Matthews, 'Some deities and Demons of the Navahos,' *The American Naturalist*, xx, pp. 846ff.

53. Graves, *The White Goddess*, passim.

54. Kramer, *The Sumerians: Their History*, p. 145.

55. Kramer, *op. cit.*, p. 146.

56. *Ibid*.

57. Kramer, *op. cit.*, p. 147.

58. *Larousse*, p. 456.

59. Briffault, *op. cit.*, ii, p. 603.

60. *Ibid*., p. 606.

61. B. Thorpe, *Northern Mythology*, i, p. 6.

62. Briffault, *op. cit.*, iii, p. 80.

63. Jacobson, *The Treasures of Darkness*, p. 121.

64. Harrison, *Themis*, pp. 192–3.

65. Campbell, *The Way of the Animal Powers*, pp. 68–9.

66. Gimbutas, *Goddesses and Gods*, p. 93.

67. Gimbutas, *op. cit.*, p. 93; 224.

68. Shakespeare, *A Midsummer Night's Dream*, V, ii, 13–4.

69. Nonnus, *Dionysiaca*, vi, 236, calls Selene *triphues*. These examples (together with the rites of Hera) should be enough to show that the idea of a threefold nature of the Moon (whether goddess or god) is not 'an evolving modern conception,' as Ronald Hutton suggests in his book, *The Triumph of the Moon*, p. 179.

70. Harrison, *Themis*, pp. 189–90.

71. Euripides, *The Bacchae*, 680ff.

72. P.D. Ouspensky, *In Search of the Miraculous*, p. 77ff.

73. Acts of the Apostles, 9:9.

74. Harold Bayley, 'Cinderella,' *The Lost Language of Symbolism*, pp. 196–231.

75. McCrickard, *Eclipse of the Sun*, pp. 37–8, observes that any trinity, whether of Sun or Moon, 'expresses a religious sense of completeness and balance.'

76. 'Arrangement in triads is an archetype in the history of religion, which in all probability formed the basis of the Christian Trinity.' Jung, *CW* 11, p. 113ff.

77. Jung, *CW* 12, p. 160.

78. Goblet d'Alviella, *The Migration of Symbols*, p. 71.

79. Knappert, *Indian Mythology*, pp. 235–6.

80. The *Homeric Hymn to Hermes*, line 28.

81. Joseph Epes Brown, *The Sacred Pipe: Black Elk's Account of the Seven Rites of the Oglala Sioux*, p. 80.

82. See Campbell, *The Wild Gander*, p. 83.

83. Plutarch, *Isis and Osiris*, 376. E. F, Loeb, p. 151.

84. Hastings, *Encyclopedia*, p. 76.

85. Carmen Blacker and Michael Loewe, eds. *Ancient Cosmologies*, London, George Allen & Unwin Ltd., 1975, p. 154.

86. Guiley, *The Lunar Almanac*, p. 87.

87. Claremont Books, *Dictionary of Proverbs*, p. 250. John Michel and Christine Rhone, *Twelve-Tribe Nations and the Science of Enchanting the Landscape*, Grand Rapids, MI., Phanes, 1991, p. 16ff.

88. Shakespeare, *Macbeth*, I, iii, 33–4.

89. Hesiod, *Theogony*, lines 60, 76;

90. The *Homeric Hymn to Demeter*, line 47.

91. See Campbell's chapter on 'nine' as 'The Mystery Number of the Goddess,' *The Mythic Dimension*, pp. 92–147.

92. Opie and Tatem, *A Dictionary of Superstitions*, p. 264.

93. *The Florentine Codex*, in *Historia de las cosas de la Neuva España*. See Krupp, pp. 57–8.

94. Plutarch, *Isis and Osiris*, 42.

95. Virgil, *Georgics*, line 285.

96. Gimbutas, *The Language of the Goddess*, pp. 286–88.

97. Brennan, *The Stars and the Stones*, p. 152.

98. Gilbert Murray, *The Rise of the Greek Epic*, Oxford: The Clarendon Press, 3rd ed., 1924, p. 211. See Campbell, *Occidental Mythology*, pp. 157–77.

99. Homer, *Odyssey*, XXIII, 102, 170.

100. Diodorus Siculus, *The Library of History*, Bk II, 35–IV, 58, Loeb, 1978, ch. 47, 41.

101. Aubrey Burl, *From Carnac to Callanish*, p. 64.

102. Alexander Thom, *Megalithic Lunar Observatories*, 1972.

103. Margaret Ponting, 'Megalithic Callanish,' *Records in Stone: Papers in Memory of Alexander Thom*, ed. C.L.N. Ruggles, pp. 423–441.

104. *Pausanias*, v. i. 4. Apollodorus, *Bibliotheka*, i, 7. In the classical version of the myth Zeus grants immortality to Endymion; whereas, in Apollodorus's version, undoubtedly the original form of the myth, immortality is the gift of the Moon. See Kerenyi, *The Gods of the Greeks*, p. 197.

105. F.M. Cornford, in Harrison, *Themis*, pp. 224–9.

106. *Pausanias*, vi. 20. 9. Loeb, p. 123.

107. Frazer, *The Golden Bough*, pt. iii, no. 4, 'The Dying God,' p. 74.

108. *Pausanias*, v.i.4; Frazer, *op. cit.*, p. 91. *Apollonius Rhodius*, 4. 57; Kerenyi, *Gods*, p. 198.

109. Cornford, in Harrison, *Themis*, p. 229.

110. Graves, *Greek Myths*, p. 65.

111. *Orphica Fragm.*, iv; Plato, *Republic*, 364 E. Brifault, *op. cit.*, iii, p. 178.

112. Cirlot, *Dictionary*, p. 216; Eliade, *Patterns*, p. 178.

113. Ted Hughes, 'New Moon in January,' *Wodwo*, p. 158; Sylvia Plath, 'The Rival,' *Ariel*, p. 48. Ancient Romans called the Moon a liar – '*Luna Mendax*'– because when it resembled a C it was waning (spelt with a D, Decrescere), and when it resembled a D it was waxing, spelt with a C, Crescere). Biedermann, *Dictionary of Symbolism*, p. 226.

114. Eliade, *Patterns*, p. 178.

115. Kazuaki Tanahashi, ed., *Moon in a Dewdrop: Writings of a Master Dogen*, p.13.

116. Kenneth Rexroth, *One Hundred More Poems from the Japanese*, p. 109.

117. Rexroth, *One Hundred Poems from the Chinese*, p. 23.

118. Pablo Neruda, *Twenty Love Poems*, translated by James Wright and Robert Bly, London, Rapp & Whiting, 1968, p. 33.

119. Shakespeare, *A Midsummer Night's Dream*, V, i.

120. Tu Fu, *Selected Poems*, trans. R. Alley, p. 31.

121. Paul Reps, compiler, *Zen Flesh, Zen Bones*, p. 23.

CHAPTER 6

1. Campbell, *The Inner Reaches of Outer Space*, p. 11. What Adolf Bastian calls 'elementary ideas,' and Jacob Burckhardt 'primordial images,' Jung calls 'archetypes of the collective unconscious,' the 'universal 'thought-forms' of humanity,' or 'the inherited possibilities of human imagination as it was from time immemorial.' He continues, 'the fact of this inheritance explains the truly amazing phenomenon that certain motifs from myths and legends repeat themselves the world over in identical forms. It also explains why it is that our mental patients can reproduce exactly the same images and associations that are known to us from the old texts.' Jung, *CW 7*, p. 65. See Anthony Stevens, *Archetype: A Natural History of the Self*, pp. 39–76. Eliade talks of the 'fundamental unity of religious phenomena and at the same time the inexhaustible newness of their expressions.' A *History of Religious Ideas*, Preface, vol. i. xv.

2. Neumann writes that one of the necessary tasks for understanding the 'psychic history of mankind' is to 'train the 'eye for the archetypal.' *The Great Mother*, p. 93.

3. Wallace Stevens, 'It must be abstract,' iv, *Selected Poems*, p. 88.

4. Job, 38:4. Literally, 'Where wast thou when I laid the foundations of the earth?'

5. Northrop Frye, *The Great Code: The Bible and Literature*, p. xviii.

6. Jung, *CW IX*, p. 6.

7. Coleridge, 'Dejection: An Ode,' IV, lines 47–50.

8. Yeats, 'The Symbolism of Poetry, *Essays and Introductions*, p. 159.

9. Yeats, 'Symbolism of Painting,' *op. cit.*, p. 149.

10. Ernst Cassirer, *The Philosophy of Symbolic Forms*, vol. ii, p. 218. See Neumann, *Origins*, p. 369.

11. Campbell, *The Hero with a Thousand Faces*, p. 249.

12. Samuel Beckett, *Worstward Ho*, London, John Calder, 1983), p.7.

13. Rilke, 'A Man Watching,' *Selected Poems of Rainer Maria Rilke*, trans. Robert Bly, p. 107.

14. Pyramid Text, Utterance 600, in R.T. Rundle Clark, *Myth and Symbol in Ancient Egypt*, p. 37.

15. Eliade, *The Myth of the Eternal Return*, pp. 4; 91f; Lao Tzu, *Tao Te Ching*, verse 1–2, p. 57.

16. *The Kalevala: Epic of the Finnish People*, trans. Eino Friberg, pp. 42–6.

17. Michael Jordan, *Encyclopedia of Gods*, p. 325; Knappert, *Pacific Mythology*, p. 93.

18. Knappert, *Pacific Mythology*, p. 291.

19. *Larousse*, p. 457.

20. *Purusa-Sukta*, or The Hymn of Man, *Rig Veda*, verse 6, p. 30.

21. *Ibid.*, verse 13, p. 30.

22. *Aitareya Upanishad* 2: 1–4, trans. Robert Ernest Hume, *The Thirteen Principal Upanishads*, p. 295.

23. Snorri Sturluson, *The Prose Edda: Tales from Norse Mythology*, pp. 34–6.

24. *Ibid.*, p. 38.

25. *The Hutchison Dictionary of World Myth*, p. 165; Cotterell, *A Dictionary of World Mythology*, p. 112.

26. *Larousse*, pp. 283–5.

27. Ngangar Mbitu and Ranchor Prime, *Essential African Mythology*, pp. 58–60; Cotterell, *A Dictionary of Mythology*, p. 211; Campbell, *Hero*, pp. 259. The wall painting of 'the Moon King and his people' is shown in ch. 12, fig. 9. (This myth is almost identical to the Moon myth of the Wahungwe Makoni tribe of Zimbabwe, where the Moon is called Mwuetsi.)

28. *Larousse*, pp. 457; 464.

29. Guiley, *The Lunar Almanac*, pp. 47–8.

30. Erdoes & Ortiz, *American Indian Myths and Legends*, pp. 147, 168.

31. *Larousse*, p. 464.

32. *Ibid.*, pp. 464–5.

33. These were the Pelasgian, the Orphic, the Homeric and the Hesiodic creation myths. Graves, *Greek Myths*, pp. 27–35.

34. Graves, *Greek Myths*, pp. 27–28.

35. Genesis, 1:1–5.

36. Lao Tzu, *Tao Te Ching*, verse 1–2, p. 57.

37. Percy Bysshe Shelley, *The Cloud*.

38. Laurens van der Post, *Jung and the Story of our Time*, p. 24. Cf. the Rev. Harley in *Moon Lore*: 'We think it will be granted that gender in the personification of inanimate objects was the result of sex in the animate subject.' (p. 87)

39. Funk & Wagnall, *Standard Dictionary of Folklore, Mythology and Legend*, p. 743.

40. Briffault, *op. cit.*, ii, p. 679.

41. With this reservation, according to the *American Bureau of Ethnology*: 'Sun goddesses and Moon gods were found mostly among the tribes of the North West Pacific Coast and the Far North – the Inuit (Eskimo), Tlingit, Chinook, Tsimshian, Nootka, Coos, Dene and others. Elsewhere the Cherokee, Maidu, Yuchi, Caddo, some Apache groups, Hopi, Jemez, Tewa and Taos. The Moon is female in Zuni,

Keresan (except Zia) and Isleta tradition. Janet McCrickard, *Eclipse of the Sun*, p. 134; Carolyne Larrington, ed., *Feminist Mythology*, p. 343.

42. McGrath, *The Sun Goddess*, p. 178.

43. Athanassakis, *The Orphic Hymns*, 'To the Moon,' no. 9, lines 3–4.

44. Plato, *The Symposium*, 190.b.

45. Briffault, *op. cit.*, ii, pp. 592–7.

46. Jacob Grimm, *Teutonic Mythology*, iii, p. 704.

47. McGrath, *Eclipse of the Sun*, pp. 54; 121. Hastings, *Encyclopaedia*, p. 707.

48. Campbell, *The Way of the Animal Powers*, pp. 258–9. Knappert, *African Mythology*, p. 166; Knappert, *Pacific Mythology*, p. 195. Funk & Wagnall, *op. cit.*, pp. 744–5.

49. Rev. George Elwes Corrie, ed., *The Works of Hugh Latimer, Bishop of Worcester (c. 1485–1555)*, the Parker Society Publications, 2 vols, Cambridge University Press, 1844–45.

50. *The Zohar*, I, 20 a.

51. Jung, *CW 12*, p. 404; Neumann, 'in its essence the moon is bound to the archetypal Feminine.' 'The Moon and Matriarchal Consciousness,' *op. cit.*, p. 71ff. Plutarch calls the Moon feminine in relation to the sun and masculine in relation to earth, but this was not known in Greece in early times. Cirlot omits the masculine dimension: 'because of its passive character - in that it receives light from the sun - it is equated with ...the passive or feminine principle.' *Dictionary*, p. 216. But originally, in those cultures where the Moon was clearly feminine, it was not because it was 'passive.'

52. Neumann, 'The Moon and Matriarchal Consciousness,' *op. cit.*, p. 78.

53. Plutarch, *Isis and Osiris*, 41, 367 D, Loeb, p. 101. See Joan Chamberlain Engelsman, *The Feminine Dimension of the Divine*, Philadelphia, Westminster Press, 1979, especially ch. 2, 'The Feminine Archetypes,' pp. 26–29.

54. A. Ungnad, ed., *Der Religion der Babylonier und Assyrer* (Jena, 1921), p. 165.

55. *Aitareya Brahmana*, in Zimmer, *Philosophies of India*, p. 71.

56. Jung's distinction between the permanent form of an archetype (when it is only a potentiality, without content) and the changing archetypal image (which responds to the outer situation) allows for archetypal images to be continually modified through the historical process. (*CW 9*: i, p. 48ff). So while the Moon might appear as an anima image to modern males, it might have been an animus image to pre-modern females. See Cashford, 'Reflecting Mirrors: Ideas of Personal and Archetypal Gender, *Harvest*, 1998.

57. Yeats, *Essays and Introductions*, p. 50.

58. *Ibid.*, p. 80.

59. Marshack, *The Origins of Civilization*, passim. Webster, *Rest Days*, p. 124ff. J.J. Bachofen, 'Extension of (the primacy of the night over the day) permits us to recognize the religious preference given to the moon over the sun, of the conceiving earth over the fecundating sea, of the dark aspect of death over the luminous aspect of growth, of the dead over the living, of mourning over rejoicing, as necessary characteristics of the predominately matriarchal age.' *Myth, Religion, and Mother Right: Selected Writings of J.J. Bachofen*, p. 77. See also: 'Conjugal mother right is always bound up with the religious pre-eminence of the moon over the sun.' (p. 115). Harrison: 'The worship of the moon naturally precedes that of the sun, because the appearances and disappearances of the moon, being at shorter intervals, naturally first arrested attention.' *Mythology*, p. 87. Briffault: 'Moon-worship has long preceded any form of sun-worship.' *The Mothers*, ii, p.

578ff. Neumann: 'Throughout the world, lunar mythology seems to have preceded solar mythology. But we also know that in the human psyche the experience of totality always precedes the experience of particulars.' *The Great Mother*, p.

56. Cirlot: 'It is generally conceded nowadays that the lunar rhythms were utilized before solar rhythms as a measure of time. *op. cit.*, p. 215.

60. Nilsson, *Primitive Time Reckoning*, pp. 241–81.

61. Reverend Timothy Harley, *Moon Lore*, p. 89.

62. Cumont, *op. cit.*, p. 69. Cf. E.B.Tylor, *Primitive Culture*, ii, p. 272: 'There are remarkable cases in which the moon is regarded as a great deity by tribes who take less account, or not at all, of the sun.'

63. Funk & Wagnall, *op. cit.*, pp. 672; 744.

64. Harrison, *Themis*, pp. 184–90. Nilsson, *op. cit.*, pp. 241–81.

65. Plutarch, *De defect. orac.*, xiii; Proclus, *Commentarius in Platonis Timaeum*, i, 23e.

66. Briffault, *op. cit.*, iii, p. 60.

67. Plutarch, *Isis and Osiris*, 41, Loeb, p. 101.

68. Zimmer, *Philosophies of India*, p. 160.

69. Cumont, *op. cit.*, p. 70.

70. Campbell, *The Mythic Image*, p. 29.

71–73. L. W. King, trans. 'The Epic of Creation,' lines 35–143, in *Babylonian Religion and Mythology*, pp. 72–8.

74. Jacobson, *The Treasures of Darkness*, p. 179.

75–76. Campbell, *Occidental Mythology*, p. 75.

77. Harding, *op. cit.*, p. 94. 'The transition from moon god to moon goddess which took place in many of the ancient religions was probably related to the rise of sun worship.' See Harrison, *Themis*, p. 388. Cf. Cirlot: 'When patriarchy superseded matriarchy, a feminine character came to be attributed to the moon and a masculine to the sun.' *Dictionary*, p. 215.

78. Neumann, *Origins*, p. 340, note 15.

79. McGrath, *The Sun Goddess*, p. 129.

80. Cumont, *op. cit.*, p. 71. 'At no other point does one perceive more clearly the ties which, in the religions of the east, united intellectual research with the evolution of belief.'

81. Neumann, 'The Moon and Matriarchal Consciousness,' *op. cit.*, p. 68.

82. Plato, *Cratylus*, 409, b.

83. Plato, *The Republic*, 508–509.

84. *Ibid.*, 'The Simile of the Cave,' Bk. 7, 512–21.

85. Aristotle, *Metaphysics*, 1072, b; *De Caelo*, I, 3, 270, b5.

86. Aristotle, *De Mundo*, 392a.

87. C. S. Lewis, *The Discarded Image*, pp. 3–5; 108–9.

88. Cicero, *Somnium Scipionis*, *De Re Publica*, VI, 17, 17. For the full passage, see ch. 13.

89. Tillyard, *The Elizabethan World Picture*, p. 46. Though, in George Chapman's poem *Hymnus in Cynthiam*, Queen Elizabeth was compared to the Moon, called Cynthia, by virtue of their mutual chastity, Quoted in Francis A. Yates, *The Occult Philosophy in the Elizabethan Age*, pp. 141–2.

90. Chaucer, *Canterbury Tales*, C 22.

91. Shakespeare, *King Lear*, V, iii, 17–19.

92. Spinoza, *Ethics*, Everyman, Dent, 1979, vii, ff.

93. Blake, 'Proverbs of Hell,' *Blake's Poetry and Prose*, p. 183.

94. Shakespeare, *Timon of Athens*, IV, iii, 339–40.

95. Shakespeare, *Troilus and Cressida*, I, iii, 88–94. ('the other' here means 'the rest'). Copernicus, in his *De Revolutionibus Orbium Coelestium* (1543) employs a similar metaphor to express the idea that the Earth and other planets move round the Sun: 'In the midst of all dwells the Sun... as if seated upon a royal throne the Sun rules the family of the

planets as they circle round him.' Eric and Tessa Hadley, *Legends of Sun and Moon.*

96. Shakespeare, *I Henry IV*, iii, 199–200.

97. McCrickard, *Eclipse of the Sun*, p. 96. Thomas, *Religion and the Decline of Magic*, pp. 456–7.

98. Ambrose, *Epistola*, 18, 24 in Hugo Ratner, 'The Christian Mystery of Sun and Moon', *Greek Myths and Christian Mystery*, pp. 89–176.

99. Warner, 'The Moon and the Stars,' *Alone of All Her Sex*, pp. 255–69.

100. Briffault, *op. cit.*, iii, p. 184.

101. Quoted in Warner, *op. cit.*, p. 259.

102. St. Bernard, *Homily no. 2*; quoted in Warner, *op. cit.*, pp. 262–3.

103. Briffault, *op. cit.*, iii, p. 184.

104. de Liguori, *op. cit.*, p. 84; in Briffault, *op. cit.*, iii, p. 184.

105. Briffault, *ibid.*

106. St. Anselm, *The Psalter of Mary*, in Warner, *op. cit.*, p. 386.

107. Warner, *op. cit.*, p. 53.

108. Revelation, 12: 1.

109. Song of Solomon, 6: 10.

110. Harrison, *Themis*, p. 200. Cf. Neumann, talking of the Aztec god Tezcatlipoca as playing the role of the obsidian knife: 'The moon as sickle-like weapon, sword and knife is an archetypal symbol of the fight of the youthful hero against the dragon of darkness, which preceded the solar mythology.' *The Great Mother*, p. 190.

111. *Satapatha-Brahmana*, xi. 9. 4. 3. *The Sacred Books of the East*, vol. xliv, p. 130.

112. K.T. Preuss, *Religion und Mythologie der Uitoto*, Leipzig, Hinrichs'sche Buchhandlung, 1921–1923, p. 52.

113. Hastings, *Encyclopaedia*, p. 68.

114. Genesis, 1: 16; *The Jewish Encyclopaedia*, vol. viii, p. 678.

115. Muhammad Abu Jafar al-Tabari, *Chroniques*, vol. i, pp. 11, 24.

116. Krupp, *Horizon*, pp. 77–8. For the story in full, see ch. 7, p. 25.

117. J. White, *Ancient History of the Maori*, vol. i, p. 37.

118. Neumann, 'The Moon and Consciousness,' *op. cit.*, p. 68.

119. Owen Barfield, *Saving the Appearances: A Study in Idolatry*, p. 42.

120. Eliade, *Patterns*, p. 246.

121. Pippa Skotnes, ed., *Miscast: Negotiating the Presence of the Bushmen*, p. 53.

122–124. C.S. Lewis, *The Discarded Image*, p. 37.

125. Shakespeare, *King Lear*, I, ii, 1.

126. Richard Tarnas, *The Passion of the Western Mind.*

127. Thomas Mann, *Joseph and His Brothers*, London, Secker & Warburg, 1956, p. 77.

128. Benedict Kiely, *Yeats's Ireland*, p. 116.

129. Yeats, *Essays and Introductions*, p. 93.

130. McCrickard, *Eclipse of the Sun* and McGrath, *The Sun Goddess.*

131. Eliade, *The Sacred and the Profane*, pp. 157–8.

132. Shakespeare, *Romeo and Juliet*, II, i, 151–3.

133. Bachofen traces this back to the literal reading of the Adam and Eve myth, which showed the masculine coming directly from God (which must be spirit), while the feminine (identified with 'soul') becomes 'merely the soul', 'merely' the highest form of an earthly and material development that stands in opposition to the 'pure spirit' that in its Apollonian-Platonic and Jewish-Christian form has led to the abstract spirituality of modern consciousness.'

Mutterrecht, vol. 2, p. 600. Neumann, *The Great Mother*, p. 57.

134. D.H. Lawrence, *Phoenix*, ii, p. 56ff.

CHAPTER 7

1. Blake, Letter to the Rev. Dr. Trusler, 23/8/1799, *Poetry and Prose of William Blake*, p. 835.

2. Iona and Peter Opie, *The Oxford Nursery Rhyme Book*, p. 264. Cf. Ted Hughes's poem, 'Moon Art' (*Moon-Whales*, p. 62), which begins:

'Whatever you want on the moon
you just draw a line round its outline
and it lumps into life – there it is.
What you draw, you get.'

3. Harley, *Moon Lore*, p. 6.

4. Numbers, XV: 32–36.

5. Jacob Grimm, *Teutonic Mythology* (1880), pp. 716–20.

6. Rev. Sabine Baring-Gould, *Curious Myths of the Middle Ages* (1866), p. 197. Grimm, the collector of fairy tales, comments that this tale must be very old, since the Full Moon is spoken of as *wadel*, which is the ancient word for a faggot or bunch of sticks. *Op. cit.*, p. 718.

7. Dante, *Inferno*, XX, 124–7. See also *Paradiso*, II, 49–51.

8. Grimm, *op. cit.*, pp. 719–20.

9. Harley, *op. cit.*, pp. 23–4.

10. Iona and Peter Opie, *op. cit.*, p. 81.

11. Quoted in Harley, *op. cit.*, pp. 28–9.

12. Chaucer, *Testament to Creseyde*, line 260–4. See also his *Troylus and Creseyde*, Book i, stanza 147:

'(Quod Pandarus) Thou hast a full great care
Lest the chorl may fall out of the moone.'

13. *A Midsummer Night's Dream*, V, i, 235–56.

14. Shakespeare, *The Tempest*, II, ii, 135–40.

15. Krzysztof Zarzycki and Eura Basiura, *Legendy Starego Krakowa* ('Legends of Old Krakow'), Krakow, 1977.

16. Harley, *op. cit.*, p. 50.

17. Grimm, *op. cit.*, p. 720.

18. Harley, *op. cit.*, p. 59.

19. Harley, *op. cit.*, p. 59. J. White, *The Ancient History of the Maori*, vol. ii, p. 64.

20. Jung, CW 5, p. 317, note 20.

22. Jung, CW 5, p. 312, note 10.

23. Henry Wadsworth Longfellow, *The Song of Hiawatha: The Courtship of Miles Standish*, Cambridge, Mass., Riverside Press, 1886, lines 122–6, p. 211. Layard comments that the Moon is also called 'grandmother' in the Pacific Ocean, in the isle of Vao, off the coast of Malekula, and also conceives children by the God of Light shining upon her; the children then come down to earth through the portal of their mothers' wombs. Layard adds that the frequent connection of grandmothers with the Moon suggests the archetype of the Old Woman. *op. cit.*, note 1, pp. 171–2.

23. Erminie A. Smith, 'Myths of the Iroquois,' Jablow, and Withers, *The Man in the Moon: Sky Tales from Many Lands*, p. 14; Bram, 'Moon,' p. 90.

24. 'The Old Man and his Fishing Line,' in W.W. Skeat, *Malay Magic*, p. 21; Jablow and Withers, *op. cit.*, pp. 21–22.

25. Jablow and Withers, *op. cit.*, p. 19.

26. Johannes Wilbert, *Folk Literature of the Selk'nam Indians*, pp. 147–58. Another version has it that the Moon disclosed the Sun's initiation rites. Hastings, *Encyclopaedia*, p. 68.

27. Version from Max Fauconnet, in *Larousse*, pp. 474–5.

28. Mbitu and Prime, *Essential African Mythology*, pp. 149–152.

29. Briffault, *The Mothers*, ii, p. 632.

30. Jablow and Withers, *op. cit.*, p. 19.

31. Briffault, *op. cit.*, ii, p. 633.

32. Baring-Gould, *op. cit.*, p. 189.

33. Snorri Sturluson, *Prose Edda*, p. 38.

34. Baring-Gould, *op. cit.*, pp. 189–90.

35. For a fuller version, see ch. 7.

36. Grant, *Viking Mythology*, p. 24. To render the Moon blameless, some versions have Mani, the Moon, taking the children up from Earth because of their father's cruelty in making them carry water all night long.

37. Lewis Spence, *Myth and Ritual in Dance, Game and Rhyme*, London, Watts & Co., 1947, pp. 178–9.

38. From Iona and Peter Opie, *op. cit.*, p. 42.

39. Iona and Peter Opie, ed., *op. cit.*, Oxford, 1951, p. 226, find it 'curious' that Baring-Gould's interpretation is so often accepted, preferring to see Jack and Jill more generally as a synonym for 'lad and lass.' However, they do not offer any arguments for or against either position, though they point out that the rhyming of 'water' with 'after' (*wachter* and *ahter*) in the first verse may indicate that the rhyme is as early as the first half of the 17th century.

40. Guiley, *The Lunar Almanac*, p. 60.

41. Funk & Wagnall, *op. cit.*, p. 672. Krupp observes that the toad can be seen 'in the bright highland features that protrude into the maria from the southeast limb of the disk.' *Beyond the Blue Horizon*, p. 73.

42. All these examples are cited in Alexander Krappe, 'The Lunar Frog,' *Folklore*, vol. LI, 1940, pp. 161–171.

43. Adapted from Birgitte Sonne, 'Mythology of the Eskimos,' in *The Feminist Companion to Mythology*, edited by Carolyn Larrington, p. 166.

44. *Ibid.*, p. 168.

45. Hartley Burr Alexander, 'North American Mythology,' *Mythology of All Races*, ed. Louis H. Gray, 1964, vol. 4, pp. 55–6.

46. Bram, *op. cit.*, p. 90. The Desano Indians of northwest Amazonia see the Moon marked with the menstrual blood of the Daughter of the Sun, who was, unusually, seduced by the Sun Father. Campbell, *Historical Atlas of World Mythology, vol. II, The Way of the Seeded Earth*, pt. 3, p. 341.

47. Harley, *op. cit.*, p. 57.

48. John Layard, *The Lady and the Hare*, p. 125.

49. Adapted from Werner, *Myths and Legends of China*, pp. 182–8.

50. Carl Hentze, *Frühchinesische Bronzen und Kultdarstellungen*, trans. Layard, *op. cit.*, pp. 131–2.

51. Eberhard, *A Dictionary of Chinese Symbols*, p. 194.

52. Harley, *op. cit.*, p. 105.

53. Bredon and Mitrophanow, *The Chinese Moon Year*, p. 401.

54. Kenneth Rexroth, *One Hundred poems from the Chinese*, p. 8.

55. Harley, *op. cit.*, p. 64. As Gubernatis says, 'the mythical hare and the moon are constantly identified.' *Zoological Mythology*, ii, p. 80. Knappert, *Pacific Mythology*, p. 107.

56. Adapted from Layard, *op. cit.*, pp. 108–10. This is one of the 'Jataka' stories of Southern (Hinayana) Buddhism. Other versions have different animals: an ape, monkey, coot or fox. See Baring-Gould, *op. cit.*, p. 191; and Harley, *op. cit.*, p. 60.

57. W.G. Black, 'The Hare in Folklore,' *Folklore Journal*, vol. i, p. 88.

58. Layard, *op. cit.*, pp. 106–7.

59. Layard, *op. cit.*, p. 115. See also Coomaraswamy, 'On

Hares and Dreams,' in *What is Civilization? And Other Essays*, Chapter 11, pp. 95–106.

60. Adapted from a compilation of several versions: 'The Elephants and the Hares,' in *The Ocean of Story*, trans. C.H. Tawney, London, 1924, vol. i, 121; and Ryder, Arthur, W., *The Panchatantra*, pp. 308–15; Baring-Gould, *op. cit.*, pp. 193–5.

61. Harley, *op. cit.*, p. 60.

62. Hares feeding on flowers from the Indus Valley civilization are shown on copper tablets from Mohenjo-daro (c. 2500–1200 BC). Quoted, with illustration, in Ann Shankar and Jenny Housego, *Bridal Durries of India*, Ahmedabad, Mapin Publishing Pvt. Ltd., 1997, p. 62.

63. Layard, *op. cit.*, p. 231.

64. Adapted from Krupp, *op. cit.*, pp. 77–78.

65. See Miller, *op. cit.*, p. 118, who says that this young Moon goddess cannot be Ixchel because Ixchel is old (though in universal moonlore the old becomes young again without contradiction). See also Hentze, *Mythes et Symboles Lunaires*, p. 172, where the rabbit is depicted coming out of the beak of the feathered serpent. The Mayans, who wrote an elementary script, also developed an accurate lunar calendar which enabled them to calculate the dates of solar and lunar eclipses, both greatly feared.

66. Krupp, *op. cit.*, p. 74.

67. Mary Ellen Miller, *Jaina Figurines: A Study of Maya Iconography*, Princeton, The Princeton Art Museum, 1975, p. 30.

68. Briffault, *op. cit.*, ii, p. 735.

69. Funk & Wagnall, *op. cit.*, p. 480.

70. Krappe, in 'Old Celtic Taboos,' *Folklore*, vol. LIII and LIV, 1942–3, pp. 200–1, writes that 'among the Algonquin and other Indian tribes the Great Hare was the moon in person.'

71. Tales of Brer Rabbit, collected in Joel Chandler Harris, *Uncle Remus: His Songs and his Sayings*, London, Nelson, 1909.

72. St. Augustine, *City of God* (413-6 AD.), cited in Warner, *op. cit.*, p. 55ff.

73. Bredon and Mitrophanow, *op. cit.*, p. 406.

74. Krappe, *op. cit.*, p. 199.

75. 'The hare, because she cheweth the cud but parteth not the hoof, she is unclean unto you.' Leviticus, xi: 6.

76. Caesar, *De Bello Gallico*, v, 12.

77. Xenophon, *Venatio*, v.14; in Briffault, *op. cit.*, ii, p. 617.

78. Briffault, *ibid*.

79. 10/5/81, in Iona Opie and Moira Tatem, ed., *A Dictionary of Superstitions*, p. 194.

80. Peter Lorie, *Superstitions: The Book of Ancient Lore*, pp. 150–3.

81. Dion Cassius, *Roman History*, LXII,b; in Layard, *op. cit.*, p. 189.

82. Writing in Latin, Bede's much-disputed words were: *Eostur-monath, qui nunc Paschalis mensis interpretatur, quondam a Dea illorum quae Eostre vocabatur, et cui in illo festa celebrabant, nomen habuit*. Chapter XV, 'De Mensibus Anglorum,' *The Complete Works of Venerable Bede*, in the Original Latin, collated by Rev. J.A. Giles, Vol. VI, p. 179.

83. Grimm, *Teutonic Mythology*, p. 291.

84. C. J. Billson, 'The Easter Hare' (1892), vol. iii, p. 447, note 4, quoting Henderson. Krappe, *Folklore*, vol. iii, quoting Mannhardt, ascribes this note to the Teutonic goddess Holda. Quoted in Layard, *op. cit.*, p. 180, note 1.

85. Grimm, *op. cit.*, p. 289.

86. *Eostre* probably gave her name to the 'east' as the place

of dawn, where the sun rises. Layard brings philological evidence from Sanskrit to Latin to suggest that Sanskrit *usra*, meaning 'dawn,' became Old Norse *austr*, meaning 'east,' and in Ionic Greek Eos, 'dawn,' and in Old Latin *Ausosa*, which becomes in classical Latin *Aurora* (Indo-European s between vowels turning in classical Latin into r), who was the Roman goddess of the Dawn.

87. Layard, *op. cit.*, p. 169.

88. R. Verstegan (pseudonym for Richard Rowlands), A Restitution of Decayed Intelligence: In *Antiquities, Concerning the most noble and renowned English nation*, Quoted, with illustration, in Layard, *op. cit.*, pp. 169–70.

89. W.G. Black, in his 'The Hare in Folk-lore,' gives a list of examples. *Folk-lore* Journal, i, p. 84. See also Billson, *op. cit.*, p. 450.

90. Frazer, *The Golden Bough*, Part V, 'Spirits of the Corn and of the Wild,' vol.i, pp. 270–80. Other animals can also embody the corn-spirit: the wolf, dog, cock, cat, goat, bull, cow, ox, horse, bird, fox, pig. Frazer points out that all these are eaten as sacraments, with particular emphasis on the animal who emerged from the last ear of corn. (pp. 303–5.)

91. Billson, *op. cit.*, pp. 442–8.

92. Billson, *op. cit.*, p. 454. The same reasoning would apply to 'bad luck' surrounding the number 13. Black, 'The Hare in Folk-lore,' *Folk-lore*, 1883, vol. i, p. 89.

93. W. Henderson, Notes on the Folk-lore of the Northern Counties of England, p. 168.

94. Frazer, *The Golden Bough*, Part VII, 'Balder the Beautiful,' vol. I, p. 316.

95. From Jeannie Robertson, in Katherine Briggs, *British Folktales*, pp. 300–1.

96. Opie and Tatem, *A Dictionary of Superstitions*, p. 190.

97–98. *Ibid.*, p. 192–3.

99. Billson, *op. cit.*, p. 441.

100. Opie and Tatem, ed., *op. cit.*, p. 192.

101. Briffault, *op. cit.*, iii, p. 184.

102. The anthropologist Frobenius constructed a map in 1929 which recorded all the countries in Africa, from west to east, where the hare was regarded as a trickster. Quoted in Layard, *op. cit.*, p. 159.

103–105. W.H.I. Bleek, *Reynard the Fox*, p. 69–74.

106. Harley, *op. cit.*, p. 72.

107. Frazer, *Folk-lore in the Old Testament*, i, p. 56. (The comparison with Aesop's Fable. Is this the distant origin of the race between the hare and the tortoise?)

108. Bleek, and Lloyd, 'The Origin of Death,' *Bushmen Folklore*, pp. 57–65.

109. Frazer, *op. cit.*, vol. I, p. 54.

110. Retold from Dorothea. F. Bleek, ed., *The Mantis and his Friends: Bushman Folklore*, pp. 5–9.

CHAPTER 8

1. Cicero, *On the Nature of the Gods*, II, 19, 50.

2. Johannes Lydus, *De Mensibus*, iv. 53; cf. Macrobius, *Saturnalia*, vii. 16.

3. Walker, *Women's Myths and Secrets*, pp. 645–6.

4. Jeanette Winter, *The Girl and the Moon Man*. See ch. 2.

5. Webster, *Rest Days*, pp. 128–9; Briffault, *The Mothers*, ii, pp. 431–9.

6. Nancy E. Auer Falk, 'Feminine Sacrality,' *Encyclopedia of Religion*, Vol. 5, p. 307. For a robust rebuttal of these claims, see Janet McCrickard, *Eclipse of the Sun*, pp. 41–49.

7. Aristotle, *Generation of Animals*, IV, 10, 20, Loeb, p. 479.

8. Adapted from Krupp, *Horizon*, pp. 70–1.

9. Briffault, *op. cit.*, ii, p. 584. Cf. A Rain-Forest tribe in Venezuela, the Cariban Makiritare, where the Moon Brother of the Water Mother is the cause of his sister's menstruation, and so of the tribe's women when the Moon passes. Campbell, *Historical Atlas of World Mythology, vol. II*, p. 330.

10. Briffault, *op. cit.*, ii, p. 432.

11. McCrickard, *op. cit.*, pp. 126; 132. Briffault, *op. cit.*, ii, pp. 432–3.

12. Huxley, *The Way of the Sacred*, p. 34.

13. Briffault, *op. cit.*, ii, p. 433.

14. McCrickard, *op. cit.*, Chs. 2 and 3, pp. 9–31.

15. Ovid, *Metamorphoses*, Bk XV, line 789. see ch. 3.

16. Briffault, *op. cit.*, ii, p. 433.

17. 'The Moon and Medicine,' *Clinical Excerpts*, 1940, vol. 14, no. 8, p.5.

18. Harding, *Woman's Mysteries*, p. 63.

19. Ellis, *The Yoruba-speaking Peoples*, p. 146.

20. Briffault, *op. cit.*, ii, p. 432.

21. Kerenyi, *Zeus and Hera*, p. 123.

22. Kerenyi, *op. cit.*, p. 118.

23. Kerenyi, *op. cit.*, p. 129. But, as Harrison points out, 'Long before her connection with Zeus, the matriarchal goddess may well have reflected the three stages of a woman's life; Teleia, full-grown, does not necessarily imply patriarchal marriage.' *Prolegomena*, p. 169.

24. Kerenyi, *op. cit.*, p. 130.

25. Kerenyi, *op. cit.*, p. 164.

26. Aristotle, *History of Animals*, IX, 2, 1, Loeb, p. 425.

27. E. Best, *Journal of the Polynesian Society*, p. 211.

28. E. Best, *Journal of the Polynesian Society*, 1905, xiv, 210, ff.

29. Harding, *op. cit.*, p. 21.

30. Adapted from Erdoes & Ortiz, *American Indian Myths and Legends*, pp. 129–136.

31. Napoleon A. Chagnon, *Yanomamo: The Last Days of Eden*, pp. 122-3.

32. Frazer, 'Balder the Beautiful,' *The Golden Bough*, Pt. I, pp. 22– 100.

33. Harding, *op. cit.*, pp. 55–63.

34. Reichel-Dolmatoff, *Rainforest Shamans*, pp. 62–3.

35. Sylvia Plath, 'Lesbos,' *Winter Trees*, p. 35.

36. Pliny, *Natural History*, Bk VII, xv, 44–6. Loeb, p. 549.

37. Talmud. Bk 7, xv. 64–xvi.67; in Frazer, *op. cit.*, VII, 1, p. 83.

38. Plato, *Gorgias*, 513.A.

39. Graves, *The White Goddess*, p. 166, note 1.

40. *Ibid.*

41. *The Sacred Books of the East*, vol. xiv, p. 133. See also George R. Elder, *The Body: An Encyclopaedia of Archetypal Symbolism*, pp. 303–5.

42. Briffault, *op. cit.*, ii, p. 429. 'There can be little doubt that the original ground for the dangerous and maleficent character universally ascribed to the moon is its direct association with the sexual functions of women.'

43. *Rig Veda*, x, 85. 40.

44. *Rig Veda*, x, 85 ff.

45. Kaushitaki Upanishad, i, 2; in *The Sacred Books of the East*, vol. i, pp. 273ff.

46. *Zend-Avesta*, yasna 9, ha 9, 22 (71); Krappe, *op. cit.*, 106.

47. *The Buddha-Karita of Asvaghosha*, IV, 75; in *The Sacred Books of the East*, vol. xlix, p. 45.

48. Shakespeare, *Hamlet*, I, iii, 36–7.

49. Frazer, *op. cit.*, , VI, 1, pp. 75–6.

50. Briffault, *op. cit.*, ii, p. 586.

51. *Ibid.* In the Greek island of Kephallonia, the tradition still exists that the sex of the unborn child can be predicted from the phase of the Moon. If the Moon is waxing at the time of conception, the child will be a girl; if waning, a boy; if the Moon is full the child will be hydrocephalic. T. B. Edwards from Kephallonia in *FLS News*, the newsletter of the Folklore Society, no. 30, November, 1999.

52. Krupp, *Horizon*, p. 71.

53. Briffault, *op. cit.*, ii, p. 589.

54. *Revues des Traditions Populaires*, xiii, p. 8.

55. Briffault, *op. cit.*, ii, p. 586.

56. Frazer, *op. cit.*, Adonis, Attis, Osiris, ii, pp. 144–8.

57. Elsworthy, *The Evil Eye*, ch. vi, pp.181–232.

58. Isaiah, 3:18.

59. Jung, *Man and His Symbols*, p. 276.

60. Shakespeare, *Anthony and Cleopatra*, II, i, 10–11.

61. Zimmer, *Man and Transformation*, Eranos, V, p. 336.

62. D.H. Lawrence, *The Rainbow*, pp. 365, 516.

63. F.M. Luzel, 'La Lune,' *Revue Celtique*, iii, p. 452;

64. Walker, *op. cit.*, p. 670.

65. Shakespeare, *The Tempest*, V, i, 294–5. II, ii, 105.

66. *The Tempest*, II, ii, 105; III, ii, 21; V, i, 294–5; V, i, 273–9.

67. For the belief that impregnation was caused by the Sun, see Frazer, *The Golden Bough*, Balder the Beautiful, i, 74ff.

68. Briffault, *op. cit.*, ii, p. 589.

69. E. Combe, *Histoire du culte de Sinn en Babylonie et en Assyrie*, p. 28.

70. Vendidad, xxi. iii. b. 9; in *The Sacred Books of the East*, vol. iv, p. 226.

71. Plutarch, *Isis and Osiris*, 43, Loeb, p. 105.

72. 'Book of Making the Spirit of Osiris,' in Wallis Budge, *Osiris and the Egyptian Resurrection*, vol. 1, p. 385. cf. Frazer, *op. cit.*, ii, p. 154f. Plutarch talks of Osiris bringing 'all generated things to their completion, contriving their birth by his skill with the aid of the rays of the moon, both those that bring increase and those that bring decrease, so that things on this earth may come into being and also perish.' 'Fragments from Other Named Works,' *Moralia*, XV, Loeb, p. 227.

73. Coffin Texts, 4, 65j, 66c, f–g; in Alison Roberts, *Hathor Rising*, p. 176.

74. Budge, *The Gods*, i, p. 448.

75. Eliade, *Patterns*, p. 165.

76. *Ibid.*

77. *Ibid.*, pp. 170–1.

78. B. Moon, ed., *Archetypal Symbolism*, p. 264.

79. Eliade, *op. cit.*, p. 166.

80. Apollodorus, *Bibliotheca*, 3.10.3; Graves, *Greek Myths*, pp. 129; 175.

81–83. McCrickard, *Eclipse of the Sun*, p. 79.

84. *Ibid.*, p. 80.

85. Birgitte Sonne, in Larrington, ed., *Feminist Mythology*, p. 166.

86. Sylvia Plath, *Ariel*, p. 73.

87. Plath, *Winter Trees*, p. 16.

88. Plath, *Winter Trees*, p. 46.

89. Opie and Tatem, *A Dictionary of Superstitions*, pp. 280–1.

90. P. Sebillot, *Traditions et Superstitions de la Haute Bretagne*, vol.i, p. 57.

91. Hazlitt, *Faiths and Folklore*, i, 191.

92. Briffault, *op. cit.*, iii, p. 120.

93. L.W. King, *The Seven Tablets of Creation*, Appendix v.

94. Buffie Johnson, *The Lady of the Beasts*, p. 166; *Knaurs Lexikon*, p. 224.

95. Aeschylus, *Suppliants*, 676.

96. Euripides, *Hippolytus*, 166.

97. Callimachus, *Hymns*, 36. 4.

98. *Orphic Hymns*, 36. 4.

99. Knappert, *Pacific Mythology*, p. 115.

100. P. J. de Arriaga, *Extirpacion de la idolatria del Piru*, Lima, 1621, p. 32.

101. W.G. Black, *Folk Medicine*, Belfast, 1883.

102. Michael Dames, *Mythic Ireland*, p. 257.

103. Plutarch, *Moralia*, VIII, p. 277. See *Symposiacs*, iii, 10.

104. Roscher, *Selene*, p. 59. *The Moon and Medicine*, *op. cit.*, pp. 6–7.

105. Guiley, *Lunar Almanac*, p. 107.

106. Claudia de Lys, *The Giant Book of Superstitions*, N.J., Citadel Press, 1979, p. 398.

107. T.F.T. Dyer, *English Folklore* (1878), p. 41.

108. Thomas Hardy, *Return of the Native* (1895), Bk.I, ch. iii, p. 24.

109. 'Collectanea: Moon Lore from West Virginia,' *Folklore*, vol. L, 1939, p. 314.

110. Yehia Gouda, *Dreams and their Meaning in the Old Arab Tradition*, p. 276.

111. Hastings, *Dictionary*, p. 65.

112. Plutarch, *Table Talk*, III, 10, 658. E; Loeb, p. 277.

113. Jacobson, *The Treasures of Darkness*, p. 126.

114. 'Hymn to Nanna–Sin,' Langdon, *Sumerian Hymns and Psalms*, p. 297.

115. Jacobson, *op. cit.*, p. 126.

116. Clyde Fisher, *The Story of the Moon*, pp. 258–9.

117. Quoted in Dames, *Mythic Ireland*, p. 108.

118. Tony Perrottet, 'Behind God's Back,' *The Sunday Times*, 3/10/99.

119. Walker, ed., *Women's Myths and Secrets*, p. 657.

119. Graves, *The White Goddess*, p. 175.

120. Graves, *Greek Myths*, I. pp. 190, 196.

121. Katzeff, *Moon Madness*, p. 6.

122. Walker, ed. *Women's Myths and Secrets*, p. 658.

123. Job 10:10.

124. Campbell, *The Mythic Image*, p. 29. (see ch. 6).

125. *Poems from the Sanskrit*, p.79.

126. Philip Larkin, 'Vers de Societe,' in *Collected Poems*, p. 181. Cf. Ted Hughes, 'The Rabbit Catcher,' *Birthday Letters*, p. 144: 'What quirky twist / Of the moon's blade had set us, so early in the day, / Bleeding each other?'

127. Bleek and Lloyd, *The Mantis and his Friends*, p. 67.

128. Birgitte Sonne, *Agayut*, p. 278.

129. Bram, *op. cit.*, 90.

130. Opie and Tatem, *op. cit.*, p. 358.

131. Sanders, tr. *The Epic of Gilgamesh*, p. 86.

132. *Antoninus Liberalis*, 15; Aeschylus, *fragment* 170.

133. Heracleitus, fr. 37. *The Fragments of Heracleitus*, p. 15.

134. Homer, *Iliad*, 21:483–4.

135. Euripides, *Iphigeneia in Tauris*, 1462 ff.

136. Callimachus, *Hymns*, 3, 127.

137. Sophocles, *Trachinian Women*, 214.

138. Lorie, *Old Wives' Tales*, p. 236.

139. Barfield, *History in English Words*, pp. 92–3. 'As time went on, Roman religious feeling quickly changed in two almost opposite ways. On the one hand it attached itself more and more to concrete and material objects, and, on the other, its gods and goddesses were felt less and less as living beings, and more and more as mere abstract intellectual conceptions.'

140. Cicero, *De Rerum Natura*, 2.27.69.

141. Ben Johnson, 'Hesperus' Hymn,' *Cynthia's Revels* (1600), Act V, sc. iii.

142. Funk & Wagnall, *Dictionary*, p. 500.

143. Reichel-Dolmatoff, *Rainforest Shamans*, pp. 65–6.

144. Sonne, in Larrington, ed., *Feminist Mythology*, pp. 31; 107.

145. Story told in full in ch. 7, pp. 14–15.

146. Sonne, *op. cit.*, p. 104.

147. Rumi, *The Mathnawi*.

CHAPTER 9

1. Nick Kollerstrom, *Planting by the Moon: A Gardeners' Calendar*, 1999.

2. John Dowson, *Supernatural: The Unseen Powers of Animals*, p. 104.

3. *Ibid.*, pp. 9, 104.

4. *Ibid.*, p. 104. See also Nigel Hawkes, 'Size of tree trunk varies with the tide,' *The Times*, 16/4/98.

5. Dowson, *op. cit.*, p. 104.

6. Plutarch, *Isis and Osiris*, 41.

7. Ptolemy, *Tetrabiblos*, I, 4.

8. Eliade, *Patterns*, p. 161.

9. Briffault, ii, p. 601.

10. Briffault, *op. cit.*, iii, p. 63.

11. *Vendidad*, xxi, III b. 9; *Sacred Books*, iii, p. 233.

12. Deuteronomy, xxxiii: 14. 'And for the precious fruits brought forth by the sun, and for the precious things put forth by the moon.'

13. Gimbutas, *Goddesses and Gods*, p. 198.

14. Porphyry, in Eusebius, *Praeparat. Evangel.*, 114.

15. Frazer, *op. cit.*, 6, p. 139.

16. Knappert, *Pacific Mythology*, p. 194.

17. Bram, 'Moon,' *op. cit.*, p. 88.

18. Langdon, *Tammuz and Ishtar*, p. 153.

19. Briffault, *op. cit.*, iii, p. 90.

20. Juan Maspero, *The Dawn of Civilization*, pp. 654–5.

21. A. Jeremias, *Handbuch*, p. 242, n. 7.

22. Neumann, *The Great Mother*, p. 102.

23. Eliade, *Patterns*, pp. 161–2.

24. K. Blind, *Folk-lore*, iii, p. 89.

25. Harley, *Moonlore*, p. 73.

26. Plutarch, *The Face on the Moon*, 939. E.F. *Moralia* XII.

27. Knappert, *African Mythology*, p. 166.

28. Briffault, *op. cit.*, ii, p. 630.

29. Briffault, *op. cit.*, ii, p. 630.

31. Harrison, *Themis*, p. 190.

32. Goblet d'Alviella, *The Migration of Symbols*, p. 157.

33. Wolkstein and Kramer, *Inanna*, p. 38.

34. Harley, *Moon Lore*, p. 178.

35. Preuss, *Religion und Mythologie der Uitoto*, i, p. 79.

36. Hesiod, *Works and Days*, 780–1.

37. Plutarch: Egyptian priests avoided the onion, 'because it is the only plant that naturally thrives and flourishes in the waning of the moon.' *Isis and Osiris*, 353 F. See Frazer, *Adonis, Attis, Osiris*, p. 362.

38. E. Taverner, 'The Roman Farmer and the Moon,' *Transactions & Proceedings of the American Philological Association*, 1918, 49, 67–82.

39. Opie and Tatem, *Superstitions*, p. 263.

40. Hazlitt, *op. cit.*, ii, 418.

41. Eric Maple, *Old Wives' Tales*, p. 82.

42. Krupp, *Horizon*, p. 69.

43. Hazlitt, *op. cit.*, ii, p. 419.

44. Hazlitt, *op. cit.*, ii, p. 418; Yeats, *Essays*, p. 10.

45. Kightly, *Almanack*, entry for March 8.

46. Pliny, *Natural History*, II, CIV, (223).

47. Jacqueline Simpson and Steve Roud, *A Dictionary of English Folklore*, p. 244;

48. Margaret Baker, *Discovering the Folklore of Plants*, p. 58.

Opie and Tatem, *Dictionary of Superstitions*, p. 266, Harrison, *Mythology*, p. 92, notes that Artemisia, a wormwood sometimes called mugwort which was the herb of Artemis, had the power of 'dispelling daemons'.

49. Aelianos (*On Animals*, 24) recommends for the cure of Moon-caused epilepsy a special kind of peony whose properties are identical to those of mandrake: it cannot be seen by day, and can only be gathered at night by tying it to a dog who pulls up the root and then dies. Bram, 'Moon,' *op. cit.*, p. 89.

50. Homer, *Odyssey*, Bk X; Funk & Wagnall, *op. cit.*, pp. 671, 741. Medea also had mandragora in her garden, and Sophocles, in a lost play called the Root-Cutters, describes her cutting her herbs by moonlight. Harrison, *Mythology*, p. 92.

51. Shakespeare, *Anthony and Cleopatra*, I, v, 1–4.

52. Genesis, xxx: 14–16; Frazer, *Folklore in the Old Testament*, ii, p. 381. *Brewer's Dictionary of Phrase and Fable*, p. 700. Funk & Wagnall, *op. cit.*, p. 671.

53. Shakespeare, *Hamlet*, IV, vii, 144.

54. *Ibid.*, III, ii, 245–6.

55. Shakespeare, *The Merchant of Venice*, V, i, 13–15.

56. Barbara Abbs, 'A Celestial Cultivation,' *The Times*, 19/12/98.

57. Nicholas Joly's Clos de la Coulee de Serrant in Savannieres, and Noel Pinguit's Le Haut Lieu; in Kollerstrom, *Planting by the Moon*, p. 58.

58. Lyall Watson, *Supernature*, pp. 24–5.

59. William Burrows, 'Periodic Spawning of Palolo Worms in Pacific Waters,' *Nature*, 1945, 155; 48.

60. Arthava-Veda, iii, 31; *Sacred Books*, xliii, p. 52.

61. *Rig Veda*, ix. 60. 4.; *Anugita*, xxviii. 16; Funk and Wagnall, *op. cit.*, p. 1032.

62. Eliade, *Patterns*, p. 163.

63. Briffault, *op. cit.*, ii, p. 629; iii, p. 54.

64. *Koji-iki, or Records of Ancient Japan*, pp. 42– 4; in Hastings, *Encyclopedia*, p. 88.

65. *Nihongi: Chronicles of Japan*, p. 32; in Hastings, *Encyclopedia*, p. 88.

66. McCrickard, *op.cit.*, p. 65. (See her analysis of the dangers of refusing the possibility that goddesses can be Suns and gods can be Moons (esp. p. 71 and footnotes).

67. Jung and Kerenyi, *Introduction to a Science of Mythology*, pp. 182– 3.

68. *Ibid.*, pp. 184–5.

69. Campbell, *Primitive Mythology*, pp. 198–9; Knappert, *Pacific Mythology*, p. 114.

70. Campbell, *op. cit.*, pp. 170–225.

71. Plutarch, *Isis and Osiris*, 35–38, Loeb, pp. 84–91.

72. Campbell, *Transformations of Myth Through Time*, Tapes, Jan. 4, 1994, vol. 1. Prog. 4.

73. Barfield, *History in English Words*, p. 121.

74. Frazer, *The Golden Bough*, Part 5, vol. i, p. 257.

75. Apuleius, *The Golden Ass*, trans. Robert Graves, p. 228.

76. Manfred Lurker, *The Gods and Symbols of Ancient Egypt*, p. 47.

77. Wallis Budge, *Osiris*, i, p. 58.

78. 'Spell for Becoming Barley,' A. de Buck, *The Egyptian Coffin Texts*, IV, Spell 269.

79. Euripides, *Bacchae*, 283–4. See also Knappert, *Indian Mythology*, p. 335. The alliance between Soma and Dionysos may account for Dionysos' 'journey' to India, in the same way that his affinity to Osiris may explain his 'visit' to Egypt.

80. Euripides, *Bacchae*, 482.

81. Harrison, *Prolegomena*, pp. 421–3. Ovid, *Fasti*, iii, 735ff.

82. Eliade, *Patterns*, p. 162.

83. Graves, *Greek Myths*, p. 58.

84. Cicero, *De Natura Deorum*, iii, 23. 58.

85. Hesychius, s.v., in Briffault, *op. cit.*, iii, p. 143; Harrison, *Prolegomena*, pp. 403–10.

86. Apollodorus, iii, 4. 3; Apollonius Rhodius, iv, 1137; Graves, *op. cit.*, p. 56.

87. Nonnos, *Dionysiaca*, vi, 155–205. *Orphica*, fragment 200.

88. Graves, *Greek Myths*, pp. 118–9.

89. Homeric Hymn to Dionysos, line 11.

90. Plutarch, *The E at Delphi*, 9, Loeb, p. 221.

91. Frederick Nietzsche, *The Birth of Tragedy*, passim.

92. Graves, *Greek Myths*, pp. 111–13.

93. *Ibid.*, p. 115.

94. Plato, *Republic*, 364 b.

95. Proclus, *Commentary on Plato's Politics*, i.3.2.

96. Apollodorus, i, 3.2.3. He concludes his history of the worship of Dionysos by saying that 'he went and fetched his mother up out of Hades, gave her the title of Thyone and went up with her into heaven.'

97. Homeric Hymn to Dionysos, line 21.

98. Elisabeth Henry, *Orpheus With His Lute*, pp. 55–6.

99. Nonnos, *Dionysiaca*, xliv, 217ff.

100. Briffault, *op. cit.*, ii, p. 121.

101. Cumont, *Le Symbolism Funéraire des Romans*, p. 181.

102. Sophocles, *Philoctetes*, 391.

103. Porphyry, *De Ant. Nym*, 18, in Gimbutas, *Goddesses and Gods*, p. 182. The Moon was often compared with a hive whose bees were the stars. W.H. Roscher, *Nektar und Ambrosia*, pp. 13ff.

104. Maarten J. Vermascren, *Cybele and Attis*, trs. A.M.H. Lemmers, p. 16.

105. Baring and Cashford, *The Myth of the Goddess*, pp. 364–90.

106. Jung and Kerenyi, *op. cit.*, p. 171.

107. Plutarch, *Quaest. de cratr. sign.*, 7. Heracleitus said that 'Hades and Dionysos are the same.' *Fragment 74, The Fragments of Heracleitus*, p. 25.

108. Mark, 14: 22–5. Jung comments that 'Anything that comes from death protects one from death. So our holy communion wine comes from the dead; we eat the dead body of Christ and drink his blood, and it gives us life. It is exactly the same as the primitive idea of soma.' *Dream Analysis*, p. 398.

109. John, 12: 24.

110. John, 15: 1; 5.

CHAPTER 10

1. Hesiod, *Theogony*, line 217. At the end of his *Theogony*, line 904, Hesiod also calls the Moirai the daughters of Zeus and Themis, but this is suggested by the translator, Dorothy Wender, to be a late addition: 'The last part of the work (perhaps from line 900) is not generally thought to be by Hesiod, and seems to have been added to provide a transition to the Catalogue of Women.' p. 153. It is interesting that the same suspect dual parentage is also given to Mnemosyne, Goddess of Memory. See also Graves on 'The Fates,' in *Greek Myths*, pp. 48–9: 'The Moirai, or Three Fates, are the Triple Moon-goddess – hence their white robes, and the linen thread which is sacred to her as Isis.'

2. Clement of Alexandria in the Stromata, quoting Epigenes, in Harrison, *Themis*, p. 189, note 4.

3. Kerenyi, *The Gods of the Greeks*, p. 32

4. Graves, *Greek Myths*, 33.3. p. 129.

5. Kerenyi, *op. cit.*, p. 32.

6. *The Hymns of Orpheus*, trans. Thomas Taylor, p. 190.

7. Eliade, *Patterns in Contemporary Religion*, p. 181.

8. Homer, *Odyssey*, 7, 197;

9. Kerenyi, *op. cit.*, p. 32.

10. Hesiod, *Theogony*, 904.

11. Homer, *Iliad*, 16, 334.

12. *Ibid.*, 8, 68. Zeus, Moira and the Erinyes, are said to bring about *ata*, a daemonic infatuation or temporary insanity, when someone cannot understand why they acted as they did. *Aisa*, another word for 'fate,' is synonymous with *moira*. See E.R. Dodds, *The Greeks and the Irrational*, p. 6.

13. Plato, *The Republic*, XI, 616, Loeb, pp. 396–7.

14. *Ibid.*, XI, 617, p. 397.

15. *Ibid.*, XI, 620, p. 400.

16. Compare Wordsworth : 'Our birth is but a sleep and a forgetting.' *Intimations of Immortality*, stanza 5.

17. Yeats's image in his poem 'He Wishes for the Cloths of Heaven' in *Collected Poems* p. 81:

> 'Had I the heaven's embroidered cloths,
> Enwrought with golden and silver light,
> The blue and the dim and the dark cloths
> Of night and light and the half-light,
> I would spread the cloths under your feet
> But I, being poor, have only my dreams...'

18. Homer, *Iliad*, 14, 190–360.

19. Pausanias, x.24.4 and i.19.2. xxx

20. Eliade, *op. cit.*, p. 180.

21. Briffault, *The Mothers*, iii, pp. 80–1.

22. Campbell, *Oriental Mythology*, p. 128.

23. Langdon, *Semitic Mythology*, pp. 63–5.

24. Langdon, *op. cit.*, p. 25. see also Ch. I, fn 99.

25. Frankfort, *Ancient Egyptian Religion*, p. 10, note 8. See Wallis Budge, *The Gods of the Egyptians*, i, pp. 416–420.

26. The lie is thereby given as 'heavy,' weighing more than a feather. Compare *Richard III*, where Shakespeare's metaphor for Richard's 'coward conscience' is also one of weight: in his visions on the night before the battle, the ghosts of Prince Edward, Clarence and Rivers say to him: 'Let me sit heavy on thy soul tomorrow.' (V, v, 71–93).

27. Homer, *Odyssey*, II, 91–114. R.B. Onians, in his *The Origins of European Thought* (to which this chapter is greatly indebted), comments: 'belief that delay in the completion of the web prolonged the life might contribute to the story of Penelope and Laertes' winding-sheet.' p. 419, note 2.

28. Homer, *Odyssey*, I, 16; and 5, 67.

29. *Ibid.*, 10, 220–242.

30. For the whole story, see Graves, *Greek Myths*, pp. 292–348. See also Kerenyi, *op. cit.*, pp. 108–111, and 268–272. For a fuller reading of this myth see Baring and Cashford, *The Myth of the Goddess*, pp. 137–143.

31. Kerenyi, *op. cit.*, p. 109.

32. Harrison calls Pasiphae the 'Moon-Queen. mother of the holy, horned Bull-Child,' in *Themis*, p. 191.

33. Frazer, *The Golden Bough*, vol. 4, The Dying God, p. 44; see Kerenyi, *op. cit.*, p. 270.

34. Catullus, *Poem LXIV*, 305–322.

35. H.R. Ellis Davidson, *Gods and Myths of Northern Europe*, p. 112.

36. Caesar, *The Gallic War*, I, 50.

37. Ellis Davidson, *op. cit.*, p. 113.

38. Briffault, *op. cit.*, iii, p. 160; Bonnefoy comp. *op.cit.*, p. 254.

39. Grant, *Viking Mythology*, p. 13.

40. Grant, *op. cit.*, p. 13.

41. Grant, *op. cit.*, p. 11; Ellis Davidson, *Myths and Symbols in Pagan Europe*, p. 164.

42. 'The Prophecy of the Seeress,' verse 20, in *The Poetic Edda*, trans., Lee M. Hollander, p. 4.

43. 'Song of the Sybil,' verse 20, in Paul B. Taylor and W.H. Auden, trans., *The Elder Edda: A Selection*, p. 147.

44. Snorri Sturluson, the *Prose Edda*, trans. Jean I. Young, pp. 45–6. Grant, *op. cit.*, p. 46.

45. 'The First Lay of Helgi,' P.B. Taylor and W.H. Auden, trans., *op. cit.*, p. 9. See also Brian Bates, *The Wisdom of the Wyrd: Teachings for today from our ancient past*, especially Chapter 6, 'Weavers of Destiny: Changing Our Life Patterns,' and Chapter 7, 'Dwarfs: Transforming With the Web of Wyrd.' Bates comments of this poem: 'Our destiny seen as a golden glittering, lacy interweaving of fibres like a rudder fastened to the moon... The Anglo-Saxon word *gewaef* means 'wove' and its cognate word *gewif* means 'fortune' (p. 112).

46. Onians, *op. cit.*, p. 355. The name Skuld appears in lists of names of Valkyries. Ellis Davidson, *Myths and Symbols in Pagan Europe*, p. 96.

47. *The Darradarjod*, trans. by N. Kershaw, *Anglo-Saxon and Norse Poems*, pp. 123f. Quoted in Onians, *op. cit.*, pp. 355–6.

48. Fernand Comte, *The Wordsworth Dictionary of Mythology*, p. 217.

49. Funk & Wagnall, p. 798. Briffault, *op. cit.*, iii, p. 12.

50. Graves, *The White Goddess*, p. 143.

51. Grant, *op. cit.*, p. 35. Compare the strikingly similar tale of Meleager and the Moirai in Campbell, *Occidental Mythology*, pp. 310–12.

52. Grant, *op. cit.*, p. 15.

53. Campbell, *Creative Mythology*, p. 121.

54. See Bates, *op. cit.*, pp. 2–3.

55. Onians, *op. cit.*, p. 356.

56. Beowulf (c. 700–800 AD.), 2419–2420.

57. Shakespeare, *The Merchant of Venice*, II, ii, 56–61. See also Grimm, *Teutonic Mythology*, pp. 405–26.

58. Shakespeare, *Macbeth*, I, i, 10–11.

59. *Ibid.*, I, iii, 38.

60. *Ibid.*, I, iii, 51–2.

61. *Mahabharata*, i. 802, 825.

62–63. Briffault, *op. cit.*, ii, 625.

64. Shakespeare, *All's Well That Ends Well*, IV, iii, 74–5.

65. Wallis Budge, *op. cit.*, vol. I, p. 454.

66. *Ibid.*, 455.

67. Plutarch, *Isis and Osiris*, 9. See Wallis Budge, *op. cit.*, pp. 451–465.

68. 'Sonnet,' *Selected Poems of Percy Bysshe Shelley*, p. 598.

69. Hyginus, *Fab.*, 140; Hesychios, quoted in Harrison, *op. cit.*, p. 399. See her discussion of the omphalos, pp. 396–444.

70. Harrison, *op. cit.*, p. 388.

71. Erminie A. Smith, 'Myths of the Iroquois,' *Annual Report, Bureau of American Ethnology*, in Jablow and Withers, *The Man in the Moon*, p. 14. (see ch. 7).

72. Krupp, *Horizon*, p. 74; *The Hutchison Dictionary*, p. 106.

73. Freya's golden necklace made by the dwarfs. Grimm suggests that Freya, daughter of the sea goddess, resembles most closely the Thracian Moon goddess whom Herodotus calls Artemis. *Kleinere Schriften*, vol. v, pp. 416ff. As goddess of fertility, love and death, she was often compared with Aphrodite and Venus (hence the naming of *Venerdi* as Friday). Briffault finds Freya, whose name means 'woman,'or 'lady,' to be but vaguely differentiated from Frigga, wife of Odin, 'the horned goddess, who is avowedly the moon.' *op. cit.*, i, 67.

74. Gerard Manley Hopkins, 'The Blessed Virgin Compared To The Air We Breathe,' lines 5–6.

75. Warner, *Alone of All Her Sex*, especially pp. 255–69.

76. *The Protoevangelion*, also called the Book of James, 2nd century AD. Eithne Wilkins, *The Rose Garden Game*, p. 94.

77. Wilkins, *op. cit.*, p. 147.

78. *Grimm's Tales for Young & Old*, no. 50, pp. 175–78.

79. Grimm, *op. cit.*, no. 188, pp. 577–9.

80. Grimm, *op. cit.*, no. 14. pp. 54–5.

81. Buffie Johnson, *op. cit.*, p. 211.

82. Zimmer, *The King and the Corpse*, p. 240.

83. Campbell, *The Mythic Image*, p. 52.

84. *Ibid*; Yeats, in T. R. Henn, Foreword to *Harban Rai Bachohan, W. B. Yeats and Occultism*, p. vii.

85. Yeats, 'Lapis Lazuli,' *Collected Poems*, p. 338.

86. Aeschylus, *Agamemnon*, 1048; 1114.

87. Sophocles, *Oedipus Rex*.

88. Aeschylus, *Agamemnon*, 1581.

89. Aeschylus, *Eumenides*, 383, 838.

90. *Ibid*, 903.

91. Euripides, *Orestes*, 12.ff.

92. Euripides, *Iphigeneia at Aulis*, 1570–6.

93. Homer, *Iliad*, XX, 70.

94. Briffault, *op. cit.*, iii, p. 140.

95. Harrison, *Prolegomena*, p. 298.

96. Aeschylus, *The Eumenides*, 577ff., 627ff.

97. Samuel Beckett, *Waiting for Godot*, pp. 42–3.

98. Fragment 787, in *Tragicorum Graecorum Fragmenta*, Vol. 4, 'Sophocles,' ed. Stefan Radt, Gottingen, Vandenhoeck & Ruprecht, 1977.

99. Plutarch, *De Fortun. Roman.* iv; Pausanias, vii, 26; in Briffault, *op. cit.*, iii, p. 162. Briffault adds that the Good Tyche was 'Good Luck,' often pictured carrying the horn of Pluto, and represented on a Roman sarcophagus as Lachesis with the two other Fates.

100. Hazlitt, *Faiths and Folklore*, ii, p. 420.

101. Miranda J. Green, *Dictionary of Celtic Myth and Legend*, pp. 225– 6; Walker, *Womens Myths and Secrets*, p. 1072.

102. Walker, *The Secrets of the Tarot*, p. 4.

103. Job, 10:7.

104. 'This, Too, Will Pass,' by Attar of Nishapur, in Idries Shah, *The Way of the Sufi*, pp. 80–1.

105. Quoted in Harding, *op. cit.*, p. 224.

106. J.E. Cirlot, *A Dictionary of Symbols*, p. 371.

107. Yeats, 'All Souls' Night,' *Collected Poems*, p. 258.

108. Yeats, 'The Cat and the Moon,' II, *Wheels and Butterflies*, p. 139.

109. Yeats, 'The Phases of the Moon,' in *A Vision*, pp. 59–64.

110. See Kathleen Raine, *Yeats the Initiate: Essays in Certain Themes in the Work of W. B. Yeats*, Dublin/London, Dolman Press, Allen & Unwin, 1986; T.R. Henn, *The Lonely Tower*; Harbans Rai Bachchan, *W.B. Yeats & Occultism*, pp. 226–257.

111. Jung: 'Whatever is born or done at this particular moment of time has the quality of this moment of time.' *CW* 15, pp. 56–7. See Liz Greene, *Saturn*, Darby Costello, *The Astrological Moon*, and Dane Rudyar, *The Phases of the Moon*.

112. Yeats, *A Vision*, pp.24–5.

113. E. M. Forster, *Aspects of the Novel*, London, Edward Arnold, 1949, ch. 2, p. 19.

114. Shakespeare, *Macbeth*, V, v, 17–23.

115. See Onians, *op. cit.*, pp. 303–466.

116. Onians, *op. cit.*, p. 333.

117. George van Driem, *A Grammar of Dumi*. Berlin, 1993.

118. Bredon and Mitrophanow, *The Moon Year*, pp. 414–6.

119. Miller and Taube, *op. cit.*, p. 110.

120. Lorie, *Superstitions*, p. 84.

121. Simon Forman, 1611, quoted in Opie and Tatem, *op. cit.*, p. 221.

122. Onians, *op. cit.*, p. 358.

123. *Artharva Veda*, VIII, 8, 4, ff. in Onians, *op. cit.*, p. 362.

124. Onians, *op. cit.*, p. 354.

125. Graham Townsley, film-maker of Kogi Indians, in private conversation.

126. John Foley, in *The Guinness Encyclopedia of Signs and Symbols*, pp. 90–8.

127. Onians, *op. cit.*, p. 325.

128. Pliny, *Natural History*, XXVIII, vii (1856, V 292).

129. Opie and Tatem, *op. cit.*, pp. 220–1; Eric Maple, *Old Wives' Tales*, p. 88.

130. Lorie, *Superstitions*, p. 89.

131. Lorie, *op. cit.*, p. 84.

132. Lorie, *op. cit.*, pp. 84–9.

133. Opie and Tatem, *op. cit.*, p. 224.

134. Opie and Tatem, *op. cit.*, pp. 220–4.

135. Capra, *The Tao of Physics and The Cosmic Web*.

136. 'The Thunder: Perfect Mind,' Nag Hammadi Library, in Jane Hirschfield, *Women in Praise of the Sacred*, New York, HarperCollins, 1994, p. 33.

CHAPTER 11

1. W. Bogoras, *Chukchee Mythology: Memoirs of the American Museum of Natural History*, New York, Trustees of the American Museum of Natural History, 1930, pp. 305, 448.

2. County Folklore, iii, *Orkney and Shetland Islands*, p. 52.

3. Frazer, *op. cit.*, part IV, vol. ii, p. 144.

4. Briffault, *op. cit.*, ii, p. 653.

5. Frazer, VI, i, pp. 75–6. Briffault, *op. cit.*, ii, p. 586. See ch. 8.

6. Opie and Tatem, ed., *A Dictionary of Superstitions*, p. 265.

7. Dames, *Mythic Ireland*, p. 80.

8. J.A. MacCulloch, *The Religion of the Ancient Celts*, London, Studio Editions, 1992, p. 206.

9. Pliny, *Natural History*, Book XVI, xcv.

10. *Brewer's Dictionary of Phrase & Fable*, p. 858.

11. *100 Selected Poems* by e. e. cummings, p. 15.

12. Plutarch, in Harding, *Women's Mysteries*, p. 114.

13. Shakespeare *A Midsummer Nights Dream*, V, i, 7–8.

14. Yeats, *Essays and Introductions*, p. 178.

15. Hesiod, *Theogony*, lines 60, 76; Kerenyi, *Gods*, pp. 103–5.

16. Homeric Hymn to the Muses and Apollo, 4–5.

17. Yeats, *Essays and Introductions*, p. 75. See Frances Yates, *The Art of Memory* and James Hillman's discussion of Memoria in his *The Myth of Analysis*, pp. 169–190.

18. Yeats, *op. cit.*, p. 79.

19. Yeats, 'Magic,' *Essays and Introductions*, pp. 50–2.

20–21. Harrison, *Themis*, p. 513.

22. Harrison, *Prolegomena*, p. 574; Kerenyi, *Gods*, pp. 103–5.

23. Homeric Hymn to Hermes, 429–430.

24. Eliade, *The Myth of the Eternal Return*, pp. 20–21ff.

25. Bram, 'Moon,' *op. cit.*, p. 86.

26. Kerenyi, *Asklepios*, p. 56.

27. *Ibid.*, pp. 92–3.

28. Bredon and Mitrophanow, *The Moon Year*, pp. 411–2.

29. Tertullian, *De Spectaculis*, ix.

30. Virgil, *Eclogues*, VIII, 69.

31. See Kevin Jackson, 'The Cultural Significance of the Moon', *The Independent*, 11/4/01.

32. Keats, 'Ode to a Nightingale', 4, 3–7. p. 234.

33. Coleridge, Notebooks, ii, 2453; 2546. Quoted in R. Holmes, *Coleridge: Darker Reflections*, HarperCollins 1998, pp. 38–9.

34. Neumann, 'The Moon', *op. cit.*, pp. 100–101.

35. Wang Wei, in Chung-yuan, *Creativity and Taoism*, London, Wildwood House, 1975, p. 189.

36. Lorca, 'The Moon Rising,' in *Selected Poems*, p. 45.

37. Lichtheim, *Ancient Egyptian Religion*, Vol 2, p. 156.

38. Elizabeth Delange, *Le Scribe Nebmeroutef*, Musée de Louvre, Service Culturelle, 1996.

39. *Mahabharata*, I, I, 74.

40. Sadguru Saut Keshavadas, *Lord Ganesha*, pp. 50–1. See also B. Moon, ed. *Archetypal Symbolism*, pp. 110–12.

41. 'The Glory of Amarnath;' in Campbell, *Baksheesh and Brahman: Indian Journal*, p. 21.

42. Lamy, *Egyptian Mysteries*, p.16 (see fig. 6).

43. Frankfort, *Ancient Egyptian Religion*, p. 4.

44. de Bucke, *Coffin Texts*, III, 343.

45. Boylan, *op. cit.*, p. 72.

46. Utterance 47, in Mercer, *The Pyramid Texts*, I, 28–9.

47. Wallis Budge, *Amulets*, passim. Elsworthy, *The Evil Eye*, pp. 124–143.

48. Partridge, *Origins*, p. 395. Cf. Gk. *meninx*, 'membrane.' Indo-European root, *re*, 'to count;' Latin, *ratus*, past participle of *reri*, count, reckon, hence to think, and reason, *ratio*.

49. Shakespeare, *Twelfth Night*, III, iv, 54.

50. John Dryden, *Amphitryon*, iv, 1.

51. *Elizabeth I: Speeches, Letters, Verses and Prayers*, p. 282.

52. Lewis, *The Discarded Image*, p. 109.

53. Rowley, *Witch of Edmonton*, II, i (1658). Brewer, p. 728.

54. Walker, ed., *Myths and Secrets*, p. 670.

55. Matthew, iv, 24. cf. Matt. xvii, 15: 'My son is lunatick. '

56. Bram, 'Moon,' *Encyclopedia of Religion*, vol. 10, p. 89.

57. Aristotle, *Historia Animalium*, IX, 12, 11.

58. John Milton, *Paradise Lost*, Bk. II, 486.

59. Marshall Cavendish, *Man, Myth and Magic*, vol. 14, 'Moon'.

60. '*News of the World*,' 15/12/1940, in Opie and Tatem, p. 265.

61. Barfield, *History in English Words*, p. 66.

62. Francis Bacon, *Works*, iii, 187.

63. Shakespeare, *As You Like It*, III, ii, 410:

64. Shakespeare, *The Winters Tale*, II, ii, 34.

65. *Brewer's Dictionary of Phrase and Fable*, p. 352.

66. Jung, CW 8, pp. 154–5.

67. Horace, *Ars. Poet.*, 453–56; Macrobius, *Saturnalia*. 1.17.11.

68. Spence, *Myth and Ritual*, p. 181; Jung, CW 5, pp. 369–70. Jung points out the relation of *mara* to *mor*, death, fate, and *mare* to sea, mother, and the idea of the child riding the mother as a horse. p. 250.

69. See William A. Whyte, 'Moon Myth in Medicine: The Moon as a Libido Symbol,' *The Psychoanalytic Review*, i, July, 1914, no. 3, pp. 241–56.

70. Unterman, *Dictionary of Jewish Lore and Legend*, p. 140.

71. Robert Louis Stevenson, *The Tale of Dr. Jekyll and Mr Hyde*.

72. Walker, *Myths and Secrets*, p. 1070ff.

73. Sprenger & Kramer, *Malleus Maleficarum*, p. 31; quoted in Opie and Tatem, *op. cit.*, p. 264. See also Michael Baigent and Richard Leigh, *The Inquisition*.

74. 'The Moon and Medicine,' *Clinical Excerpts*, 1940, vol. 14, no. 8, pp. 8–9.

75. Song by E.Y. Harburg, 1898–1981.

76. Opie and Tatem, *op. cit.*, p. 265.

77. Funk & Wagnall, *op. cit.*, p. 744.

78. Opie and Tatem, *op. cit.*, p. 59.

79. Adapted from Marguerite Poland, *The Mantis and the Moon: Stories for the Children of Africa*, pp. 1–5.

80. Krupp, *Horizon*, pp. 63–4, and Katzeff, *Moon Madness*, may be taken as representative of these two positions.

81. van der Post, *The Seed and the Sower*, p.15. *Jung and the Story of our Time*, p.26.

82. Hillman, Foreword to Inscapes, in *The Essential James Hillman: A Blue Fire*, ed. Thomas Moore, p. 234.

83. Blake, *op. cit.*, p. 835.

84. Harrison, *Themis*, p. 138.

85. *Artharva-Veda*, iv, p. 94.

86. Bram, *Moon*, p. 89. Graves points out that 'witch' and 'wicked' are both derived from the ancient word for 'willow,' which also gives 'wicker.' Under the entry for willow, the plant above all others that loves water, Nicholas Culpepper in his *Complete Herbal* says simply: 'The Moon owns it.' *The White Goddess*, p. 173.

87. Funk & Wagnall, *Dictionary*, p. 500.

88. Briffault, *op. cit.*, ii, p. 599.

89. Briffault, *op. cit.*, p. 302.

90. John Clare, 'January: A Cottage Evening,' *The Shepherd's Calendar*, p. 14.

91. Coleridge, *Essays*, I, 40–1. Opie and Tatem, *op. cit.*, p. 58

92. Briffault, *op. cit.*, ii, p. 598.

93. *Pausanias*, x, 12. 6.; Plutarch, *De ser. num. vindict*, xxii; Virgil, *Aeneid*, v. 735. See Harrison, *Themis*, pp. 388–9.

94. Lydus, B, *Magical Power*, 295, abridged.

95. Agrippa, *De Occulta Philosophia* (1510), p. ccxxv.

96. Elsworthy, *The Evil Eye*, p. 202.

97. *Ibid.*, pp. 196; 260; Shakespeare, *Much Ado About Nothing*, II, i. p. 47.

98. Personal conversation with Brian White of Somerset, whose mother-in-law told him he had nailed the horse shoe to the door the 'wrong way up' (points downwards) so the luck would fall out; upon which he changed it. Elsworthy, also from Somerset, wrote a century earlier: 'We may without discussion assume that the horse shoe wherever used is the handy conventional representative of the crescent.' Elsworthy, *op. cit.*, (1895) p. 217.

99. B. Moon, ed., *Archetypal Symbolism*, pp. 194–7.

100. Eliade, *Shamanism*, p. 62.

101. *Ibid.*, p. 292.

102. The Koran, 54: 1; *Concise Encyclopaedia of Islam*, p. 274.

103. Brewer, *op. cit.*, p. 738.

104. Coomaraswamy, *What is Civilization?* p. 102.

105. Cooper, *Symbolism*, p. 113.

106. Bachchan, *W.B. Yeats & Occultism*, p. 231.

107. Brewer, *op. cit.*, p. 1018.

108. de Lys, *The Giant Book of Superstitions*, pp. 375–77.

109. Eric Maple, *Old Wives' Tales*, pp. 78; 46.

110. *Oxford English Dictionary*, pp. 2598–9.

111. Funk & Wagnall, *op. cit.*, p. 743.

112. Briffault, *op. cit.*, ii, p. 679.

113. Plutarch, *Isis and Osiris*, 370F.

114. Graves, *The White Goddess*, p. 445.

115. Shakespeare, *Macbeth*, III, v, 23–5.

116. Shakespeare, *Macbeth*, IV, i, 27–8.

117. Apollonius Rhodius, The Voyage of Argo IV, 56–62. p. 148.

118. Shakespeare, *The Tempest*, V, i, 272–3.

119. Shakespeare, *Othello*, V, ii, 109–111.

120. Plato, *Georgias*, 513:A.

121. Pliny, *Natural History*, VIII, Bk. XXX, 7., Loeb, p. 283.

122. Kerenyi, *Gods*, pp. 81–2.

123. Guiley, *Lunar Almanac*, pp. 121–2.

124. *Kaushitaki Upanishad*, ii, 9.

125. Thomas Cahill, *How the Irish Saved Civilization*, p. 65.

126. Gerald Gardner, *Witchcraft Today* (1954), cited in Ronald Hutton, *The Triumph of the Moon*, pp. 245, 292.

127. See Margot Adler, *Drawing Down the Moon*, pp. 19–20, et passim, for a sympathetic understanding of how modern witches think about their craft.

128. *Ibid.*, p. 20.

129. See Plutarch, 'The Face of the Moon', quoted in ch. 12.

130. Werner, *Myths and Legends of China*, p. 188.

131. Rose Quong, *op. cit.*, pp. 19–20.

132. Harrison, *Themis*, p. 200.

133. Homeric Hymn to Selene, 14–16.

134. Kerenyi, *Gods of the Greeks*, p. 196.

135. See chapter 7.

136. Plutarch, *The Face of the Moon*, 944.

137. Campbell, *Occidental Mythology*, pp. 163–4.

138. Rilke, *Duino Elegies*, I, 10–13.

139. Blake, *op. cit.*, p. 183.

140. Neumann, *op. cit.*, p. 118.

141. Eliade, *Man and Time*, p. 197. For the ceremony of worshipping the Moon see Zimmer, *Artistic Form and Yoga in the Sacred Images of India*, pp. 136–137, and Coomaraswamy, *Traditional Art and Symbolism*, p. 132 ff.

142. Roger Cook, *The Tree of Life*, p. 114.

143. Warner, *Alone of All Her Sex*, pp. 255–69.

144. Rahner, *op. cit.*, p. 175.

145. *Gospel of Thomas*, Logion 22.

146. See Jung, *CW* 12; Fabricius, *Alchemy: The Medieval Alchemists and their Royal Art*.

147. Jung, *CW* 9:i, p. 304; *CW* 16, pp. 273–82.

148. Campbell, *Creative Mythology*, p. 291.

149. Fabricius, *op. cit.*, p. 152.

150. Jung, *CW* 12, p. 293.

151. Spence, *op. cit.*, pp. 188–9.

152. Jung, *CW* 12, pp. 463–4; 293–5.

153. Lamy, *Egyptian Mysteries*, p. 16.

154. *Ibid.*

155. Adapted from Su Tung-P'o, 'Thoughts Suggested by the Red Wall: Summer,' in *Taoist Tales*, ed., Raymond van Over, pp. 183–5.

CHAPTER 12

1. Bleek, *Reynard the Fox*, pp. 71–4. (See ch. 7).

2. Briffault, *The Mothers*, ii, pp. 646–7.

3. Hollis, *The Nandi*, p. 98.

4. Briffault, *op. cit.*, ii, pp. 641–51. Codrington, *op. cit.*, pp. 260–5.

5. *Gilgamesh*; African tribes; in Briffault, *op. cit.*, pp. 645–8.

6. Adam and Eve in Genesis, 3: 1–24. Epimetheus in Hesiod, *Works and Days*, lines 52–105.

7. Bleek, and Lloyd, *op. cit.*, pp. 57–65.

8. Frazer, *Adonis, Attis, Osiris*, vol. ii, p. 142.

9. Harrison, *Themis*, p. 178.

10. Frazer, *Folk–lore in the Old Testament*, i, p. 45

11. Briffault, *op. cit.*, ii, pp. 653–4.

12. *Ibid.*, p. 659.

13. Frazer, *Folk-lore*, p. 72.

14. Briffault, *op. cit.*, ii, p. 659.

15. Frazer, *Folklore*, i, p. 73.

16. See footnotes 1 and 7. Stories told in full in ch. 7.

17. Frazer, *op. cit.*, p. 65.

18. Bleek, *Reynard the Fox*, p. 74. Frazer, *op. cit.*, pp. 64–5.

19. Hollis, *The Nandi*, p. 98.

20. Briffault, *op. cit.*, ii, p. 651.

21. *Ibid.*, pp. 655; 661.

22. Frazer, *op. cit.*, p. 69.

23. *Ibid.*, pp. 69–70.

24. Codrington, *op. cit.*, p. 156.

25. Aristotle, *Histor. Animal.*, vii, 18.

26. Apollodorus, *Bibliotheka*, iii, 3.

27. Wallis Budge, *Gods*, ii, p. 377.

28. N.K. Sanders, trans. *The Epic of Gilgamesh*, p. 70.

29. Frazer, *op. cit.*, p. 76.

30. John A. Phillips, *Eve: The History of an Idea*, p. 41.

31. Dylan Thomas, 'Do not go gentle...' a poem in memory of his father. *Collected Poems*.

32. Layard, *The Stone Men of Malekula*, chapter 13.

33. Briffault, *op. cit.*, iii, p. 133. Khons is addressed as 'the raging one, the Lord of Lords...' *Coffin Texts*, 660–p; in Roberts, *Hathor Rising*, p. 176.

34. Shakespeare, *Pericles*, II, i, 17.

35. *Oxford Dictionary of English Etymology*, p. 991.

36. White, *op. cit.*, ii, p. 90.

37. Webster, *op. cit.*, p. 136.

38. Briffault, *op. cit.*, ii, p. 576.

39. L. Spence, 'Brazil,' in Hastings' *Encyclopaedia*, ii, p. 837.

40. Eliade, *Shamanism*, p. 327.

41. White, *op. cit.*, i, p. 142.

42. Knappert, *Pacific Mythology*, pp. 142–3; 194.

43. Chapter 1, pp. 14–15.

44. See ch. 7.

45. Plutarch, quoted in Harding, *Woman's Mysteries*, p. 28.

46. Codrington, *The Melanesians*, pp. 168–9.

47. Briffault, *op. cit.*, ii, p. 679.

48. Unterman, *Dictionary of Jewish Lore and Legend*, p. 140.

49. Opie and Tatem, *Dictionary*, pp. 406–7.

50. Robert Burns; see Yeats's discussion of these lines in 'The Symbolism of Poetry,' *Essays and Introductions*, pp. 155–6.

51. John Keats, 'Lamia,' lines 136–7.

52. *The Oxford Dictionary of English Etymology*, p. 991. *The New Shorter Oxford English Dictionary*, p. 3619.

53. Shakespeare, *I Henry IV*, I, i, 1.

54. Partridge, *Origins*, pp. 756–7.

55. Frazer, *op. cit.*, *Adonis, Attis, Osiris*, vol. ii, pp. 140–50.

56. Briffault, *op. cit.*, iii, 175.

57. Hesiod, *Works and Days*, 42–105.

58. Plutarch, *Isis and Osiris*, 16; Homeric Hymn to Demeter, lines 242–75.

59. Larrington, ed., *op. cit.*, pp. 262–3.

60. Frazer, *Folklore in the Old Testament*, i, p. 72.

61. Briffault, *op. cit.*, ii, p. 654.

62. *Ibid.*, p. 652.

63. *Larousse*, p. 465.

64. Langdon, *Mythology*, vol. v, Semitic, pp. 286–7; 305

65. Krupp, *Beyond the Blue Horizon*, pp. 70–1. See ch. 7.

66. See ch. 9, p. 17.

67. Dryden (1631–1700), *Collected Poetry*.

68. Knappert, *Indian Mythology*, p. 235. (See ch. 5).

69. *Oxford Dictionary of English Etymology*, p. 990; Weekley, *Etymological Dictionary*, p. 1612.

70. *Rig Veda*, x, lxxxv, 5.

71. Krappe, *La Genèse des Mythes*, p. 112. (See ch. 11).

72. Krupp, *Horizon*, p. 70.

73. See ch. 8.

74. See ch. 1.

75. Knappert, *Pacific Mythology*, p. 115. (See ch. 3).

76. See ch. 3.

77. Knappert, *Pacific Mythology*, pp. 194–5.

78. Wallis Budge, *Gods*, ii, p. 27.

79. Plutarch, *Isis and Osiris*, 39.

80. Bleek and Lloyd, *op. cit.*, pp. 50–1; note, pp. 38–9.

81. Frazer, *Adonis, Attis, Osiris*, vol. ii, p. 130.

82. Wolfram von Eschenbach, *Parzival*. Campbell, *Creative Mythology*, pp. 409–10.

83. McCrickard, *Eclipse of the Sun*, p. 79.

84. *Ibid.*, pp. 79–80.

85. Coyolxauhqui was probably an Aztec version of the older Moon deity, Metzli, who was usually represented as male.

86. Comte, *Wordsworth Dictionary of Mythology*, p. 108.

87. Eduardo Matos Moctezuma, *Treasures of the Great Temple*, La Jolla, California, 1990, pp. 122–125.

88. George R. Elder, *Archetypal Body*, p. 422.

89. Jung, *CW* 8, p. 393.

90. The Aztecs, descendants of nomadic peoples, were the last to rule in Mexico, following the Toltec culture which began about 900 AD, and ended what is known as the Classic Period (150–900 AD), during which the Mayans ruled in the Yucatan and Chiapas, and the Teotihuacanians ruled in the city of Teotihuacan. The Aztecs in turn were conquered by the Spaniards in 1519. The tale was collected in 1580 by Spaniards after the Spanish conquest of Mexico in Book Three ('The Origin of the Gods') of the Florentine Codex, a compilation of Aztec life and legends in a book called *Historia de las cosas de la Nueva Espana* ('History of the Things of New Spain'). See Krupp, *op. cit*, pp. 57–8.

91. Elder, *Archetypal Body*, p. 423.

92. Cotterell, *A Dictionary of World Mythology*, p. 175.

93. Campbell, *Occidental Mythology*, p. 55.

94. Hesiod, *Theogony*, 977; Hyginus, *Fabula*, 181; *Pausanias*, ix.2.3; quoted in Graves, *Greek Myths*, pp. 84–5.

95. Kerenyi, *The Gods of the Greeks*, p. 149.

96. *Ibid.*, p. 146. Graves suggests that Aktaion, whose name means 'shore-dweller,' was 'a sacred king of the pre-Hellenic stag cult, torn to pieces at the end of his 50 month reign, namely half a Great Year.' Graves, *op. cit.*, pp. 85; 124.

97. Harrison, *Themis*, p. 199; Kerenyi, *Gods*, p. 36. In *Prolegomena*, Harrison comments that 'all the canonical denizens of the underworld are heroic or divine figures of the older stratum of the population. Hades has become a sort of decent Lower-house to which are relegated the divinities of extinct or dying cults.' (pp. 605–6).

98. Eliade, *The Myth of the Eternal Return*, p. 20.

99. Shakespeare, *Hamlet*, II, ii, 97–8.

100. Coleridge, *Biographia Literaria*, ch. XIV, p. 169.

101. Yeats, 'Sailing to Byzantium,' in *Collected Poems*, p. 218.

102. T. S. Eliot, 'Burnt Norton,' lines 65–68, *Four Quartets*, p. 16.

CHAPTER 13

1. Briffault, *The Mothers*, iii, p. 9.

2. Krupp, *Horizon*, p. 165.

3. Krupp, *Skywatchers, Shamans and Kings*, p. 229.

4. *The Times*, 25/10/95.

5. Funk & Wagnall, *Dictionary*, pp. 337–8; Krupp, *Horizon*, pp. 158–72; Harley, *Moon Lore*, pp. 152–75.

6. Hollander, trans. *The Poetic Edda*, p. 61.

7. Snorri Sturluson, *Prose Edda*, p. 39.

8. Guiley, *The Lunar Almanac*, p. 28.

9. Guiley, *op. cit.*, p. 149.

10. Funk & Wagnall, *op. cit.*, p. 337.

11. Zimmer, *Myths and Symbols*, pp. 175–6. (At least by the 5th c. AD, it was known in India that the Earth rotated on its axis and moved around the Sun, and these discoveries were later brought by the Arabs to Europe).

12. Krupp, *op. cit.*, p. 168.

13. *Ibid.*, p. 163.

14. Nicholson, *Heavenly Bodies*, pp. 58–65; Kim Long, *The Moon Book*, pp. 43–9.

15. Wallis Budge, *Osiris*, i, p. 382.

16. Krupp, *op. cit.*, p. 164.

17. Fisher, *The Story of the Moon*, pp. 253–4.

18. Thucydides, vii. 50; Plutarch, *Nicias*, 23.

19. Shakespeare, *King Lear*, I, ii, 103–10.

20. Matthew, 24:29. See also Mark, 13:24–25.

21. Revelations, 6:12–14.

22. Guiley, *op. cit.*, p. 109.

23. *Richard II*, II, iv, 7–15.

24. Ovid, *Metamorphoses*, Bk XV, line 789. A red or a pale Moon in ancient China, was an omen of great ill luck. (Werner, *Myths and Legends of China*, p. 176).

25. Campbell, *The Way of the Animal Powers*, p. 163.

26. Garcia Lorca, *Deep Song and Other Prose*, p. 31.

27. Funk & Wagnall, *op. cit.*, p. 338. According to Eduard Seler's account (Hastings, *Encyclopedia*, VIII, pp. 615f), a young woman in Mexico was decapitated in order to renew the Moon-goddess; she was then skinned and a young man clothed himself in the skin to represent the risen goddess-Moon. See Jung, *CW* 11, p. 228.

28. Layard, 'The Making of Man in Malekula,' in *Eranos-Jahrbuch*, p. 235; in Campbell, *Primitive Mythology*, p. 446. For a fuller account see Layard, 'The Malekulan Journey of the Dead,' in Campbell, ed., *Spiritual Disciplines, Eranos*, pp. 115–150; and Layard, *Stone Men of Malekula*.

29. Leo Frobenius, in Campbell, *Primitive Mythology*, p. 166.

30. Frobenius, *Monumenta Africana*, pp. 318–22.

31. Campbell, *op. cit.*, p. 421.

32. Frobenius, *Erythraa*, p. 309, text to Plates 34–5.

33. Campbell, *Primitive Mythology*, p. 409.

34. *Ibid.*, p. 411.

35. Campbell, *Oriental Mythology*, p. 89.

36. Campbell, *The Inner Reaches of Outer Space*, p. 72.

37. Frazer, *The Spirits of the Corn and the Wild, The Golden Bough*, vol. 8, pp. 261–2. Frazer writes that human beings have a natural instinct of immortality, which may arise from: 'the sense of life which every man feels in his own breast...Arguing apparently from his own sensations he conceives of life as an indestructible kind of energy, which when it disappears in one form must necessarily reappear in another, though in the new form it need not be immediately perceptible by us; in other words he infers that death does not destroy the vital principle not even the conscious personality, but it merely transforms both of them into other shapes, which are not the less real because they commonly elude the evidence of our senses.'

38. *Kaushitaki Upanishad*, i, 2, in *Sacred Books*, vol. i, p. 274.

39. Genesis, 12:1–3. Briffault, *op. cit.*, iii, p. 108.

40. On the mythical ancestor originating in the Moon, see W. Koppers, 'Der Hund in der Mythologie der zirkumpazifischen Volker,' *WBKL*, 1930, vol. i, pp. 359 ff.

41. Wallis Budge, *Osiris*, i, p. 300, and Frankfort, *Ancient Egyptian Religion*, pp. 6–7.

42. Larousse, *Mythology*, p. 465. See also Eliade, *The Quest*, pp. 136–7, who describes the mythical ancestor of the Calinas, Caraibes of the northern coast of Guyana, as living in the luminous part of the Moon, where the souls of the pious go to rejoin him.

43. *Black Elk Speaks*, as told to John G. Neihardt, Lincoln and London, University of Nebraska Press, 1985, p. 43.

44. Walker, *Secrets*, pp. 679–1.

45. Briffault, *op. cit.*, p. 746.

46. See Chapter 7, note 22.

47. Funk & Wagnall, *op. cit.*, p. 1032. Knappert, *Indian Mythology*, p. 66.

48. Wendy O'Flaherty, *Hindu Myths*, p. 30, note 12; pp. 60–70. In the *Nirukta* and the *Brhaddevata*, Manu was born of the union of the Sun, Vivasrat, and the 'identical female' created by Saranyu, which O' Flaherty suggests is 'reminiscent of the image of the sun placed in the moon.' (p. 60). Tacitus mentions a mythic ancestor of the West Germans called *Mannus*. *Sanskrit Dictionary*, p. 784.

49. Knappert, *African Mythology*, p. 166.

50. Harding, in Jung, *Dream Analysis*, p. 369.

51. The Yanomami Indians of Brazil, for example.

52. Dames, *Mythic Ireland*, p. 147.

53. Sonne, *Agayut*, p. 118.

54. Krappe, *Genèse des Mythes*, pp. 116–9.

55. Cumont, *Symbolism Funéraire des Romains*, p. 181.

56. Kramer, *The Sumerians*, p. 132.

57. Jacobson, *The Treasures of Darkness*, pp. 122–3.

58. Kramer, *From the Poetry of Sumer*, p. 86.

59. Wallis Budge, *Osiris*, ii, pp. 305–47.

60. *Ibid.* ii, p. 274.

61. Plutarch, 'Face', *Moralia*, XII, 28 A–C, 943.

62. de Vries, *Dictionary of Symbols and Imagery*, p. 326.

63. Homer, *Odyssey*, XIV, 161–4.

64. *Ibid.*, XXIV, 1–10.

65. See E. Siecke, *Hermes der Mondgott*.

66. Krappe, *op. cit.*, p. 116; Kerenyi, *Hermes*, pp. 64–69 et passim. The Homeric *Hymn to Hermes*, passim.

67. Graves, *Greek Myths*, pp. 190–3.

68. Kerenyi, *op. cit.*, p. 65.

69. Hazlitt, *Faiths and Folklore*, p. 419.

70. *Kaushitaki Upanishad*, i. 2, *Sacred Books*, vol. i, pp. 273ff.

71. See Harley, *Moon Lore*, pp. 49–50; Cumont, *Symbolism Funéraire*, Chapter III, 'La Lune Séjour des Morts,' pp. 177–252; Eliade, *Patterns*, p. 174; de Vries, *Dictionary*, p. 326. McGrath, *The Sun Goddess*, p. 127.

72. Harley, *op. cit.*, p. 49.

73. R.V. Lanzone, *Dizionario di mitologia egizia*, p. 85.

74. Plutarch, 'Of Isis and Osiris', *Moralia*, V, 368.C. See Wallis Budge, *Osiris*, ii, p. 250.

75. Tylor, *Primitive Culture*, London, 1929, vol. ii, p. 70. Krappe, *Mythes*, p. 117.

76. A. Mariette, *Abydos*, i, 51a.

77. Plutarch, 'Face' 944.C. Cumont, *op. cit.*, p. 184, n. 4. (Kerenyi writes that according to the Pythagoreans, 'the image of the unique mixture of elements that produced the individual passes to the moon, never to be replaced.' *Pythagoras und Orpheus*, 2nd ed., p. 59).

78. Iamblichus, *Vit. Pythag.*, vi, 30. See also Cumont, *Astrology and Religion among the Greeks and Romans*, p. 96.

79. Jung, *CW* 5, p. 318, note 21.

80. Cumont, *Symbolisme Funéraire*, p. 190.

81. *Ibid.*, pp. 213–17; 246–50.

82. *Ibid.*, p. 242.

83. BBC booklet on Stonehenge, programme on BBC2 in the series *Ancient Voices*, first broadcast in May 1998. Spawforth speculates that the third stage of megalithic building, oriented to the midsummer and midwinter solstices, may even have performed a similar function in relation to the Sun. The beam of the Sun at its limit on the winter solstice might also have opened a point in time where the dead could journey to the realm of their ancestors. (p. 17).

84. Bleek and Lloyd, *Specimens of Bushmen Folklore*, p. 399.

85. Telegram to Laurens van der Post from Japanese Sea Captain Mori on the death of William Plomer; in van der Post, *Yet Being Someone Other*, p. 337.

86. Lorca, *Deep Song and Other Prose*, p. 121.

87. *Brihadaranyaka-Upanishad*, vi, 2, 16; *op. cit.*, vol. 15, p. 209

88. *Khandogya Upanishad*, v, 10, 4. *op. cit.*, vol. I, p. 80.

89. *Brihadaranyaka-Upanishad*, vi, 2, 15; *op. cit.*, vol. 15, p. 208.

90. Bram, *op. cit.*, p. 89.

91. De Vries, *op. cit.*, p. 326.

92. Cumont, *op. cit.*, pp. 179–80.

93. D.H. Lawrence, 'The Ship of Death,' appendix of his *Last Poems*.

94. For a discussion of bridges as symbolizing the passing from one state of being to another, see Beverley Moon, ed., *Archetypal Symbolism*, pp. 368–9.

95. Eliade, *op. cit.*, p. 172.

96. Bram, *op. cit.*, p. 89.

97. Walker, *Woman's Myths and Secrets*, p. 672.

98. Mary Magdalene, lines 1350–1356. See Malvern, *Venus in Sackcloth*, p. 121;

99. *Kaushitaki Upanishad*, i, 2. *Sacred Books*, vol. I, p. 274.

100. Jung, *CW* 5, p. 318, note 21. de Vries, *op. cit.*, p. 326.

101. Cotterell, *Dictionary*, p. 145; Cirlot, *Dictionary*, p. 216.

102. Cicero, *De Re Publica*, VI, 17, 17.

103. Aristotle, *De Caelo*, I, 3, 270, b5. Cf. Macrobius: 'The moon, being the boundary of ether and air, is also the demarcation between the divine and the mortal.' *Commentary on the Dream of Scipio*, I, xxi, p. 181.

104. Plutarch, *op. cit.*, 943.A, *Nous* usually translated as 'mind,' has more the sense of 'true self' or 'reason and understanding,' Plato's 'rational soul,' the highest level of divinity. See Loeb, p. 215, note d.

105. Plutarch, *op. cit.*, 943.B.

106. Plutarch, *ibid.*, 944.B.

107. Plutarch, *ibid.*, 943.E.

108. Plutarch, *ibid.*, 944.E.

109. Plutarch, *ibid.*, 945.C.

110. Plutarch, *ibid.*, 945.C.

111. Plato, *Republic*, 508.E.

112. Plato, *Symposium*, 190.B.

113. Walter Wili, 'The History of the Spirit in Antiquity,' in Campbell, ed., *Spirit and Nature, Eranos*, pp. 93–4.

114. Cicero, 'Dream of Scipio Africanus the Younger,' *De Re Publica*, VI.IX. See also pp. 261–283.

115. Cicero, *op. cit.*, VI. XIV.

116. Cicero, *op. cit.*, VI. XVII.

117. Shakespeare, *The Merchant of Venice*, V, i, 54–66.

118. *Ibid.*, V, i, 108–9.

119. Shakespeare, *Henry VIII*, III, ii, 134.

120. John D. Sinclair, trans. Dante, *The Divine Comedy: 3: Paradiso*, Preface, p. 7.

121. Dante, *Paradiso*, Canto II, 121–3, trans. Sinclair, *op. cit.*, p. 39.

122. Dante, *Paradiso*, Canto II, 49–51, *op. cit.*, p. 35. See John Pope–Hennessy, *Paradiso: Illuminations to Dante's Divine Comedy* by Giovanni di Paolo, pp. 36, 41, 74–76.

123. Dante, *Paradiso*, Canto II, 34–6. *op. cit.*, p. 35.

124. Dante, *Paradiso*, Canto III, 10–18, trans. Sinclair, *op. cit.*, p. 49.

125. Sinclair, trans. *op. cit.*, Commentary on Canto III, p. 57.

126. Dante, *Paradiso*, Canto III, 70–3, *op. cit.*, p. 53.

127. Zimmer, *Man and Transformation, Eranos*, p. 348.

128. Zimmer, *op. cit.*, pp. 349–52.

129. J. Bronowski, *The Ascent of Man*, p. 222.

130. Alfred Lord Tennyson, 'Locksley Hall sixty years after,'

line 172.

131. Conversation with Mary Aver, 1999.

132. Ludovico Ariosto, *Orlando Furioso*, 1532, Bk. XXXIV; in *Brewer's Book of Myth and Legend*, p. 189.

133. Alexander Pope, *The Rape of the Lock* (1711), Canto V, line 109.

134. *Ibid.*, Canto V, lines 113–22.

135. Giacomo Leopardi, *Opere*, I, 240–1. In Krappe, *Genèse des Mythes*, p. 118.

136. *Brewer's Dictionary of Phrase and Fable*, p. 745.

137–140. P. D. Ouspensky, *In Search of the Miraculous*, pp. 85–6.

CHAPTER 14

1. John, 19: 31-42; 20:1. See Rahner, *Greek Myths and Christian Mystery*, pp. 109-34.

2. Apostles' Creed, *The Book of Common Prayer*, Oxford University Press, p. 49.

3. Krappe, *Genèse des Mythes*, p. 113.

4. Jonah, 1:17.

5. Matthew, 12:40.

6. Acts, 9:9.

7. Dante, *The Divine Comedy*.

8. See Ch. 1. pp. 27–9.

9. See Ch. 11, pp. 280–81.

10. See Ch. 12, p. 312.

11. See Ch. 9, p. 234-5.

12. See Ch. 3, p. 88–90; Ch 13, pp. 337–8.

13. B. Moon, ed., *Archetypal Symbolism*, p. 368.

14. Eliade, *Shamanism*, p. 36.

15. 'The Cattle Raid of Cooley,' The Ulster Cycle.

16. Van der Post, *The Heart of the Hunter*, p. 221:

17. Frazer, *The Golden Bough*, Pt. IV: Adonis, Attis, Osiris, vol. 1. pp. 2-56.

18. Eliade, *The Myth of the Eternal Return*, p. 72.

19. Joan Halifax, *Shaman: The Wounded Healer*, pp. 12-13.

20. *Ibid.*, p. 13.

21. Yeats, *Essays and Introductions*, p. 91.

22. Goethe, 'Holy Longing,' in *News of the Universe*, ed. Robert Bly, p. 70.

23. John, 3: 3-5.

24. Gospel of Thomas, Logion 113, *op. cit.*, pp. 55-7.

25. Galatians, 2: 20.

26. Jung, *CW* 14, pp. 7-37.

27. Von Franz, *Alchemy*, p. 163.

28. St. John of the Cross, *The Dark Night of the Soul*.

29. T. S. Eliot, 'East Coker,' *The Four Quartets*, III.

30. Quoted in Rundle Clark, *op. cit.*, p. 88.

31. Jung, in *CW* 11, writes: 'The numinous experience of the individuation process is, on the archaic level, the prerogative of shamans and medicine men; later, of the physician, prophet, and priest; and finally, at the civilized stage, of philosophy and religion. The shaman's experience of sickness, torture, death, and regeneration implies, at a higher level, the idea of being made whole through sacrifice, of being changed by transubstantiation and exalted to the pneumatic man – in a word, of apotheosis.'(pp. 294-5).

32. Max Cade, *The Awakened Mind*, Shaftesbury, Dorset, Element Books, 1989.

33. Yeats, *Collected Poems*, p. 308.

34. Cf. Frankfort, *Kingship and the Gods*, p. 67.

35. Blake, *op. cit.*, p. 580.

36. Eliade, *A History of Religious Ideas*, vol. 1, Preface.

37. Jung, *CW* 8, p. 375.

38. Joseph Conrad, *Heart of Darkness*, Penguin Books, 1989, p. 32

39. Origen, *Homiliae in Leviticum*, V, 2; in Jung, *CW* 16, p. 197.

40. Zimmer, *op. cit.*, pp. 351.

41. Blake, *op. cit.*, p. 860; see Ch. 4, p. 98.

42. Campbell, *Hero*, p. 19.

43. Jung, *CW* 9:i, p. 7.

44. Shakespeare, *The Tempest*, 1, ii, 48.

45. Campbell, 'The Perennial Philosophies of the East,' *Transformations of Myth through Time*, Tapes no. 5. Vol. 1. Prog. 5; Aldous Huxley, *The Perennial Philosophy*, London, Chatto and Windus, 1969.

46. Coomaraswamy, *Traditional Art and Symbolism*, p. 458.

47. Eliot, 'Hamlet,' *Selected Essays*, p. 145: 'The only way of expressing emotion in the form of art is by finding an "objective correlative"; in other words, a set of objects, a situation, a chain of events which shall be the formula of that particular emotion; such that when the external facts, which must terminate in sensory experience, are given, the emotion is immediately evoked.'

48. Wallace Stevens, *The Necessary Angel*, p. 83.

49. Campbell, *The Inner Reaches of Outer Space*, p. 17.

50. Fred Hoyle, *The Nature of the Universe*, Oxford, Basil Blackwell, 1953, p. 9. (slightly differently phrased; perhaps the original for the more popular version quoted above?).

51. *The Daily Telegraph, The Independent*, etc. quoted in *The Week*, Talking Points, July 20, 1999.

52. Stevens, 'Angel Surrounded by Paysans,' *Selected Poems*, p. 127.

53. Barfield, *Saving the Appearances*, pp. 144-7.

54. Thomas Mann, 'Freud and the Future,' *Life and Letters Today*, Vol. 15, 1936, pp. 89-90.

55. Jung, *CW* IX:1, para. 271.

56. Logion 77, *op. cit.*, p. 43. See also Capra, *The Tao of Physics*, London, Wildwood House, 1975.

57. Jung, *CW* 6, p. 185.

58. Shakespeare, *Hamlet*, II, i, 63.

59. Thomas Berry, 1/1/01, Notes for a Conference on Earth Jurisprudence, Washington, April, 2001. See also his *The Great Work*.

60. Einstein, *The Expanded Quotable Einstein*, p. 316.

61. Yeats, 'Byzantium,' *Collected Poems*, p. 281.

62. Tarnas, *The Passion of the Western Mind*, p. 439. The whole of his Epilogue is essential reading: pp. 416-445.

63. Coleridge, *Biographia Literaria*, XIV, pp. 173-4. For further discussion, see Baring and Cashford, *The Myth of the Goddess*, pp. 659-681.

64. James Lovelock, *Gaia: A New Look at Life on Earth*, Oxford, OUP, 1979.

65. 'New Moon, Hilal,' in *Rumi: Lion of the Heart*, trans. Coleman Barks with John Moyne, p. 50.

66. Yeats, 'William Blake and the Imagination,' *Essays and Introductions*, pp. 112-3.

67. *Ibid.*, p. 112.

68. Yeats, 'The Symbolism of Poetry,' *op. cit.*, pp. 161-2. Yeats's quotations are from Blake.

69. Keats, *Endymion*, III, 44-57.

SELECTED BIBLIOGRAPHY

Adler, Margot, *Drawing Down the Moon*, New York, Penguin Books USA Inc., 1986.

Apuleius, Lucius, *The Golden Ass*, trans. Robert Graves, Harmondsworth, Penguin Books Ltd., 1950.

Athanassakis, Apostolos N., *The Orphic Hymns: Text, Translation, and Notes*, Missoula, Montana, Scholars Press for the Society of Biblical Literature, 1977.

Aristotle, *On the Heavens*, trans. W. K. C. Guthrie, Loeb Classical Library, Cambridge, Mass. and London, Harvard University Press and William Heinemann Ltd., 1986.

Awakawa, Yasuichi, *Zen Painting: Brushmarks of Infinity*, trans. John Besten, Kodansta International Ltd. 1997.

Bachchan, Harbens Rai, *W. B. Yeats and Occultism: A study of his works in relation to Indian lore, the Cabbala, Swedenborg, Boehme and Theosophy*, Delhi, Motilal Banarsidass, 1965.

Bachofen, Johann Jakob, *Myth, Religion and Mother Right*, trans. Ralph Manheim, Bollingen Series LXXXIV, Princeton, N.J., Princeton University Press, 1967.

Baker, Margaret, *Discovering The Folklore of Plants*, Princes Risborough, Buckinghamshire, Shire Publications Ltd., 1969.

Bancroft, Anne, *Zen: Direct Pointing to Reality*, London, Thames and Hudson, 1979.

Barfield, Owen, *History in English Words*, Edinburgh, Floris Books, 1985.

    Poetic Diction, London, Faber and Faber Ltd., 1928.

    Saving the Appearances, A Study in Idolatry, rev. edn, Hanover, New Hampshire, Wesleyan University Press, 1989.

    Speakers Meaning: Fresh Light on Language and Meaning, Middletown, Wesleyan University Press, 1984.

Baring, Anne and Cashford, Jules, *The Myth of the Goddess: Evolution of an Image*, Harmondsworth, Viking Arkana, Penguin Books, 1991.

Baring-Gould, Sabine Rev., *Curious Myths of the Middle Ages*, London, Messrs. Rivington, 1866.

Bates, Brian, *The Wisdom of the Wyrd: Teachings for Today from our Ancient Past*, London, Random House, 1996.

Bayley, Harold, *The Lost Language of Symbolism: an Inquiry into the Origin of Certain Letters, Words, Names, Fairy-tales, Folklore, and Mythologies*, London, Williams and Norgate Ltd., 1912.

Begg, Ean, *The Cult of the Black Virgin*, London, Arkana, Routledge & Kegan Paul, 1985.

Bernot, Denise, et al. ed., *La Lune: Mythes et Rites*, Paris, du Seuil, 1962.

Berry, Thomas, *The Great Work: Our Way into the Future*, New York, Bell Tower, 1999.

Bible, The, Authorized King James Version, Oxford, Oxford University Press.

Biedermann, Hans, *Dictionary of Symbolism: Cultural Icons and the Meanings behind them*, trans. James Hulbert, New York and London, Meridian, Penguin Books, 1994.

Blake, William, *Complete Poetry and Prose*, ed. Geoffrey Keynes, London, Nonesuch Press, 1961.

Bleek, Wilhelm H.I. and Lloyd, Lucy C., *Bushmen Folklore*, London, George Allen & Co., Ltd., 1911.

Bleek, Wilhelm, H. I., *Reynard the Fox in South Africa; or Hottentot Fables and Tales*, chiefly translated from original manuscripts in the library of His Excellency Sir George Grey, KCB., London, Trubner and Co., 1864.

Bleeker, Claas J., *Hathor and Thoth: Two key figures of the Ancient Egyptian Religion*, Leiden, Brill Publishers, 1973.

Bly, Robert, *News of the Universe: Poems of Twofold Consciousness*, San Francisco, Sierra Club Books, 1980.

    The Kabir Book: Forty-four of the Ecstatic Poems of Kabir, Versions by Robert Bly, Boston, A Seventies Press Book, Beacon Press, 1977.

    Selected Poems of Rainer Maria Rilke, A translation from the German and commentary by Robert Bly, New York, Harper, Colophon Books, 1981.

Bonnefoy, Yves, comp., *Greek and Egyptian Mythologies*, trans. under the direction of Wendy Doniger, Chicago and London, University of Chicago Press, 1992.

    Roman and European Mythologies, trans. under the direction of Wendy Doniger, Chicago and London, University of Chicago Press, 1992.

Boylan, Patrick, *Thoth, the Hermes of Egypt*, Chicago, Ares Publishers, Inc., 1987.

Bram, Jean Rhys, The Moon, in Eliade, ed., *The Encyclopaedia of Religion*, vol. 10, New York, Macmillan, 1987.

Bredon, Juliet, and Mitrophanow, Igor, *The Moon Year: A Record of Chinese Customs and Festivals*, Shanghai, Kelly & Walsh, Ltd., 1927.

Brennan, Martin, *The Stars and the Stones: Ancient Art and Astronomy in Ireland*, London, Thames and Hudson, 1983.

Brewer's Dictionary of Phrase and Fable, 14th edition, revised by Ivor H. Evans, London, Cassell Publishers Ltd., 1989.

Briffault, Henri, *The Mothers: A Study of Sentiments and Institutions*, 3 vols., London and New York, George Allen & Unwin Ltd., 1927.

Briggs, Katherine, *British Folktales*, New York, Pantheon Books, 1991.

Bronowski, J., *The Ascent of Man*, London, Science Horizons Inc. 1973.

Brough, John, trans., *Poems from the Sanskrit*, Harmondsworth, Penguin Books, 1987

Brueton, Diana, *Many Moons: The Myth and Magic, Fact and Fantasy of Our Nearest Heavenly Body*, New York, Prentice Hall Press, 1991.

Budge, E. A. Wallis, *The Gods of the Egyptians: Studies in Egyptian Mythology*, 2 vols., New York, Dover Publications, 1969.

    Osiris and the Egyptian Resurrection, 2 vols., 1911. Reprint. New York, Dover Publications, 1973.

Amulets and Superstitions, New York, Dover Publications, 1978.

Burkert, Walter, *Structure and History in Greek Mythology and Ritual*, Berkeley, Los Angeles and London, University of California Press, 1979.

Burl, Aubrey, *From Carnac to Callanish: The Prehistoric Stone Rows and Avenues of Britain, Ireland and Brittany*, London and New Haven, Yale University Press, 1993.

Campbell, Joseph, *The Hero With a Thousand Faces*, Bollingen Series XVII, 2nd edn., Princeton, New Jersey, Princeton University Press, 1968.

    The Masks of God: Oriental Mythology, Harmondsworth, Penguin Books Ltd., 1970.

    The Masks of God: Primitive Mythology, Harmondsworth, Penguin Books Ltd., 1976.

    The Masks of God: Occidental Mythology, Harmondsworth, Penguin Books Ltd., 1976.

    The Masks of God: Creative Mythology, Harmondsworth, Penguin Books Ltd., 1976.

    The Mythic Image, Princeton, New Jersey, Princeton University Press, 1975.

    The Inner Reaches of Outer Space: Metaphor as Myth and as Religion, New York, Harper & Row, Publishers, Inc., 1988.

    Historical Atlas of World Mythology, Volume I: The Way of the Animal Powers, New York, Alfred van der Marck Editions, 1983.

    Historical Atlas of World Mythology, Volume II: The Way of the Seeded Earth, Part 1: The Sacrifice, New York, Harper & Row Publishers Inc., 1988.

    Historical Atlas of World Mythology, Volume III: The Way of the Seeded Earth, Part 2: Mythologies of the Primitive Planters: The Northern Americas, New York, Harper & Row, Publishers, Inc., 1989.

Campbell, Joseph, ed., *Papers from the Eranos Yearbooks*, 6 vols. Bollingen Series XXX, 4, Princeton, New Jersey, Princeton University Press, 1970.

Cashford, Jules, trans. *The Homeric Hymns* (Introduction by Nicholas Richardson), Penguin Classics, 2003.

    with Anne Baring, *The Myth of the Gosdess: Evolution of and Image*, Harmondsworth, Penguin Books, 1991.

    Joseph Campbell and the Grail Myth, in John Matthews, ed., *The Household of the Grail*, Wellingborough, Aquarian Press, Thorsons, 1990.

    The Myth of Isis and Osiris, Bath, Barefoot Books, 1995.

    Theseus and the Minotaur, Bath, Barefoot Books, 1996.

    Reflecting Mirrors: Ideas of Personal and Archetypal Gender, London, *Harvest: Journal for Jungian Studies*, 1998.

Cassirer, Ernst, *The Philosophy of Symbolic Forms*, trans. Ralph Manheim, 3 vols, New Haven, Yale University Press, 1953-57.

Cicero, Marcus Tullius, *De Republica de Legibus*, ed. T.E. Page, et al, trans. Clinton Walker Keyes, *Loeb Classical Library*, Cambridge, Mass. and London, Harvard University Press and William Heinemann Ltd., 1952.

Cirlot, J. E., *A Dictionary of Symbols*, London and Henley, Routledge & Kegan Paul, 1978.

Clarke, Lindsay, *Lindsay Clarke's Traditional Celtic Stories*, Thorsons, HarperCollins, 1999.

Codrington, R. H., *The Melanesians: Studies in Their Anthropology and Folklore*, Oxford, Clarendon Press, 1891. Reprint: New York, Dover Publications, 1982.

Coleridge, Samuel T., *Biographia Literaria*, Oxford, Oxford University Press, 1907.

> *The Portable Coleridge*, Harmondsworth, Penguin Books Ltd., 1977.

Collon, Dominique, *Catalogue of the Western Asiatic Seals in the British Museum: Cylinder Seals III, Isis-Larsa and Old Babylonian Periods*, London, British Museum Publications Ltd., 1986.

Comte, Ferdinand, ed., *The Wordsworth Dictionary of Mythology*, Ware, Wordsworth, 1994.

Cook, Roger, *The Tree of Life: Image for the Cosmos*, London, Thames and Hudson, 1974.

Coomaraswamy, Ananda K., *Time and Eternity*, New Delhi, Manoharlal Publishers Ltd., 1993.

> *What is Civilisation? And Other Essays*, Oxford, Oxford University Press, 1989.

Cooper, J. C., *An Illustrated Encyclopedia of Traditional Symbols*, London, Thames and Hudson, 1978.

> *Symbolism: The Universal Language*, Wellingborough, Aquarian Press, 1982.
> *Symbolic and Mythological Animals*, London, Aquarian Press, HarperCollins, 1992.

Cornford, F. M. *From Religion to Philosophy: A Study in the Origins of Western Speculation*, Sussex, The Harvester Press, 1980.

Costello, Darby, *The Astrological Moon*, CPA Seminar Series, 6, Centre for Psychological Astrology Press, 1996.

Cotterell, Arthur, *A Dictionary of World Mythology*, New York, G. P. Putman's Sons, 1980.

> *The Macmillan Illustrated Encyclopedia of Myths and Legends*, New York, Macmillan Publishing Company, 1989.

Cummings, e. e., *100 Selected Poems*, New York, Grove Press, Inc., 1954.

Cumont, Franz, *Recherches sur le Symbolisme Funéraire des Romains*, Paris, Geuthner, 1942.

> *Astrology and Religion among the Greeks and Romans*, trans. J. B. Baker, New York, Dover Publications, 1960.
> *The Mysteries of Mithra*, trans. Thomas J. McCormack, New York, Dover Publications, Inc., 1956.

Dames, Michael, *Mythic Ireland*, London, Thames and Hudson Ltd., 1992.

> *The Silbury Treasure: The Great Goddess Rediscovered*, London, Thames and Hudson, 1976.

Dante, *The Divine Comedy*, Italian text with translation and comment by John D. Sinclair, London, Oxford, New York, Oxford University Press, 1971.

David, Julian, *Interweaving Symbols of Individuation: A Jungian Perspective*, Cape Town, Kaggen Press, 1991.

David, Rosalie, *A Guide to the Religious Ritual at Abydos*, Warminster, Aris & Phillips, 1981.

Davidson, H. R. Ellis, *Gods and Myths of Northern Europe*, Harmondsworth, Penguin Books, 1964.

> *Myths and Symbols in Pagan Europe: Early Scandinavian and Celtic Religions*, Syracuse, New York, Syracuse University Press, 1988.

Dodds, E. R. *The Greeks and the Irrational*, Berkeley, University of California Press, 1951.

Downer, John, *Supernatural: The Unseen Powers of Animals*, London, BBC Worldwide Ltd. 1999.

Eberhard, Wolfram, ed., *A Dictionary of Chinese Symbols: Hidden Symbols in Chinese Life and Thought*, London, Routledge, 1986.

Elder, George, R, *The Body: An Encyclopedia of Archetypal Symbolism*, Boston, Shambhala, 1996.

Eliade, Mircea, *A History of Religious Ideas*, 3 vols., trans. Willard R. Trask, Chicago, University of Chicago Press, 1975.

> *Patterns in Comparative Religion*, London, Sheed & Ward Publishers, 1958.
> *Shamanism: Archaic Techniques of Ecstasy*, trans. Willard R. Trask, Bollingen Series LXXVI, Princeton, New Jersey, Princeton University Press, 1972.
> *The Myth of the Eternal Return or, Cosmos and History*, trans. Willard R. Trask, Bollingen Series XLVI, Princeton, New Jersey, Princeton University Press, 1971.
> *Images and Symbols: Studies in Religious Symbolism*, trans. Philip Mairet, Princeton, New Jersey, Princeton University Press, 1991.

Eliot, T. S., *Collected Poems: 1909-1962*, London, Faber & Faber Ltd., 1963.

Elsworthy, Fredrick Thomas, *The Evil Eye: The Origins and Practices of Superstition*, New York, Julian Press, 1958.

Erdoes, Richard and Ortiz, Alfonso, eds. *American Indian Myths and Legends*, New York, Pantheon Books, 1984.

Eschenbach, Wolfram von, *Parzival*, trans. A. T. Hatto, Harmondsworth, Penguin Books, 1980.

Fabricius, Johannes, *Alchemy; the Medieval Alchemists and their Royal Art*, Wellingborough, Northamptonshire, The Aquarian Press, 1989.

Falck, Colin, *Myth, Truth and Literature: Towards a true post-modernism*, New York and Cambridge, Cambridge University Press, 1994.

Faulkner, R. O., *The Ancient Egyptian Pyramid Texts*, 3 vols. Oxford, Oxford University Press, 1969.

Fisher, Clyde, *The Story of the Moon*, New York, Doubleday, Doran and Co., 1945.

Folklore, a quarterly review of myth, tradition, institution and custom: incorporating the Archaeological review and the Folk-lore Journal, London, the Folk-lore Society, 1890-2002.

Folley, Tom, *The Book of the Moon*, London, Courage Books, 1997.

Fowden, Garth, *The Egyptian Hermes: a Historical Approach to the Late Pagan Mind*, Princeton, New Jersey, Princeton University Press, 1986.

Frankfort, Henri, *et al*, *The Intellectual Adventure of Ancient Man*, Chicago, University of Chicago Press, 1946.

> *Ancient Egyptian Religion: An Interpretation*, New York, Harper & Row, Torch Books, 1961.
> *Kingship and the Gods*, Chicago, University of Chicago Press, 1948.

Franz, Marie-Louise von, *Time: Rhythm and Repose*, London, Thames and Hudson, 1978.

> *Alchemy: An Introduction to the Symbolism and the Psychology*, Toronto, Inner City Books, 1980.

Frazer, Sir James George, *Folk-lore in the Old Testament*, 3 vols. London, Macmillan and Co., Ltd., 1918.

> *The Belief in Immortality and the Worship of the Dead*, London, Macmillan and Co., Ltd., 1913.
> *The Golden Bough, A Study in Magic and Religion*, 13 vols. London, Macmillan and Co., Ltd., 1911-15.

Frye, Northrop, *The Great Code: the Bible and Literature*, New York and London, Harcourt, Brace Jovanovich, 1982.

Funk & Wagnall's Standard Dictionary of Folklore, Mythology, and Legend, ed. Maria Leach, San Francisco, HarperSanFrancisco, Harper & Row, 1984.

Getty, Adele, *Goddess: Mother of Living Nature*, London, Thames and Hudson, 1990.

The Epic of Gilgamesh, an English version with an introduction by N. K. Sandars, Harmondsworth, Penguin Books Ltd., 1972.

Gimbutas, Marija, *The Goddesses and Gods of Old Europe, 6500-3500 B.C.: Myths and Cult Images*, London, Thames and Hudson, 1982.

> *The Language of the Goddess*, London, Thames and Hudson, 1989.

Goblet d'Alviella, Eugene, *The Migration of Symbols*, Wellingborough, Northants, Aquarian Press, 1979.

The Gospel According to Thomas, Coptic Text established and translated by A. Guillaumont et al, Leiden, E. J. Brill, 1976.

Grant, John, *An Introduction to Viking Mythology*, London, New Burlington Books, 1990.

Grant, Michael, *Myths of the Greeks and Romans*, Cleveland, Ohio, The World Publishing Company, 1962.

Graves, Robert, *The Greek Myths*, London, Cassell, 1955.

> *The White Goddess: a Historical Grammar of Poetic Myth*, London, Faber & Faber, 1977.

Gray, John, *Near-Eastern Mythology*, London, Hamlyn, 1982.

Green, Miranda J., *Dictionary of Celtic Myth and Legend*, London, Thames and Hudson, 1992.

Greene, Liz, *Saturn: A New Look at an Old Devil*, Arkana, 1990.

Grene, David and Lattimore, Richmond, eds., *Greek Tragedies*, 3 vols., Chicago, University of Chicago Press, 1963.

Grimm, Jacob, *Teutonic Mythology*, 4 vols. trans. J.S. Stallybrass, London, George Bell & Sons, 1883.

Grimm, Jakob and Wilhelm, *Grimm's Fairy Tales*, New York, Nelson Doubleday, Inc., 1954.

Gubernatis, Angelo de, *Zoological Mythology: or The*

Legends of Animals, 2 vols., London, Truebner & Co., 1872.

Guiley, Rosemary E., *The Lunar Almanac*, London, Judy Piatkus (Publishers), 1991.

Hadley, Eric, *Legends of the Sun and Moon*, Cambridge, Cambridge University Press, 1990.

Halifax, Joan, *Shaman: the Wounded Healer*, London, Thames and Hudson, 1982.

Harding, Esther, *Woman's Mysteries: Ancient and Modern*, London, Rider, 1982.

Harley, Rev. Timothy, *Moon Lore*, Rutland, Vermont, Charles E. Tuttle Co., Publishers, 1970.

Harrison, Jane E., *Mythology*, New York and London, Harcourt Brace Jovanovich, 1963.

　Prolegomena to the Study of Greek Religion, London, Merlin Press, 1980.

　Themis: A Study of the Social Origins of Greek Religion, London, Merlin Press, 1977.

Harvey, Andrew and Baring, Anne, *The Mystic Vision*, New Alresford, Hampshire, Godsfield Press, 1995.

　The Divine Feminine: Exploring the Feminine Face of God Throughout the World, New Alresford, Hampshire, Godsfield Press, 1996.

Hastings, James, ed., with the assistance of J. A. Selbie, et al., *Encyclopaedia of Religion and Ethics*, 13 vols., Edinburgh, T. and T. Clark, New York, C. Scribner's Sons, 1908-1926.

Hazlitt, W. Carew, *Faiths and Folklore of the British Isles: A Descriptive and Historical Dictionary*, 2 vols., New York, Benjamin Blom, 1965.

Henderson, Joseph L. and Oakes, Maud, *The Wisdom of the Serpent: the Myths of Death, Rebirth, and Resurrection*, Princeton, New Jersey, Princeton University Press, 1990.

Henn, T. R., *The Lonely Tower: Studies in the Poetry of W. B. Yeats*, London, Methuen & Co., 1950.

Hentze, Carl Philipp, *Mythes et Symboles Lunaires*, Antwerp, De Sikkel, 1932.

　Frühchinesische Bronzen und Kultdarstellungen, Antwerp, De Sikkel, 1938.

Heraclitus, *The Fragments of Heraclitus*, Bray, the Guild Press, 1976.

Hesiod, *Theogony and Works and Days*, trans. Dorothea Wender. Harmondsworth, Penguin Books, 1973.

Hesiod, *The Homeric Hymns and Homerica*, trans. H. G. Evelyn-White, Loeb Classical Library, Cambridge, Mass. and London, Harvard University Press and William Heinemann Ltd., 1914.

Hillman, James, *The Myth of Analysis: Three Essays in Archetypal Psychology*, New York, Harper & Row, Harper, Colophon Books, 1978.

　Revisioning Psychology, New York, Harper & Row, Harper, Colophon Books, 1977.

　Healing Fiction, Barrytown, New York, Station Hill Press, 1983.

　The Essential Hillman: A Blue Fire, ed. Thomas Moore, London, Routledge, 1990.

Hollander, Lee. M., trans. *The Poetic Edda*, Austin, Texas, University of Austin, 1990.

Homer, *The Iliad*, trans. Richmond Lattimore, Chicago, Phoenix Books, 1961.

　The Odyssey, trans. Robert Fagels, New York, Penguin Books Inc., 1996.

Hornung, Erik, *The Valley of the Kings: Horizon of Eternity*, New York, Timken Publishers, 1990.

Hughes, Ted, *Selected Poems: 1957-1981*, London, Faber and Faber, 1982.

　Moon-Whales, London and Boston, Faber and Faber, 1991.

　Birthday Letters, London, Faber and Faber, 1998.

Hume, Robert Earnest, trans., *The Thirteen Principal Upanishads*, Oxford, 1921.

The Hutchison Dictionary of World Myth, ed. Peter Bently, London, Helicon in association with Duncan Baird Publishers, 1996.

Hutton, Ronald, *The Triumph of the Moon: A History of Modern Pagan Witchcraft*, Oxford and New York, Oxford University Press, 1999.

Huxley, Francis, *The Way of the Sacred*, Garden City, New York, Doubleday & Company, Inc., 1974.

Ions, Veronica, *Egyptian Mythology*, London, The Hamlyn Publishing Group Ltd., 1986.

　Indian Mythology, London, The Hamlyn Publishing Group Ltd., 1967.

Jablow, Alta and Withers, Carl, *The Man in the Moon: Sky Tales from Many Lands*, New York, Chicago and San Francisco, Holt, Rinehart and Winston, 1969.

Jacobson, Thorkild, *The Treasures of Darkness: a History of Mesopotamian Religion*, New Haven, Connecticut, Yale University Press, 1976.

Johnson, Buffie, *Lady of the Beasts: Ancient Images of the Goddess and Her Sacred Animals*, San Francisco, Harper & Row, 1988.

Jung, C. G., *Collected Works*, 20 vols., eds. Sir Herbert Read, Gerhard Adler, Michael Fordham, William McGuire, trans. R.F.C. Hull, London, Routledge & Kegan Paul, 1957-79.

　Modern Man in Search of a Soul, trans. W.S. Dell and Cary F. Baynes, London, Routledge & Kegan Paul, 1981.

　Man and His Symbols, London, Pan Books, 1978.

　Dream Analysis: Notes of a Seminar given 1928-1930, ed. William McGuire, Bollingen Series XCIX, Princeton, New Jersey, Princeton University Press, 1984.

Jung, C. G. and Kerenyi, Carl, *Introduction to a Science of Mythology: The Myth of the Divine Child and the Mysteries of Eleusis*, trans. R. F. C. Hull, London, Routledge & Kegan Paul, 1951.

The Kalevala: Epic of the Finnish People, trans. Eino Friberg, Helsinki, Otava Publishing Company Ltd., 1988.

Katzeff, Paul, *Moon Madness, and Other Effects of the Full Moon*, London, Robert Hale, 1990.

Keats, John, *Poems*, London, Bell & Hyman Ltd., 1979.

Kenton, Warren, *Astrology: The Celestial Mirror*, London, Thames and Hudson, 1974

Kerenyi, Carl, *Eleusis: Archetypal Image of Mother and Daughter*, New York, Schocken Books, 1967.

　Zeus and Hera: Archetypal Image of Father, Husband and Wife, trans. Christopher Holme, Bollingen Series LXV, Princeton, New Jersey, Princeton University Press, 1975.

　Dionysos: Archetypal Image of Indestructible Life, trans. Ralph Manheim, Bollingen Series LXV:2, Princeton, NJ, Princeton University Press, 1976.

The Gods of the Greeks, trans. Norman Cameron, London, Thames and Hudson, 1979.

　Hermes: Guide of Souls, Dallas, Texas, Spring Publications, 1986.

　Goddesses of Sun and Moon, trans. Murray Stein, Dallas, Texas, Spring Publications, Inc., 1987.

Kershaw, Nora, trans., *Darradarjod, Anglo-Saxon and Norse Poems*, Cambridge, Cambridge University Press, 1922.

Kightly, Charles, *The Perpetual Almanack of Folklore*, London, Thames and Hudson, 1994.

King, Leonard William, *The Seven Tablets of Creation; or, the Babylonian Legends concerning the Creation of the World and of Mankind*, London, Luzac, 1902.

Knappert, Jan, *Indian Mythology: An Encyclopedia of Myth and Legend*, London, Diamond Books, 1995.

　The Aquarian Guide to African Mythology, Wellingborough, Northamptonshire, Aquarian Press, 1990.

　Pacific Mythology: An Encyclopedia of Myth and Legend, London, Aquarian Press, Harper Collins, 1992.

Kollerstrom, Nick, *Planting by the Moon: a Gardener's Calendar, 1999*, Devon, Prospect Books, 1998.

Kramer, Samuel N., *The Sumerians, Their History, Culture and Character*, Chicago and London, University of Chicago Press, 1971.

Krappe, Alexander H., The Lunar Frog, *Folk-lore*, vol. LI, 1940, pp. 161-171.

　La Genèse des Mythes, Paris, Payot, 1938.

Krupp, Edward C., *Beyond the Blue Horizon: Myths & Legends of the Sun, Moon, Stars, & Planets*, Oxford and New York, Oxford University Press, 1992.

　Skywatchers, Shamans & Kings, Chichester, John Wiley & Sons, Inc., 1997.

Lajard, Felix, *Recherches sur le culte publique et les mystères de mithra en Orient et en Occident*, Paris, 1867.

Lamy, Lucie, *Egyptian Mysteries: New Light on Ancient Knowledge*, London, Thames and Hudson, 1981.

Langdon, Stephen H., *Oxford Editions of Cuneiform Inscriptions*, edited under the direction of S. Langdon, London, New York [etc.], Oxford University Press, H. Milford, 1923.

　Semitic Mythology, The Mythology of all Races, vol. 5, Marshall Jones Company, Inc., 1931.

Larousse Dictionary of World Folklore, comp. Alison Jones, Larousse plc, 1995.

Larrington, Carolyne, ed. *The Feminist Companion to Mythology*, London, Pandora Press, 1992.

Lawrence, D. H., *The Complete Poems of D. H. Lawrence*, Vivian De Sola Pinto and Warren Roberts, eds., London, Heinemann, 1972.

　Women in Love, London, Everyman, 1993.

Layard, John, *The Stone Men of Malekula*, London, Chatto & Windus, 1942.

　The Lady of the Hare, London, Faber & Faber, 1944.

Lewis, C. S., *The Discarded Image: An Introduction to Medieval and Renaissance Literature*, Cambridge,

Cambridge University Press, 1964.

Long, Kim, *The Moon Book: The meaning of methodical movements of the magnificent, mysterious moon and other interesting facts about the earth's nearest neighbor,* Boulder, Colorado, Johnson Publishing Company, 1988.

Lorca, *The Selected Poems of Federico Garcia Lorca,* trans. W. S. Merwin, ed. Francisco Garcia Lorca and Donald M. Allen, New Directions Paperback, New York, 1961.

Lorie, Peter, *Superstition: The Book of Ancient Lore,* London, Simon and Schuster, 1992.

Lovejoy, Arthur O., *The Great Chain of Being: A Study of the History of an Idea,* Cambridge, Mass. and London, Harvard University Press, 1964.

Mackenzie, Donald A., *Myths from China & Japan,* London, The Gresham Publishing Company Ltd.

Macrobius, Ambrosius, *Saturnalia,* trans. Percival Vaughn Davies, New York, Columbia Universty Press, 1969.

Maple, Eric, *Old Wives' Tales,* London, Robert Hale, 1981.

March, Jenny, *Dictionary of Classical Mythology,* London, Cassell, 1998.

Marshack, Alexander, *The Roots of Civilization,* London, Weidenfeld & Nicholson, 1991.

Mbitu, Ngangar and Prime, Ranchor, *Essential African Mythology,* London and San Francisco, Thorsons, HarperCollins, 1997.

McCrickard, Janet, *Eclipse of the Sun: An Investigation into Sun and Moon Myths,* Somerset, Gothic Image Publications, 1990.

McGrath, Sheena, *The Sun Goddess: Myth, Legend and History,* London, Blandford, 1997.

Miller, Mary Ellen and Taube, Karl, *An Illustrated Dictionary of The Gods and Symbols of Ancient Mexico and the Maya,* London, Thames and Hudson, 1993.

Monier-Williams, M, *A Sanskrit-English Dictionary,* Delhi, Motilal Banarsidas Publishers Private Ltd., 1995.

Moon, Beverly, ed. *An Encyclopedia of Archetypal Symbolism,* The Archive for Research in Archetypal Symbolism, Boston and London, Shambhala, 1991.

Muller, F. Max, ed., *The Sacred Books of the East,* 50 vols. Delhi, India, Motilal Banarsidass, 1992.

Neumann, Erich, *The Origins and History of Consciousness,* Bollingen Series XLII, trans. R. F. C. Hull, Princeton, New Jersey, Princeton University Press, 1954.

    The Great Mother, Bollingen Series XLVII, trans. Ralph Mannheim, Princeton, New Jersey, Princeton University Press, 1955.

    The Fear of the Feminine and other essays on feminine psychology, Bollingen Series LXI.4, Princeton, new Jersey, Princeton University Press, 1994.

New Larousse Encyclopedia of Mythology, trans. Richard Aldington and Delano Ames (intro. by Robert Graves), The Hamlyn Publishing Group Ltd., 1959.

Nicolson, Iain, *Heavenly Bodies: A Beginner's Guide to Astronomy,* London, BBC Books, 1994.

Nilsson, Martin P., *Primitive Time-reckoning : a study*

in the origins and first development of the art of counting time among the primitive and early culture peoples, Lund, C. W. K. Gleerup, 1920.

O'Flaherty, Wendy Doniger, *Hindu Myths: A Sourcebook,* translated from the Sanskrit, Harmondsworth, Penguin Books, 1978.

O'Hara, Gwydion, *Moon Lore: Myths and Folklore from Around the World,* St. Paul, Minnesota, Llewellyn Publications, 1996.

Onians, Richard B., *The Origins of European Thought: About the Body, the Mind, the Soul, the World, Time and Fate,* Cambridge, Cambridge University Press, 1984.

Opie, Iona and Peter, *The Oxford Nursery Rhyme Book,* Oxford, Clarendon Press, 1955.

Opie, Iona and Tatem, Moira, eds., *A Dictionary of Superstitions,* Oxford and New York, Oxford University Press, 1989.

Otto, Rudolf, *The Idea of the Holy: an inquiry into the non-rational factor in the idea of the divine and its relation to the rational,* trans. John W. Harvey, Oxford, OUP, 1958.

Ouspensky, P.D., *In Search of the Miraculous: Fragments of an Unknown Teaching,* London, Routledge & Kegan Paul, 1975.

Ovid, *Metamorphosis,* 6 vols., trans. Frank Justus Miller, Loeb Classical Library, Cambridge, Mass. and London, Harvard University Press and William Heinemann Ltd., 1977.

Oxford Dictionary of English Etymology, ed. C. T. Onians, Oxford, Oxford University Press, 1966.

Palmer, Martin & Xiaomin, Zhao, *Essential Chinese Mythology,* Thorsons, HarperCollins, 1997.

Partridge, Eric, *Origins: A Short Etymological Dictionary of Modern English,* London, Melbourne, Henley, Routledge & Kegan Paul, 1979.

Pausanias, *Description of Greece,* 4 vols., trans. W. H. S. Jones, Cambridge, Massachusetts, Harvard University Press, London, William Heinemann Ltd., 1988.

Phillips, John A, *Eve: The History of an Idea,* San Francisco, Harper & Row, 1984.

Plath, Sylvia, *The Colossus,* London, Faber & Faber, 1968.

    Winter Trees, London, Faber & Faber, 1971.

Plato, *The Collected Dialogues,* ed. Hamilton, Edith and Crains, Huntington, Bollingen Series LXXI, Princeton, New Jersey, Princeton University Press, 1989.

Pliny, *Natural History,* vol. 1, trans. H. Rackham, Loeb Classical Library, Cambridge, Mass. and London, Harvard University Press, 1997.

Plutarch, Isis and Osiris, *Moralia,* V, trans. F.C. Babbit, Loeb Classical Library, London, William Heinemann Ltd., 1969.

    On the Face of the Moon, *Moralia,* XII, trans. Harold Cherniss and William Helmbold, Loeb Classical Library, Cambridge, Mass. and London, Harvard University Press and William Heinmann Ltd., 1957.

Pope-Hennessy, John, *Paradiso: the Illuminations to Dante's Divine Comedy by Giovanni di Paolo,* London, Thames and Hudson, 1993.

Ptolemy, *Tetrabiblos,* trans. F.E. Robbins, Loeb Classical Library, Cambridge, Mass. and London, Harvard University Press, 1998.

Purce, Jill, *The Mystic Spiral: Journey of the Soul,* London, Thames and Hudson, 1974.

Rahner, Hugo, *Greek Myths and Christian Mystery,* trans. Brian Battershaw, London, Burns & Oates, 1963, pp. 154-176.

Ray, Jean Dorothy, *Eskimo Masks: Art and Ceremony,* Seattle, University of Washington Press, 1967.

Reichel-Dolmatof, Gerardo, *Rainforest Shamans: Essays on the Tukano Indians of the Northwest Amazon,* Totnes, Devon, Themis Books in association with the COAMA Programme, Colombia, and the Gaia Foundation, London.

    Astronomical Models of Social Behavior Among Some Indians of Colombia, *Annals of the New York Academy of Sciences,* vol. 385, 1982, pp. 165-181.

Reps, Paul, with Nyogen Senzaki, *Zen Flesh Zen Bones: A Collection of Zen & Pre-Zen Writings,* Tokyo, Tuttle, 1957.

Rexroth, Kenneth, *One Hundred Poems from the Chinese,* Toronto and New York, New Directions Books, 1971.

    One Hundred More Poems from the Japanese, Toronto and New York, New Directions Books, 1976.

The Rig Veda: An Anthology, one hundred and eight hymns, selected, translated and annotated by Wendy Doniger O'Flaherty, Harmondsworth, Penguin Books, 1981.

Rilke, Rainer Maria, *Selected Poetry,* ed. and trans. Stephen Marshall, London, Picador, Pan Books Ltd., 1987.

Roberts, Alison, *Hathor Rising: The Power of the Goddess in Ancient Egypt,* Rochester, Vermont, Inner Traditional International Ltd., 1997.

Roscher, Wilhelm H., *Ausfuehrliches Lexikon der Griechischen und Roemischen Mythologie,* 5 vols, Leipzig, Teubner, 1884-1937.

    Nektar und Ambrosia, Leipzig, Druck und Verlag von B. G. Teubner, 1883.

    Uber Selene und Verwandtes, Leipzig, Druck und Verlag von B. G. Teubner, 1890.

Ruggles, Clive L. N., ed., *Records in Stone: Papers in Memory of Alexander Thom,* Cambridge, Cambridge University Press, 1988.

Rundle Clark, R.T., *Myth and Symbol in Ancient Egypt,* London, Thames and Hudson, 1978.

Sachs, Maryam, *The Moon,* New York, London, Paris, Abbeville Press Publishers, 1998.

Schele, Linda and Miller, Mary E., *The Blood of Kings: Dynasty and Ritual in Maya Art,* New York, George Brazilier, Inc., in association with the Kimbell Art Museum, Fort Worth, 1986.

Segal, Robert A., *Encountering Jung: Jung on Mythology,* Princeton, Princeton University Press, 1998.

Shah, Idries, *The Pleasantries of the Incredible Mulla Nasrudin,* London, Pan Books, Picador, 1975.

    Tales of the Dervishes, London, Jonathon Cape, 1967.

Shakespeare, William, *The Riverside Shakespeare*, Boston and London, Houghton Mifflin Company, 1974.

Shapiro, Max S. and Hendricks, Rhoda A., *A Dictionary of Mythologies*, London, Toronto, Sydney, New York, Paladin, Granada, 1981.

Shearer, Ann, *Athene: Image and Energy*, Harmondsworth, Viking Arkana, 1996.

Sheldrake, Rupert, *A New Science of Life: The Hypothesis of Formative Causation*, Los Angeles, Tarcher, 1981.

Shelley, Percy Bysshe, *Poems and Prose*, London, Everyman, 1995.

Simpson, Jacqueline and Roud, Steve, *A Dictionary of English Folklore*, Oxford, Oxford University Press, 2000.

Singh, Madanjeet, comp., *The Sun in Myth and Art*, London, Thames and Hudson, 1993.

Skolimowsky, Henryk, *The Participatory Mind*, London, Arkana, 1994.

Sonne, Birgitte, *Agayut: Nunivak Eskimo Masks from The 5th Thule Expedition*, Copenhagen, Gyldendal, 1988.

> *Mythology of the Eskimos*, in Carolyne Larrington, ed., *The Feminist Companion to Mythology*, London, Pandora Press, 1992.

Spengler, Oswald, *The Decline of the West*, New York, The Modern Library, abridged by Helmut Werner, 1962.

Stevens, Anthony, *Archetype: A Natural History of the Self*, Routledge & Kegan Paul Ltd., 1982.

> *Ariadne's Clue: a Guide to the Symbols of Humankind*, Harmondsworth, Allen Lane, The Penguin Press, 1998.

Stevens, Wallace, *Selected Poems*, London and Boston, Faber & Faber, 1965.

> *The Necessary Angel: Essays on Reality and the Imagination*, London and Boston, Faber & Faber, 1984.

Sturluson, Snorri, *The Prose Edda: Tales from Norse Mythology*, trans. Jean I. Young, Berkeley, Los Angeles, London, University of California Press, 1978.

Tanahashi, Kazuaki, ed., *Moon in a Dewdrop: Writings of Zen Master Dogen*, New York, North Point Press, Farrar, Straus and Giroux, 1985.

Tarnas, Richard, *The Passion of the Western Mind: Understanding the Ideas That Have Shaped Our World View*, New York, Harmony Books, 1991.

Taylor, Paul B. and Auden W. H., trans. *The Elder Edda: a Selection*, New York, Random House, 1967.

Thom, Alexander, *Megalithic Lunar Observatories*, Oxford, Clarendon Press, 1978.

Thomas, Keith, *Religion and the Decline of Magic*, Harmondsworth, Penguin Books Ltd., 1991.

Tillyard, E., *The Elizabethan World Picture*, Harmondsworth, Penguin Books Ltd., 1990.

Tompkins, Peter and Bird, Christopher, *The Secret Life of Plants*, Harmondsworth, Penguin Books, 1974.

Tsu, Lao, *Tao Te Ching*, Harmondsworth, Penguin Books, 1963.

Tu Fu *Selected Poems*, trans. R. Alley. Peking, Foreign Language Press, 1964.

Unterman, Alan, *Dictionary of Jewish Lore and Legend*, Thames and Hudson, London, 1991.

Van der Post, Laurens, *The Seed and the Sower*, London, Hogarth Press, 1963.

> *Jung and the Story of our Time*, Harmondsworth, Penguin Books, 1975.

> *The Heart of the Hunter*, Harmondsworth, Penguin Books, 1978.

> *Yet Being Someone Other*, London, Hogarth Press, 1982.

Van Over, Raymond, ed., *Taoist Tales*, New York and London, Mentor Book, The New American Library, 1973.

Vermaseren, M. J., *Cybele and Attis*, trans. A. M. H. Lemmers, London, Thames and Hudson, 1977.

Virgil, *The Georgics*, trans. C. Day Lewis, London, Jonathan Cape, 1940.

> *Eclogues, Georgics, Aeneid 1-6*, vol 1, trans. H. Rushton Fairclough, Loeb Classical Library, Cambridge, Mass. and London, Harvard University Press, 1999.

Vries, Ad de, *Dictionary of Symbols and Imagery*, Amsterdam, Elsevier Science Publishers, 1984.

Waley, Arthur, *Chinese Poems*, London, Unwin Books, 1961.

> *170 Chinese Poems*, London, Constable & Co. Ltd., 1977.

Walker, Barbara, ed., *The Woman's Encyclopedia of Myth and Secrets*, San Francisco, Harper & Row, 1983.

> *The Woman's Dictionary of Symbols and Sacred Objects*, San Francisco, Harper Collins, 1998.

Ward, William Hayes, *Seal Cylinders of Western Asia*, New York, J. P. Morgan Library /AMS Press, 1910.

Warner, Marina, *Alone of All her Sex: The Myth and the Cult of the Virgin Mary*, London, Weidenfeld and Nicolson, 1976.

Watson, Lyall, *Supernature: The Natural History of the Supernatural*, London, Coronet Books, Hodder Paperbacks, Ltd., 1974.

Watts, Alan, *Myth and Ritual in Christianity*, London, Thames and Hudson, 1954.

Webster, Hutton, *Rest Days: the Christian Sunday, the Jewish Sabbath, and their Historical and Anthropological Prototypes*, New York, Macmillan, 1916.

Weekley, Ernest, *An Etymological Dictionary of Modern English*, 2 vols., New York, Dover Publications, Inc., 1967.

Werner, Edward T. C., *Myths and Legends of China*, London, George G. Harrap & Co. Ltd., 1958.

Westwood, Jennifer, *Albion, a Guide to Legendary Britain*, London, Grafton Books, 1985.

White, J., *The Ancient History of the Maori*, 4 vols., Wellington, 1886-89.

Winter, Jeannette, *The Girl and the Moon Man*, New York, Pantheon Books, 1984.

Wolkstein, Diane and Kramer, Samuel Noah, *Inanna, Queen of Heaven and Earth: Her Stories and Hymns from Sumer*, London, Rider & Co., 1983.

Yates, Frances A., *The Art of Memory*, Harmondsworth, Peregrine Books, Penguin Books, 1966.

> *The Occult Philosophy in the Elizabethan Age*, London, Boston and Henley, Routledge & Kegan Paul, 1979.

Yeats, W. B., *A Vision*, London, Macmillan, 1962.

> *The Collected Poems*, London, Macmillan, 1952.

> *The Celtic Twilight*, Bridport, Prism Press, 1990.

> *Essays and Introductions*, London and Basingstoke, Macmillan Press Ltd., 1961.

> *Wheels and Butterflies*, London, Macmillan and Co., Ltd., 1934.

Zimmer, Heinrich, *Myths and Symbols in Indian Art and Civilization*, ed. Joseph Campbell, Bollingen Series VI, Princeton New Jersey, Princeton University Press, 1946.

> *Philosophies of India*, ed. Joseph Campbell, Bollingen Series XXVI, Princeton, New Jersey, Princeton University Press, 1951.

> *The Art of Indian Asia*, 2 vols, completed and edited by Joseph Campbell. Bollingen Series XXXIX, Princeton, New Jersey, Princeton University Press, 1983.

> *The King and the Corpse: Tales of the Soul's Conquest of Evil*, ed. Joseph Campbell, Bollingen Series XI, Princeton, New Jersey, Princeton University Press, 1973.

INDEX